TCP/IP Tutorial and Technical Overview

Sixth Edition

ISBN 0-13-020130-8

90000

9 780130 201300

The ITSO Networking Series

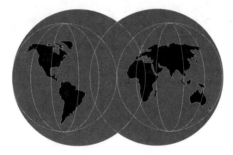

TCP/IP Tutorial and Technical Overview

Sixth Edition

MARTIN W. MURHAMMER ■ ORCUN ATAKAN ■
STEFAN BRETZ ■ LARRY R. PUGH ■
KAZUNARI SUZUKI ■ DAVID H. WOOD

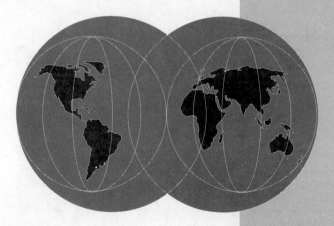

PRENTICE HALL PTR, UPPER SADDLE RIVER, NEW JERSEY 07458
http://www.phptr.com

For information about redbooks:
http://www.redbooks.ibm.com

Send comments to:
redbooks@us.ibm.com

Published by Prentice Hall PTR
Prentice-Hall, Inc.
A Simon & Schuster Company
Upper Saddle River, NJ 07458

Prentice Hall books are widely used by corporations and government agencies for training, marketing, and resale. The publisher offers discounts on this book when ordered in bulk quantities. For more information, contact

    Corporate Sales Department,
    Phone 800-382-3419; FAX: 201-236-7141
    E-mail (Internet): corpsales@prenhall.com

Or Write: Prentice Hall PTR
    Corporate Sales Department
    One Lake Street
    Upper Saddle River, NJ 07458

Take Note! Before using this information and the product it supports, be sure to read the general information under Appendix A, "Special Notices" on page 857.

Printed in the United States of America
10 9 8 7 6 5 4 3 2

ISBN 0-13-020130-8

Prentice-Hall International (UK) Limited, *London*
Prentice-Hall of Australia Pty. Limited, *Sydney*
Prentice-Hall Canada Inc., *Toronto*
Prentice-Hall Hispanoamericana, S.A., *Mexico*
Prentice-Hall of India Private Limited, *New Delhi*
Prentice-Hall of Japan, Inc., *Tokyo*
Simon & Schuster Asia Pte. Ltd., *Singapore*
Editora Prentice-Hall do Brasil, Ltda., *Rio de Janeiro*

Contents

Chapter 4. Application Protocols 193

Preface

This redbook provides an introduction as well as a reference to the Transmission Control Protocol/Internet Protocol (TCP/IP) suite of protocols and applications, which provide the foundation and framework for many computer networks, among them the world's largest, the Internet. This redbook explains the basics of TCP/IP and also includes an overview of the latest developments in the world of TCP/IP and the Internet. Special areas of interest are security (IPSec, VPN, certificate and key management, etc.), Java, IP mobility and address management, multicasting, priority and bandwidth reservation, IPv6, directory protocols and, last but not least, the latest hardware and software developments.

To provide a comprehensive presentation of the topics, this book is structured as follows:

- Part 1 describes the history, architecture and standards of TCP/IP and also includes the core network, transport, routing and application protocols of the TCP/IP suite.

- Part 2 introduces new architectures and special purpose protocols, such as IP Version 6, IP security, quality of service, load balancing and Internet protocols.

- Part 3 discusses network connections and platform implementations of TCP/IP.

It has always been the purpose of this redbook to provide an introduction and overview that is valuable to the TCP/IP novice to find the bearings in the world of heterogeneous connectivity. For the benefit of readers who are new to TCP/IP, this basic information has been included with this edition in Part 1.

It is the main intention of the authors of this edition, however, to provide in-depth information on the most current protocols, technologies and implementations of TCP/IP available today and which are actually used and deployed throughout the Internet as well as in private TCP/IP networks. This material has been compiled as both an overview as well as a technical reference for advanced TCP/IP users and experts in this area who want to broaden their scope of knowledge.

The Team That Wrote This Redbook

This redbook was produced by a team of specialists from around the world working at the International Technical Support Organization, Raleigh Center. The leader of this project was Martin W. Murhammer.

Martin W. Murhammer is a Senior I/T Availability Professional at the International Technical Support Organization Raleigh Center. Before joining the ITSO in 1996, he was a Systems Engineer in the Systems Service Center at IBM Austria. He has 13 years of experience in the personal computing environment including such areas as heterogeneous connectivity, server design, system recovery, and Internet solutions. He is an IBM Certified OS/2 Engineer and a Certified LAN Server Engineer and has previously coauthored nine redbooks during projects at the ITSO Raleigh and Austin Centers.

Orcun Atakan is an Internet Specialist at the Information Systems Technical Support help desk in IBM Turkey, where he has been working for three years. His areas of expertise is IP security, Internet, Java, Firewalls and the IBM eNetwork range of products.

Stefan Bretz is a Support Specialist at IBM Network Service Software in Germany. He has two years of experience in the MVS TCP/IP field with a focus on FTP and Sockets. His areas of expertise include IP multicasting, RTP and RSVP. He holds a Bachelor's Degree in Computer Engineering from the Berufsakademie (University of Applied Studies) in Mannheim.

Larry R. Pugh has worked for IBM for 25 years. His career at IBM includes jobs as a Systems Programmer, Systems Engineer, and Telecommunications Analyst. He has worked in networking for the past 20 years. In his early networking career he assisted IBM customers with configuring and implementing SNA networks. Ten years ago he joined IBM Education, where he is currently working as an Instructor/Developer. He developed and taught SNA courses before he switched to TCP/IP courses and lab configurations for TCP/IP networks six years ago. Larry graduated from Grambling State University in Grambling, La., in 1973 with a degree in Applied Mathematics and Computer Science.

Kazunari Suzuki is an Advisory I/T Specialist working for the Network Design Support Office at IBM Japan. He has five years of experience supporting IBM networking hardware products, focusing on TCP/IP and SNA connectivity. His areas of expertise also include MVS and DB2.

David H. Wood is a Senior Software Specialist with IBM UK. He has 10 years experience in networking software. His current areas of expertise include OS/2, LAN/WARP Server, WorkSpace On-Demand, Network Computers, Dynamic IP, NetWare, DCE and Windows NT.

Thanks to the following people for their invaluable contributions to this project:

Karl Wozabal, Marco Pistoia, Harry J. Dutton, Linda Robinson, Gail
Christensen, Kathryn Casamento
International Technical Support Organization, Raleigh Center

Fant Steele
International Technical Support Organization, Rochester Center

Uwe Zimmermann
International Technical Support Organization, Austin Center

Edward Britton, Alfred Christensen, Charlotte Davis, Ed Ellesson, Chris
Gage, Pratik Gupta, Brian K. Haberman, Ricardo Haragutchi, Lap Huynh, David
Jacobson, Charles Kunzinger, Acee Lindem, Calvin Stacy Powers, Laura
Rademacher, Catherine M. Rossi, Bill Stephenson, Glenn Stump, John Tavs
IBM Research Triangle Park

Christopher Metz
IBM New York

Brian Carpenter, Member of the IAB and Co-Chair of the IETF Working
Group for Differentiated Services
IBM United Kingdom

Pete Russell, Lynda Linney
IBM United Kingdom

Nagatsugu Yamanouchi, Yuhji Mori, Tatsuji Namatsu, Kohji Yokoe
Atsushi Itoh, Atsuhiko Iwamura, Kunihiko Tejima
IBM Japan

Scott S. Gass
International Network Services

Thanks to the authors and contributors of previous editions of this redbook:

Peter Frick, Gerard Bourbigot, Frank Vandewiele
Authors of first edition

Peter Frick, Lesia Antonowytsch Cox, Ricardo Haragutchi
Authors of second edition

Philippe Beaupied, Frederic Debulois
Authors of third edition

Philippe Beaupied, Francis Li
Authors of fourth edition

Eamon Murphy, Matthias Enders, Steve Hayes
Authors of fifth edition

Antonius Bekker, Paul D. Bosco, Bob Botts, Edward Britton, Alfred
Christensen, Niels Christiansen, Jim Curran, Pete Haverlock, Barry
Nusbaum, Richard Ryniker, Bruce Wilder;
TCP/IP Development Team, Raleigh;
International Technical Support Organization Rochester Center;
Telecommunications Education Center, Raleigh;
Contributors to previous editions

Part 1. Architecture and Core Protocols

Chapter 1. Introduction to TCP/IP - History, Architecture and Standards

Today, the Internet, World Wide Web, and Information Super Highway are familiar terms to millions of people all over the world. Transmission Control Protocol/Internet Protocol (TCP/IP) is the protocol suite developed for the Internet. In this chapter we describe how the Internet was formed, how it developed and how it is likely to develop in the future. We also look at the basic properties of TCP/IP.

1.1 Internet History - Where It All Came From

Networks have become a fundamental, if not the most important, part of today's information systems. They form the backbone for information sharing in enterprises, governmental and scientific groups. That information can take several forms. It can be notes and documents, data to be processed by another computer, files sent to colleagues, and even more exotic forms of data.

Most of these networks were installed in the late 60s and 70s, when network design was the "state of the art" topic of computer research and sophisticated implementers. It resulted in multiple networking models such as packet-switching technology, collision-detection local area networks, hierarchical enterprise networks, and many other excellent technologies.

From the early 70s on, another aspect of networking became important: protocol layering, which allows applications to communicate with each other. A complete range of architectural models were proposed and implemented by various research teams and computer manufacturers.

The result of all this great know-how is that today any group of users can find a physical network and an architectural model suitable for their specific needs. This ranges from cheap asynchronous lines with no other error recovery than a bit-per-bit parity function, through full-function wide area networks (public or private) with reliable protocols such as public packet-switching networks or private SNA networks, to high-speed but limited-distance local area networks.

The down side of this exploding information sharing is the rather painful situation when one group of users wants to extend its information system to another group of users who happen to have a different network technology and different network protocols. As a result, even if they could agree on a type of network technology to physically interconnect the two locations, their applications (such as mailing systems) still would not be able to communicate with each other because of the different protocols.

This situation was recognized rather early (beginning of the 70s) by a group of researchers in the U.S. who came up with a new principle: *internetworking*. Other official organizations became involved in this area of interconnecting networks, such as ITU-T (formerly CCITT) and ISO. All were trying to define a set of protocols, layered in a well-defined suite, so that applications would be able to talk to other applications, regardless of the underlying network technology and the operating systems where those applications run.

1.1.1 Internetworks

Those original designers, funded by the *Defense Advanced Research Projects Agency* (DARPA), of the *ARPANET protocol suite* introduced fundamental concepts such as *layering* and *virtualizing* in the world of networking, well before ISO even took an interest in networking.

The official organization of those researchers was the ARPANET Network Working Group, which had its last general meeting in October 1971. DARPA continued its research for an internetworking protocol suite, from the early *NCP (Network Control Program)* host-to-host protocol to the TCP/IP protocol suite, which took its current form around 1978. At that time, DARPA was well known for its pioneering of packet-switching over radio networks and satellite channels. The first real implementations of the *Internet* were found around 1980 when DARPA started converting the machines of its research network (ARPANET) to use the new TCP/IP protocols. In 1983, the transition was completed and DARPA demanded that *all* computers willing to connect to its ARPANET use TCP/IP.

DARPA also contracted Bolt, Beranek, and Newman (BBN) to develop an implementation of the TCP/IP protocols for Berkeley UNIX on the VAX and funded the University of California at Berkeley to distribute that code free of charge with their UNIX operating system. The first release of the *Berkeley Software Distribution* to include the TCP/IP protocol set was made available in 1983 (4.2BSD). From that point on, TCP/IP spread rapidly among universities and research centers and has become the standard communications subsystem for all UNIX connectivity. The second release (4.3BSD) was distributed in 1986, with updates in 1988 (4.3BSD Tahoe) and 1990 (4.3BSD Reno). 4.4BSD was released in 1993. Due to funding constraints, 4.4BSD was the last release of the BSD by the Computer Systems Research Group of the University of California at Berkeley.

As TCP/IP internetworking spread rapidly, new wide area networks were created in the U.S. and connected to ARPANET. In turn, other networks in the rest of the world, not necessarily based on the TCP/IP protocols, were added to the set of interconnected networks. The result is what is described as *The Internet*. Some examples of the different networks that have played key roles in this development are described in the next sections.

1.1.2 The Internet

What exactly is the Internet? First, the word *internet* (also *internetwork*) is simply a contraction of the phrase *interconnected network*. However, when written with a capital "I" the Internet refers to a worldwide set of interconnected networks, so the Internet is an internet, but the reverse does not apply. The Internet is sometimes called the *connected Internet*.

The Internet consists of the following groups of networks (see the following sections for more information on some of these):

- Backbones: large networks that exist primarily to interconnect other networks. Currently the backbones are NSFNET in the US, EBONE in Europe, and large commercial backbones.

- Regional networks connecting, for example, universities and colleges.

- Commercial networks providing access to the backbones to subscribers, and networks owned by commercial organizations for internal use that also have connections to the Internet.

- Local networks, such as campus-wide university networks.

In many cases, particularly for commercial, military and government networks, traffic between these networks and the rest of the Internet is restricted (see also 5.3, "Firewalls" on page 359).

1.1.3 ARPANET

Sometimes referred to as the "grand-daddy of packet networks," the ARPANET was built by DARPA (which was called ARPA at that time) in the late 60s to accommodate research equipment on packet-switching technology and to allow resource sharing for the Department of Defense's contractors. The network interconnected research centers, some military bases and government locations. It soon became popular with researchers for collaboration through electronic mail and other services. It was developed into a research utility run by the Defense Communications Agency (DCA) by the end of 1975 and split in 1983 into MILNET for interconnection of military sites and ARPANET for interconnection of research sites. This formed the beginning of the "capital I" Internet.

In 1974, the ARPANET was based on 56 Kbps leased lines that interconnected *packet-switching nodes* (PSN) scattered across the continental U.S. and western Europe. These were minicomputers running a protocol known as *1822* (after the number of a report describing it) and dedicated to the packet-switching task. Each PSN had at least two connections to other PSNs (to allow alternate routing in case of circuit failure) and up to 22 ports for user computer (*host*) connections. These 1822 systems offered reliable, flow-controlled delivery of a packet to a destination node. This is the reason why the original *NCP* protocol was a rather simple protocol. It was replaced by the TCP/IP protocols, which do not assume reliability of the underlying network hardware and can be used on other-than-1822 networks. This 1822 protocol did not become an industry standard, so DARPA decided later to replace the 1822 packet switching technology with the *CCITT X.25* standard.

Data traffic rapidly exceeded the capacity of the 56 Kbps lines that made up the network, which were no longer able to support the necessary throughput. Today the ARPANET has been replaced by new technologies in its role of backbone on the research side of the connected Internet (see NSFNET later in this chapter), whereas MILNET continues to form the backbone of the military side.

1.1.4 NSFNET

NSFNET, the National Science Foundation Network, is a three-level internetwork in the United States consisting of:

- The *backbone*: a network that connects separately administered and operated mid-level networks and NSF-funded supercomputer centers. The backbone also has transcontinental links to other networks such as EBONE, the European IP backbone network.
- *Mid-level networks*: of three kinds (regional, discipline-based and supercomputer consortium networks).
- *Campus networks*: whether academic or commercial, connected to the mid-level networks.

First Backbone

Originally established by the National Science Foundation (NSF) as a communications network for researchers and scientists to access the NSF supercomputers, the first NSFNET backbone used six DEC LSI/11 microcomputers as packet switches, interconnected by 56 Kbps leased lines. A primary interconnection between the NSFNET backbone and the ARPANET existed at Carnegie Mellon, which allowed routing of datagrams between users connected to each of those networks.

Second Backbone

The need for a new backbone appeared in 1987, when the first one became overloaded within a few months (estimated growth at that time was 100% per year). The NSF and MERIT, Inc., a computer network consortium of eight state-supported universities in Michigan, agreed to develop and manage a new, higher-speed backbone with greater transmission and switching capacities. To manage it they defined the *Information Services* (IS) which is comprised of an Information Center and a Technical Support Group. The Information Center is responsible for information dissemination, information resource management and electronic communication. The Technical Support Group provides support directly to the field. The purpose of this is to provide an integrated information system with easy-to-use-and-manage interfaces accessible from any point in the network supported by a full set of training services.

Merit and NSF conducted this project in partnership with IBM and MCI. IBM provided the software, packet-switching and network-management equipment, while MCI provided the long-distance transport facilities. Installed in 1988, the new network initially used 448 Kbps leased circuits to interconnect 13 *nodal switching systems* (NSS) supplied by IBM. Each NSS was composed of nine IBM RISC systems (running an IBM version of 4.3BSD UNIX) loosely coupled via two IBM Token-Ring Networks (for redundancy). One Integrated Digital Network Exchange (IDNX) supplied by IBM was installed at each of the 13 locations, to provide:

- Dynamic alternate routing
- Dynamic bandwidth allocation

Third Backbone

In 1989, the NSFNET backbone circuits topology was reconfigured after traffic measurements and the speed of the leased lines increased to T1 (1.544 Mbps) using primarily fiber optics.

Due to the constantly increasing need for improved packet switching and transmission capacities, three NSSs were added to the backbone and the link speed was upgraded. The migration of the NSFNET backbone from T1 to T3 (45Mbps) was completed in late 1992. The subsequent migration to gigabit levels has already started and will continue through the late 1990s.

In April 1995 the US government discontinued its funding of NSFNET. This was in part a reaction to growing commercial use of the network. About the same time, NSFNET gradually migrated the main backbone traffic in the U.S. to commercial network service providers, and NSFNET reverted to being a network for the research community. The main backbone network is now run in cooperation with MCI and is known as the vBNS (very high speed Backbone Network Service).

NSFNET has played a key role in the development of the Internet. However, many other networks have also played their part and/or also make up a part of the Internet today.

1.1.5 Commercial Use of the Internet

In recent years the Internet has grown in size and range at a greater rate than anyone could have predicted. A number of key factors have influenced this growth. Some of the most significant milestones have been the free distribution of Gopher in 1991, the first posting, also in 1991, of the specification for hypertext and, in 1993, the release of Mosaic, the first graphics-based browser. Today the vast majority of the hosts now connected to the Internet are of a commercial nature. This is an area of potential and actual conflict with the initial aims of the Internet, which were to foster open communications between academic and research institutions. However, the continued growth in commercial use of the Internet is inevitable so it will be helpful to explain how this evolution is taking place.

One important initiative to consider is that of the *Acceptable Use Policy (AUP)*. The first of these policies was introduced in 1992 and applies to the use of NSFNET. A copy of this can be obtained at *nic.merit.edu/nsfnet/acceptable.use.policy*. At the heart of this AUP is a commitment "to support open research and education". Under "Unacceptable Uses" is a prohibition of "use for for-profit activities", unless covered by the General Principle or as a specifically acceptable use. However, in spite of this apparently restrictive stance the NSFNET was increasingly used for a broad range of activities, including many of a commercial nature, before reverting to its original objectives in 1995.

The provision of an AUP is now commonplace among Internet Service Providers, although the AUP has generally evolved to be more suitable for commercial use. Some networks still provide services free of any AUP.

Let us now focus on the Internet service providers who have been most active in introducing commercial uses to the Internet. Two worth mentioning are PSINet and UUNET, which began in the late 80s to offer Internet access to both businesses and individuals. The California-based CERFnet provided services free of any AUP. An organization to interconnect PSINet, UUNET and CERFnet was formed soon after, called the Commercial Internet Exchange (CIX), based on the understanding that the traffic of any member of one network may flow without restriction over the networks of the other members. As of July 1997, CIX had grown to more than 146 members from all over the world connecting member internets. At about the same time that CIX was formed, a non-profit company, Advance Network and Services (ANS), was formed by IBM, MCI and Merit, Inc. to operate T1 (subsequently T3) backbone connections for NSFNET. This group was active in increasing the commercial presence on the Internet.

ANS formed a commercially oriented subsidiary called ANS CO+RE to provide linkage between commercial customers and the research and education domains. ANS CO+RE provides access to NSFNET as well as being linked to CIX. In 1995 ANS was acquired by America Online.

In 1995, as the NSFNET was reverting to its previous academic role, the architecture of the Internet changed from having a single dominant backbone in the U.S. to having a number of commercially operated backbones. In order for the different backbones to be able to exchange data, the NSF set up four Network Access Points (NAPs) to serve as data interchange points between the backbone service providers.

Another type of interchange is the Metropolitan Area Ethernet (MAE). Several MAEs have been set up by Metropolian Fiber Systems (MFS), who also have their own backbone network. NAPs and MAEs are also referred to as public exchange points (IXPs). Internet Service Providers (ISPs) typically will have connections to a number of IXPs for performance and backup.

Similar to CIX in the United States, European Internet providers formed the RIPE (Réseaux IP Européens) organization to ensure technical and administrative coordination. RIPE was formed in 1989 to provide a uniform IP service to users throughout Europe. Currently, more than 1000 organizations participate in RIPE, and close to 6 million hosts (as of February 1998) could be reached via RIPE-coordinated networks.

Today, the largest Internet backbones run at OC3 (155 Mbps) or OC12 (622 Mbps). By late 1998 OC12 should be the standard speed for major backbones.

1.1.6 Information Superhighway

One recent and important initiative was the creation of the U.S. Advisory Council on the National Information Infrastructure (NIIAC) headed by U.S. Vice President Al Gore (who has been credited with coining the phrase "information superhighway"). The Advisory Council, which was made up of representatives from many areas of industry, government, entertainment and education, met for a period of two years from

1994-6. At the end of their term, they concluded their work with the publishing of two major reports:

- Kickstart Initiative: Connecting America's Communities to the Information Superhighway

- A Nation of Opportunity: Realizing the Promise of the Information Superhighway

Among the findings in these reports are the goal that every person in the U.S. should have access to the Internet by the year 2005, with all schools and libraries being connected by the year 2000.

Although the reports do not specify direct government funding for expansion of the Internet, preferring "commercial and competitive initiatives" to be the driving force, it does give a responsibility to all levels of government to ensure fair access and remove regulatory obstacles. Both reports may be found at:

`http://www.benton.org/contents.html`

From a more international perspective, the Group of Seven (G7) ministers met in Brussels in February 1995 to discuss the emerging Global Information Infrastructure (GII). The conference was attended by science, technology and economic ministers of Canada, the United Kingdom, France, Japan, Germany, Italy and the United States, and focused on technological, cultural and economic issues regarding the development of an international infrastructure.

Both the NIIAC and the GII described above were important initiatives which increased acceptance, and encouraged further growth, of the Internet.

The most recent and substantive government affirmation for the Internet came, in 1996, in the form of the Next Generation Internet initiative. This was launched by the Clinton administration with the goals of:

- Connecting universities and national labs with networks that are 100-1000 times faster than today's (as of October 1996) Internet.

- Promote expermentation with the next generation of networking technologies.

- Demonstrate new applications that meet important national goals and missions.

The initiative included funding of $100 million for 1998.

1.1.7 Internet2

The success of the Internet and the subsequent frequent congestion of the NSFNET and its commercial replacement led to some frustration among the research community who had previously enjoyed exclusive use of the Internet. The university community, therefore, together with government and industry partners, and encouraged by the funding component of the NGI, have formed the *Internet2* project.

Internet2 has the following principle objectives:

- To create a high bandwidth, leading-edge network capability for the research community in the U.S.

- To enable a new generation of applications and communication technologies to fully exploit the capabilities of broadband networks.

- To rapidly transfer newly developed technologies to all levels of education and to the broader Internet community, both in the U.S. and abroad.

For further information, please refer to 8.9, "Internet2" on page 587.

1.1.8 The Open Systems Interconnect (OSI) Model

Around the same time that DARPA was researching for an internetworking protocol suite in response to the requirement for the establishment of networking standards, which eventually led to TCP/IP and the Internet (see 1.1, "Internet History - Where It All Came From" on page 3), an alternative standards approach was being led by the CCITT (Comité Consultatif International Telephonique et Telegraphique, or Consultative Committee on International Telephony and Telegraphy), and the ISO (International Organization for Standardization). The CCITT has since become the ITU-T (International Telecommunications Union - Telecommunication Standardization Sector).

This effort resulted in the OSI (Open Systems Interconnect) Reference Model (ISO 7498), which defined a seven-layer model of data communication with physical transport at the lower layer and application protocols at the upper layers. This model, shown in Figure 1 on page 12, is widely accepted as a basis for the understanding of how a network protocol stack should operate and as a reference tool for comparing network stack implementations.

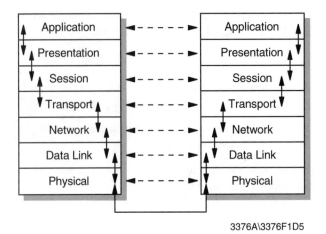

3376A\3376F1D5

Figure 1. *The OSI Reference Model*

The OSI Reference Model has seven layers; each layer provides a set of functions to the layer above and, in turn, relies on the functions provided by the layer below. Although messages can only pass vertically through the stack from layer to layer, from a logical point of view, each layer communicates directly with its peer layer on other nodes.

The seven layers are:

Application
   Network applications such as terminal emulation and file transfer

Presentation
   Formatting of data and encryption

Session
   Establishment and maintenance of sessions

Transport
   Provision of reliable and unreliable end-to-end delivery

Network
   Packet delivery, including routing

Data Link
   Framing of units of information and error checking

Physical
   Transmission of bits on the physical hardware

The two standards processes approach standardization from two different perspectives. The OSI approach started from a clean slate and defined standards, adhering tightly to their own model, using a formal committee process without requiring implementations. The Internet uses a less formal engineering approach, where anybody can propose and comment on RFCs, and implementations are required to verify feasibility. The OSI protocols developed slowly, and because running the full protocol stack is resource intensive, they have not been widely deployed, especially in the desktop and small computer market. In the meantime, TCP/IP and the Internet were developing rapidly and being put into use.

1.1.8.1 X.500: The Directory Service Standard

The OSI protocols did, however, address issues important in large distributed systems that were developing in an ad hoc manner in the desktop and Internet marketplace. One such important area was directory services. The CCITT created the X.500 standard in 1988, which became ISO 9594, Data Communications Network Directory, Recommendations X.500-X.521 in 1990, though it is still commonly referred to as X.500.

X.500 organizes directory entries in a hierarchical name space capable of supporting large amounts of information. It also defines powerful search capabilities to make retrieving information easier. Because of its functionality and scalability, X.500 is often used together with add-on modules for interoperation between incompatible directory services. X.500 specifies that communication between the directory client and the directory server uses the Directory Access Protocol (DAP). For further information on X.500 and directories, please see Chapter 12, "Directory Protocols and Distributed Computing" on page 717.

1.2 TCP/IP Architectural Model - What It Is All About

The TCP/IP protocol suite is named for two of its most important protocols: Transmission Control Protocol (TCP) and Internet Protocol (IP). Another name for it is the Internet Protocol Suite, and this is the phrase used in official Internet standards documents. The more common term TCP/IP is used to refer to the entire protocol suite in this book.

1.2.1 Internetworking

The first design goal of TCP/IP was to build an interconnection of networks that provided universal communication services: an *internetwork*, or *internet*. Each physical network has its own technology-dependent communication interface, in the form of a programming interface that provides basic communication functions (primitives). Communication services are provided by software that runs between the physical network and the user applications and that provides a common interface for these applications, independent of the underlying physical network. The architecture of the physical networks is hidden from the user.

The second aim is to *interconnect* different physical networks to form what appears to the the user to be one large network. Such a set of interconnected networks is called an *internetwork* or an *internet*.

To be able to interconnect two networks, we need a computer that is attached to both networks and that can forward packets from one network to the other; such a machine is called a *router*. The term *IP router* is also used because the routing function is part of the IP layer of the TCP/IP protocol suite (see 1.2.2, "The TCP/IP Protocol Stack" on page 15).

Figure 2 shows two examples of internets.

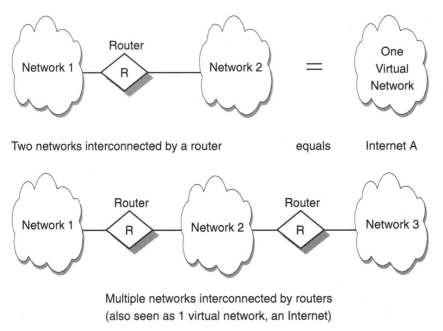

3376a\3376F1D1

Figure 2. Internet Examples. Two interconnected sets of networks, each seen as one logical network.

The basic properties of a router are:

- From the network standpoint, a router is a normal host.

- From the user standpoint, routers are invisible. The user sees only one large internetwork.

To be able to identify a host on the internetwork, each host is assigned an address, the *IP address*. When a host has multiple network adapters (interfaces), each interface has a unique IP address. The IP address consists of two parts:

```
IP address = <network number><host number>
```

The *network number* part of the IP address is assigned by a central authority and is unique throughout the Internet. The authority for assigning the *host number* part of the IP address resides with the organization that controls the network identified by the network number. The addressing scheme is described in detail in 2.1.1, "IP Addressing" on page 36.

1.2.2 The TCP/IP Protocol Stack

The TCP/IP protocol suite has evolved over a period of some 30 years. Like most networking software, TCP/IP is modelled in layers. This layered representation leads to the term *protocol stack*, which is synonymous with protocol suite. It can be used for positioning (but *not* for comparing functionally) the TCP/IP protocol suite against others, such as SNA and the Open System Interconnection (OSI) model (see Figure 1 on page 12). Functional comparisons cannot easily be extracted from this, as there are basic differences in the layered models used by the different protocol suites.

The Internet protocols are modeled in four layers:

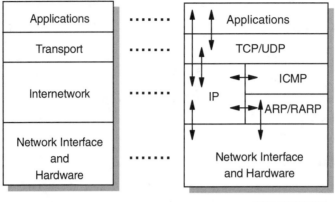

Figure 3. The TCP/IP Protocol Stack. Each layer represents a "package" of functions.

Application Layer

The application layer is provided by the program that uses TCP/IP for communication. An application is a user process cooperating with another process on the same or a different host. Examples of applications are Telnet, FTP, SMTP, and Gopher. The interface between the application and transport layers is defined by port numbers and sockets, which is described in more detail in 2.6, "Ports and Sockets" on page 94.

Transport Layer

The transport layer provides the end-to-end data transfer. Multiple applications can be supported simultaneously. The transport layer is responsible for providing a reliable exchange of information. The main transport layer protocol is TCP which is discussed in more detail in 2.8, "Transmission Control Protocol (TCP)" on page 100.

Another transport layer protocol is User Datagram Protocol (UDP, discussed in 2.7, "User Datagram Protocol (UDP)" on page 97), which provides a connectionless service in comparison to TCP, which provides a connection-oriented service. That means that applications using UDP as the transport protocol have to provide their own end-to-end flow control. Usually, UDP is used by applications that need a fast transport mechanism.

Internetwork Layer

The internetwork layer, also called the *internet layer* or the *network layer*, provides the "virtual network" image of an internet (that is, this layer shields the higher levels from the physical network architecture below it). Internet Protocol (IP) is the most important protocol in this layer. It is a *connectionless* protocol that doesn't assume reliability from the lower layers. IP does *not* provide reliability, flow control or error recovery. These functions must be provided at a higher level.

Part of communicating messages between computers is a routing function that ensures that messages will be correctly delivered to their destination. IP provides this routing function. IP is discussed in detail in 2.1, "Internet Protocol (IP)" on page 35. A message unit in an IP network is called an *IP datagram*. This is the basic unit of information transmitted across TCP/IP networks. Other internetwork layer protocols are IP, ICMP, IGMP, ARP and RARP.

Network Interface Layer

The network interface layer, also called the *link layer* or the *data-link layer*, is the interface to the actual network hardware. This interface may or may not provide reliable delivery, and may be packet or stream oriented. In fact, TCP/IP does not specify any protocol here, but can use almost any network interface available, which illustrates the flexibility of the IP layer. Examples are IEEE 802.2, X.25 (which is reliable in itself), ATM, FDDI and even SNA. Possible physical networks and interfaces that IBM TCP/IP products can connect to are discussed in Chapter 13, "Connection Protocols" on page 757.

Note that the RFCs actually do not describe or standardize any network layer protocols per se; they only standardize ways of accessing those protocols from the internetwork layer.

The actual interactions between the layers are shown by the arrows in Figure 3 on page 16. A more detailed "layering model" is shown in Figure 4.

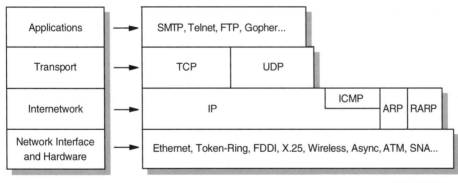

3376a\3376F1D3

Figure 4. Detailed Architectural Model

1.2.3 TCP/IP Applications

The highest-level protocols within the TCP/IP protocol stack are application protocols. They communicate with applications on other internet hosts and are the user-visible interface to the TCP/IP protocol suite.

All application protocols have some characteristics in common:

- They can be user-written applications or applications standardized and shipped with the TCP/IP product. Indeed, the TCP/IP protocol suite includes application protocols such as:

  - TELNET for interactive terminal access to remote internet hosts.

  - FTP (file transfer protocol) for high-speed disk-to-disk file transfers.

  - SMTP (simple mail transfer protocol) as an internet mailing system.

  These are some of the most widely implemented application protocols, but many others exist. Each particular TCP/IP implementation will include a lesser or greater set of application protocols.

- They use either UDP or TCP as a transport mechanism. Remember that UDP is unreliable and offers no flow-control, so in this case the application has to provide its own error recovery and flow-control routines. It is often easier to build applications on top of TCP, a reliable, connection-oriented protocol. Most application protocols will use TCP, but there are applications built on UDP to provide better performance through reduced protocol overhead.

- Most of them use the client/server model of interaction.

1.2.3.1 The Client/Server Model

TCP is a peer-to-peer, connection-oriented protocol. There are no master/slave relations. The applications, however, use a client/server model for communications.

A *server* is an application that offers a service to internet users; a *client* is a requester of a service. An application consists of both a server and a client part, which can run on the same or on different systems.

Users usually invoke the client part of the application, which builds a *request* for a particular service and sends it to the server part of the application using TCP/IP as a transport vehicle.

The server is a program that receives a request, performs the required service and sends back the results in a *reply*. A server can usually deal with multiple requests (multiple clients) at the same time.

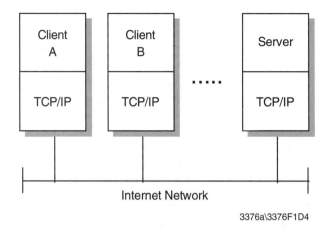

Figure 5. The Client/Server Model of Applications

Some servers wait for requests at a *well-known port* so that their clients know to which IP socket they must direct their requests. The client uses an arbitrary port for its communication. Clients that wish to communicate with a server that does not use a well-known port must have another mechanism for learning to which port they must address their requests. This mechanism might employ a registration service such as Portmap, which uses a well-known port.

For detailed information on TCP/IP application protocols, please refer to Chapter 4, "Application Protocols" on page 193.

1.2.4 Bridges, Routers and Gateways

Forming an internetwork by interconnecting multiple networks is done by *routers*. It is important to distinguish between a router, a bridge and a gateway.

Bridge   Interconnects LAN segments at the network interface layer level and forwards frames between them. A bridge performs the function of a MAC relay, and is independent of any higher layer protocol (including the Logical Link protocol). It provides MAC layer protocol conversion, if required. Examples of bridges are:

- A PC running the IBM Token-Ring Network Bridge program
- The IBM 8229 LAN bridge

A bridge can be said to be *transparent* to IP. That is, when an IP host sends an IP datagram to another host on a network connected by a bridge, it sends the datagram directly to the host and the datagram "crosses" the bridge without the sending IP host being aware of it.

Router   Interconnects networks at the internetwork layer level and routes packets between them. The router must understand the addressing structure associated with the networking protocols it supports and take decisions on whether, or how, to forward packets. Routers are able to select the best transmission paths and optimal packet sizes. The basic routing function is implemented in the IP layer of the TCP/IP protocol stack, so any host or workstation running TCP/IP over more than one interface could, in theory and also with most of today's TCP/IP implementations, forward IP datagrams. However, dedicated routers provide much more sophisticated routing than the minimum functions implemented by IP.

Because IP provides this basic routing function, the term "IP router," is often used. Other, older, terms for router are "IP gateway," "Internet gateway" and "gateway." The term *gateway* is now normally used for connections at a higher layer than the internetwork layer.

A router can be said to be *visible* to IP. That is, when a host sends an IP datagram to another host on a network connected by a router, it sends the datagram to the router and not directly to the target host.

Gateway   Interconnects networks at higher layers than bridges or routers. A gateway usually supports address mapping from one network to another, and may also provide transformation of the data between the environments to support end-to-end application connectivity. Gateways typically limit the interconnectivity of two networks to a subset of the application protocols supported on either one. For example, a VM host running TCP/IP may be used as an SMTP/RSCS mail gateway.

Note: The term "gateway," when used in this sense, is *not* synonymous with "IP gateway."

A gateway can be said to be *opaque* to IP. That is, a host cannot send an IP datagram through a gateway; it can only send it *to* a gateway. The higher-level protocol information carried by the datagrams is then passed on by the gateway using whatever networking architecture is used on the other side of the gateway.

Closely related to routers and gateways is the concept of a *firewall* or *firewall gateway*, which is used to restrict access from the Internet to a network or a group of networks controlled by an organization for security reasons. See 5.3, "Firewalls" on page 359 for more information on firewalls.

1.3 Finding Standards for TCP/IP and the Internet

TCP/IP has been popular with developers and users alike because of its inherent openness and perpetual renewal. The same holds true for the Internet as an open communications network. On the other hand, this openness could easily turn into a sword with two edges if it were not controlled in some way. Although there is no overall governing body to issue directives and regulations for the Internet — control is mostly based on mutual cooperation — the Internet Society (ISOC) serves as the standardizing body for the Internet community. It is organized and managed by the Internet Architecture Board (IAB).

The IAB itself relies on the Internet Engineering Task Force (IETF) for issuing new standards, and on the Internet Assigned Numbers Authority (IANA) for coordinating values shared among multiple protocols. The RFC Editor is responsible for reviewing and publishing new standards documents.

The IETF itself is governed by the Internet Engineering Steering Group (IESG) and is further organized in the form of Areas and Working Groups where new specifications are discussed and new standards are propsoed.

The Internet Standards Process, described in *RFC2026 — The Internet Standards Process - Revision 3*, is concerned with all protocols, procedures, and conventions that are used in or by the Internet, whether or not they are part of the TCP/IP protocol suite.

The overall goals of the Internet Standards Process are:

- Technical excellence

- Prior implementation and testing

- Clear, concise, and easily understood documentation

- Openness and fairness

- Timeliness

The process of standardization is summarized below:

- In order to have a new specification approved as a standard, applicants have to submit that specification to the IESG where it will be discussed and reviewed for technical merit and feasibility and also published as an Internet draft document. This should take no shorter than two weeks and no longer than six months.

- Once the IESG reaches a positive conclusion, it issues a last-call notification to allow the specification to be reviewed by the whole Internet community.

- After the final approval by the IESG, an Internet draft is recommended to the Internet Engineering Taskforce (IETF), another subsidiary of the IAB, for inclusion into the standards track and for publication as a Request for Comment (RFC; see 1.3.1, "Request For Comments (RFC)" on page 22).

- Once published as an RFC, a contribution may advance in status as described in 1.3.2, "Internet Standards" on page 24. It may also be revised over time or phased out when better solutions are found.

- If the IESG does not approve of a new specification after, of if a document has remained unchanged within, six months of submission, it will be removed from the Internet drafts directory.

1.3.1 Request For Comments (RFC)

The Internet protocol suite is still evolving through the mechanism of *Request For Comments* (RFC). New protocols (mostly application protocols) are being designed and implemented by researchers, and are brought to the attention of the Internet community in the form of an Internet draft (ID).[1] The largest source of IDs is the Internet Engineering Task Force (IETF) which is a subsidiary of the IAB. However, anyone may submit a memo proposed as an ID to the RFC Editor. There are a set of rules which RFC/ID authors must follow in order for an RFC to be accepted. These rules are themselves described in an RFC (RFC 2223) which also indicates how to submit a proposal for an RFC.

Once an RFC has been published, all revisions and replacements are published as new RFCs. A new RFC which revises or replaces an existing RFC is said to "update" or to "obsolete" that RFC. The existing RFC is said to be "updated by" or "obsoleted by" the new one. For example RFC 1542, which describes the BOOTP protocol, is a "second edition," being a revision of RFC 1532 and an amendment to RFC 951. RFC 1542 is therefore labelled like this: "Obsoletes RFC 1532; Updates RFC 951." Consequently, there is never any confusion over whether two people are referring to different versions of an RFC, since there is never more than one current version.

Some RFCs are described as *information documents* while others describe Internet protocols. The Internet Architecture Board (IAB) maintains a list of the RFCs that describe the protocol suite. Each of these is assigned a *state* and a *status*.

An Internet protocol can have one of the following states:

---

[1] Some of these protocols, particularly those dated April 1, can be described as impractical at best. For instance, RFC 1149 (dated 1990 April 1) describes the transmission of IP datagrams by carrier pigeon and RFC 1437 (dated 1993 April 1) describes the transmission of people by electronic mail.

Standard

The IAB has established this as an official protocol for the Internet. These are separated in two groups:

1. IP protocol and above, protocols that apply to the whole Internet.
2. Network-specific protocols, generally specifications of how to do IP on particular types of networks.

Draft standard

The IAB is actively considering this protocol as a possible standard protocol. Substantial and widespread testing and comments are desired. Comments and test results should be submitted to the IAB. There is a possibility that changes will be made in a draft protocol before it becomes a standard.

Proposed standard

These are protocol proposals that may be considered by the IAB for standardization in the future. Implementations and testing by several groups are desirable. Revision of the protocol is likely.

Experimental

A system should not implement an experimental protocol unless it is participating in the experiment and has coordinated its use of the protocol with the developer of the protocol.

Informational

Protocols developed by other standard organizations, or vendors, or that are for other reasons outside the purview of the IAB may be published as RFCs for the convenience of the Internet community as informational protocols. Such protocols may in some cases also be recommended for use on the Internet by the IAB.

Historic

These are protocols that are unlikely to ever become standards in the Internet either because they have been superseded by later developments or due to lack of interest.

Definitions of protocol status:

Required

A system must implement the required protocols.

Recommended

A system should implement the recommended protocol.

Elective

A system may or may not implement an elective protocol. The general notion is that if you are going to do something like this, you must do exactly this.

Limited use

These protocols are for use in limited circumstances. This may be because of their experimental state, specialized nature, limited functionality, or historic state.

Not recommended

These protocols are not recommended for general use. This may be because of their limited functionality, specialized nature, or experimental or historic state.

1.3.2 Internet Standards

Proposed standard, draft standard and standard protocols are described as being on the *Internet Standards Track*. When a protocol reaches the standard state it is assigned a standard number (STD). The purpose of STD numbers is to clearly indicate which RFCs describe Internet standards. STD numbers reference multiple RFCs when the specification of a standard is spread across multiple documents. Unlike RFCs, where the number refers to a specific document, STD numbers do not change when a standard is updated. STD numbers do not, however, have version numbers since all updates are made via RFCs and the RFC numbers are unique. Thus to clearly specify which version of a standard one is referring to, the standard number and all of the RFCs which it includes should be stated. For instance, the Domain Name System (DNS) is STD 13 and is described in RFCs 1034 and 1035. To reference the standard, a form like "STD-13/RFC1034/RFC1035" should be used.

For some standards track RFCs the status category does not always contain enough information to be useful. It is therefore supplemented, notably for routing protocols by an *applicability statement* which is given either in STD 1 or in a separate RFC.

References to the RFCs and to STD numbers will be made throughout this book, since they form the basis of all TCP/IP protocol implementations.

The following Internet standards are of particular importance:

STD 1 — Internet Official Protocol Standards

This standard gives the state and status of each Internet protocol or standard, and defines the meanings attributed to each different state or status. It is issued by the IAB approximately quarterly. At the time of writing this standard is in RFC 2400 (September 1998).

STD 2 — Assigned Internet Numbers

This standard lists currently assigned numbers and other protocol parameters in the Internet protocol suite. It is issued by the Internet Assigned Numbers Authority (IANA). The current edition at the time of writing is RFC1700 (October 1994).

STD 3 — Host Requirements

This standard defines the requirements for Internet host software (often by reference to the relevant RFCs). The standard comes in three parts: *RFC1122 — Requirements for Internet hosts – communications layer*, *RFC1123 — Requirements for Internet hosts – application and support*, and *RFC 2181 — Clarifications to the DNS Specification.*

STD 4 — Router Requirements

This standard defines the requirements for IPv4 Internet gateway (router) software. It is defined in *RFC 1812 — Requirements for IPv4 Routers.*

1.3.2.1 For Your Information (FYI)

A number of RFCs that are intended to be of wide interest to Internet users are classified as *For Your Information (FYI)* documents. They frequently contain introductory or other helpful information. Like STD numbers, an FYI number is not changed when a revised RFC is issued. Unlike STDs, FYIs correspond to a single RFC document. For example, *FYI 4 – FYI on Questions and Answers - Answers to Commonly asked "New Internet User" Questions* is currently in its fourth edition. The RFC numbers are 1177, 1206, 1325 and 1594.

1.3.2.2 Obtaining RFCs

RFC and ID documents are available publicly and online and may be best obtained from the IETF Web site:

```
http://www.ietf.org
```

1.3.3 Major Internet Protocols

To give an idea of the importance of the major protocols, we list some of them together with their current state and status and STD number where applicable in Table 1. The complete list can be found in *RFC2400 — Internet Official Protocol Standards.*

Protocol	Name	State	Status	STD
Table 1 (Page 1 of 2). Current State, Status and STD Numbers of Important Internet Protocols				
IP	Internet Protocol	Std.	Req.	5
ICMP	Internet Control Message Protocol	Std.	Req.	5
Legend: **State:** Std. = Standard; Draft = Draft Standard; Prop. = Proposed Standard; Info. = Informational; Hist. = Historic **Status:** Req. = Required; Rec. = Recommended; Ele. = Elective; Not = Not Recommended				

Table 1 (Page 2 of 2). *Current State, Status and STD Numbers of Important Internet Protocols*

Protocol	Name	State	Status	STD
UDP	User Datagram Protocol	Std.	Rec.	6
TCP	Transmission Control Protocol	Std.	Rec.	7
TELNET	TELNET Protocol	Std.	Rec.	8
FTP	File Transfer Protocol	Std.	Rec.	9
SMTP	Simple Mail Transfer Protocol	Std.	Rec.	10
MAIL	Format of Electronic Mail Messages	Std.	Rec.	11
DOMAIN	Domain Name System	Std.	Rec.	13
MIME	Multipurpose Internet Mail Extensions	Draft	Ele.	
SNMP	Simple Network Management Protocol	Std.	Rec.	15
SMI	Structure of Management Information	Std.	Rec.	16
MIB-II	Management Information Base-II	Std.	Rec.	17
NETBIOS	NetBIOS Services Protocol	Std.	Ele.	19
TFTP	Trivial File Transfer Protocol	Std.	Ele.	33
RIP	Routing Information Protocol	Hist.	Not	34
RIP2	Routing Information Protocol V2	Draft	Ele.	
ARP	Address Resolution Protocol	Std.	Ele.	37
RARP	Reverse Address Resolution Protocol	Std.	Ele.	38
BGP4	Border Gateway Protocol 3	Draft	Ele.	
PPP	Point-to-Point Protocol	Std.	Ele.	51
POP3	Post Office Protocol V3	Std.	Ele.	53
OSPF2	Open Shortest Path First Protocol V2	Std.	Ele.	54
BOOTP	Bootstrap Protocol	Draft	Rec.	
DHCP	Dynamic Host Configuration Protocol	Draft	Ele.	
IMAPV4	Interactive Mail Access Protocol V4	Prop.	Ele.	
GOPHER	The Internet Gopher Protocol	Info.		
SUN-NFS	Network File System Protocol	Info.		
IPV6	Internet Protocol Version 6	Prop.	Ele.	
HTTP-1.1	Hypertext Transfer Protocol 1.1	Prop.	Ele.	

Legend:
State: Std. = Standard; Draft = Draft Standard; Prop. = Proposed Standard; Info. = Informational; Hist. = Historic
Status: Req. = Required; Rec. = Recommended; Ele. = Elective; Not = Not Recommended

1.4 Future of the Internet

Trying to predict the future of the Internet is not an easy task. Few would have imagined even say, three years ago, the extent to which the Internet has now become a part of everyday life in business, homes and schools. There are a number of things, however, about which we can be fairly certain.

Bandwidth requirement will continue to increase at massive rates; not only is the number of Internet users growing rapidly, but the applications being used are becoming more advanced and therefore need more bandwidth. This is the reason why the number of core (backbone) service providers has grown from four in 1995 to around 48 today (whereas the number of Internet connection providers has grown only moderately). However, new technologies such as Dense Wave Division Multiplexing (DWDM) will help to get the most bandwidth from currently installed fiber.

Today it is possible to hear radio stations from almost any part of the globe via the Internet. Today this is at around AM quality. Soon FM-quality radio and video-on-demand will be driving the bandwidth requirement.

Many businesses have already completed an experimental period of Internet access and are moving towards using the Internet for serious business use both intra- and inter-company. This has been made possible by the rapid advances in TCP/IP security technologies made in only the last one to two years. In the not too distant future, the availability of private, secure high bandwidth networking from Internet providers may well make many companies question the feasibility of their current in-house wide area networks.

Today we already have Voice over IP technology. As this technology matures we are almost certain to see a sharing of bandwidth between voice and data across the Internet. This raises some interesting questions for phone companies. The cost to a user of an Internet connection between New York and Japan is the same as a connection within New York - not so a phone connection. This, and the fact that the Internet is deregulated, will raise many interesting questions in the years to come.

1.5 IBM and the Internet

To the casual observer of a decade or so ago, it may have appeared that IBM had little interest in the Internet or TCP/IP. It is true that for a long period of time, certain parts of IBM involved in the development and marketing of SNA networks and protocols did consider TCP/IP to be a competitor. In fact, IBM has been practically involved in the development of the Internet for a long time, supplying software and hardware to

NSFNET, for example. More importantly, IBM has long been involved in the various organizations, committees and task forces responsible for establishing open standards. IBM is currently represented on over 130 IETF Working Groups, helping to shape the future development of TCP/IP.

In March 1992, IBM introduced the *Networking Blueprint* (later expanded to become the Open Blueprint). The Open Blueprint is a framework, based on open and industry standards, for creating network solutions without concern for underlying networking components and services. It allows the incorporation of multiple network protocols (including TCP/IP and SNA) into a single network. For details on the Open Blueprint, please refer to the Open Blueprint homepage at:

`http://www.software.ibm.com/openblue`

1.5.1 The Network Computing Framework

Today, Network Computing, the Internet and TCP/IP are at the core of IBM's strategy. IBM has developed a model for designing business solutions in the network computing environment - the *Network Computing Framework for e-business* (NCF). NCF is based on an n-tier distributed environment where any number of tiers of application logic and business services are separated into components that communicate with each other across a network. In its most basic form, NCF can be depicted as a "logical" three-tier computing model, meaning that there is a logical, but not necessarily physical, separation of processes. This model is designed to support "thin clients" with high-function Web application and enterprise servers.

A prototypical NCF three-tier architecture consists of:

1. A client tier containing logic related to the presentation of information (that is, the graphical user interface) and requests to applications through a browser or Java applet.

2. Web application servers containing the business logic and processes that control the reading and writing of data.

3. Servers that provide the data storage and transactional applications used by the Web application server processes.

The application elements residing in these three logical tiers are connected through a set of industry-standard protocols, services, and software connectors.

1.5.1.1 NCF Architecture

The NCF architecture provides a full range of services for developing and deploying e-business applications. Because it is based on industry standards, NCF has the ability to plug-and-play multiple components provided by any vendor. The NCF architecture is shown graphically in Figure 6 on page 29.

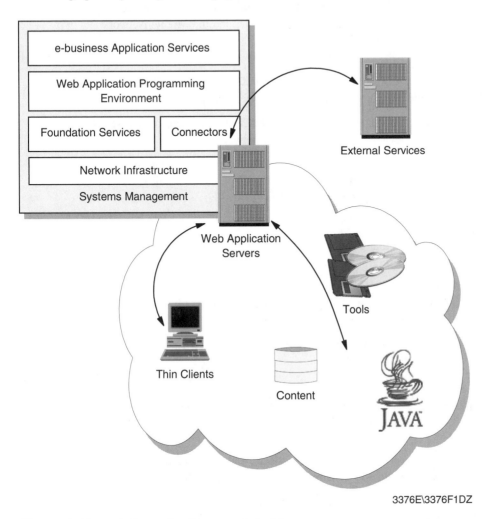

Figure 6. Network Computing Framework Architecture

The NCF architecture is composed of the following key elements:

Clients

NCF clients are "thin clients", meaning that little or no application logic is executed on the client and therefore relatively little software is required to be installed on the client. In this model, applications are managed on the server and dynamically downloaded "on-demand" to requesting clients. As such, the client portions of new applications should be implemented in HTML, Dynamic HTML, XML, and Java applets. NCF supports a broad range of fixed, mobile, and "Tier 0" clients from IBM and other industry leaders, based on industry initiatives such as the Network Computer Profile, and the Mobile Network Computer Reference Specification.

Network infrastructure

The NCF network infrastructure provides a platform for the entire framework. It includes the following services, all based on open standards:

- TCP/IP and network services, such as DHCP, that dynamically assign IP addresses as devices enter and leave the network.

- Security services based on public key technology that support user identification and authentication, access control, confidentiality, data integrity, and non-repudiation of transactions.

- Directory services that locate users, services, and resources in the network.

- Mobile services that provide access to valuable corporate data to the nomadic computing user.

- Client management services that support the setup, customization, and management of network computers, managed PCs, and in the future Tier 0 devices such as smartcards, digital cellphones, etc.

- File and print services that are accessed and managed via a standard Web browser interface.

Foundation Services

NCF foundation services provide the core functionality required to develop and support the business logic of e-business applications running on the Web application server. It includes the following services:

- An HTTP server that coordinates, collects, and assembles Web pages composed of static and dynamic content and delivers them to NCF clients.

- Mail and community services that provide e-mail messaging, calendaring and group scheduling, chat, and newsgroup discussions.

- Groupware services that provide a rich shared virtual workspace and support the coordination of business workflow processes.

- Database services that integrate the features and functions of an object-relational database with those of the Web application server.

- Transaction services that extend the Web application server by providing a highly available, robust, expandable and secure transactional application execution environment.

- Messaging services that provide robust, asynchronous communication and message brokering facilities that support a publish/subscribe model of communication and message transformations.

Connectors

The bulk of today's critical data and application (especially transactional) programs reside on and use existing enterprise systems. NCF connectors allow existing data and application programs to work together with Web clients and servers, seamlessly linking the strength of the Internet with the strength of the enterprise. At the core, connectors are software that provide linkage between the NCF Web server programming model environment and systems, applications, and services that are reached through the use of application specific protocols.

Web Application Programming Environment

The NCF Web application programming environment, based on Java servlets, Enterprise Java services and Enterprise JavaBean components, provides an environment for writing dynamic, transactional, secure business applications on Web application servers. Services are provided that promote separation of business and presentation logic enabling applications to dynamically adapt and tailor content based on user interests and client device.

e-business Application Services

NCF e-business application services are building blocks that facilitate the creation of e-business solutions. They are higher level application-oriented components that conform to the NCF programming model. They build on and extend the underlying NCF infrastructure and foundation services with functions required for specific types of applications, for example, e-commerce applications. As a result, e-business solutions can be developed faster with higher quality. Examples of NCF e-business application services include payment services, catalog services, and order management services.

Systems Management

Within an enterprise, NCF systems management services provide the core functionality that supports end-to-end management across networks, systems, middleware and applications. NCF provides the tools and services that support management of the complete lifecycle of an application from installation and configuration, to the monitoring of its operational characteristics such as availability and security, to the controlled update of changes. Across multiple enterprises, NCF provides a collaborative management approach for establishing and following procedures to share information and coordinate problem resolution with business partners. This collaborative approach includes policy management, data repository, scheduling and report generation.

Development Tools

NCF provides a broad range of tools to enable creation, deployment and management of e-business applications for Internet, extranet and intranet environments. It also supports integrating third-party tools into the development process. NCF supports the different skill sets involved in developing Web applications, providing tools that target specific skill sets, and facilitates collaboration among members of the development team.

1.5.1.2 API and Protocol Support

The following table summarizes the standard protocols and APIs supported by each component of the NCF architecture. While IBM will provide a complete and competitive set of products that implement the framework, other implementations can also work within it. Thus, customers can choose from providers that support these open standards. Likewise, solution providers can build their solutions using a variety of software products sourced from different vendors.

Table 2 (Page 1 of 2). NCF - API and Protocol Support		
Service	**Protocol Standard**	**API**
Network Infrastructure		
Directory	LDAP	JNDI
Security	CDSA, SSL, IPsec, x.509v3 certificates	JSSL, JCE
Network	TCP/IP	JDK java.net
File	AFS/DFS	JDK java.io
Print	IPP	JDK java.2d, JNPAPI
Mobile	MNCRP	n/a
Foundation Services		
Mail and Community	SMTP, POP3, IMAP4, IRC, NNTP, FTP, iCalendar	Java Notes API
Groupware	n/a	Java Notes API
Data	ODBC, DRDA	JDBC, JSQL, EJB
Transactions	CORBA OTS/IIOP	EJB, JTS
Message Queuing	BMQS	JMS
Web Application Programming Environment		
Web Server	HTTP, HTML, XML	Servlets, Server-side-includes
Web Browser	HTTP, HTML, XML	Applets, DOM Level 1
Component Model	CORBA IIOP	JavaBeans

Table 2 (Page 2 of 2). NCF - API and Protocol Support

Service	Protocol Standard	API
Business Component Model	CORBA IIOP	EJB, RMI
Scripting	ECMAScript	JSP (Java Server Pages)
Systems Management		
Distribution (Install/Config)	DMTF-CIM	AMS
Operations (Fix/Change)	DMTF-CIM	AMS
Performance (Monitor)	SNMP	ARM
Events (Alarms)	SNMP	TEC
Development Tools		
Authoring and Versioning	WebDAV	n/a

For a discussion of some of the protocols mentioned in Table 2 on page 32 and IBM e-business solutions based upon them, please refer to Chapter 8, "Internet Protocols and Applications" on page 555.

For further details on NCF, please refer to the following IBM redbooks:

- *SG24-5296 IBM Network Computing Framework for e-business Guide*
- *SG24-5220 Internet Security in the Network Computing Framework*
- *SG24-5205 Publishing Tools in the Network Computing Framework*
- *SG24-2119 Network Computing Framework Component Guide*

or refer to the Network Computing Framework home page at:

`http://www.software.ibm.com/ebusiness`

Chapter 2. Internetworking and Transport Layer Protocols

This chapter provides an overview of the most important and common protocols of the TCP/IP internetwork and transport layers, which are the following:

- Internet Protocol (IP)

- Internet Control Message Protocol (ICMP)

- Address Resolution Protocol (ARP)

- Reverse Address Resolution Protocol (RARP)

- User Datagram Protocol (UDP)

- Transmission Control Protocol (TCP)

These protocols perform datagram addressing, routing and delivery, provide connection-oriented and connectionless services to applications, and resolve internetwork layer addresses to network interface layer addresses and vice versa.

2.1 Internet Protocol (IP)

IP is a *standard protocol* with STD number 5. That standard also includes ICMP (see 2.2, "Internet Control Message Protocol (ICMP)" on page 74) and IGMP (see 9.2, "Internet Group Management Protocol (IGMP)" on page 596). Its status is *required*.

The current IP specification can be found in RFCs 791, 950, 919 and 922, with updates in RFC 1349.

IP is the protocol that hides the underlying physical network by creating a *virtual network* view. It is an unreliable, best-effort and connectionless packet delivery protocol. Note that best-effort means that the packets sent by IP may be lost, out of order, or even duplicated, but IP will not handle these situations. It is up to the higher layer protocols to deal with these situations.

One of the reasons for using a connectionless network protocol was to minimize the dependency on specific computing centers that used hierarchical connection-oriented networks. The DoD intended to deploy a network that would still be operational if parts of the country were destroyed. During earthquakes, this has been proved to be true for the Internet.

2.1.1 IP Addressing

IP addresses are represented by a 32-bit unsigned binary value which is usually expressed in a dotted decimal format. For example, 9.167.5.8 is a valid Internet address. The numeric form is used by the IP software. The mapping between the IP address and an easier-to-read symbolic name, for example myhost.ibm.com, is done by the *Domain Name System* discussed in 4.2, "Domain Name System (DNS)" on page 194. We first look at the numeric form, which is called the IP address.

2.1.1.1 The IP Address

The standards for IP addresses are described in *RFC 1166 – Internet Numbers*.

To be able to identify a host on the Internet, each host is assigned an address, the *IP address*, or *Internet Address*. When the host is attached to more than one network, it is called *multi-homed* and it has one IP address for each network interface. The IP address consists of a pair of numbers:

IP address = <network number><host number>

The *network number* part of the IP address is centrally administered by the Internet Network Information Center (the InterNIC) and is unique throughout the Internet.[2]

IP addresses are 32-bit numbers usually represented in a *dotted decimal* form (as the decimal representation of four 8-bit values concatenated with dots). For example, *128.2.7.9* is an IP address with 128.2 being the network number and 7.9 being the host number. The rules used to divide an IP address into its network and host parts are explained below.

The binary format of the IP address 128.2.7.9 is:

10000000 00000010 00000111 00001001

IP addresses are used by the IP protocol to uniquely identify a host on the Internet. (Strictly speaking, an IP address identifies an interface that is capable of sending and receiving IP datagrams, and one system can have multiple such interfaces. However, both hosts and routers must have at least one IP address, so this simplified definition is acceptable.) IP datagrams (the basic data packets exchanged between hosts) are transmitted by a physical network attached to the host and each IP datagram contains a *source IP address* and a *destination IP address*. To send a datagram to a certain IP destination, the target IP address must be translated or mapped to a physical address.

---

[2] Prior to 1993, the NIC function was performed by the DDN NIC (nic.ddn.mil). See RFC 1400 for more information about this transition.

This may require transmissions on the network to find out the destination's physical network address. (For example, on LANs the Address Resolution Protocol, discussed in 2.4, "Address Resolution Protocol (ARP)" on page 87, is used to translate IP addresses to physical MAC addresses.).

The first bits of the IP address specify how the rest of the address should be separated into its network and host part.

The terms *network address* and *netID* are sometimes used instead of network number, but the formal term, used in RFC 1166, is network number. Similarly, the terms *host address* and *hostID* are sometimes used instead of host number.

There are five classes of IP addresses. These are shown in Figure 7.

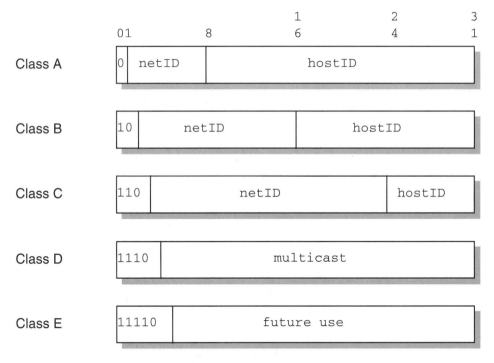

Figure 7. IP - Assigned Classes of IP Addresses

- Class A addresses use 7 bits for the <network> and 24 bits for the <host> portion of the IP address. That allows for 2^7-2 (126) networks with $2^{24}-2$ (16777214) hosts each; a total of over 2 billion addresses.

- Class B addresses use 14 bits for the <network> and 16 bits for the <host> portion of the IP address. That allows for $2^{14}-2$ (16382) networks with $2^{16}-2$ (65534) hosts each; a total of over 1 billion addresses.

- Class C addresses use 21 bits for the <network> and 8 bits for the <host> portion of the IP address. That allows for $2^{21}-2$ (2097150) networks with $2^{8}-2$ (254) hosts each; a total of over half a billion addresses.

- Class D addresses are reserved for multicasting (a sort of broadcasting, but in a limited area, and only to hosts using the same class D address).

- Class E addresses are reserved for future use.

It is clear that a Class A address will only be assigned to networks with a huge number of hosts, and that class C addresses are suitable for networks with a small number of hosts. However, this means that medium-sized networks (those with more than 254 hosts or where there is an expectation that there may be more than 254 hosts in the future) must use Class B addresses. The number of small- to medium-sized networks has been growing very rapidly in the last few years and it was feared that, if this growth had been allowed to continue unabated, all of the available Class B network addresses would have been used by the mid-1990s. This is termed the IP Address Exhaustion problem. The problem and how it is being addressed are discussed in 2.1.5, "The IP Address Exhaustion Problem" on page 54.

One point to note about the split of an IP address into two parts is that this split also splits the responsibility for selecting the IP address into two parts. The network number is assigned by the InterNIC, and the host number by the authority which controls the network. As we shall see in the next section, the host number can be further subdivided: this division is controlled by the authority which owns the network, and *not* by the InterNIC.

2.1.1.2 Special IP Addresses

Any component of an IP address with a value all bits 0 or all bits 1 has a special meaning:

all bits 0

Stands for *this*: this host (IP address with <host address>=0) or this network (IP address with <network address>=0). When a host wants to communicate over a network, but does not yet know the network IP address, it may send packets with <network address>=0. Other hosts on the network will interpret the address as meaning *this network*. Their reply will contain the fully qualified network address, which the sender will record for future use.

all bits 1

Stands for *all*: all networks or all hosts. For example, the following means all hosts on network 128.2 (class B address):

128.2.255.255

This is called a directed broadcast address because it contains both a valid <network address> and a broadcast <host address>.

Loopback

The class A network 127.0.0.0 is defined as the loopback network. Addresses from that network are assigned to interfaces that process data inside the local system and never access a physical network (loopback interfaces).

2.1.2 IP Subnets

Due to the explosive growth of the Internet, the principle of assigned IP addresses became too inflexible to allow easy changes to local network configurations. Those changes might occur when:

- A new type of physical network is installed at a location.
- Growth of the number of hosts requires splitting the local network into two or more separate networks.
- Growing distances require splitting a network into smaller networks, with gateways between them.

To avoid having to request additional IP network addresses in these cases, the concept of subnets was introduced. The assignment of subnets can be done locally, as the whole network still appears to be one IP network to the outside world.

The host number part of the IP address is subdivided again into a network number and a host number. This second network is termed a *subnetwork* or *subnet*. The main network now consists of a number of subnets and the IP address is interpreted as:

<network number><subnet number><host number>

The combination of the subnet number and the host number is often termed the *local address* or the *local part*. *Subnetting* is implemented in a way that is transparent to remote networks. A host within a network that has subnets is aware of the subnetting but a host in a different network is not; it still regards the local part of the IP address as a host number.

The division of the local part of the IP address into subnet number and host number parts can be chosen freely by the local administrator; any bits in the local part can be used to form the subnet. The division is done using a *subnet mask* which is a 32 bit number. Zero bits in the subnet mask indicate bit positions ascribed to the host number, and ones indicate bit positions ascribed to the subnet number. The bit positions in the subnet mask belonging to the network number are set to ones but are not used. Subnet masks are usually written in dotted decimal form, like IP addresses.

The special treatment of all bits zero and all bits one applies to each of the three parts of a subnetted IP address just as it does to both parts of an IP address that has not been subnetted (see 2.1.1.2, "Special IP Addresses" on page 38). For example, a subnetted Class B network, which has a 16-bit local part, could use one of the following schemes:

- The first byte is the subnet number; the second byte is the host number. This gives us 2^8-2 (254 with the values 0 and 255 being reserved) possible subnets, each having up to 2^8-2 (254) hosts. The subnet mask is 255.255.255.0.

- The first 12 bits are used for the subnet number and the last four for the host number. This gives us 2^{12}-2 (4094) possible subnets but only 2^4-2 (14) hosts per subnet. The subnet mask is 255.255.255.240.

  There are many other possibilities. In fact, the number of subnets and hosts and future requirements should be taken into consideration before defining a subnet. In the above example, for a subnetted Class B network, there are 16 bits left for the subnet number and the host number fields. The administrator has the choice of defining either a larger number of subnets with a small number of hosts in each, or a smaller number of subnets with many hosts.

While the administrator is completely free to assign the subnet part of the local address in any legal fashion, the objective is to assign a *number* of bits to the subnet number and the remainder to the local address. Therefore, it is normal to use a contiguous block of bits at the beginning of the local address part for the subnet number because this makes the addresses more readable. (This is particularly true when the subnet occupies 8 or 16 bits.) With this approach, either of the subnet masks above are "good" masks, but masks such as 255.255.252.252 and 255.255.255.15 are not. (In fact, hardly any TCP/IP implementation supports non-contiguous subnet masks, and their use is commonly discouraged, especially in CIDR environments that would become non-functional by choosing non-conventional subnet masks or network prefixes.)

2.1.2.1 Types of Subnetting

There are two types of subnetting: static and variable length. Variable length is the more flexible of the two. Which type of subnetting is available depends upon the routing protocol being used; native IP routing supports only static subnetting, as does the widely used RIP protocol. However, RIP Version 2 supports variable length subnetting as well. See 3.3.1, "Routing Information Protocol (RIP)" on page 138 for a description of RIP and RIP2. Chapter 3, "Routing Protocols" on page 123 discusses routing protocols in detail.

Static Subnetting: Static subnetting means that all subnets in the subnetted network use the same subnet mask. This is simple to implement and easy to maintain, but it implies wasted address space for small networks. For example, a network of four hosts that uses a subnet mask of 255.255.255.0 wastes 250 IP addresses. It also makes the network more difficult to reorganize with a new subnet mask. All hosts and routers are required to support static subnetting.

Variable Length Subnetting: When variable length subnetting is used, the subnets that make up the network can use different subnet masks. A small subnet with only a few hosts needs a subnet mask that accommodates only these few hosts. A subnet with many hosts attached may need a different subnet mask to accommodate the large number of hosts. The possibility to assign subnet masks according to the needs of the individual subnets will help conserve network addresses. Also, a subnet can be split into two parts by adding another bit to the subnet mask. Other subnets in the network are unaffected by the change. Variable length subnetting allows you to divide the network so that it is possible to define adequate hosts for each subnet by changing the subnet mask for each network. This can be achieved by configuring the routers accordingly. Please note that not every host and router supports variable length subnetting. With static subnetting each subnet has the same number of hosts. If it is required to have different numbers of hosts for each network, then variable length subnetting should be used.

Only networks of the size needed will be allocated and routing problems will be solved by isolating networks with routers that support variable subnetting. A host that does not support this kind of subnetting would have to route to a router that supports variable subnetting.

Mixing Static and Variable Length Subnetting: At first sight, it appears that the presence of a host that only supports static subnetting would prevent variable length subnetting from being used anywhere in the network. Fortunately this is not the case. Provided that the routers between subnets with different subnet masks are using variable length subnetting, the routing protocols employed are able to hide the difference between subnet masks from the hosts in a subnet. Hosts can continue to use basic IP routing and offload all of the complexities of the subnetting to dedicated routers.

2.1.2.2 A Static Subnetting Example

Recall that an IP address consists of the pair <network address><host address>. For example, let us take a class A network; the address format is shown in Figure 8 on page 42:

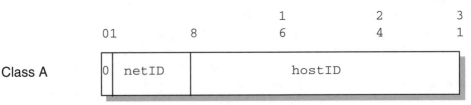

Figure 8. IP - Class A Address without Subnets

Let us use the following IP address:

```
00001001 01000011 00100110 00000001      a 32-bit address
    9        67       38       1         decimal notation (9.67.38.1)

       9.67.38.1          is an IP address  (class A)  having

       9                  as the <network address>
          67.38.1         as the <host address>
```

Subnets are an extension to this by considering a part of the <host address> to be a subnetwork address. IP addresses are then interpreted as <network address><subnetwork address><host address>.

For example, you may wish to choose the bits from 8 to 25 of a class A IP address to indicate the subnet addresses, and the bits from 26 to 31 to indicate the actual host addresses. Figure 9 shows the subnetted address that has thus been derived from the original class A address:

Class A
Subnet

```
                          1           2           3
01              8         6           4           1
 ┌──┬──────────┬────────────────────────┬──────┐
 │0 │ netID    │ subnet number          │ host │
 │  │          │                        │ ID   │
 └──┴──────────┴────────────────────────┴──────┘
```

Figure 9. IP - Class A Address with Subnet Mask and Subnet Address

We normally use a bit mask, known as the subnet mask, to identify which bits of the original host address field should indicate the subnet number. In the above example, the subnet mask is 255.255.255.192 in decimal notation (or 11111111 11111111

11111111 11000000 in bit notation). Note that, by convention, the <network address> is masked as well.

For each of these subnet values, only 2^{18}-2 addresses (from 1 to 262143) are valid because of the all bits 0 and all bits 1 number restrictions. This split will therefore give 262142 subnets each with a maximum of 2^6-2 or 62 hosts.

You will notice that the value applied to the subnet number takes the value of the full byte with non-significant bits being set to zero. For example, the hexadecimal value 01 in this subnet mask assumes an 8-bit value 01000000 and gives a subnet value of 64 and not 1 as it might seem.

Applying this mask to our sample class A address 9.67.38.1 would break the address down as follows:

```
00001001 01000011 00100110 00000001 = 9.67.38.1 (class A address)
11111111 11111111 11111111 11------   255.255.255.192 (subnet mask)
==================================== logical_AND
00001001 01000011 00100110 00------ = 9.67.38  (subnet base address)
```

This leaves a host address of:

```
-------- -------- -------- --000001 = 1         (host address)
```

IP will recognize all host addresses as being on the local network for which the logical_AND operation described above produces the same result. This is important for routing IP datagrams in subnet environments (see 2.1.3, "IP Routing" on page 45).

Note that the actual subnet number would be:

```
-------- 01000011 00100110 00------ = 68760     (subnet number)
```

You will notice that the subnet number shown above is a relative number. That is, it is the 68760th subnet of network 9 with the given subnet mask. This number bears no resemblance to the actual IP address that this host has been assigned (9.67.38.1) and has no meaning in terms of IP routing.

The division of the original <host address> part into <subnet> and <host> parts can be chosen freely by the local administrator, except that the values of all zeroes and all ones in the <subnet> field are reserved for special addresses.

Note: Because the range of available IP addresses is decreasing rapidly, many routers do support the use of all zeroes and all ones in the <subnet> field, though this is not coherent with the standards.

2.1.2.3 A Variable Length Subnetting Example

Consider a corporation that was assigned a Class C network 165.214.32.0, and it has the requirement to split this address range into five separate networks. The required number of hosts for each subnet are following:

- 1. Subnet: 50 hosts

- 2. Subnet: 50 hosts

- 3. Subnet: 50 hosts

- 4. Subnet: 30 hosts

- 5. Subnet: 30 hosts

This cannot be achieved by using static subnetting. For this case, the static subnetting can only divide the network into four subnets with 64 hosts each or eight subnet with 32 hosts each. This method would not meet the requirement.

To be able to divide the network into five subnets, multiple masks should be defined. Using a mask of 255.255.255.192, the network will be divided into four subnets with 64 hosts each. After that, the last subnet can be further divided into two subnets with 32 hosts each by using a mask of 255.255.255.224. There will be three subnets with 64 hosts each and two subnets with 32 hosts each. This would meet the requirements.

2.1.2.4 Obtaining a Subnet Mask

Usually, hosts will store the subnet mask to be used in a configuration file. However, sometimes this cannot be done, as for example in the case of a diskless workstation. The ICMP protocol includes two messages, address mask request and address mask reply, that allow hosts to obtain the correct subnet mask from a server. See 2.2.1.10, "Address Mask Request (17) and Address Mask Reply (18)" on page 85 for more information.

2.1.2.5 Addressing Routers and Multi-homed Hosts

Whenever a host has a physical connection to multiple networks or subnets, it is described as being *multi-homed*. All routers are multi-homed since their purpose is to join networks or subnets. A multi-homed host always has different IP addresses associated with each network adapter, since each adapter is in a different subnet or network.

2.1.3 IP Routing

An important function of the IP layer is *IP routing*. It provides the basic mechanism for routers to interconnect different physical networks. This means that a host can function as a normal host and a router simultaneously.

A basic router of this type is referred to as a *router with partial routing information*, because the router only has information about four kinds of destinations:

- Hosts that are directly attached to one of the physical networks to which the router is attached

- Hosts or networks for which the router has been given explicit definitions

- Hosts or networks for which the router has received an ICMP redirect message

- A default destination for everything else

The last two items allow a basic router to begin with a very limited amount of information and to increase its information because a more sophisticated router will issue an ICMP redirect message if it receives a datagram and it knows of a better router on the same network for the sender to use. This process is repeated each time a basic router of this type is restarted.

Additional protocols are needed to implement a full-function router that can exchange information with other routers in remote network. Such routers are essential except in small networks. The protocols they use are discussed in Chapter 3, "Routing Protocols" on page 123.

There are two types of IP routing: direct and indirect.

2.1.3.1 Direct Routing

If the destination host is attached to a physical network to which the source host is also attached, an IP datagram can be sent directly, simply by encapsulating the IP datagram in the physical network frame. This is called direct delivery and is referred to as direct routing.

2.1.3.2 Indirect Routing

Indirect routing occurs when the destination host is not on a network directly attached to the source host. The only way to reach the destination is via one or more IP gateways. (Note that in TCP/IP terminology, the terms gateway and router are used interchangeably for a system that actually performs the duties of a router.) The address of the first of these gateways (the first hop) is called an indirect route in the context of the IP routing algorithm. The address of the first gateway is the only information needed by the source host.

In some cases there are multiple subnets defined on the same network. Even if the destination host is on the same network with the source host, if the they are on different subnets, then indirect routing is used. Thus, there is a need for a router that forwards the traffic between subnets.

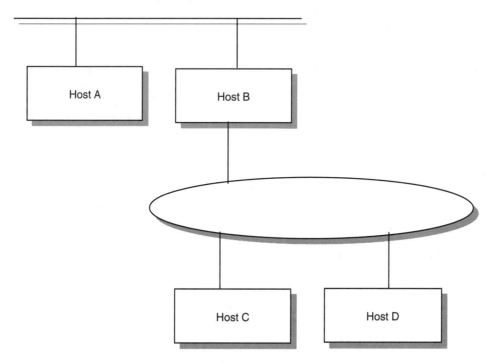

Figure 10. IP - Direct and Indirect Routes. (Host C has a *direct* route to hosts B and D, and an *indirect* route to host A via gateway B.)

2.1.3.3 IP Routing Table

The determination of available direct routes is derived from the list of local interfaces available to IP and is composed by IP automatically at initialization. A list of networks and associated gateways (indirect routes) needs to be configured to be used with IP routing if required. Each host keeps the set of mappings between the following:

- Destination IP network address(es)
- Route(s) to next gateway(s)

These are stored in a table called the IP routing table. Three types of mappings can be found in this table:

1. The direct routes, for locally attached networks

2. The indirect routes, for networks reachable via one or more gateways

3. The default route, which contains the (direct or indirect) route to be used in case the destination IP network is not found in the mappings of type 1 and 2 above

See the network in Figure 11 for an example configuration.

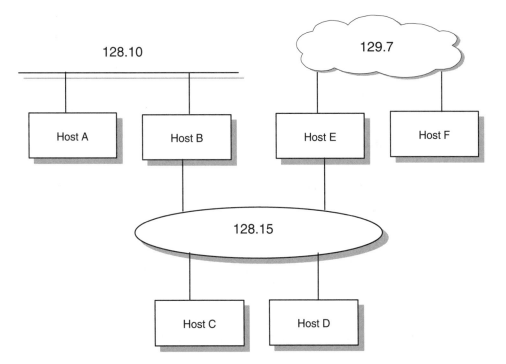

Figure 11. *IP - Routing Table Scenario*

The routing table of host D might contain the following (symbolic) entries:

```
destination      router    interface

   129.7.0.0     E         lan0
   128.15.0.0    D         lan0
   128.10.0.0    B         lan0
   default       B         lan0
   127.0.0.1     loopback  lo
```

Figure 12. IP - Routing Table Example 1

The routing table of host F might contain the following (symbolic) entries:

```
destination      router    interface

   129.7.0.0     F         wan0
   default       E         wan0
   127.0.0.1     loopback  lo
```

Figure 13. IP - Routing Table Example 2

2.1.3.4 IP Routing Algorithm

IP uses a unique algorithm to route an IP datagram, called the IP routing algorithm. To send an IP datagram on the network, the general IP routing algorithm has the following form:

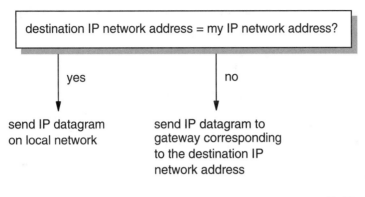

Figure 14. IP - IP Routing without Subnets

To be able to differentiate between subnets, the IP routing algorithm changes and has the following form:

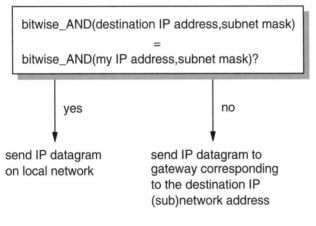

Figure 15. IP - IP Routing with Subnets

Some implications of this algorithm are:

- It is a change to the general IP algorithm. Therefore, to be able to operate this way, the particular gateway must contain the new algorithm. Some implementations may still use the general algorithm, and will not function within a subnetted network, although they can still communicate with hosts in other networks that are subnetted.

- As IP routing is used in all of the hosts (and not just the routers), all of the hosts in the subnet must have:

  1. An IP routing algorithm that supports subnetting.
  2. The same subnet mask (unless subnets are formed within the subnet).

- If the IP implementation on any of the hosts does not support subnetting, that host will be able to communicate with any host in its own subnet but not with any machine on another subnet within the same network. This is because the host sees only one IP network and its routing cannot differentiate between an IP datagram directed to a host on the local subnet and a datagram that should be sent via a router to a different subnet.

In case one or more hosts do not support subnetting, an alternative way to achieve the same goal exists in the form of *proxy-ARP*, which doesn't require any changes to the IP routing algorithm for single-homed hosts, but does require changes on routers between subnets in the network. This is explained in more detail in 2.4.4, "Proxy-ARP or Transparent Subnetting" on page 92.

The entire IP routing algorithm is illustrated in the figure below, including support of subnets:

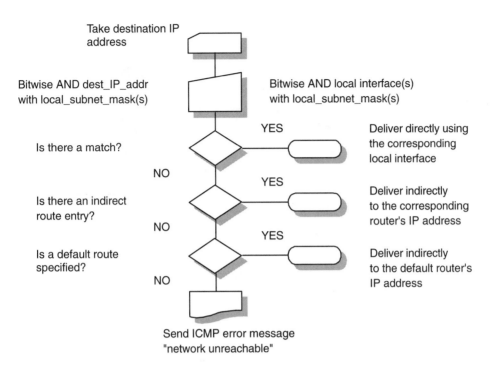

Take destination IP address

Bitwise AND dest_IP_addr with local_subnet_mask(s)

Bitwise AND local interface(s) with local_subnet_mask(s)

Is there a match?

YES — Deliver directly using the corresponding local interface

NO

Is there an indirect route entry?

YES — Deliver indirectly to the corresponding router's IP address

NO

Is a default route specified?

YES — Deliver indirectly to the default router's IP address

NO

Send ICMP error message "network unreachable"

Figure 16. *IP - Routing Algorithm (with Subnets)*

Notes:

1. This is an iterative process. It is applied by every host handling a datagram, except for the host to which the datagram is finally delivered.

2. Routing tables and the routing algorithm are local to any host in an IP network. In order to be able to forward IP datagrams on behalf of other hosts, routers need to exchange their routing table information with other routers in the network. This is done using special routing protocols, some of which are discussed in Chapter 3, "Routing Protocols" on page 123.

2.1.4 Methods of Delivery - Unicast, Broadcast, Multicast and Anycast

The majority of IP addresses refer to a single recipient, called *unicast* addresses. Unicast connections are one-to-one connections. Additionally, there are three special types of IP addresses that are used for addressing multiple recipients: broadcast addresses, multicast addresses and anycast addresses. As you see in Figure 17 on page 52, a broadcast serves all, multicast only some and anycast only one specific availbale host.

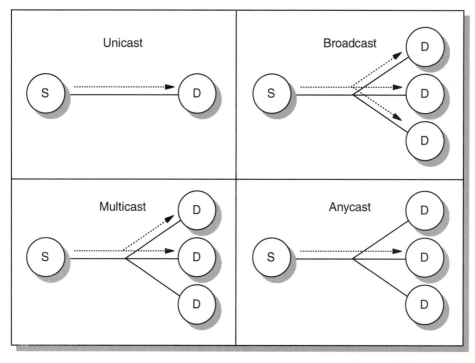

Figure 17. *IP - Packet Delivery Modes*

Any protocol that is *connectionless* can send broadcast, multicast or anycast messages as well as unicast messages. A protocol that is *connection-oriented* can only use unicast addresses because the connection exists between a specific pair of hosts.

2.1.4.1 Broadcasting

There are a number of addresses that are used for IP broadcasting. All use the convention that all-bits 1 indicates all. Broadcast addresses are never valid as source addresses, only as destination addresses. The different types of broadcast addresses are listed here:

Limited Broadcast Address

> The address 255.255.255.255 (all bits 1 in all parts of the IP address) is used on networks that support broadcasting, such as LANs, and it refers to all hosts on the subnet. It does not require the host to know any IP configuration information at all. All hosts on the local network will recognize the address, but routers will never forward it.

There is one exception to this rule, called *BOOTP forwarding*. The BOOTP protocol uses the limited broadcast address to allow a diskless workstation to contact a boot server. BOOTP forwarding is a configuration option available on some routers, including the IBM 2210 Nways Multiprotocol Router and the IBM 2216 Nways Multiaccess Connector to make an exception for UDP datagrams for ports 67 (used by the BOOTP protocol). Without this facility, a separate BOOTP server would be required on each subnet. However, this is not simple forwarding because the router also plays a part in the BOOTP protocol. See 7.1, "Bootstrap Protocol (BOOTP)" on page 511 for more information about BOOTP forwarding and 2.7, "User Datagram Protocol (UDP)" on page 97 for an explanation of UDP ports.

Network-Directed Broadcast Address

If the network number is a valid network number, the network is not subnetted and the host number is all ones (for example, 128.2.255.255), then the address refers to all hosts on the specified network. Routers should forward these broadcast messages unless configured otherwise. This is used in ARP requests (see 2.4, "Address Resolution Protocol (ARP)" on page 87) on unsubnetted networks.

Subnet-Directed Broadcast Address

If the network number is a valid network number, the subnet number is a valid subnet number and the host number is all ones, then the address refers to all hosts on the specified subnet. Since the sender's subnet and the target subnet may have different subnet mask, the sender must somehow find out the subnet mask in use at the target. The actual broadcast is performed by the router that receives the datagram into the subnet.

All-Subnets-Directed Broadcast Address

If the network number is a valid network number, the network is subnetted and the local part is all ones (for example, 128.2.255.255), then the address refers to all hosts on all subnets in the specified network. In principle routers may propagate broadcasts for all subnets but are not required to do so. In practice, they do not; there are few circumstances where such a broadcast would be desirable, and it can lead to problems, particularly if a host has been incorrectly configured with no subnet mask. Consider the wasted resource involved if a host 9.180.214.114 in the subnetted Class A network 9 thought that it was not subnetted and used 9.255.255.255 as a local broadcast address instead of 9.180.214.255 and all of the routers in the network respected the request to forward the request to all clients.

If routers do respect all-subnets-directed broadcast address, they use an algorithm called *reverse path forwarding* to prevent the broadcast messages from multiplying out of control. See RFC 922 for more details on this algorithm.

2.1.4.2 Multicasting

Broadcasting has a major disadvantage; its lack of selectivity. If an IP datagram is broadcast to a subnet, every host on the subnet will receive it, and have to process it to determine whether the target protocol is active. If it is not, the IP datagram is discarded. Multicasting avoids this overhead by using groups of IP addresses.

Each group is represented by a 28-bit number, which is included in a Class D address. So *multicast group addresses* are IP addresses in the range 224.0.0.0 to 239.255.255.255. For each multicast address there is a set of zero or more hosts that are listening to it. This set is called the *host group*. There is no requirement for any host to be a member of a group to send to that group. Packets that are sent to a multicast address, are forwarded only to the members of the corresponding host group. So multicast makes it possible to establish a one to some connection. See 9.1, "Multicasting" on page 593 for detailed information about IP multicasting.

2.1.4.3 Anycasting

Sometimes, the same IP services are provided by different hosts. For example, a user wants to download a file via FTP and the file is available on different FTP servers. But the user doesn't know which connection is the fastest. So it is possible that the connection to the server from which he or she downloads the file is slower than the other ones.

Hosts that provide the same IP service could serve an anycast address to other hosts that may require the service. The connection is made to the first host in the anycast address group that responds. This process guarantees that the service is provided by the host that has the best connection to the receiver.

The anycast service will be part of IPV6. Please see Anycast Address on page 475 for further details about anycasting.

2.1.5 The IP Address Exhaustion Problem

The number of networks on the Internet has been approximately doubling annually for a number of years. However, the usage of the Class A, B and C networks differs greatly. Nearly all of the new networks assigned in the late 1980s were Class B, and in 1990 it became apparent that if this trend continued, the last Class B network number would be assigned during 1994. On the other hand, Class C networks were hardly being used.

The reason for this trend was that most potential users found a Class B network to be large enough for their anticipated needs, since it accommodates up to 65534 hosts, whereas a class C network, with a maximum of 254 hosts, severely restricts the potential growth of even a small initial network. Furthermore, most of the class B networks being assigned were small ones. There are relatively few networks that would need as many as 65,534 host addresses, but very few for which 254 hosts would be an adequate limit. In summary, although the Class A, Class B and Class C divisions of the IP address are logical and easy-to-use (because they occur on byte boundaries), with hindsight they are not the most practical because Class C networks are too small to be useful for most organizations while Class B networks are too large to be densely populated by any but the largest organizations.

In May 1996, there were all of Class A addresses either allocated or assigned, as well as 61.95 percent of Class B and 36.44 percent of Class C IP network addresses. The terms assigned and allocated in this context have the following meanings:

Assigned
>   The number of network numbers in use. The Class C figures are somewhat inaccurate, because the figures do not include many class C networks in Europe, which were allocated to RIPE and subsequently assigned but which are still recorded as allocated.

Allocated
>   This includes all of the assigned networks and additionally, those networks that have either been reserved by IANA (for example, the 63 class A networks are all reserved by IANA) or have been allocated to regional registries by IANA and will subsequently be assigned by those registries.

Another way to look at these numbers is to examine the proportion of the address space that has been used. The figures in the table do not show for example that the Class A address space is as big as the rest combined, or that a single Class A network can theoretically have as many hosts as 66,000 Class C networks.

Since 1990, the number of assigned Class B networks has been increasing at a much lower rate than the total number of assigned networks and the anticipated exhaustion of the Class B network numbers has not yet occurred. The reason for this is that the policies of the InterNIC on network number allocation were changed in late 1990 to preserve the existing address space, in particular to avert the exhaustion of the Class B address space. The new policies can be summarized as follows.

- The upper half of the Class A address space (network numbers 64 to 127) is reserved indefinitely to allow for the possibility of using it for transition to a new numbering scheme.

- Class B networks are only assigned to organizations that can clearly demonstrate a need for them. The same is, of course, true for Class A networks. The requirements for Class B networks are that the requesting organization:

- Has a subnetting plan that documents more than 32 subnets within its organizational network

- Has more than 4096 hosts

Any requirements for a Class A network would be handled on an individual case basis.

- Organizations that do not fulfill the requirements for a Class B network are assigned a consecutively numbered block of Class C network numbers.

- The lower half of the Class C address space (network numbers 192.0.0 through 207.255.255) is divided into eight blocks, which are allocated to regional authorities as follows:

192.0.0 - 193.255.255   Multi-regional

194.0.0 - 195.255.255   Europe

196.0.0 - 197.255.255   Others

198.0.0 - 199.255.255   North America

200.0.0 - 201.255.255   Central and South America

202.0.0 - 203.255.255   Pacific Rim

204.0.0 - 205.255.255   Others

206.0.0 - 207.255.255   Others

The ranges defined as Others are to be where flexibility outside the constraints of regional boundaries is required. The range defined as multi-regional includes the Class C networks that were assigned before this new scheme was adopted. The 192 networks were assigned by the InterNIC and the 193 networks were previously allocated to RIPE in Europe.

The upper half of the Class C address space (208.0.0 to 223.255.255) remains unassigned and unallocated.

- Where an organization has a range of class C network numbers, the range provided is assigned as a *bit-wise contiguous* range of network numbers, and the number of networks in the range is a power of 2. That is, all IP addresses in the range have a common prefix, and every address with that prefix is within the range. For example, a European organization requiring 1500 IP addresses would be assigned eight Class C network numbers (2048 IP addresses) from the number space reserved for European networks (194.0.0 through 195.255.255) and the first of these network numbers would be divisible by eight. A range of addresses satisfying these rules would be 194.32.136 through 194.32.143, in which case the range would consist of all of the IP addresses with the 21-bit prefix 194.32.136, or B'110000100010000010001'.

The maximum number of network numbers assigned contiguously is 64, corresponding to a prefix of 18 bits. An organization requiring more than 4096 addresses but less than 16,384 addresses can request either a Class B or a range of Class C addresses. In general, the number of Class C networks assigned is the minimum required to provide the necessary number of IP addresses for the organization on the basis of a two-year outlook. However, in some cases, an organization can request multiple networks to be treated separately. For example, an organization with 600 hosts would normally be assigned four class C networks. However, if those hosts were distributed across 10 token-ring LANs with between 50 and 70 hosts per LAN, such an allocation would cause serious problems, since the organization would have to find 10 subnets within a 10-bit local address range. This would mean at least some of the LANs having a subnet mask of 255.255.255.192 which allows only 62 hosts per LAN. The intent of the rules is not to force the organization into complex subnetting of small networks, and the organization should request 10 different Class C numbers, one for each LAN.

The current rules are to be found in *RFC 2050 — INTERNET REGISTRY IP ALLOCATION GUIDELINES* which updates RFC 1466. The reasons for the rules for the allocation of Class C network numbers will become apparent in the following sections. The use of Class C network numbers in this way has averted the exhaustion of the Class B address space, but it is not a permanent term solution to the overall address space constraints that are fundamental to IP. A long-term solution is discussed in Chapter 6, "IP Version 6" on page 457.

Today, there are three registries that handle world-wide IP address assignments:

APNIC (Asia-Pacific Network Information Center)
> Handles IP address allocation for Asia-Pacific. APNIC can be contacted at the following URL:
>
> `http://www.apnic.net`

ARIN (American Registry for Internet Numbers)
> Handles IP address allocation for North and South America, the Caribbean, and sub-Saharan Africa. ARIN can be contacted at the following URL:
>
> `http://www.arin.net`

RIPE NCC (Reseau IP Europeens)
> Handles IP address allocation for Europe and surrounding areas. RIPE NCC can be contacted at the following URL:
>
> `http://www.ripe.net`

2.1.6 Intranets (Private IP Addresses)

Another approach to conservation of the IP address space is described in *RFC 1918 —
Address Allocation for Private Internets.* Briefly, it relaxes the rule that IP addresses
are globally unique by reserving part of the address space for networks that are used
exclusively within a single organization and that do not require IP connectivity to the
Internet. There are three ranges of addresses that have been reserved by IANA for this
purpose:

10 A single Class A network

172.16 through 172.31 16 contiguous Class B networks

192.168.0 through 192.168.255 256 contiguous Class C networks

Any organization can use any addresses in these ranges without reference to any other
organization. However, because these addresses are not globally unique, they cannot
be referenced by hosts in another organization and they are not defined to any external
routers. Routers in networks not using private addresses, particularly those operated
by Internet service providers, are expected to quietly discard all routing information
regarding these addresses. Routers in an organization using private addresses are
expected to limit all references to private addresses to internal links; they should
neither advertise routes to private addresses to external routers nor forward IP
datagrams containing private addresses to external routers. Hosts having only a private
IP address do not have IP layer connectivity to the Internet. This may be desirable
and may even be a reason for using private addressing. All connectivity to external
Internet hosts must be provided with application gateways (please see 5.3.4,
"Application Level Gateway (Proxy)" on page 363).

2.1.7 Classless Inter-Domain Routing (CIDR)

It has been mentioned in 2.1.1, "IP Addressing" on page 36 that due to the impacts of
growth, the IP address space will near exhaustion very soon if addresses are assigned
as they are requested or as they used to be assigned. IPv6 will easily overcome that
problem (see Chapter 6, "IP Version 6" on page 457), but what can be done until
IPv6 will be fully deployed?

One idea was to use a range of Class C addresses instead of a single Class B address.
The problem there is that each network must be routed separately because standard IP
routing understands only class A, B and C network addresses (see 2.1.3, "IP Routing"
on page 45).

Within each of these types of network, subnetting can be used to provide better
granularity of the address space within each network, but there is no way to specify
that multiple Class C networks are actually related (see 2.1.2, "IP Subnets" on

page 39). The result of this is termed the *routing table explosion* problem: A Class B network of 3000 hosts requires one routing table entry at each backbone router, whereas the same network, if addressed as a range of Class C networks, would require 16 entries.

The solution to this problem is a scheme called Classless Inter-Domain Routing (CIDR). CIDR is described in RFCs 1518 to 1520.

CIDR does not route according to the class of the network number (hence the term classless) but solely according to the high order bits of the IP address, which are termed the IP prefix. Each CIDR routing table entry contains a 32-bit IP address and a 32-bit network mask, which together give the length and value of the IP prefix. This can be represented as <IP_address network_mask>. For example, to address a block of eight Class C addresses with one single routing table entry, the following representation would suffice: <192.32.136.0 255.255.248.0>. This would, from a backbone point of view, refer to the Class C network range from 192.32.136.0 to 192.32.143.0 as one single network because of the identical IP prefix, as illustrated in Figure 18:

```
11000000 00100000 10001000 00000000 = 192.32.136.0 (class C address)
11111111 11111111 11111--- -------- = 255.255.248.0 (network mask)
==================================== logical_AND
11000000 00100000 10001--- -------- = 192.32.136 (IP prefix)

11000000 00100000 10001111 00000000 = 192.32.143.0 (class C address)
11111111 11111111 11111--- -------- = 255.255.248.0 (network mask)
==================================== logical_AND
11000000 00100000 10001--- -------- = 192.32.136 (same IP prefix)
```

Figure 18. Classless Inter-Domain Routing - IP Supernetting Example

This process of combining multiple networks into a single entry is referred to as supernetting because routing is based on network masks that are shorter than the natural network mask of an IP address, in contrast to subnetting (see 2.1.2, "IP Subnets" on page 39) where the subnet masks are longer than the natural network mask.

The current Internet address allocation policies and the assumptions on which those policies were based, are described in *RFC 1518 — An Architecture for IP Address Allocation with CIDR*. They can be summarized as follows:

- IP address assignment reflects the physical topology of the network and not the organizational topology; wherever organizational and administrative boundaries do not match the network topology, they should *not* be used for the assignment of IP addresses.

- In general, network topology will closely follow continental and national boundaries and therefore IP addresses should be assigned on this basis.

- There will be a relatively small set of networks that carry a large amount of traffic between routing domains and which will be interconnected in a non-hierarchical way and that will cross national boundaries. These are referred to as *transit routing domains (TRDs)*. Each TRD will have a unique IP prefix. TRDs will not be organized in a hierarchical way where there is no appropriate hierarchy. However, wherever a TRD is wholly within a continental boundary, its IP prefix should be an extension of the continental IP prefix.

- There will be many organizations that have attachments to other organizations that are for the private use of those two organizations and that do not carry traffic intended for other domains (transit traffic). Such private connections do not have a significant effect on the routing topology and can be ignored.

- The great majority of routing domains will be single-homed. That is, they will be attached to a single TRD. They should be assigned addresses that begin with that TRD's IP prefix. All of the addresses for all single-homed domains attached to a TRD can therefore be aggregated into a single routing table entry for all domains outside that TRD.

  Note: This implies that if an organization changes its Internet service provider, it should change all of its IP addresses. This is not the current practice, but the widespread implementation of CIDR is likely to make it much more common.

- There are a number of address assignment schemes that can be used for multi-homed domains. These include:

  - The use of a single IP prefix for the domain. External routers must have an entry for the organization that lies partly or wholly outside the normal hierarchy. Where a domain is multi-homed but all of the attached TRDs themselves are topologically nearby, it would be appropriate for the domain's IP prefix to include those bits common to all of the attached TRDs. For example, if all of the TRDs were wholly within the United States, an IP prefix implying an exclusively North American domain would be appropriate.

  - The use of one IP prefix for each attached TRD, with hosts in the domain having IP addresses containing the IP prefix of the most appropriate TRD. The organization appears to be a set of routing domains.

- Assigning an IP prefix from one of the attached TRDs. This TRD becomes a default TRD for the domain but other domains can explicitly route by one of the alternative TRDs.

- The use of IP prefixes to refer to sets of multi-homed domains having the TRD attachments. For example, there may be an IP prefix to refer to single-homed domains attached to network A, one to refer to single-homed domains attached to network B and one to refer to dual-homed domains attached to networks A and B.

- Each of these has various advantages, disadvantages and side effects. For example, the first approach tends to result in inbound traffic entering the target domain closer to the sending host than the second approach, and therefore a larger proportion of the network costs are incurred by the receiving organization.

Because multi-homed domains can vary greatly in character and none of the above schemes is suitable for all such domains, there is no single policy that is best and RFC 1518 does not specify any rules for choosing between them.

2.1.7.1 CIDR Implementation

The implementation of CIDR in the Internet is primarily based on *Border Gateway Protocol Version 4* (see 3.4.2, "Border Gateway Protocol (BGP-4)" on page 177). The implementation strategy, described in *RFC 1520 — Exchanging Routing Information Across Provider Boundaries in the CIDR Environment* involves a staged process through the routing hierarchy beginning with backbone routers. Network service providers are divided into four types:

Type 1
> Those that cannot employ any default inter-domain routing.

Type 2
> Those that use default inter-domain routing but require explicit routes for a substantial proportion of the assigned IP network numbers.

Type 3
> Those that use default inter-domain routing and supplement it with a small number of explicit routes.

Type 4
> Those that perform all inter-domain routing using only default routes.

The CIDR implementation involves an implementation beginning with the Type 1 network providers, then the Type 2 and finally the Type 3 ones. CIDR has already been widely deployed in the backbone and over 9,000 class-based routes have been replaced by approximately 2,000 CIDR-based routes.

2.1.8 IP Datagram

The unit of transfer of a data packet in TCP/IP is called an IP datagram. It is made up of a header containing information for IP and data that is only relevant to the higher level protocols.

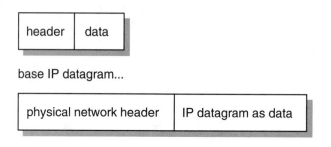

base IP datagram...

encapsulated within the physical network's frame

3376\3376F203

Figure 19. IP - Format of a Base IP Datagram

IP can handle fragmentation and re-assembly of IP datagrams. The maximum length of an IP datagram is 65,535 bytes (or octets). There is also a requirement for all TCP/IP hosts to support IP datagrams of size up to 576 bytes without fragmentation.

Fragments of a datagram all have a header, basically copied from the original datagram, and data following it. They are treated as normal IP datagrams while being transported to their destination. Note, however, that if one of the fragments gets lost, the complete datagram is considered lost since IP does not provide any acknowledgment mechanism, so the remaining fragments will simply be discarded by the destination host.

2.1.8.1 IP Datagram Format

The IP datagram header is a minimum of 20 bytes long:

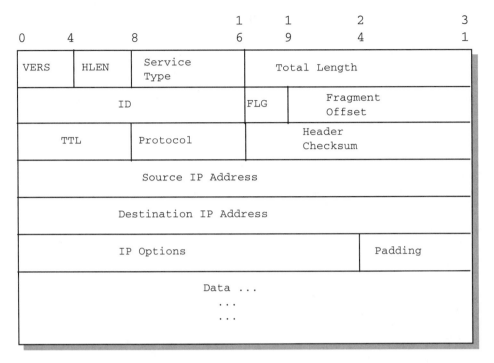

Figure 20. *IP - Format of an IP Datagram Header*

Where:

VERS

   The version of the IP protocol. The current version is 4. 5 is experimental and 6 is IPv6 (see 6.2, "The IPv6 Header Format" on page 459).

HLEN

   The length of the IP header counted in 32-bit quantities. This does not include the data field.

Service Type

   The service type is an indication of the quality of service requested for this IP datagram.

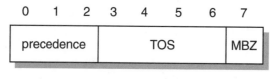

3376\3376F205

Figure 21. *IP - Service Type*

Where:

Precedence

Is a measure of the nature and priority of this datagram:

000 Routine

001 Priority

010 Immediate

011 Flash

100 Flash override

101 Critical

110 Internetwork control

111 Network control

TOS Specifies the *type of service* value:

1000 Minimize delay

0100 Maximize throughput

0010 Maximize reliability

0001 Minimize monetary cost

0000 Normal service

MBZ

Reserved for future use (must be zero unless participating in an Internet protocol experiment, which makes use of this bit).

A detailed description of the *type of service* can be found in the RFC 1349 (please also refer to 10.1, "Why QoS?" on page 643 for more details).

Total Length

The total length of the datagram, header and data, specified in bytes.

Identification

A unique number assigned by the sender to aid in reassembling a fragmented datagram. Fragments of a datagram will have the same identification number.

Flags

Various control flags:

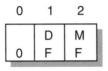

Figure 22. IP - Flags

Where:

0   Reserved, must be zero.

DF   Don't Fragment: 0 means allow fragmentation, 1 means do not allow fragmentation.

MF   More Fragments: 0 means that this is the last fragment of this datagram, 1 means that this is not the last fragment.

Fragment Offset

Used with fragmented datagrams, to aid in reassembly of the full datagram. The value is the number of 64-bit pieces (header bytes are not counted) that are contained in earlier fragments. In the first (or only) fragment, this value is always zero.

Time to Live

Specifies the time (in seconds) this datagram is allowed to travel. Each router where this datagram passes is supposed to subtract from this field its processing time for this datagram. Actually a router is able to process a datagram in less than 1 second; thus it will subtract one from this field, and the TTL becomes a hop-count metric rather than a time metric. When the value reaches zero, it is assumed that this datagram has been traveling in a closed loop and it is discarded. The initial value should be set by the higher level protocol that creates the datagram.

Protocol Number

Indicates the higher level protocol to which IP should deliver the data in this datagram. Some important values are:

0   Reserved

1   Internet Control Message Protocol (ICMP)

2	Internet Group Management Protocol (IGMP)
3	Gateway-to-Gateway Protocol (GGP)
4	IP (IP encapsulation)
5	Stream
6	Transmission Control Protocol (TCP)
8	Exterior Gateway Protocol (EGP)
9	Private Interior Routing Protocol
17	User Datagram Protocol (UDP)
41	IP Version 6 (IPv6)
50	Encap Security Payload for IPv6 (ESP)
51	Authentication Header for IPv6 (AH)
89	Open Shortest Path First

The full list can be found in *STD 2 — Assigned Internet Numbers*.

Header Checksum

Is a checksum on the header only. It does not include the data. The checksum is calculated as the 16-bit one's complement of the one's complement sum of all 16-bit words in the header. For the purpose of this calculation, the checksum field is assumed to be zero. If the header checksum does not match the contents, the datagram is discarded because at least one bit in the header is corrupt, and the datagram may even have arrived at the wrong destination.

Source IP Address

The 32-bit IP address of the host sending this datagram.

Destination IP Address

The 32-bit IP address of the destination host for this datagram.

Options

Variable length. An IP implementation is not required to be capable of generating options in the datagrams it creates, but all IP implementations are required to be able to process datagrams containing options. The Options field is variable in length. There may be zero or more options. There are two option formats. The format for each is dependent on the value of the option number found in the first byte.

- A type byte alone.

1 byte

Figure 23. IP - A Type Byte

- A type byte, a length byte and one or more option data bytes.

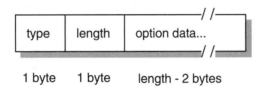

1 byte   1 byte   length - 2 bytes

Figure 24. IP - A Type Byte, a Length Byte and One or More Option Data Bytes

The type byte has the same structure in both cases:

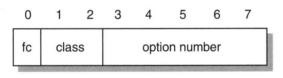

3376\3376F209

Figure 25. IP - The Type Byte Structure

Where:

fc   Flag copy indicates whether (1) or not (0) the option field is to be copied when the datagram is fragmented.

class The option class is a 2-bit unsigned integer:

   0   control

   1   reserved

   2   debugging and measurement

   3   reserved

option number

   The option number is a 5-bit unsigned integer.

0   End of option list. It has a class of 0, the fc bit is set to zero, and it has no length byte or data. That is, the option list is terminated by a X'00' byte. It is only required if the IP header length (which is a multiple of 4 bytes) does not match the actual length of the options.

1   No operation. It has a class of 0, the fc bit is not set and there is no length byte or data. That is, a X'01' byte is a NOP. It may be used to align fields in the datagram.

2   Security. It has a class of 0, the fc bit is set and there is a length byte with a value of 11 and 8 bytes of data). It is used for security information needed by U.S. Department of Defense requirements.

3   Loose source routing. It has a class of 0, the fc bit is set and there is a variable length data field. This option is discussed in more detail below.

4   Internet time stamp. It has a class of 2, the fc bit is not set and there is a variable length data field. The total length may be up to 40 bytes. This option is discussed in more detail below.

7   Record route. It has a class of 0, the fc bit is not set and there is a variable length data field. This option is discussed in more detail below.

8   Stream ID. It has a class of 0, the fc bit is set and there is a length byte with a value of 4 and one data byte. It is used with the SATNET system.

9   Strict source routing. It has a class of 0, the fc bit is set and there is a variable length data field. This option is discussed in more detail below.

length
Counts the length (in bytes) of the option, including the type and length fields.

option data
Contains data relevant to the option.

padding
If an option is used, the datagram is padded with all-zero bytes up to the next 32-bit boundary.

data   The data contained in the datagram is passed to a higher level protocol, as specified in the *protocol* field.

2.1.8.2 Fragmentation

When an IP datagram travels from one host to another it can cross different physical networks. Physical networks have a maximum frame size, called the *maximum transmission unit (MTU)*, that limits the length of a datagram that can be placed in one physical frame. Therefore, a scheme has been put in place to fragment long IP datagrams into smaller ones, and to reassemble them at the destination host. IP requires that each link has an MTU of at least 68 bytes, so if any network provides a lower value than this, fragmentation and re-assembly must be implemented in the network interface layer in a way that is transparent to IP. 68 is the sum of the maximum IP header length of 60 bytes and the minimum possible length of data in a non-final fragment (8 bytes). IP implementations are not required to handle unfragmented datagrams larger than 576 bytes, but most implementations will handle larger values, typically slightly more than 8192 bytes or higher, and rarely less than 1500.

An unfragmented datagram has all-zero fragmentation information. That is, the more fragments flag bit is zero and the fragment offset is zero. When fragmentation is to be done, the following steps are performed:

- The DF flag bit is checked to see if fragmentation is allowed. If the bit is set, the datagram will be discarded and an error will be returned to the originator using ICMP.

- Based on the MTU value, the data field is split into two or more parts. All newly created data portions must have a length that is a multiple of 8 bytes, with the exception of the last data portion.

- All data portions are placed in IP datagrams. The header of these datagrams are copies of the original one, with some modifications:

  - The more fragments flag bit is set in all fragments except the last.

  - The fragment offset field in each is set to the location this data portion occupied in the original datagram, relative to the beginning of the original unfragmented datagram. The offset is measured in 8-byte units.

  - If options were included in the original datagram, the high order bit of the option type byte determines whether or not they will be copied to all fragment datagrams or just to the first one. For instance, source route options have to be copied in all fragments and therefore they have this bit set.

  - The header length field of the new datagram is set.

  - The total length field of the new datagram is set.

  - The header checksum field is re-calculated.

- Each of these fragmented datagrams is now forwarded as a normal IP datagram. IP handles each fragment independently, that is, the fragments can traverse different routers to the intended destination, and can be subject to further fragmentation if they pass through networks that have smaller MTUs.

At the destination host, the data has to be reassembled into one datagram. The identification field of the datagram was set by the sending host to a unique number (for the source host, within the limits imposed by the use of a 16-bit number). As fragmentation doesn't alter this field, incoming fragments at the receiving side can be identified if this ID field is used together with the source and destination IP addresses in the datagram.

In order to reassemble the fragments, the receiving host allocates a buffer in storage as soon as the first fragment arrives. A timer routine is then started. When the timer times out and not all of the fragments have been received, the datagram is discarded. The initial value of this timer is called the IP datagram time-to-live (TTL) value. It is implementation-dependent, and some implementations allow it to be configured; for example, IBM AIX Version 4.3 provides an *ipfragttl* option with a default value of 60 seconds.

When subsequent fragments of the datagram arrive before the timer expires, the data is simply copied into the buffer storage at the location indicated by the fragment offset field. As soon as all fragments have arrived the complete original unfragmented datagram is restored, and processing continues just as for unfragmented datagrams.

Note: IP does not provide the reassembly timer. It will treat each and every datagram, fragmented or not, the same way, that is, as individual messages. It is up to the higher layer to implement a timeout and to look after any missing fragments. The higher layer could be TCP for a connection-oriented transport network or the application for connectionless transport networks based upon UDP and IP.

The netstat command can be used on some TCP/IP hosts to list details of fragmentation that is occurring. An example of this is the `netstat -i` command in TCP/IP for OS/2.

2.1.8.3 IP Datagram Routing Options

The IP datagram Options field allows two methods for the originator of an IP datagram to explicitly provide routing information and one method for an IP datagram to determine the route that it travels.

Loose Source Routing: The Loose Source Routing option, also called the Loose Source and Record Route (LSRR) option, provides a means for the source of an IP datagram to supply explicit routing information to be used by the routers in forwarding the datagram to the destination, and to record the route followed.

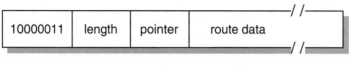

Figure 26. IP - Loose Source Routing Option

1000011
(Decimal 131) is the value of the option type byte for loose source routing.

length
Contains the length of this option field, including the type and length fields.

pointer
Points to the option data at the next IP address to be processed. It is counted relative to the beginning of the option, so its minimum value is four. If the pointer is greater than the length of the option, the end of the source route is reached and further routing is to be based on the destination IP address (as for datagrams without this option).

route data
Is a series of 32-bit IP addresses.

Whenever a datagram arrives at its destination and the source route is not empty (pointer < length) the receiving host will:

- Take the next IP address in the route data field (the one indicated by the pointer field) and put it in the destination IP address field of the datagram.

- Put the local IP address in the source list at the location pointed to by the pointer field. The IP address for this is the local IP address corresponding to the network on which the datagram will be forwarded. (Routers are attached to multiple physical networks and thus have multiple IP addresses.)

- Increment pointer by 4.

- Transmit the datagram to the new destination IP address.

This procedure ensures that the return route is recorded in the route data (in reverse order) so that the final recipient uses this data to construct a loose source route in the reverse direction. This is a *loose* source route because the forwarding router is allowed to use any route and any number of intermediate routers to reach the next address in the route.

Note: The originating host puts the IP address of the first intermediate router in the destination address field and the IP addresses of the remaining routers in the path, including the target destination are placed in the source route option. The recorded route in the datagram when it arrives at the target contains the IP addresses of each of the routers that forwarded the datagram. Each router has moved one place in the source route, and normally a different IP address will be used, since the routers record the IP address of the outbound interface but the source route originally contained the IP address of the inbound interface.

Strict Source Routing: The Strict Source Routing option, also called the Strict Source and Record Route (SSRR) option, uses the same principle as loose source routing except that the intermediate router *must* send the datagram to the next IP address in the source route via a directly connected network and not via an intermediate router. If it cannot do so it reports an error with an ICMP Destination Unreachable message.

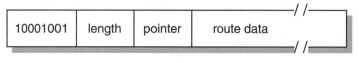

3376\3376F2OU

Figure 27. IP - Strict Source Routing Option

1001001
 (Decimal 137) is the value of the option type byte for strict source routing.

length
 Has the same meaning as for loose source routing.

pointer
 Has the same meaning as for loose source routing.

route data
 Is a series of 32-bit IP addresses.

Record Route: This option provides a means to record the route of an IP datagram. It functions similarly to the source routing discussed above, but this time the source host has provided an empty routing data field, which will be filled in as the datagram traverses routers. Note that sufficient space for this routing information must be provided by the source host: if the data field is filled before the datagram reaches its destination, the datagram is forwarded with no further recording of the route.

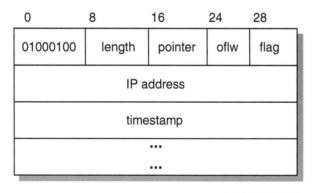

3376\3376F2OV

Figure 28. IP - Record Route Option

0000111
(Decimal 7) is the value of the option type byte for record route

length.
Has the same meaning as for loose source routing.

pointer
Has the same meaning as for loose source routing.

route data
Is a multiple of four bytes in length chosen by the originator of the datagram.

2.1.8.4 Internet Time Stamp

A time stamp is an option forcing some (or all) of the routers on the route to the destination to put a time stamp in the option data. The time stamps are measured in seconds and can be used for debugging purposes. They cannot be used for performance measurement for two reasons:

- They are insufficiently precise because most IP datagrams will be forwarded in less than one second.

- They are insufficiently accurate because IP routers are not required to have synchronized clocks.

3376\3376F2OW

Figure 29. IP - Internet Time Stamp Option

Where:

01000100

(Decimal 68) is the value of the option type for the internet time stamp option.

length

Contains the total length of this option, including the type and length fields.

pointer

Points to the next time stamp to be processed (first free time stamp).

oflw (overflow)

Is a 4 bit unsigned integer of the number of IP modules that cannot register time stamps due to a lack of space in the data field.

flag   Is a 4-bit value which indicates how time stamps are to be registered. Values are:

> *0* Time stamps only, stored in consecutive 32-bit words.
> *1* Each time stamp is preceded by the IP address of the registering module.
> *2* The IP address fields are pre-specified, and an IP module only registers when it finds its own address in the list.

Time stamp

A 32-bit time stamp recorded in milliseconds since midnight UT (GMT).

The originating host must compose this option with a large enough data area to hold all the time stamps. If the time stamp area becomes full, no further time stamps are added.

2.2 Internet Control Message Protocol (ICMP)

ICMP is a *standard protocol* with STD number 5. That standard also includes IP (see 2.1, "Internet Protocol (IP)" on page 35) and IGMP (see 9.2, "Internet Group Management Protocol (IGMP)" on page 596). Its status is *required*. It is described in RFC 792 with updates in RFC 950.

Path MTU Discovery is a *draft standard protocol* with a status of *elective*. It is described in RFC 1191.

ICMP Router Discovery is a *proposed standard protocol* with a status of *elective*. It is described in RFC 1256.

When a router or a destination host must inform the source host about errors in datagram processing, it uses the Internet Control Message Protocol (ICMP). ICMP can be characterized as follows:

- ICMP uses IP as if ICMP were a higher level protocol (that is, ICMP messages are encapsulated in IP datagrams). However, ICMP is an integral part of IP and must be implemented by every IP module.

- ICMP is used to report some errors, *not* to make IP reliable. Datagrams may still be undelivered without any report on their loss. Reliability must be implemented by the higher level protocols that use IP.

- ICMP can report errors on any IP datagram with the exception of ICMP messages, to avoid infinite repetitions.

- For fragmented IP datagrams, ICMP messages are only sent about errors on fragment zero. That is, ICMP messages never refer to an IP datagram with a non-zero fragment offset field.

- ICMP messages are never sent in response to datagrams with a destination IP address that is a broadcast or a multicast address.

- ICMP messages are never sent in response to a datagram that does not have a source IP address that represents a unique host. That is, the source address cannot be zero, a loopback address, a broadcast address or a multicast address.

- ICMP messages are never sent in response to ICMP error messages. They can be sent in response to ICMP query messages (ICMP types 0, 8, 9, 10 and 13 through 18).

- RFC 792 states that ICMP messages can be generated to report IP datagram processing errors, *not* must. In practice, routers will almost always generate ICMP messages for errors, but for destination hosts, the number of ICMP messages generated is implementation dependent.

2.2.1 ICMP Messages

ICMP messages are described in RFC 792 and RFC 950, belong to STD 5 and are mandatory.

ICMP messages are sent in IP datagrams. The IP header will always have a Protocol number of 1, indicating ICMP and a type of service of zero (routine). The IP data field will contain the actual ICMP message in the format shown in Figure 30.

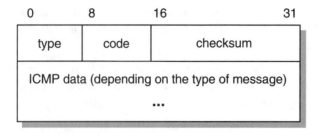

3376\3376F2A1

Figure 30. ICMP - Message Format

Where:

Type   Specifies the type of the message:

0 Echo reply
3 Destination unreachable
4 Source quench
5 Redirect
8 Echo
9 Router advertisement
10 Router solicitation
11 Time exceeded
12 Parameter problem
13 Time Stamp request
14 Time Stamp reply
15 Information request (obsolete)
16 Information reply (obsolete)
17 Address mask request
18 Address mask reply
30 Traceroute
31 Datagram conversion error
32 Mobile host redirect
33 IPv6 Where-Are-You
34 IPv6 I-Am-Here
35 Mobile registration request
36 Mobile registration reply
37 Domain name request
38 Domain name reply
39 SKIP
40 Photuris

Code	Contains the error code for the datagram reported on by this ICMP message. The interpretation is dependent upon the message type.
Checksum	Contains the 16-bit one's complement of the one's complement sum of the ICMP message starting with the ICMP Type field. For computing this checksum, the checksum field is assumed to be zero. This algorithm is the same as that used by IP for the IP header. Compare this with the algorithm used by UDP and TCP (see 2.7, "User Datagram Protocol (UDP)" on page 97 and 2.8, "Transmission Control Protocol (TCP)" on page 100), which also include a *pseudo-IP* header in the checksum.
Data	Contains information for this ICMP message. Typically it will contain a part of the original IP message for which this ICMP message was generated. The length of the data can be determined from the length of the IP datagram that contains the message less the IP header length.

Each of the messages is explained below.

2.2.1.1 Echo (8) and Echo Reply (0)

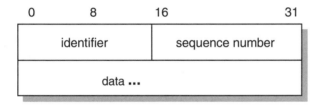

3376\3376F2A6

Figure 31. *ICMP - Echo and Echo Reply*

Echo is used to detect if another host is active on the network. The sender initializes the identifier and sequence number (which is used if multiple echo requests are sent), adds some data to the data field and sends the ICMP echo to the destination host. The ICMP header code field is zero. The recipient changes the type to Echo Reply and returns the datagram to the sender. This mechanism is used by the Ping command to determine if a destination host is reachable (see 2.2.2.1, "Ping" on page 85).

2.2.1.2 Destination Unreachable (3)

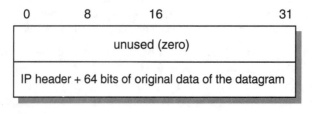

3376\3376F2A2

Figure 32. ICMP - Destination Unreachable

If this message is received from an intermediate router, it means that the router regards the destination IP address as unreachable.

If this message is received from the destination host, it means that the protocol specified in the protocol number field of the original datagram is not active, or that protocol is not active on this host or the specified port is inactive. (See 2.7, "User Datagram Protocol (UDP)" on page 97 for an introduction to the port concept.)

The ICMP header code field will have one of the following values:

0 Network unreachable
1 Host unreachable
2 Protocol unreachable
3 Port unreachable
4 Fragmentation needed but the *Do Not Fragment* bit was set
5 Source route failed
6 Destination network unknown
7 Destination host unknown
8 Source host isolated (obsolete)
9 Destination network administratively prohibited
10 Destination host administratively prohibited
11 Network unreachable for this type of service
12 Host unreachable for this type of service
13 Communication administratively prohibited by filtering
14 Host precedence violation
15 Precedence cutoff in effect

If a router implements the Path MTU Discovery protocol, the format of the destination unreachable message is changed for code 4 to include the MTU of the link that could not accept the datagram.

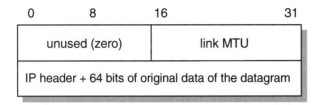

3376\3376F2A3

Figure 33. ICMP - Fragmentation Required with Link MTU

2.2.1.3 Source Quench (4)

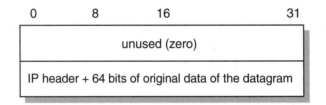

3376\3376F2A4

Figure 34. ICMP - Source Quench

If this message is received from an intermediate router, it means that the router does not have the buffer space needed to queue the datagrams for output to the next network.

If this message is received from the destination host, it means that the incoming datagrams are arriving too quickly to be processed.

The ICMP header code field is always zero.

2.2.1.4 Redirect (5)

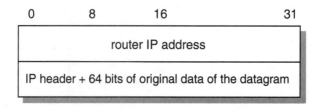

```
0          8          16                    31
┌──────────────────────────────────────────────┐
│                router IP address              │
├──────────────────────────────────────────────┤
│ IP header + 64 bits of original data of the datagram │
└──────────────────────────────────────────────┘
```

3376\3376F2A5

Figure 35. ICMP - Redirect

If this message is received from an intermediate router, it means that the host should send future datagrams for the network to the router whose IP address is given in the ICMP message. This preferred router will always be on the same subnet as the host that sent the datagram and the router that returned the IP datagram. The router will forward the datagram to its next hop destination. If the router IP address matches the source IP address in the original datagram header it indicates a routing loop. This ICMP message will not be sent if the IP datagram contains a source route.

The ICMP header code field will have one of the following values:

0 Network redirect
1 Host redirect
2 Network redirect for this type of service
3 Host redirect for this type of service

2.2.1.5 Router Advertisement (9) and Router Solicitation (10)

ICMP messages 9 and 10 are optional. They are described in RFC 1256 which is elective.

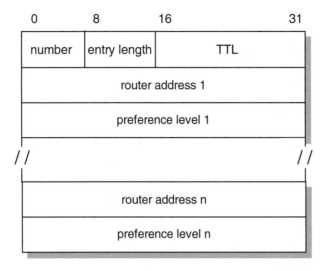

3376\3376F2A7

Figure 36. ICMP - Router Advertisement

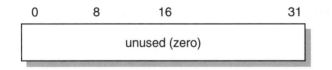

3376\3376F2A8

Figure 37. ICMP - Router Solicitation

Where:

number

The number of entries in the message.

entry length

The length of an entry in 32-bit units. This is 2 (32 bits for the IP address and 32 bits for the preference value).

TTL The number of seconds that an entry will be considered valid.

router address

One of the sender's IP addresses.

preference level

A signed 32-bit level indicating the preference to be assigned to this address when selecting a default router for a subnet. Each router on a subnet is responsible for advertising its own preference level. Larger values imply higher preference; smaller values imply lower. The default is zero, which is in the middle of the possible range. A value of X'80000000' -2^{31} indicates that the router should never be used as a default router.

The ICMP header code field is zero for both of these messages.

These two messages are used if a host or a router supports the router discovery protocol. The use of multicasting is recommended, but broadcasting may be used if multicasting is not supported on an interface. Routers periodically advertise their IP addresses on those subnets where they are configured to do so. Advertisements are made on the all-systems multicast address (224.0.0.1) or the limited broadcast address (255.255.255.255). The default behavior is to send advertisements every 10 minutes with a TTL value of 1800 (30 minutes). Routers also reply to solicitation messages they receive. They may reply directly to the soliciting host, or they may wait a short random interval and reply with a multicast.

Hosts can send solicitation messages when they start until they receive a response. Solicitation messages are sent to the all-routers multicast address (224.0.0.2) or the limited broadcast address (255.255.255.255). Typically, three solicitation messages are sent at 3-second intervals. Alternatively a host may wait for periodic advertisements. Each time a host receives an advertisement, it updates its default router if the new advertisement has one with a higher preference value and sets the TTL timer for the entry to match the value in the advertisement. When the host receives a new advertisement for its current default router, it resets the TTL value to that in the new advertisement. This also provides a mechanism for routers to declare themselves unavailable. They send an advertisement with a TTL value of zero.

2.2.1.6 Time Exceeded (11)

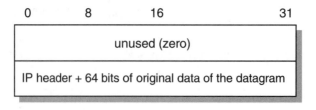

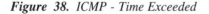

Figure 38. ICMP - Time Exceeded

If this message is received from an intermediate router, it means that the time-to-live field of an IP datagram has expired.

If this message is received from the destination host, it means that the IP fragment reassembly time-to-live timer has expired while the host is waiting for a fragment of the datagram. The ICMP header code field may have the one of the following values:

0 transit TTL exceeded
1 reassembly TTL exceeded

2.2.1.7 Parameter Problem (12)

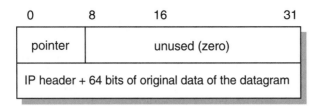

3376\3376F2AA

Figure 39. ICMP - Parameter Problem

Indicates that a problem was encountered during processing of the IP header parameters. The pointer field points to the byte in the original IP datagram where the problem was encountered. The ICMP header code field may have the one of the following values:

0 unspecified error
1 required option missing

2.2.1.8 Time Stamp Request (13) and Time Stamp Reply (14)

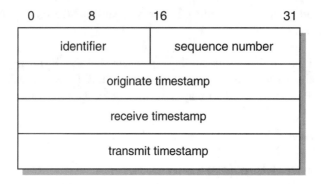

3376\3376F2AB

Figure 40. ICMP - Time Stamp Request and Time Stamp Reply

These two messages are for performance measurements and for debugging. They are not used for clock synchronization.

The sender initializes the identifier and sequence number (which is used if multiple time stamp requests are sent), sets the originate time stamp and sends it to the recipient. The receiving host fills in the receive and transmit time stamps, changes the type to time stamp reply and returns it to the recipient. The receiver has two time stamps in case there is a perceptible time difference between the receipt and transmit times, but in practice, most implementations will perform the two (receipt and reply) in one operation and will set the two time stamps to the same value. Time Stamps are the number of milliseconds elapsed since midnight UT (GMT).

2.2.1.9 Information Request (15) and Information Reply (16)

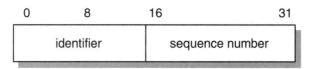

3376\3376F2AC

Figure 41. ICMP - Information Request and Information Reply

An information request is issued by a host to obtain an IP address for an attached network. The sender fills in the request with the destination IP address in the IP header set to zero (meaning this network) and waits for a reply from a server authorized to assign IP addresses to other hosts. The ICMP header code field is zero. The reply will contain IP network addresses in both the source and destination fields of the IP header. This mechanism is now obsolete (see also 2.5, "Reverse Address Resolution Protocol (RARP)" on page 93).

2.2.1.10 Address Mask Request (17) and Address Mask Reply (18)

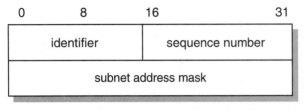

Figure 42. ICMP - Address Mask Request and Reply

An address mask request is used by a host to determine the subnet mask in use on an attached network. Most hosts will be configured with their subnet mask(s), but some, such as diskless workstations, must obtain this information from a server. A host uses RARP (see 2.5, "Reverse Address Resolution Protocol (RARP)" on page 93) to obtain its IP address. To obtain a subnet mask, the host broadcasts an address mask request. Any host on the network that has been configured to send address mask replies will fill in the subnet mask, convert the packet to an address mask reply and return it to the sender. The ICMP header code field is zero.

2.2.2 ICMP Applications

There are two simple and widely used applications that are based on ICMP: Ping and Traceroute. Ping uses the ICMP Echo and Echo Reply messages to determine whether a host is reachable. Traceroute sends IP datagrams with low TTL values so that they expire en route to a destination. It uses the resulting ICMP Time Exceeded messages to determine where in the internet the datagrams expired and pieces together a view of the route to a host. These applications are discussed in the following sections.

2.2.2.1 Ping

Ping is the simplest of all TCP/IP applications. It sends one or more IP datagrams to a specified destination host requesting a reply and measures the round trip time. The word *ping*, which is used as a noun and a verb, is taken from the sonar operation to locate an underwater object. It is also an abbreviation for *Packet InterNet Groper*.

Traditionally, if you could ping a host, other applications such as Telnet or FTP could reach that host. With the advent of security measures on the Internet, particularly firewalls (see 5.3, "Firewalls" on page 359), which control access to networks by application protocol and/or port number, this is no longer strictly true. Nonetheless, the first test of reachability for a host is still to attempt to ping it.

The syntax that is used in different implementations of ping varies from platform to platform. The syntax here is for the OS/2 implementation:

```
ping [-switches] host [size [packets]]
```

Where:

switches

> Switches to enable various ping options

host The destination, either a symbolic name or an IP address

size The size of the data portion of the packet

packets

> The number of packets to send

Ping uses the ICMP Echo and Echo Reply messages, as described in 2.2.1.1, "Echo (8) and Echo Reply (0)" on page 77. Since ICMP is required in every TCP/IP implementation, hosts do not require a separate server to respond to pings.

Ping is useful for verifying a TCP/IP installation. Consider the following four forms of the command; each requires the operation of an additional part of the TCP/IP installation:

ping loopback

> Verifies the operation of the base TCP/IP software.

ping my-IP-address

> Verifies whether the physical network device can be addressed.

ping a-remote-IP-address

> Verifies whether the network can be accessed.

ping a-remote-host-name

> Verifies the operation of the name server (or the flat namespace resolver, depending on the installation).

Ping is implemented in all IBM TCP/IP products.

2.2.2.2 Traceroute

The Traceroute program can be useful when used for debugging purposes. Traceroute enables determination of the route that IP datagrams follow from host to host.

Traceroute is based upon ICMP and UDP. It sends an IP datagram with a TTL of 1 to the destination host. The first router to see the datagram will decrement the TTL to 0 and return an ICMP Time Exceeded message as well as discarding the datagram. In this way, the first router in the path is identified. This process can be repeated with successively larger TTL values in order to identify the series of routers in the path to the destination host. Traceroute actually sends UDP datagrams to the destination host which reference a port number that is outside the normally used range. This enables Traceroute to determine when the destination host has been reached, that is, when an ICMP Port Unreachable message is received.

Traceroute is implemented in all IBM TCP/IP products.

2.3 Internet Group Management Protocol (IGMP)

IGMP is a *standard protocol* with STD number 5. That standard also includes IP (see 2.1, "Internet Protocol (IP)" on page 35) and ICMP (see 2.2, "Internet Control Message Protocol (ICMP)" on page 74). Its status is *recommended*. It is described in RFC 1112 with updates in RFC 2236.

Similar to ICMP, the Internet Group Management Protocol (IGMP) is also an integral part of IP. It serves the purpose of allowing hosts to participate in IP multicasts and to cancel such participation. IGMP further provides routers with the capability to check if any hosts on a local subnet are at all interested in a particular multicast.

Please see 9.2, "Internet Group Management Protocol (IGMP)" on page 596 for a more detailed discussion of IGMP.

2.4 Address Resolution Protocol (ARP)

The ARP protocol is a *network-specific standard protocol*. The address resolution protocol is responsible for converting the higher level protocol addresses (IP addresses) to physical network addresses. It is described in RFC 826.

2.4.1 ARP Overview

On a single physical network, individual hosts are known on the network by their physical hardware address. Higher level protocols address destination hosts in the form of a symbolic address (IP address in this case). When such a protocol wants to send a datagram to destination IP address w.x.y.z, the device driver does not understand this address.

Therefore, a module (ARP) is provided that will translate the IP address to the physical address of the destination host. It uses a lookup table (sometimes referred to as the *ARP cache*) to perform this translation.

When the address is not found in the ARP cache, a broadcast is sent out on the network, with a special format called the *ARP request*. If one of the machines on the network recognizes its own IP address in the request, it will send an *ARP reply* back to the requesting host. The reply will contain the physical hardware address of the host and source route information (if the packet has crossed bridges on its path). Both this address and the source route information are stored in the ARP cache of the requesting host. All subsequent datagrams to this destination IP address can now be translated to a physical address, which is used by the device driver to send out the datagram on the network.

An exception to the rule constitutes the Asynchronous Transfer Mode (ATM) technology where ARP cannot be implemented in the physical layer as described previously. Therefore, an ARP server is used with which every host has to register upon initialization in order to be able to resolve IP addresses to hardware addresses (please also see 13.3, "Asynchronous Transfer Mode (ATM)" on page 761).

ARP was designed to be used on networks that support hardware broadcast. This means, for example, that ARP will not work on an X.25 network.

2.4.2 ARP Detailed Concept

ARP is used on IEEE 802 networks as well as on the older DIX Ethernet networks to map IP addresses to physical hardware addresses *see 13.1, "Ethernet and IEEE 802.x Local Area Networks (LANs)" on page 757). To do this, it is closely related to the device driver for that network. In fact, the ARP specifications in RFC 826 only describe its functionality, not its implementation. The implementation depends to a large extent on the device driver for a network type and they are usually coded together in the *adapter microcode*.

2.4.2.1 ARP Packet Generation

If an application wishes to send data to a certain IP destination address, the IP routing mechanism first determines the IP address of the next hop of the packet (it can be the destination host itself, or a router) and the hardware device on which it should be sent. If it is an IEEE 802.3/4/5 network, the ARP module must be consulted to map the <protocol type, target protocol address> to a physical address.

The ARP module tries to find the address in this ARP cache. If it finds the matching pair, it gives the corresponding 48-bit physical address back to the caller (the device driver), which then transmits the packet. If it doesn't find the pair in its table, it *discards the packet* (assumption is that a higher level protocol will retransmit) and generates a network *broadcast* of an ARP request.

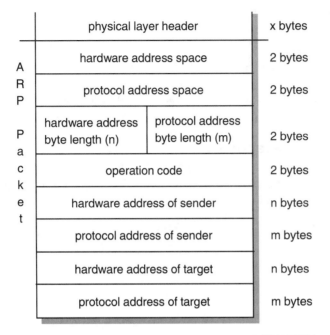

physical layer header		x bytes
hardware address space		2 bytes
protocol address space		2 bytes
hardware address byte length (n)	protocol address byte length (m)	2 bytes
operation code		2 bytes
hardware address of sender		n bytes
protocol address of sender		m bytes
hardware address of target		n bytes
protocol address of target		m bytes

3376\3376F2AH

Figure 43. ARP - Request/Reply Packet

Where:

Hardware address space
  Specifies the type of hardware; examples are Ethernet or Packet Radio Net.

Protocol address space
  Specifies the type of protocol, same as the EtherType field in the IEEE 802 header (IP or ARP).

Hardware address length
  Specifies the length (in bytes) of the hardware addresses in this packet. For IEEE 802.3 and IEEE 802.5 this will be 6.

Protocol address length
  Specifies the length (in bytes) of the protocol addresses in this packet. For IP this will be 4.

Operation code

> Specifies whether this is an ARP request (1) or reply (2).

Source/target hardware address

> Contains the physical network hardware addresses. For IEEE 802.3 these are 48-bit addresses.

Source/target protocol address

> Contains the protocol addresses. For TCP/IP these are the 32-bit IP addresses.

For the ARP request packet, the target hardware address is the only undefined field in the packet.

2.4.2.2 ARP Packet Reception

When a host receives an ARP packet (either a broadcast request or a point-to-point reply), the receiving device driver passes the packet to the ARP module which treats it as shown in Figure 44 on page 91.

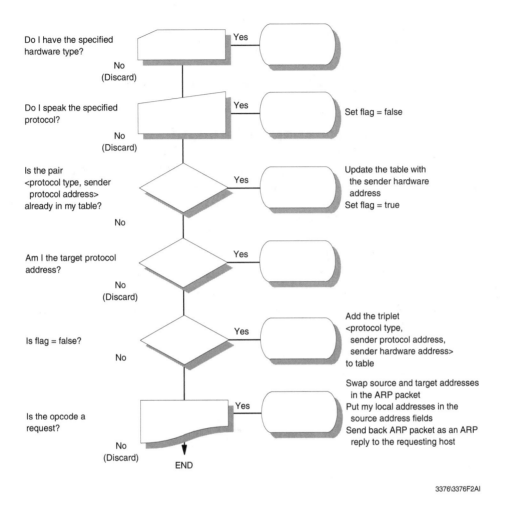

Do I have the specified hardware type?

Yes

No (Discard)

Do I speak the specified protocol?

Yes

Set flag = false

No (Discard)

Is the pair <protocol type, sender protocol address> already in my table?

Yes

Update the table with the sender hardware address
Set flag = true

No

Am I the target protocol address?

Yes

No (Discard)

Is flag = false?

Yes

Add the triplet <protocol type, sender protocol address, sender hardware address> to table

No

Is the opcode a request?

Yes

Swap source and target addresses in the ARP packet
Put my local addresses in the source address fields
Send back ARP packet as an ARP reply to the requesting host

No (Discard)

END

3376\3376F2AI

Figure 44. ARP - Packet Reception

The requesting host will receive this ARP reply, and will follow the same algorithm to treat it. As a result of this, the triplet <protocol type, protocol address, hardware address> for the desired host will be added to its lookup table (ARP cache). The next time a higher level protocol wants to send a packet to that host, the ARP module will find the target hardware address and the packet will be sent to that host.

Note that because the original ARP request was a broadcast on the network, all hosts on that network will have updated the sender's hardware address in their table (only if it was already in the table).

2.4.3 ARP and Subnets

The ARP protocol remains unchanged in the presence of subnets. Remember that each IP datagram first goes through the IP routing algorithm. This algorithm selects the hardware device driver that should send out the packet. Only then, the ARP module associated with that device driver is consulted.

2.4.4 Proxy-ARP or Transparent Subnetting

Proxy-ARP is described in *RFC 1027 — Using ARP to Implement Transparent Subnet Gateways*, which is in fact a subset of the method proposed in *RFC 925 — Multi-LAN Address Resolution*. It is another method to construct local subnets, without the need for a modification to the IP routing algorithm, but with modifications to the routers that interconnect the subnets.

2.4.4.1 Proxy-ARP Concept

Consider one IP network that is divided into subnets and interconnected by routers. We use the "old" IP routing algorithm, which means that no host knows about the existence of multiple physical networks. Consider hosts A and B which are on different physical networks within the same IP network, and a router R between the two subnetworks:

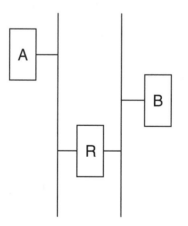

Figure 45. ARP - Hosts Interconnected by a Router

When host A wants to send an IP datagram to host B, it first has to determine the physical network address of host B through the use of the ARP protocol.

As host A cannot differentiate between the physical networks, its IP routing algorithm thinks that host B is on the local physical network and sends out a broadcast ARP request. Host B doesn't receive this broadcast, but router R does. Router R understands subnets, that is, it runs the subnet version of the IP routing algorithm and it will be able to see that the destination of the ARP request (from the target protocol address field) is on another physical network. If router R's routing tables specify that the next hop to that other network is through a different physical device, it will reply to the ARP *as if it were host B*, saying that the network address of host B is that of the router R itself.

Host A receives this ARP reply, puts it in its cache and will send future IP packets for host B to the router R. The router will forward such packets to the correct subnet.

The result is transparent subnetting:

- Normal hosts (such as A and B) don't know about subnetting, so they use the "old" IP routing algorithm.
- The routers between subnets have to:
  1. Use the subnet IP routing algorithm.
  2. Use a modified ARP module, which can reply on behalf of other hosts.

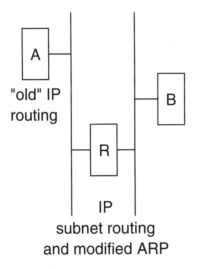

Figure 46. ARP - Proxy-ARP Router

2.5 Reverse Address Resolution Protocol (RARP)

The RARP protocol is a *network-specific standard protocol*. It is described in RFC 903.

Some network hosts, such as diskless workstations, do not know their own IP address when they are booted. To determine their own IP address, they use a mechanism similar to ARP, but now the hardware address of the host is the known parameter, and the IP address the queried parameter. It differs more fundamentally from ARP in the fact that a RARP server must exist on the network that maintains that a database of mappings from hardware address to protocol address must be pre-configured.

2.5.1 RARP Concept

The reverse address resolution is performed the same way as the ARP address resolution. The same packet format (see Figure 43 on page 89) is used as for ARP.

An exception is the operation code field that now takes the following values:

3 For the RARP request
4 For the RARP reply

And of course, the physical header of the frame will now indicate RARP as the higher-level protocol (8035 hex) instead of ARP (0806 hex) or IP (0800 hex) in the EtherType field. Some differences arise from the concept of RARP itself:

- ARP only assumes that every host knows the mapping between its own hardware address and protocol address. RARP requires one or more server hosts on the network to maintain a database of mappings between hardware addresses and protocol addresses so that they will be able to reply to requests from client hosts.

- Due to the size this database can take, part of the server function is usually implemented outside the adapter's microcode, with optionally a small cache in the microcode. The microcode part is then only responsible for reception and transmission of the RARP frames, the RARP mapping itself being taken care of by server software running as a normal process in the host machine.

- The nature of this database also requires some software to create and update the database manually.

- In case there are multiple RARP servers on the network, the RARP requester only uses the first RARP reply received on its broadcast RARP request, and discards the others.

2.6 Ports and Sockets

This section introduces the concepts of *port* and *socket*, which are necessary to exactly determine which local process at a given host actually communicates with which process at which remote host using which protocol. If this sounds confusing, consider the following:

- An application process is assigned a process identifier number (process ID) which is likely to be different each time that process is started.

- Process IDs differ between operating system platforms, hence they are not uniform.

- A server process can have multiple connections to multiple clients at a time, hence simple connection identifiers would not be unique.

The concept of ports and sockets provides a way to uniformly and uniquely identify connections and the programs and hosts that are engaged in them, irrespective of specific process IDs.

2.6.1 Ports

Each *process* that wants to communicate with another process identifies itself to the TCP/IP protocol suite by one or more *ports*. A port is a 16-bit number, used by the host-to-host protocol to identify to which higher level protocol or application program (process) it must deliver incoming messages. There are two types of port:

well-known
> Well-known ports belong to standard servers, for example Telnet uses port 23. Well-known port numbers range between 1 and 1023 (prior to 1992, the range between 256 and 1023 was used for UNIX-specific servers). Well-known port numbers are typically odd, because early systems using the port concept required an odd/even pair of ports for duplex operations. Most servers require only a single port. Exceptions are the BOOTP server, which uses two: 67 and 68 (see 7.1, "Bootstrap Protocol (BOOTP)" on page 511) and the FTP server, which uses two: 20 and 21 (see 4.4, "File Transfer Protocol (FTP)" on page 226).
>
> The well-known ports are controlled and assigned by the Internet central authority (IANA) and on most systems can only be used by system processes or by programs executed by privileged users. The reason for well-known ports is to allow clients to be able to find servers without configuration information. The well-known port numbers are defined in *STD 2 — Assigned Internet Numbers*.

ephemeral
> Clients do not need well-known port numbers because they initiate communication with servers and the port number they are using is contained in the UDP datagrams sent to the server. Each client process is allocated a port number as long as it needs it by the host it is running on. Ephemeral port numbers have values greater than 1023, normally in the range 1024 to 65535. A client can use any number allocated to it, as long as the combination of <transport protocol, IP address, port number> is unique.

Ephemeral ports are not controlled by IANA and on most systems can be used by ordinary user-developed programs.

Confusion due to two different applications trying to use the same port numbers on one host is avoided by writing those applications to request an available port from TCP/IP. Because this port number is dynamically assigned, it may differ from one invocation of an application to the next.

UDP, TCP and ISO TP-4 all use the same port principle (please see Figure 50 on page 101). To the extent possible, the same port numbers are used for the same services on top of UDP, TCP and ISO TP-4.

Note: Normally, a server will use either TCP or UDP, but there are exceptions. For example, domain name servers (see 4.2, "Domain Name System (DNS)" on page 194) use both UDP port 53 and TCP port 53.

2.6.2 Sockets

The socket interface is one of several *application programming interfaces (APIs)* to the communication protocols. Designed to be a generic communication programming interface, it was first introduced by the 4.2 BSD UNIX system. Although it has not been standardized, it has become a *de facto* industry standard.

4.2 BSD allowed two different communication domains: Internet and UNIX. 4.3 BSD has added the Xerox Network System (XNS) protocols and 4.4 BSD will add an extended interface to support the ISO OSI protocols.

Let us consider the following terminologies:

- A *socket* is a special type of *file handle*, which is used by a process to request network services from the operating system.

- A *socket address* is the triple:

      {*protocol, local-address, local-process*}

   In the TCP/IP suite, for example:

      {*tcp, 193.44.234.3, 12345*}

- A *conversation* is the communication link between two processes.

- An *association* is the 5-tuple that completely specifies the two processes that comprise a connection:

      {*protocol, local-address, local-process, foreign-address, foreign-process*}

   In the TCP/IP suite, the following could be a valid association:

{*tcp, 193.44.234.3, 1500, 193.44.234.5, 21*}

- A *half-association* is either:

   {*protocol, local-address, local-process*}

   or

   {*protocol, foreign-address, foreign-process*}

   which specify each half of a connection.

- The half-association is also called a *socket* or a *transport address*. That is, a socket is an endpoint for communication that can be named and addressed in a network.

Two processes communicate via *TCP sockets*. The socket model provides a process with a full-duplex byte stream connection to another process. The application need not concern itself with the management of this stream; these facilities are provided by TCP.

TCP uses the same port principle as UDP to provide multiplexing. Like UDP, TCP uses well-known and ephemeral ports. Each side of a TCP connection has a *socket* that can be identified by the triple <TCP, IP address, port number>. If two processes are communicating over TCP, they have a *logical connection* that is uniquely identifiable by the two sockets involved, that is by the combination <TCP, local IP address, local port, remote IP address, remote port> (see Figure 50). Server processes are able to manage multiple conversations through a single port. Please refer to 4.19.1, "The Socket API" on page 319 for more information about socket APIs.

2.7 User Datagram Protocol (UDP)

UDP is a *standard protocol* with STD number 6. UDP is described by *RFC 768 — User Datagram Protocol*. Its status is *recommended*, but in practice every TCP/IP implementation that is not used exclusively for routing will include UDP.

UDP is basically an application interface to IP. It adds no reliability, flow-control or error recovery to IP. It simply serves as a *multiplexer/demultiplexer* for sending and receiving datagrams, using *ports* to direct the datagrams as shown in Figure 47 on page 98. For a more detailed discussion of ports refer to 2.6, "Ports and Sockets" on page 94.

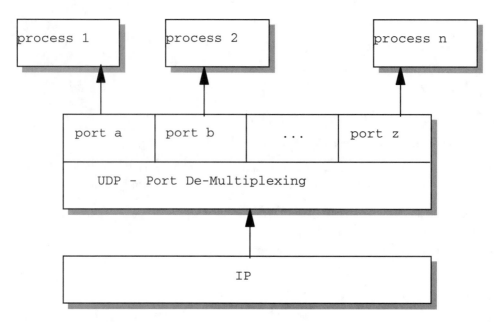

Figure 47. *UDP - Demultiplexing Based on Ports*

UDP provides a mechanism for one application to send a datagram to another. The UDP layer can be regarded as being extremely thin and consequently has low overheads, but it requires the application to take responsibility for error recovery and so on.

Applications sending datagrams to a host need to identify a target that is more specific than the IP address, since datagrams are normally directed to certain processes and not to the system as a whole. UDP provides this by using *ports*.

The port concept is discussed in 2.6, "Ports and Sockets" on page 94.

2.7.1 UDP Datagram Format

Each UDP datagram is sent within a single IP datagram. Although, the IP datagram may be fragmented during transmission, the receiving IP implementation will re-assemble it before presenting it to the UDP layer. All IP implementations are required to accept datagrams of 576 bytes, which means that, allowing for maximum-size IP header of 60 bytes, a UDP datagram of 516 bytes is acceptable to all implementations. Many implementations will accept larger datagrams, but this is not guaranteed. The UDP datagram has a 16-byte header that is described in Figure 48.

Source Port	Destination Port
Length	Checksum
Data...	

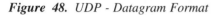

3376B\3376F2AM

Figure 48. UDP - Datagram Format

Where:

Source Port
Indicates the port of the sending process. It is the port to which replies should be addressed.

Destination Port
Specifies the port of the destination process on the destination host.

Length
Is the length (in bytes) of this user datagram including the header.

Checksum
Is an optional 16-bit one's complement of the one's complement sum of a pseudo-IP header, the UDP header and the UDP data. The pseudo-IP header contains the source and destination IP addresses, the protocol and the UDP length:

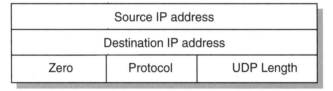

Source IP address		
Destination IP address		
Zero	Protocol	UDP Length

3376B\3376F2AN

Figure 49. UDP - Pseudo-IP Header

The pseudo-IP header effectively extends the checksum to include the original (unfragmented) IP datagram.

2.7.2 UDP Application Programming Interface

The application interface offered by UDP is described in RFC 768. It provides for:

- The creation of new receive ports.

- The receive operation that returns the data bytes and an indication of source port and source IP address.

- The send operation that has as parameters the data, source and destination ports and addresses.

The way this should be implemented is left to the discretion of each vendor.

Be aware that UDP and IP do not provide guaranteed delivery, flow-control or error recovery, so these must be provided by the application.

Standard applications using UDP include:

- Trivial File Transfer Protocol (TFTP)
- Domain Name System (DNS) name server
- Remote Procedure Call (RPC), used by the Network File System (NFS)
- Simple Network Management Protocol (SNMP)
- Lightweight Directory Access Protocol (LDAP)

2.8 Transmission Control Protocol (TCP)

TCP is a *standard protocol* with STD number 7. TCP is described by *RFC 793 — Transmission Control Protocol*. Its status is *recommended*, but in practice every TCP/IP implementation that is not used exclusively for routing will include TCP.

TCP provides considerably more facilities for applications than UDP, notably error recovery, flow control and reliability. TCP is a *connection-oriented* protocol unlike UDP which is *connectionless*. Most of the user application protocols, such as Telnet and FTP, use TCP.

The two processes communicate with each other over a TCP connection (InterProcess Communication - IPC), as shown in Figure 50 on page 101. Please see 2.6, "Ports and Sockets" on page 94 for more details about ports and sockets.

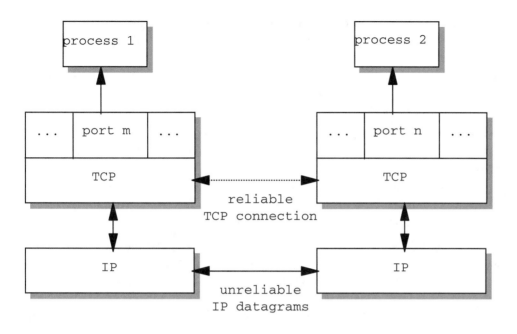

Figure 50. *TCP - Connection between Processes.* (Processes 1 and 2 communicate over a TCP connection carried by IP datagrams.)

2.8.1 TCP Concept

As noted above, the primary purpose of TCP is to provide reliable logical circuit or connection service between pairs of processes. It does *not* assume reliability from the lower-level protocols (such as IP), so TCP must guarantee this itself.

TCP can be characterized by the following facilities it provides for the applications using it:

Stream Data Transfer

From the application's viewpoint, TCP transfers a contiguous stream of bytes through the network. The application does not have to bother with chopping the data into basic blocks or datagrams. TCP does this by grouping the bytes in TCP segments, which are passed to IP for transmission to the destination. Also, TCP itself decides how to segment the data and it can forward the data at its own convenience.

Sometimes, an application needs to be sure that all the data passed to TCP has actually been transmitted to the destination. For that reason, a push function is

defined. It will push all remaining TCP segments still in storage to the
destination host. The normal close connection function also pushes the data to
the destination.

Reliability

TCP assigns a sequence number to each byte transmitted and expects a positive
acknowledgment (ACK) from the receiving TCP. If the ACK is not received
within a timeout interval, the data is retransmitted. Since the data is transmitted
in blocks (TCP segments) only the sequence number of the first data byte in the
segment is sent to the destination host.

The receiving TCP uses the sequence numbers to rearrange the segments when
they arrive out of order, and to eliminate duplicate segments.

Flow Control

The receiving TCP, when sending an ACK back to the sender, also indicates to
the sender the number of bytes it can receive beyond the last received TCP
segment, without causing overrun and overflow in its internal buffers. This is
sent in the ACK in the form of the highest sequence number it can receive
without problems. This mechanism is also referred to as a window-mechanism
and we discuss it in more detail later in this chapter.

Multiplexing

Is achieved through the use of ports, just as with UDP.

Logical Connections

The reliability and flow control mechanisms described above require that TCP
initializes and maintains certain status information for each data stream. The
combination of this status, including sockets, sequence numbers and window
sizes, is called a logical connection. Each connection is uniquely identified by
the pair of sockets used by the sending and receiving processes.

Full Duplex

TCP provides for concurrent data streams in both directions.

2.8.1.1 The Window Principle

A simple transport protocol might use the following principle: send a packet and then
wait for an acknowledgment from the receiver before sending the next packet. If the
ACK is not received within a certain amount of time, retransmit the packet.

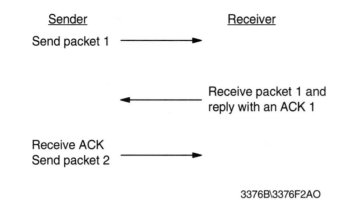

Figure 51. *TCP - The Window Principle*

While this mechanism ensures reliability, it only uses a part of the available network bandwidth.

Consider now a protocol where the sender groups its packets to be transmitted as in Figure 52 and uses the following rules:

- The sender can send all packets within the window without receiving an ACK, but must start a timeout timer for each of them.

- The receiver must acknowledge each packet received, indicating the sequence number of the last well-received packet.

- The sender slides the window on each ACK received.

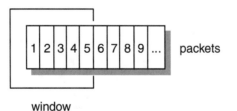

Figure 52. *TCP - Message Packets*

In our example, the sender can transmit packets 1 to 5 without waiting for any acknowledgment:

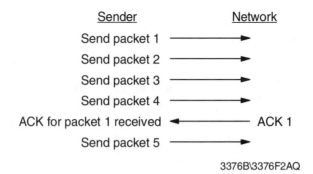

Figure 53. *TCP - Window Principle*

At the moment the sender receives ACK 1 (acknowledgment for packet 1), it can slide its window one packet to the right:

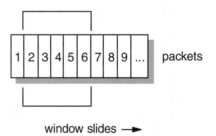

Figure 54. *TCP - Message Packets*

At this point, the sender may also transmit packet 6.

Imagine some special cases:

Packet 2 gets lost

   The sender will not receive ACK 2, so its window will remain in position 1 (as in Figure 54). In fact, since the receiver did not receive packet 2, it will acknowledge packets 3, 4 and 5 with an ACK 1, since packet 1 was the last one received in sequence. At the sender's side, eventually a timeout will occur for packet 2 and it will be retransmitted. Note that reception of this packet by the receiver will generate ACK 5, since it has now successfully received all packets 1 to 5, and the sender's window will slide four positions upon receiving this ACK 5.

Packet 2 did arrive, but the acknowledgment gets lost:

> The sender does not receive ACK 2, but will receive ACK 3. ACK 3 is an acknowledgment for *all* packets up to 3 (including packet 2) and the sender can now slide its window to packet 4.

This window mechanism ensures:

- Reliable transmission.
- Better use of the network bandwidth (better throughput).
- Flow-control, since the receiver may delay replying to a packet with an acknowledgment, knowing its free buffers available and the window-size of the communication.

2.8.1.2 The Window Principle Applied to TCP

The above window principle is used in TCP, but with a few differences:

- Since TCP provides a byte-stream connection, sequence numbers are assigned to each byte in the stream. TCP divides this contiguous byte stream into TCP segments to transmit them. The window principle is used at the byte level; that is, the segments sent and ACKs received will carry byte-sequence numbers and the window size is expressed as a number of bytes, rather than a number of packets.

- The window size is determined by the receiver when the connection is established, and is variable during the data transfer. Each ACK message will include the window size that the receiver is ready to deal with at that particular time.

The sender's data stream can now be seen as follows:

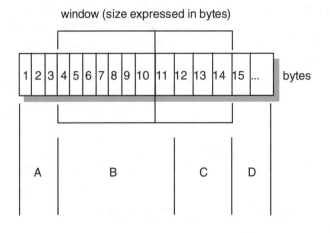

Figure 55. *TCP - Window Principle Applied to TCP*

Where:

A Bytes that are transmitted and have been acknowledged.
B Bytes that are sent but not yet acknowledged.
C Bytes that can be sent without waiting for any acknowledgment.
D Bytes that cannot yet be sent.

Remember that TCP will block bytes into segments, and a TCP segment only carries the sequence number of the first byte in the segment.

2.8.1.3 TCP Segment Format

The TCP segment format is shown in Figure 56 on page 107.

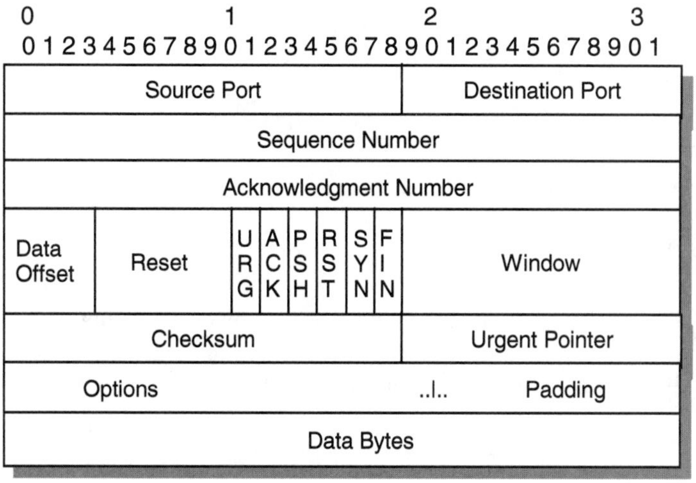

```
 0               1               2               3
 0 1 2 3 4 5 6 7 8 9 0 1 2 3 4 5 6 7 8 9 0 1 2 3 4 5 6 7 8 9 0 1
┌───────────────────────────────┬───────────────────────────────┐
│          Source Port          │        Destination Port       │
├───────────────────────────────┴───────────────────────────────┤
│                        Sequence Number                         │
├────────────────────────────────────────────────────────────────┤
│                     Acknowledgment Number                      │
├─────────┬───────────┬─┬─┬─┬─┬─┬─┬──────────────────────────────┤
│         │           │U│A│P│R│S│F│                              │
│  Data   │   Reset   │R│C│S│S│Y│I│            Window            │
│ Offset  │           │G│K│H│T│N│N│                              │
├─────────┴───────────┴─┴─┴─┴─┴─┴─┼──────────────────────────────┤
│            Checksum             │        Urgent Pointer        │
├────────────────────────┬────────┴──────────────────────────────┤
│        Options         │        ..|..        Padding           │
├────────────────────────┴────────────────────────────────────────┤
│                          Data Bytes                            │
└────────────────────────────────────────────────────────────────┘
```

Figure 56. TCP - Segment Format

Where:

Source Port
The 16-bit source port number, used by the receiver to reply.

Destination Port
The 16-bit destination port number.

Sequence Number
The sequence number of the first data byte in this segment. If the SYN control bit is set, the sequence number is the initial sequence number (n) and the first data byte is n+1.

Acknowledgment Number
If the ACK control bit is set, this field contains the value of the next sequence number that the receiver is expecting to receive.

Data Offset
The number of 32-bit words in the TCP header. It indicates where the data begins.

Reserved
Six bits reserved for future use; must be zero.

URG
Indicates that the urgent pointer field is significant in this segment.

ACK

Indicates that the acknowledgment field is significant in this segment.

PSH Push function.

RST Resets the connection.

SYN Synchronizes the sequence numbers.

FIN No more data from sender.

Window

Used in ACK segments. It specifies the number of data bytes beginning with the one indicated in the acknowledgment number field which the receiver (= the sender of this segment) is willing to accept.

Checksum

The 16-bit one's complement of the one's complement sum of all 16-bit words in a pseudo-header, the TCP header and the TCP data. While computing the checksum, the checksum field itself is considered zero.

The pseudo-header is the same as that used by UDP for calculating the checksum. It is a pseudo-IP-header, only used for the checksum calculation, with the format shown in Figure 57:

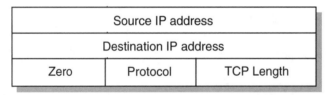

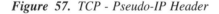

3376B\3376F2AT

Figure 57. TCP - Pseudo-IP Header

Urgent Pointer

Points to the first data octet following the urgent data. Only significant when the URG control bit is set.

Options

Just as in the case of IP datagram options, options can be either:

- A single byte containing the option number, or
- A variable length option in the following format:

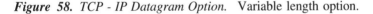

3376B\3376F2AU

Figure 58. TCP - IP Datagram Option. Variable length option.

There are currently seven options defined:

Kind	Length	Meaning
Table 3. TCP - IP Datagram Options		
0	-	End of Option List
1	-	No-Operation
2	4	Maximum Segment Size
3	3	Window Scale
4	2	Sack-Permitted
5	X	Sack
8	10	Time Stamps

Maximum Segment Size Option

This option is only used during the establishment of the connection (SYN control bit set) and is sent from the side that is to receive data to indicate the maximum segment length it can handle. If this option is not used, any segment size is allowed.

3376B\3376F2AV

Figure 59. TCP - Maximum Segment Size Option

Window Scale Option

This option is not mandatory. Both sides must send the Windows Scale Option in their SYN segments to enable windows scaling in their direction. The Window Scale expands the definition of the TCP window to 32 bits. It defines the 32-bit window size by using scale factor in the SYN segment over standard 16-bit window size. The receiver rebuild the the 32-bit window size by using the 16-bit window size and scale factor.

This option is determined while handshaking. There is no way to change
it after the connection has been established.

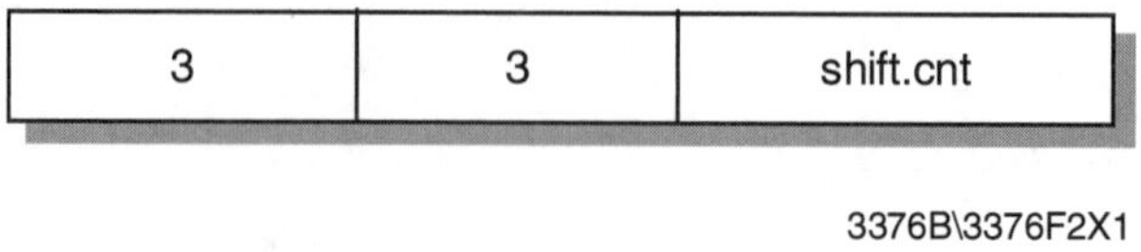

3376B\3376F2X1

Figure 60. TCP - Window Scale Option

SACK-Permitted Option

This option is set when selective acknowledgment is used in that TCP
connection.

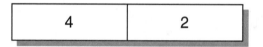

Figure 61. TCP - Sack-Permitted Option

SACK Option

Selective Acknowledgment (SACK) allows the receiver to inform the
sender about all the segments which are received successfully. Thus, the
sender will only send the segments that actually got lost. If the number of
the segments which are lost since the last SACK, is much, the next SACK
option contains long data. To reduce this, the SACK option should be
used for the most recent received data.

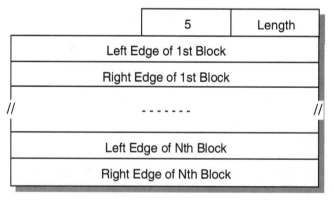

3376B\3376F2X3

Figure 62. TCP - Sack Option

Time Stamps Option

The time stamps option sends a time stamp value that indicates the current value of the time stamp clock of the TCP sending the option. Time Stamp Echo Value can only be used if the ACK bit is set in the TCP header.

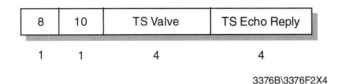

Figure 63. TCP - Time Stamps Option

Padding

All zero bytes used to fill up the TCP header to a total length that is a multiple of 32 bits.

2.8.1.4 Acknowledgments and Retransmissions

TCP sends data in variable length segments. Sequence numbers are based on a byte count. Acknowledgments specify the sequence number of the next byte that the receiver expects to receive.

Consider that a segment gets lost or corrupted. In this case, the receiver will acknowledge all further well-received segments with an acknowledgment referring to the first byte of the missing packet. The sender will stop transmitting when it has sent all the bytes in the window. Eventually, a timeout will occur and the missing segment will be retransmitted.

Figure 64 on page 112 illustrates and example where a window size of 1500 bytes and segments of 500 bytes are used.

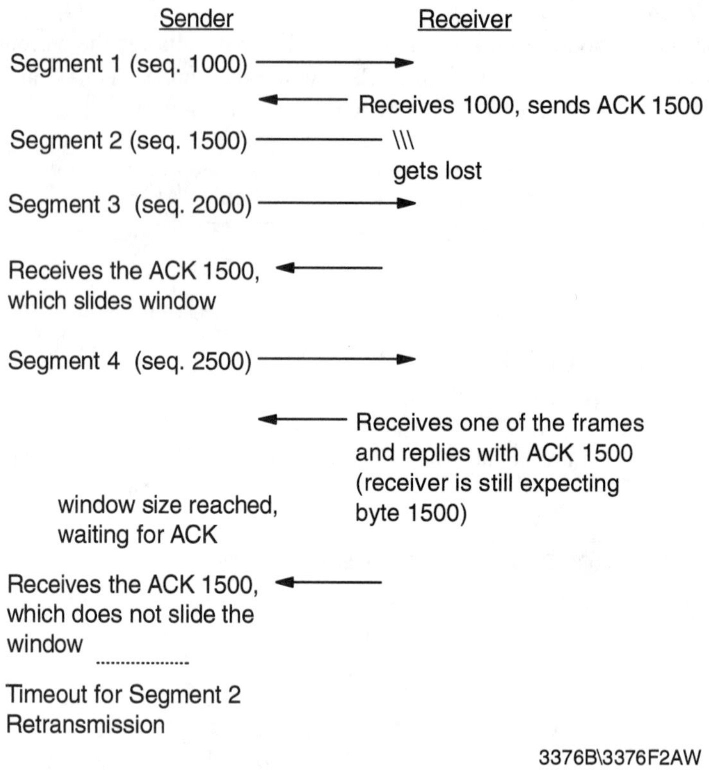

```
        Sender                    Receiver
Segment 1 (seq. 1000) ─────────────▶

                      ◀───────── Receives 1000, sends ACK 1500
Segment 2 (seq. 1500) ───────── \\\
                                gets lost
Segment 3  (seq. 2000) ─────────▶


Receives the ACK 1500, ◀─────────
which slides window


Segment 4  (seq. 2500) ─────────▶


                      ◀───────── Receives one of the frames
                                and replies with ACK 1500
                                (receiver is still expecting
      window size reached,       byte 1500)
      waiting for ACK

Receives the ACK 1500, ◀─────────
which does not slide the
window       ·················
Timeout for Segment 2
Retransmission
                                       3376B\3376F2AW
```

Figure 64. TCP - Acknowledgment and Retransmission Process

A problem now arises, since the sender does know that segment 2 is lost or corrupted, but doesn't know anything about segments 3 and 4. The sender should at least retransmit segment 2, but it could also retransmit segments 3 and 4 (since they are within the current window). It is possible that:

1. Segment 3 has been received, and for segment 4 we don't know. It could be received, but ACK didn't reach us yet, or it could be lost also.
2. Segment 3 was lost, and we received the ACK 1500 upon the reception of segment 4.

Each TCP implementation is free to react to a timeout as the implementers wish. It could retransmit only segment 2, but in case 2 above, we will be waiting again until segment 3 times out. In this case, we lose all of the throughput advantages of the window mechanism. Or TCP might immediately resend all of the segments in the current window.

Whatever the choice, maximal throughput is lost. This is because the ACK does not contain a second acknowledgment sequence number indicating the actual frame received.

Variable Timeout Intervals: Each TCP should implement an algorithm to adapt the timeout values to be used for the round trip time of the segments. To do this, TCP records the time at which a segment was sent, and the time at which the ACK is received. A weighted average is calculated over several of these round trip times, to be used as a timeout value for the next segment(s) to be sent.

This is an important feature, because delays can vary in IP network, depending on multiple factors, such as the load of an intermediate low-speed network or the saturation of an intermediate IP gateway.

2.8.1.5 Establishing a TCP Connection

Before any data can be transferred, a connection has to be established between the two processes. One of the processes (usually the server) issues a *passive OPEN* call, the other an *active OPEN* call. The passive OPEN call remains dormant until another process tries to connect to it by an active OPEN.

On the network, three TCP segments are exchanged:

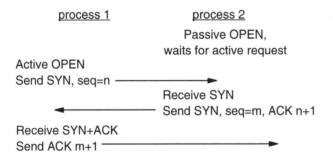

The connection is now established and the two data streams
(one in each direction) have been initialized (sequence numbers)

3376B\3376F2AY

Figure 65. TCP - Connection Establishment

This whole process is known as a *three-way handshake*.

Note that the exchanged TCP segments include the initial sequence numbers from both sides, to be used on subsequent data transfers.

Closing the connection is done implicitly by sending a TCP segment with the FIN bit (no more data) set. Since the connection is full-duplex (that is, there are two independent data streams, one in each direction), the FIN segment only closes the data transfer in one direction. The other process will now send the remaining data it still has to transmit and also ends with a TCP segment where the FIN bit is set. The connection is deleted (status information on both sides) once the data stream is closed in both directions.

2.8.2 TCP Application Programming Interface

The TCP application programming interface is not fully defined. Only some base functions it should provide are described in *RFC 793 - Transmission Control Protocol*. As is the case with most RFCs in the TCP/IP protocol suite, a great degree of freedom is left to the implementers, thereby allowing for optimal (operating system-dependent) implementations, resulting in better efficiency (greater throughput).

The following function calls are described in the RFC:

Open   To establish a connection takes several parameters, such as:
- Active/passive
- Foreign socket
- Local port number
- Timeout value (optional)

This returns a local connection name, which is used to reference this particular connection in all other functions.

Send   Causes data in a referenced user buffer to be sent over the connection. Can optionally set the URGENT flag or the PUSH flag.

Receive Copies incoming TCP data to a user buffer.

Close   Closes the connection; causes a push of all remaining data and a TCP segment with FIN flag set.

Status   Is an implementation-dependent call that could return information such as:
- Local and foreign socket
- Send and receive window sizes
- Connection state
- Local connection name

Abort   Causes all pending Send and Receive operations to be aborted, and a RESET to be sent to the foreign TCP.

Full details can be found in *RFC 793 - Transmission Control Protocol*.

2.8.3 TCP Congestion Control Algorithms

One big difference between TCP and UDP is the congestion control algorithm. The TCP congestion algorithm prevents a sender from overrunning the capacity of the network (for example, slower WAN links). TCP can adapt the sender's rate to network capacity and attempt to avoid potential congestion situations. In order to understand the difference between TCP and UDP, understanding basic TCP congestion control algorithms is very helpful.

Several congestion control enhancements have been added and suggested to TCP over the years. This is still an active and ongoing research area. But modern implementations of TCP contain four intertwined algorithms as basic Internet standards:

- Slow start

- Congestion avoidance

- Fast retransmit

- Fast recovery

2.8.3.1 Slow Start

Old implementations of TCP would start a connection with the sender injecting multiple segments into the network, up to the window size advertised by the receiver. While this is ok when the two hosts are on the same LAN, if there are routers and slower links between the sender and the receiver, problems can arise. Some intermediate routers could not handle it, packets were dropped, retransmission resulted and performance was degraded.

The algorithm to avoid this is called slow start. It operates by observing that the rate at which new packets should be injected into the network is the rate at which the acknowledgments are returned by the other end. Slow start adds another window to the sender's TCP: the congestion window, called cwnd. When a new connection is established with a host on another network, the congestion window is initialized to one segment (for example, the segment size announced by the other end, or the default, typically 536 or 512). Each time an ACK is received, the congestion window is increased by one segment. The sender can transmit the lower value of the congestion window or the advertised window. The congestion window is flow control imposed by the sender, while the advertised window is flow control imposed by the receiver. The former is based on the sender's assessment of perceived network congestion; the latter is related to the amount of available buffer space at the receiver for this connection.

The sender starts by transmitting one segment and waiting for its ACK. When that ACK is received, the congestion window is incremented from one to two, and two segments can be sent. When each of those two segments is acknowledged, the congestion window is increased to four. This provides an exponential growth, although it is not exactly exponential because the receiver may delay its ACKs, typically sending one ACK for every two segments that it receives.

At some point the capacity of the IP network (for example, slower WAN links) can be reached, and an intermediate router will start discarding packets. This tells the sender that its congestion window has gotten too large. Please see Figure 66 for an overview of slow start in action.

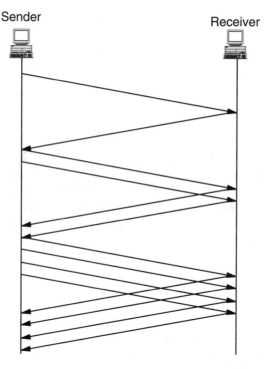

3376a\3376F2KA

Figure 66. TCP Slow Start in Action

2.8.3.2 Congestion Avoidance

The assumption of the algorithm is that packet loss caused by damage is very small (much less than 1%), therefore the loss of a packet signals congestion somewhere in the network between the source and destination. There are two indications of packet loss:

1. A timeout occurs.

2. Duplicate ACKs are received.

Congestion avoidance and slow start are independent algorithms with different objectives. But when congestion occurs TCP must slow down its transmission rate of packets into the network, and then invoke slow start to get things going again. In practice they are implemented together.

Congestion avoidance and slow start require that two variables be maintained for each connection:

- A congestion window, cwnd

- A slow start threshold size, ssthresh

The combined algorithm operates as follows:

1. Initialization for a given connection sets cwnd to one segment and ssthresh to 65535 bytes.

2. The TCP output routine never sends more than the lower value of cwnd or the receiver's advertised window.

3. When congestion occurs (time out or duplicate ACK), one-half of the current window size is saved in ssthresh. Additionally, if the congestion is indicated by a timeout, cwnd is set to one segment.

4. When new data is acknowledged by the other end, increase cwnd, but the way it increases depends on whether TCP is performing slow start or congestion avoidance. If cwnd is less than or equal to ssthresh, TCP is in slow start; otherwise TCP is performing congestion avoidance.

Slow start continues until TCP is halfway to where it was when congestion occurred (since it recorded half of the window size that caused the problem in step 2), and then congestion avoidance takes over. Slow start has cwnd begin at one segment, and incremented by one segment every time an ACK is received. As mentioned earlier, this opens the window exponentially: send one segment, then two, then four, and so on.

Congestion avoidance dictates that cwnd be incremented by segsize*segsize/cwnd each time an ACK is received, where segsize is the segment size and cwnd is maintained in bytes. This is a linear growth of cwnd, compared to slow start's exponential growth.

The increase in cwnd should be at most one segment each round-trip time (regardless of how many ACKs are received in that round trip time), whereas slow start increments cwnd by the number of ACKs received in a round-trip time. Many implementations incorrectly add a small fraction of the segment size (typically the segment size divided by 8) during congestion avoidance. This is wrong and should not be emulated in future releases. Please see Figure 67 for an example of TCP slow start and congestion avoidance in action.

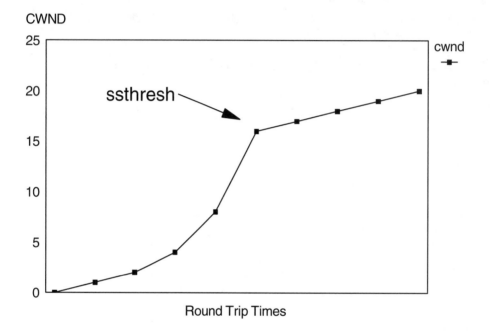

Figure 67. TCP Slow Start and Congestion Avoidance Behavior in Action

2.8.3.3 Fast Retransmit

Fast retransmit avoids TCP having to wait for a timeout to resend lost segments.

Modifications to the congestion avoidance algorithm were proposed in 1990. Before describing the change, realize that TCP may generate an immediate acknowledgment (a duplicate ACK) when an out-of-order segment is received. This duplicate ACK should not be delayed. The purpose of this duplicate ACK is to let the other end know that a segment was received out of order, and to tell it what sequence number is expected.

Since TCP does not know whether a duplicate ACK is caused by a lost segment or just a reordering of segments, it waits for a small number of duplicate ACKs to be received. It is assumed that if there is just a reordering of the segments, there will be only one or two duplicate ACKs before the reordered segment is processed, which will then generate a new ACK. If three or more duplicate ACKs are received in a row, it is a strong indication that a segment has been lost. TCP then performs a retransmission of what appears to be the missing segment, without waiting for a retransmission timer to expire. Please see Figure 68 for an overview of TCP fast retransmit in action.

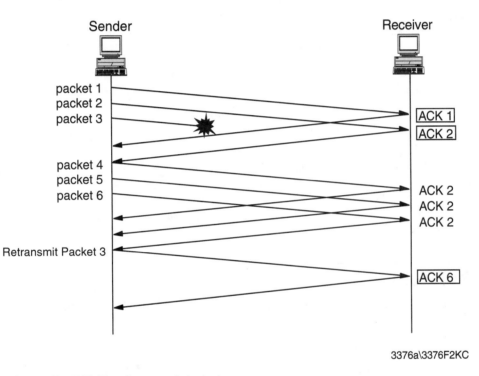

3376a\3376F2KC

Figure 68. TCP Fast Retransmit in Action

2.8.3.4 Fast Recovery

After fast retransmit sends what appears to be the missing segment, congestion avoidance, but not slow start, is performed. This is the fast recovery algorithm. It is an improvement that allows high throughput under moderate congestion, especially for large windows.

The reason for not performing slow start in this case is that the receipt of the duplicate ACKs tells TCP more than just a packet has been lost. Since the receiver can only generate the duplicate ACK when another segment is received, that segment has left the network and is in the receiver's buffer. That is, there is still data flowing between the two ends, and TCP does not want to reduce the flow abruptly by going into slow start. The fast retransmit and fast recovery algorithms are usually implemented together as follows.

1. When the third duplicate ACK in a row is received, set ssthresh to one-half the current congestion window, cwnd, but no less than two segments. Retransmit the missing segment. Set cwnd to ssthresh plus 3 times the segment size. This inflates the congestion window by the number of segments that have left the network and the other end has cached (3).

2. Each time another duplicate ACK arrives, increment cwnd by the segment size. This inflates the congestion window for the additional segment that has left the network. Transmit a packet if allowed by the new value of cwnd.

3. When the next ACK arrives that acknowledges new data, set cwnd to ssthresh (the value set in step 1). This ACK should be the acknowledgment of the retransmission from step 1, one round-trip time after the retransmission. Additionally, this ACK should acknowledge all the intermediate segments sent between the lost packet and the receipt of the first duplicate ACK. This step is congestion avoidance, since TCP is down to one-half the rate it was at when the packet was lost.

2.9 References

Please refer to the following RFCs for more information on TCP/IP internetwork and transport layer protocols:

- *RFC 768 — User Datagram Protocol*
- *RFC 791 — Internet Protocol*
- *RFC 792 — Internet Control Message Protocol*
- *RFC 793 — Transmission Control Protocol*
- *RFC 826 — Ethernet Address Resolution Protocol*
- *RFC 903 — Reverse Address Resolution Protocol*
- *RFC 919 — Broadcasting Internet Datagrams*
- *RFC 922 — Broadcasting Internet datagrams in the presence of subnets*
- *RFC 950 — Internet Standard Subnetting Procedure*

- *RFC 1112 — Host extensions for IP multicasting*

- *RFC 1166 — Internet numbers*

- *RFC 1191 — Path MTU discovery*

- *RFC 1256 — ICMP Router Discovery Messages*

- *RFC 1323 — TCP Extensions for High Performance*

- *RFC 1466 — Guidelines for Management of IP Address Space*

- *RFC 1518 — An Architecture for IP Address Allocation with CIDR*

- *RFC 1519 — Classless Inter-Domain Routing (CIDR): an Address Assignment and Aggregation Strategy*

- *RFC 1520 — Exchanging Routing Information Across Provider Boundaries in the CIDR Environment*

- *RFC 1918 — Address Allocation for Private Internets*

- *RFC 2001 — TCP Slow Start, Congestion Avoidance, Fast Retransmit, and Fast Recovery Algorithms*

- *RFC 2018 — TCP Selective Acknowledgement Options*

- *RFC 2050 — INTERNET REGISTRY IP ALLOCATION GUIDELINES*

- *RFC 2236 — Internet Group Management Protocol, Version 2*

Chapter 3. Routing Protocols

One of the basic functions of IP is its ability to form connections between different physical networks. This is due to the flexibility of IP to use almost any physical network below it, and to the IP routing algorithm. A system that does this is termed a *router*, although the older term *IP gateway* is also used.

Note: In other sections of the book, we show the position of each protocol in the layered model of the TCP/IP protocol stack. The routing function is part of the internetwork layer, but the primary function of a routing protocol is to *exchange* routing information with other routers, and in this respect the protocols behave more like application protocols. Therefore, we do not attempt to represent the position of these protocols in the protocol stack with a diagram as we do with the other protocols.

3.1 Basic IP Routing

The fundamental function for routers is present in *all* IP implementations:

> An *incoming* IP datagram that specifies a destination IP address other than one of the local host's IP address(es), is treated as a normal *outgoing* IP datagram.

This outgoing IP datagram is subject to the IP routing algorithm (see 2.1.3.4, "IP Routing Algorithm" on page 48) of the local host, which selects the *next hop* for the datagram (the next host to send it to). This new destination can be located on any of the physical networks to which the intermediate host is attached. If it is a physical network other than the one on which the host originally received the datagram, then the net result is that the intermediate host has *forwarded* the IP datagram from one physical network to another.

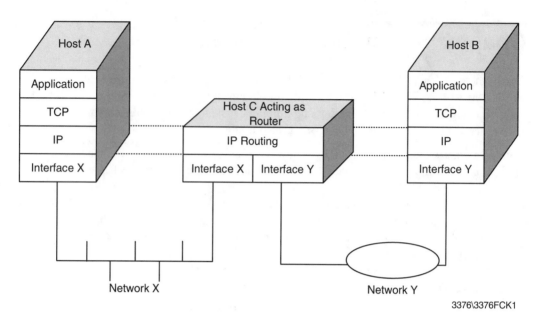

3376\3376FCK1

Figure 69. *Router Operation of IP*

The normal IP routing table contains information about the locally attached networks and the IP addresses of other routers located on these networks, plus the networks they attach to. It can be extended with information on IP networks that are farther away, and can also contain a default route, but it still remains a table with limited information; that is, it represents only a part of the whole IP networks. That is why this kind of router is called a *router with partial routing information*.

Some considerations apply to these routers with partial information:

- They do not know about all IP networks.
- They allow local sites autonomy in establishing and modifying routes.
- A routing entry error in one of the routers can introduce inconsistencies, thereby making part of the network unreachable.

Some error reporting should be implemented by routers with partial information via the Internet Control Message Protocol (ICMP) described in 2.2, "Internet Control Message Protocol (ICMP)" on page 74. They should be able to report the following errors back to the source host:

- Unknown IP destination network by an ICMP *Destination Unreachable* message.
- Redirection of traffic to more suitable routers by sending ICMP *Redirect* messages.

- Congestion problems (too many incoming datagrams for the available buffer space) by an ICMP *Source Quench* message.
- The Time-to-Live field of an IP datagram has reached zero. This is reported with an ICMP *Time Exceeded* message.
- Also, the following base ICMP operations and messages should be supported:
  - Parameter problem
  - Address mask
  - Time stamp
  - Information request/reply
  - Echo request/reply

A more intelligent router is required if:

- The router has to know routes to *all* possible IP networks, as was the case for the Internet backbone routers.
- The router has to have dynamic routing tables, which are kept up-to-date with minimal or no manual intervention.
- The router has to be able to advertise local changes to other routers.

These more advanced forms of routers use additional protocols to communicate with each other. A number of protocols of this kind exist, and descriptions of the important ones will be given in the following sections. The reasons for this multiplicity of different protocols are basically fourfold:

- Using Internet terminology, there is a concept of a group of networks, called an *autonomous system (AS)* (see AS in 3.1.2, "Autonomous Systems" on page 126), which is administered as a unit. The AS concept arose because the TCP/IP protocols were developed with the ARPANET already in place.

  Routing within an AS and routing outside an AS are treated as different issues and are addressed by different protocols.

- Over two decades several routing protocols were tested in the Internet. Some of them performed well; others had to be abandoned.

- The emergence of ASs of different sizes called for different routing solutions. For small to medium-sized ASs a group of routing protocols based upon Distance Vector, such as RIP, became very popular. However, such protocols do not perform well for large interconnected networks. Link State protocols, such as OSPF, are much better suited for such networks.

- To exchange routing information between ASs border gateway protocols were developed.

3.1.1 Routing Processes

In TCP/IP software operating systems, routing protocols are often implemented using one of two daemons:[3]

routed

> Pronounced "route D." This is a basic routing daemon for interior routing supplied with the majority of TCP/IP implementations. It uses the RIP protocol (see 3.3.1, "Routing Information Protocol (RIP)" on page 138).

gated

> Pronounced "gate D." This is a more sophisticated daemon on UNIX-based systems for interior and exterior routing. It can employ a number of additional protocols such as OSPF (see 3.3.4, "Open Shortest Path First (OSPF)" on page 146) and BGP (see 3.4.2, "Border Gateway Protocol (BGP-4)" on page 177).

In TCP/IP hardware implementations, mainly in dedicated router operating systems such as the Common Code for IBM routers or Cisco's Internetworking Operating System (IOS), the routing protocols are implemented in the operating system.

For Multicast Roting Protocols such as DVMRP and MOSPF, please see 9.3, "Multicast Routing Protocols" on page 600.

3.1.2 Autonomous Systems

The dynamic routing protocols can be divided into two groups:

- Interior Gateway Protocols (IGPs)

  Examples of these protocols are Open Short Path First (OSPF) and Routing Information Protocol (RIP).

- Exterior Gateway Protocols (EGPs):

  An example of these routing protocols is Border Gateway Protocol Verson 4 (BGP-4).

In this book, the term gateway is frequently used to imply an IP router.

---

[3] Daemon, pronounced "demon," is a UNIX term for a background server process. Usually, daemons have names ending with a d. An analogous concept for MVS is a server running in a separate address space from TCP/IP; for VM it is a separate service virtual machine, for OS/2 it is a separate OS/2 process, and so on. Although TCP/IP servers are often implemented differently on different platforms, the *routed* daemon is implemented like this on each of these platforms.

Gateway protocols are referred to as interior or exterior depending on whether they are used within or between autonomous systems (ASs).

Interior gateway protocols allow routers to exchange routing information within an AS. Exterior gateway protocols allow the exchange of summary reachability information between separately administered ASs.

An autonomus system (AS) is defined as a logical portion of larger IP networks that are administered by a single authority. The AS would normally comprise the internetwork within an organization, and would be designated as such to allow communication over public IP networks with ASs belonging to other organizations. It is mandatory to register an organization's internetwork as an AS in order to use these public IP services (see Figure 70).

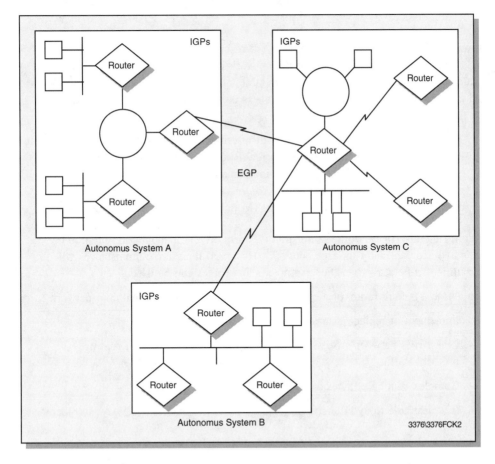

Figure 70. *Autonomous Systems*

Figure 70 illustrates three interconnected ASs. It shows that IGPs are used within each AS, and an EGP is used between the three ASs.

3.2 Routing Algorithms

Dynamic routing algorithms allow routers to exchange route or link information, from which the best paths to reach destinations in an internetwork are calculated.

Static routing can also be used to supplement dynamic routing.

3.2.1 Static Routing

Static routing requires that routes be configured manually for each router, which constitutes one major reason why system administrators shy away from this technique if they have a choice.

Static routing has the disadvantage that network reachability in this case is not dependent on the existence and state of the network itself. If a destination is down, the static routes would remain in the routing table, and traffic would still be sent toward that destination in vain without awareness of an alternate path to the destination if any.

Note: There are solutions to overcome this disadvantage including standard RFC 2338 VRRP (see VRRP in 11.1, "Virtual Router Redundancy Protocol (VRRP)" on page 682) and product implementation such as nexthop awareness parameter (see *Nways Multiprotocol Routing Services Protocol Configuration and Monitoring Reference Volume 1*, IBM publication number SC30-3680-07).

To simplify the task of network administrators, normally the manual configuration of routes is avoided especially in large network. However, there are circumstances when static routing can be attractive. For example, static routes can be used:

- To define a default route, or a route that is not being advertised within a network

- To supplement or replace exterior gateway protocols when:

    - Line tariffs between ASs make it desirable to avoid the cost of routing protocol traffic.

    - Complex routing policies are to be implemented.

    - It is desirable to avoid disruption caused by faulty exterior gateways in other ASs.

3.2.2 Distance Vector Routing

The principle behind *distance vector* routing is very simple. Each router in an internetwork maintains the distance from itself to every known destination in a *distance vector table*. Distance vector tables consist of a series of destinations (vectors) and costs (distances) to reach them and define the lowest costs to destinations at the time of transmission.

The distances in the tables are computed from information provided by neighbor routers. Each router transmits its own distance vector table across the shared network. The sequence of operations for doing this is as follows:

- Each router is configured with an identifier and a cost for each of its network links. The cost is normally fixed at 1, reflecting a single hop, but can reflect some other measurement taken for the link such as the traffic, speed, etc.

- Each router initializes with a distance vector table containing zero for itself, one for directly attached networks, and infinity for every other destination.

- Each router periodically (typically every 30 seconds) transmits its distance vector table to each of its neighbors. It can also transmit the table when a link first comes up or when the table changes.

- Each router saves the most recent table it receives from each neighbor and uses the information to calculate its own distance vector table.

- The total cost to each destination is calculated by adding the cost reported to it in a neighbor's distance vector table to the cost of the link to that neighbor.

- The distance vector table (the routing table) for the router is then created by taking the lowest cost calculated for each destination.

Figure 71 on page 130 shows the distance vector tables for three routers within a simple internetwork.

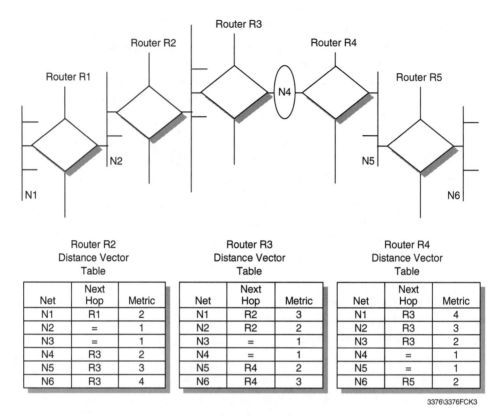

Router R2
Distance Vector
Table

Net	Next Hop	Metric
N1	R1	2
N2	=	1
N3	=	1
N4	R3	2
N5	R3	3
N6	R3	4

Router R3
Distance Vector
Table

Net	Next Hop	Metric
N1	R2	3
N2	R2	2
N3	=	1
N4	=	1
N5	R4	2
N6	R4	3

Router R4
Distance Vector
Table

Net	Next Hop	Metric
N1	R3	4
N2	R3	3
N3	R3	2
N4	=	1
N5	=	1
N6	R5	2

3376\3376FCK3

Figure 71. Distance Vector - Routing Table Calculation

The distance vector algorithm produces a stable routing table after a period directly related to the number of routers across the network. This period is referred to as the *convergence time* and represents the time it takes for distance vector information to traverse the network. In a large internetwork, this time may become too long to be useful.

Routing tables are recalculated if a changed distance vector table is received from a neighbor, or if the state of a link to a neighbor changes. If a network link goes down, the distance vector tables that have been received over it are discarded and the routing table is recalculated.

The chief advantage of distance vector is that it is very easy to implement. There are also the following significant disadvantages:

- The instability caused by old routes persisting in an internetwork

- The long convergence time on large internetworks

- The limit to the size of an internetwork imposed by maximum hop counts

- The fact that distance vector tables are always transmitted even if their contents have not changed

Enhancements to the basic algorithm have evolved to overcome the first two of these problems. They are described in the following subsections.

3.2.2.1 The Count to Infinity Problem

The basic distance vector algorithm will always allow a router to correctly calculate its distance vector table.

Using the example shown in Figure 72 on page 132 you can see one of the problems of distance vector protocols known as *counting to infinity*.

Counting to infinity occurs when a network becomes unreachable, but erroneous routes to that network persist because of the time for the distance vector tables to converge.

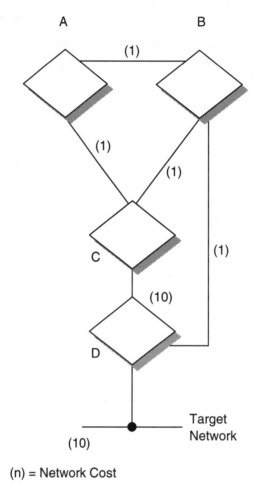

Figure 72. *Counting to Infinity - Example Network*

The example network shows four routers interconnected by five network links. The networks all have a cost of 1 except for that from C to D, which has a cost of 10.

Each of the routers A, B, C and D has routes to all networks. If we show only the routes to the target network, we will see they are as follows:

For D : Directly connected network. Metric 1.

For B : Route via D. Metric 2.

For C : Route via B. Metric 3.

For A : Route via B. Metric 3.

If the link from B to D fails, then all routes will be adjusted in time to use the link from C to D. However, the convergence time for this can be considerable.

Distance vector tables begin to change when B notices that the route to D has become unavailable. Figure 73 shows how the routes to the target network will change, assuming all routers send distance vector table updates at the same time.

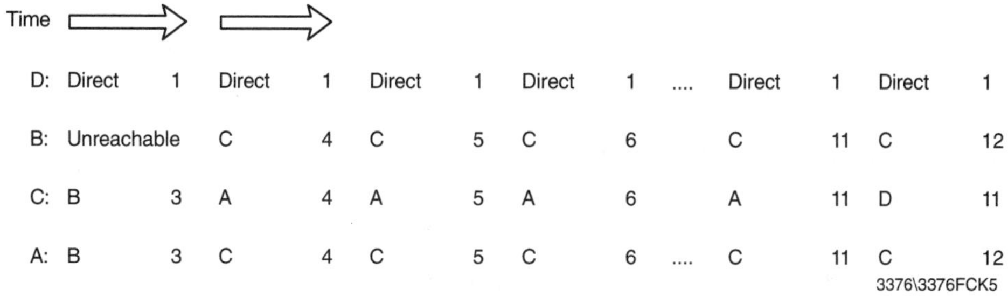

Time ⇒ ⇒

D:	Direct	1	Direct	1	Direct	1	Direct	1	....	Direct	1	Direct	1
B:	Unreachable		C	4	C	5	C	6		C	11	C	12
C:	B	3	A	4	A	5	A	6		A	11	D	11
A:	B	3	C	4	C	5	C	6	....	C	11	C	12

3376\3376FCK5

Figure 73. Counting to Infinity

The problem can be seen clearly. B is able to remove the failed route immediately because it times out the link. Other routers, however, have tables that contain references to this route for many update periods after the link has failed.

1. Initially A and C have a route to D via B.

2. Link from D to B fails.

3. A and C then send updates based on the route to D via B even after the link has failed.

4. B then believes it has a route to D via either A or C. But, in reality it does not have such a route, as the routes are vestiges of the previous route via B, which has failed.

5. A and C then see that the route via B has failed, but believe a route exists via one another.

Slowly the distance vector tables converge, but not until the metrics have counted up, in theory, to infinity. To avoid this happening, practical implementations of distance vector have a low value for infinity; for example, RIP uses a maximum metric of 16.

The manner in which the metrics increment to infinity gives rise to the term *counting to infinity*. It occurs because A and C are engaged in an extended period of mutual deception, each claiming to be able to get to the target network D via one another.

3.2.2.2 Split Horizon

Counting to infinity can easily be prevented if a route to a destination is never reported back in the distance vector table that is sent to the neighbor from which the route was learned. *Split horizon* is the term used for this technique.

The incorporation of split horizon would modify the sequence of distance vector table changes to that shown in Figure 74. The tables can be seen to converge considerably faster than before (see Figure 73 on page 133).

Time

D:	Direct	1	Direct	1	Direct	1	Direct	1
B:	Unreachable		Unreachable		Unreachable		C	12
C:	B	3	A	4	D	11	D	11
A:	B	3	C	4	Unreachable		C	12

Note: Faster Routing Table Convergence

3376\3376FCK6

Figure 74. Split Horizon

3.2.2.3 Split Horizon with Poison Reverse

Poison reverse is an enhancement to split horizon, whereby routes learned from a neighbor router are reported back to it but with a metric of infinity (that is, network unreachable).

The use of poison reverse is safer than split horizon alone because it breaks erroneous looping routes immediately.

If two routers receive routes pointing at each other, and they are advertised with a metric of infinity, the routes will be eliminated immediately as unreachable. If the routes are not advertised in this way, they must be eliminated by the timeout that results from a route not being reported by a neighbor router for several periods (for example, six periods for RIP).

Poison reverse does have one disadvantage. It significantly increases the size of distance vector tables that must be exchanged between neighbor routers because all routes are included in the distance vector tables. While this is generally not a problem on LANs, it can cause real problems on point-to-point connections in large internetworks.

3.2.2.4 Triggered Updates

Split horizon with poison reverse will break routing loops involving two routers. It is still possible, however, for there to be routing loops involving three or more routers. For example, A may believe it has a route through B, B through C, and C through A. This loop can only be eliminated by the timeout that results from counting to infinity.

Triggered updates are designed to reduce the convergence time for routing tables, and hence reduce the period during which such erroneous loops are present in an internetwork.

When a router changes the cost for a route in its distance vector table, it must send the modified table immediately to neighbor routers. This simple mechanism ensures that topology changes in a network are propagated quickly, rather than at a rate dependent on normal periodic updates.

3.2.3 Link State Routing

The growth in the size of internetworks in recent years has necessitated the replacement of distance vector routing algorithms with alternatives that address the shortcomings identified in 3.2.2, "Distance Vector Routing" on page 129.

These new protocols have been based on *link state* or shortest path first (see 3.2.3.1, "Shortest-Path First (SPF)" on page 137) algorithms. The best example is the OSPF Interior Gateway Protocol.

The principle behind link state routing is straightforward, although its implementation can be complex:

- Routers are responsible for contacting neighbors and learning their identities.

- Routers construct link state packets which contain lists of network links and their associated costs.

- Link state packets are transmitted to all routers in a network.

- All routers therefore have an identical list of links in a network, and can construct identical topology maps.

- The maps are used to compute the best routes to all destinations.

Routers contact neighbors by sending *hello* packets on their network interfaces. Hello packets are sent directly to neighbors on point-to-point links and non-broadcast networks. On LANs, hello packets are sent to a predefined group or multicast IP address that can be received by all routers. Neighbors who receive hellos from a router should reply with hello packets that include the identity of that originating router.

Once neighbors have been contacted in this way, link state information can be exchanged.

Link state information is sent in the form of *link state packets* (LSPs), also known as link state advertisements. LSPs provide the database from which network topology maps can be calculated at each router. LSPs are normally sent only under the following specific circumstances:

- When a router discovers a new neighbor

- When a link to a neighbor goes down

- When the cost of a link changes

- Basic refresh packets are sent every 30 minutes

Once a router has generated an LSP it is critical that it is received successfully by all other routers in a network. If this does not happen, routers on the network will calculate network topology based on incorrect link state information.

Distribution of LSPs would normally be on the basis of each router's routing tables. However, this leads to a *chicken and egg* situation. Routing tables would rely on LSPs for their creation and LSPs would rely on routing tables for their distribution. A simple scheme called *flooding* overcomes this, and ensures that LSPs are successfully distributed to all routers in a network.

Flooding requires that a router that receives an LSP transmits it to all neighbors except the one from which it was received. All LSPs must be explicitly acknowledged to ensure successful delivery, and they are sequenced and time stamped to ensure duplicates are not received and retransmitted.

When a router receives an LSP it looks in its database to check the sequence number of the last LSP from the originator. If the sequence number is the same as, or earlier than, the sequence number of the LSP in its database, then the LSP is discarded. Otherwise the LSP is added to the database.

The flooding process ensures that all routers in a network have the same link state information. All routers are then able to compute the same shortest path tree (see shortest path tree in 3.2.3.1, "Shortest-Path First (SPF)" on page 137) topology map for the network, and hence select best routes to all destinations.

3.2.3.1 Shortest-Path First (SPF)

SPF is an algorithm that each router in the same AS has an identical link-state database, leading to an identical graphical replesentation by calculating a tree of shortest paths with the router itself as root. The tree is called the shortest-path tree giving an entire path to any destination network or host. Figure 75 shows the shortest-path tree example from router A. Each router, A, B, C, D and E has an identical link-state database as shown. Router A generate its own shortest-path tree by calculating a tree of shortest paths with router A itself as root.

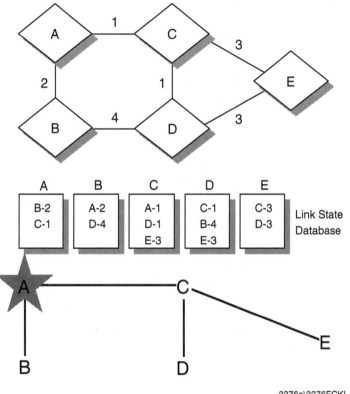

3376a\3376FCKL

Figure 75. Shortest-Path First (SPF) Example

3.3 Interior Gateway Protocols (IGP)

There are many standard and proprietary interior gateway protocols. IBM products such as operating systems and routers support only standard IGP protocols (see

Chapter 14, "Platform Implementations" on page 813). This section describes the following IGPs:

- Routing Information Protocol (RIP)

- Routing Information Protocol, Version 2 (RIP-2)

- Open Shortest Path Fist (OSPF)

3.3.1 Routing Information Protocol (RIP)

RIP is an IAB standard protocol; its status is elective. This means that it is one of several interior gateway protocols available, and it may or may not be implemented on a system. If a system does implement it, however, the implementation should be in line with the RFC 1058.

RIP is based on the Xerox PUP and XNS routing protocols. The RFC was issued after many RIP implementations had been completed. For this reason some do not include all the enhancements to the basic distance vector routing protocol (such as poison reverse and triggered updates).

RIP is a distance vector routing protocol suitable for small networks as compared to OSPF (see OSPF in 3.3.4, "Open Shortest Path First (OSPF)" on page 146). This is because of the shortcomings of distance vector routing identified in 3.2.2, "Distance Vector Routing" on page 129.

There are two versions of RIP. Version 1 (RIP-1) is a widely deployed protocol with a number of known limitations. Version 2 (RIP-2) is an enhanced version designed to alleviate the limitations of RIP while being highly compatible with it. The term RIP is used to refer to Version 1, while RIP-2 refers to Version 2. Whenever the reader encounters the term RIP in TCP/IP literature, it is safe to assume that it is referring to Version 1 unless explicitly stated otherwise. We use this nomenclature in this section except when the two versions are being compared, when we use the term RIP-1 to avoid possible confusion.

RIP is very widely used because the code (known as *ROUTED*) was incorporated on the Berkeley Software Distribution (BSD) UNIX operating system, and in other UNIX systems based on it.

3.3.1.1 Protocol Description

RIP packets are transmitted onto a network in *User Datagram Protocol* (UDP) datagrams, which in turn are carried in IP datagrams. RIP sends and receives datagrams using UDP port 520. RIP datagrams have a maximum size of 512 octets and tables larger than this must be sent in multiple UDP datagrams.

RIP datagrams are normally broadcast onto LANs using the LAN MAC all-stations broadcast address and the IP network or subnetwork broadcast address. They are specifically addressed on point-to-point and multi-access non-broadcast networks, using the destination router IP address.

Routers normally run RIP in *active mode*; that is, advertising their own distance vector tables and updating them based on advertisements from neighbors. End nodes, if they run RIP, normally operate in *passive (or silent) mode*; that is, updating their distance vector tables on the basis of advertisements from neighbors, but not in turn advertising them.

RIP specifies two packet types: *request* and *response*.

A request packet is sent by routers to ask neighbors to send part of their distance vector table (if the packet contains destinations), or all their table (if no destinations have been specified).

A response packet is sent by routers to advertise their distance vector table in the following circumstances:

- Every 30 seconds

- In response to a request packet

- When distance vector tables change (if triggered updates are supported)

Active and passive systems listen for all response packets and update their distance vector tables accordingly. A route to a destination, computed from a neighbor's distance vector table, is kept until an alternate is found with lower cost, or it is not re-advertised in six consecutive RIP responses. In this case the route is timed out and deleted.

When RIP is used with IP, the address family identifier is 2 and the address fields are 4 octets. To reduce problems of counting to infinity the maximum metric is 16 (unreachable) and directly connected networks are defined as having a metric of one.

The RIP packet format for IP is shown in Figure 76 on page 140.

Number of Octets

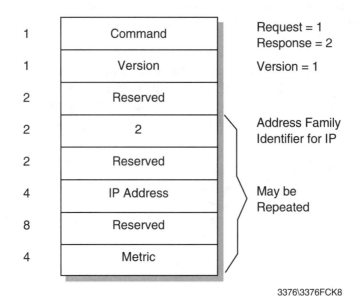

Figure 76. RIP Message

RIP makes no provision for passing subnet masks with its distance vector tables. A router receiving a RIP response must already have subnet mask information to allow it to interpret the network identifier and host identifier portions of the IP address correctly.

In the absence of subnet mask information a router will interpret routes as best as it can. If it knows an IP network has a specific subnet mask, it will interpret all other route information for that network on the basis of that single mask. If it receives a packet with bits set in the field that it regards as the host field, it will interpret it as a route to a host with a mask of *255.255.255.255*.

The above makes it impossible for RIP to be used in an internetwork with variable length subnet masks.

3.3.2 Routing Information Protocol Version 2 (RIP-2)

RIP-2 is a *draft standard protocol*. Its status is *elective*. It is described in RFC 1723.

RIP-2 extends RIP-1. It is less powerful than other recent IGPs such as OSPF (see 3.3.4, "Open Shortest Path First (OSPF)" on page 146) but it has the advantages of easy implementation and lower overheads. The intention of RIP-2 is to provide a straightforward replacement for RIP that can be used on small to medium-sized networks, can be employed in the presence of variable subnetting (see 2.1.2.1, "Types of Subnetting" on page 40) or supernetting (see 2.1.7, "Classless Inter-Domain Routing (CIDR)" on page 58) and importantly, can interoperate with RIP-1. In fact, the major reason for developing and deploying RIP-2 was the use of CIDR, which cannot be used in conjunction with RIP-1.

RIP-2 takes advantage of the fact that half of the bytes in a RIP-1 message are reserved (must be zero) and that the original RIP-1 specification was well designed with enhancements in mind, particularly in the use of the version field. One notable area where this is not the case is in the interpretation of the metric field. RIP-1 specifies it as being a value between 0 and 16 stored in a four-*byte* field. For compatibility, RIP-2 preserves this definition, meaning that it agrees with RIP-1 that 16 is to be interpreted as infinity, and wastes most of this field.

Note: Neither RIP-1 nor RIP-2 are properly suited for use as an IGP in an AS where a value of 16 is too low to be regarded as infinity, because high values of infinity exacerbate the counting to infinity problem. The more sophisticated link-state protocol used in OSPF provides a much better routing solution when the AS is large enough to have a legitimate hop count close to 16.

Provided that a RIP-1 implementation obeys the specification in RFC 1058, RIP-2 can interoperate with RIP-1. The RIP message format is extended as shown in Figure 77 on page 142.

Number of Octets

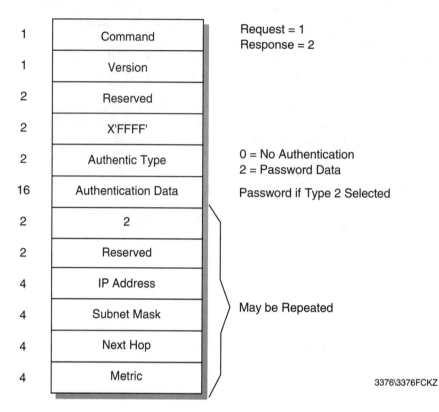

Figure 77. RIP-2 Message

The first entry in the message can be an authentication entry, as shown here, or it can be a route as in a RIP-1 message. If the first entry is an authentication entry, only 24 routes can be included in a message; otherwise the maximum is 25 as in RIP-1.

The fields in a RIP-2 message are the same as for a RIP-1 message except as follows:

Version

Is 2. This tells RIP-1 routers to ignore the fields designated as "must be zero." (If the value is 1, RIP-1 routers are required to discard messages with non-zero values in these fields since the messages originate with a router claiming to be RIP-1-compliant but sending non-RIP-1 messages.)

Address Family

May be X'FFFF' in the first entry only, indicating that this entry is an authentication entry.

Authentication Type

Defines how the remaining 16 bytes are to be used. The only defined types are 0 indicating no authentication and 2 indicating that the field contains password data.

Authentication Data

The password is 16 bytes, plain text ASCII, left adjusted and padded with ASCII NULLs (X'00').

Route Tag

Is a field intended for communicating information about the origin of the route information. It is intended for interoperation between RIP and other routing protocols. RIP-2 implementations must preserve this tag, but RIP-2 does not further specify how it is to be used.

Subnet Mask

The subnet mask associated with the subnet referred to by this entry.

Next Hop

A recommendation about the next hop that the router should use to send datagrams to the subnet or host given in this entry.

To ensure safe interoperation with RIP, RFC 1723 specifies the following restrictions for RIP-2 routers sending over a network interface where a RIP-1 router may hear and operate on the RIP messages.

1. Information internal to one network must never be advertised into another network.

2. Information about a more specific subnet cannot be advertised where RIP-1 routers would consider it a host route.

3. *Supernet* routes (routes with a subnet mask shorter than the natural or unsubnetted network mask) must not be advertised where they could be misinterpreted by RIP-1 routers.

RIP-2 also supports the use of multicasting (see 9.1, "Multicasting" on page 593) rather than simple broadcasting. This can reduce the load on hosts that are not listening for RIP-2 messages. This option is configurable for each interface to ensure optimum use of RIP-2 facilities when a router connects mixed RIP-1/RIP-2 subnets to RIP-2-only subnets. Similarly, the use of authentication in mixed environments can be configured to suit local requirements.

RIP-2 is implemented in recent versions of the *gated* daemon, often termed *gated Version 3*.

3.3.3 RIPng for IPv6

RIPng is intended to allow routers to exchange information for computing routes through an IPv6-based network and documented in RFC2080 (see IPv6 in Chapter 6, "IP Version 6" on page 457).

3.3.3.1 Protocol Description

RIPng is a distance vector protocol and similar to RIP-2 in IPv4 (see 3.2.2, "Distance Vector Routing" on page 129). RIPng is a UDP-based protocol and sends and receives datagrams on UDP port number 521. RIPng should be implemented only in routers; IPv6 provides other mechanisms for router discovery. Any router that uses RIPng is assumed to have interfaces to one or more networks, otherwise it isn't really a router (see router discovery in 6.3, "Internet Control Message Protocol Version 6 (ICMPv6)" on page 476). RIPng has the following limitations, just as RIP-2 in IPv4, which are specific to a distance vector protocol.

- Limited number of networks where longest path is 15.

- RIPng depends on counting to infinity. The resolution of the loop would require much more time (see counting to infinity in 3.2.2.1, "The Count to Infinity Problem" on page 131).

- Fixed metric. It is not appropriate for situations where routers need to be chosen based on real-time applications.

The RIPng message format is extended as shown in Figure 78.

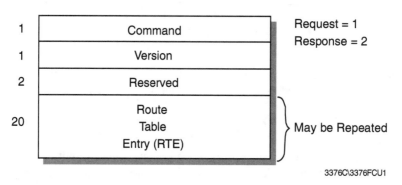

3376C\3376FCU1

Figure 78. RIPng Message

The basic blocks of a RIPng message are the following:

Command

It is the same idea as in RIP-1 and RIP-2 in IPv4 (see Figure 76 on page 140 and Figure 77 on page 142 also).

Route Table Entry (RTE)

It is a different idea from RIP-1 and RIP-2. RIPng provides the ability to specify the immediate next hop IPv6 address to which packets to a destination specified by an RTE should be forwarded in much the same way as RIP-1 and RIP-2 (see RTE in Figure 79 on page 145).

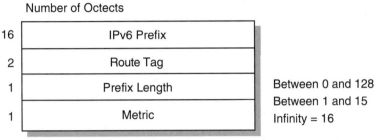

3376C\3376FCU2

Figure 79. RIPng Route Table Entry (RTE)

In RIP-2, each route table entry has a next hop field. Including a next hop field for each RTE in RIPng would nearly double the size of the RTE. Therefore, in RIPng, the next hop is specified by a special RTE and applies to all of the address RTEs following the next hop RTE until the end of the message or until another next hop RTE is encountered.

Next Hop Route Table Entry (RTE)

The next hop RTE is identified by a value of 0xFF in the metric field of an RTE. The prefix field specifies the IPv6 address of the next hop.

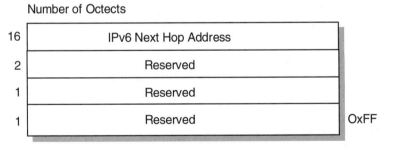

3376C\3376FCU3

Figure 80. RIPng Next Hop Route Table Entry (RTE)

3.3.4 Open Shortest Path First (OSPF)

The Open Shortest Path First (OSPF) V2 Protocol is an interior gateway protocol defined in RFC 2328. A report on the use of OSPF V2 is contained in RFC 1246 *Experience with the OSPF Protocol.*

It is an IAB standard protocol; its status is elective. However, RFC 1812 *Requirements for IPv4 Routers*, lists OSPF as the only required dynamic routing protocol.

OSPF is important because it has a number of features not found in other interior gateway protocols. Support for these additional features makes OSPF the preferred choice for new IP internetwork implementations especially in large networks. The following features are covered within OSPF:

- Support for *type of service (TOS)* routing[4]

- Provides *load balancing* (see 11.6, "OSPF Equal-Cost Multipath" on page 714)

- Allows site partitioning into subsets by using *areas*

- Information exchange between routers requires *authentication* (also in RIP-2, see RIP-2 in 3.3.2, "Routing Information Protocol Version 2 (RIP-2)" on page 140)

- Support for *host-specific routes* as well as network-specific routes

- Reduces table maintenance overhead to a minimum by implementing a *designated router*

- Allows definition of *virtual links* to provide support to a non-contiguous area

- Allows the usage of *variable length subnet masks*(also in RIP-2, see RIP-2 in 3.3.2, "Routing Information Protocol Version 2 (RIP-2)" on page 140)

- Will *import* RIP and EGP routes into its database

3.3.4.1 OSPF Terminology

OSPF uses specific terminology which must be understood before the protocol can be described.

Areas: OSPF internetworks are organized into *areas*. An OSPF area consists of a number of networks and routers that are logically grouped together. Areas can be defined on a per location or a per region basis, or they can be based on administrative boundaries. All OSPF networks consist of at least one area, the backbone, plus as

---

4 The use of TOS has been dropped in recent OSPF implementations.

many additional areas as are demanded by network topology and other design criteria. Within an OSPF area all routers maintain the same topology database, exchanging link state information to maintain their synchronization. This ensures that all routers calculate the same network map for the area.

Information about networks outside an area is summarized by an *area border* or *AS boundary routers* (see "Intra-Area, Area Border and AS Boundary Routers") and flooded into the area. Routers within an area have no knowledge of the topology of networks outside the area, only of routes to destinations provided by area borders and AS boundary routers.

The importance of the area concept is that it limits the size of the topology database that must be held by routers. This has direct impact on the processing to be carried out by each router, and on the amount of link state information that must be flooded into individual networks.

The OSPF Backbone: All OSPF networks must contain at least one area, the *backbone*, which is assigned an area identifier of 0.0.0.0. (This is different definition from IP address 0.0.0.0.) The backbone has all the properties of an area, but has the additional responsibility of distributing routing information between areas attached to it. Normally an OSPF backbone should be contiguous, that is with all backbone routers attached one to another. This may not be possible because of network topology, in which case backbone continuity must be maintained by the use of *virtual links* (see below). Virtual links are backbone router-to-backbone router connections that traverse a non-backbone area.

Routers within the backbone operate identically to other intra-area routers and maintain full topology databases for the backbone area.

Intra-Area, Area Border and AS Boundary Routers: There are three possible types of routers in an OSPF network. Figure 81 on page 148 shows the location of intra-area, area border and AS boundary routers within an OSPF internetwork.

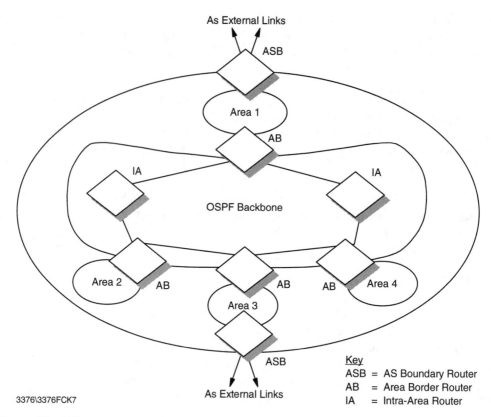

Figure 81. *OSPF Network*

Intra-Area Routers

Routers that are situated entirely within an OSPF area are called *intra-area routers*. All intra-area routers flood router links advertisements into the area to define the links they are attached to. If they are elected designated or backup-designated routers (see "Designated and Backup Designated Router" on page 152), they also flood network links advertisements to define the identity of all routers attached to the network. Intra-area routers maintain a topology database for the area in which they are situated.

Area Border Routers

Routers that connect two or more areas are referred to as *area border routers*. Area border routers maintain topology databases for each area to which they are attached, and exchange link state information with other routers in those areas. Area border routers also flood summary link state advertisements into each area to inform them of inter-area routes.

AS Boundary Routers

Routers that are situated at the periphery of an OSPF internetwork and exchange reachability information with routers in other ASs using exterior gateway protocols are called *AS boundary routers*. Routers that import static routes or routes from other IGPs, such as RIP, into an OSPF network are also AS boundary routers. AS boundary routers are responsible for flooding AS external link state advertisements into all areas within the AS to inform them of external routes.

Virtual Link: A virtual link is part of the backbone. Its endpoints are two area border routers that share a common non-backbone area. The link is treated as a point-to-point link with metrics cost equal to the intra-area metrics between the endpoints of the links. The routing through the virtual link is done using normal intra-area routing (see Figure 82 on page 150). Virtual endpoints are area border routers (ABRs) that share Area 2 as a transit area.

Transit Area: An area through which a virtual route is physically connected. In Figure 82 on page 150, Area 2 is transit area. In Figure 82 on page 150, virtual endpoints are ABRs that share Area 2 as a transit area.

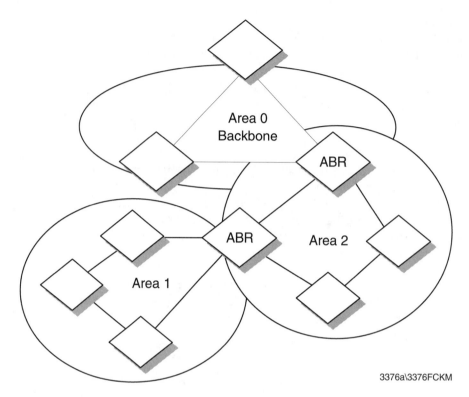

Figure 82. OSPF Virtual Link, Transit Area

Stub Area: An area configured to use default routing for inter-AS routing. A stub area can be configured where there is only a single exit from the area, or where any exit can be used without preference for routing to destinations outside the autonomous system. By default inter-AS routes are copied to all areas, so the use of stub areas can reduce the storage requirements of routers within those areas for autonomous systems where a lot of inter-AS routes are defined.

Neighbor Routers: Two routers that have interfaces to a common network. On multiaccess networks, neighbors are dynamically discovered by the Hello protocol.

Each neighbor is described by a state machine, which describes the conversation between this router and its neighbor. A brief outline of the meaning of the states follows. See the section immediately following for a definition of the terms *adjacency* and *designated router*.

Down

    Initial state of a neighbor conversation. It indicates that there has been no recent information received from the neighbor.

Attempt

    A neighbor on a non-broadcast network appears down and an attempt should be made to contact it by sending regular Hello packets.

Init A Hello packet has recently been received from the neighbor. However, bidirectional communication has not yet been established with the neighbor. (That is, the router itself did not appear in the neighbor's Hello packet.)

2-way

    In this state, communication between the two routers is bidirectional. Adjacencies can be established, and neighbors in this state or higher are eligible to be elected as (backup) designated routers.

ExStart

    The two neighbors are about to create an adjacency.

Exchange

    The two neighbors are telling each other what they have in their topological databases.

Loading

    The two neighbors are synchronizing their topological databases.

Full The two neighbors are now fully adjacent; their databases are synchronized.

Various events cause a change of state. For example, if a router receives a Hello packet from a neighbor that is down, the neighbor's state changes to init, and an inactivity timer is started. If the timer fires (that is, no further OSPF packets are received before it expires), the neighbor will return to the down state. Refer to RFC 2173 for a complete description of the states and information on the events which cause state changes.

Adjacent Router: Neighbor routers can become *adjacent*. They are said to be adjacent when they have synchronized their topology databases through the exchange of link state information.

Link state information is exchanged only between adjacent routers, not between neighbor routers.

Not all neighbor routers become adjacent. Neighbors on point-to-point links do so, but on multi-access networks adjacencies are only formed between individual routers and the designated and backup designated routers.

The exchange of link state information between neighbors can create significant amounts of network traffic. Limiting the number of adjacencies on multi-access networks in this way achieves considerable reductions in network traffic.

Designated and Backup Designated Router: All multi-access networks have a *designated* and a *backup designated* router. These routers are elected automatically for each network once neighbor routers have been discovered by the Hello protocol.

The designated router performs two key roles for a network:

- It generates network links advertisements that list the routers attached to a multi-access network.

- It forms adjacencies with all routers on a multi-access network and therefore becomes the focal point for forwarding of all link state advertisements.

The backup designated router forms the same adjacencies as the designated router. It therefore has the same topology database and is able to assume designated router functions should it detect that the designated router has failed.

Physical Network Types: All OSPF areas consist of aggregates of networks linked by routers. OSPF categorizes networks into the following different types.

Point-to-point Network
>   Point-to-point networks directly link two routers.

Multi-Access Network
>   Multi-access networks are those that support the attachment of more than two routers. They are further subdivided into two types:
>
>   - Broadcast
>
>   - Non-broadcast

Point-to-Multipoint Network
>   Point-to-multipoint networks describe a special case of multiaccess non-broadcast where not every router has a direct connection to any other router (also referred to as partial mesh).

Broadcast networks have the capability of directing OSPF packets to all attached routers, using an address that is recognized by all of them. An Ethernet LAN and token-ring LAN are examples of a broadcast multi-access network.

Non-broadcast networks do not have this capability and all packets must be specifically addressed to routers on the network. This requires that routers on a non-broadcast network be configured with the addresses of neighbors. Examples of a non-broadcast multi-access network are the X.25 public data network or a frame relay network

Interface: The connection between a router and one of its attached networks. Each interface has state information associated with it that is obtained from the underlying lower-level protocols and the OSPF protocol itself. A brief description of each state is given here. Please refer to RFC 2173 for more details, and for information on the events that will cause an interface to change its state.

Down
> The interface is unavailable. This is the initial state of an interface.

Loopback
> The interface is looped back to the router. It cannot be used for regular data traffic.

Waiting
> The router is trying to determine the identity of the designated router or its backup.

Point-to-Point
> The interface is to a point-to-point network or is a virtual link. The router forms an adjacency with the router at the other end.

> **Note:** The interfaces do not need IP addresses. Since the remainder of the internetwork has no practical need to see the routers' interfaces to the point-to-point link, just the interfaces to other networks, any IP addresses for the link would be needed only for communication between the two routers. To conserve the IP address space, the routers can dispense with IP addresses on the link. This has the effect of making the two routers appear to be one to IP but this has no ill effects. Such a link is called an *unnumbered* link.

DR Other
> The interface is on a multiaccess network but this router is neither the designated router nor its backup. The router forms adjacencies with the designated router and its backup.

Backup
> The router is the backup designated router. It will be promoted to designated router if the present designated router fails. The router forms adjacencies with every other router on the network.

DR The router itself is the designated router. The router forms adjacencies with every other router on the network. The router must also originate a network links advertisement for the network node.

Type of Service (TOS) Metrics: In each type of link state advertisement, different metrics can be advertised for each IP Type of Service. A metric for TOS 0 (used for OSPF routing protocol packets) must always be specified. Metrics for other TOS values can be specified; if they are not, these metrics are assumed equal to the metric specified for TOS 0.[5]

Link State Database: Also called the *directed graph* or the *topological database*. It is created from the link state advertisements generated by the routers in the area.

Note: RFC 2328 uses the term link state database in preference to topological database. The former term has the advantage that it describes the contents of the database, the latter is more descriptive of the purpose of the database, to describe the topology of the area. We have previously used the term topological database for this reason, but for the remainder of this section where we discuss the operation of OSPF in more detail, we refer to it as the link state database.

Shortest-Path Tree: Each router runs the SPF (see SPF in 3.2.3.1, "Shortest-Path First (SPF)" on page 137) algorithm on the link state database to obtain its shortest-path tree. The tree gives the route to any destination network or host as far as the area boundary. It is used to build the routing table.

Note: Because each router occupies a different place in the area's topology, application of the SPF algorithm gives a different tree for each router, even though the database is identical.

Area border routers run multiple copies of the algorithm but build a single routing table.

Routing table: The routing table contains entries for each destination: network, subnet or host. For each destination, there is information for one or more types of service (TOS). For each combination of destination and type of service, there are entries for one or more optimum paths to be used.

Area ID: A 32-bit number identifying a particular area. The backbone has an area ID of zero.

Router ID: A 32-bit number identifying a particular router. Each router within the AS has a single router ID. One possible implementation is to use the lowest numbered IP address belonging to a router as its router ID.

---

[5] The use of TOS has been dropped in recent OSPF implementations.

Router Priority: An 8-bit unsigned integer, configurable on a per-interface basis indicating this router's priority in the selection of the (backup) designated router. A router priority of zero indicates that this router is ineligible to be the designated router.

Link State Advertisements: Link state information is exchanged by adjacent OSPF routers to allow area topology databases to be maintained, and inter-area and inter-AS routes to be advertised.

Link state information consists of five types of link state advertisement. Together these provide all the information needed to describe an OSPF network and its external environment:

1. Router links

2. Network links

3. Summary links (type 3 and 4)

4. AS External links

Router link advertisements

> *Router link* advertisements are generated by all OSPF routers and describe the state of the router's interfaces (links) within the area. They are flooded throughout a single area only.

Network link advertisements

> *Network link* advertisements are generated by the designated router on a multi-access network and list the routers connected to the network. They are flooded throughout a single area only.

Summary link advertisements

> *Summary link* advertisements are generated by area border routers. There are two types: one describes routes to destinations in other areas; the other descirbes routes to AS boundary routers. They are flooded throughout a single area only.

AS external link advertisements

> *AS external link* advertisements are generated by AS boundary routers and describe routes to destinations external to the OSPF network. They are flooded throughout all areas in the OSPF network.

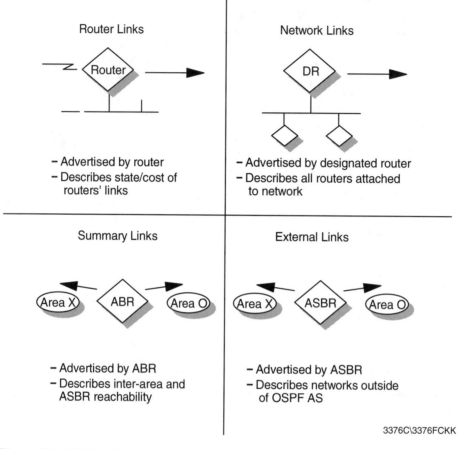

Figure 83. OSPF Link State Advertisements

3.3.4.2 Protocol Description

The OSPF protocol is an implementation of a *link state* routing protocol, as described in 3.2.3, "Link State Routing" on page 135.

OSPF packets are transmitted directly in IP datagrams. IP datagrams containing OSPF packets can be distinguished by their use of *protocol identifier 89* in the IP header. OSPF packets are not, therefore, contained in TCP or UDP headers. OSPF packets are always sent with IP type of service set to 0, and the IP precedence field set to internetwork control. This is to aid them in getting preference over normal IP traffic. (To see further details on IP protocol identifiers, type of service and precedence, refer to 10.2, "Integrated Services" on page 644.)

OSPF packets are sent to a standard multicast IP address on point-to-point and broadcast networks. This address is 224.0.0.5, referred to as AllSPFRouters in the RFC. They are sent to specific IP addresses on non-broadcast networks using neighbor network address information that must be configured for each router. All OSPF packets share a common header, which is shown in Figure 84 on page 158. This header provides general information such as area identifier and originating router identifier, and also includes a checksum and authentication information. A type field defines each OSPF packet as one of five possible types:

1. Hello

2. Database description

3. Link state request

4. Link state update

5. Link state acknowledgement

The router identifier, area identifier, and authentication information are configurable for each OSPF router.

Number of Octets

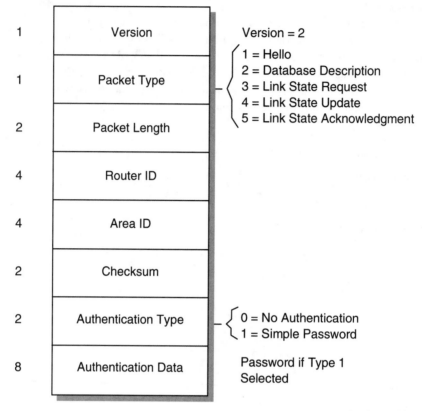

Figure 84. OSPF Common Header

The OSPF protocol defines a number of stages which must be executed by individual routers. They are as follows:

- Discovering neighbors
- Electing the designated router
- Initializing neighbors
- Propagating link state information
- Calculating routing tables

The use of the five OSPF packet types to implement stages of the OSPF protocol are described in the following subsection.

During OSPF operation a router cycles each of its interfaces through a number of to DR Other, BackupDR or DR (DR stands for designated router) depending on the status of each attached network and the identity of the designated router elected for each of them. (See a detailed description of these states in "Interface" on page 153.)

At the same time a router cycles each neighbor interface (interaction) through a number of states as it discovers them and then becomes adjacent. These states are: Down, Attempt, Init, 2-Way, ExStart, Exchange, Loading and Full. (See a detailed description of these states in "Neighbor Routers" on page 150.)

Discovering Neighbors - The OSPF Hello Protocol: The Hello protocol is responsible for discovering neighbor routers on a network, and establishing and maintaining relationships with them. Hello packets are sent out periodically on all router interfaces. The format of these is shown in Figure 85 on page 160.

Number of Octets

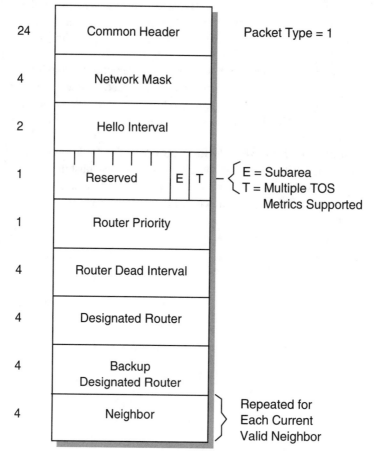

Figure 85. OSPF Hello Packet

Hello packets contain the identities of neighbor routers whose hello packets have already been received over a specific interface. They also contain the network mask, router priority, designated router identifier and backup designated router identifier. The final three parameters are used to elect the designated router on multi-access networks.

The network mask, router priority, hello interval and router dead interval are configurable for each interface on an OSPF router.

A router interface changes state from Down to Point-to-Point (if the network is point-to-point), to DR Other (if the router is ineligible to become designated router), or otherwise to Waiting as soon as hello packets are sent over it.

A router receives hello packets from neighbor routers via its network interfaces. When this happens the neighbor interface state changes from Down to Init. Bidirectional communication is established between neighbors when a router sees itself listed in a hello packet received from another router. Only at this point are the two routers defined as true neighbors, and the neighbor interface changes state from Init to 2-Way.

Electing the Designated Router: All multi-access networks have a designated router. There is also a backup designated router that takes over in the event that the designated router fails. The use of a backup, which maintains an identical set of adjacencies and an identical topology database to the designated router, ensures that there is no extended loss of routing capability if the designated router fails. The designated router performs two major functions on a network:

- It originates network link advertisements on behalf of the network.

- It establishes adjacencies with all other routers on the network. Only routers with adjacencies exchange link state information and synchronize their databases.

The designated router and backup designated router are elected on the basis of the router identifier, router priority, designated router and backup designated router fields in hello packets. Router priority is a single octet field that defines the priority of a router on a network. The lower the value of the priority field the more likely the router is to become the designated router, hence the higher its priority. A zero value means the router is ineligible to become a designated or backup designated router.

The process of designated router election is as follows:

1. The current values for designated router and backup designated router on the network are initialized to 0.0.0.0.

2. The current values for router identifier, router priority, designated router and backup designated router in hello packets from neighbor routers are noted. Local router values are included.

3. Backup designated router election:

    Routers that have been declared as designated router are ineligible to become a backup designated router.

    The backup designated router will be declared to be:

- The highest priority router that has been declared as a backup designated router

- The highest priority router if no backup designated router has been declared

If equal priority routers are eligible, the one with the highest router identifier is chosen.

4. Designated router election:

    The designated router will be declared to be:

    - The highest priority router that has been declared designated router

    - The highest priority router if no designated router has been declared

5. If the router carrying out the above determination is declared the designated or backup designated router, then the above steps are re-executed. This ensures that no router can declare itself both designated and backup designated router.

Once designated and backup designated routers have been elected for a network, they proceed to establish adjacencies with all routers on the network.

Completion of the election process for a network causes the router interface to change state from Waiting to DR, BackupDR, or DR Other depending on whether the router is elected the designated router, the backup designated router or none of these.

Establishing Adjacencies - Database Exchange: A router establishes adjacencies with a subset of neighbor routers on a network.

Routers connected by point-to-point networks and virtual links always become *adjacent*. Routers on multi-access networks form adjacencies with the designated and backup designated routers only.

Link state information flows only between adjacent routers. Before this can happen it is necessary for them to have the same topological database, and to be synchronized. This is achieved in OSPF by a process called *database exchange*.

Database exchange between two neighbor routers occurs as soon as they attempt to bring up an adjacency. It consists of the exchange of a number of database description packets that define the set of link state information present in the database of each router. The link state information in the database is defined by the list of link state headers for all link state advertisement in the database. (See Figure 90 on page 167 for information on the link state header.)

The format of database description packets is shown in Figure 86 on page 163.

Number of Octets

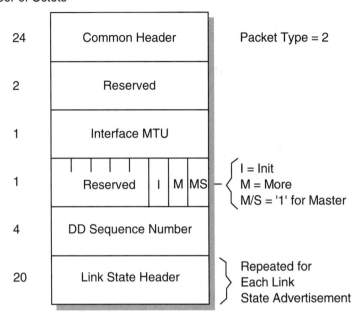

Figure 86. OSPF Database Description Packet

During the database exchange process the routers form a *master/slave* relationship, the master being the first to transmit. The master sends database description packets to the slave to describe its database of link state information. Each packet is identified by a sequence number and contains a list of the link state headers in the master's database. The slave acknowledges each packet by sequence number and includes its own database of headers in the acknowledgements.

Flags in database description packets indicate whether they are from a master or slave (the M/S bit), the first such packet (the I bit) and if there are more packets to come (the M bit). Database exchange is complete when a router receives a database description packet from its neighbor with the M bit off.

During database exchange each router makes a list of the link state advertisements for which the adjacent neighbor has a more up-to-date instance (all advertisements are sequenced and time stamped). Once the process is complete each router requests these more up-to-date instances of advertisements using link state requests.

The format of link state request packets is shown in Figure 87 on page 164.

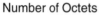

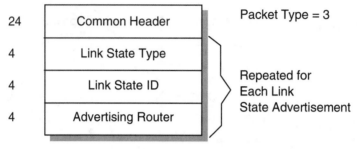

Figure 87. OSPF Link State Request Packet

The database exchange process sequences the neighbor interface state from 2-Way through:

- ExStart as the adjacency is created and the master agreed upon
- Exchange as the topology databases are being described
- Loading as the link state requests are being sent and responded to
- And finally to Full when the neighbors are fully adjacent

In this way, the two routers synchronize their topology databases and are able to calculate identical network maps for their OSPF area.

Link State Propagation: Information about the topology of an OSPF network is passed from router to router in link state advertisements.

Link state advertisements pass between adjacent routers in the form of *link state update* packets, the format of which is shown in Figure 88 on page 165.

Number of Octets

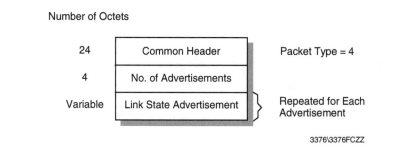

Figure 88. *OSPF Link State Update Packet*

Link state advertisements are of five types: router links, network links, summary links (two types) and AS external links as noted earlier in this section.

Link state updates pass as a result of link state requests during database exchange, and also in the normal course of events when routers wish to indicate a change of network topology. Individual link state update packets can contain multiple link state advertisements.

It is essential that each OSPF router in an area has the same network topology database, and hence the integrity of link state information must be maintained.

For that reason link state update packets must be passed without loss or corruption throughout an area. The process by which this is done is called *flooding*.

A link state update packet floods one or more link state advertisements one hop further away from their originator. To make the flooding procedure reliable each link state advertisement must be acknowledged separately. Multiple acknowledgements can be grouped together into a single *link state acknowledgement packet*. The format of the link state acknowledgement packet is shown in Figure 89.

Number of Octets

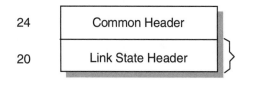

Figure 89. *OSPF Link State Acknowledgement Packet*

In order to maintain database integrity it is essential that all link state advertisements are rigorously checked to ensure validity.

The following checks are applied and the advertisement discarded if:

- The link state checksum is incorrect.
- The link state type is invalid.
- The advertisement's age has reached its maximum.
- The advertisement is older than or the same as one already in the database.

If an advertisement passes the above checks, then an acknowledgement is sent back to the originator. If no acknowledgement is received by the originator, then the original link state update packet is retransmitted after a timer has expired.

Once accepted an advertisement is flooded onward over the router's other interfaces until it has been received by all routers within an area.

Advertisements are identified by their link state type, link state ID and the advertising router. They are further qualified by their link state sequence number, link state age and link state checksum number.

The age of a link state advertisement must be calculated to determine if it should be installed into a router's database. Only a more recent advertisement should be accepted and installed. Valid link state advertisements are installed into the topology database of the router. This causes the topology map or graph to be recalculated and the routing table to be updated.

Link state advertisements all have a common 20-byte header. This is shown in Figure 90 on page 167. The four link state advertisement types are shown in Figure 91 on page 170, in Figure 92 on page 173, in Figure 93 on page 173, and in Figure 94 on page 175.

Number of Octets

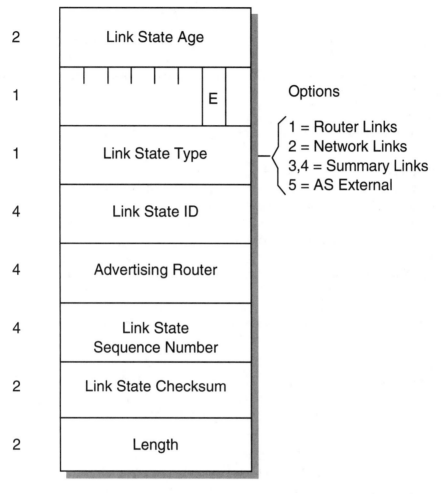

3376\3376FCKF

Figure 90. OSPF Link State Header

The fields in the link state advertisement header are:

Link Stage Age
A 16-bit number indicating the time in seconds since the origin of the
advertisement. It is increased as the link state advertisement resides in a router's
database and with each hop it travels as part of the flooding procedure. When it
reaches a maximum value, it ceases to be used for determining routing tables
and is discarded unless it is still needed for database synchronization. The age

is also to determine which of two otherwise identical copies of an advertisement a router should use.

Options

One bit that describes optional OSPF capabilitiy. The E-bit indicates an external routing capability. It is set unless the advertisement is for a router, network link or summary link in a stub area. The E-bit is used for information only and does not affect the routing table.

Link State Type

The types of the link state advertisement are (see "Link State Advertisements" on page 155):

1. Router links - These describe the states of a router's interfaces.
2. Network links - These describe the routers attached to a network.
3. Summary links - These describe inter-area, intra-AS routes. They are created by area border routers and allow routes to networks within the AS but outside the area to be described concisely.
4. Summary links - These describe routes to the boundary of the AS (that is, to AS boundary routers). They are created by area border routers. They are very similar to type 3.
5. AS external links - These describe routes to networks outside the AS. They are created by AS boundary routers. A default route for the AS can be described this way.

Link State ID

A unique ID for the advertisement that is dependent on the link state type. For types 1 and 4 it is the router ID, for types 3 and 5 it is an IP network number, and for type 2 it is the IP address of the designated router.

Advertising Router

The router ID of the router that originated the link state advertisement. For type 1 advertisements, this field is identical to the link state ID. For type 2, it is the router ID of the network's designated router. For types 3 and 4, it is the router ID of an area border router. For type 5, it is the router ID of an AS boundary router.

LS Sequence Number

Used to allow detection of old or duplicate link state advertisements.

Link State Sequence Checksum

Checksum of the complete link state advertisement excluding the link state age field.

Routing Table Calculation: Each router in an OSPF area builds up a topology database of validated link state advertisements and uses them to calculate the network map for the area. From this map the router is able to determine the best route for each destination and insert it into its routing table.

Each advertisement contains an age field which is incremented while the advertisement is held in the database. An advertisement's age is never incremented past MaxAge. When age reaches MaxAge, it is excluded from routing table calculation, and re-flooded through the area as a newly originated advertisement.

Note: MaxAge is an architecture constant and the maximum age an LSA can attain. The value of MaxAge is set to 1 hour.

Routers build up their routing table from the database of link state advertisements in the following sequence:

1. The shortest path tree is calculated from router and network links advertisements allowing best routes within the area to be determined.

2. Inter-area routes are added by examination of summary link advertisements.

3. AS external routes are added by examination of AS external link advertisements.

The topology graph or map constructed from the above process is used to update the routing table. The routing table is recalculated each time a new advertisement is received.

Number of Octets

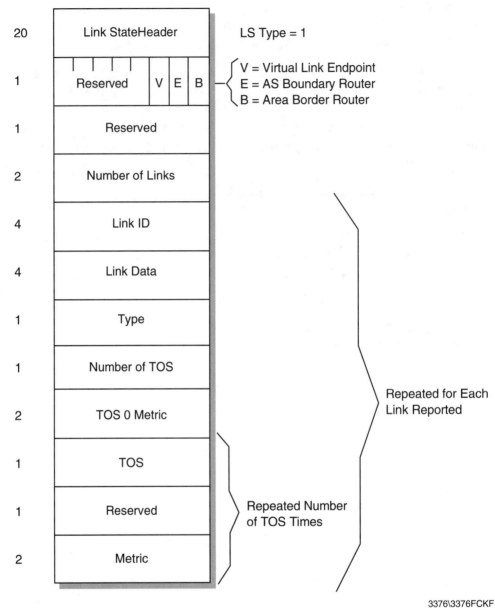

Figure 91. OSPF Router Links Advertisement

The field in the router link advertisement header are:

V Bit

> When set, this router is the endpoint of a virtual link that is using this area as a transit area.

E Bit

> When set, the router is an AS boundary router.

B Bit

> When set, the router is an area border router.

Number of Links

> The number of links described by this advertisement.

Link ID

> Identifies the object that this link connects to. The value depends upon the type field (see below).
>
> 1. Neighboring router's router ID
> 2. IP address of the designated router
> 3. IP network/subnet number. This value depends on what the inter area route is to:
>   > For a stub network it is the IP network/subnet number.
>   > For a host it is X'FFFFFFFF'.
>   > For the AS-external default route it is X'00000000'.
> 4. Neighboring router's router ID

Link Data

> This value also depends upon the type field (see RFC 2328 for details).

Type What this link connects to.

> 1. Point-to-point connection to another router
> 2. Connection to a transit network
> 3. Connection to a stub network or to a host
> 4. Virtual link

Number of TOS

> The number of different TOS metrics given for this link in addition to the metric for TOS 0.

TOS 0 Metric

> The cost of using this outbound link for TOS 0. All OSPF routing protocol packets are sent with the IP TOS field set to 0.

TOS For backward compatibility with previous versions of the OSPF specification.

> **Note:** In RFC 2328 the TOS routing option has been deleted from OSPF. This action was required by the Internet standards process, due to lack of

implementation experience with OSPF's TOS routing. However, for backward compatibility the formats of OSPF's various LSAs remain unchanged, maintaining the ability to specify TOS metrics in router-LSAs, summary-LSAs, ASBR-summary-LSAs, and AS-external-LSAs (see RFC 2328 for detail).

Metric

The cost of using this outbound router link for traffic of the specified Type of Service.

As an example, suppose the point-to-point link between routers RT1 (IP address: 192.1.2.3) and RT6 (IP address: 6.5.4.3) is a satellite link. To encourage the use of this line for high-bandwidth traffic, the AS administrator can set an artificially low metric for that TOS. Router RT1 would then originate the following router links advertisement (assuming RT1 is an area border router and is not an AS boundary router):

```
; RT1's router links advertisement

LS age = 0                      ; always true on origination
LS type = 1                     ; indicates router links
Link State ID = 192.1.2.3       ; RT1's Router ID
Advertising Router = 192.1.2.3  ; RT1
bit E = 0                       ; not an AS boundary router
bit B = 1                       ; area border router
#links = 1
        Link ID = 6.5.4.3       ; neighbor router's Router ID
        Link Data = 0.0.0.0     ; interface to unnumbered SL
        Type = 1                ; connects to router
        # other metrics = 1
        TOS 0 metric = 8
            TOS = 2             ; high bandwidth
            metric = 1          ; traffic preferred
```

The format of a network links advertisement (type 2) is shown in Figure 92 on page 173.

Number of Octets

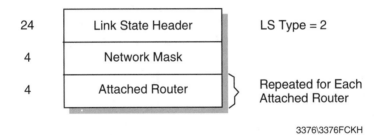

Figure 92. *OSPF Network Links Advertisement*

The fields in the network link advertisement header are:

Network Mask
> The IP address mask for the network. For example a CIDR prefix length /20 network would have the mask 255.255.240.0 (dotted-decimal) and the mask 1111 1111 1111 1111 1110 0000 0000 0000 (binary), (see 2.1.7, "Classless Inter-Domain Routing (CIDR)" on page 58).

Attached Router
> The router IDs of each of the routers attached to the network that are adjacent to the designated router (including the sending router). The number of routers in the list is deduced from the length field in the header.

Number of Octets

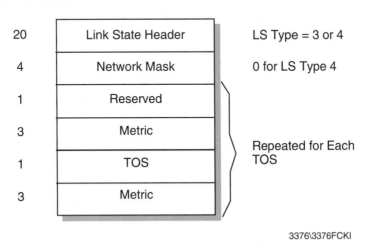

Figure 93. *OSPF Summary Links Advertisement*

The fields in the summary link advertisement header are:

Network Mask

For a type 3 link state advertisement, this is the IP address mask for the network. For a type 4 link state advertisement, this is not meaningful and must be zero.

Reserved

All zero.

Metric

The cost of this route for this type of service in the same units used for TOS metrics in type 1 advertisements.

TOS Zero or more entries for additional types of service. The number of entries can be determined from the length field in the header.

Number of Octets

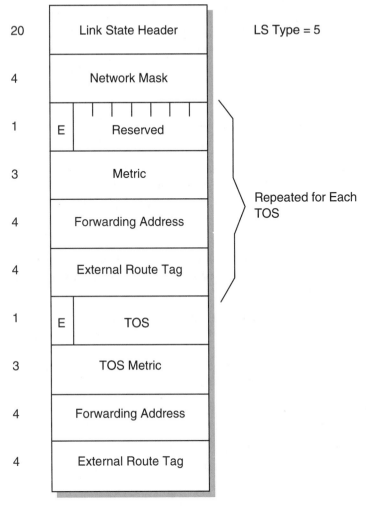

Figure 94. *OSPF External Links Advertisement*

The fields in the external link advertisement header are:

Network Mask
    The IP address mask for the network.

Bit E

> The type of external metric. If set, the type is 2, otherwise it is 1.

> 1. The metric is directly comparable to OSPF link state metrics
> 2. The metric is considered larger than all OSPF link state metrics

Reserved

> All zero.

Metric

> The cost of this route. Interpretation depends on the E-bit.

Forwarding Address

> The IP address that data traffic for this type of service intended for the advertised destination is to be forwarded to. The value 0.0.0.0 indicates that traffic should be forwarded to the AS boundary router that originated the advertisement.

External Route Tag

> A 32-bit value attached to the external route by an AS boundary router. This is not used by the OSPF itself. It can be used to communicate information between AS boundary routers.

TOS Zero or more entries for additional types of service. The number of entries can be determined from the length field in the header.

3.4 Exterior Routing Protocols

Exterior Routing Protocols or Exterior Gateway Protocols (EGPs) are used to exchange routing information between routers in different autonomous systems.

Note: The term exterior routing protocol has no abbreviation commonly used, so we shall use the abbreviation EGP as is usual in TCP/IP literature.

Two EGPs are commonly used:

- Exterior Gateway Protocol (see 3.4.1, "Exterior Gateway Protocol (EGP)")
- Border Gateway Protocol (see 3.4.2, "Border Gateway Protocol (BGP-4)" on page 177)

3.4.1 Exterior Gateway Protocol (EGP)

EGP is a *historic protocol* and described in RFC 904. Interestingly, its status is still listed as *recommended*.

The Exterior Gateway Protocol is a protocol used for exchange of routing information between *exterior* gateways (not belonging to the same autonomous system). EGP assumes a single backbone, and therefore only one single path between any two ASs. Therefore, the practical use of EGP today is virtually restricted to someone who wants to build a private Internet. In the real world, EGP is being replaced progressively by BGP.

EGP is based on periodic polling using Hello/I Hear You message exchanges, to monitor neighbor reachability and poll requests to solicit update responses. EGP restricts exterior gateways by allowing them to advertise only those destination networks reachable entirely within that gateway's autonomous system. Thus, an exterior gateway using EGP passes along information to its EGP neighbors but does not advertise reachability information about its EGP neighbors (gateways are neighbors if they exchange routing information) outside the autonomous system. The routing information from inside an AS must be collected by this EGP gateway, usually via an Interior Gateway Protocol (IGP). This is shoen in Figure 70 on page 127.

3.4.2 Border Gateway Protocol (BGP-4)

The Border Gateway Protocol (BGP) is a draft standard protocol. Its status is elective. It is described in RFC 1771.

The Border Gateway Protocol is an exterior gateway protocol used to exchange network reachability information among ASs (see Figure 70 on page 127).

BGP-4 was introduced in the Internet in the loop-free exchange of routing information between autonomous systems. Based on Classless Inter-Domain Routing (CIDR), BGP has since evolved to support the aggregation and reduction of routing information.

In essence, CIDR is a strategy designed to address the following problems:

- Exhaustion of Class B address space

- Routing table growth

CIDR eliminates the concept of address classes and provides a method for summarizing n different routes into single routes. This significantly reduces the amount of routing information that BGP routers must store and exchange. (See 2.1.7, "Classless Inter-Domain Routing (CIDR)" on page 58 for details.)

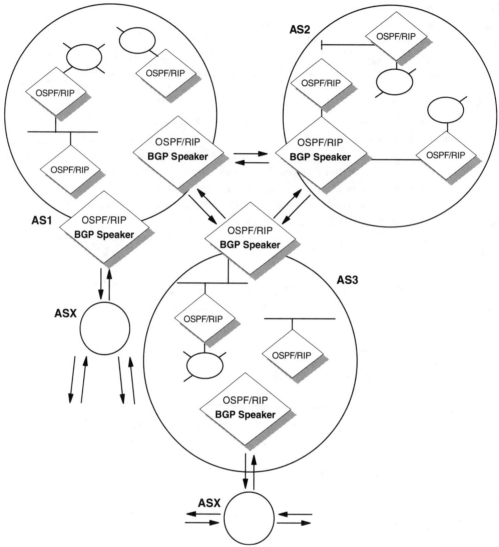

3376\3376FCZD

Figure 95. BGP Speaker and AS Relationship

Before giving an overview of the BGP protocol, we define some terms used in BGP:

BGP speaker

A system running BGP (see Figure 95).

BGP neighbors

A pair of BGP speakers exchanging inter-AS routing information. BGP neighbors may be of two types:

Internal   A pair of BGP speakers in the same autonomous system. Internal BGP neighbors must present a consistent image of the AS to their external BGP neighbors. This is explained in more detail below.

External   A pair of BGP neighbors in different autonomous systems. External BGP neighbors must be connected by a BGP connection as defined below. This restriction means that in most cases where an AS has multiple BGP inter-AS connections, it will also require multiple BGP speakers.

BGP session

A TCP session between BGP neighbors that are exchanging routing information using BGP. The neighbors monitor the state of the session by sending a *keepalive* message regularly. (The recommended interval is 30 seconds.)[6]

AS border router (ASBR)

A router that has a connection to multiple autonomous systems.

Note: The nomenclature for this type of router is somewhat varied. RFC 2328, which describes OSPF, uses the term *AS boundary router*. RFC 1771 and 1772, which describe BGP, use the terms *border router* and *border gateway*. We use the first term consistently when describing both OSPF and BGP. BGP defines two types of AS border routers, depending on its topological relationship to the BGP speaker that refers to it.

Internal   A next hop router in the same AS as the BGP speaker.

External   A next hop router in a different AS from the BGP speaker.

The IP address of a border router is specified as a next hop destination when BGP advertises an AS path (see below) to one of its external neighbors. Next hop border routers must share a physical connection (see below) with both the sending and receiving BGP speakers. If a BGP speaker advertises an external border router as a next hop, that router must have been learned of from one of that BGP speaker's peers.

AS connection

BGP defines two types of inter-AS connections:

---

6 This keepalive message is implemented in the application layer, and is independent of the keepalive message available in many TCP implementations.

Physical connection

An AS shares a physical network with another AS, and this network is connected to at least one border router from each AS. Since these two routers share a network, they can forward packets to each other without requiring any inter-AS or intra-AS routing protocols. (That is, they require neither an IGP nor an EGP to communicate.)

BGP connection

A BGP connection means that there is a BGP session between a pair of BGP speakers, one in each AS. This session is used to communicate the routes through the physically connected border routers that can be used for specific networks. BGP requires that the BGP speakers must be on the same network as the physically connected border routers so that the BGP session is also independent of all inter-AS or intra-AS routing protocols. The BGP speakers do not need to be border routers, and vice versa.

Note: The term BGP connection can be used to refer to a session between two BGP speakers in the same AS.

Traffic type

BGP categorizes traffic in an AS as one of two types:

local   Local traffic is traffic that either originates in or terminates in that AS. That is, either the source or the destination IP address is in the AS.

transit   Transit traffic is all non-local traffic.

One of the goals of BGP is to minimize the amount of transit traffic.

AS type

An AS is categorized as one of three types:

stub   A stub AS has a single inter-AS connection to one other AS. A stub AS only carries local traffic.

multihomed

A multihomed AS has connections to more than one other AS but refuses to carry transit traffic.

transit   A transit AS has connections to more than one other AS and carries both and local transit traffic. The AS may impose policy restrictions on what transit traffic will be carried.

AS number

A 16-bit number uniquely identifying an AS. This is the same AS number used by EGP.

AS path

A list of all of the AS numbers traversed by a route when exchanging routing information. Rather than exchanging simple metric counts, BGP communicates entire paths to its neighbors.

Routing policy

A set of rules constraining routing to conform to the wishes of the authority that administers the AS. Routing policies are not defined in the BGP protocol, but are selected by the AS authority and presented to BGP in the form of implementation-specific configuration data. Routing policies can be selected by the AS authority in whatever way that authority sees fit. For example:

- A multihomed AS can refuse to act as a transit AS. It does this by not advertising routes to networks other than those directly connected to it.

- A multihomed AS can limit itself to being a transit AS for a restricted set of adjacent ASs. It does this by advertising its routing information to this set only.

- An AS can select which outbound AS should be used for carrying transit traffic.

An AS can also apply performance-related criteria when selecting outbound paths:

- An AS can optimize traffic to use short AS paths rather than long ones.

- An AS can select transit routes according to the service quality of the intermediate hops. This service quality information could be obtained using mechanisms external to BGP.

It can be seen from the definitions above that a stub AS or a multihomed AS has the same topological properties as an AS in the ARPANET architecture. That is, it never acts as an intermediate AS in an inter-AS route. In the ARPANET architecture, EGP was sufficient for such an AS to exchange reachability information with its neighbors, and this remains true with BGP. Therefore, a stub AS or a multihomed AS can continue to use EGP (or any other suitable protocol) to operate with a transit AS. However, RFC 1772 recommends that BGP is used instead of EGP for these types of AS because it provides an advantage in bandwidth and performance. Additionally, in a multihomed AS, BGP is more likely to provide an optimum inter-AS route than EGP, since EGP only addresses reachability and not distance.

3.4.2.1 Path Selection

Each BGP speaker must evaluate different paths to a destination from the border router(s) for an AS connection, select the best one that complies with the routing policies in force and then advertise that route to all of its BGP neighbors at that AS connection.

BGP is a vector-distance protocol but, unlike traditional vector-distance protocols such as RIP where there is a single metric, BGP determines a preference order by applying a function mapping each path to a preference value and selects the path with the highest value. The function applied is generated by the BGP implementation according to configuration information. However, BGP does not keep a cost metric to any path which is sometimes thought of as a shortcoming, but there is no mechanism in place for BGP to collect a uniform cost for paths across the multitude of today's service provider networks.

Where there are multiple viable paths to a destination, BGP maintains all of them but only advertises the one with the highest preference value. This approach allows a quick change to an alternate path should the primary path fail.

3.4.2.2 Routing Policies

RFC 1772 includes a recommended set of policies for all implementations:

- A BGP implementation should be able to control which routes it announces. The granularity of this control should be at least at the network level for the announced routes and at the AS level for the recipients. For example, BGP should allow a policy of announcing a route to a specific network to a specific adjacent AS. Care must be taken when a BGP speaker selects a new route that cannot be announced to a paticular external peer, while the previously selected route was announced to that peer. Specifically, the local system must explicitly indicate to the peer that the previous route is now infeasible.

- BGP should allow a weighting policy for paths. Each AS can be assigned a weight and the preferred path to a destination is then the one with the lowest aggregate weight.

- BGP should allow a policy of excluding an AS from all possible paths. This can be done with a variant of the previous policy; each AS to be excluded is given an *infinite* weight and the route selection process refuses to consider paths of infinite weight.

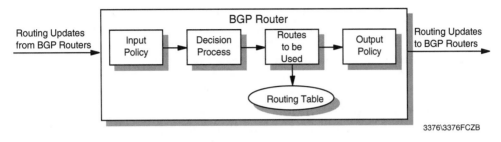

Figure 96. *BGP Process and Routing Policies*

See Figure 96 regarding the BGP process and routing policies:

1. Routing updates are received from other BGP routers.

2. Input policy engine filters routes and performs attribute manipulation.

3. Decision process decides what routes the BGP router will use.

4. Output policy engine filters routes and performs attribute manipulation for routes to be advertised.

5. Routing updates are advertised to other BGP routers.

3.4.2.3 AS Consistency

BGP requires that a transit AS present the same view to every AS using its services. If the AS has multiple BGP speakers, they must agree on two aspects of topology: intra-AS and inter-AS. Since BGP does not deal with intra-AS routing at all, a consistent view of intra-AS topology must be provided by the interior routing protocol(s) employed in the AS. Naturally, a protocol such as OSPF (see 3.3.4, "Open Shortest Path First (OSPF)" on page 146) that implements synchronization of router databases lends itself well to this role. Consistency of the external topology *may* be provided by all BGP speakers in the AS having BGP sessions with each other, but BGP does not require that this method be used, only that consistency be maintained.

3.4.2.4 Routing Information Exchange

BGP only advertises routes that it uses itself to its neighbors. That is, BGP conforms to the normal Internet hop-by-hop paradigm, even though it has additional information in the form of AS paths and theoretically could be capable of informing a neighbor of a route it would not use itself.

When two BGP speakers form a BGP session, they begin by exchanging their entire routing tables. Routing information is exchanged via UPDATE messages (see below for the format of these messages). Since the routing information contains the complete AS path to each listed destination in the form of a list of AS numbers in addition to the usual reachability and next hop information used in traditional vector distance protocols, it can be used to suppress routing loops and to eliminate the *counting-to-infinity* problem found in RIP. After BGP neighbors have performed their initial exchange of their complete routing databases, they only exchange updates to that information.

3.4.2.5 Protocol Description

BGP runs over a reliable transport layer connection between neighbor routers. BGP relies on the transport connection for fragmentation, retransmission, acknowledgement and sequencing. It assumes that the transport connection will close in an orderly fashion, delivering all data, in the event of an error notification.

Practical implementations of BGP use TCP as the transport mechanism. Therefore, BGP protocol data units are contained within TCP packets. Connections to the BGP service on a router use TCP port 179.

The BGP protocol comprises four main stages:

- Opening and confirming a BGP connection with a neighbor router

- Maintaining the BGP connection

- Sending reachability information

- Notification of error conditions

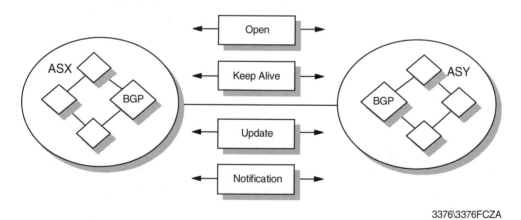

3376\3376FCZA

Figure 97. BGP Messages Flow between BGP Speakers

Opening and Confirming a BGP Connection: BGP communication between two routers commences with the TCP transport protocol connection being established.

Once the connection has been established, each router sends an *open* message to its neighbor.

The BGP open message, like all BGP messages, consists of a standard header plus packet-type specific contents. The standard header consists of a 16-octet maker field, which is set to all ones when the autentication code is 0, the length of the total BGP packet, and a type field that specifies the packet to be one of four possible types:

1. OPEN[7]
2. UPDATE
3. NOTIFICATION
4. KEEPALIVE

The format of the BGP header is shown in Figure 98.

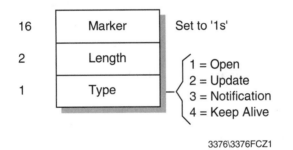

Figure 98. *BGP Message Header*

The open message defines the originating router's AS number, its BGP router identifier and the hold time for the connection. If no keepalive, update or notification messages are received for a period of hold time, the originating router assumes an error, sends a notification message, and closes the connection.

The open message also provides an optional parameter length and optional parameters. These fields may be used to authenticate a BGP peer.

---

[7] RFC 1771 uses uppercase to name BGP messages, so we do the same in this section.

The format of the open message is shown in Figure 99 on page 186.

Number of Octets

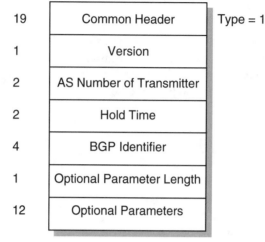

3376\3376FCZ2

Figure 99. BGP Open Message

An acceptable open message is acknowledged by a *keepalive* message. Once neighbor routers have sent keepalive messages in response to opens, they can proceed to exchange further keepalives, notifications and updates.

Maintaining the BGP Connection: BGP messages must be exchanged periodically between neighbors. If no messages have been received for the period of the hold timer calculated by using the smaller of its configured hold time and the hold time received in the OPEN message, then an error on the connection is assumed.

BGP uses keepalive messages to maintain the connection between neighbors. Keepalive messages consist of the BGP packet header only, with no data. The RFC recommends that the hold time timer is 90 seconds and keepalive timer is 30 seconds.

Sending Reachability Information: Reachability information is exchanged between BGP neighbors in update messages.

An update message is used to advertise a single feasible route to a peer, or to withdraw infeasible routes from service. An update may simultaneously advertise a feasible route and withdraw multiple infeasible routes from service. The following are the basic blocks of an UPDATE message:

- Network Layer Reachability Information (NLRI)

- Path attributes

- Withdrawn routes

The format of these is shown in Figure 100.

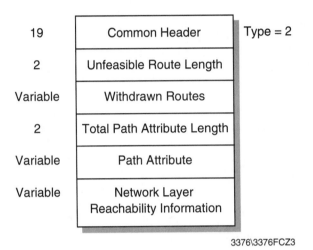

Figure 100. BGP Update Message

Network Layer Reachability Information (NLRI): NLRI is the mechanism by which BGP-4 supports classless routing. NLRI is an variable field indication, in the form of an IP prefix route, of the networks being advertised. The NLRI is also represented by the tuple <length,prefix>. A tuple of the form <14,220.24.106.0>indicates a route to be reachable of the form 220.24.106.0 255.252.0.0 or 220.24.106.0/14 in the CIDR format (see Figure 101 on page 188).

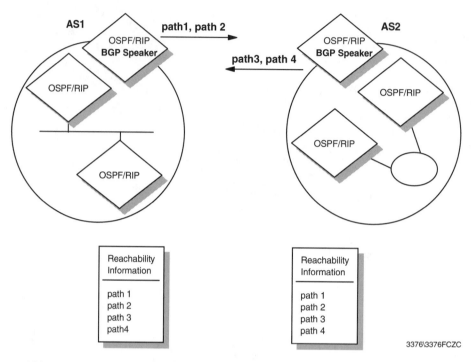

Figure 101. BGP Exchanging NLRI

Path Attributes: Each path attribute consists of a triple set of values: attribute flag, attribute type and attribute value. Three of the attribute flags provide information about the status of the attribute types, and may be optional or well-known, transitive or non-transitive and partial or complete.

Attribute flags must be read in conjunction with their associated attribute types. There are seven attribute types that together define an advertised route:

- Origin, which is a well-known mandatory attribute (type code 1), and defines the origin of the route as an IGP, an EGP or INCOMPLETE (for example a static route).

- AS path is a well-known mandatory attribute (type code 2), and defines the ASs which must be crossed to reach the network being advertised. It is a sequence of AS numbers a route has traversed to reach a destination. The AS that originates the route adds its own AS number when sending the route to its external BGP peer. Each AS that receives the route and passes it on to other BGP peer will prepend its own AS number as the last element of the sequence.

- Next hop is a well-known mandatory attribute (type code 3), and defines the IP address of the ASBR that is next hop on the path to the listed destnation(s).

- Multi_exit_disc which is an optional non-transitive attribute (type code 4), used by a BGP speaker's decision process to discriminate among multiple exit points to a neighboring autonomous system.

- Local_pref which is a well-known discretionary attribute (type code 5), and used by a BGP speaker to inform other BGP speakers in its own autonomous system of the originating speaker's degree of preference for an advertised route.

- Atomic_aggregate, which is a well-known discretionary attribute (type code 6), and used by a BGP speaker to inform other BGP speakers that the local system selected a less specific route without selecting a more specific route which is included in it.

- Aggregator, which is an optional transitive attribute (type code 7), and indicates the last AS number that formed the aggregate route, followed by the IP address of the BGP speaker that formed the aggregate route.

The format of BGP path attributes is shown in Figure 102.

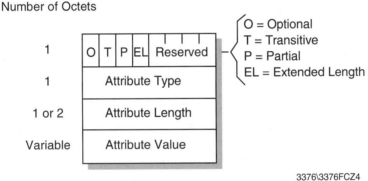

3376\3376FCZ4

Figure 102. BGP Path Attributes

Withdrawn Routes: An infeasible route length indicates the total length of the withdrawn routes field in octets. A value of it equaling 0 indicates that no routes are being withdrawn from service, and that the Withdrawn Routes field is not present in this update message.

Withdrawn routes is a variable length field. Updates that are not feasible or that are no longer in service and need to be withdrawn from BGP routing table. The withdrawn routes have the same formats as the NLRI. Withdrawn routes are also

represented by the tuple <length,prefix>. A tuple of the form
<15,220.24.106.0>indicates a route to be withdrawn of the form 220.24.106.0
255.254.0.0 or 220.24.106.0/15 in the CIDR format (see Figure 103 on page 190).

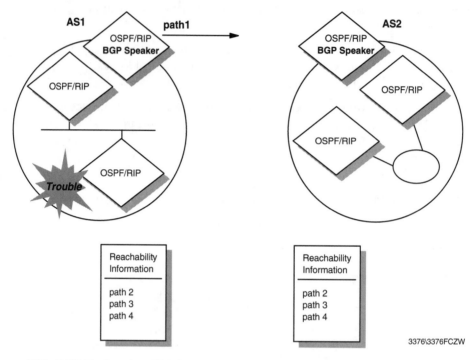

Figure 103. BGP Exchanging Withdraw Routes

Notifying Errors: Notification messages are sent to a neighbor router when error
conditions are detected. The BGP transport connection is closed immediately after a
notification message has been sent.

Notification messages consist of an *error code* and an *error subcode*, which further
qualifies the main error. The format of notification messages is shown in Figure 104
on page 191.

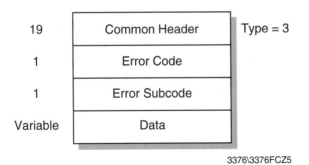

3376\3376FCZ5

Figure 104. *BGP Notification Message*

Error codes that are provided by BGP are as follows:

- Message Header Error
- Open Message Error
- Update Message Error
- Hold Timer Expired
- Finite State Machine Error
- Cease

A data field is included in the notification message to provide additional diagnostic information.

3.5 References

For more information on IP routing protocols, please see the following RFCs:

- *RFC 904 — Exterior Gateway Protocol Formal Specification*
- *RFC 1058 — Routing Information Protocol*
- *RFC 1245 — OSPF Protocol Analysis*
- *RFC 1246 — Experience with the OSPF Protocol*
- *RFC 1721 — RIP Version 2 Protocol Analysis*
- *RFC 1722 — RIP Version 2 Protocol Applicability Statement*
- *RFC 1723 — RIP Version 2 – Carrying Additional Information*

- *RFC 1724 — RIP Version 2 MIB Extension*
- *RFC 1771 — A Border Gateway Protocol 4 (BGP-4)*
- *RFC 1772 — Application of the Border Gateway Protocol in the Internet*
- *RFC 1812 — Requirements for IP Version 4 Routers*
- *RFC 1850 — OSPF Version 2: Management Information Base*
- *RFC 2080 — RIPng for IPv6*
- *RFC 2328 — OSPF Version 2*

Chapter 4. Application Protocols

The highest level protocols are called *application protocols*. They communicate with applications on other hosts and are the user-visible interface to the TCP/IP protocol suite.

4.1 Characteristics of Applications

All of the higher level protocols have some characteristics in common:

- They can be user-written applications or applications standardized and shipped with the TCP/IP product. Indeed, the TCP/IP protocol suite includes application protocols such as:

  - TELNET for interactive terminal access to remote hosts.

  - FTP (file transfer protocol) for high-speed disk-to-disk file transfers.

  - SMTP (simple mail transfer protocol) as an Internet mailing system.

  These are the most widely implemented application protocols, but a lot of others exist. Each particular TCP/IP implementation will include a more or less restricted set of application protocols.

- They use either UDP or TCP as a transport mechanism. Remember that UDP (see 2.7, "User Datagram Protocol (UDP)" on page 97) is unreliable and offers no flow-control, so in this case the application has to provide its own error recovery and flow-control routines. It is often easier to build applications on top of TCP (see 2.8, "Transmission Control Protocol (TCP)" on page 100), a reliable, connection-oriented protocol. Most application protocols will use TCP, but there are applications built on UDP to provide better performance through reduced protocol overhead.

- Most of them use the client/server model of interaction.

4.1.1 Client/Server Model

TCP is a peer-to-peer, connection-oriented protocol. There are no master/slave relations. The applications, however, use a client/server model for communications.

A *server* is an application that offers a service to users; a *client* is a requester of a service. An application consists of both a server and a client part, which can run on the same or on different systems.

Users usually invoke the client part of the application, which builds a *request* for a particular service and sends it to the server part of the application using TCP/IP as a transport vehicle.

The server is a program that receives a request, performs the required service and sends back the results in a *reply*. A server can usually deal with multiple requests (multiple clients) at the same time.

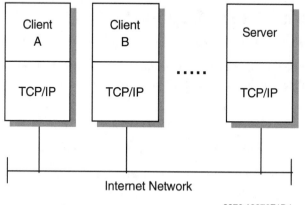

3376a\3376F1D4

Figure 105. *The Client/Server Model of Applications*

Some servers wait for requests at a well-known port (see 2.6, "Ports and Sockets" on page 94) so that their clients know to which IP socket they must direct their requests. The client uses an arbitrary port for its communication. Clients that wish to communicate with a server that does not use a well-known port must have another mechanism for learning to which port they must address their requests. This mechanism might employ a registration service such as Portmap, which uses a well-known port.

The next sections discuss the most widely used application protocols.

4.2 Domain Name System (DNS)

The Domain Name System is a *standard protocol* with STD number 13. Its status is *recommended*. It is described in RFC 1034 and RFC 1035. This section explains the implementation of the Domain Name System, and the implementation of name servers.

The early internet configurations required users to use only numeric IP addresses. Very quickly, this evolved to the use of symbolic host names. For example, instead of typing TELNET 128.12.7.14 one could type TELNET eduvm9, and eduvm9 is then translated in some way to the IP address 128.12.7.14. This introduces the problem of maintaining the mappings between IP addresses and high-level machine names in a coordinated and centralized way.

Initially, host names to address mappings were maintained by the Network Information Center (NIC) in a single file (HOSTS.TXT), which was fetched by all hosts using FTP. This is called a *flat namespace*.

Due to the explosive growth in the number of hosts, this mechanism became too cumbersome (consider the work involved in the addition of just one host to the Internet) and was replaced by a new concept: *Domain Name System*. Hosts can continue to use a local flat namespace (the HOSTS.LOCAL file) instead of or in addition to the Domain Name System, but outside small networks, the Domain Name System is practically essential. The Domain Name System allows a program running on a host to perform the mapping of a high-level symbolic name to an IP address for any other host without the need for every host to have a complete database of host names.

4.2.1 The Hierarchical Namespace

Consider the internal structure of a large organization. As the chief executive cannot do everything, the organization will probably be partitioned into divisions, each of them having autonomy within certain limits. Specifically, the executive in charge of a division has authority to make direct decisions, without permission from his or her chief executive.

Domain names are formed in a similar way, and will often reflect the hierarchical delegation of authority used to assign them. For example, consider the name:

small.itso.raleigh.ibm.com

Here, itso.raleigh.ibm.com is the lowest level domain name, a subdomain of raleigh.ibm.com, which again is a subdomain of ibm.com, a subdomain of com. We can also represent this naming concept by a hierarchical tree (see Figure 106 on page 196).

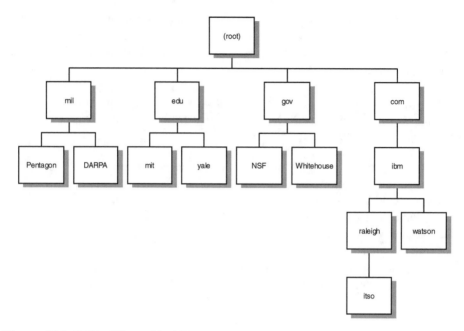

Figure 106. *DNS - Hierarchical Namespace*

The complete structure is explained in the following sections.

4.2.2 Fully Qualified Domain Names (FQDNs)

When using the Domain Name System, it is common to work with only a part of the domain hierarchy, for example, the ral.ibm.com domain. The Domain Name System provides a simple method of minimizing the typing necessary in this circumstance. If a domain name ends in a dot (for example, wtscpok.itsc.pok.ibm.com.), it is assumed to be complete. This is termed a *fully qualified domain ame (FQDN)* or an *absolute domain name*. However, if it does not end in a dot (for example, wtscpok.itsc), it is incomplete and the DNS resolver (see below) may complete this, for example, by appending a suffix such as .pok.ibm.com to the domain name. The rules for doing this are implementation-dependent and locally configurable.

4.2.3 Generic Domains

The three-character top-level names are called the *generic* domains or the *organizational* domains. Table 4 on page 197 shows some of the top-level domains of today's Internet domain namespace.

Table 4. DNS - Some Top-Level Internet Domains

Domain Name	Meaning
com	Commercial organizations
edu	Educational institutions
gov	Government institutions
int	International organizations
mil	U.S. Military
net	Major network support centers
org	Non-profit organizations
country code	ISO standard 2-letter identifier for country-specific domains

Since the Internet began in the United States, the organization of the hierarchical namespace initially had only U.S. organizations at the top of the hierarchy, and it is still largely true that the generic part of the namespace contains US organizations. However, only the .gov and .mil domains are restricted to the US.

At the time of writing, the U.S. Department Of Commerce - National Telecommunications and Information Administration is looking for a different organization for .us domains. As a result of this, it has been decided to change the status of the Internet Assigned Numbers Authority (IANA), which will no longer be funded and run by the U.S. Government. A new non-profit organization with an international Board of Directors will be funded by domain registries instead. On the other hand, there are some other organizations that have already begun to register new top-level domains. For current information see the IANA Web site at the URL below:

```
http://www.iana.org
```

4.2.4 Country Domains

There are also top-level domains named for the each of the ISO 3166 international 2-character country codes (from ae for the United Arab Emirates to zw for Zimbabwe). These are called the *country* domains or the *geographical* domains. Many countries have their own second-level domains underneath which parallel the generic top-level domains. For example, in the United Kingdom, the domains equivalent to the generic domains .com and .edu are .co.uk and .ac.uk (ac is an abbreviation for academic). There is a .us top-level domain, which is organized geographically by state (for example, .ny.us refers to the state of New York). See RFC 1480 for a detailed description of the .us domain.

4.2.5 Mapping Domain Names to IP Addresses

The mapping of names to addresses consists of independent, cooperative systems called name servers. A name server is a server program that holds a master or a copy of a name-to-address mapping database, or otherwise points to a server that does, and that answers requests from the client software, called a name resolver.

Conceptually, all Internet domain servers are arranged in a tree structure that corresponds to the naming hierarchy in Figure 106 on page 196. Each leaf represents a name server that handles names for a single subdomain. Links in the conceptual tree do not indicate physical connections. Instead, they show which other name server a given server can contact.

4.2.6 Mapping IP Addresses to Domain Names — Pointer Queries

The Domain Name System provides for a mapping of symbolic names to IP addresses and vice versa. While it is a simple matter in principle to search the database for an IP address given its symbolic name because of the hierarchical structure, the reverse process cannot follow the hierarchy. Therefore, there is another namespace for the reverse mapping. It is found in the domain in-addr.arpa (arpa because the Internet was originally the ARPAnet).

Because IP addresses are normally written in dotted decimal format, there is one layer of domains for each hierarchy. However, because domain names have the least-significant parts of the name first but dotted decimal format has the most significant bytes first, the dotted decimal address is shown in reverse order. For example, the domain in the domain name system corresponding to the IP address 129.34.139.30 is 30.139.34.129.in-addr.arpa. Given an IP address, the Domain Name System can be used to find the matching host name. A domain name query to find the host names associated with an IP address is called a *pointer query*.

4.2.7 The Distributed Name Space

The Domain Name System uses the concept of a *distributed name space*. Symbolic names are grouped into *zones of authority*, or more commonly *zones*. In each of these zones, one or more hosts has the task of maintaining a database of symbolic names and IP addresses and providing a server function for clients who wish to translate between symbolic names and IP addresses. These local name servers are then (through the internetwork on which they are connected) logically interconnected into a hierarchical tree of *domains*. Each zone contains a part or a *subtree* of the hierarchical tree and the names within the zone are administered independently of names in other zones. Authority over zones is vested in the name servers.

Normally, the name servers that have authority for a zone will have domain names belonging to that zone, but this is not required. Where a domain contains a subtree that falls in a different zone, the name server(s) with authority over the superior domain are said to *delegate authority* to the name server(s) with authority over the subdomain. Name servers can also delegate authority to themselves; in this case, the domain name space is still divided into zones moving down the domain name tree, but authority for two zones is held by the same server. The division of the domain name space into zones is accomplished using resource records stored in the Domain Name System.

4.2.8 Domain Name Resolution

The domain name resolution process can be summarized in the following steps:

1. A user program issues a request such as the gethostbyname() sockets call. (This particular call is used to ask for the IP address of a host by passing the hostname.)
2. The resolver formulates a query to the name server. (Full resolvers have a local name cache to consult first, stub resolvers do not.)
3. The name server checks to see if the answer is in its local authoritative database or cache, and if so, returns it to the client. Otherwise, it will query other available name server(s), starting down from the root of the DNS tree or as high up the tree as possible.
4. The user program will finally be given a corresponding IP address (or host name, depending on the query) or an error if the query could not be answered. Normally, the program will not be given a list of all the name servers that have been consulted to process the query.

The query/reply messages are transported by either UDP or TCP.

Domain name resolution is a client/server process. The client function (called the *resolver* or *name resolver*) is transparent to the user and is called by an application to resolve symbolic high-level names into real IP addresses or vice versa. The name server (also called a *domain name server*) is a server application providing the translation between high-level machine names and the IP addresses.

4.2.8.1 Domain Name Full Resolver

Figure 107 on page 200 shows a program called a *full resolver*, which is a program distinct from the user program, which forwards all queries to a name server for processing. Responses are cached by the name server for future use, and often by the name server.

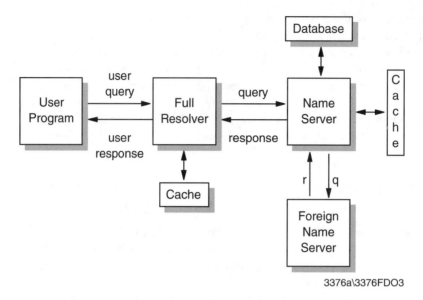

3376a\3376FDO3

Figure 107. DNS - Using a Full Resolver for Domain Name Resolution

4.2.8.2 Domain Name Stub Resolver

Figure 108 on page 201 shows a *stub resolver*, a routine linked with the user program, which forwards the queries to a name server for processing. Responses are cached by the name server but not usually by the resolver although this is implementation-dependent. On UNIX, the stub resolver is implemented by two library routines: gethostbyname() and gethostbyaddr() for converting host names to IP addresses and vice versa. Other platforms have the same or equivalent routines. Stub resolvers are much more common than full resolvers.

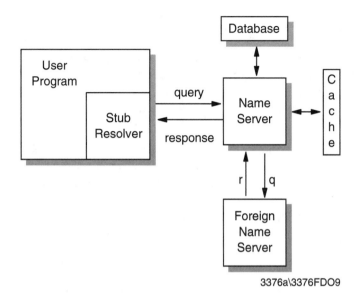

Figure 108. *DNS - Using a Stub Resolver for Domain Name Resolution*

4.2.8.3 Domain Name Resolver Operation

Domain name queries can be one of two types: *recursive* or *iterative* (also termed *non-recursive*). A flag bit in the domain name query specifies whether the client desires a recursive query and a flag bit in the response specifies whether the server supports recursive queries. The difference between a recursive and an iterative query arises when the server receives a request for which it cannot supply a complete answer by itself. A recursive query requests that the server should issue a query itself to determine the requested information and return the complete answer to the client. An iterative query means that the name server should return what information it has available and also a list of additional servers for the client to contact to complete the query.

Domain name responses can be one of two types: *authoritative* and *non-authoritative*. A flag bit in the response indicates which type a response is. When a name server receives a query for a domain in a zone over which it has authority, it returns all of the requested information in a response with the authoritative answer flag set. When it receives a query for a domain over which it does not have authority, its actions depend upon the setting of the recursion desired flag in the query.

- If the recursion desired flag is set and the server supports recursive queries, it will direct its query to another name server. This will either be a name server with authority for the domain given in the query, or it will be one of the root name servers. If the second server does not return an authoritative answer (for example, if it has delegated authority to another server), the process is repeated.

When a server (or a full resolver program) receives a response, it will cache it to improve the performance of repeat queries. The cache entry is stored for a maximum length of time specified by the originator in a 32-bit *time-to-live (TTL)* field contained in the response. 172,800 seconds (two days) is a typical TTL value.

- If the recursion desired flag is not set or the server does not support recursive queries, it will return whatever information it has in its cache and also a list of additional name servers to be contacted for authoritative information.

4.2.8.4 Domain Name Server Operation

Each name server has *authority* for zero or more zones. There are three types of name servers:

Primary

A primary name server loads a zone's information from disk, and has authority over the zone.

Secondary

A secondary name server has authority for a zone, but obtains its zone information from a primary server using a process called *zone transfer*. To remain synchronized, the secondary name servers query the primary on a regular basis (typically every three hours) and re-execute the zone transfer if the primary has been updated.

A name server can operate as a primary or a secondary name server for multiple domains, or a primary for some domains and as a secondary for others. A primary or secondary name server performs all of the functions of a caching only name server.

Caching-only

A name server that does not have authority for any zone is called a caching-only name server. A caching-only name server obtains all of its data from primary or secondary name servers as required. It requires at least one NS record to point to a name server from which it can initially obtain information.

When a domain is registered with the root and a separate zone of authority established, the following rules apply:

- The domain must be registered with the root administrator.

- There must be an identified administrator for the domain.

- There must be at least two name servers with authority for the zone that are accessible from outside and inside the domain to ensure no single point of failure.

It is also recommended that name servers that delegate authority also apply these rules, since the delegating name servers are responsible for the behavior of name servers under their authority.

4.2.9 Domain Name System Resource Records

The Domain Name System's distributed database is composed of *resource records (RRs)* which are divided into classes for different kinds of networks. We only discuss the Internet class of records. Resource records provide a mapping between domain names and *network objects*. The most common network objects are the addresses of Internet hosts, but the Domain Name System is designed to accommodate a wide range of different objects.

The start of a zone, marked by a Start of Authority (SOA) record, is closer to the root of the tree than the end. A Name Server Record (NS) marks the end of a zone started by an SOA record and points to a name server having authority for the next zone. At the root, there can be no higher name servers to delegate authority. Authority for the zone encompassing the root of the name space is vested in a set of *root name servers*.[8]

As a result of this scheme:

- Rather than having a central server for the database, the work that is involved in maintaining this database is off-loaded to hosts throughout the name space.
- Authority for creating and changing symbolic host names and responsibility for maintaining a database for them is delegated to the organization owning the zone (within the name space) containing those host names.
- From the user's standpoint, there is a single database that deals with these address resolutions. The user may be aware that the database is distributed, but generally need not be concerned about this.

Note: Although domains within the namespace will frequently map in a logical fashion to networks and subnets within the IP addressing scheme, this is not a requirement of the Domain Name System. Consider a router between two subnets. It has two IP addresses, one for each network adapter, but it would not normally have two symbolic names.

The general format of a resource record is:

---

[8] At the time of writing there were thirteen root servers. The current list is available by anonymous FTP from ftp.rs.internic.net in the file netinfo/root-servers.txt.

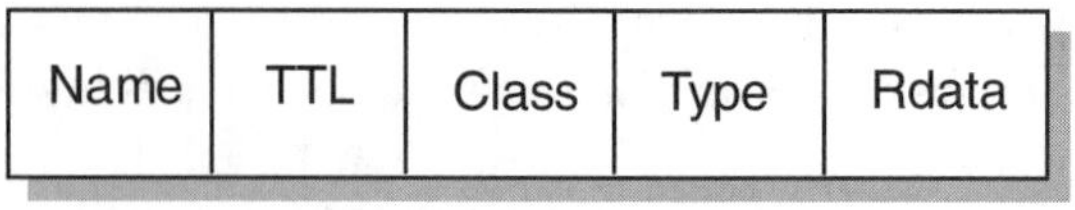

Name	TTL	Class	Type	Rdata

Figure 109. DNS - General Resource Record Format

where:

name

> Is the domain name to be defined. The Domain Name System is very general in its rules for the composition of domain names. However, it recommends a syntax for domain names which will minimize the likelihood of applications that use a DNS resolver (that is, nearly all TCP/IP applications) from misinterpreting a domain name. A domain name adhering to this recommended syntax will consist of a series of labels consisting of alphanumeric characters or hyphens, each label having a length of between 1 and 63 characters, starting with an alphabetic character. Each pair of labels is separated by a dot (period) in human readable form, but not in the form used within DNS messages. Domain names are not case-sensitive.

ttl

> Is the *time-to-live (TTL)* time in seconds that this resource record will be valid in a name server cache. This is stored in the DNS as an unsigned 32-bit value. 86400 (one day) is a typical value for records pointing to IP addresses.

class

> Identifies the protocol family. The only commonly used value is:
>
> *IN*   The Internet system

type

> Identifies the type of the resource in this resource record.
>
> The different types are described in detail in RFCs 1034, 1035 and 1706. Each type has a name and a value. Commonly used types include:

Type	Value	Meaning
A	1	A host address.
CNAME	5	Canonical name of an alias; specifies an alias name for a host.
HINFO	13	The CPU and OS used by the host; this is only a comment field.

Type	Value	Meaning
MX	15	A mail exchange for the domain; specifies a domain name for a mailbox. This is used by SMTP (see 4.7.2, "SMTP and the Domain Name System" on page 247 for more information).
NS	2	The authoritative name server for a domain.
PTR	12	A pointer to another part of the domain name space.
SOA	6	The start of a zone of authority in the domain name space.
WKS	11	Well-known services; specifies that certain services (for instance SMTP) are expected to be always active on this host.

Rdata

The value depends on the type, for example:

A	A 32-bit IP address (if the class is IN)
CNAME	A domain name
MX	A 16-bit preference value (low values being preferred) followed by a domain name
NS	A host name
PTR	A domain name

Please refer to 7.3, "Dynamic Domain Name System" on page 526 for additional resource record types.

4.2.10 Domain Name System Messages

All messages in the Domain Name System protocol use a single format. This format is shown in Figure 110 on page 206. This frame is sent by the resolver to the name server. Only the header and the question section are used to form the query. Replies and/or forwarding of the query use the same frame, but with more sections filled in (the answer/authority/additional sections).

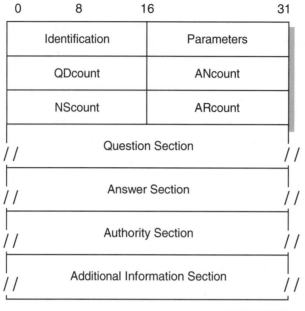

Figure 110. DNS - DNS Message Format

4.2.10.1 Header Format

The header section is always present and has a fixed length of 12 bytes. The other sections are of variable length.

ID   A 16-bit identifier assigned by the program. This identifier is copied in the corresponding reply from the name server and can be used for differentiation of responses when multiple queries are outstanding at the same time.

Parameters

A 16-bit value in the following format:

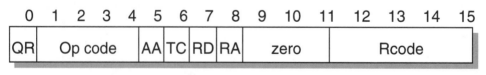

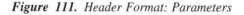

3376a\3376FDO4

Figure 111. Header Format: Parameters

QR Flag identifying a query (0) or a response(1)

Op code

    4-bit field specifying the kind of query:

    0 standard query (QUERY)
    1 inverse query (IQUERY)
    2 server status request (STATUS)
    Other values are reserved for future use

AA Authoritative answer flag. If set in a response, this flag specifies that the responding name server is an authority for the domain name sent in the query.

TC Truncation flag. Set if message was longer than permitted on the physical channel.

RD Recursion desired flag. This bit signals to the name server that recursive resolution is asked for. The bit is copied to the response.

RA Recursion available flag. Indicates whether the name server supports recursive resolution.

zero

    3 bits reserved for future use. Must be zero.

Rcode

    4-bit response code. Possible values are:

    0 No error.
    1 Format error. The server was unable to interpret the message.
    2 Server failure. The message was not processed because of a problem with the server.
    3 Name error. The domain name in the query does not exist. This is only valid if the AA bit is set in the response.
    4 Not implemented. The requested type of query is not implemented by name server.
    5 Refused. The server refuses to respond for policy reasons.
    Other values are reserved for future use.

QDcount An unsigned 16-bit integer specifying the number of entries in the question section.

ANcount An unsigned 16-bit integer specifying the number of RRs in the answer section.

NScount An unsigned 16-bit integer specifying the number of name server RRs in the authority section.

ARcount　　An unsigned 16-bit integer specifying the number of RRs in the additional records section.

4.2.10.2 Question Section

The next section contains the queries for the name server. It contains QDcount (usually 1) entries, each in the format shown in Figure 112.

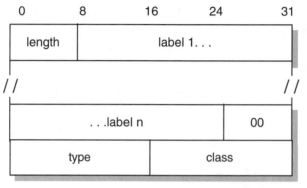

Figure 112. DNS - Question Format. All of the fields are byte-aligned. The alignment of the Type field on a 4-byte boundary is for example purposes and is not required by the format.

length　　A single byte giving the length of the next label.

label　　One element of the domain name characters (for example ibm from ral.ibm.com). The domain name referred to by the question is stored as a series of these variable length labels, each preceded by a 1-byte length.

00　　X'00' indicates the end of the domain name and represents the null label of the root domain.

Type　　2 bytes specifying the type of query. It can have any value from the Type field in a resource record.

Class　　2 bytes specifying the class of the query. For Internet queries, this will be IN.

For example, the domain name raleigh.ibm.com would be encoded with the following fields:

```
X'07'
"raleigh"
X'03'
"ibm"
X'03'
"com"
X'00'
```

Thus the entry in the question section for raleigh.ibm.com would require 21 bytes: 17 to store the domain name and 2 each for the Qtype and Qclass fields.

4.2.10.3 Answer, Authority and Additional Resource Sections

These three sections contain a variable number of resource records. The number is specified in the corresponding field of the header. The resource records are in the format shown in Figure 113.

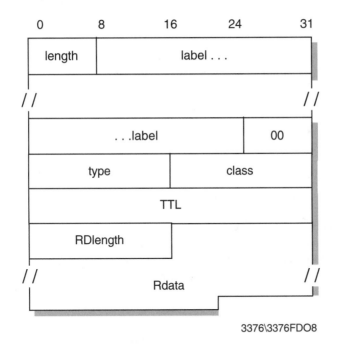

3376\3376FDO8

Figure 113. DNS - Answer Record Entry Format. All of the fields are byte-aligned. The alignment of the Type field on a 4-byte boundary is for example purposes and is not required by the format.

Where the fields before the TTL field have the same meanings as for a question entry and:

TTL   A 32-bit time-to-live value in seconds for the record. This defines how long it can be regarded as valid.

RDlength   A 16-bit length for the Rdata field.

Rdata   A variable length string whose interpretation depends on the Type field.

4.2.10.4 Message Compression

In order to reduce the message size, a compression scheme is used to eliminate the repetition of domain names in the various RRs. Any duplicate domain name or list of labels is replaced with a pointer to the previous occurrence. The pointer has the form of a 2-byte field:

- The first 2 bits distinguish the pointer from a normal label, which is restricted to a 63-byte length plus the length byte ahead of it (which has a value of <64).
- The offset field specifies an offset from the start of the message. A zero offset specifies the first byte of the ID field in the header.
- If compression is used in an Rdata field of an answer, authority or additional section of the message, the preceding RDlength field contains the real length after compression is done.

Please refer to 7.3, "Dynamic Domain Name System" on page 526 for additional message formats.

4.2.11 A Simple Scenario

Consider a stand-alone network (no outside connections), consisting of two physical networks: one has an internet network address 129.112, the other has a network address 194.33.7, interconnected by an IP gateway (VM2).

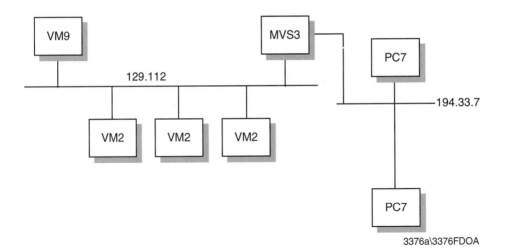

Figure 114. DNS - A Simple Configuration. Two networks connected through an IP gateway.

Let us assign the name server function to VM1. Remember that the domain hierarchical tree forms a logical tree, completely independent of the physical configuration. In this simple scenario, there is only one level in the domain tree. Let's give this configuration the domain name test.example.

The zone data for the name server will then be as shown in Figure 115.

```
;note: an SOA record has no TTL field
;
$origin test.example.                                      ;note 1
;
@           IN SOA VM1.test.example. ADM.VM1.test.example.
                  (870611          ;serial number for data
                   1800            ;secondary refreshes every 30 mn
                   300             ;secondary reties every 5 mn
                   604800          ;data expire after 1 week
                   86400)          ;minimum TTL for data is 1 week
;
@     99999 IN NS   VM1.test.example.                      ;note 2
;
VM1   99999 IN A    129.112.1.1                            ;note 3
      99999 IN WKS 129.112.1.1 TCP (SMTP                   ;note 4
                                    FTP
                                    TELNET
                                    NAMESRV)
;
RT1   99999 IN A     129.112.1.2
            IN HINFO IBM RT/PC-AIX                         ;note 5
RT2   99999 IN A     129.112.1.3
            IN HINFO IBM RT/PC-AIX
PC1   99999 IN A     129.112.1.11
PC2   99999 IN A     194.33.7.2
PC3   99999 IN A     194.33.7.3
;
;VM2 is an IP gateway and has 2 different IP addresses
;
VM2   99999 IN A     129.112.1.4
      99999 IN A     194.33.7.1
      99999 IN WKS   129.112.1.4 TCP (SMTP FTP)
            IN HINFO IBM-3090-VM/CMS
;
4.1.112.129.in-addr.arpa.  IN  PTR  VM2                    ;note 6
;
;Some mailboxes
;
central 10   IN MX  VM2.test.example.                      ;note 7 and 8
;
;a second definition for the same mailbox, in case VM2 is down
;
central 20   IN MX  VM1.test.example.
waste   10   IN MX  VM2.test.example.
```

Figure 115. *DNS - Zone Data for the Name Server*

Notes:

1 The $origin statement sets the @ variable to the zone name (test.example.). Domain names that do not end with a period are suffixed with the zone name. Fully qualified domain names (those ending with a period) are unaffected by the zone name.

2 Defines the name server for this zone.

3 Defines the Internet address of the name server for this zone.

4 Specifies well-known services for this host. These are expected to always be available.

5 Gives information about the host.

6 Used for inverse mapping queries (see 4.2.6, "Mapping IP Addresses to Domain Names — Pointer Queries" on page 198).

7 Will allow mail to be addressed to user@central.test.example.

8 See 4.7.2, "SMTP and the Domain Name System" on page 247 for the use of these definitions.

4.2.12 Extended Scenario

Consider the case where a connection is made to a third network (129.113), which has an existing name server with authority for that zone.

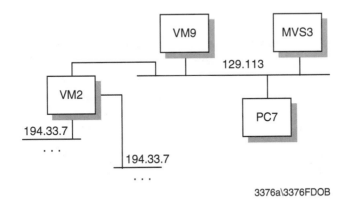

3376a\3376FDOB

Figure 116. DNS - Extended Configuration. A third network is connected to the existing configuration.

Let us suppose that the domain name of the other network is tt.ibm.com and that its name server is located in VM9.

All we have to do is add the address of this name server to our own name server database, and to reference the other network by its own name server. The following two lines are all that is needed to do that:

```
tt.ibm.com.          99999  IN NS    VM9.tt.ibm.com.
VM9.tt.ibm.com.      99999  IN A     129.113.1.9
```

This simply indicates that VM9 is the authority for the new network, and that all queries for that network will be directed to that name server.

4.2.13 Transport

Domain Name System messages are transmitted either as datagrams (UDP) or via stream connection (TCP).

UDP usage: Server port 53 (decimal).

Messages carried by UDP are restricted to 512 bytes. Longer messages are truncated and the TC bit is set in the header. Since UDP frames can be lost, a retransmission strategy is required.

TCP usage: Server port 53 (decimal).

In this case, the message is preceded by a 2-byte field indicating the total message frame length.

STD 3 — Host Requirements requires that:

- A Domain Name System resolver or server that is sending a non-zone-transfer query *must* send a UDP query first. If the answer section of the response is truncated and if the requester supports TCP, it should try the query again using TCP. UDP is preferred over TCP for queries because UDP queries have much lower overhead, and the use of UDP is essential for a heavily loaded server. Truncation of messages is rarely a problem given the current contents of the Domain Name System database, since typically 15 response records can be accommodated in the datagram, but this may change as new record types are added to the Domain Name System.
- TCP must be used for zone transfer activities because the 512-byte limit for a UDP datagram will always be inadequate for a zone transfer.
- Name servers must support both types of transport.

4.2.13.1 Dynamic DNS (DDNS)

The Dynamic Domain Name System (DDNS) is a protocol that defines extensions to the Domain Name System to enable DNS servers to accept requests to add, update and delete entries in the DNS database dynamically. Because DDNS offers a functional superset to existing DNS servers, a DDNS server can serve both static and dynamic domains at the same time, a welcome feature for migration and overall DNS design.

DDNS is currently available in a non-secure and a secure flavor, defined in RFC 2136 and RFC 2137, respectively. Rather than allowing any host to update its DNS records, the secure version of DDNS uses public key security and digital signatures to authenticate update requests from DDNS hosts. IBM, for instance, has fully implemented secure DDNS on its OS/2 Warp Server, AIX, OS/390 and AS/400 platforms as well as on Windows NT.

Without client authentication, another host could impersonate an unsuspecting host by remapping the address entry for the unsuspecting host to that of its own. Once the remapping occurs, important data, such as logon passwords and mail intended for the host would unfortunately be sent to the impersonating host instead.

Please see also 7.3, "Dynamic Domain Name System" on page 526 for more information on how DDNS works together with DHCP to perform seamless updates of reverse DNS mapping entries and see 6.4, "DNS in IPv6" on page 493 for more information about DNS with IPv6.

4.2.14 DNS Applications

Three common utilities for querying name servers are provided with many DNS implementations:

host   Obtains an IP address associated with a host name or a host name associated with an IP address.

nslookup   Allows you to locate information about network nodes, examine the contents of a name server database and establish the accessibility of name servers.

dig   Allows you to exercise name servers, gather large volumes of domain name information and execute simple domain name queries. DIG stands for Domain Internet Groper.

4.2.15 References

The following RFCs define the Domain Name System standard and the information kept in the system:

- *RFC 1032 — Domain Administrator's Guide*
- *RFC 1033 — Domain Administrator Operations Guide*
- *RFC 1034 — Domain Names – Concepts and Facilities*

- *RFC 1035 — Domain Names – Implementation and Specification*
- *RFC 1101 — DNS Encoding of Networks Names and Other Types*
- *RFC 1183 — New DNS RR Definitions*
- *RFC 1480 — The US Domain*
- *RFC 1591 — Domain Name System Structure and Delegation*
- *RFC 1706 — DNS NSAP Resource Records*

4.3 TELNET

TELNET is a *standard protocol* with STD number 8. Its status is *recommended*. It is described in RFC 854 *TELNET Protocol Specifications* and RFC 855 *TELNET Option Specifications.*

The TELNET protocol provides a standardized interface, through which a program on one host (the TELNET client) can access the resources of another host (the TELNET server) as though the client were a local terminal connected to the server.

For example, a user on a workstation on a LAN may connect to a host attached to the LAN as though the workstation were a terminal attached directly to the host. Of course, TELNET can be used across WANs as well as LANs.

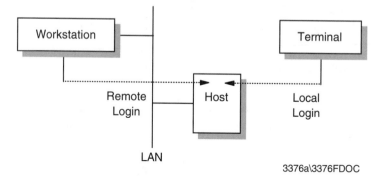

Figure 117. TELNET - Remote Login Using TELNET

Most TELNET implementations do not provide you with graphics capabilities.

4.3.1 TELNET Operation

TELNET protocol is based on three ideas:

1. The Network Virtual Terminal (NVT) concept. An NVT is an imaginary device having a basic structure common to a wide range of real terminals. Each host

maps its own terminal characteristics to those of an NVT, and assumes that every other host will do the same.

2. A symmetric view of terminals and processes.

3. Negotiation of terminal options. The principle of negotiated options is used by the TELNET protocol, because many hosts wish to provide additional services, beyond those available with the NVT. Various options may be negotiated. Server and client use a set of conventions to establish the operational characteristics of their TELNET connection via the "DO, DON'T, WILL, WON'T" mechanism discussed later in this chapter.

The two hosts begin by verifying their mutual understanding. Once this initial negotiation is complete, they are capable of working on the minimum level implemented by the NVT. After this minimum understanding is achieved, they can negotiate additional options to extend the capabilities of the NVT to reflect more accurately the capabilities of the real hardware in use. Because of the symmetric model used by TELNET, both the host and the client may propose additional options to be used.

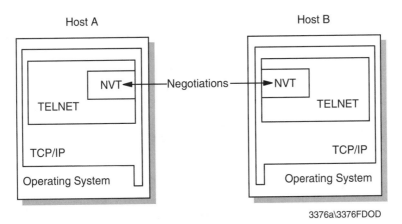

Figure 118. TELNET - The Symmetric TELNET Model

4.3.1.1 Network Virtual Terminal

The NVT has a printer (or display) and a keyboard. The keyboard produces outgoing data, which is sent over the TELNET connection. The printer receives the incoming data. The basic characteristics of an NVT, unless they are modified by mutually agreed options are:

- The data representation is 7-bit ASCII transmitted in 8-bit bytes.

- The NVT is a half-duplex device operating in a line-buffered mode.

- The NVT provides a local echo function.

All of these can be negotiated by the two hosts. For example, a local echo is preferred because of the lower network load and superior performance but there is an option for using a remote echo, although no host is required to use it.

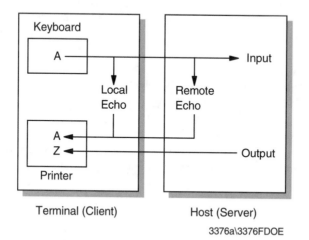

Figure 119. TELNET - Echo Option

An NVT printer has an unspecified carriage width and page length. It can handle printable ASCII characters (ASCII code 32 to 126) and understands some ASCII control characters such as:

Command	ASCII	Action
NULL (NUL)	0	No Operation.
Line Feed (LF)	10	Moves the printer to the next print line, keeping the same horizontal position.
Carriage Return (CR)	13	Moves the printer to the left margin.
BELL (BEL)	7	Produces an audible or visible signal.
Back Space (BS)	8	Moves the print head one character position toward the left margin.
Horizontal Tab (HT)	9	Moves the printer to the next horizontal tab stop.
Vertical Tab (VT)	11	Moves the printer to the next vertical tab stop.
Form Feed (FF)	12	Moves the printer to the top of the next page, keeping the same horizontal position.

4.3.1.2 TELNET Options

There is an extensive set of TELNET options, and the reader should consult *STD 1 — Official Internet Protocol Standards* for the standardization state and status for each of them. At the time of writing, the following options were defined:

Table 5 (Page 1 of 2). TELNET Options

Num	Name	State	RFC	STD
0	Binary Transmission	Standard	856	27
1	Echo	Standard	857	28
3	Suppress Go Ahead	Standard	858	29
5	Status	Standard	859	30
6	Timing Mark	Standard	860	31
255	Extended-Options-List	Standard	861	32
34	Linemode	Draft	1184	
2	Reconnection	Proposed		
4	Approx Message Size Negotiation	Proposed		
7	Remote Controlled Trans and Echo	Proposed	726	
8	Output Line Width	Proposed		
9	Output Page Size	Proposed		
10	Output Carriage-Return Disposition	Proposed	652	
11	Output Horizontal Tabstops	Proposed	653	
12	Output Horizontal Tab Disposition	Proposed	654	
13	Output Formfeed Disposition	Proposed	655	
14	Output Vertical Tabstops	Proposed	656	
15	Output Vertical Tab Disposition	Proposed	657	
16	Output Linefeed Disposition	Proposed	658	
17	Extended ASCII	Proposed	698	
18	Logout	Proposed	727	
19	Byte Macro	Proposed	735	
20	Data Entry Terminal	Proposed	1043	
21	SUPDUP	Proposed	736	

Table 5 (Page 2 of 2). TELNET Options

Num	Name	State	RFC	STD
22	SUPDUP Output	Proposed	749	
23	Send Location	Proposed	779	
24	Terminal Type	Proposed	1091	
25	End of Record	Proposed	885	
26	TACACS User Identification	Proposed	927	
27	Output Marking	Proposed	933	
28	Terminal Location Number	Proposed	946	
29	TELNET 3270 Regime	Proposed	1041	
30	X.3 PAD	Proposed	1053	
31	Negotiate About Window Size	Proposed	1073	
32	Terminal Speed	Proposed	1079	
33	Remote Flow Control	Proposed	1372	
35	X Display Location	Proposed	1096	
39	TELNET Environment Option	Proposed	1572	
40	TN3270 Enhancements	Proposed	1647	
37	TELNET Authentication Option	Experimental	1416	
41	Telnet XAUTH	Experimental		
42	Telnet CHARSET	Experimental	2066	
43	Telnet Remote Serial Port	Experimental		
44	Telnet Com Port Control	Experimental	2217	

All of the standard options have a status of *recommended* and the remainder have a status of *elective*. There is a historic version of the TELNET Environment Option which is *not* recommended; it is TELNET option 36 and was defined in RFC 1408.

Full-Screen Capability: Full-screen TELNET is possible provided the client and server have compatible full-screen capabilities. For example, VM and MVS provide a TN3270-capable server. To use this facility, a TELNET client must support TN3270.

4.3.1.3 TELNET Command Structure

The communication between client and server is handled with internal commands, which are not accessible by users. All internal TELNET commands consist of 2 or 3-byte sequences, depending on the command type.

The Interpret As Command (IAC) character is followed by a command code. If this command deals with option negotiation, the command will have a third byte to show the code for the referenced option.

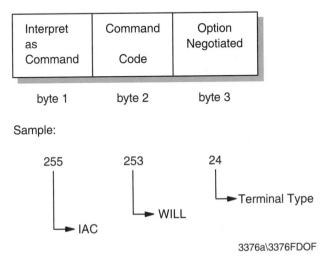

3376a\3376FDOF

Figure 120. TELNET - Internal TELNET Command Structure. This command proposes negotiation about terminal type.

Command name	Code	Comments
SE	240	End of sub-negotiation parameters.
NOP	241	No operation.
Data Mark	242	The data stream portion of a synch. This should always be accompanied by a TCP urgent notification.
Break	243	NVT character BRK.
Go ahead	249	The GA signal.
SB	250	Indicates that what follows is sub-negotiation of the option indicated by the immediately following code.
WILL	251	Shows the desire to use, or confirmation that you are now using, the option indicated by the code immediately following.
WON'T	252	Shows the refusal to use, or to continue to use, the option indicated by the code immediately following.

Command name	Code	Comments
DO	253	Requests that the other party uses, or confirms that you are expecting the other party to use, the option indicated by the code immediately following.
DON'T	254	Demands that the other party stop using, or confirms that you are no longer expecting the other party to use, the option indicated by the code immediately following.
IAC	255	Interpret As Command. Indicates that what follows is a TELNET command, not data.

4.3.1.4 Option Negotiation

Using internal commands, TELNET in each host is able to negotiate options. The starting base of negotiation is the NVT capability: each host to be connected must agree to this minimum. Every option can be negotiated by the use of the four command codes WILL, WON'T, DO, DON'T described above.

In addition, some options have sub-options: if both parties agree to the option, they use the SB and SE commands to manage the sub-negotiation. Here is a simplified example of how option negotiation works.

Send	Reply	Meaning
DO transmit binary	WILL transmit binary	
DO window size	WILL window size	Can we negotiate window size?
SB Window Size 0 80 0 24 SE		Specify window size.
DO terminal type	WILL terminal type	Can we negotiate terminal type?
SB terminal type SE		Send me your terminal characteristics.
	SB terminal type IBM-3278-2 SE	My terminal is a 3278-2.
DO echo	WON'T echo	

The terminal types are defined in *STD 2 — Assigned Numbers*.

4.3.1.5 TELNET Basic Commands

The primary goal of the TELNET protocol is the provision of a standard interface for hosts over a network. To allow the connection to start, the TELNET protocol defines a standard representation for some functions:

IP	Interrupt Process
AO	Abort Output
AYT	Are You There
EC	Erase Character
EL	Erase Line
SYNCH	Synchronize

4.3.2 Terminal Emulation (Telnet 3270)

Telnet may be used to make a TCP/IP connection to an SNA host. However, telnet 3270 is used to provide 3270 telnet emulation (TN3270). The following differences between traditional telnet and 3270 terminal emulation make it necessary for additional telnet options specifically for TN3270 to be defined:

- 3270 terminal emulation uses block mode rather than line mode.

- 3270 terminal emulation uses the EBCDIC character set rather than the ASCII character set.

- 3270 terminal emulation uses special key functions such as ATTN and SYSREQ.

The TN3270 connection over telnet is accomplished by the negotiation of the following three different telnet options;

1. Terminal Type

2. Binary Transmission

3. End of Record

A TN3270 server must support these characteristics during initial client/server session negotiations. Binary transmission and end of record options can be sent in any order during the TN3270 negotiation. Please note that TN3270 does not use any additional option during the TN3270 negotiation; it uses normal telnet options. After a TN3270 connection is established, additional options can be used. These options are TELNET-REGIME, SUPPRESS-GO-AHEAD, ECHO and TIMING-MARK.

Terminal type option is a string that specifies the terminal type for the host such as IBM 3278-3. The -3 following 3278 indicates the use of an alternate screen size other than the standard screen size which is 24x80. Binary transmission telnet option states that the connection will be other than initial mode which is NVT. If the client or server want to switch to NVT mode, they should send a command that disables binary option. A 3270 data stream consists of a command and related data. Since the length of the data associated with the command may vary, every command and its related data must be separated with the IAC EOR sequence. For this purpose, the EOR telnet option is used during the negotiation.

Other important issues for a TN3270 connection are the correct handling of the ATTN and SYSREQ functions. The 3270 ATTN key is used in SNA environments to interrupt the current process. The 3270 SYSREQ key is used in SNA environments to terminate the session without closing the connection. However, SYSREQ and ATTN commands cannot be sent directly to the TN3270 server over a telnet connection. Most of the TN3270 server implementations convert the BREAK command to an ATTN request to the host via the SNA network. On the client side, a key or combination of keys are mapped to BREAK for this purpose. For the SYSREQ key, either a telnet Interrupt Process command can be sent or a SYSREQ command can be sent imbedded into a TN3270 data stream. Similarly, on the client side, a key or combination of keys are mapped for SYSREQ.

There are some functions that cannot be handled by traditional TN3270. Some of these issues are;

1. TN3270 does not support 328x types of printers.

2. TN3270 cannot handle SNA BIND information.

3. There is no support for the SNA positive/negative reponse process.

4. The 3270 ATTN and SYSREQ keys are not supported by all implementations.

5. TN3270 cannot define telnet sessions into SNA device names.

4.3.3 TN3270 Enhancements (TN3270E)

The 3270 structured field allows non-3270 data to be carried in 3270 data. Therefore, it is possible to send graphics, IPDS printer data streams and others. The structured field consists of a structured field command and one or more blocks following the command. However, not every TN3270 client can support all types of data. In order for clients to be able to support any of these functions, the supported range of data types should be determined when the telnet connection is established. This process requires additions to TN3270. To overcome the shortcomings of traditional TN3270, TN3270 extended attributes are defined. Please refer to RFC 2355 for detailed information about TN3270 enhancements (TN3270E).

In order to use the extended attributes of TN3270E, both the client and server should support TN3270E. If either side does not support TN3270E, traditional TN3270 can be used. Once both sides have agreed to use TN3270E, they begin to negotiate the subset of TN3270E options. These options are device-type and a set of supported 3270 functions which are:

- Printer data stream type

- Device status information

- The passing of BIND information from server to client

- Positive/negative response exchanges

4.3.3.1 Device-Type Negotiation

Device-type names are NVT ASCII strings and all uppercase. When the TN3270E server issues the DEVICE-TYPE SEND command to the client, the server replies with a device type, a device name or a resource name followed by the DEVICE-TYPE REQUEST command. The device-types are:

Table 6. TN3270E Device-Types - Terminals

Terminal	Terminal-E	Screen Size
IBM-3278-2	IBM-3278-2-E	24 row x 80 col display
IBM-3278-3	IBM-3278-3-E	32 row x 80 col display
IBM-3278-4	IBM-3278-4-E	43 row x 80 col display
IBM-3278-5	IBM-3278-5-E	27 row x 132 col display
IBM-DYNAMIC	n/a	n/a

Table 7. TN3270E Device-Types - Printers

Printer
IBM-3287-1

Since the 3278 and 3287 are commonly used devices, device-types are restricted to 3278 and 3287 terminal and printer types to simplify the negotiation. This does not mean that other types of devices cannot be used. Simply, the device-type negotiation determines the generic characteristic of the 3270 device that will be used. More advanced functions of 3270 data stream supported by the client are determined by the combination of read partition query and query reply.

The -E suffix indicates the use of extended attributes such as partition, graphics, extended colors and alternate character sets. If the client and the server have agreed to use extended attributes and negotiated on a device with the -E suffix, IBM-DYNAMIC device or printer, both sides must be able to handle the 3270 structured field. The structured field also allows 3270 telnet clients to issue specific 3270 data stream to host applications that the client is capable of using.

From the point of TN3270E client, it is not always possible or easy to know device names available on the network. The TN3270E server should assign the proper device to the client. This is accomplished by using a device pool that is defined on the TN3270E server. Basically, these device pools contain SNA network devices such as terminals and printers. In other words, The TN3270E implementation maps TN3270 sessions to specific SNA logical unit (LU) names thus effectively turning them into SNA devices. The device pool not only defines SNA network devices but also provides some other important functions for a TN3270E session. Some of these are:

- It is possible to assign one or more printers to a specific terminal device.

- It is possible to assign a group of devices to a specific organization.

- A pool can be defined that has access to only certain types of applications on the host.

The TN3270E client can issue CONNECT or ASSOCIATE commands to connect or associate the sessions to certain types of resources. However, this resource must not conflict with the definition on the server and the device-type determined during the negotiation.

4.3.4 References

Please refer to the following RFCs for more information on telnet:

- *RFC 854 — TELNET Protocol Specifications*

- *RFC 855 — TELNET Option Specifications.*

- *RFC 2355 — TN3270 Enhancements*

4.4 File Transfer Protocol (FTP)

FTP is a *standard protocol* with STD Number 9. Its status is *recommended*. It is described in RFC 959 *File Transfer Protocol (FTP)* and updated in RFC 2228 *FTP Security Extensions*.

Copying files from one machine to another is one of the most frequently used operations. The data transfer between client and server can be in either direction. The client can send a file to the server machine. It can also request a file from this server.

To access remote files, the user must identify himself or herself to the server. At this point the server is responsible for authenticating the client before it allows the file transfer.

From an FTP user's point of view, the link is connection-oriented. In other words, it is necessary to have both hosts up and running TCP/IP to establish a file transfer.

4.4.1 Overview of FTP

FTP uses TCP as a transport protocol to provide reliable end-to-end connections. The FTP server listens to connections on port 20 and 21. Two connections are used: the first is for login and follows the TELNET protocol and the second is for managing the data transfer. As it is necessary to log into the remote host, the user must have a user name and a password to access files and directories. The user who initiates the connection assumes the client function, while the server function is provided by the remote host.

On both sides of the link the FTP application is built with a protocol interpreter (PI), a data transfer process (DTP), and a user interface (see Figure 121 on page 228).

The user interface communicates with the protocol interpreter, which is in charge of the control connection. This protocol interpreter has to communicate the necessary information to its own file system.

On the opposite side of the link, the protocol interpreter, besides its function of responding to the TELNET protocol, has to initiate the data connection. During the file transfer, the data management is performed by DTPs. After a user's request is completed, the server's PI has to close the control connection.

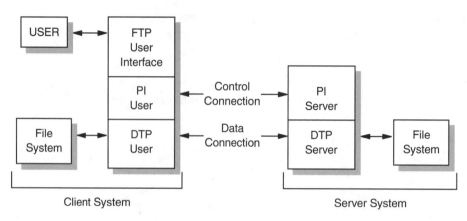

Figure 121. *FTP - FTP Principle*

4.4.2 FTP Operations

When using FTP, the user will perform some or all of the following operations:

- Connect to a remote host
- Select a directory
- List files available for transfer
- Define the transfer mode
- Copy files to or from the remote host
- Disconnect from the remote host

4.4.2.1 Connecting to a Remote Host

To execute a file transfer, the user begins by logging into the remote host. This is the primary method of handling the security. The user must have a user ID and password for the remote host, unless using anonymous FTP which is described in 4.4.6, "Anonymous FTP" on page 233.

There are four commands that are used:

Open   Selects the remote host and initiates the login session

User   Identifies the remote user ID

Pass   Authenticates the user

Site   Sends information to the foreign host that is used to provide services
              specific to that host

4.4.2.2 Selecting a Directory

When the control link is established, the user can use the cd (change directory)
subcommand to select a remote directory to work with. Obviously, the user can only
access directories for which the remote user ID has the appropriate authorization. The
user can select a local directory with the lcd (local change directory) command. The
syntax of theses commands depends upon the operating system in use.

4.4.2.3 Listing Files Available for Transfer

This task is performed using the dir or ls subcommands.

4.4.2.4 Specifying the Transfer Mode

Transferring data between dissimilar systems often requires transformations of the data
as part of the transfer process. The user has to decide on two aspects of the data
handling:

- The way the bits will be moved from one place to another

- The different representations of data upon the system's architecture

This is controlled using two subcommands:

Mode   Specifies whether the file is to be treated as having a record structure in a
              byte stream format.

        Block   Logical record boundaries of the file are preserved.

        Stream   The file is treated as a byte stream. This is the default, and
                    provides more efficient transfer but may not produce the
                    desired results when working with a record-based file system.

Type   Specifies the character sets used for the data.

        ASCII   Indicates that both hosts are ASCII-based, or that if one is
                    ASCII-based and the other is EBCDIC-based, that
                    ASCII-EBCDIC translation should be performed.

        EBCDIC   Indicates that both hosts use an EBCDIC data representation.

        Image   Indicates that data is to be treated as contiguous bits packed in
                    8-bit bytes.

Because these subcommands do not cover all possible differences between systems, the
SITE subcommand is available to issue implementation-dependent commands.

4.4.2.5 Transferring Files

The following commands can be used to copy files between FTP clients and servers:

Get   Copies a file from the remote host to the local host.

Mget   Copies multiple files from the remote to the local host.

Put   Copies a file from the local host to the remote host.

Mput   Copies multiple files from the local host to the remote host.

4.4.2.6 Using Passive Mode

Passive mode reverses the direction of data transfer, so that the FTP server on the remote host selects a port and informs the FTP client program which port to use when the client connects to the server on the remote host. Since, passive mode allows the FTP server to create a port for the connection, it will be relatively easy to ensure that no dangerous service goes on a given port. This approach makes it easier to configure filtering rules for firewalls. Therefore, this mode is also referred to as firewall-friendly mode. Please see 5.3.4.2, "An Example: FTP Proxy Server" on page 366 for more detail about FTP proxy server and passive mode.

4.4.2.7 Using Proxy Transfer

Proxy transfer allows the clients that have slow a connection to use a third-party transfer between two remote servers. A client that is connected to a server opens an FTP connection to another server using that server by issuing the proxy open command. For example, client A wants to download a file from server B but the connection is slow. In this case, client A can first connect to server C and then issue the proxy open server_B command to log into server B. Client A sends proxy get file_name to transfer the file from server B to server C.

4.4.2.8 Terminating the Transfer Session

The following commands are used to end an FTP session:

Quit   Disconnects from the remote host and terminates FTP. Some implementations use the BYE subcommand.

Close   Disconnects from the remote host but leaves the FTP client running. An open command can be issued to work with a new host.

4.4.3 Reply Codes

In order to manage these operations, the client and server conduct a dialog using the TELNET convention. The client issues commands, and the server responds with *reply codes*. The responses also include comments for the benefit of the user, but the client program uses only the codes.

Reply codes are three digits long, with the first digit being the most significant.

Table 8. FTP Reply Codes. The second and third digits provide more details about the response.

Reply code	Description
1xx	Positive preliminary reply.
2xx	Positive completion reply.
3xx	Positive intermediate reply.
4xx	Transient negative completion reply.
5xx	Permanent negative completion reply.

Example: For each user command, shown like **this**, the FTP server responds with a message beginning with a 3-digit reply code, shown like this:

```
FTP foreignhost
220 service ready
USERNAME cms01
331 user name okay
PASSWORD xyxyx
230 user logged in
TYPE Image
200 command okay
```

4.4.4 FTP Scenario

A LAN user has to transfer a file from a workstation to a system running VM. The file has to be transferred from the workstation's disk drive to the minidisk 191 owned by CMS user cms01. There is no Resource Access Control Facility (RACF) installed. The symbolic name corresponding to an Internet address is host01.itsc.raleigh.ibm.com.

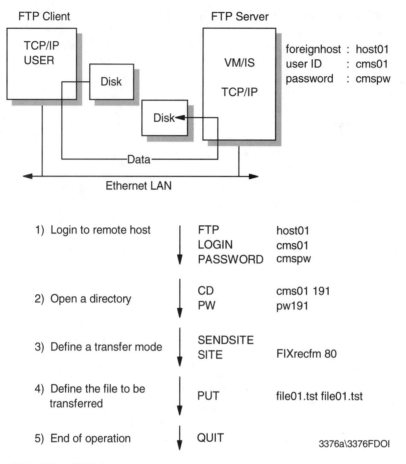

Figure 122. FTP - FTP Scenario

4.4.5 A Sample FTP Session

Figure 123 on page 233 illustrates an FTP session as seen from an FTP client program:

```
[C:\SAMPLES]ftp host01.itsc.raleigh.ibm.com
Connected to host01.itsc.raleigh.ibm.com.
220 host01 FTP server (Version 4.1 Sat Nov 23 12:52:09 CST 1991) ready.
Name (rs60002): cms01
331 Password required for cms01.
Password: xxxxxx
230 User cms01 logged in.
ftp> put file01.tst file01.tst
200 PORT command successful.
150 Opening data connection for file01.tst (1252 bytes).
226 Transfer complete.
local: file01.tst remote: file01.tst
1285 bytes received in 0.062 seconds (20 Kbytes/s)
ftp> close
221 Goodbye.
ftp> quit
```

Figure 123. FTP - A Sample FTP Session

4.4.6 Anonymous FTP

Many TCP/IP sites implement what is known as *anonymous FTP*, which means that these sites allow public access to some file directories. The remote user only needs to use the login name *anonymous* and password *guest* or some other common password conventions, for example the user's Internet e-mail ID. The password convention used on a system is explained to the user during the login process.

4.4.7 Remote Job Entry Using FTP

The FTP server on MVS allows sending job control language (JCL) to the internal reader. With this feature a kind of remote job entry (RJE) for TCP/IP can be implemented. It uses the site filetype=jes subcommand to indicate that the file sent is not really a file but a job. The FTP server on MVS then transfers the job to the job entry system (JES) for spooling and execution. The individual spool files can be received with the get subcommand of FTP.

4.5 Trivial File Transfer Protocol (TFTP)

The TFTP protocol is a *standard protocol* with STD number 33. Its status is *elective* and it is described in RFC 1350 *The TFTP Protocol (Revision 2)*. Updates to TFTP can be found in the following RFCs: 1785, 2347, 2348, and 2349.

TCP/IP file transfer is a disk-to-disk data transfer, as opposed to, for example, the VM SENDFILE command, a function that is considered in the TCP/IP world as a mailing function, where you send out the data to someone's mailbox (reader in the case of VM).

TFTP is an extremely simple protocol to transfer files. It is implemented on top of UDP (User Datagram Protocol). The TFTP client initially sends read/write request via port 69, then the server and the client determines the port that they will use for the rest of the connection. TFTP lacks most of the features of FTP (see 4.4, "File Transfer Protocol (FTP)" on page 226). The only thing it can do is read/write a file from/to a server.

Note: TFTP has no provisions for user authentication; in that respect, it is an unsecure protocol.

4.5.1 TFTP Usage

The command TFTP <hostname> takes you to the interactive prompt where you can enter subcommands, such as the following:

`Connect <host>`
> Specify destination host ID

`Mode <ascii/binary>`
> Specify the type of transfer mode

`Get <remote filename> [<local filename>]`
> Retrieve a file

`Put <remote filename> [<local filename>]`
> Store a file

`Verbose`

> Toggle verbose mode, which displays additional information during file transfer, on or off

`Quit`
> Exit TFTP

For a full list of these commands, see the user's guide of your particular TFTP implementation.

4.5.2 Protocol Description

Any transfer begins with a request to read or write a file. If the server grants the request, the connection is opened and the file is sent in blocks of 512 bytes (fixed length). Blocks of the file are numbered consecutively, starting at 1. Each data packet must be acknowledged by an acknowledgment packet before the next one can be sent. Termination of the transfer is assumed on a data packet of less than 512 bytes.

Almost all errors will cause termination of the connection (lack of reliability). If a packet gets lost in the network, a timeout will occur, after which a retransmission of the last packet (data or acknowledgment) will take place.

There was a serious bug, known as the Sorcerer's Apprentice Syndrome, in RFC 783. It may cause excessive retransmission by both sides in some network delay scenarios. It was documented in RFC 1123 and was corrected in RFC 1350. OACK packet was added to the TFTP packets as an extension. This is described in RFC 2347. For details, please refer to the RFCs.

4.5.2.1 TFTP Packets

There are six types of packets:

Opcode	Operation
1	Read Request (RRQ)
2	Write Request (WRQ)
3	Data (DATA)
4	Acknowledgment (ACK)
5	Error (ERROR)
6	Option Acknowledgment (OACK)

The TFTP header contains the *opcode* associated with the packet.

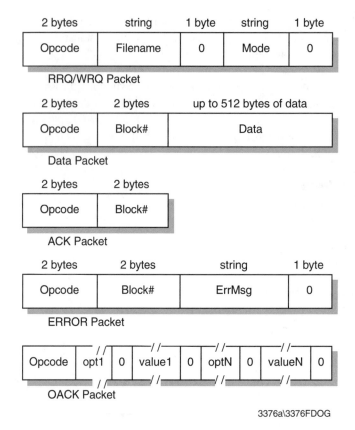

Figure 124. TFTP - TFTP Packets

4.5.2.2 Data Modes

Three modes of transfer are currently defined in RFC 1350:

NetASCII US-ASCII as defined in *USA Standard Code for Information Interchange* with modifications specified in RFC 854 *Telnet Protocol Specification* and extended to use the high order bit. That is, it is an 8-bit character set, unlike US-ASCII, which is 7-bit.

Octet Raw 8-bit bytes, also called binary.

Mail This mode was originally defined in RFC 783 and was declared obsolete by RFC 1350. It allowed for sending mail to a user rather than transferring to a file.

The mode used is indicated in the Request for Read/Write packet (RRQ/WRQ).

4.5.3 TFTP Multicast Option

This option allows multiple clients to get files simultaneously from the server using the multicast packets. As an example, when two similar machines are remotely booted, they can retrieve the same config file simultaneously by adding the multicast option to the TFTP option set. TFTP Multicast Option is described in RFC 2090.

Here is the TFTP read request packet, which is modified to include the multicast option.

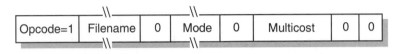

Figure 125. TFTP - Read Request Packet with Multicast Option

If the server accepts the multicast, it sends an Option Acknowledgment (OACK) packet to the server including the multicast option. This packet (OACK) consists of the multicast address and a flag that specifies whether the client should send acknowledgments (ACK).

4.5.4 Security Issue

Since TFTP does not have any authentication mechanism, the server should protect the host files. Generally, TFTP servers does not allow write access and only allow read access to public directories. Some server implementations also have a host access list.

4.6 Remote Execution Command Protocol (REXEC and RSH)

Remote EXEcution Command Daemon (REXECD) is a server that allows execution of the REXEC or Remote Shell Protocol (RSH) command from a remote host over the TCP/IP network. The client function is performed by the REXEC process.

4.6.1 Principle of Operation

REXECD is a server (or daemon). It handles commands issued by foreign hosts, and transfers orders to slave virtual machines for job execution. The daemon performs automatic login, and user authentication when user ID and password are entered.

The REXEC command is used to define user ID, password, host address, and the process to be started on the remote host. On the other hand, RSH does not require you to send a username and password; it uses a host access file instead. Both server and client are linked over the TCP/IP network. REXEC uses TCP port 512 and RSH uses TCP port 514.

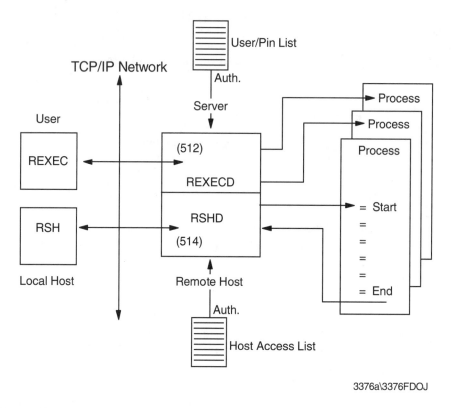

3376a\3376FDOJ

Figure 126. REXEC - REXECD Principle

4.7 Simple Mail Transfer Protocol (SMTP)

Electronic mail (e-mail) is probably the most widely used TCP/IP application. The basic Internet mail protocols provide mail (note) and message exchange between TCP/IP hosts; facilities have been added for the transmission of data that cannot be represented as 7-bit ASCII text.

There are three standard protocols that apply to mail of this kind. Each is *recommended*. The term SMTP is frequently used to refer to the combined set of protocols, since they are so closely inter-related, but strictly speaking SMTP is just one of the three. Normally, it is evident from the context which of the three protocols is being referred to. Whenever some doubt might exist, we refer to the STD or RFC numbers to avoid ambiguity. The three standards are:

- A standard for exchange of mail between two computers (STD 10/RFC 821), which specifies the protocol used to send mail between TCP/IP hosts. This standard is SMTP itself.

- A standard (STD 11) on the format of the mail messages, contained in two RFCs. RFC 822 describes the syntax of mail header fields and defines a set of header fields and their interpretation. RFC 1049 describes how a set of document types other than plain text ASCII can be used in the mail body (the documents themselves are 7-bit ASCII containing imbedded formatting information: PostScript, Scribe, SGML, TEX, TROFF and DVI are all listed in the standard).

  The official protocol name for this standard is MAIL.

- A standard for the routing of mail using the Domain Name System, described in RFC 974. The official protocol name for this standard is DNS-MX.

The STD 10/RFC 821 dictates that data sent via SMTP is 7-bit ASCII data, with the high-order bit cleared to zero. This is adequate in most instances for the transmission of English text messages, but is inadequate for non-English text or non-textual data. There are two approaches to overcoming these limitations:

- Multipurpose Internet Mail Extensions (MIME), defined in RFCs 2045 to 2049, which specifies a mechanism for encoding text and binary data as 7-bit ASCII within the mail envelope defined by RFC 822. MIME is described in 4.8, "Multipurpose Internet Mail Extensions (MIME)" on page 250.

- SMTP Service Extensions, which define a mechanism to extend the capabilities of SMTP beyond the limitations imposed by RFC 821. There are three current RFCs that describe SMTP Service Extensions:

  - A standard for a receiver SMTP to inform a sender SMTP which service extensions it supports (RFC 1869).

    RFC 1869 modifies RFC 821 to allow a client SMTP agent to request that the server respond with a list of the service extensions that it supports at the start of an SMTP session. If the server SMTP does not support RFC 1869, it will respond with an error and the client can either terminate the session or attempt to start a session according to the rules of RFC 821. If the server does support RFC 1869, it can also respond with a list of the service extensions that it supports. A registry of services is maintained by IANA. The initial list defined in RFC 1869 contains those commands listed in RFC 1123 *Requirements for Internet Hosts — Application and Support* as optional for SMTP servers.

Other service extensions are defined via RFCs in the usual manner. The next two RFCs define specific extensions:

- A protocol for 8-bit text transmission (RFC 1652) that allows an SMTP server to indicate that it can accept data consisting of 8-bit bytes. A server that reports that this extension is available to a client must leave the high order bit of bytes received in an SMTP message unchanged if requested to do so by the client.

  The MIME and SMTP Service Extension approaches are complementary rather than competing standards. In particular, RFC 1652 is titled *SMTP Service Extension for 8-bit-MIMEtransport*, since the MIME standard allows messages to be declared as consisting of 8-bit data rather than 7-bit data. Such messages cannot be transmitted by SMTP agents that strictly conform to RFC 821, but can be transmitted when both the client and the server conform to RFCs 1869 and 1652. Whenever a client SMTP attempts to send 8-bit data to a server that does not support this extension, the client SMTP must either encode the message contents into a 7-bit representation compliant with the MIME standard or return a permanent error to the user.

  This service extension does not permit the sending of arbitrary binary data because RFC 821 defines the maximum length of a line that an SMTP server is required to accept as 1000 characters. Non-text data could easily have sequences of more than 1000 characters without a <CRLF> sequence.

  Note: The service extension specifically limits the use of non-ASCII characters (those with values above decimal 127) to message bodies. They are *not* permitted in RFC 822 message headers.

- A protocol for message size declaration (RFC 1870) that allows a server to inform a client of the maximum size message it can accept. Without this extension, a client can only be informed that a message has exceeded the maximum size acceptable to the server (either a fixed upper limit or a temporary limit imposed by a lack of available storage space at the server) after transmitting the entire message. When this happens, the server discards the failing message. If both client and server support the Message Size Declaration extension, the client may declare an estimated size of the message to be transferred and the server will return an error if the message is too large.

Each of these SMTP Service Extensions is a *draft standard protocol* and each has a status of *elective*.

4.7.1 How SMTP Works

SMTP (that is, STD 11/RFC 821) is based on *end-to-end delivery*; an SMTP client will contact the destination host's SMTP server directly to deliver the mail. It will keep the mail item being transmitted until it has been successfully copied to the recipient's SMTP. This is different from the store-and-forward principle that is common in many mailing systems, where the mail item may pass through a number of intermediate hosts in the same network on its way to the destination and where successful transmission from the sender only indicates that the mail item has reached the first intermediate hop.

In various implementations, there is a possibility to exchange mail between the TCP/IP SMTP mailing system and the locally used mailing systems. These applications are called *mail gateways* or *mail bridges*. Sending mail through a mail gateway can alter the end-to-end delivery specification, since SMTP will only guarantee delivery to the mail-gateway host, not to the real destination host, which is located beyond the TCP/IP network. When a mail gateway is used, the SMTP end-to-end transmission is host-to-gateway, gateway-to-host or gateway-to-gateway; the behavior beyond the gateway is not defined by SMTP. CSNET provides an interesting example of mail gateway service. Started as a low-cost facility to interconnect scientific and corporate research centers, CSNET operates a mail gateway service that allows subscribers to send and receive mail across the Internet using only a dial-up modem. The mail gateway polls the subscribers at regular times, delivers mail that was addressed to them and picks up the outgoing mail. Although this is not a direct end-to-end delivery, it has proven to be a very useful system.

Each message has:

- A header, or envelope, the structure of which is strictly defined by RFC 822.

  The mail header is terminated by a null line (that is, a line with nothing preceding the <CRLF> sequence). However, some implementations (for example VM, which does not support zero-length records in files) may interpret this differently and accept a blank line as a terminator.

- Contents

  Everything after the null (or blank) line is the message body which is a sequence of lines containing ASCII characters (that is, characters with a value less than 128 decimal).

RFC 821 defines a client/server protocol. As usual, the client SMTP is the one that initiates the session (that is, the sending SMTP) and the server is the one that responds (the receiving SMTP) to the session request. However, since the client SMTP frequently acts as a server for a user mailing program, it is often simpler to refer to the client as the sender SMTP and to the server as the receiver SMTP.

4.7.1.1 Mail Header Format

The user normally doesn't have to worry about the message header, since it is taken care of by SMTP itself. A short reference is included below for completeness.

RFC 822 contains a complete lexical analysis of the mail header. The syntax is written in a form known as the augmented Backus-Naur Form (BNF). RFC 822 contains a description of augmented BNF, and many RFCs that are related to RFC 822 use this format. RFC 822 describes how to parse a mail header to a *canonical representation*, unfolding continuation lines, deleting insignificant spaces, removing comments and so on. The syntax is powerful, but relatively difficult to parse. A basic description is given here, which should be adequate for the reader to interpret the meaning of simple mail headers that he or she encounters. However, this description is too great a simplification to understand the details workings of RFC 822 mailers; for a full description, refer to RFC 822.

Briefly, the header is a list of lines, of the form:

`field-name: field-value`

Fields begin in column 1. Lines beginning with white space characters (SPACE or TAB) are continuation lines that are unfolded to create a single line for each field in the canonical representation. Strings enclosed in ASCII quotation marks indicate single tokens within which special characters such as the colon are not significant. Many important field values (such as those for the To and From fields) are *mailboxes*. The most common forms for these are:

```
octopus@garden.under.the.sea
The Octopus <octopus@garden.under.the.sea>
"The Octopus" <octopus@garden.under.the.sea>
```

The string The Octopus is intended for human recipients and is the name of the mailbox owner. The string octopus@garden.under.the.sea is the machine-readable address of the mailbox. (The angle brackets are used to delimit the address but are not part of it.) One can see that this form of addressing is closely related to the Domain Name System concept. In fact, the client SMTP uses the Domain Name System to determine the IP address of the destination mailbox.

Some frequently used fields are:

keyword	value
to	Primary recipients of the message.

cc	Secondary (carbon-copy) recipients of the message.
from	Identity of sender.
reply-to	The mailbox to which responses are to be sent. This field is added by the originator.
return-path	Address and route back to the originator. This field is added by the final transport system that delivers the mail.
Subject	Summary of the message. This is usually provided by the user.

4.7.1.2 Mail Exchange

The SMTP design is based on the model of communication shown in Figure 127. As a result of a user mail request, the sender SMTP establishes a two-way connection with a receiver SMTP. The receiver SMTP can be either the ultimate destination or an intermediate (mail gateway). The sender SMTP will generate commands that are replied to by the receiver SMTP.

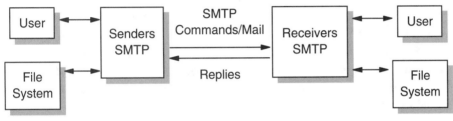

3376a\3376FDOM

Figure 127. SMTP - Model for SMTP

SMTP Mail Transaction Flow: Although mail commands and replies are rigidly defined, the exchange can easily be followed in Figure 128 on page 245. All exchanged commands/replies/data are text lines, delimited by a <CRLF>. All replies have a numeric code at the beginning of the line.

1. The sender SMTP establishes a TCP connection with the destination SMTP and then waits for the server to send a 220 Service ready message or a 421 Service not available message when the destination is temporarily unable to proceed.

2. HELO (HELO is an abbreviation for hello) is sent, to which the receiver will identify himself or herself by sending back its domain name. The sender-SMTP can use this to verify if it contacted the right destination SMTP.

   If the sender SMTP supports SMTP Service Extensions as defined in RFC 1869, it may substitute an EHLO command in place of the HELO command. A receiver SMTP that does not support service extensions will respond with a 500 Syntax error, command unrecognized message. The sender SMTP should then retry with

HELO, or if it cannot transmit the message without one or more service extensions, it should send a QUIT message.

If a receiver-SMTP supports service extensions, it responds with a multi-line 250 OK message, which includes a list of service extensions that it supports.

3. The sender now initiates the start of a mail transaction by sending a MAIL command to the receiver. This command contains the reverse-path which can be used to report errors. Note that a path can be more than just the user mailbox@host domain name pair. In addition, it can contain a list of routing hosts. Examples of this are when we pass a mail bridge, or when we provide explicit routing information in the destination address. If accepted, the receiver replies with a 250 OK.

4. The second step of the actual mail exchange consists of providing the server SMTP with the destinations for the message. There can be more than one recipient.) This is done by sending one or more RCPT TO:<forward-path> commands. Each of them will receive a reply 250 OK if the destination is known to the server, or a 550 No such user here if it isn't.

5. When all RCPT commands are sent, the sender issues a DATA command to notify the receiver that the message contents are following. The server replies with 354 Start mail input, end with <CRLF>.<CRLF>. Note the ending sequence that the sender should use to terminate the message data.

6. The client now sends the data line by line, ending with the 5-character sequence <CRLF>.<CRLF> line upon which the receiver acknowledges with a 250 OK or an appropriate error message if anything went wrong.

7. We now have several possible actions:

   • The sender has no more messages to send. He or she will end the connection with a QUIT command, which will be answered with a 221 Service closing transmission channel reply.
   • The sender has no more messages to send, but is ready to receive messages (if any) from the other side. He or she will issue the TURN command. The two SMTPs now switch their role of sender/receiver and the sender (previously the receiver) can now send messages by starting with step 3 above.
   • The sender has another message to send, and simply goes back to step 3 to send a new MAIL command.

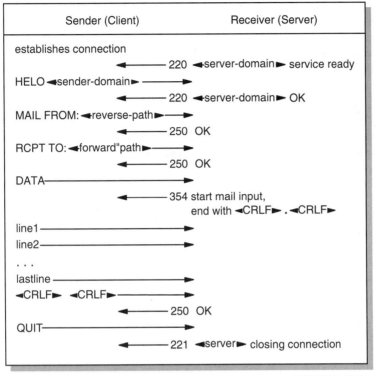

Sender (Client)   Receiver (Server)

establishes connection
                                     ◄———————— 220 ◄server-domain► service ready
HELO ◄sender-domain► ————————►
                                     ◄———————— 220 ◄server-domain► OK
MAIL FROM: ◄reverse-path►————►
                                     ◄———————— 250 OK
RCPT TO: ◄forward"path►————►
                                     ◄———————— 250 OK
DATA————————————————————►
                                     ◄———————— 354 start mail input,
                                                   end with ◄CRLF► . ◄CRLF►
line1 ————————————————————►
line2 ————————————————————►
. . .
lastline ————————————————►
◄CRLF► ◄CRLF►————————————►
                                     ◄———————— 250 OK
QUIT————————————————————►
                                     ◄———————— 221 ◄server► closing connection

3376a\3376FDON

Figure 128. SMTP - Normal SMTP Data Flow. One mail message is delivered to one destination mailbox.

The SMTP Destination Address (Mailbox Address): Its general form is local-part@domain-name and can take several forms:

user@host   For a direct destination on the same TCP/IP network.

user%remote-host@gateway-host
                          For a user on a non-SMTP destination remote-host, via the mail gateway gateway-host.

@host-a,@host-b:user@host-c
                          For a relayed message. This contains explicit routing information. The message will first be delivered to host-a, who will resend (relay) the message to host-b. Host-b will then forward the message to the real destination host-c. Note that the message is stored on each of the intermediate hosts, so we don't have an end-to-end delivery in this case.

In the above description, only the most important commands were mentioned. All of them are commands that must be recognized in each SMTP implementation. Other commands exist, but most of those are only optional; that is, the RFC standard does not require them to be implemented everywhere. However, they implement very interesting functions such as relaying, forwarding, mailing lists, etc.

For a full list of command verbs, see RFC 821 *Simple Mail Transfer Protocol* and RFC 1123 *Requirements for Internet Hosts — Application and Support*. For details of SMTP service extensions, see RFC 1869 *SMTP Service Extensions*, RFC 1652 *SMTP Service Extension for 8-bit-MIMEtransport* and RFC 1870 *SMTP Service Extension for Message Size Declaration*.

Example: In the following scenario, user abc at host vm1.stockholm.ibm.com sends a note to users xyz, opq and rst at host delta.aus.edu. The lines preceded by R: are lines sent by the receiver; the S: lines are sent by the sender.

```
R: 220 delta.aus.edu Simple Mail Transfer Service Ready
S: HELO stockholm.ibm.com
R: 250 delta.aus.edu

S: MAIL FROM:<abc@stockholm.ibm.com>
R: 250 OK

S: RCPT TO:<xyz@delta.aus.edu>
R: 250 OK
S: RCPT TO:<opq@delta.aus.edu>
R: 550 No such user here
S: RCPT TO:<rst@delta.aus.edu>
R: 250 OK

S: DATA
R: 354 Start mail input, end with <CRLF>.<CRLF>
S: Date: 23 Jan 89  18:05:23
S: From: Alex B. Carver <abc@stockholm.ibm.com>
S: Subject: Important meeting
S: To:  <xyz@delta.aus.edu>
S: To:  <opq@delta.aus.edu>
S: cc:  <rst@delta.aus.edu>
S:
S: Blah blah blah
S: etc.....
S: .
R: 250 OK

S: QUIT
R: 221 delta.aus.edu Service closing transmission channel
```

Figure 129. *SMTP - An Example Scenario*

Note that the message header is part of the data being transmitted.

4.7.2 SMTP and the Domain Name System

If the network is using the domain concept, an SMTP cannot simply deliver mail sent to TEST.IBM.COM by opening a TCP connection to TEST.IBM.COM. It must first query the name server to find out to which host (again a domain name) it should deliver the message.

For message delivery, the name server stores resource records (RRs) known as MX RRs. They map a domain name to two values:

- A preference value. As multiple MX resource records may exist for the same domain name, a preference (priority) is assigned to them. The lowest preference value corresponds to the most preferred record. This is useful whenever the most preferred host is unreachable; the sending SMTP then tries to contact the next (less preferred) host.
- A host name.

It is also possible that the name server responds with an empty list of MX RRs. This means that the domain name is in the name server's authority, but has no MX assigned to it. In this case, the sending SMTP may try to establish the connection with the host name itself.

An important recommendation is given in RFC 974. It recommends that after obtaining the MX records, the sending SMTP should query for Well-Known Services (WKS) records for this host, and should check that the referenced host has SMTP as a WKS-entry.

Note: This is only an option of the protocol but is already widely implemented.

Here is an example of MX resource records:

```
fsc5.stn.mlv.fr.        IN    MX 0   fsc5.stn.mlv.fr.
                        IN    MX 2   psfred.stn.mlv.fr.
                        IN    MX 4   mvs.stn.mlv.fr.
                        IN    WKS    152.9.250.150 TCP (SMTP)
```

In the above example, mail for fsc5.stn.mlv.fr should by preference, be delivered to the host itself, but in case the host is unreachable, the mail might also be delivered to psfred.stn.mlv.fr or to mvs.stn.mlv.fr (if psfred.stn.mlv.fr is unreachable, too).

4.7.2.1 Addressing Mailboxes on Server Systems

When a user employs a server system for all mail functions, the mailbox address seen by other SMTP users refers exclusively to the mail server system. For example if two OS/2 systems are named:

```
hayes.itso.ral.ibm.com
```

and

```
itso180.itso.ral.ibm.com
```

with the first one being used as an UltiMail client and the second as an UltiMail server, the mailbox address might be:

```
hayes@itso180.itso.ral.ibm.com
```

This mailbox address would appear in the From: header field of all outgoing mail and in the SMTP commands to remote servers issued by the UltiMail server system.

When the user uses a POP server, however, the mailbox address on outbound mail items contains the workstation's hostname (for example, steve@hayes.itso.ral.ibm.com). In this case, the sender should include a Reply-To: field in the mail header to indicate that replies should *not* be sent to the originating mailbox. For example, the mail header might look like this:

```
Date: Fri, 10 Feb 95 15:38:23
From: steve@hayes.itso.ral.ibm.com
To: "Steve Hayes" <tsgsh@gford1.warwick.uk.ibm.com>
Reply-To: hayes@itso180.itso.ral.ibm.com
Subject: Test Reply-To: header field
```

The receiving mail agent is expected to send replies to the Reply-To: address and not the From: address.

Using the Domain Name System to Direct Mail: An alternative approach to using the Reply-To: header field is to use the Domain Name System to direct mail to the correct mailbox. The administrator for the domain name server with authority for the domain containing the user's workstation and the name server can add MX resource records to the Domain Name System to direct mail appropriately, as described in 4.7.2, "SMTP and the Domain Name System" on page 247. For example, the following MX records indicate to client SMTPs that if the SMTP server on hayes.itso.ral.ibm.com is not available, there is a mail server on itso.180.ral.ibm.com (9.24.104.180) that should be used instead.

```
itso180.itso.ral.ibm.com.   IN    WKS  9.24.104.180 TCP (SMTP)

hayes.itso.ral.ibm.com.     IN    MX 0 hayes.itso.ral.ibm.com.
                            IN    MX 1 itso180.itso.ral.ibm.com.
```

4.7.3 References

A detailed description of the SMTP, MAIL and DNS-MX standards can be found in the following RFCs:

- *RFC 821 — Simple Mail Transfer Protocol*
- *RFC 822 — Standard for the format of ARPA Internet text messages*
- *RFC 974 — Mail Routing and the Domain System*

- *RFC 1049 — A Content Type Header Field for Internet messages*
- *RFC 1652 — SMTP Service Extension for 8-bit-MIMEtransport*

4.8 Multipurpose Internet Mail Extensions (MIME)

MIME is a *draft-standard protocol*. Its status is *elective*.

Electronic mail (as described in 4.7, "Simple Mail Transfer Protocol (SMTP)" on page 238) is probably the most widely used TCP/IP application. However, SMTP (that is, an STD 10/RFC 821-compliant mailing system) is limited to 7-bit ASCII text with a maximum line length of 1000 characters, which results in a number of limitations:

- SMTP cannot transmit executable files or other binary objects. There are a number of ad hoc methods of encapsulating binary items in SMTP mail items, for example:

    - Encoding the file as pure hexadecimal

    - The UNIX UUencode and UUdecode utilities that are used to encode binary data in the UUCP mailing system to overcome the same limitations of 7-bit transport

    - The Andrew Toolkit representation

    None of these can be described as a de facto standard. UUencode is perhaps the most pervasive due to the pioneering role of UNIX systems in the Internet.

- SMTP cannot transmit text data that includes national language characters since these are represented by code points with a value of 128 (decimal) or higher in all character sets based on ASCII.

- SMTP servers may reject mail messages over a certain size. Any given server may have permanent and/or transient limits on the maximum amount of mail data it can accept from a client at any given time.

- SMTP gateways that translate from ASCII to EBCDIC and vice versa do not use a consistent set of code page mappings, resulting in translation problems.

- Some SMTP implementations or other mail transport agents (MTAs) in the Internet do not adhere completely to the SMTP standards defined in RFC 821. Common problems include:

    - Removal of trailing white space characters (TABs and SPACEs)

    - Padding of all lines in a message to the same length

    - Wrapping of lines longer than 76 characters

- Changing of new line sequences between different conventions. (For instance <CR> characters may be converted to <CRLF> sequences.)

- Conversion of TAB characters to multiple SPACEs.

MIME is a standard that includes mechanisms to solve these problems in a manner that is highly compatible with existing RFC 822 standards. Because mail messages are frequently forwarded through mail gateways, it is not possible for an SMTP client to distinguish between a server that manages the destination mailbox and one that acts as a gateway to another network. Since mail that passes through a gateway may be tunnelled through further gateways, some or all of which may be using a different set of messaging protocols, it is not possible in general for a sending SMTP to determine the lowest common denominator capability common to all stages of the route to the destination mailbox. For this reason, MIME assumes the worst: 7-bit ASCII transport, which may not strictly conform to or be compatible with RFC 821. It does not define any extensions to RFC 821, but limits itself to extensions within the framework of RFC 822. Thus, a MIME message is one which can be routed through any number of networks that are loosely compliant with RFC 821 or are capable of transmitting RFC 821 messages.

MIME is a *draft-standard protocol* with a status of *elective*. It is described in five parts:

- Protocols for including objects other than US ASCII text mail messages within the bodies of messages conforming to RFC 822. These are described in RFC 2045.

- General structure of the MIME media typing system and defines an initial set of media types. This is described in RFC 2046.

- A protocol for encoding non-US ASCII text in the header fields of mail messages conforming to RFC 822. This is described in RFC 2047.

- Various IANA registration procedures for MIME-related facilities. This is described in RFC 2048.

- MIME conformance criteria. This is described in RFC 2049.

Although RFC 2045 provides a mechanism suitable for describing non-textual data from X.400 messages in a form that is compatible with RFC 822, it does not say how X.400 message parts are to be mapped to MIME message parts. The conversion between X.400 and MIME is defined in RFCs 1494, 2156 and 1496 which update the protocols for the conversion between RFC 822 and X.400.

The MIME standard was designed with the following general order of priorities:

1. Compatibility with existing standards such as RFC 822.

There are two areas where compatibility with previous standards is not complete.

- RFC 1049 (which is part of STD 11) described a Content-Type: field used to indicate the type of (ASCII text) data in a message body. PostScript or SGML would allow a user mail agent to process it accordingly. MIME retains this field, but changes the values that are defined for it. Since the correct response for a mail agent on encountering an unknown value in this field is basically to ignore it, this does not raise any major compatibility concerns.

- RFC 934 discussed encapsulation of messages in the context of message forwarding and defined encapsulation boundaries: lines indicating the beginning and end of an encapsulated message. MIME retains broad compatibility with RFC 934, but does not include the quoting mechanism used by RFC 934 for lines in encapsulated messages that could otherwise be misinterpreted as boundaries.[9]

The most important compatibility issue is that the standard form of a MIME message is readable with an RFC 821-compliant mail reader. This is, of course, the case. In particular the default encoding for MIME message bodies is no encoding at all, just like RFC 822.

2. Robustness across existing practice. As noted above, there are many widely deployed MTAs in the Internet that do not comply with STD 10/RFC 821. The encoding mechanisms specified in RFC 2045 are designed to always circumvent the most common of these (folding of lines as short as 76 characters and corruption of trailing white space characters) by only transmitting short lines with no trailing white space characters, and allowing encoding of any data in a mail safe fashion.

Note: MIME does *not* require mail items to be encoded; the decision is left to the user and/or the mail program. For binary data transmitted across (7-bit) SMTP, encoding is invariably required, but for data consisting mostly of text, this may not be the case.

The preferred encoding mechanism for mostly text data is such that, at a minimum, it is mail-safe with any compliant SMTP agent on an ASCII system and at maximum is mail-safe with all known gateways and MTAs. The reason why MIME does not require maximum encoding is that the

---

[9] The reason for this departure is that MIME allows for deeply nested encapsulation, but encodes text in such a way as to reversibly spill text lines at or before column 76 to avoid the lines being spilled irreversibly by non-conforming SMTP agents. The RFC 934 quoting mechanism can result in lines being lengthened with each level of encapsulation, possibly past column 76.

encoding hampers readability when the mail is transmitted to non-MIME compliant systems.

3. Ease of extension. RFC 2045 categorizes elements of mail bodies into seven *content-types*, which have *subtypes*. The content-type/subtype pairs in turn have parameters that further describe the object concerned. The RFC defines a mechanism for registering new values for these and other MIME fields with the Internet Assigned Numbers Authority (IANA). This process is itself updated by RFC 2048.

   For the current list of all MIME values, consult *STD 2 — Assigned Internet Numbers*. The remainder of this chapter describes only the values and types given in RFC 2045.

One consequence of this approach is that, to quote RFC 2045, "some of the mechanisms [used in MIME] may seem somewhat strange or even baroque at first. In particular, compatibility was always favored over elegance."

Because RFC 822 defines the syntax of message headers (and deliberately allows for additions to the set of headers it describes) but not the composition of message bodies, the MIME standard is largely compatible with RFC 822, particularly the RFC 2045 part that defines the structure of message bodies and a set of header fields that are used to describe that structure.

MIME can be seen as a high-level protocol; since it works entirely within the boundaries of STD 10 and STD 11, it does not involve the transport layer (or lower layers) of the protocol stack at all.

4.8.1 How MIME Works

A MIME-compliant message must contain a header field with the following verbatim text:

MIME-Version: 1.0

As is the case with RFC 822 headers, the case of MIME header field names are never significant but the case of field values may be, depending on the field name and the context. For the MIME fields described below, the values are case-insensitive unless stated otherwise.

The general syntax for MIME header fields is the same as that for RFC 822, so the following field is valid since parenthetical phrases are treated as comments and ignored.

MIME-Version: 1.0 (this is a comment)

The following five header fields are defined for MIME:

MIME-Version
> As noted above, this must have the value 1.0.

Content-Type
> This describes how the object within the body is to be interpreted. The default value is text/plain; charset=us-ascii, which indicates unformatted 7-bit ASCII text data (which is a message body by the RFC 822 definition).

Content-Transfer-Encoding
> This describes how the object within the body was encoded so that it could be included in the message in a mail-safe form.

Content-Description
> A plain text description of the object within the body, which is useful when the object is not readable (for example, audio data).

Content-ID
> A world-unique value specifying the content of this part of this message.

The first two of these fields are described in more detail in the following sections.

4.8.2 The Content-Type Field

The body of the message is described with a *Content-Type* field of the form:

```
Content-Type: type/subtype ;parameter=value ;parameter=value
```

The allowable parameters are dependent on the type and subtype. Some type/subtype pairs have no parameters, some have optional ones, some have mandatory ones and some have both. The subtype parameter *cannot* be omitted, but the whole field can, in which case the default value is text/plain.

There are seven standard content-types:

text
> A single subtype is defined:

> *plain*   Unformatted text. The character set of the text may be specified with the charset parameter. The following values are permitted:

>> *us-ascii* The text consists of ASCII characters in the range 0 to 127 (decimal). This is the default (for compatibility with RFC 822).

>> *iso-8859-x* where x is in the range 1 to 9 for the different parts of the ISO-8859 standard. The text consists of ISO characters in the range 0 to 255 (decimal). All of the ISO-8859 character sets are

ASCII-based with national language characters and so on in the range 128 to 255. Note that, if the text contains no characters with values above 127, the character set should be specified as us-ascii because it can be adequately represented in that character set.

Further subtypes may be added to describe other readable text formats (such as word processor formats) which contain formatting information for an application to enhance the appearance of the text, provided that the correct software is not required to determine the meaning of the text.

multipart

The message body contains multiple objects of independent data types. In each case, the body is divided into parts by lines called encapsulation boundaries. The contents of the boundary are defined with a parameter in the content-type field, for example:

```
Content-Type: multipart/mixed; boundary="1995021309105517"
```

The boundary should not appear in any of the parts of the message. It is case-sensitive and consists of 1-70 characters from a set of 75 which are known to be very robust through mail gateways, and it may not end in a space. (The example uses a 16-digit decimal timestamp.) Each encapsulation boundary consists of the boundary value prefixed by a <CRLF> sequence and two hyphens (for compatibility with RFC 934). The final boundary that marks the end of the last part also has a suffix of two hyphens. Within each part there is a MIME header, which like ordinary mail headers is terminated by the sequence <CRLF><CRLF> but may be blank. The header fields define the content of the encapsulated message.

Four subtypes are defined:

mixed The different parts are independent but are to be transmitted together. They should be presented to the recipient in the order that they appear in the mail message.

parallel This differs from the mixed subtype only in that no order is ascribed to the parts and the receiving mail program can, for example, display all of them in parallel.

alternative The different parts are alternative versions of the same information. They are ordered in increasing faithfulness to the original, and the recipient's mail system should display the best version to the user.

digest   This is a variant on multipart/mixed where the default type/subtype is message/rfc822 (see below) instead of text/plain. It is used for the common case where multiple RFC 822 or MIME messages are transmitted together.

An example of a complex multipart message is shown in Figure 130.

```
MIME-Version: 1.0
From: Steve Hayes <steve@hayessj.bedfont.uk.ibm.com>
To:   Matthias Enders <enders@itso180.itso.ral.ibm.com>
Subject: Multipart message
Content-type: multipart/mixed; boundary="1995021309105517"

This section is called the preamble.  It is after the header but before the
first boundary.  Mail readers which understand multipart messages must
ignore this.
--1995021309105517

The first part.  There is no header, so this is text/plain with
charset=us-ascii by default.  The immediately preceding <CRLF> is part of
the <CRLF><CRLF> sequence that ends the null header.  The one at the end is
part of the next boundary, so this part consists of five lines of text with
four <CRLF>s.
--1995021309105517
Content-type: text/plain; charset=us-ascii
Comments: this header explicitly states the defaults

One line of text this time, but it ends in a line break.

--1995021309105517
Content-Type: multipart/alternative; boundary=_
Comments:     An encapsulated multipart message!

Again, this preamble is ignored.  The multipart body contains a still image
and a video image encoded in Base64.  See4.8.3.5, "Base64 Encoding" on page 264
One feature is that the character "_" which is allowed in multipart
boundaries never occurs in Base64 encoding so we can use a very simple
boundary!
--_
Content-type: text/plain
```

Figure 130 (Part 1 of 2). MIME - A Complex Multipart Example

This message contains images which cannot be displayed at your terminal.
This is a shame because they're very nice.

```
--_
Content-type: image/jpeg
Content-transfer-encoding: base64
Comments: This photograph is to be shown if the user's system cannot display
          MPEG videos.  Only part of the data is shown in this book because
          the reader is unlikely to be wearing MIME-compliant spectacles.
```

```
Qk1OAAAAAAAAAE4EAABAAAAAAQAEAAPAAAAABAAgAAAAAAAAAAAAAAAAAAAAAAABAAAAAQAAAAA
AAAAAAAAAAAAAAAAAAAAAAB4VjQSAAAAAAAAgAAAkgAAAJKAAKoAAACqAIAAqpIAAMHBwQDJyckA
/9uqAKpJAAD/SQAAAG0AAFVtAACqbQAA/20AAAAkAABVkgAAqiQAAP+SAAAAtgAAVbYAAKq2AAD/
<base64 data continues for another 1365 lines>
```

```
--_
Content-type: video/mpeg
Content-transfer-encoding: base64
```

```
AAABswoAeBn//+CEAAABsgAAAOgAAAG4AAAAAAAAAQAAT/////wAAAGy//8AAAEBQ/Zl IwwBGWCX
+pqMiJQDjAKywS/1NRrtXcTCLgzVQymqqHAf0sL1sMgMq4SWLCwOTYRdgyAyrhNYsLhhF3DLjAGg
BdwDXBv3yMV8/4tzrp3zsAWIGAJg1IBKTeFFI2IsgutIdfuSaAGCTsBVnWdz8afdMMAMgKgMEkPE
<base64 data continues for another 1839 lines>
```

```
-- --
That was the end of the nested multipart message.  This is the epilogue.
Like the preamble it is ignored.
--1995021309105517--
And that was the end of the main multipart message.  That's all folks!
```

Figure 130 (Part 2 of 2). *MIME - A Complex Multipart Example*

message

The body is an encapsulated message, or part of one. Three subtypes are defined:

rfc822   The body itself is an encapsulated message with the syntax of an RFC 822 message. It is required that at least one of From:, Subject: or Date: must be present.

    Note: rfc822 refers to the syntax of the encapsulated message envelopes and does not preclude MIME messages for example.

partial   This type is used to allow fragmentation of large mail items in a similar way to IP fragmentation. Because SMTP agents may impose upper limits on maximum mail sizes, it may be necessary to send large items as fragments. The intent of the message/partial mail items is that the fragmentation is transparent to the recipient. The receiving user agent should re-assemble the fragments to create a new message with identical semantics to the original. There are three parameters for the Content-Type: field:

id= A unique identifier common to all parts of the message.

number= The sequence number of this part, with the first part being numbered 1.

total= The total number of parts. This is optional on all but the last part. The last part is identified by the fact that it has the same value for the number and total parameters.

The original message is always a message according to RFC 822 rules. The first part is syntactically equivalent to a message/rfc822 message (that is the body itself contains message headers), and the subsequent parts are syntactically equivalent to text/plain messages. When re-building the message, the RFC 822 header fields are taken from the top-level message, not from the enclosed message, with the exception of those fields that cannot be copied from the inner message to the outer when fragmentation is performed (for example, the Content-Type: field).

Note: It is explicitly permitted to fragment a message/partial message further. This allows mail gateways to freely fragment messages in order to ensure that all parts are small enough to be transmitted. If this were not the case, the mail agent performing the fragmentation would have to know the smallest maximum size limit that the mail items would encounter en route to the destination.

external-body This type contains a pointer to an object that exists elsewhere. It has the syntax of the message/rfc822 type. The top-level message header defines how the external object is to be accessed, using the access-type: parameter of the Content-Type: field and a set of additional parameters that are specific to the access type. The intent is for the mail reader to be able to synchronously access the external object using the specified access type. The following access types are defined:

ftp File Transfer Protocol. The recipient will be expected to supply the necessary user ID and password. For security reasons, these are never transmitted with the message.

tftp Trivial File Transfer Protocol.

anon-ftp Anonymous FTP.

local-file The data is contained in a file accessible directly via the recipient's local file system.

mail-server The data is accessible via a mail server. Unlike the others, this access is necessarily asynchronous.

When the external object has been received, the desired message is obtained by appending the object to the message header encapsulated within the body of the message/external-body message. This encapsulated message header defines how the resulting message is to be interpreted. (It is required to have a Content-ID: and will normally have a Content-Type: field.) The encapsulated message body is not used (the real message body is elsewhere, after all) and it is therefore termed the phantom body. There is one exception to this: if the access-type is mail-server the phantom body contains the mail server commands necessary to extract the real message body. This is because mail server syntaxes vary widely so it is much simpler to use the otherwise redundant phantom body than to codify a syntax for encoding arbitrary mail server commands as parameters on the Content-Type: field.

image

The body contains image data requiring a graphical display or some other device such as a printer to display it. Two subtypes are defined initially:

jpeg The image is in JPEG format, JFIF encoding.

gif GIF format.

video

The body contains moving image data (possibly with synchronized audio) requiring an intelligent terminal or multimedia workstation to display it. A single subtype is defined initially:

mpeg MPEG format.

audio

The body contains image data requiring a speaker and sound card (or similar hardware) to display it. A single subtype is defined initially:

basic   A lowest common denominator format in the absence of any de facto standards for audio encoding. Specifically, it is single-channel 8-bit ISDN mu-law encoding at a sample rate of 8kHz.

application

This type is intended for types that do not fit into other categories, and particularly for data to be processed by an application program before being presented to the user, such as spreadsheet data. It is also intended for application programs that are intended to be processed as part of the mail reading process (for example, see the PostScript type below). This type of usage poses serious security risks unless an implementation ensures executable mail messages are run in a safe or *padded cell* environment.

Two subtypes are defined initially:

PostScript   Adobe Systems PostScript (Level 1 or Level 2).

> **Security Issues:** Although PostScript is often thought of as a format for printer data, it is a programming language and the use of a PostScript interpreter to process application/PostScript types poses serious security problems. Any mail reader that automatically interprets PostScript programs is equivalent, in principle, to one that automatically runs executable programs it receives. RFC 2045 outlines the issues involved.

octet-stream This subtype indicates general binary data consisting of 8-bit bytes. It is also the subtype that a mail reader should assume on encountering an unknown type or subtype. Any parameters are permitted, and RFC mentions two: a type= parameter to inform the recipient of the general type of the data and padding= to indicate a bit stream encoded in a byte stream. (The padding value is the number of trailing zero bits added to pad the stream to a byte boundary.)

> Implementations are recommended to offer the user the option of using the data as input to a user program or of storing it in a file. (There is no standard for the default name of such a file, although RFC 2045 does mention a "Content-Disposition:" field to be defined in a later RFC.)

> **Security Issues:** RFC strongly recommends against an implementation executing an application/octet-stream part automatically or using it as input to a program specified in the mail header. To do so would expose the receiving system to serious

security risks and could impact the integrity of any networks that the system is connected to.

Obviously, there are many types of data that do not fit into any of the subtypes above. Co-operating mail programs may, in keeping with the rules of RFC 822, use types and/or subtypes beginning with X- as private values. No other values are permitted unless they have first been registered with the Internet Assigned Numbers Authority (IANA). See RFC 2048 for more details. The intention is that few, if any, additional types will be needed, but that many subtypes will be added to the set.

4.8.3 The Content-Transfer-Encoding Field

As already noted, SMTP agents and mail gateways can severely constrain the contents of mail messages that can be transmitted safely. The MIME types described above list a rich set of different types of objects which can be included in mail messages and the majority of these do not fall within these constraints. Therefore, it is necessary to encode data of these types in a fashion that can be transmitted, and to decode them on receipt. RFC 2045 defines two forms of encoding that are mail safe. The reason for two forms rather than one is that it is not possible, given the small set of characters known to be mail safe, to devise a form that can both encode text data with minimal impact to the readability of the text and yet can encode binary data that consists of characters distributed randomly across all 256 byte values compactly enough to be practical.

These two encodings are used only for bodies and not for headers. Header encoding is described in 4.8.4, "Using Non-ASCII Characters in Message Headers" on page 266. The Content-Transfer-Encoding: field defines the encoding used. Although cumbersome, this field name emphasizes that the encoding is a feature of the transport process and not an intrinsic property of the object being mailed. Although there are only two encodings defined, this field can take on *five* values. (As usual, the values are case-insensitive.) Three of the values actually specify that no encoding has been done; where they differ is that they imply different reasons why this is the case. This is a subtle but important point. MIME is not restricted to SMTP as a transport agent, despite the prevalence of (broadly) SMTP-compliant mail systems on the Internet. It therefore allows a mail agent to transmit data that is not mail-safe by the standards of SMTP (that is STD 10/RFC 821). If such a mail item reaches a gateway to a more restrictive system, the encoding mechanism specified allows the gateway to decide on an item-by-item basis whether the body must be encoded to be transmitted safely.

The five encodings are:

- 7-bit (the default if the Content-Transfer-Encoding: header is omitted)

- 8-bit

- Binary

- Quoted-Printable

- Base64

These are described in the sections that follow.

4.8.3.1 7-bit Encoding

7-bit encoding means that no encoding has been done and the body consists of lines of ASCII text with a length of no more than 1000 characters. It is therefore known to be mail-safe with any mail system that *strictly* conforms with STD 10/RFC 821. This is the default, since these are the restrictions which apply to pre-MIME STD 11/RFC 822 messages.

Note: 7-bit encoding does *not* guarantee that the contents are truly mail safe for two reasons. First, gateways to EBCDIC networks have a smaller set of mail-safe characters, and secondly because of the many non-conforming SMTP implementations. The Quoted-Printable encoding is designed to overcome these difficulties for text data.

4.8.3.2 8-bit Encoding

8-bit encoding implies that lines are short enough for SMTP transport, but that there may be non-ASCII characters (that is, octets with the high-order bit set). Where SMTP agents support the SMTP Service Extension for 8-bit-MIMEtransport, described in RFC 1652, 8-bit encoding is possible. Otherwise, SMTP implementations should set the high-order bit to zero, so 8-bit encoding is not valid.

4.8.3.3 Binary Encoding

Binary encoding indicates that non-ASCII characters may be present and that the lines may be too long for SMTP transport. (That is, there may be sequences of 999 or more characters without a CRLF sequence.) There are currently no standards for the transport of unencoded binary data by mail based on the TCP/IP protocol stack, so the only case where it is valid to use binary encoding in a MIME message sent on the Internet or other TCP/IP based network is in the header of an external-body part (see the message/external-body type above). Binary encoding would be valid if MIME were used in conjunction with other mail transport mechanisms, or with a hypothetical SMTP Service Extension that did support long lines.

4.8.3.4 Quoted-Printable Encoding

This is the first of the two real encodings and it is intended to leave text files largely readable in their encoded form.

- It represents non-mail safe characters by the hexadecimal representation of their ASCII characters.

- It introduces reversible (soft) line breaks to keep all lines in the message to a length of 76 characters or less.

Quoted-Printable encoding uses the equal sign as a quote character to indicate both of these cases. It has five rules which are summarized as follows:

1. Any character except one that is part of a new line sequence (that is, a X'0D0A' sequence on a text file) can be represented by =XX, where XX are two uppercase hexadecimal digits. If none of the other rules apply, the character must be represented like this.

2. Any character in the range X'21' to X'7E' except X'3D' ("=") can be represented as the ASCII character.

3. ASCII TAB (X'09') and SPACE (X'20') can be represented as the ASCII character except when it is the last character on the line.

4. A line break must be represented by a <CRLF> sequence (X'0D0A'). When encoding binary data, X'0D0A' is not a line break and should be coded, according to rule 1, as =0D=0A.

5. Encoded lines cannot be longer than 76 characters (excluding the <CRLF>). If a line is longer than this, a soft line break must be inserted at or before column 75. A soft line break is the sequence =<CRLF> (X'3D0D0A').

This scheme is a compromise between readability, efficiency and robustness. Since rules 1 and 2 use the phrase "may be encoded," implementations have a fair degree of latitude on how many characters are quoted. If as few characters are quoted as possible within the scope of the rules, then the encoding will work with well-behaved ASCII SMTP agents. Adding the following set of ASCII characters to the list of those to be quoted is adequate for well-behaved EBCDIC gateways:

! " # $ @ [\ ] ^ ` { ¦ } ~

For total robustness, it is better to quote *every* character except for the 73-character set known to be invariant across all gateways, that is the letters and digits (A-Z, a-z and 0-9) and the following 11 characters:

' ( ) + , - . / : = ?

Note: This invariant list does not even include the SPACE character. For practical purposes, when encoding text files, only a SPACE at the end of a line should be quoted. Otherwise readability is severely impacted.

4.8.3.5 Base64 Encoding

This encoding is intended for data that does not consist mainly of text characters. Quoted-Printable replaces each non-text character with a 3-byte sequence which is grossly inefficient for binary data. Base64 encoding works by treating the input stream as a bit stream, regrouping the bits into shorter bytes, padding these short bytes to 8 bits and then translating these bytes to characters that are known to be mail-safe. As noted in the previous section, there are only 73 safe characters, so the maximum byte length usable is 6 bits which can be represented by 64 unique characters (hence the name Base64). Since the input and output are both byte streams, the encoding has to be done in groups of 24 bits (that is 3 input bytes and 4 output bytes). The process can be seen as follows:

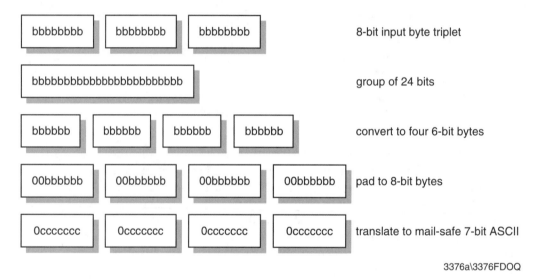

bbbbbbbb bbbbbbbb bbbbbbbb		8-bit input byte triplet
bbbbbbbbbbbbbbbbbbbbbbbb		group of 24 bits
bbbbbb bbbbbb bbbbbb bbbbbb		convert to four 6-bit bytes
00bbbbbb 00bbbbbb 00bbbbbb 00bbbbbb		pad to 8-bit bytes
0ccccccc 0ccccccc 0ccccccc 0ccccccc		translate to mail-safe 7-bit ASCII

3376a\3376FDOQ

Figure 131. MIME - Base64 Encoding. How 3 input bytes are converted to 4 output bytes in the Base64 encoding scheme.

The translate table used is called the *Base64 Alphabet*.

Base64 value	ASCII char.	Base64 value	ASCII char.	Base64 value	ASCII char.	Base64 value	ASCII char.
0	A	16	Q	32	g	48	w
1	B	17	R	33	h	49	x
2	C	18	S	34	i	50	y
3	D	19	T	35	j	51	z
4	E	20	U	36	k	52	0
5	F	21	V	37	l	53	1
6	G	22	W	38	m	54	2
7	H	23	X	39	n	55	3
8	I	24	Y	40	o	56	4
9	J	25	Z	41	p	57	5
10	K	26	a	42	q	58	6
11	L	27	b	43	r	59	7
12	M	28	c	44	s	60	8
13	N	29	d	45	t	61	9
14	O	30	e	46	u	62	+
15	P	31	f	47	v	63	/

Figure 132. MIME - The Base64 Alphabet

One additional character (the = character) is needed for padding. Because the input is a byte stream that is encoded in 24-bit groups it will be short by zero, 8 or 16 bits, as will the output. If the output is of the correct length, no padding is needed. If the output is 8 bits short, this corresponds to an output quartet of two complete bytes, a short byte and a missing byte. The short byte is padded with two low-order zero bits. The missing byte is replaced with an = character. If the output is 16 bits short, this corresponds to an output quartet of one complete byte, a short byte and two missing bytes. The short byte is padded with 6 low-order zero bits. The two missing bytes are replaced with an = character. If zero characters (that is As) were used, the receiving agent would not be able to tell when decoding the input stream if trailing X'00' characters in the last or last two positions of the output stream were data or padding. With pad characters, the number of "="s (0, 1 or 2) gives the length of the input stream modulo 3 (0, 2 or 1 respectively).

4.8.3.6 Conversion between Encodings

The Base64 encoding can be freely translated to and from the binary encoding without ambiguity since both treat the data as an octet-stream. This is also true for the conversion from Quoted-Printable to either of the other two (in the case of the Quoted-Printable to Binary conversion the process can be viewed as involving an intermediate binary encoding) by converting the quoted character sequences to their 8-bit form, deleting the soft line breaks and replacing hard line breaks with <CRLF> sequences. This is not strictly true of the reverse process since Quoted-Printable is actually a record-based system. There is a semantic difference between a hard line break and an imbedded =0D=0A sequence. (For example when decoding Quoted-Printable on a EBCDIC record-based system such as VM, hard line breaks map to record boundaries but =0D=0A sequences map to X'0D25' sequences.)

4.8.3.7 Multiple Encodings

MIME does *not* allow nested encodings. Any Content-Type that recursively includes other Content-Type fields (notably the multipart and message types) cannot use a Content-Transfer-Encoding other than 7-bit, 8-bit or binary. All encodings must be done at the innermost level. The purpose of this restriction is to simplify the operation of user mail agents. If nested encodings are not permitted, the structure of the entire message is always visible to the mail agent without the need to decode the outer layer(s) of the message.

This simplification for user mail agents has a price: complexity for gateways. Because a user agent can specify an encoding of 8-bit or binary, a gateway to a network where these encodings are not safe must encode the message before passing it to the second network. The obvious solution, to simply encode the message body and to change the Content-Transfer-Encoding: field, is not allowed for the multipart or message types since it would violate the restriction described above. The gateway must therefore correctly parse the message into its components and re-encode the innermost parts as necessary.

There is one further restriction: messages of type message/partial must *always* have 7-bit encoding. (8-bit and binary are also disallowed.) The reason for this is that if a gateway needs to re-encode a message, it requires the entire message to do so, but the parts of the message may not all be available together. (Parts may be transmitted serially because the gateway is incapable of storing the entire message at once or they may even be routed independently via different gateways.) Therefore message/partial body parts must be mail safe across lowest common denominator networks; that is, they must be 7-bit encoded.

4.8.4 Using Non-ASCII Characters in Message Headers

All of the mechanisms above refer exclusively to bodies and not to headers. The contents of message headers must still be coded in US-ASCII. For header fields that include human-readable text, this is not adequate for languages other than English. A mechanism to include national language characters is defined by the second part of MIME (RFC 2047). This mechanism differs from the Quoted-Printable encoding, which would be used in a message body for the following reasons:

- The format of message headers is strictly codified by RFC 822, so the encoding used by MIME for header fields must work within a narrower set of constraints than that used for bodies.

- Message relaying programs frequently change message headers, for example re-ordering header fields, deleting some fields but not others, re-ordering mailboxes within lists or spilling fields at different positions than the original message.

- Some message handling programs do not correctly handle some of the more arcane features of RFC 822 (such as the use of the \ character to quote special characters such as < and >).

The approach used by MIME is to reserve improbable sequences of legal ASCII characters that are not syntactically important in RFC 822 for use with this protocol. Words in header fields that need national characters are replaced by *encoded words* which have the form:

`=?charset?encoding?word?=`

where:

charset   The value allowed for the charset parameter used with text/plain MIME type, that is: "us-ascii" or "iso-8859-1" through "iso-8859-9."

encoding   B or Q. B is identical to the Base64 encoding used in message bodies. Q is similar to the Quoted-Printable encoding but uses _ to represent X'20' (ASCII SPACE).[10] Q encoding requires the encoding of _ characters and does not allow line breaks. Any printable ASCII character other than _, = and SPACE may be left unquoted within an encoded word unless it would be syntactically meaningful when the header field is parsed according to RFC 822.

           charset and encoding are both case-insensitive.

word   A string of ASCII text characters other than SPACE, which conforms to the rules of the encoding given.

An encoded word must have no imbedded white space characters (SPACE or TAB), can be up to 75 characters long, and cannot be on a line that is greater than 76 characters long (excluding the <CRLF>). These rules ensure that gateways will not fold encoded words in the middle of the word. Encoded words can generally be used

---

[10] The underscore character is not strictly mail-safe, but it is used because the use of any other character to indicate a SPACE would seriously hamper readability.

in the human-readable parts of header fields. For example, if a mailbox is specified in the following form:

```
The Octopus <octopus@garden.under.the.sea>
```

an encoded word could be used in the The Octopus section but not in the address part between the < and the>). RFC 2047 specifies precisely where encoded words can be used with reference to the syntax of RFC 822.

4.8.5 References

A detailed description of MIME can be found in the following RFCs:

- *RFC 2045 – MIME (Multipurpose Internet Mail Extensions) Part One: Format of Internet Message Bodies*
- *RFC 2046 – MIME (Multipurpose Internet Mail Extensions) Part Two: Media Types*
- *RFC 2047 – MIME (Multipurpose Internet Mail Extensions) Part Three: Message Header Extensions for Non-ASCII Text*
- *RFC 2048 – MIME (Multipurpose Internet Mail Extensions) Part Four: Registration Procedures*
- *RFC 2049 – MIME (Multipurpose Internet Mail Extensions) Part Five: Conformance Criteria and Examples*
- *RFC 2156 — MIXER (MIME Internet X.400 Enhanced Relay): Mapping between X.400 and RFC 822/MIME*

4.9 Post Office Protocol (POP)

The Post Office Protocol, Version 3 is a *standard protocol* with STD number 53. Its status is *elective*. It is described in RFC 1939. The older Post Office Protocol Version 2 is an *historic protocol* with a status of *not recommended*.

The Post Office Protocol is an electronic mail protocol with both client (sender/receiver) and server (storage) functions. POP3 supports basic functions (download and delete) for electronic mail retrieval. More advanced functions are supported by IMAP4 (see 4.10, "Internet Message Access Protocol Version 4 (IMAP4)" on page 270).

POP3 clients establish a TCP connection to the server using port 110. When the connection is established, the POP3 server sends a greeting message to the client. The session then enters the *authentication state*. The client must send its identification to the server while the session is in this state. If the server verifies the ID successfully, the session enters the *transaction state*. In this state, the client can access the mailbox.

When the client sends the QUIT command, the session enters the *Update state* and the connection is then closed.

4.9.1 POP3 Commands and Responses

POP3 commands consist of a keyword and possibly one or more arguments following the keyword. Keywords are three or four characters long and separated by one space character from arguments. Each argument must be up to 40 characters long.

The server sends a response to the command that was issued by the client. This response must be up to 512 characters and begin with a status indicator which shows whether the reply is positive or negative. These indicators are (+OK) or (-ERR). The server must send these indicators in upper case.

Here are the three states for a POP3 session:

Authorization state

In this state, the client sends identification to the server. This is implemented in two ways. More information on authentication is described in RFC 1734.

1. Using USER and PASS commands.

2. Using APOP command.

Transaction state

In this state, the client can issue commands for listing, retrieving and deleting. Please note that the deleting action is not taken in this state. The client must send the QUIT command and then the server goes to the update state.

Update state

In this state, the server updates the mailbox according to the commands received from the client in the transaction state and the TCP connection ends. If the connection is broken for any reason before quit command is received from the client, the server does not enter the update state. Thus, the server will not update anything.

Important POP3 Commands

USER name   User name for authentication.

PASS password   Password for authentication.

STAT   To get the number of messages and total size of the messages.

LIST [msg]   If a message number is specified, the size of this mail is listed (if it exists). If not, all messages will be listed with the message sizes.

RETR msg   This command sends the whole message to the client.

DELE msg   This command deletes the specified message.

NOOP   The server does not do anything, just sends a positive response.

RSET   This command cancels previous delete requests if they exist.

QUIT   If entered in the authorization state, it merely ends the TCP connection. If entered in the transaction state, it first updates the mailbox (deletes any messages requested previously) and then ends the TCP connection.

4.9.2 References

A detailed description of the Post Office Protocol can be found in the following RFCs:

- *RFC 937 — Post Office Protocol – Version 2*
- *RFC 1939 — Post Office Protocol – Version 3*

4.10 Internet Message Access Protocol Version 4 (IMAP4)

The Internet Message Access Protocol, Version 4 is a *proposed standard protocol*. Its status is *elective*. It is described in RFC 2060.

IMAP4 is an electronic messaging protocol with both client and server functions. Similar to POP, IMAP4 servers store messages for multiple users to be retrieved upon client requests, but IMAP4 clients have more capabilities in doing so than POP clients. IMAP4 allows clients to have multiple remote mailboxes to retrieve messages from and to choose any of those at any time. IMAP4 clients can specify criteria for downloading messages, such as not to transfer large messages over slow links. Also, IMAP4 always keeps messages on the server and replicates copies to the clients. Transactions performed by disconnected clients are effected on server mailboxes by periodic re-synchronization of client and server. Let us discuss the underlying electronic mail models of IMAP4 first, to understand the IMAP4 functions clearly. These are described in detail in RFC 1733 *Distributed Electronic Mail Models In IMAP4*.

4.10.1 IMAP4 Underlying Electronic Mail Models

IMAP4 supports all three major electronic mail models. These models are offline, online and disconnected use models.

In the offline model, a client periodically connects to the server and downloads the mail messages. Mail messages are deleted on the server. Therefore, mail is processed locally on the client. An example of a mail protocol that uses this model is POP3. Please see 4.9, "Post Office Protocol (POP)" on page 268 for further information.

In the online model, clients make changes on the server. In other words, mail is processed remotely on the server. An example of a mail protocol that uses this model is NFS. Please see 4.13, "Network File System (NFS)" on page 297 for further information.

The disconnected use model is composite of offline and online models. In this model, a client downloads the data and makes changes on it locally, then at a later time uploads it to server. An example of a mail program which that this model is Lotus Notes Mail.

These three models have some advantages and disadvantages. Since IMAP4 supports all these models, the client is able to switch to another model. As an example, if the connection is too slow and there is a large message in the mailbox. An IMAP4 client can retrieve a small part of the message, change that part and then reconnect to the server and upload that part again.

4.10.2 IMAP4 Commands and Responses

Similar to the POP3 (see, 4.9, "Post Office Protocol (POP)" on page 268), IMAP4 clients establish a TCP connection to the server using port 143. When the connection is established, the server sends a greeting message. After that, the client and the server exchange data interactively. Whenever the client sends a command, the server sends a completion result response to this command. The server can also send data for any other reason. All commands and responses are in the form of lines ending with CRLF.

All client commands begin with a different identifier which is called a *tag*. The server may not respond to the commands in order in which they were received. Let us say a command that has the tag ABC005 is sent and then another command which has tag ABC006 is sent. If it takes less time to process the second command, the server responds to the ABC006 command first with a line beginning with the relevant tag (In this case, ABC006). As this example shows, a unique tag must be used for every command sent. In two cases, the client command is not sent completely. In these cases, the client sends the second part of the command without any tag and the server responds to this command with a line beginning with (+). The client must finish sending the whole command before sending another command.

All data responses and status responses begin with (*), which are called untagged responses. These responses may not be requested by the client. The server can send data without any request. As an example, if a new mail message arrives during the session, the server sends the relevant flag to notify the client. The server sends a command completion response to the command that was issued by the client. This response begins with the same tag of the relevant command and a status indicator following by the tag, which shows either the operation result is positive or negative. These indicators are OK, NO or BAD.

4.10.3 Message Numbers

There are two types of method used to identify the messages: the unique identifier and the message sequence number. Here are the some of the attributes. Please refer to RFC 2060 for details.

4.10.3.1 Unique Identifier (UID) Message Attribute

Every message has a 32-bit identifier, which when it is combined with a unique identifier validity value forms a 64-bit value. When a new message is added to the mailbox, a higher UID is assigned to that message than those added previously. Unique identifiers do not have to be contiguous. Unique identifiers also persist in to other sessions. In this way, if the clients disconnect, in the next session the client can use the same values from the previous session.

Each mailbox has a unique identifier validity value. If it is not possible to use the same value for the next session, then a new value must be greater than the value that was used in the previous session. As an example, if a mailbox is deleted in one session and a new one created with the same name in the next session, since the mailbox name is the same, the client may not realize that this is a new mailbox. In this case, the unique identifier validity value should be changed. The unique identifier validity value is sent with the mailbox selection to the client as *UIDVALIDITY*.

4.10.3.2 Message Sequence Number Message Attribute

The message sequence number shows the relative position of the message in the mailbox. It must be in ascending order. The message sequence number is subject to change during the session or in the next session. If a new message is added, the number of total messages (including the new message) is assigned to that message. The total number of the messages and the message sequence number of the newest message must always be kept the same, in order to correctly assign the message sequence number to each new mail message. If a message is removed permanently, then the message sequence numbers must be recalculated accordingly in that session.

4.10.3.3 Flags Message Attribute

Flags are used to show the current status of the message. There are two types of flags: permanent and session-only. Here are the current flags at the time of writing this book. Please refer to RFC 2060 for the latest details.

\seen   Message has been read.

\Answered   Message has been answered.

\Flagged   Message is marked for special attention.

\Deleted   Message is deleted for later permanent removal.

\Draft   Message has been completed.

\Recent   Message has arrived recently and this is the first session after its arrival. This flag cannot be changed by the client.

4.10.4 IMAP4 States

Similar to POP3 (see, 4.9, "Post Office Protocol (POP)" on page 268), the IMAP4 session works in different states. Some commands are valid for certain states and some of the commands are valid for all states. If the client sends a command that is not appropriate for that state, the server responds with an error message. This error message may vary. The server might send either BAD or NO depending on the implementation. Here are the four states for IMAP4.

Non-Authenticated State
> In this state, the client sends identification to the server.

Authenticated State
> In this state, the client must select a mailbox to proceed.

Selected State
> In this state, a mailbox has been selected successfully.

Logout State
> In this state, connection is ended with either the client request or any other reason.

Flow diagram of an IMAP4 session.

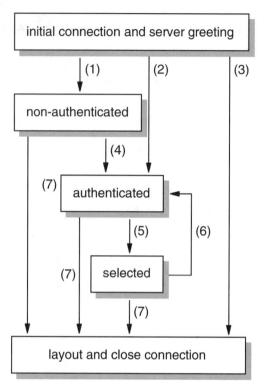

Figure 133. IMAP4 - Flow Diagram

(1)   Connection without pre-authentication (OK greeting)

(2)   Pre-authenticated connection (PREAUTH greeting)

(3)   Rejected connection (BYE greeting)

(4)   Successful LOGIN or AUTHENTICATE command

(5)   Successful SELECT or EXAMINE command

(6)   CLOSE command, or failed SELECT or EXAMINE command

(7)   LOGOUT command, server shutdown, or connection closed

4.10.5 Client Commands

Most of the IMAP4 commands must be used in the corresponding state. Some of them can be used in more than one state. The following list shows the commands and the states in which they are used:

In Any State

The following commands are valid for this state:

CAPABILITY This command sends a request a list of functions that the server supports.

NOOP This command does nothing. It can be used to reset the inactivity autologout timer on the server.

LOGOUT This command sends a request to end the connection.

In Non-Authenticated State

All commands in any state and the following commands are valid for this state:

AUTHENTICATE This command requests a special authentication mechanism with an argument from the server. If the server does not support that mechanism, the server sends an error message.

LOGIN This command sends the username and password in plain text.

In Authenticated State

All commands in Any State and the following commands are valid for this state:

SELECT This command selects a mailbox.

EXAMINE This command also selects a mailbox but access to the mailbox with this command is read-only.

CREATE This command creates a mailbox with a given name. It is not allowed to create INBOX or any other existing mailbox.

DELETE This command permanently removes the mailbox with the given name.

RENAME This command changes the name of the mailbox.

SUBSCRIBE This command adds the specified mailbox to the subscription list which can be obtained by the LSUB command.

UNSUBSCRIBE This command removes the specified mailbox name from the subscription list.

LIST This command requests a subset of names from the complete set of all names available from the server.

LSUB This command requests a subset of names from the subscription list.

STATUS This command requests the status of the given mailbox name. The server checks the flags and send the status according to the status of the flags.

APPEND This command appends a message text to the given mailbox as a new message.

In Selected State

All commands in any state, all commands in authenticated state and the following commands are valid for this state:

CHECK This command requests resolution of the state of the selected mailbox in the memory and the disk.

CLOSE This command permanently removes all messages from the currently selected mailbox that were previously marked as deleted and returns to authenticated state from selected state.

EXPUNGE This command permanently removes all messages from the currently selected mailbox that were previously marked as deleted.

SEARCH This command searches the mailbox for the messages that match given searching criteria.

FETCH This command retrieves data associated with a message in the selected mailbox.

STORE This command updates the message with the data which was retrieved by a FETCH command.

COPY This command copies the specified message to the end of the specified destination mailbox.

UID This command returns unique identifier instead of message sequence numbers. This command is used with other commands.

4.10.6 References

A detailed description of the IMAP protocol can be found in the following RFCs:

- *RFC 1733 — DISTRIBUTED ELECTRONIC MAIL MODELS IN IMAP4*
- *RFC 2060 — INTERNET MESSAGE ACCESS PROTOCOL - VERSION 4rev1*

4.11 Network Management

With the growth in size and complexity of the TCP/IP-based internetworks the need for network management became very important. The current network management framework for TCP/IP-based internetworks consists of:

1. SMI (RFC 1155) - Describes how managed objects contained in the MIB are defined. (It is discussed in 4.11.3, "Structure and Identification of Management Information (SMI)" on page 278.)

2. MIB-II (RFC 1213) - Describes the managed objects contained in the MIB. (It is discussed in 4.11.4, "Management Information Base (MIB)" on page 279.)

3. SNMP (RFC 1157) - Defines the protocol used to manage these objects. (It is discussed in 4.11.5, "Simple Network Management Protocol (SNMP)" on page 284.)

The Internet Architecture Board issued an RFC detailing its recommendation, which adopted two different approaches:

- In the short term SNMP should be used.

  The IAB recommends that all IP and TCP implementations be network manageable. At the current time, this implies implementation of the Internet MIB-II (RFC 1213), and at least the recommended management protocol SNMP (RFC 1157).

  Note that the historic protocols *Simple Gateway Monitoring Protocol* (SGMP , RFC 1028) and MIB-I (RFC-1156) are not recommended for use.

SNMP uses the basic concept of describing and defining management information called *Structure and Identification of Management Information* (SMI) described in RFC 1155 and *Management Information Base* (MIB) described in RFC 1156.

4.11.1 Standards

SNMP is an *Internet standard protocol*. Its status is *recommended*. Its current specification can be found in RFC 1157 *Simple Network Management Protocol (SNMP)*.

MIB-II is an *Internet standard protocol*. Its status is *recommended*. Its current specification can be found in RFC 1213 *Management Information Base for Network Management of TCP/IP-based Internets: MIB-II*.

4.11.2 Bootstrap Protocol (BOOTP)

The BOOTstrap Protocol (BOOTP) enables a client workstation to initialize with a minimal IP stack and request its IP address, a gateway address and the address of a name server from a BOOTP server. Once again, a good example of a client that requires this service is a diskless workstation. If BOOTP is to be used in your network, then you must make certain that both the server and client are on the same physical LAN segment. BOOTP can only be used across bridged segments when source-routing bridges are being used, or across subnets if you have a router capable of BOOTP forwarding, also known as a BOOTP relay agent. This is discussed in detail in 7.1, "Bootstrap Protocol (BOOTP)" on page 511

4.11.3 Structure and Identification of Management Information (SMI)

The SMI defines the rules for how managed objects are described and how management protocols can access these objects. The description of managed objects is made using a subset of the ASN.1 (Abstract Syntax Notation 1, ISO standard 8824), a data description language. The object type definition consists of five fields:

- Object: A textual name, termed the *object descriptor*, for the object type along with its corresponding *object identifier* defined below.

- Syntax: The abstract syntax for the object type. It can be a choice of SimpleSyntax (Integer, Octet String, Object Identifier, Null) or an ApplicationSyntax (NetworkAddress, Counter, Gauge, TimeTicks, Opaque) or other application-wide types (see RFC 1155 for more details).

- Definition: A textual description of the semantics of the object type.

- Access: One of read-only, read-write, write-only or not-accessible.

- Status: One of mandatory, optional, or obsolete.

As an example, we can have:

```
OBJECT
        sysDescr { system 1 }
Syntax  OCTET STRING
Definition This value should include the full name and version
        identification of the system's hardware type, software
        operating system, and networking software. It is
        mandatory that this contain only printable ASCII
        characters.
Access  read-only.
Status  mandatory.
```

This example shows the definition of an object contained in the Management Information Base (MIB). Its name is sysDescr and it belongs to the system group (see 4.11.4, "Management Information Base (MIB)" on page 279).

A managed object not only has to be described but identified, too. This is done using the ASN.1 Object Identifier in the same way as a telephone number, reserving group of numbers to different locations. In the case of TCP/IP-based network management the number allocated was 1.3.6.1.2 and SMI uses it as the base for defining new objects.

The number 1.3.6.1.2 is obtained by joining groups of numbers with the following meaning:

- The first group defines the node administrator:
  - (1) for ISO
  - (2) for CCITT
  - (3) for the joint ISO-CCITT
- The second group for the ISO node administrator defines (3) for use by other organizations.
- The third group defines (6) for the use of the U.S. Department of Defense (DoD).
- In the fourth group the DoD has not indicated how it will manage its group so the Internet community assumed (1) for its own.
- The fifth group was approved by IAB to be:
  - (1) for the use of OSI directory in the Internet
  - (2) for objects identification for management purposes
  - (3) for objects identification for experimental purposes
  - (4) for objects identification for private use.

In the example the {system 1} beside the object name means that the object identifier is 1.3.6.1.2.1.1.1. It is the first object in the first group (system) in the Management Information Base (MIB).

4.11.4 Management Information Base (MIB)

The MIB defines the objects that may be managed for each layer in the TCP/IP protocol. There are two versions: MIB-I and MIB-II. MIB-I was defined in RFC 1156, and is now classified as a *historic* protocol with a status of *not recommended*.

Table 9 (Page 1 of 2). Management Information Base II (MIB-II). Group definition.

Group	Objects for	#
System	Basic system information	7
Interfaces	Network attachments	23
AT	Address translation	3
IP	Internet protocol	38
ICMP	Internet control message protocol	26
TCP	Transmission control protocol	19
UDP	User datagram protocol	7

Legend:
#=Number of objects in the group

Table 9 (Page 2 of 2). *Management Information Base II (MIB-II). Group definition.*

Group	Objects for	#
EGP	Exterior gateway protocol	18
SNMP	SNMP applications entities	30
Legend: #=Number of objects in the group		

Each managed node supports only those groups that are appropriate. For example, if there is no gateway, the EGP group need not be supported. But if a group is appropriate, all objects in that group must be supported.

The list of managed objects defined has been derived from those elements considered essential. This approach of taking only the essential objects is not restrictive, since the SMI provides extensibility mechanisms such as definition of a new version of the MIB and definition of private or non-standard objects.

Below are some examples of objects in each group. The complete list is defined in RFC 1213. Please also refer to RFC 2011, RFC 2012 and RFC 2013 for updated information of IP, TCP and UDP.

- System Group

    - sysDescr - Full description of the system (version, HW, OS)
    - sysObjectID - Vendor's object identification
    - sysUpTime - Time since last re-initialization
    - sysContact - Name of contact person
    - sysServices - Services offered by device

- Interfaces Group

    - ifIndex - Interface number
    - ifDescr - Interface description
    - ifType - Interface type
    - ifMtu - Size of the largest IP datagram
    - ifAdminisStatus - Status of the interface
    - ifLastChange - Time the interface entered in the current status
    - ifINErrors - Number of inbound packets that contained errors
    - ifOutDiscards - Number of outbound packets discarded

- Address Translation Group

    - atTable - Table of address translation

- atEntry - Each entry containing one network address to physical address equivalence
- atPhysAddress - The media-dependent physical address
- atNetAddress - The network address corresponding to the media-dependent physical address

- **IP Group**

  - ipForwarding - Indication of whether this entity is an IP gateway
  - ipInHdrErrors - Number of input datagrams discarded due to errors in their IP headers
  - ipInAddrErrors - Number of input datagrams discarded due to errors in their IP address
  - ipInUnknownProtos - Number of input datagrams discarded due to unknown or unsupported protocol
  - ipReasmOKs - Number of IP datagrams successfully re-assembled

- **ICMP Group**

  - icmpInMsgs - Number of ICMP messages received
  - icmpInDestUnreachs - Number of ICMP destination-unreachable messages received
  - icmpInTimeExcds - Number of ICMP time-exceeded messages received
  - icmpInSrcQuenchs - Number of ICMP source-quench messages received
  - icmpOutErrors - Number of ICMP messages not sent due to problems within ICMP

- **TCP Group**

  - tcpRtoAlgorithm - Algorithm to determine the timeout for retransmitting unacknowledged octets
  - tcpMaxConn - Limit on the number of TCP connections the entity can support
  - tcpActiveOpens - Number of times TCP connections have made a direct transition to the SYN-SENT state from the CLOSED state
  - tcpInSegs - Number of segments received, including those received in error
  - tcpConnRemAddress - The remote IP address for this TCP connection
  - tcpInErrs - Number of segments discarded due to format error
  - tcpOutRsts - Number of resets generated

- **UDP Group**

  - udpInDatagrams - Number of UDP datagrams delivered to UDP users
  - udpNoPorts - Number of received UDP datagrams for which there was no application at the destination port
  - udpInErrors - Number of received UDP datagrams that could not be delivered for reasons other than the lack of an application at the destination port

- udpOutDatagrams - Number of UDP datagrams sent from this entity
- EGP Group
    - egpInMsgs - Number of EGP messages received without error
    - egpInErrors - Number of EGP messages with errors
    - egpOutMsgs - Number of locally generated EGP messages
    - egpNeighAddr - The IP address of this entry's EGP neighbor
    - egpNeighState - The EGP state of the local system with respect to this entry's EGP neighbor

This is not the complete MIB definition but it is presented as an example of the objects defined in each group. These modules currently support IPv4.

To illustrate this, the Interfaces Group contains two top-level objects: the number of interface attachments on the node (ifNumber) and a table containing information on those interfaces (ifTable). Each entry (ifEntry) in that table contains the objects for a particular interface. Among those, the interface type (ifType) is identified in the MIB tree using the ASN.1 notation by 1.3.6.1.2.1.2.2.1.3. and for a token-ring adapter the value of the corresponding variable would be 9, which means iso88025-tokenRing (see Figure 134 on page 283).

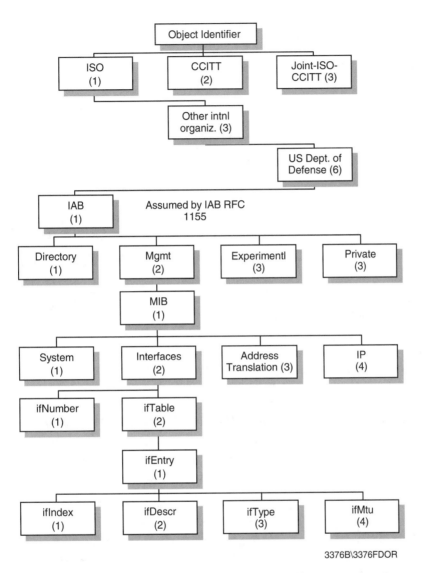

Figure 134. MIB-II - Object Identifier Allocation for TCP/IP-based Network

4.11.4.1 IBM-Specific MIB Part

IBM has added the following objects in the MIB-II database:

```
* IBM SNMP agent DPI UDP port
DPI_port                    1.3.6.1.4.1.2.2.1.1.    number          2

* IBM "ping" round-trip-time table
RTTaddr                     1.3.6.1.4.1.2.2.1.3.1.  internet        60
minRTT                      1.3.6.1.4.1.2.2.1.3.2.  number          60
maxRTT                      1.3.6.1.4.1.2.2.1.3.3.  number          60
aveRTT                      1.3.6.1.4.1.2.2.1.3.4.  number          60
RTTtries                    1.3.6.1.4.1.2.2.1.3.5.  number          60
RTTresponses                1.3.6.1.4.1.2.2.1.3.6.  number          60
```

Where:

- DPI_port returns the port number between the agent and the subagent.

- *RTT* allows an SNMP manager to ping remote hosts. RTT stands for Round Trip Table.

    - RTTaddr: host address
    - minRTT: minimum round trip time
    - maxRTT: maximum round trip time
    - aveRTT: average round trip time
    - RTTtries: number of pings yet to be performed
    - RTTresponses: number of responses received

4.11.5 Simple Network Management Protocol (SNMP)

The SNMP added the improvement of many years of experience in SGMP and allowed it to work with the objects defined in the MIB with the representation defined in the SIM.

RFC 1157 defines the Network Management Station (NMS) as the one that executes network management applications (NMA) that monitor and control network elements (NE) such as hosts, gateways and terminal servers. These network elements use a management agent (MA) to perform the network management functions requested by the network management stations. The Simple Network Management Protocol (SNMP) is used to communicate management information between the network management stations and the agents in the network elements.

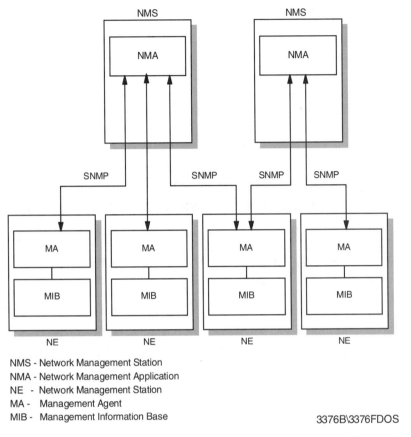

NMS - Network Management Station
NMA - Network Management Application
NE - Network Management Station
MA - Management Agent
MIB - Management Information Base

3376B\3376FDOS

Figure 135. SNMP - Components of the Simple Network Management Protocol

All the management agent functions are only alterations (set) or inspections (get) of variables limiting the number of essential management functions to two and avoiding more complex protocols. In the other direction, from NE to NMS, a limited number of unsolicited messages (traps) are used to indicate asynchronous events. In the same way, trying to preserve the simplicity, the interchange of information requires only an unreliable datagram service and every message is entirely and independently represented by a single transport datagram. This means also that the mechanisms of the SNMP are generally suitable for use with a wide variety of transport services. The RFC 1157 specifies the exchange of messages via the UDP protocol, but a wide variety of transport protocols can be used.

The entities residing at management stations and network elements that communicate with one another using the SNMP are termed SNMP application entities. The peer processes that implement it are the protocol entities. An SNMP agent with some arbitrary set of SNMP application entities is called an SNMP community, where each one is named by a string of octets that need to be unique only to the agent participating in the community.

A message in the SNMP protocol consists of a version identifier, an SNMP community name and a protocol data unit (PDU). It is mandatory that all implementations of the SNMP support the five PDUs:

- GetRequest: Retrieve the values of a specific object from the MIB.

- GetNextRequest: Walk through portions of the MIB.

- SetRequest: Alter the values of a specific object from the MIB.

- GetResponse: Response from a GetRequest, a GetNextRequest and a SetRequest.

- Trap: Capability of the network elements to generate events to network management stations such as agent initialization, agent restart and link failure. There are seven trap types defined in RFC 1157: coldStart, warmStart, linkDown, linkUp, authenticationFailure, egpNeighborLoss and enterpriseSpecific.

The formats of these messages are as follows:

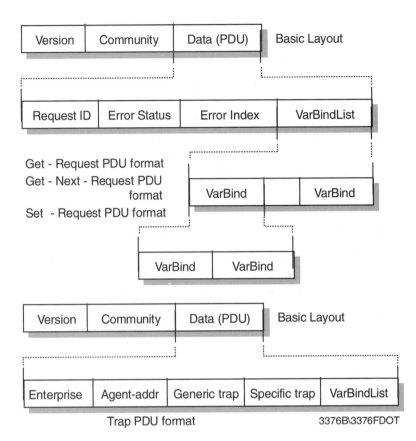

Figure 136. SNMP Message Format - Request, Set and Trap PDU format

4.11.6 Simple Network Management Protocol Version 2 (SNMPv2)

The framework of Version 2 of the Simple Network Management Protocol (SNMPv2) was published in April 1993 and consists of 12 RFCs including the first, RFC 1441, which is an introduction. In August 1993 all 12 RFCs became a proposed standard with the status elective.

This framework consists of the following disciplines:

- Structure of Management Information (SMI)

    Definition of the OSI ASN.1 subset for creating MIB modules. See RFC 1902 for a description.
- Textual conventions

Definition of the initial set of textual conventions available to all MIB modules. See RFC 1903 for a description.

- Protocol operations

  Definition of protocol operations with respect to the sending and receiving of PDUs. See RFC 1905 for a description.

- Transport mappings

  Definition of mapping SNMPv2 onto an initial set of transport domains because it can be used over a variety of protocol suites. The mapping onto UDP is the preferred mapping. The RFC also defines OSI, DDP, IPX etc. See RFC 1906 for a description.

- Protocol instrumentation

  Definition of the MIB for SNMPv2. See RFC 1907 for a description.

- Administrative framework

  Definition of the administrative infrastructure for SNMPv2, the user-based security model for SNMPv2 and the community-based SNMPv2. See RFCs 1909, 1910 and 1901 for descriptions.

- Conformance statements

  Definition of the notation compliance or capability of agents. See RFC 1904 for a description.

The following sections describe the major differences and improvements from SNMPv1 to SNMPv2.

4.11.6.1 SNMPv2 Entity

An SNMPv2 entity is an actual process that performs network management operations by generating and/or responding to SNMPv2 protocol messages by using the SNMPv2 protocol operations. All possible operations of an entity can be restricted to a subset of all possible operations that belong to a particular administratively defined party (please refer to 4.11.6.2, "SNMPv2 Party" on page 289 below). An SNMPv2 entity could be member of multiple SNMPv2 parties. The following local databases are maintained by an SNMPv2 entity:

- One database for all parties known by the SNMPv2 entity which could be:

  - Operation realized locally

  - Operation realized by proxy interactions with remote parties or devices

  - Operation realized by other SNMPv2 entities

- Another database that represents all managed object resources that are known to that SNMPv2 entity.

- And at least a database that represents an access control policy that defines the access privileges accorded to known SNMPv2 parties

An SNMPv2 entity can act as an SNMPv2 agent or manager.

4.11.6.2 SNMPv2 Party

An SNMPv2 party is a conceptual, virtual execution environment whose operation is restricted, for security or other purposes, to an administratively defined subset of all possible operations of a particular SNMPv2 entity (please refer to 4.11.6.1, "SNMPv2 Entity" on page 288 above). Architecturally, each SNMPv2 party comprises:

- A single, unique party identity

- A logical network location at which the party executes, characterized by a transport protocol domain and transport addressing information

- A single authentication protocol and associated parameters by which all protocol messages originated by the party are authenticated as to origin and integrity

- A single privacy protocol and associated parameters by which all protocol messages received by the party are protected from disclosure

4.11.6.3 GetBulkRequest

The GetBulkRequest is defined in RFC 1905 and is thus part of the protocol operations. A GetBulkRequest is generated and transmitted as a request of an SNMPv2 application. The purpose of the GetBulkRequest is to request the transfer of a potentially large amount of data, including, but not limited to, the efficient and rapid retrieval of large tables. The GetBulkRequest is more efficient than the GetNextRequest in case of retrieval of large MIB object tables. The syntax of the GetBulkRequest is:

```
GetBulkRequest [ non-repeaters = N, max-repetitions = M ]
              ( RequestedObjectName1,
                RequestedObjectName2,
                RequestedObjectName3 )
```

Where:

RequestedObjectName1, 2, 3

MIB object identifier such as sysUpTime etc. The objects are in a lexicographically ordered list. Each object identifier has a binding to at least one variable. For example, the object identifier ipNetToMediaPhysAddress has a variable binding for each IP address in the ARP table and the content is the associated MAC address.

N	Specifies the non-repeaters value, which means that you request only the contents of the variable next to the object specified in your request of the first N objects named between the parentheses. This is the same function as provided by the GetNextRequest.

M	Specifies the max-repetitions value, which means that you request from the remaining (number of requested objects - N) objects the contents of the M variables next to your object specified in the request. Similar to an iterated GetNextRequest but transmitted in only one request.

With the GetBulkRequest you can efficiently get the contents of only the next variable or the next M variables in only one request.

Assume the following ARP table in a host that runs an SNMPv2 agent:

```
Interface-Number  Network-Address  Physical-Address  Type

       1             10.0.0.51      00:00:10:01:23:45  static
       1             9.2.3.4        00:00:10:54:32:10  dynamic
       2             10.0.0.15      00:00:10:98:76:54  dynamic
```

An SNMPv2 manager sends the following request to retrieve the sysUpTime and the complete ARP table:

```
GetBulkRequest [ non-repeaters = 1, max-repetitions = 2 ]
               ( sysUpTime,
                 ipNetToMediaPhysAddress,
                 ipNetToMediaType )
```

The SNMPv2 entity acting in an agent role responds with a response PDU:

```
Response (( sysUpTime.0 =  "123456" ),
         ( ipNetToMediaPhysAddress.1.9.2.3.4 =
                              "000010543210" ),
         ( ipNetToMediaType.1.9.2.3.4 =  "dynamic" ),
         ( ipNetToMediaPhysAddress.1.10.0.0.51 =
                              "000010012345" ),
         ( ipNetToMediaType.1.10.0.0.51 =  "static" ))
```

The SNMPv2 entity acting in a manager role continues with:

```
GetBulkRequest [ non-repeaters = 1, max-repetitions = 2 ]
               ( sysUpTime,
                 ipNetToMediaPhysAddress.1.10.0.0.51,
                 ipNetToMediaType.1.10.0.0.51 )
```

The SNMPv2 entity acting in an agent role responds with:

```
Response (( sysUpTime.0 =  "123466" ),
         ( ipNetToMediaPhysAddress.2.10.0.0.15 =
                                "000010987654" ),
         ( ipNetToMediaType.2.10.0.0.15 =
                                        "dynamic" ),
         ( ipNetToMediaNetAddress.1.9.2.3.4 =
                                        "9.2.3.4" ),
         ( ipRoutingDiscards.0 =  "2" ))
```

This response signals the end of the table to the SNMPv2 entity acting in a manager role. With the GetNextRequest you would have needed four requests to retrieve the same information. If you had set the max-repetition value of the GetBulkRequest to three, in this example, you would have needed only one request.

4.11.6.4 InformRequest

An InformRequest is generated and transmitted as a request from an application in an SNMPv2 manager entity that wishes to notify another application, acting also in an SNMPv2 manager entity, of information in the MIB view[11] of a party local to the sending application. The packet is used as an indicative assertion to the manager of another party about information accessible to the originating party (manager-to-manager communication across party boundaries). The first two variables in the variable binding list of an InformRequest are sysUpTime.0 and snmpEventID.i[12] respectively. Other variables may follow.

4.11.7 MIB for SNMPv2

This MIB defines managed objects that describe the behavior of the SNMPv2 entity.

Note: This is not a replacement of the MIB-II.

Following are some object definitions to get an idea of the contents:

```
sysName OBJECT-TYPE
    SYNTAX     DisplayString (SIZE (0..255))
    MAX-ACCESS read-write
    STATUS     current
    DESCRIPTION
            "An administratively-assigned name for this managed node.
```

---

[11] A MIB view is a subset of the set of all instances of all object types defined according to SMI.

[12] snmpEventID.i is an SNMPv2 manager-to-manager MIB object that shows the authoritative identification of an event.

```
                 By convention, this is the node's fully-qualified domain
                 name.  If the name is unknown, the value is the zero-length
                 string."
       ::= { system 5 }

warmStart NOTIFICATION-TYPE
     STATUS  current
     DESCRIPTION
                 "A warmStart trap signifies that the SNMPv2
                 entity, acting in an agent role, is reinitializing
                 itself such that its configuration is unaltered."
       ::= { snmpTraps 2 }
```

4.11.8 Single Authentication and Privacy Protocol

The authentication protocol provides a mechanism by which SNMPv2 management communications, transmitted by a party, can be reliably identified as having originated from that party.

The privacy protocol provides a mechanism by which SNMPv2 management communications transmitted to a party are protected from disclosure.

Principal threats against which the SNMPv2 security protocol provides protection are:

- Modification of information

- Masquerade

- Message stream modification

- Disclosure

The following security services provide protection against the above threats:

- Data integrity

  Provided by the MD5 message digest algorithm. A 128-bit digest is calculated over the designated portion of a SNMPv2 message and included as part of the message sent to the recipient.

- Data origin authentication

  Provided by prefixing each message with a secret value shared by the originator of that message and its intended recipient before digesting.

- Message delay or replay

  Provided by including a time stamp value in each message.

- Data confidentiality

Provided by the symmetric privacy protocol which encrypts an appropriate portion of the message according to a secret key known only to the originator and recipient of the message. This protocol is used in conjunction with the symmetric encryption algorithm, in the cipher block chaining mode, which is part of the Data Encryption Standard (DES). The designated portion of an SNMPv2 message is encrypted and included as part of the message sent to the recipient.

4.11.9 The New Administrative Model

It is the purpose of the Administrative Model for SNMPv2 to define how the administrative framework is applied to realize effective network management in a variety of configurations and environments.

The model entails the use of distinct identities for peers that exchange SNMPv2 messages. Thus, it represents a departure from the community-based administrative model of the original SNMPv1. By unambiguously identifying the source and intended recipient of each SNMPv2 message, this new strategy improves upon the historical community scheme both by supporting a more convenient access control model and allowing for effective use of asymmetric (public key) security protocols in the future. Please refer to Figure 137 for the new message format.

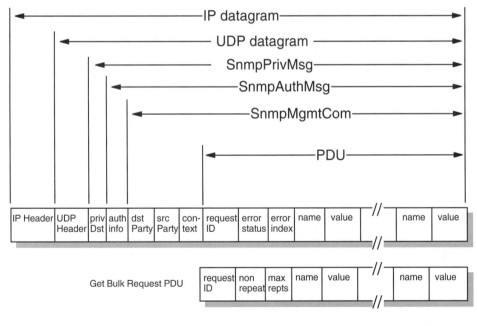

3376B\3376FDOV

Figure 137. SNMP Version 2 Message Format

PDU   Includes one of the following protocol data units:

- GetNextRequest
- GetRequest
- Inform
- Report
- Response
- SNMPv2-Trap
- SetRequest

The GetBulkRequest has a different PDU format as shown above (please also refer to 4.11.6.3, "GetBulkRequest" on page 289).

Note: The SNMP trap now has the same format as all the other requests.

SnmpMgmtCom (SNMP Management Communication)
Adds the source party ID (srcParty), the destination party ID (dstParty) and the context to the PDU. The context specifies the SNMPv2 context containing the management information referenced by the communication.

SnmpAuthMsg
This field is used as authentication information from the authentication protocol used by that party. The SnmpAuthMsg is serialized according to ASN.1 BER[13] and can then be encrypted.

SnmpPrivMsg SNMP Private Message
An SNMPv2 private message is an SNMPv2 authenticated management communication that is (possibly) protected from disclosure. A private destination (privDst) is added to address the destination party.

The message is then encapsulated in a normal UDP/IP datagram and sent to the destination across the network.

For further information please refer to the above mentioned RFCs.

4.11.10 Simple Network Management Protocol Version 3 (SNMPv3)

At the time of writing, the framework of SNMPv3 is not specified entirely. SNMPv3 will probably have the same architecture with some more functions and components. Actually, SNMP applications are specified to support SNMPv3. According to the

---

[13] ASN.1 BER specifies the Basic Encoding Rules according to ISO 8825 which are used in OSI Abstract Syntax Notation one.

current draft documents, SNMPv3 is an extensible SNMP framework that is added to SNMPv2. SNMPv3 is supposed to support the following;

- A new SNMP message format

- Security for messages

- Access control

Since SNMP has a modular structure, the need of changing a module, most of the time does not impact the other modules directly. This allows you to define SNMPv3 over existing model easily. For example, to add a new SNMP message format, it will be enough to upgrade message processing model. Furthermore, since it is needed to support SNMPv1 and SNMPv2 messages as well, it can be achieved to add the new SNMPv3 message module in to message processing subsystem. The following figure illustrates this structure.

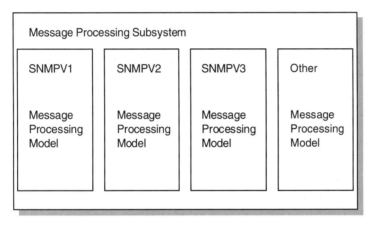

3376B\3376FDOW

Figure 138. SNMP - Message Processing Subsystem

4.11.11 References

The following RFCs define the Simple Network Management Protocol and the information kept in a system:

- *RFC 1052 - IAB Recommendations for the Development of Internet Network Management Standards*
- *RFC 1085 - ISO Presentation Services on Top of TCP/IP-Based Internets*
- *RFC 1155 - Structure and Identification of Management Information for TCP/IP-Based Internets*

- *RFC 1157 - A Simple Network Management Protocol (SNMP)*
- *RFC 1213 - Management Information Base for Network Management of TCP/IP-Based Internets: MIB-II*
- *RFC 1215 - Convention for Defining Traps for Use with the SNMP*
- *RFC 1228 - SNMP-DPI: Simple Network Management Protocol Distributed Programming Interface*
- *RFC 1239 - Reassignment of Experimental MIBs to Standard MIBs*
- *RFC 1351 - SNMP Administrative Model*
- *RFC 1352 - SNMP Security Protocols*
- *RFC 1441 - Introduction to Version 2 of the Internet-Standard Network Management Framework*
- *RFC 1592 - Simple Network Management Protocol Distributed Protocol Interface Version 2.0*
- *RFC 1748 - IEEE 802.5 Token-Ring MIB*
- *RFC 1901 - Introduction to Community-Based SNMPv2*
- *RFC 1902 - Structure of Management Information for Version 2 of the Simple Network Management Protocol (SNMPv2)*
- *RFC 1903 - Textual Conventions for Version 2 of the Simple Network Management Protocol (SNMPv2)*
- *RFC 1904 - Conformance Statements for Version 2 of the Simple Network Management Protocol (SNMPv2)*
- *RFC 1905 - Protocol Operations for Version 2 of the Simple Network Management Protocol (SNMPv2)*
- *RFC 1906 - Transport Mappings for Version 2 of the Simple Network Management Protocol (SNMPv2)*
- *RFC 1907 - Management Information Base for Version 2 of the Simple Network Management Protocol (SNMPv2)*
- *RFC 1909 - An Administrative Infrastructure for SNMPv2*
- *RFC 1910 - User-Based Security Model for SNMPv2*
- *RFC 2011 - SNMPv2 Management Information Base for the Internet Protocol Using SMIv2*
- *RFC 2012 - SNMPv2 Management Information Base for the Transmission Control Protocol Using SMIv2*
- *RFC 2013 - SNMPv2 Management Information Base for the User Datagram Protocol Using SMIv2*
- *RFC 2271 - An Architecture for Describing SNMP Management Frameworks*
- *RFC 2273 - SNMPv3 Applications*

4.12 Remote Printing (LPR and LPD)

The line printer requester (LPR) allows access to printers on other computers running
the line printer daemon (LPD) as though they were on your computer. The clients
provided (LPR, LPQ, LPRM or LPRMON or LPRPORTD) allow the user to send files
or redirect printer output to a remote host running a remote print server (LPD). Some
of these clients can also be used to query the status of a job, as well as to delete a job.
For more information about remote printing, see RFC 1179.

4.13 Network File System (NFS)

The SUN Microsystems Network File System (NFS) protocol enables machines to
share file systems across a network. The NFS protocol is designed to be machine-,
operating system-, and transport protocol-independent. This is achieved through
implementation on top of Remote Procedure Call (see 4.19.2, "Remote Procedure Call
(RPC)" on page 323). RPC establishes machine independence by using the External
Data Representation convention.

SUN-NFS is a *proposed standard protocol*. Its status is *elective*. The current NFS
specification can be found in RFC 1813 *NFS: NFS Version 3 Protocol Specification*.

4.13.1 NFS Concept

NFS allows authorized users to access files located on remote systems as if they were
local. Two protocols serve this purpose:

1. The Mount protocol to specify the remote host and file system to be accessed and
   where to locate them in the local file hierarchy
2. The NFS protocol to do the actual file I/O to the remote file system

Both the Mount and NFS protocols are RPC applications (caller/server concept) and
are transported by both TCP and UDP.

4.13.1.1 Mount Protocol

The Mount protocol is an RPC application shipped with NFS. It is program number
100005. The Mount protocol is transported by both TCP and UDP. Mount is an RPC
server program and provides a total of six procedures:

NULL	Does nothing. Useful for server response testing.
MNT	Mount function Returns a file handle pointing to the directory.
DUMP	Returns the list of all mounted file systems.
UMNT	Removes a mount list entry.
UMNTALL	Removes all mount list entries for this client.

EXPORT Returns information about the available file systems.

The MOUNT call returns a file handle to the directory. The file handle is a variable-length array of 64 bytes maximum, which will be used subsequently by the client to access files. File handles are a fundamental part of NFS because each directory and file will be referenced through a handle. Some implementations will encrypt the handles for security reasons. (For example, NFS on VM can optionally use the VM encryption programs to provide this.)

The user interface to this RPC application is provided through the MOUNT command. The user issues a MOUNT command to locate the remote file system in his or her own file hierarchy.

For example, consider a VM NFS server. The concept of subdirectories (hierarchical file system) does not exist here; there are only minidisks (to be considered as one directory each). Now consider an AIX client. (AIX does have a subdirectory file system.) The client can access the user 191 VM minidisk as its local subdirectory /u/vm/first by issuing the MOUNT command:

```
MOUNT -o options
      host:user.191,ro,pass=password,record=type,names=action
      /u/vm/first
```

Where:

options	System options such as message size.
host	The TCP/IP name of the remote host.
user	VM user ID.
191	Minidisk address.
pass=	Link password that will allow the NFS machine to access the minidisk.
record=	Specifies what translation processing is to be done on the CMS records:

> *binary* No processing performed.
>
> *text* Code conversion between EBCDIC (server) and ASCII (client).
>
> *nl* EBCDIC-to-ASCII translation, and new line characters are interpreted as CMS record boundaries.

names=	Specifies the handling of a file name:

> *fold* File names supplied by the client are translated to uppercase.
>
> *mixed* File names are used as supplied by the client.
>
> If no name translation option is specified, case folding is performed and, in addition, client names that are not valid in CMS will be converted into valid CMS names.

The result is that the VM minidisk is now seen by the client machine as a local subdirectory:

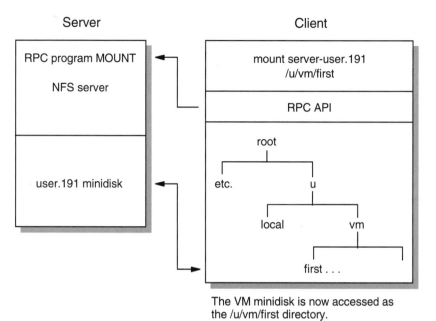

The VM minidisk is now accessed as
the /u/vm/first directory.

3376a\3376FDOK

Figure 139. NFS - Mount Command. The client *mounts* the VM minidisk user.191 as
its local directory */u/vm/first*.

Obviously, the previous command:

```
MOUNT -o options host:user.191,ro,pass=password,record=type,names=action
/u/vm/first
```

has three parts:

1. -o options is the client part. It has to be understood by the NFS client only. This
   means, it depends on the client host and is documented in the client's
   documentation.
2. host:user.191,ro,....,names=action is the server part. The syntax depends on the
   server's file system. (Obviously, user.191 does not mean anything to an MVS
   NFS server.) Refer to the documentation of the NFS server to know what
   parameters it will accept.
3. /u/vm/first is a client part and is called the *mount point*, that is, where the remote
   file system will be hooked on the local file system.

The UMOUNT command removes the remote file system from the local file hierarchy.
Following the example abovem the following command will remove the /u/vm/first
directory:

UMOUNT /u/vm/first

4.13.1.2 NFS Protocol

NFS is the RPC application program providing file I/O functions to a remote host, once it has been requested through a MOUNT command. It has program number 100003 and sometimes uses IP port 2049. As this is not an officially assigned port and several versions of NFS (and mount) already exist, port numbers may change. It is advised to go to Portmap (port number 111) (see "Portmap or Portmapper" on page 327) to obtain the port numbers for both the Mount and NFS protocols. The NFS protocol is transported by both TCP and UDP.

The NFS program supports 22 procedures, providing for all basic I/O operations such as:

ACCESS	Resolves the access rights, according to the set of permissions of the file for that user.
LOOKUP	Searches for a file in the current directory and if found, returns a file handle pointing to it plus information on the file's attributes.
READ and WRITE	Basic read/write primitives to access the file.
RENAME	Renames a file.
REMOVE	Deletes a file.
MKDIR and RMDIR	Creation/deletion of subdirectories.
GET and SET-ATTR	Gets or sets file attributes.

Other functions are also provided.

These correspond to most of the file I/O primitives used in the local operating system to access local files. In fact, once the remote directory is mounted, the local operating system just has to re-route the file I/O primitives to the remote host. This makes all file I/Os look alike, regardless of whether the file is located locally or remotely. The user can operate his or her normal commands and programs on both kinds of files; in other words, this NFS protocol is completely transparent to the user (see Figure 140 on page 301).

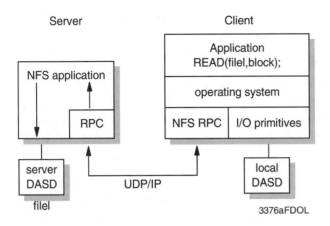

Server   Client

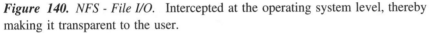

Figure 140. NFS - File I/O. Intercepted at the operating system level, thereby
making it transparent to the user.

4.13.1.3 File Integrity

Since NFS is a stateless protocol, there is a need to protect the file integrity of the
NFS-mounted files. Many implementations have the Lock Manager protocol for this
purpose. Sometimes, multiple processes might open the same file simultaneously. If
the file is opened for merely read access, every process will get the most current data.
If there is more than one processes writing to the file at one time, the changes made
by writers should be coordinated and at the same time the most accurate changes
should be given to the readers. If some part of the file is cached on each client's local
system, it becomes a more complicated job to synchronize the writers and readers
accordingly. Though they might not occur so frequently, these incidents should be
taken into consideration.

Lock Manager Protocol: This protocol allows client and server processes to
exclude the other processes when they are writing to the file. When a process locks the
file for exclusive access, no other process can access the file. When a process locks
the file for shared access, the other processes can share the file but cannot initiate an
exclusive access lock. If any other process request conflicts with the locking state,
either the process waits until the lock is removed or it may return an error message.

4.13.1.4 NFS File System

NFS assumes a hierarchical file system (directories). Files are unstructured streams of
uninterpreted bytes; that is, files are seen as a contiguous byte stream, without any
record-level structure.

This is the kind of file system used by AIX and PC/DOS, so these environments will easily integrate an NFS client extension in their own local file system. File systems used in VM and MVS lend themselves less readily to this kind of extension.

With NFS, all file operations are *synchronous*. This means that the file-operation call only returns when the server has completed all work for this operation. In case of a write request, the server will physically write the data to disk and if necessary, update any directory structure, before returning a response to the client. This ensures file integrity.

NFS also specifies that servers should be *stateless*. That is, a server does not need to maintain any extra information about any of its clients in order to function correctly. In case of a server failure, clients only have to retry a request until the server responds, without having to reiterate a mount operation.

4.13.1.5 Cache File System

The Cache File System (CacheFS) provides the ability to cache one file system on another. CacheFS accomplishes caching by mounting remote directories on the local system. Whenever the client needs a mounted file, it first refers to local cache. If the requested file exists, it is accessed locally. Otherwise, the file is retrieved from the server using NFS. In case of reading the file sequentially, the future data is retrieved for future access to the cache. This procedure increases the file access speed. It depends on the implementation to store the cache on Random Access Memory (RAM) or disk. If the amount of the data is not too large, it is better to use RAM for much faster access to the cache.

CacheFS periodically checks the cached data for the data accuracy, sweeps out the inaccurate data from the cache and retrieves the current data from the server to the cache. CacheFS is proper for the cases in which the files are not changed frequently. In other circumstances, CacheFS reduces server and network loads and improves performance for clients on slow links.

4.13.2 WebNFS

WebNFS is an enhanced version of the standard NFS. WebNFS allows the clients to access files over wide area networks (WANs). Since as a transport protocol UDP is fast for local area networks (LANs), many implementations use UDP for the standard NFS. However, a TCP connection is much more reliable for wide area networks. Most of the new NFS implementations support TCP and UDP. WebNFS clients first attempt to use a TCP connection. If it fails or refused, it then uses a UDP connection. WebNFS can easily recover from dropped lines and recover the lost data.

4.13.2.1 Pathname Evaluation

The standard NFS version 3 is designed for LANs. The amount of time for each LOOKUP requests is not significant. As a result of this, the NFS protocol permits only one single pathname request at a time. When we consider a WAN or the Internet, to request the pathname and evaluate the pathname might cause significant delays. This process is very expensive, especially for files that are several directories away. WebNFS can handle retrieving the entire pathname and evaluate it.

4.13.2.2 NFS URL

This scheme allows the NFS clients to go over Internet just like other Internet applications. The URL scheme is based on the common Internet scheme syntax. The NFS URL is described in RFC 2224. The general form of the NFS URL scheme is the following:

```
nfs://<host>:<port><url-path>
```

The port is optional. If it is not specified, the default value is 2049. The WebNFS server evaluates the path using a multi-component lookup relative to the public file handle.

4.13.3 References

The following RFCs provide detailed information on NFS:

- *RFC 1813 — NFS Version 3 Protocol Specification*

- *RFC 2054 — WebNFS Client Specification*

- *RFC 2055 — WebNFS Server Specification*

- *RFC 2224 — NFS URL Scheme*

4.14 X Window System

The X Window System (hereafter referred to as X) is one of the most widely used *graphical user interface (GUI)*, or bitmapped-window display systems. It is supported by all major workstation vendors, and is used by a large and growing number of users worldwide. The X Window System offers more than just a raw environment. It also offers a platform for uniquely incorporated commercial packages. In addition to writing application software, some industry groups have created proprietary software packages and standards for interfaces that leverage the display capabilities of the X Window System. These packages are then integrated into applications to improve the look and feel of them.

The two most significant commercial packages in this area are the Open Software Foundation's *MOTIF* and UNIX International's *Open Look*. X was the brainchild of Robert Scheifler, Jim Gettys, and others at MIT, as part of *Project Athena*, a research project devoted to the examination of very large networks of personal computers and workstations. (For an overview of the Project Athena, please refer to *Project Athena: Supporting Distributed Computing at MIT*.) As part of this study, a unifying window system environment extending over all systems was deemed necessary. X was envisioned as this window system, one that could be used among the varied heterogeneous computers and networks.

As Project Athena progressed, X evolved into a portable network-based window system. Much of the early work on X was derived from an existent Stanford window system called W. In fact the name X was simply a play on the previous name W. The MIT X Consortium, founded in 1988, is dedicated to the advancement of the X Window System and to the promotion of cooperation within the computer industry in standardizing the X Window System interfaces.

Current X releases contain two numbers: the *version number* indicating major protocol or standards revisions, and a *release number* indicating minor changes. At the time of writing, the latest version is X11 Release 6.4, also known as X11R6.4. The latest release of OSF/MOTIF is V2.1.10 (based on X11R5). Major revisions of X are incompatible, but there is backward compatibility with minor releases within major revision categories.

The aim of X was to allow the user to control all sessions from one screen, with applications either running in a window, or in separate virtual terminals but with an icon on the primary screen reminding him or her of the existence of that application (the same function as OS/2 Presentation Manager).

The X Window System provides the capability of managing both local and remote windows. Remote windows are established through TCP/IP, and local windows through the use of BSD *sockets*. Some of the important features of X11R6.4 is that it provides access to remote applications over the Internet. Since the internet connections are relatively slow, there is a need to compress the data and send accordingly. For this purpose the Low Bandwidth X (LBX) extension is added in the latest release. Another issue that comes with the Internet is security. The latest X window release has security function to overcome this problem.

4.14.1 Functional Concept

Basically there are two parts communicating with each other:

1. The application, which gets input from the user, executes code and sends output back to the user. Instead of reading and writing directly to a display, the application uses the Xlib programming interface to send and receive data to/from the user's terminal. The application part is also called the X client.

2. The user's terminal, running a display-managing software which receives/sends data from/to the application and is called the X server.

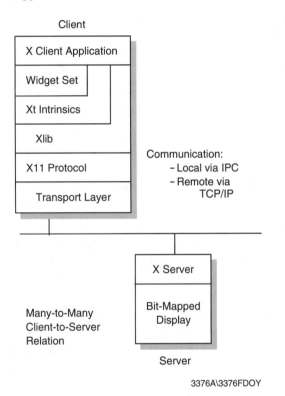

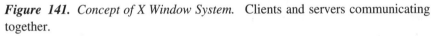

3376A\3376FDOY

Figure 141. *Concept of X Window System.* Clients and servers communicating together.

Terminology:

- **X Server**: This is a dedicated program that provides display services on a graphic terminal, on behalf of a user, at the request of the user's X client program. It controls the screen and handles the keyboard and the mouse (or other input devices) for one or more X clients. Equally, it is responsible for output to the display, the mapping of colors, the loading of fonts and the keyboard mapping. Typically X server programs run on high-performance graphic PCs and workstations, as well as X terminals, which are designed to run only the X server program.

An X Font Service Protocol is available to allow the X servers to delegate the task of managing fonts to a font server. The X11R6.4 X server supports LBX, security, printing and AddGroup extensions.

- **X Client**: This is the actual *application* and is designed to employ a graphical user interface to display its output. Typically, many X clients compete for the service of one X server per display per user. Conflict for services are resolved by the X Window Manager, a separate entity altogether. *Xterm* and *Xclock* are two examples of X clients.

  Since the X11R6 release, X client uses the MIT-KERBEROS-5 authorization scheme. Once the connection is established, Xdm initiates the authentication over Xlib to authorize the client to the server.

- **X Window Manager**: This is an X client program located on the workstation where the X server runs. While windows can be created without a window manager in place, a window manager permits windows to be resized, moved, and otherwise modified on demand.

- **X Protocol**: This runs within the network connection, and allows requests and responses between client and server. It uses a reliable byte stream connection (that is TCP) and describes the format of messages exchanged between client and server over this connection.

- **Xlib**: The rudimentary application programming interface is contained in the Xlib. It is a collection of C primitive subroutines embedded in all X clients, which gives the lowest level access to the X protocol. The procedures in Xlib translate client requests to X protocol requests, parse incoming messages (events, replies, and errors) from the X server, and provide several additional utilities, such as storage management and operating system-independent operations. It is possible to write application programs entirely with Xlib. In fact, most existing X clients are or were developed in this fashion. Other significant functions of Xlib are device-independent color, international languages, local customs and character string encodings support.

- **X Toolkits**: The complexity of the low-level Xlib interface and of the underlying X protocol is handled by an increasing variety of available X *toolkits*. The X toolkits are software libraries that provide high-level facilities for implementing common user-interface *objects* such as buttons, menus, and scroll bars, as well as layout tools for organizing these objects on the display. The basis for a family of toolkits is provided with the standard X releases from MIT. The library, called the X Intrinsics or Xt, forms the building blocks for sets of user interface objects called *widgets*.

- **Widgets**: For toolkits based on the X Intrinsics, a common interface mechanism called a *widget* is used. A widget is essentially an X window plus some additional data and a set of procedures for operating on that data. Widgets are a client-side notion only. Neither the X server nor the X protocol understand widgets. A sample widget set, *Xaw*, more commonly referred to as the *Athena Widget Set*, is distributed by MIT with the X11 source.

4.14.1.1 Functionality

The following paragraphs outline the functional operation of the X Window System.

- X client and X server can be on different hosts. Then they use the TCP/IP protocol to communicate over the network. They can also be on the same machine, using IPC (inter-process communication) to communicate (through sockets).

- There is only one X server per terminal. Multiple X client applications can communicate with this one X server. The duty of the X server is to display the application windows and to send the user input to the appropriate X client application.

- It is up to the X client to maintain the windows that it created. It is notified by *events* from the X server whenever something is changed on the display by other clients. However, they don't have to care about which part of their windows are visible when they are drawing or redrawing their windows.

- The X server keeps track of the visibility of the windows, by maintaining *stacks*. A stack contains all *"first generation" children* of a parent window. A child window can also be a parent window by having one or more child windows itself, which are again held in a *substack*. The *primary stack* is the stack that holds all the windows located directly below the root. See Figure 142 on page 308 for an illustration. Subwindows can only be fully visible when their parent is on the top of its respective stack and mapped to the display.

- X server itself has no management functions; it only performs window clipping according to its stacks. Every client is responsible for its own windows. There is a *window manager* which manipulates the top-level windows of all the clients. The window manager is not part of the X server but is itself a client. As soon as the window manager changes something on the screen (for instance, resizing a window), it makes the X server send out an exposure event to all the other clients.

- The client applications send *request messages* to the X server, which replies with a *reply message* or an *error message*. The X server can also send *event messages* to the applications. Event messages indicate changes to the windows (and their visibility), and user input (mouse and keyboard).

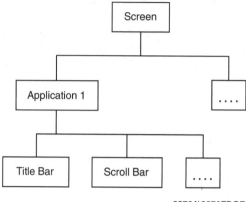

3376A\3376FDOZ

Figure 142. *X Window System Window Structure.* Each window is a child of another window, the whole display being the root.

Applying this client/server concept gives the following advantages:

- Applications don't have to know the hardware characteristics of the terminal.

- Applications don't have to be on the same computer as the terminal.

- Programs written to Xlib are portable.

- New terminal types can be added by providing an appropriate X server.

- The programmers do not have to deal with the communications. They just write graphic applications to Xlib, regardless of whether the users will be remote or local.

4.14.2 Protocol

An X Window System protocol can be implemented on top of any reliable byte stream transport mechanism. It uses a simple block protocol on top of the stream layer. Four kinds of messages are used:

- Request format. Requests flow from the client application to the X server.

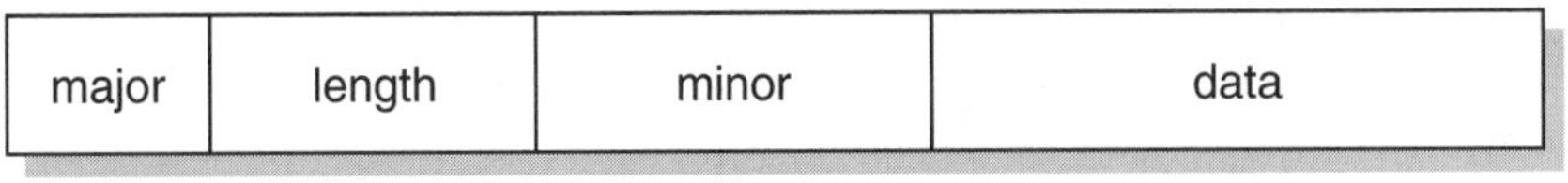

major	length	minor	data

Figure 143. *X Window Request Format*

Where:

> Major and minor are opcodes, each 1-byte long.
> Length is 2-bytes long.
> Data can be zero or more bytes, depending on the request.

- Reply format: 32-byte block.

- Error format: 32-byte block.

- Event format: 32-byte block.

Reply, error and event messages are sent by the X server to the X client applications.

Displays are always numbered from zero. For TCP connections, display number N is associated with port 5800+N (hex 5800) and port 5900+N. The X server treats connections on the 58xx ports as connections with hosts that use the low-order byte first format, and the 59xx ports as high-order byte first.

There are more than a hundred different possible requests, each corresponding to an Xlib application call. As this document is not a programmer's guide, we will not deal with the Xlib functions. RFC 1013 *X Window System Protocol, Version 11* contains the 1987 alpha update of the X11 protocol. For documentation on the current release X11R6, please contact either MIT or a commercial computer books publisher.

4.15 Finger Protocol

Finger is a *draft-standard protocol*. Its status is *elective*. The current finger specification can be found in *RFC 1288 — The Finger User Information Protocol*.

The finger command displays information about users of a remote host. Finger is a UNIX command. Its format is:

```
finger user@host
or
finger @host
```

The information provided by the finger command about a user depends on the implementation of the finger server. If a user is not specified, the information will typically be a list of all users currently logged on to this host.

Connections are established through TCP port 79 (decimal). The client sends an ASCII command string, ending with <CRLF>. The server responds with one or more ASCII strings, until the server closes the connection.

4.16 NETSTAT

The NETSTAT command is used to query TCP/IP about the network status of the local host. The exact syntax of this command is very implementation-dependent. See the *User's Guide* or the *Command Reference Manual* of your implementation for full details. It is a useful tool for debugging purposes.

In general, NETSTAT will provide information on:

- Active TCP connections at this local host

- State of all TCP/IP servers on this local host and the sockets used by them

- Devices and links used by TCP/IP

- The IP routing tables (gateway tables) in use at this local host

The NETSTAT command is implemented in all IBM software TCP/IP products.

4.17 Network Information System (NIS)

The Network Information System (NIS) is not an Internet standard. It was developed by Sun Microsystems, Inc. It was originally known as the Yellow Pages.

NIS is a distributed database system which allows the sharing of system information in an AIX- or UNIX-based environment. Examples of system information that can be shared include the /etc/passwd, /etc/group and /etc/hosts files. NIS has the following advantages:

- Provides a consistent user ID and group ID name space across a large number of systems

- Reduces the time and effort by users in managing their user IDs, group IDs and NFS file system ownerships

- Reduces the time and effort by system administrators in managing user IDs, group IDs and NFS file system ownerships

NIS is built on the SUN-RPC. It employs the client/server model. An NIS domain is a collection of systems consisting of:

NIS master server   Maintains *maps*, or databases, containing the system information such as passwords and host names.

NIS slave server(s)   Can be defined to offload the processing from the master NIS server or when the NIS master server is unavailable.

NIS client(s)   Are the remaining systems that are served by the NIS servers.

The NIS clients do not maintain NIS maps; they query NIS servers for system information. Any changes to an NIS map is done only to the NIS master server (via RPC). The master server then propagates the changes to the NIS slave servers.

Note that the speed of a network determines the performance and availability of the NIS maps. When using NIS, the number of slave servers should be tuned in order to achieve these goals.

4.18 NetBIOS over TCP/IP

For some time, the NetBIOS service has been a dominant mechanism for networking of personal computers in a LAN environment. NetBIOS is a vendor-independant software interface (API), not a protocol. There is no official NetBIOS specification, although in practice, the NetBIOS version described in the IBM publication *SC30-3587 LAN Technical Reference: 802.2 and NetBIOS APIs* is used as reference.

The NetBIOS service has some specific characteristics that limit its use in certain wide area network environments:

- NetBIOS workstations address each other using NetBIOS names. NetBIOS relies on the broadcast technique to register and find NetBIOS names on the network.

- NetBIOS uses a flat name space, which bears no relationship to the domain name system.

- NetBIOS generally uses the 802.2 interface, so it is not routable.

One solution to overcome these limitations is found in *RFC 1001 — Protocol Standard for a NetBIOS Service on a TCP/UDP Transport: Concepts and Methods* and *RFC 1002 — Protocol Standard for a NetBIOS Service on a TCP/UDP Transport: Detailed Specifications.*

As the titles suggest, these RFCs define a method of implementing NetBIOS services on top of the Transmission Control Protocol (TCP) and User Datagram Protocol (UDP).

RFCs 1001/1002 do not define an encapsulation technique; they define the mapping of NetBIOS services to UDP/IP and TCP/IP. For example, once a NetBIOS session has been established, sockets-send commands will be used over a TCP connection to send NetBIOS session data.

From the point of view of a network application, written to the NetBIOS interface, there is no change to the NetBIOS service. An application is unaware of the change in the underlying protocol.

The NetBIOS service running over TCP and UDP is logically represented in Figure 144.

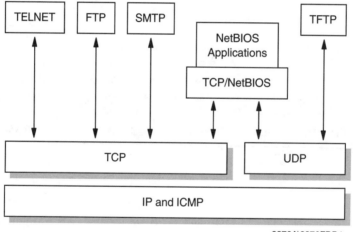

3376A\3376FDD1

Figure 144. TCP/IP and NetBIOS

RFC 1001 introduces a number of new concepts to facilitate NetBIOS operation in a TCP/IP environment:

NetBIOS Scope
The NetBIOS scope is a group of computers across which a NetBIOS name is known. In a standard NetBIOS configuration, using broadcast techniques, all the computers in this group would be able to contact each other. The NetBIOS over TCP/IP implementation must provide an alternative method for this group to communicate with each other, particularly as they may be spread across subnets. An internet may support multiple, non-intersecting NetBIOS scopes. Each

NetBIOS scope has a *scope identifier*, which is a character string in a format compatible with the domain name system.

NetBIOS End Node

Computers using NetBIOS over TCP/IP are known as NetBIOS end nodes. RFC 1001 defines the following three types of end node:

Broadcast (B) node

> Uses local broadcast UDP datagrams to establish connections and distribute datagrams. Because broadcast datagrams cannot typically cross routers, B nodes (as defined in RFC 1001) can only establish communications within a single network segment.

Point-to-Point (P) node

> Relies on a NetBIOS name server (NBNS) to establish connections with other nodes and on a NetBIOS datagram distributor (NBDD) for datagram distribution. P nodes neither generate, nor listen for, broadcast UDP packets, and use directed unicast packets only.

Mixed (M) node

> A mixed node is a combination of both B and P nodes. It uses both unicast (to a NBNS) and broadcast packets

A fourth node type, the hybrid (H) node, although not defined in the RFCs, is also widely implemented:

Hybrid (H) Node

> The hybrid node is also a combination of B and P nodes. However, the H node will always attempt to contact a NetBIOS name server initially, using unicast packets, and will only resort to broadcast packets in the event that this is unsuccessful. The H node has an advantage over the M node in that it limits the generation of unwanted broadcast packets.

NetBIOS Name Server (NBNS)

The NBNS registers the NetBIOS name/IP address of each P, M or H node when it is initialized. Whenever a node wishes to contact another node by means of its NetBIOS name, it uses the NBNS to obtain the corresponding IP address for that node. NetBIOS names are combined with their scope identifiers and stored in an encoded form (which is a valid domain system name) in the NBNS.

NetBIOS Datagram Distributor (NBDD)

The NBDD extends the NetBIOS datagram distribution service to the internet environment. When an end node wishes to broadcast a datagram, the node sends a unicast datagram, which contains the scope of the broadcast to the NBDD.

The NBDD sends a NetBIOS datagram to each end node within the specified NetBIOS scope, using the services of the NBNS to obtain the relevant IP addresses. (In practice it is likely that the NBNS and NBDD will be implemented on the same device.)

4.18.1 NetBIOS over TCP/IP in IBM OS/2 Warp 4

IBM OS/2 NetBIOS over TCP/IP can be configured in a B node (default), P node or H node implementation.

For B-node operations the NetBIOS over TCP/IP contains routing extensions, not defined in the RFCs, that allow communication between networks over IP routers and bridges. The use of these extensions is optional, but if they are not active the NetBIOS over TCP/IP will operate only on the local LAN segment. The following are the three routing extensions for the IBM NetBIOS over TCP/IP:

Names File Routing Extension

> This routing extension is implemented through the use of a names file, x:\IBMCOM\RFCNAMES.LST which contains NetBIOS name and IP address pairs. This implementation requires an entry in the names file for every other workstation with which a workstation needs to communicate. This file is conceptually similar to the TCP/IP hosts file.

> The advantage of using a names file is in the reduction of name query broadcasts, because before the NetBIOS over TCP/IP program broadcasts to the network for NetBIOS name to IP address resolution, it searches this local file.

> If an address in the file is given, not as an IP address, but as a host name string, it is translated to an IP address by the TCP/IP GetHostByName() function by looking it up in the local hosts file or by querying the Internet domain name server. The host name string must therefore be in the same form here as it is in the hosts file or on the domain name server.

Broadcast File Routing Extension

> This routing extension is implemented through the use of a broadcast file, x:\IBMCOM\RFCBCST.LST. A TCP/IP is normally limited to a single subnet unless the broadcast file exists. The broadcast file contains a list of host names (such as deptsrvr), host IP addresses (such as 9.67.60.80) or subnet broadcast addresses (such as ausvm1.austin.ibm.com). The file is read once at startup and each valid address is added to the set of destination addresses for broadcast packets. Any host or network accessible by these addresses becomes part of the local NetBIOS broadcast domain; that is, they receive all name lookup and registration packets as

well as all broadcast and group NetBIOS datagrams. These addresses can be on other networks and accessed through the appropriate router or bridge by the IBM TCP/IP program. The remote node is treated as if it were a node on the local network.

Each line of the broadcast file is either an IP address in dotted decimal notation (for example, 89.0.0.1) or a host name string that occurs in either the local hosts file used by the IBM TCP/IP program or on an Internet domain name server. If an address is given as a host name string, it is translated to an IP address by the TCP/IP GetHostByName() function by looking it up in the local hosts file or by querying an Internet domain name server. The host name string must be in the same form here as it is in the hosts file or on the domain name server.

A maximum of 32 entries is allowed in the broadcast file.

Domain Name Server (DNS) Routing Extension

This routing extension uses a TCP/IP domain name server (DNS) as a central repository for NetBIOS name and IP address pairs, so that the NetBIOS over TCP/IP clients can obtain the IP address of other workstations. This extension requires that the network administrator enters the NetBIOS name (in an encoded format) and the IP address of every NetBIOS over TCP/IP workstation into the domain name server. The NetBIOS names must be entered into the DNS in an encoded format. An encoded format is necessary, because NetBIOS names are 16 bytes of any bit pattern and the domain name server accepts a limited character set. The NetBIOS over TCP/IP program encodes them into the 32-byte, reversible, half-ASCII format that is specified in RFC 1001. A MAPNAME utility is available to encode and decode NetBIOS names. (The MAPNAME utility can also be used to enter encoded NetBIOS name/IP address pairs into the local HOSTS file at the workstation.)

If B node operation is configured with one or more of the routing extensions, an OS/2 client uses the different methods of resolving NetBIOS names in the following order:

1. Look up the local name cache (NetBIOS names that have already been resolved by any method are stored in this cache)
2. Look up the local names file x:\IBMCOM\RFCNAMES.LST
3. Search the domain name server
4. Check the x:\MPTN\ETC\HOSTS file
5. Use the broadcast file x:\IBMCOM\RFCBCST.LST
6. Broadcast to local subnet

The routing extensions to the B node usefully extend the range of NetBIOS clients in a TCP/IP environment. However, whatever extension is used, a considerable amount of configuration is necessary either at the client, or at the DNS. Also, the extensions have no value in a Dynamic IP environment, when an administrator will not be able to tell in advance which IP address should be mapped to which NetBIOS name.

A superior solution is always to use a dedicated NetBIOS name server that maps NetBIOS names to IP addresses dynamically (see 4.18.3, "NetBIOS Name Server (NBNS) Implementations" on page 317).

4.18.2 NetBIOS over TCP/IP in Microsoft Windows Systems

Whenever Windows NT 4.0, Windows 95, or Windows 98 clients are configured to use the TCP/IP protocol, client-to-server or peer-to-peer file or printer sharing is actually conducted using NetBIOS over TCP/IP.

NetBIOS over TCP/IP in a Windows environment is also based on RFCs 1001/1002, with routing extensions.

Windows 95, Windows 98 and Windows NT can use a file called LMHOSTS to perform NetBIOS name to IP address resolution. Under Windows 95 and Windows 98, the file should be located in the \WINDOWS subdirectory, while under NT, it is located in \WINNT\SYSTEM32\DRIVERS\ETC. LMHOSTS performs a similar function to the RFCNAMES.LST file on an OS/2 workstation. At its simplest, the file contains NetBIOS name and IP address pairs. Additional options are available to enhance the configuration.

Unlike OS/2 clients, Windows clients do not support the domain name server routing extension using names encoded to the RFC 1001/1002 specification. However, Microsoft's Service Pack 3 for Windows NT 4.0 introduces a new way of NetBIOS name resolution, using non-RFC-encoded names in the DNS. This technique requires the *node status request* frame (defined in RFC 1001/1002) and can be implemented on both Windows NT Workstation clients and Windows NT Server.

Note: A fix (APAR IC20646) is available for IBM OS/2 Warp Server to support node status request frames, but OS/2 Warp clients do not yet support this new technique.

In the DNS domain file, the Windows NT Server computer name, also known as server name, is appended as a pure ASCII name with an A record that points to the server's static IP address. In addition, the domain name is included with an alias, CNAME, to the server's name. For a domain controller SERVER-A in the domain

DOMAIN-A, the entries in the DNS domain file would look like the following two lines:

```
SERVER-A IN A 9.53.4.5
DOMAIN-A IN CNAME SERVER-A.
```

The logon sequence would use the following steps:

1. The Windows NT Workstation client queries the DNS server for hostname DOMAIN-A.
2. The DNS server returns the information that DOMAIN-A is the alias to SERVER-A. The Windows NT Workstation client receives the IP address of the Windows NT Server.
3. Since the Windows NT Workstation client is not sure whether or not the target IP address is really a NetBIOS node, which has certain NetBIOS names registered, it sends a node status request frame to the received IP address (which is the Windows NT Server). This node status request frame passes a resource record name of * (asterisk).
4. The Windows NT Server responds to the node status request by sending a complete list of NetBIOS names registered in the node.
5. The Windows NT Workstation client now selects the target IP address for the correct server name and domain name, then it starts the logon sequence through an SMB session.

This technique might be called *DNS-Only* or *Use of non-RFC-encoded names* NetBIOS name resolution, but it actually is a combination of DNS name resolution and the use of the node status request frame defined in the RFC 1001/1002.

Windows NT, Windows 95, and Windows 98 workstations can also resolve NetBIOS names to IP addresses by using a NetBIOS name server.

4.18.3 NetBIOS Name Server (NBNS) Implementations

NetBIOS name servers dynamically register NetBIOS-to-IP mappings for P, H and M node workstations as they are initialized and respond to requests for those mappings. The NBNS is the simplest NetBIOS over IP solution to manage, as it removes the requirement for manual configuration of files, either on the client workstations, or on the DNS.

4.18.3.1 Microsoft Windows Internet Name Service (WINS)

Windows Internet Name Service (WINS) is Microsoft's implementation of an NBNS. WINS only supports Microsoft's proprietary clients with its implementation of native NetBIOS and NetBIOS over TCP/IP

Each Microsoft client needs to be configured with the IP address of a primary WINS server, and optionally with the IP address of a secondary WINS server. Whenever a client starts, it will attempt to register its NetBIOS name and IP address with the primary WINS server. The registration occurs when services or applications are started (for example, Workstation or Messenger), and is sent directly to the primary WINS server. If the name is not already registered to another client, the server responds with a message detailing the NetBIOS name that has been registered, and the name time-to-live (TTL). If the client attempts three times to register its name with the primary server and fails, the client will attempt to register its name with the secondary server. If the secondary server also fails to respond, the client will revert to broadcasting in order to register its name.

The name registrations are made on a temporary basis, and the client is responsible for maintaining the lease of the registered name. At one-eighth of the TTL, the client will attempt to refresh its name registration with the primary WINS server. If the client does not receive a response from the server, it will continue to attempt to refresh the registration every two minutes until half the TTL has expired. At this point it will repeat the procedure, but this time using the secondary WINS server.

With WINS enabled, the client acts as an H node client for name registration. For resolution, it is H node with a few modifications. The sequence used by a WINS client for name resolution is:

1. Check to see if it is the local machine name.
2. Check the local cache. (Any resolved name is placed in a cache for 10 minutes.)
3. Try to use the primary WINS server. (Use the secondary server if the primary does not answer after three attempts).
4. Try a name query broadcast.
5. Check the LMHOSTS file. (If the computer is configured to use LMHOSTS).
6. Try the HOSTS file.
7. Try the DNS.

WINS Limitations: According to RFC 1001/1002, a NetBIOS name server should support all NetBIOS group names. WINS, however, only keeps a list of IP addresses for group names ending in 0x1C. IBM OS/2 Warp Server domains, for example, are registered with a 0x00 suffix and, as such, are not stored by a WINS server. The WINS NBNS only supports Windows 9x and NT clients.

4.18.3.2 Network TeleSystems (NTS) Shadow IPserver

Shadow IPserver is a software system for managing name and address assignments and desktop configuration information within a TCP/IP network. IPserver includes a robust set of network services offered through standards-based protocol interactions, such as:

- DHCP service

- DNS service

- NBNS and NBDD services

The Shadow IPserver NBNS service is an integrated NetBIOS name server and datagram distributor. The IPserver NBNS service fully implements RFCs 1001 and 1002. The NBNS service provides name resolution services similar to those provided by Microsoft WINS, but supports any client configured for P, H or M node operation. Microsoft Windows 9x and Windows NT protocol stacks do not support datagram distribution, however. The Shadow IPserver supports up to 16,000 names on a single server and is the NBNS recommended by IBM for use in OS/2 networks.

For further information on NetBIOS over TCP/IP, please refer to RFC 1001 and RFC 1002. For information on the IBM OS/2 and Microsoft Windows implementations, please refer to the IBM redbooks SG24-2009 *Network Clients for OS/2 Warp Server* and SG24-5280 *Beyond DHCP - Work Your TCP/IP Internetwork with Dynamic IP*.

4.19 Application Programming Interfaces (APIs)

Application programming interfaces allow developers to write applications that can make use of TCP/IP services. The following sections provide an overview of the most common APIs for TCP/IP applications.

4.19.1 The Socket API

The socket interface is one of several application programming interfaces (APIs) to the communication protocols. Designed to be a generic communication programming interface, it was first introduced by the 4.2BSD UNIX system. Although it has not been standardized, it has become a de facto industry standard.

The socket interface is differentiated by the services that are provided to applications: stream sockets (connection-oriented), datagram sockets (connectionless), and raw sockets (direct access to lower layer protocols) services. Please see 2.6, "Ports and Sockets" on page 94 for more detail about ports and sockets.

A variation of the BSD sockets interface is provided by the Winsock interface developed by Microsoft and other vendors to support TCP/IP applications on Windows operating systems. Winsock 2.0, the latest version, provides a more generalized interface allowing applications to communicate with any available transport layer protocol and underlying network services, including, but no longer limited to, TCP/IP. Please see 4.19.3, "Windows Sockets Version 2 (Winsock V2.0)" on page 328 for more information about Winsock.

4.19.1.1 Basic Socket Calls

The following lists some basic socket interface calls. In the next section we see an example scenario of using these socket interface calls.

- Initialize a socket.

  FORMAT:

  ```
  int sockfd = socket(int family, int type, int protocol)
  ```

  Where:

  - family stands for addressing family. It can take on values such as AF_UNIX, AF_INET, AF_NS, AF_OS2 and AF_IUCV. Its purpose is to specify the method of addressing used by the socket.
  - type stands for the type of socket interface to be used. It can take on values such as SOCK_STREAM, SOCK_DGRAM, SOCK_RAW, and SOCK_SEQPACKET.
  - protocol can be UDP, TCP, IP or ICMP.
  - sockfd is an integer (similar to a file descriptor) returned by the socket call.

- Bind (register) a socket to a port address.

  FORMAT:

  ```
  int bind(int sockfd, struct sockaddr *localaddr, int addrlen)
  ```

  Where:

  - sockfd is the same integer returned by the socket call.
  - localaddr is the local address returned by the bind call.

  Note that after the bind call, we now have values for the first three parameters inside our 5-tuple association:

  ```
  {protocol, local-address, local-process, foreign-address, foreign-process}
  ```

- Indicate readiness to receive connections.

  FORMAT:

  ```
  int listen(int sockfd, int queue-size)
  ```

  Where:

  - sockfd is the same integer returned by the socket call.

- queue-size indicates the number of connection requests that can be queued by the system while the local process has not yet issued the accept call.

- Accept a connection.

  FORMAT:

  ```
  int accept(int sockfd, struct sockaddr *foreign-address, int addrlen)
  ```

  Where:

  - sockfd is the same integer returned by the socket call.
  - foreign-address is the address of the foreign (client) process returned by the accept call.

  Note that this accept call is issued by a server process rather than a client process. If there is a connection request waiting on the queue for this socket connection, accept takes the first request on the queue and creates another socket with the same properties as sockfd; otherwise, accept will block the caller process until a connection request arrives.

- Request connection to the server.

  FORMAT:

  ```
  int connect(int sockfd, struct sockaddr *foreign-address, int addrlen)
  ```

  Where:

  - sockfd is the same integer returned by the socket call.
  - foreign-address is the address of the foreign (server) process returned by the connect call.

  Note that this call is issued by a client process rather than a server process.

- Send and/or receive data.

  The read(), readv(sockfd, char *buffer int addrlen), recv(), readfrom(), send(sockfd, msg, len, flags) and write() calls can be used to receive and send data in an established socket association (or connection).

  Note that these calls are similar to the standard read and write file I/O system calls.

- Close a socket.

  FORMAT:

  ```
  int close(int sockfd)
  ```

  Where:

  - sockfd is the same integer returned by the socket call.

For more details, please refer to the literature listed in Appendix B, "Related Publications" on page 861.

4.19.1.2 An Example Scenario

As an example, consider the socket system calls for a connection-oriented protocol.

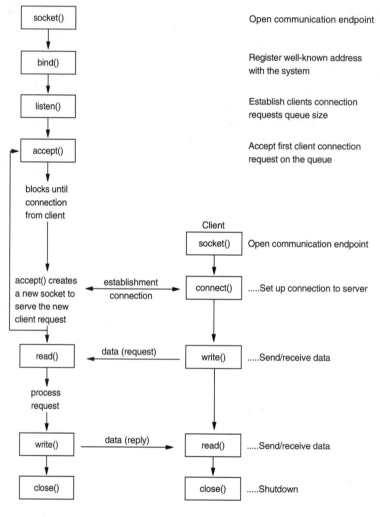

Figure 145. Socket System Calls for Connection-Oriented Protocol

Consider the previous socket system calls in terms of specifying the elements of the association:

	Protocol	Local Address ,	Local Process	Foreign Address ,	Foreign Process
connection-oriented server	socket()	bind()		listen() accept()	
connection-oriented client	socket()	connect()			
connectionless server	socket()	bind()		recvfrom()	
connectionless client	socket()	bind()		sendto()	

Figure 146. Socket System Calls and Association

The socket interface is differentiated by the different services that are provided. Stream, datagram, and raw sockets each define a different service available to applications.

- **Stream socket interface** (SOCK_STREAM): It defines a reliable connection-oriented service (over TCP for example). Data is sent without errors or duplication and is received in the same order as it is sent. Flow control is built-in to avoid data overruns. No boundaries are imposed on the exchanged data, which is considered to be a stream of bytes. An example of an application that uses stream sockets is the File Transfer Program (FTP).

- **Datagram socket interface** (SOCK_DGRAM): It defines a connectionless service (over UDP for example). Datagrams are sent as independent packets. The service provides no guarantees; data can be lost or duplicated, and datagrams can arrive out of order. No disassembly and reassembly of packets is performed. An example of an application that uses datagram sockets is the Network File System (NFS).

- **Raw socket interface** (SOCK_RAW): It allows direct access to lower layer protocols such as IP and ICMP. This interface is often used for testing new protocol implementations. An example of an application that uses raw sockets is the Ping command.

4.19.2 Remote Procedure Call (RPC)

Remote Procedure Call is a standard developed by Sun Microsystems and used by many vendors of UNIX systems.

RPC is an application programming interface (API) available for developing distributed applications. It allows programs to call subroutines that are executed at a remote system. The caller program (called client) sends a call message to the server process, and waits for a reply message. The call message includes the procedure's parameters and the reply message contains the procedure's results. RPC also provides a standard way of encoding data in a portable fashion between different systems called External Data Representation (XDR).

4.19.2.1 RPC Concept

The concept of RPC is very similar to that of an application program issuing a procedure call:

- The caller process sends a call message and waits for the reply.
- On the server side, a process is dormant awaiting the arrival of call messages. When one arrives, the server process extracts the procedure parameters, computes the results and sends them back in a reply message.

See Figure 147 on page 325 for a conceptual model of RPC.

This is only a possible model, as the Sun RPC protocol doesn't put restrictions on the concurrency model. In the model above, the caller's execution blocks until a reply message is received. Other models are possible; for instance, the caller may continue processing while waiting for a reply, or the server may dispatch a separate task for each incoming call so that it remains free to receive other messages.

The remote procedure calls differ from local procedure calls in the following ways:

- Use of global variables as the server has no access to the caller program's address space.
- Performance may be affected by the transmission times.
- User authentication may be necessary.
- Location of server must be known.

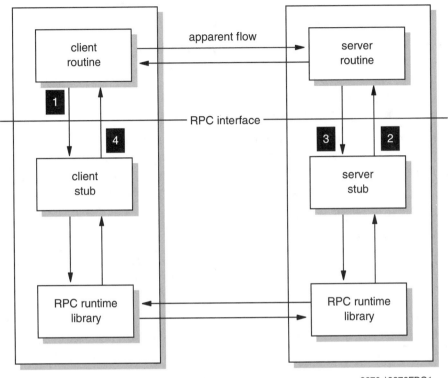

Figure 147. RPC - Remote Procedure Call Model

Transport: The RPC protocol can be implemented on any transport protocol. In the case of TCP/IP, it can use either TCP or UDP as the transport vehicle. The type of the *transport* is a parameter of the RPCGEN command. In case UDP is used, remember that this does not provide reliability, so it will be up to the caller program itself to ensure this (using timeouts and retransmissions, usually implemented in RPC library routines). Note that even with TCP, the caller program still needs a timeout routine to deal with exceptional situations such as a server crash.

The call and reply message data is formatted to the XDR standard.

RPC Call Message: The RPC call message consists of several fields:

- Program and procedure numbers

  Each call message contains three fields (unsigned integers): that uniquely identify the procedure to be executed:

  – Remote program number

- Remote program version number
- Remote procedure number

The remote program number identifies a functional group of procedures, for instance a file system, which would include individual procedures such as read and write. These individual procedures are identified by a unique procedure number within the remote program. As the remote program evolves, a version number is assigned to the different releases.

Each remote program is attached to an internet port. The number of this port can be freely chosen, except for the reserved well-known-services port numbers. It is evident that the caller will have to know the port number used by this remote program.

Assigned program numbers:

00000000 - 1FFFFFFF	defined by Sun
20000000 - 3FFFFFFF	defined by user
40000000 - 5FFFFFFF	transient (temporary numbers)
60000000 - FFFFFFFF	reserved

- Authentication fields

    Two fields, *credentials* and *verifier*, are provided for the authentication of the caller to the service. It is up to the server to use this information for user authentication. Also, each implementation is free to choose the varieties of supported authentication protocols. Some authentication protocols are:

    - Null authentication.
    - UNIX authentication. The callers of a remote procedure may identify themselves as they are identified on the UNIX system.
    - DES authentication. In addition to user ID, a timestamp field is sent to the server. This timestamp is the current time, enciphered using a key known to the caller machine and server machine only (based on the *secret key* and *public key* concept of DES).

- Procedure parameters

    Data (parameters) passed to the remote procedure.

RPC Reply Message: Several replies exist, depending on the action taken:

- SUCCESS: Procedure results are sent back to the client.
- RPC_MISMATCH: Server is running another version of RPC than the caller.
- AUTH_ERROR: Caller authentication failed.
- PROG_MISMATCH: If program is unavailable or if the version asked for does not exist or if the procedure is unavailable.

For a detailed description of the call and reply messages, see RFC 1057 *RPC: Remote Procedure Call Protocol Specification Version 2*, which also contains the type definitions (typedef) for the messages in XDR language.

Portmap or Portmapper: The Portmap or Portmapper is a server application that will map a program number and its version number to the Internet port number used by the program. Portmap is assigned the reserved (well-known service) port number 111.

Portmap only knows about RPC programs on the host it runs on. In order for Portmap to know about the RPC program, every RPC program should register itself with the local Portmapper when it starts up.

The RPC client (caller) has to ask the Portmap service on the remote host about the port used by the desired server program.

Normally, the calling application would contact Portmap on the destination host to obtain the correct port number for a particular remote program, and then send the call message to this particular port. A variation exists when the caller also sends the procedure data along to Portmap and then the remote Portmap directly invokes the procedure.

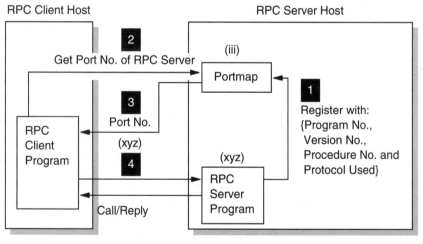

3376a\3376FDO2

Figure 148. RPC - Portmap

RPCGEN: RPCGEN is a tool that generates C code to implement an RPC protocol. The input to RPCGEN is a file written in a language similar to C, known as the RPC language. Assuming that an input file named proto.x is used, RPCGEN produces the following output files:

- A header file called proto.h that contains common definitions of constants and macros
- Client stub source file, protoc.c
- Server stub source file, protos.c
- XDR routines source file, protox.c

4.19.3 Windows Sockets Version 2 (Winsock V2.0)

Winsock V2.0 is a network programming interface. It is basically a version of Berkeley Sockets adapted for Microsoft Windows operating systems with more functions and enhancements. The previous version of the Winsock API, Windows Sockets V1.1, is widely implemented. Therefore, Winsock V2.0 retains backwards compatibility with Winsock V1.1 but provides many more functions. One of the most significant aspects of Winsock V2.0 is that it provides a protocol-independent transport interface supporting various networking capabilities. Besides, Winsock V2.0 also supports the coexistence of multiple protocol stacks. The new functions of Winsock V2.0 can be summarized as follows:

- Support for multiple protocols
- Protocol-independent name resolution
- Quality of Service
- Protocol-independent multicast and multipoint
- Overlapped I/O and event objects
- Socket sharing
- Layered service providers

The Winsock V1.1 architecture permits only one Dynamic Link Library (DLL), WINSOCK.DLL or WSOCK32.DLL, on a system at a time, which provides the Winsock API with a way to communicate with an underlying transport protocol. This approach restricts the use of different types of Winsock implementations in conjunction with Winsock V1.1. For systems that have more than one network interface, this can become a hindrance. Winsock V2.0 provides a better solution to this problem. The new Winsock V2.0 architecture allows for simultaneous support of multiple protocol stacks, interfaces, and service providers. Figure 149 on page 329 illustrates the Winsock V2.0 structure.

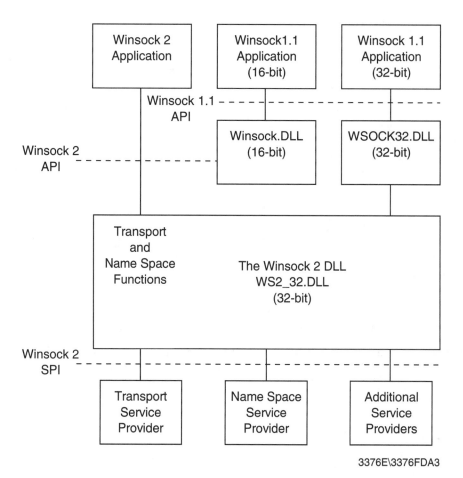

Figure 149. Winsock V2.0 Architecture

4.19.4 SNMP Distributed Programming Interface (SNMP DPI)

SNMP defines a protocol that permits operations on a collection of variables. This set of variables (MIB) and a core set of variables have previously been defined. However, the design of the MIB makes provision for extension of this core set. Unfortunately, conventional SNMP agent implementations provide no means for an end user to make new variables available. The SNMP DPI addresses this issue by providing a light-weight mechanism that permits end users to dynamically add, delete, or replace management variables in the local MIB without requiring recompilation of the SNMP agent. This is achieved by writing the so-called subagent that communicates with the agent via the SNMP DPI. It is described in RFC 1592.

The SNMP DPI allows a process to register the existence of a MIB variable with the SNMP agent. When requests for the variable are received by the SNMP agent, it will pass the query on to the process acting as a subagent. This subagent then returns an appropriate answer to the SNMP agent. The SNMP agent eventually packages an SNMP response packet and sends the answer back to the remote network management station that initiated the request. None of the remote network management stations have any knowledge that the SNMP agent calls on other processes to obtain an answer.

Communication between the SNMP agent and its clients (subagents) takes place over a stream connection. This is typically a TCP connection, but other stream-oriented transport mechanisms can be used. (As an example, the VM SNMP agent allows DPI connections over IUCV.)

The SNMP Agent DPI can:

- Create and delete subtrees in the MIB
- Create a register request packet for the subagent to inform the SNMP agent
- Create response packet for the subagent to answer the SNMP agent's request
- Create a TRAP request packet.

The following figure shows the flow between an SNMP agent and a subagent.

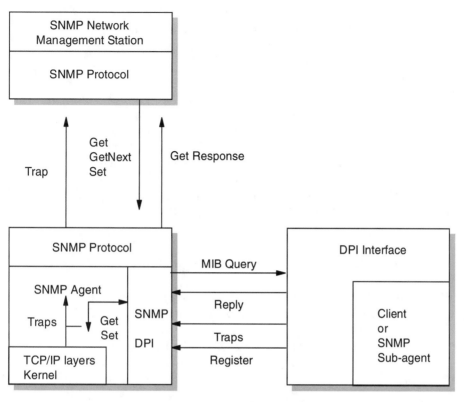

3376B\3376FDOU

Figure 150. SNMP DPI Overview

- The SNMP agent communicates with the SNMP manager via the SNMP protocol.
- The SNMP agent communicates with some statically linked-in instrumentation (potentially for the MIB II), which in turn talks to the TCP/IP layers and kernel (operating system) in an implementation-dependent manner.
- An SNMP sub-agent, running as a separate process (potentially on another machine), can set up a connection with the agent. The sub-agent has an option to communicate with the SNMP agent through UDP or TCP sockets, or even through other mechanisms.
- Once the connection is established, the sub-agent issues a DPI OPEN and one or more REGISTER requests to register one or more MIB subtrees with the SNMP agent.
- The SNMP agent responds to DPI OPEN and REGISTER requests with a RESPONSE packet, indicating success or failure.

- The SNMP agent will decode SNMP packets. If such a packet contains a Get or GetNext request for an object in a subtree registered by a sub-agent, it sends a corresponding DPI packet to the sub-agent. If the request is for a GetBulk, then the agent translates it into multiple DPI GETNEXT packets and sends those to the sub-agent. However, the sub-agent can request (in the REGISTER packet) that a GETBULK be passed to the sub-agent. If the request is for a Set, then the agent uses a 2-phase commit scheme and sends the sub-agent a sequence of SET/COMMIT, SET/UNDO or SET/COMMIT/UNDO DPI packets.
- The SNMP sub-agent sends responses back via a RESPONSE packet.
- The SNMP agent then encodes the reply into an SNMP packet and sends it back to the requesting SNMP manager.
- If the sub-agent wants to report an important state change, it sends a DPI TRAP packet to the SNMP agent which will encode it into an SNMP trap packet and send it to the manager(s).
- If the sub-agent wants to stop operations, it sends a DPI UNREGISTER and a DPI CLOSE packet to the agent. The agent sends a response to an UNREGISTER request.
- There is no RESPONSE to a CLOSE; the agent just closes the DPI connection. A CLOSE implies an UNREGISTER for all registrations that exist for the DPI connection being CLOSED.
- An agent can send DPI UNREGISTER (if a higher priority registration comes in or for other reasons) to the sub-agent. The sub-agent then responds with a DPI RESPONSE packet.
- An agent can also (for whatever reason) send a DPI CLOSE to indicate it is terminating the DPI connection.
- A sub-agent can send an ARE_YOU_THERE to verify that the connection is still open. If so, the agent sends a RESPONSE with no error, otherwise, it may send a RESPONSE with an error.

4.19.5 FTP API

The file transfer protocol (FTP) API is supplied as part of TCP/IP for OS/2. It allows applications to have a client interface for file transfer. Applications written to this interface can communicate with multiple FTP servers at the same time. It allows up to 256 simultaneous connections and enables third-party proxy transfers between pairs of FTP servers. Consecutive third-party transfers are allowed between any sequence of pairs of FTP servers. An example of such an application is FTPPM.

The FTP API tracks the servers to which an application is currently connected. When a new request for FTP service is requested, the API checks whether a connection to the server exists and establishes one if it does not exist. If the server has dropped the connection since last use, the API re-establishes it.

Note: The FTP API is not re-entrant. In a multithreaded program, the access to the APIs must be serialized. For example, without serialization, the program may fail if it has two threads running concurrently and each thread has its own connection to a server.

4.19.6 CICS Socket Interface

Customer Information Control System (CICS) is a high-performance transaction-processing system. It was developed by IBM and has product implementations in MVS/ESA, MVS, VSE, OS/400, OS/2 and AIX/6000.

CICS is the most widely used Online Transaction Processing (OLTP) system in the marketplace today. It provides a rich set of CICS *command level* APIs to the application transaction programs for data communications (using SNA) and database (using VSAM, IMS or DB2).

Given the need for interoperability among heterogeneous network protocols, there is a requirement to enhance the CICS data communications interface to include support for TCP/IP in addition to SNA. The *IBM Sockets Interface for CICS* is a first step towards addressing this requirement.

4.19.7 IMS Socket Interface

The IMS socket interface is implemented in TCP/IP for OS/390 V2R5.

The IMS to TCP/IP sockets interface allows you to develop IMS message processing programs that can conduct a conversation with peer programs in other TCP/IP hosts. The applications can be either client or server applications. The IMS to TCP/IP sockets interface includes socket interfaces for IBM C/370, assembler language, COBOL, and PL/I languages to use datagram (connectionless) and stream (connection-oriented) sockets. It also provides ASCII-EBCDIC conversion routines, an ASSIST module that permits the use of conventional IMS calls for TCP/IP communications, and a Listener function to listen for and accept connection requests and start the appropriate IMS transaction to service those requests.

4.19.8 Sockets Extended

The Sockets Extended information described here is related to the implementation in MVS only.

Sockets Extended provides programmers writing in assembler language, COBOL, or PL/I with an application program interface that may be used to conduct peer-to-peer conversations with other hosts in the TCP/IP networks. You can develop applications for TSO, batch, CICS, or IMS using this API. The applications may be designed to be reentrant and multithreaded depending upon the application requirements. Typically server applications will be multithreaded while client applications might not be.

4.19.9 REXX Sockets

REXX sockets allow you to develop REXX applications that communicate over a TCP/IP network. Calls are provided to initialize sockets, exchange data via sockets, perform management activities, and close the sockets.

The REXX Socket APIs are implemented in TCP/IP for MVS and OS/2.

Part 2. Special Purpose Protocols and New Technologies

Chapter 5. TCP/IP Security Overview

This chapter discusses security issues regarding TCP/IP networks and provides an overview of solutions to resolve security problems before they can occur. The field of network security in general and of TCP/IP security in particular is too wide to be dealt with in an all encompassing way in this book, so the focus of this chapter is on the most common security exposures and measures to counteract them. Because many, if not all, security solutions are based on cryptographic algorithms, we also provide a brief overview of this topic for the better understanding of concepts presented throughout this chapter.

5.1 Security Exposures and Solutions

This section gives an overview of some of the most common attacks on computer security, and it presents viable solutions to those exposures and lists actual implementations thereof.

5.1.1 Common Attacks Against Security

For thousands of years, people have been guarding the gates to where they store their treasures and assets. Failure to do so usually resulted in being robbed, neglected by society or even killed. Though things are usually not as dramatic anymore, they can still become very bad. Modern day I/T managers have realized that it is equally important to protect their communications networks against intruders and saboteurs from both inside and outside. One does not have to be overly paranoid to find some good reasons as to why this is the case:

- Tapping the wire: to get access to cleartext data and passwords

- Impersonation: to get unauthorized access to data or to create unauthorized e-mails, orders, etc.

- Denial-of-service: to render network resources non-functional

- Replay of messages: to get access to and change information in transit

- Guessing of passwords: to get access to information and services that would normally be denied (dictionary attack)

- Guessing of keys: to get access to encrypted data and passwords (brute-force attack)

- Viruses: to destroy data

Though these attacks are not exclusively specific to TCP/IP networks, they should be considered potential threats to anyone who is going to base their network on TCP/IP, which is what the majority of enterprises, organizations and small businesses around the world are doing today. Hackers do likewise and hence find easy prey.

5.1.2 Solutions to Network Security Problems

With the same zealousness that intruders search for a way to get into someone's computer network, the owners of such networks should, and most likely will, try to protect themselves. Taking on the exposures mentioned before, here are some solutions to effectively defend oneself against an attack. It has to be noted that any of those solutions only solve a single or just a very limited number of security problems. Therefore, a combination of several such solutions should be considered in order to guarantee a certain level of safety and security.

- Encryption: to protect data and passwords

- Authentication and authorization: to prevent improper access

- Integrity checking and message authentication codes: to protect against improper alteration of messages

- Non-repudiation: to make sure that an action cannot be denied by the person who performed it

- Digital signatures and certificates: to ascertain a party's identity

- One-time passwords and two-way random number handshakes: to mutually authenticate parties of a conversation

- Frequent key refresh, strong keys and prevention of deriving future keys: to protect against breaking of keys (cryptanalysis)

- Address concealment: to protect against denial-of-service attacks

Table 10 matches common problems and security exposures to the solutions listed above:

Table 10 (Page 1 of 2). Security Exposures and Protections

Problem / Exposure	Remedy
How to prevent wire tappers from reading messages?	Encrypt messages, typically using a shared secret key. (Secret keys offer a tremendous performance advantage over public/private keys.)
How to distribute the keys in a secure way?	Use a different encryption technique, typically public/private keys.

Table 10 (Page 2 of 2). Security Exposures and Protections

Problem / Exposure	Remedy
How to prevent keys from becoming stale, and how to protect against guessing of future keys by cracking current keys?	Refresh keys frequently and do not derive new keys from old ones (use perfect forward secrecy).
How to prevent retransmission of messages by an impostor (replay attack)?	Use sequence numbers. (Time stamps are usually unreliable for security purposes.)
How to make sure that a message has not been altered in transit?	Use message digests (hash or one-way functions).
How to make sure that the message digest has not also been compromised?	Use digital signatures by encrypting the message digest with a secret or private key (origin authentication, non-repudiation).
How to make sure that the message and signature originated from the desired partner?	Use two-way handshakes involving encrypted random numbers (mutual authentication).
How to make sure that handshakes are exchanged with the right partners (man-in-the-middle attack)?	Use digital certificates (binding of public keys to permanent identities).
How to prevent improper use of services by otherwise properly authenticated users?	Use a multi-layer access control model.
How to protect against viruses?	Restrict access to outside sources; run anti-virus software on every server and workstation that has contact to outside data, and update that software frequently.
How to protect against unwanted or malicious messages (denial-of-service attacks)?	Restrict access to internal network using filters, firewalls, proxies, packet authentication, conceal internal address and name structure, etc.

In general, keep your network tight towards the outside but also keep a watchful eye at the inside because most attacks are mounted from inside a corporate network.

5.1.3 Implementations of Security Solutions

The following protocols and systems are commonly used to provide various degrees of security services in a computer network. They are introduced in detail later in this chapter.

- IP filtering
- Network Address Translation (NAT)
- IP Security Architecture (IPSec)
- SOCKS
- Secure Sockets Layer (SSL)

- Application proxies

- Firewalls

- Kerberos and other authentication systems (AAA servers)

- Secure Electronic Transactions (SET)

Figure 151 illustrates where those security solutions fit within the TCP/IP layers:

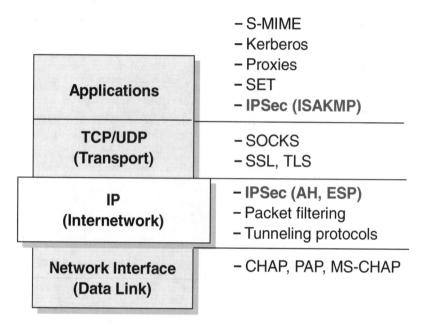

Figure 151. *Security Solutions in the TCP/IP Layers*

Table 11 summarizes the characteristics of some of the security solutions mentioned before and compares them to each other. This should help anyone who needs to devise a security strategy to determine what combination of solutions would achieve a desired level of protection.

Table 11 (Page 1 of 2). *Security Solution Implementations - A Comparison*							
	Access Control	Encryption	Authenti-cation	Integrity Checking	PFS	Address Conceal-ment	Session Monitoring
IP Filtering	y	n	n	n	n	n	n

Table 11 (Page 2 of 2). Security Solution Implementations - A Comparison

	Access Control	Encryption	Authenti-cation	Integrity Checking	PFS	Address Conceal-ment	Session Monitoring
NAT	y	n	n	n	n	y	y (connection)
IPSec	y	y (packet)	y (packet)	y (packet)	y	y	n
SOCKS	y	n	y (client/user)	n	n	y	y (connection)
SSL	y	y (data)	y (system/ user)	y		n	y
Application Proxy	y	normally no	y (user)	y	normally no	y	y (connection and data)
AAA servers	y (user)	n	y (user)	n	n	n	n

As mentioned earlier, an overall security solution can, in most cases, only be provided by a combination of the listed options, for instance by using a firewall. However, what one's particular security requirements are needs to be specified in a security policy.

5.1.4 Network Security Policy

An organization's overall security policy must be determined according to security analysis and business needs analysis. Since a firewall relates to network security only, a firewall has little value unless the overall security policy is properly defined.

Network security policy defines those services that will be explicitly allowed or denied, how these services will be used and the exceptions to these rules. Every rule in the network security policy should be implemented on a firewall and/or remote access server (RAS). Generally, a firewall uses one of the following methods.

Everything not specifically permitted is denied

This approach blocks all traffic between two networks except for those services and applications that are permitted. Therefore, each desired service and application should be implemented one by one. No service or application that might be a potential hole on the firewall should be permitted. This is the most secure method, denying services and applications unless explicitly allowed by the administrator. On the other hand, from the point of users, it might be more restrictive and less convenient.

Everything not specifically denied is permitted

> This approach allows all traffic between two networks except for those services and applications that are denied. Therefore, each untrusted or potentially harmful service or application should be denied one by one. Although this is a flexible and convenient method for the users, it could potentially cause some serious security problems.

Remote access servers should provide authentication of users and should ideally also provide for limiting certain users to certain systems and/or networks within the corporate intranet (authorization). Remote access servers must also determine if a user is considered roaming (can connect from multiple remote locations) or stationary (can connect only from a single remote location), and if the server should use call-back for particular users once they are properly authenticated.

Generally, anonymous access should at best be granted to servers in a demilitarized zone (DMZ, see 5.3.6.4, "Screened Subnet Firewall (Demilitarized Zone)" on page 373). All services within a corporate intranet should require at least password authentication and appropriate access control. Direct access from the outside should always be authenticated and accounted.

5.2 A Short Introduction to Cryptography

The purpose of this chapter is to introduce the terminology and give a brief overview of the major cryptographic concepts that relate to TCP/IP security implementations. The information presented here only scratches the surface. Some issues are left open or not mentioned at all.

5.2.1 Terminology

Let's start with defining some very basic concepts.

Cryptography

> Put simply, cryptography is the science of keeping your data and communications secure. To achieve this goal, techniques such as *encryption, decryption* and *authentication* are used. With the recent advances in this field, the frontiers of cryptography have become blurred. Every procedure consisting of transforming data based on methods that are difficult to reverse can be considered cryptography. The key factor to strong cryptography is the difficulty of reverse engineering. You would be amazed to know that breaking simple methods such as password-scrambled word processor documents or compressed archives is a matter of minutes for a hacker using an ordinary PC. *Strong* cryptography means that the computational effort needed to retrieve your

cleartext messages without knowing the proper procedure makes the retrieval infeasible. In this context, infeasible means something like this: if all the computers in the world were assigned to the problem, they would have to work tens of thousands of years until the solution was found. The process of retrieval is called *cryptanalysis*. An attempted cryptanalysis is an *attack*.

Encryption and Decryption - Cryptographic Algorithms

Encryption is the transformation of a cleartext message into an unreadable form in order to hide its meaning. The opposite transformation, which retrieves the original cleartext, is the decryption. The mathematical function used for encryption and decryption is the *cryptographic algorithm* or *cipher*.

The security of a cipher might be based entirely on keeping how it works secret, in which case it is a *restricted* cipher. There are many drawbacks to restricted ciphers. It is very difficult to keep in secret an algorithm used by many people. If it is incorporated in a commercial product, then it is only a matter of time and money to get it reverse engineered. For these reasons, the currently used algorithms are *keyed*, that is, the encryption and decryption makes use of a parameter, the *key*. The key can be chosen from a set of possible values, called the *keyspace*. The keyspace usually is huge, the bigger the better. The security of these algorithms rely entirely on the key, not on their internal secrets. In fact the algorithms themselves are public and are extensively analyzed for possible weaknesses.

Note: As a general rule, be conservative. Do not trust brand new, unknown or unpublished algorithms. The principle of the keyed ciphers is shown in Figure 152.

Secret Key   **Secret Key**

Encryption   Decryption

Cleartext   Ciphertext   Original Cleartext

Alice   **Bob**

Figure 152. Keyed Encryption and Decryption

Note: It is common in the cryptographic literature to denote the first participant in a protocol as Alice and the second one as Bob. They are the "crypto couple".

Authentication, Integrity, and Non-Repudiation

Encryption provides confidentiality to your messages. When communicating over an untrusted medium, such as the Internet, besides confidentiality, you need more:

- *Authentication* - A method for verifying that the sender of a message is really who he or she claims to be. Any intruder masquerading as someone else is detected by authentication.

- *Integrity checking* - A method for verifying that a message has not been altered along the communication path. Any tampered message sent by an intruder is detected by integrity check. As a side effect, communication errors are also detected.

- *Non-repudiation* - The possibility to prove that the sender has really sent the message. When algorithms providing non-repudiation are used, the sender is not able to later deny the fact that he or she sent the message in question.

5.2.2 Symmetric or Secret-Key Algorithms

The symmetric algorithms are keyed algorithms where the decryption key is the same as the encryption key. These are the conventional cryptographic algorithms where the sender and the receiver must agree on the key *before* any secured communication can take place between them. Figure 152 on page 343 illustrates a symmetric algorithm. There are two types of symmetric algorithms: *block algorithms*, which operate on the cleartext in blocks of bits, and *stream algorithms*, which operate on a single bit (or byte) of cleartext at a time.

Block ciphers are used in several *modes*. *Electronic Codebook Mode (ECB)* is the simplest; each block of cleartext is encrypted independently. Given a block length of 64 bits, there are 2^{64} possible input cleartext blocks, each of them corresponding to exactly one out of 2^{64} possible ciphertext blocks. An intruder might construct a codebook with known cleartext-ciphertext pairs and mount an attack. Because of this vulnerability, often the *Cipher Block Chaining (CBC)* mode is used, where the result of the encryption of the previous block is used in the encryption of the current block, thus each ciphertext block is dependent not just on the corresponding plaintext block, but on all previous plaintext blocks.

The algorithms often make use of *initialization vectors (IVs)*. These are variables independent of the keys and are good for setting up the initial state of the algorithms.

A well-known block algorithm is DES, a worldwide standard cipher developed by IBM. DES is an acronym for Data Encryption Standard. DES operates on 64-bit blocks and has a key length of 56 bits, often expressed as a 64-bit number, with every eighth bit serving as parity bit. From this key 16 subkeys are derived, which are used in the 16 rounds of the algorithm.

DES produces ciphertexts of the same length as the cleartext and the decryption algorithm is exactly the same as the encryption, the only difference being the subkey schedule. These properties makes it very suitable for hardware implementations.

Although DES is aging (its origins dates back to the early '70s), after more then 20 years of analysis the algorithm itself is still considered secure. The most practical attack against it is *brute-force*: try the decryption with all possible keys and look for a meaningful result. The problem is the key length. Given enough money and time, a brute-force attack against the 56-bit key might be feasible; that's why recently a new mode of DES, called triple-DES or 3DES has gained popularity. With triple-DES, the original DES algorithm is applied in three rounds, with two or three different keys. This encryption is thought to be unbreakable for a long time, even with the foreseeable technological advances taken into account.

An exportable version of DES is IBM's Commercial Data Masking Facility or CDMF, which uses a 40-bit key.

Another, more recent block algorithm is the *International Data Encryption Algorithm (IDEA)*. This cipher uses 64-bit blocks and 128-bit keys. It was developed in the early '90s and aimed to replace DES. It is cryptographically strong and faster than DES. Despite this, there is no widespread commercial acceptance, mainly because it is relatively new and not fully analyzed. The most significant use of IDEA is in the freeware secure e-mail package Pretty Good Privacy (PGP).

An example of a stream algorithm is A5, which is used to encrypt digital cellular telephony traffic in the GSM standard, widely used in Europe.

The advantage of the symmetric algorithms is their efficiency. They can be easily implemented in hardware. A major disadvantage is the difficulty of key management. A secure way of exchanging the keys must exist, which is often very hard to implement.

5.2.3 Asymmetric or Public-Key Algorithms

These algorithms address the major drawback of the symmetric ones, the requirement of the secure key-exchange channel. The idea is that two different keys should be used: a public key, which as the name implies, is known to everyone, and a private key, which is to be kept in tight security by the owner. The private key cannot be determined from the public key. A cleartext encrypted with the public key can only be decrypted with the corresponding private key, and vice versa. A cleartext encrypted with the private key can only be decrypted with the corresponding public key. Thus, if someone sends a message encrypted with the recipient's public key, it can be read by the intended recipient only. The process is shown in Figure 153, where Alice sends an encrypted message to Bob.

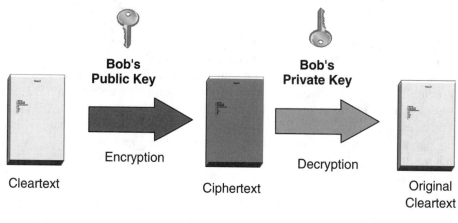

Alice   **Bob**

Figure 153. Encryption Using the Recipient's Public Key

As the public key is available to anyone, privacy is assured without the need for a secure key-exchange channel. Parties who wish to communicate retrieve each other's public key.

5.2.3.1 Authentication and Non-Repudiation

An interesting property of the public-key algorithms is that they can provide authentication. Use the private key for encryption. Since anyone has access to the corresponding public key and can decrypt the message, this provides no privacy. However, it authenticates the message. If one can successfully decrypt it with the claimed sender's public key, then the message has been encrypted with the corresponding private key, which is known by the real sender only. Thus, the sender's identity is verified. The encryption with the private key is used in *digital signatures*. In Figure 154 on page 347 the principle is shown. Alice encrypts her message with her private key ("signs" it), in order to enable Bob to verify the authenticity of the message.

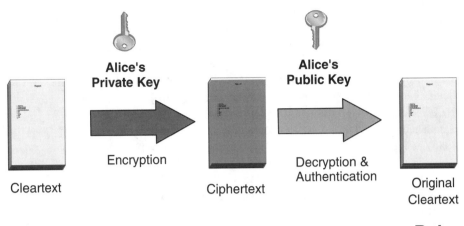

Alice's Private Key

Alice's Public Key

Cleartext — Encryption — Ciphertext — Decryption & Authentication — Original Cleartext

Alice

Bob

Figure 154. Authentication by Encrypting with a Private Key

Going a step forward, encrypting with the private key gives non-repudiation too. The mere existence of such an encrypted message testifies that the originator has really sent it, because only he or she could have used the private key to generate the message. Additionally, if a timestamp is included, then the exact date and time can also be proven. There are protocols involving trusted third parties that prevent the sender from using phony timestamps.

Note: Inspired by the "stamping" idea, the IPSec architecture makes use of sequence numbers (instead of timestamps), to achieve replay protection.

5.2.3.2 Examples of Public-Key Algorithms

Algorithms based on public keys can be used for a variety of purposes. Two common applications are:

1. Encryption (see "RSA Public Key Algorithm" on page 348)
2. Generation of shared keys for use with symmetric key algorithms (see "Diffie-Hellman Key Exchange" on page 349)

The most popular public-key algorithm is the de-facto standard *RSA*, named after the three inventors: Ron Rivest, Adi Shamir and Leonard Adleman. The security of RSA relies on the difficult problem of factoring large numbers. The public and private keys are functions of two very large (200 digits or even more) prime numbers. Given the public key and the ciphertext, an attack would be successful if it could factor the product of the two primes. RSA has resisted many years of extensive attacks. As computing power grows, keeping RSA secure is a matter of increasing the key length. (As opposed to DES, where the key length is fixed.)

Another public-key algorithm, actually the very first ever invented, is *Diffie-Hellman*. This is a key-exchange algorithm; that is, it is used for securely establishing a shared secret over an insecure channel. The communicating parties exchange public information from which they derive a key. An eavesdropper cannot reconstruct the key from the information that went through the insecure channel. (More precisely, the reconstruction is computationally infeasible.) The security of Diffie-Hellman relies on the difficulty of calculating discrete logarithms in finite fields. After the shared secret has been established, it can then be used to derive keys for use with symmetric key algorithms such as DES.

Diffie-Hellman makes possible the secure derivation of a shared secret key, but it does not authenticate the parties. For authentication another public-key algorithm must be used, such as RSA.

Unfortunately, public-key algorithms while providing for easier key management, privacy, authentication and non-repudiation also have some disadvantages. The most important one is that they are slow and difficult to implement in hardware. For example, RSA is 100 to 10000 times slower than DES, depending on implementation. Because of this, public-key algorithms generally are not used for bulk encryption. Their most important use is key exchange and authentication. Another notable disadvantage is that they are susceptible to certain cryptanalytic attacks to which symmetric algorithms are resistant.

Therefore, a good cryptographic system (*cryptosystem*) makes use of both worlds. It uses public-key algorithms in the session establishment phase for authentication and key exchange, then a symmetric one for encrypting the consequent messages.

For the interested reader, below we give more detailed information of the two most important asymmetric algorithms. Both of them involve modular arithmetics. An arithmetic operation modulo m means that the result of that operation is divided by m and the remainder is taken. For example: $3 * 6 \bmod 4 = 2$, since $3 * 6 = 18$ and dividing 18 by 4 gives us 2 as the remainder.

RSA Public Key Algorithm: RSA is used in the ISAKMP/Oakley framework as one of the possible authentication methods. The principle of the RSA algorithm is as follows:

1. Take two large primes, p and q.

2. Find their product $n = pq$; n is called the modulus.

3. Choose a number, e, less than n and relatively prime to $(p-1)(q-1)$ which means that e and $(p-1)(q-1)$ have no common factor other than 1.

4. Find its inverse, d mod (p-1)(q-1) which means that ed = 1 mod (p-1)(q-1).

e and d are called the public and private exponents, respectively. The public key is the pair (n,e); the private key is d. The factors p and q must be kept secret or destroyed.

A simplified example of RSA encryption would be the following:

1. Suppose Alice wants to send a private message, m, to Bob. Alice creates the ciphertext c by exponentiating:

   $c = m^e \bmod n$

   where e and n are Bob's public key.

2. Alice sends c to Bob.

3. To decrypt, Bob exponentiates:

   $m = c^d \bmod n$

   and recovers the original message; the relationship between e and d ensures that Bob correctly recovers m. Since only Bob knows d, only Bob can decrypt the ciphertext.

A simplified example of RSA authentication would be the following:

1. Suppose Alice wants to send a signed message, m, to Bob. Alice creates a digital signature s by exponentiating:

   $s = m^d \bmod n$

   where d and n belong to Alice's private key.

2. She sends s and m to Bob.

3. To verify the signature, Bob exponentiates and checks if the result, compares to m:

   $m = s^e \bmod n$

   where e and n belong to Alice's public key.

Diffie-Hellman Key Exchange: The Diffie-Hellman key exchange is a crucial component of the ISAKMP/Oakley framework. In the earliest phase of a key negotiation session there is no secure channel in place. The parties derive shared secret keys using the Diffie-Hellman algorithm. These keys will be used in the next steps of the key negotiation protocol.

The outline of the algorithm is the following:

1. The parties (Alice and Bob) share two public values, a modulus m and an integer g; m should be a large prime number.

2. Alice generates a large random number a and computes:

$$X = g^a \bmod m$$

3. Bob generates a large random number b and computes:

$$Y = g^b \bmod m$$

4. Alice sends X to Bob.

5. Bob computes:

$$K1 = X^b \bmod m$$

6. Bob sends Y to Alice.

7. Alice computes:

$$K2 = Y^a \bmod m$$

Both K1 and K2 are equal to $g^{ab} \bmod m$. This is the shared secret key. No one is able to generate this value without knowing a or b. The security of the exchange is based on the fact that is extremely difficult to inverse the exponentiation performed by the parties. (In other words, to find out discrete logarithms in finite fields of size m.) Similar to RSA, advances in adversary computing power can be countered by choosing larger initial values, in this case a larger modulus m.

Please see Chapter 11, "Availability, Scalability and Load Balancing" on page 681 for more details on how ISAKMP/Oakley uses Diffie-Hellman exchanges.

5.2.4 Hash Functions

Hash functions (also called message digests) are fundamental to cryptography. A hash function is a function that takes variable-length input data and produces fixed length output data (the hash value), which can be regarded as the "fingerprint" of the input. That is, if the hashes of two messages match, then we get a high assurance that the messages are the same.

Cryptographically useful hash functions must be *one-way*, which means that they should be easy to compute, but infeasible to reverse. An everyday example of a one-way function is mashing a potato; it is easy to do, but once mashed, reconstructing the original potato is rather difficult. A good hash function should be *collision-resistant*. It should be hard to find two different inputs that hash to the same value. As any hash function maps an input set to a smaller output set, theoretically it is possible to find collisions. The point is to provide a unique digital "fingerprint" of the message, that identifies it with high confidence, much like a real fingerprint identifying a person.

A hash function that takes a key as a second input parameter and its output depends on both the message and the key is called a *Message Authentication Code (MAC)*, as shown in Figure 155.

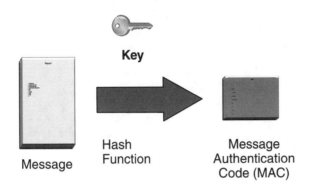

Key

Message Hash Function Message Authentication Code (MAC)

Figure 155. *Generating a Message Authentication Code (MAC)*

Put simply, if you encrypt a hash, it becomes a MAC. If you add a secret key to a message, then hash the concatenation, the result is a MAC. Both symmetric and asymmetric algorithms can be used to generate MACs.

Hash functions are primarily used in integrity check and authentication techniques. Let's see how integrity and authentication is assured with hash functions:

- The sender calculates the hash of the message and appends it to the message.

- The recipient calculates the hash of the received message and then compares the result with the transmitted hash.

- If the hashes match, the message was not tampered with.

- In case of MACs where the encryption key (symmetric or asymmetric) should have been used by a trusted sender only, a successful MAC decryption indicates that the claimed and actual senders are identical. (Unless, of course, your keys have been compromised.)

See Figure 156 on page 352 for an illustration of the procedure. The Message* and MAC* notations reflect the fact that the message might have been altered while crossing the untrusted channel.

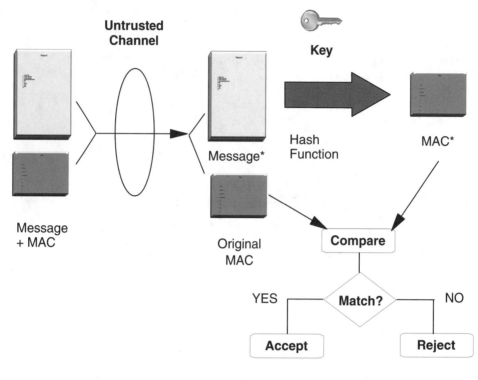

Alice   **Bob**

Figure 156. Checking Integrity and Authenticity with MAC

One could argue that the same result can be obtained with any kind of encryption, because if an intruder modifies an encrypted message, the decryption will result in nonsense, thus tampering can be detected. The answer is that many times only integrity and/or authentication is needed, maybe with encryption on some of the fields of the message. And encryption is very processor-intensive. (Examples are the personal banking machine networks, where only the PINs are encrypted, however MACs are widely used. Encrypting all the messages in their entirety would not yield noticeable benefits and performance would dramatically decrease.)

The encryption of a hash with the private key is called a *digital signature*. It can be thought of as a special MAC. Using digital signatures instead of encrypting the whole message with the private key leads to considerable performance gains and a remarkable new property. The authentication part can be decoupled from the document itself. This property is used for example in the Secure Electronic Transactions (SET) protocol.

The encryption of a secret key with a public key is called a *digital envelope*. This is a common technique used to distribute secret keys for symmetric algorithms.

5.2.4.1 Examples of Hash Functions

The most widely used hash functions are MD5 and Secure Hash Algorithm 1 (SHA-1). MD5 was designed by Ron Rivest (co-inventor of RSA). SHA-1 is largely inspired from MD5 and was designed by the National Institute of Standards and Technology (NIST) and the National Security Agency (NSA) for use with the Digital Signature Standard (DSS). MD5 produces a 128-bit hash, while SHA-1 produces a 160-bit hash. Both functions encode the message length in their output. SHA-1 is regarded as more secure, because of the larger hashes it produces.

Note: Neither MD5 nor SHA-1 takes a key as input parameter, hence in their original implementation they cannot be used for MAC calculation. However, for this purpose it is easy to concatenate a key with the input data and apply the function to the result. In practice, for example in IPSec, often more sophisticated schemes are used.

Keyed MD5 and Keyed SHA-1: Using MD5 and SHA-1 in keyed mode is simple. The shared secret key and the datagram to be protected are both input to the hash algorithm and the output (the hash value) is placed in the Authentication Data field of the AH Header, as it is shown in Figure 157.

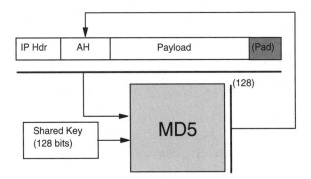

Figure 157. Keyed MD5 Processing

Keyed SHA-1 operates in the same way, the only difference being the larger 160-bit hash value.

HMAC-MD5-96 and HMAC-SHA-1-96: A stronger method is the Hashed Message Authentication Code (HMAC), proposed by IBM. HMAC itself is not a hash function, rather a cryptographically strong way to use a specific hash function for MAC calculation.

Here is how HMAC works, considering MD5 as an example. The base function is applied twice in succession. In the first round the input to MD5 is the shared secret key and the datagram. The 128-bit output hash value and the key is input again to the hash function in the second round. The leftmost 96 bits of the resulting hash value are used as the MAC for the datagram. See Figure 158 for an illustration.

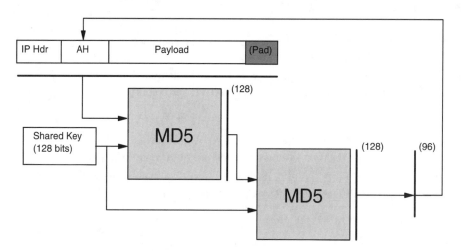

Figure 158. HMAC-MD5-96 Processing

HMAC-SHA-1-96 operates in the same way, except that the intermediary results are 160 bits long.

Digital Signature Standard (DSS): As mentioned previously, a hash value encrypted with the private key is called a *digital signature* and is illustrated in Figure 159 on page 355.

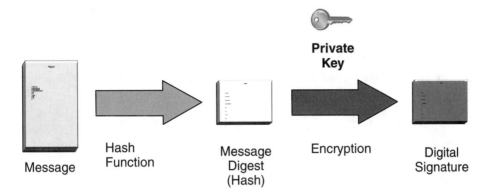

Private
Key

Message   Hash
Function   Message
Digest
(Hash)   Encryption   Digital
Signature

Figure 159. *Generating a Digital Signature*

One authentication method that can be used with ISAKMP/Oakley is DSS which was selected by NIST and NSA to be the digital authentication standard of the U.S. government. The standard describes the Digital Signature Algorithm (DSA) used to sign and verify signatures of message digests produced with SHA-1.

A brief description of DSA is given below:

1. Choose a large prime number, p, usually between 512 and 1024 bits long.

2. Find a prime factor q of (p-1), 160 bits long.

3. Compute:

    $g = h^{(p-1)/q} \bmod p$

    where h is a number less than (p-1) and the following is true:

    $h^{(p-1)/q} > 1$

4. Choose another number x, less than q, as the sender's private key.

5. Compute:

    $y = g^x \bmod p$

    and use that as the sender's public key. The pair (x,y) is sometimes referred to as the long-term key pair.

6. The sender signs the message as follows:

    a. Generate a random number, k, less than q.
    b. Compute:

    $r = (g^k \bmod p) \bmod q$

    $s = (k^{-1}(SHA1(m) + xr)) \bmod q$

The pair (k,r) is sometimes referred to as the per-session key pair, and the signature is represented by the pair (r,s).

7. The sender sends (m,r,s).

8. The receiver verifies the signature as follows:

    a. Compute:

       ```
       w=s⁻¹ mod q
       ```

       ```
       u1=(SHA1(m)*w) mod q
       ```

       ```
       u2=(rw) mod q
       ```

       ```
       v=((gᵘ¹yᵘ²) mod p) mod q
       ```

9. If v=r, then the signature is verified.

5.2.5 Digital Certificates and Certification Authorities

As we said before in 5.2.3.1, "Authentication and Non-Repudiation" on page 346, with public-key cryptography, the parties retrieve each other's public key. There are security exposures here. An intruder could change some real public keys with his or her own public key, and then mount a so-called *man-in-the-middle attack*. It works like this. The intruder places himself between Alice and Bob. He can trick Bob by sending him one of his own public keys as if it were Alice's. The same applies to Alice. She thinks she uses Bob's public key, but the sour reality is that she actually uses the intruder's. So the clever intruder can decrypt the confidential traffic between the two and remain undetected. For example, a message sent by Alice and encrypted with "Bob's" public key lands at the intruder, who decrypts it, learns its content, then re-encrypts it with Bob's real public key. Bob has no way to realize that Alice is using a phony public key.

An intruder could also use impersonation, claiming to be somebody else, for example an online shopping mall, fouling innocent shoppers.

The solution to these serious threats is the *digital certificate*. A digital certificate is a file that binds an identity to the associated public key. This binding is validated by a trusted third party, the *certification authority (CA)*. A digital certificate is signed with the private key of the certification authority, so it can be authenticated. It is only issued after a verification of the applicant. Apart from the public key and identification, a digital certificate usually contains other information too, such as:

- Date of issue

- Expiry date

- Miscellaneous information from issuing CA (for example, serial number)

Note: There is an international standard in place for digital certificates: the ISO X.509 protocols.

Now the picture looks different. The parties retrieve each other's digital certificate and authenticate it using the public key of the issuing certification authority. They have confidence that the public keys are real, because a trusted third party vouches for them. The malicious online shopping mall is put out of business.

It easy to imagine that one CA cannot cover all needs. What happens when Bob's certificate is issued by a CA unknown to Alice? Can she trust that unknown authority? Well, this is entirely her decision, but to make life easier, CAs can form a hierarchy, often referred to as the *trust chain*. Each member in the chain has a certificate signed by it superior authority. The higher the CA is in the chain, the tighter security procedures are in place. The root CA is trusted by everyone and its private key is top secret.

Alice can traverse the chain upwards until she finds a CA that she trusts. The traversal consists of verifying the subordinate CA's public key and identity using the certificate issued to it by the superior CA.

When a trusted CA is found up in the chain, Alice is assured that Bob's issuing CA is trustworthy. In fact this is all about delegation of trust. We trust your identity card if somebody who we trust signs it. And if the signer is unknown to us, we can go upward and see who signs for the signer, etc.

An implementation of this concept can be found in the SET protocol, where the major credit card brands operate their own CA hierarchies that converge to a common root. Lotus Notes authentication, as another example, is also based on certificates, and it can be implemented using hierarchical trust chains. PGP also uses a similar approach, but its trust chain is based on persons and it is rather a distributed Web than a strict hierarchical tree.

5.2.6 Random-Number Generators

An important component of a cryptosystem is the random-number generator. Many times random session keys and random initialization variables (often referred to as initialization vectors) are generated. For example, DES requires an explicit initialization vector and Diffie-Hellman relies on picking random numbers which serve as input for the key derivation.

The quality, that is the randomness of these generators, is more important than you would think. The ordinary random function provided with most programming language libraries is good enough for games, but not for cryptography. Those random-number generators are rather predictable; if you rely on them, be prepared for happy cryptanalysts finding interesting correlations in your encrypted output.

The fundamental problem faced by the random-number generators is that the computers are ultimately deterministic machines, so real random sequences cannot be produced. As John von Neumann ironically said: "Anyone who considers arithmetical methods of producing random digits is, of course, in a state of sin". (Quoted by Donald Knuth.) That's why the term *pseudorandom generator* is more appropriate.

Cryptographically strong pseudorandom generators must be unpredictable. It must be computationally infeasible to determine the next random bit, even with total knowledge of the generator.

A common practical solution for pseudorandom generators is to use hash functions. This approach provides sufficient randomness and it can be efficiently implemented. Military-grade generators use specialized devices that exploit the inherent randomness in physical phenomena. An interesting solution can be found in the PGP software. The initial seed of the pseudorandom generator is derived from measuring the time elapsed between the keystrokes of the user.

5.2.7 Export/Import Restrictions on Cryptography

U.S. export regulations changed in 1996, which put cryptography under the control of the Commerce Department. It had formerly been treated as a munition. This is a significant step in liberalizing the export of cryptographic products.

According to the new export regulations a license may be granted to export a 56-bit key encryption algorithm if a company has an approved key recovery plan. The key recovery plan must be implemented in 2 years and the license is granted on a 6 month basis.

In 1997 IBM was granted the license to export DES as long as it was used similar to other products that have been approved. Recently, the export of triple-DES has been allowed for banking applications.

In September 1998, the White House announced further liberalization of U.S. export restrictions on cryptographic material and key recovery requirements which can be sumarized as follows:

- The key recovery requirement for export of 56-bit DES and equivalent products is eliminated. This includes products that use 1024-bit asymmetric key exchanges together with 56-bit symmetric key algorithms.

- Export of unlimited strength encryption (for example, 3DES) under license exceptions (with or without key recovery) is now broadened to include others besides the financial industry for 45 countries. This includes subsidiaries of U.S firms, insurance, health and medical (excluding biochemical and pharmaceutical manufacturers), and online merchants for the purpose of securing online transactions (excluding distributors of items considered munitions).

  For the latter, revocerable products will be granted exceptions world wide (excluding terrorist countries) without requiring a review of foreign key recovery agents.

- Export of recoverable products will be granted to most most commercial firms for a broad range of countries in the major commercial markets (excluding items on the U.S. munitions list).

- Export licenses to end users may be granted on a case-by-case basis.

These regulations are expected to be formally published by the U.S. Export Regulation Office in November 1998.

In France, according to the law, any product capable of enciphering/deciphering user data should be granted a license from the French government before being marketed. Then customers need to be authorized to use them on a case-by-case basis. In reality, two major and useful exceptions exist:

1. Routinely, licenses are granted that allow banks to use DES products on a global basis (no case-by-case authorization required).
2. Routinely, global licenses are granted that allow anybody to use weak encryption (RC2/RC4 with 40-bit keys).

5.3 Firewalls

Firewalls have significant functions in an organization's security policy. Therefore, it is important to understand these functions and apply them to the network properly. This chapter explains the firewall concept, network security, firewall components and firewall examples.

5.3.1 Firewall Concept

A firewall is a system (or group of systems) that enforces a security policy between a secure internal network and an untrusted network such as the Internet. Firewalls tend to be seen as a protection between the Internet and a private network. But generally speaking a firewall should be considered as a means to divide the world into two or more networks: one or more secure networks and one or more non-secure networks.

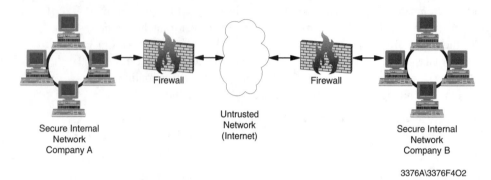

Figure 160. *A Firewall Illustration*

A firewall can be a PC, a router, a midrange, a mainframe, a UNIX workstation, or a combination of these that determines which information or services can be accessed from the outside and who is permitted to use the information and services from outside. Generally, a firewall is installed at the point where the secure internal network and untrusted external network meet which is also known as a *choke point*.

In order to understand how a firewall works, consider the network to be a building to which access must be controlled. The building has a lobby as the only entry point. In this lobby, receptionists welcome visitors, security guards watch visitors, video cameras record visitor actions and badge readers authenticate visitors who enter the building.

Although these procedures may work well to control access to the building, if an unauthorized person succeeds in entering, there is no way to protect the building against this intruder's actions. However, if the intruder's movements are monitored, it may be possible to detect any suspicious activity.

Similarly, a firewall is designed to protect the information resources of the organization by controlling the access between the internal secure network and the untrusted external network (please see Figure 161 on page 361). However, it is important to note that even if the firewall is designed to permit the trusted data to pass through, deny the vulnerable services and prevent the internal network from outside attacks, a newly created attack may penetrate the firewall at any time. The network administrator must examine all logs and alarms generated by the firewall on a regular basis. Otherwise, it is not possible to protect the internal network from outside attacks.

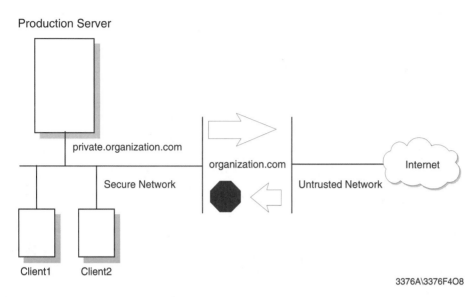

Figure 161. A Firewall Controls Traffic Between the Secure Network and the Internet

5.3.2 Components of A Firewall System

As mentioned previously, a firewall can be a PC, a midrange, a mainframe, a UNIX workstation, a router, or combination of these. Depending on the requirements, a firewall can consist of one or more of the following functional components:

1. Packet-filtering router

2. Application level gateway (Proxy)

3. Circuit level gateway

Each of these components has different functions and shortcomings. Generally, in order to build an effective firewall, these components are used together.

5.3.3 Packet-Filtering Router

Most of the time, packet-filtering is accomplished by using a router that can forward packets according to filtering rules. When a packet arrives at the packet-filtering router, the router extracts certain information from the packet header and makes decisions according to the filter rules as to whether the packet will pass through or be discarded (please see Figure 162 on page 362). The following information can be extracted from the packet header:

- Source IP address
- Destination IP address
- TCP/UDP source port
- TCP/UDP destination port
- ICMP message type
- Encapsulated protocol information (TCP, UDP, ICMP or IP tunnel)

The packet-filtering rules are based on the network security policy (please see 5.1.4, "Network Security Policy" on page 341). Therefore, packet-filtering is done by using these rules as input. When determining the filtering rules, outsider attacks must be taken into consideration as well as service level restrictions and source/destination level restrictions.

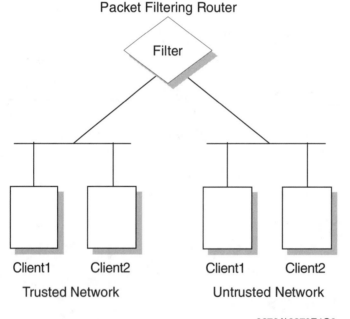

3376A\3376F4O9

Figure 162. Packet Filtering Router

Service Level Filtering

Since most services use well-known TCP/UDP port numbers, it is possible to allow or deny services by using related port information in the filter. For example, an FTP server listens for connections on TCP port 20 and 21. Therefore, to permit FTP connections to pass through to a secure network, the router should be configured to permit packets which contain 20 and 21 as the TCP port in its header. On the other hand, there are some applications, such as NFS, which use RPC and use different ports for each connection. Allowing these kind of services might cause security problems.

Source/Destination Level Filtering

The packet-filtering rules allow a router to permit or deny a packet according to the destination or the source information in the packet header. In most cases, if a service is available, only that particular server is permitted to outside users. Other packets that have another destination or no destination information in their headers are discarded.

Advanced Filtering

As mentioned previously (please see 5.1.1, "Common Attacks Against Security" on page 337), there are different types of attacks that threaten the privacy and network security. Some of them can be discarded by using advanced filtering rules such as checking IP options, fragment offset and so on.

Packet-Filtering Limitations: Packet-filtering rules are sometimes very complex. When there are exceptions to existing rules, it becomes much more complex. Although, there are a few testing utilities available, it is still possible to leave some holes in the network security. Packet filters do not provide an absolute protection for a network. For some cases, it might be necessary to restrict some set of information (for example, a command) from passing through to the internal secure network. It is not possible to control the data with packet filters because they are not capable of understanding the contents of a particular service. For this purpose, an application level control is required.

5.3.4 Application Level Gateway (Proxy)

An application level gateway is often referred to as a *proxy*. Actually, an application level gateway provides higher level control on the traffic between two networks in that the contents of a particular service can be monitored and filtered according to the network security policy. Therefore, for any desired application, corresponding proxy code must be installed on the gateway in order to manage that specific service passing through the gateway (please see Figure 163 on page 364).

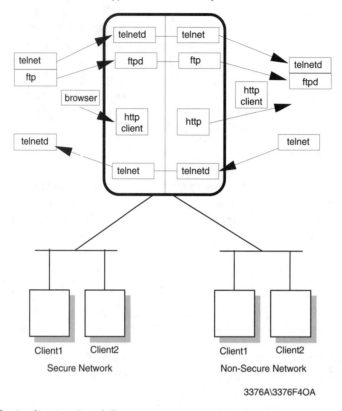

Figure 163. Application Level Gateway

A proxy acts as a server to the client and as a client to the destination server. A virtual connection is established between the client and the destination server. Though the proxy seems to be *transparent* from the point of view of the client and the server, the proxy is capable of monitoring and filtering any specific type of data, such as commands, before sending it to the destination. For example, an FTP server is permitted to be accessed from outside. In order to protect the server from any possible attacks the FTP proxy in the firewall can be configured to deny PUT and MPUT commands.

A proxy server is an application-specific relay server that runs on the host that connects a secure and a non-secure network. The purpose of a proxy server is to control exchange of data between the two networks at an application level instead of an IP level. By using a proxy server, it is possible to disable IP routing between the secure and the non-secure network for the application protocol the proxy server is able to handle, but still be able to exchange data between the networks by relaying it in the proxy server. Figure 164 on page 365 shows an FTP proxy server.

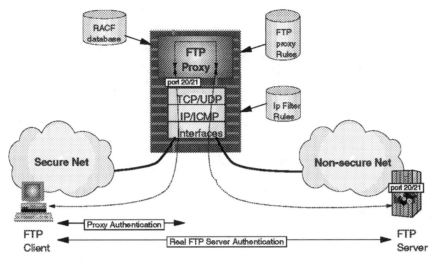

Figure 164. *FTP Proxy Server*

Please note that in order for any client to be able to access the proxy server, the client software must be specifically modified. In other words, the client and server software should support the proxy connection. In the previous example, the FTP client must authenticate itself to the proxy first. If it is successfully authenticated, the FTP session starts based on the proxy restrictions. Most proxy server implementations use more sophisticated authentication methods such as security ID cards. This mechanism generates a unique key which is not reusable for another connection. Two security ID cards are supported by IBM Firewall: the SecureNet card from Axent and the SecureID card from Security Dynamics.

Compared with IP filtering, application level gateways provide much more comprehensive logging based on the application data of the connections. For example, an HTTP proxy can log the URLs visited by users. Another feature of application level gateways is that they use strong user authentication. For example, when using FTP and TELNET services from the unsecure network, users have to authenticate themselves to the proxy. Figure 165 on page 366 shows a proxy server TCP segment flow example.

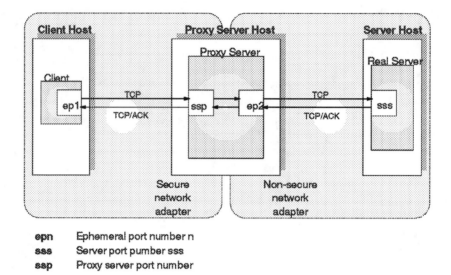

epn	Ephemeral port number n
sss	Server port pumber sss
ssp	Proxy server port number

Figure 165. *Proxy Server TCP Segment Flow*

5.3.4.1 Application Level Gateway Limitations

A disadvantage of application level gateways is that in order to achieve a connection via a proxy server, the client software should be changed to support that proxy service. This can sometimes be achieved by some modifications in user behavior rather than software modification. For example, to connect to a TELNET server over a proxy, the user first has to be authenticated by the proxy server then by the destination TELNET server. This requires two user steps to make a connection rather than one. However, a modified TELNET client can make the proxy server transparent to the user by specifying the destination host rather than proxy server in the TELNET command.

5.3.4.2 An Example: FTP Proxy Server

Most of the time, in order to use the FTP proxy server, users must have a valid user ID and password. On UNIX systems, users also should be defined as users of the UNIX system.

FTP can be used in one of two modes:

1. Normal mode

2. Passive mode

In *normal* mode, the FTP client first connects to the FTP server port 21 to establish a control connection. When data transfer is required (for example, as the result of a

DIR, GET, or PUT command), the client sends a PORT command to the server instructing the server to establish a data connection from the server's data port (port 20) to a specified ephemeral port number on the client host.

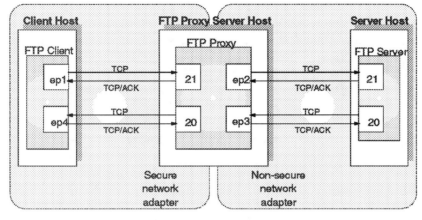

Figure 166. *Normal Mode FTP Proxy*

In an FTP proxy server situation, normal mode means that we have to allow inbound TCP connections from the non-secure network to the FTP proxy host. Notice in Figure 166 how a connection is established from the FTP server port 20 in the non-secure network to the FTP proxy server's ephemeral port number. To allow this to happen, IP filtering rules are used that allow inbound connection requests from port 20 to an ephemeral port number on the FTP proxy host. This is normally not an IP filter rule. It is sometimes better to add a custom filter rule configuration, because it would allow a cracker to run a program on port 20 and scan all the port numbers above 1023, which in its simplest form might result in a denial of service situation.

A much more firewall-friendly mode is the passive mode of operation, as shown in Figure 165 on page 366. This mode has actually been dubbed firewall-friendly FTP, and is described in RFC 1579 *Firewall-Friendly FTP*.

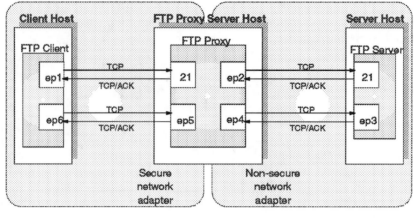

epn   Ephemeral port number n

Figure 167. Passive Mode FTP Proxy (Firewall-Friendly FTP)

In *passive* mode, the FTP client again establishes a control connection to the server's port 21. When data transfer has to start, the client sends a PASV command to the server. The server responds with a port number for the client to contact in order to establish the data connection, and the client then initiates the data connection.

In this setup, to establish connections to both port 21 and any ephemeral port number in the non-secure network, an ephemeral port number is used on the FTP proxy host. However, adding a rule that allows inbound connections to ephemeral port numbers on the FTP proxy server might cause security problems.

5.3.5 Circuit Level Gateway

A circuit level gateway relays TCP and also UDP connections and does not provide any extra packet processing or filtering. A circuit level gateway can be said to be a special type of application level gateway. This is because the application level gateway can be configured to pass all information once the user is authenticated, just as the circuit level gateway (please see Figure 168 on page 369). However, in practice, there are significant differences between them such as:

- Circuit level gateways can handle several TCP/IP applications as well as UDP applications without any extra modifications on the client side for each application. Thus, this makes circuit level gateways a good choice to satisfy user requirements.

- Circuit level gateways do not provide packet processing or filtering. Thus, a circuit level gateway is generally referred to as a *transparent* gateway.

- Application level gateways have a lack of support for UDP.

- Circuit level gateways are often used for outbound connections, whereas application level gateways (proxy) are used for both inbound and outbound connections. Generally, in cases of using both types combined, circuit level gateways can be used for outbound connections and application level gateways can be used for inbound connections to satisfy both security and user requirements.

A well known example of a circuit level gateway is SOCKS (please refer to 5.6, "SOCKS" on page 417 for more information). Because the data flows over SOCKS are not monitored or filtered, a security problem may arise. To minimize the security problems, trusted services and resources should be used on the outside network (untrusted network).

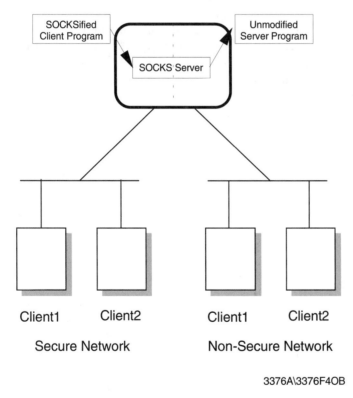

Circuit Level Gateway

Figure 168. *Circuit Level Gateway*

5.3.6 Firewall Examples

A firewall consists of one or more software elements that run on one or more hosts. The hosts may be general purpose computer systems or specialized such as routers. There are four important examples to firewalls. These are the following:

1. Packet-Filtering Firewall

2. Dual-Homed Gateway Firewall

3. Screened Host Firewall

4. Screened Subnet Firewall

These firewall examples are commonly used firewall types and are described below.

5.3.6.1 Packet-Filtering Firewall

The packet-filtering firewall is commonly used and an inexpensive firewall type. In this type of firewall, there is one router between the external network and internal secure network (please see Figure 169 on page 371). A packet-filtering router forwards the traffic between networks using packet-filtering rules to permit or deny traffic (please see 5.3.3, "Packet-Filtering Router" on page 361). A packet-filtering router has the same disadvantages of the packet-filtering router. Generally, a packet-filtering router is configured to deny any service if it is not explicitly permitted. Although this approach prevents some potential attacks, it is still open to attacks which result from improper configurations on filter rules.

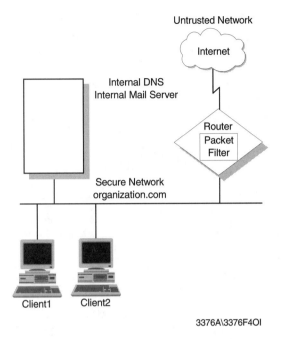

Untrusted Network

Internet

Internal DNS
Internal Mail Server

Router
Packet
Filter

Secure Network
organization.com

Client1   Client2

3376A\3376F4OI

Figure 169. Packet-Filtering Firewall

Since each host can be directly accessed from the external network, each host in the
internal network should have their own authorization mechanism and need to be
updated regularly in case of any attacks.

5.3.6.2 Dual-Homed Gateway Firewall

A dual-homed host has at least two network interfaces and therefore at least two IP
addresses. Since the IP forwarding is not active, all IP traffic between the two
interfaces is broken at the firewall (please see Figure 170 on page 372). Thus, there
is no way for a packet to pass the firewall unless the related proxy service or Socks
are defined on the firewall. Compared to the packet filtering firewalls, dual-homed
gateway firewalls make sure that any attack that comes from unknown services will be
blocked. A dual-homed gateway implements the method in which everything not
specifically permitted is denied.

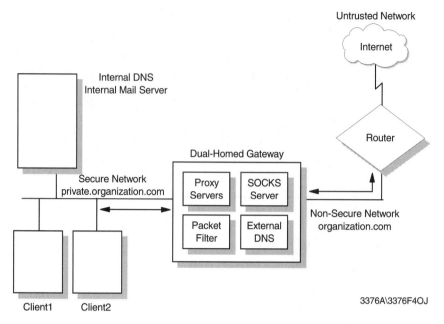

Figure 170. Dual-Homed Firewall

If an information server (such as a Web or FTP server) is needed to be located to give access to the outside users, it can either be installed inside the protected network or it can be installed between the firewall and the router which is relatively insecure. If it is installed beyond the firewall, the firewall must have the related proxy services to give access to the information server from inside the secure network. If the information server is installed between the firewall and the router, the router should be capable of packet filtering and configured accordingly. This type of firewall is called a screened host firewall and discussed in 5.3.6.3, "Screened Host Firewall."

5.3.6.3 Screened Host Firewall

This type of firewall consists of a packet filtering router and an application level gateway. The router is configured to forward all traffic to the bastion host (application level gateway) and in some cases also to the information server (please see Figure 171 on page 373). Since the internal network is on the same subnet as the bastion host, the security policy may allow internal users to access outside directly or force them to use proxy services to access the outside network. This can be achieved by configuring the router filter rules so that the router only accepts traffic originating from the bastion host.

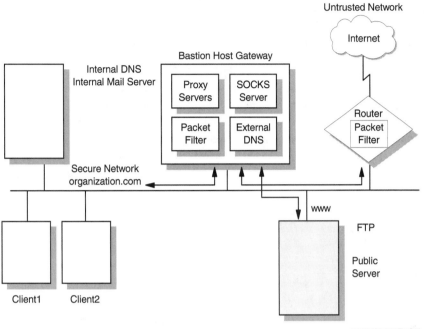

Figure 171. Screened Host Firewall

This configuration allows an information server to be placed between the router and the bastion host. Again, the security policy determines whether the information server will be accessed directly by either outside users or internal users or if it will be accessed via bastion host. If strong security is needed, both traffic from internal network to the information server and from outside to the information server can go through the bastion host.

In this configuration the bastion host can be a standard host or if a more secure firewall system is needed it can be a dual-homed host. In this case, all internal traffic to the information server and to the outside through the router is automatically forced to pass the proxy server on the dual-homed host. Since, the bastion host is the only system that can be accessed from the outside, it should not be permitted to log on to the bastion host. Otherwise an intruder may easily log on the system and change the configuration to pass the firewall easily.

5.3.6.4 Screened Subnet Firewall (Demilitarized Zone)

This type of firewall consists of two packet filtering routers and a bastion host. Screened subnet firewalls provide the highest level security among the firewall examples (please see Figure 172 on page 374). This is achieved by creating a demilitarized zone (DMZ) between the external network and internal network so that the outer router only permits access from the outside to the bastion host (possibly to the information server) and the inner router only permits access from internal network to the bastion host. Since the outer router only advertises the DMZ to the external network, the system on the external network cannot reach internal network. Similarly, the inner router advertises the DMZ to the internal network; the systems in the internal network cannot reach the Internet directly. This provides strong security in that an intruder has to penetrate three separate systems to reach the internal network.

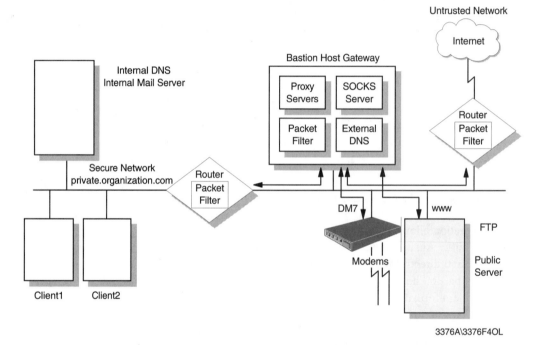

3376A\3376F4OL

Figure 172. *Screened Subnet Firewall*

One of the significant benefit of the DMZ is that since the routers force the systems on both external and internal networks to use the bastion host, there is no need for the bastion host to be a dual-homed host. This provides much faster throughput than achieved by a dual-homed host. Of course this is more complicated and some security problems could be caused by improper router configurations.

5.4 Network Address Translation (NAT)

This section explains Network Address Translation (NAT). Originally NAT was suggested as a short-term solution to the problem of IP address depletion. In order to be assured of any-to-any communication in the Internet, all IP addresses have to be officially assigned by the Internet Assigned Numbers Authority (IANA). This is becoming increasingly difficult to achieve, because the number of available address ranges is now severely limited. Also many organizations have in the past used locally assigned IP addresses, not expecting to require Internet connectivity.

NAT is defined in RFC 1631.

5.4.1 NAT Concept

The idea of NAT is based on the fact that only a small part of the hosts in a private network are communicating outside of that network. If each host is assigned an IP address from the official IP address pool only when they need to communicate, then only a small number of official addresses are required.

NAT might be a solution for networks that have private address ranges or illegal addresses and want to communicate with hosts on the Internet. In fact, most of the time, this can also be achieved by implementing a firewall. Hence, clients that communicate with the Internet by using a proxy or SOCKS server do not expose their addresses to the Internet, so their addresses do not have to be translated anyway. However, for any reason, when proxy and SOCKS are not available or do not meet specific requirements, NAT might be used to manage the traffic between the internal and external network without advertising the internal host addresses.

Consider an internal network that is based on the private IP address space, and the users want to use an application protocol for which there is no application gateway; the only option is to establish IP-level connectivity between hosts in the internal network and hosts on the Internet. Since the routers in the Internet would not know how to route IP packets back to a private IP address, there is no point in sending IP packets with private IP addresses as source IP addresses through a router into the Internet.

As shown in Figure 173 on page 376 NAT handles this by taking the IP address of an outgoing packet and dynamically translates it to an official address. For incoming packets it translates the official address to an internal address.

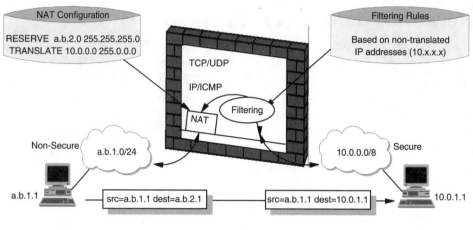

3376E\3376F4OM

Figure 173. *Network Address Translation (NAT)*

From the point of two hosts that exchange IP packets with each other, one in the secure network and one in the non-secure network, NAT looks like a standard IP router that forwards IP packets between two network interfaces (please see Figure 174).

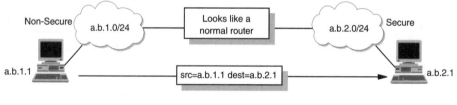

3376E\3376F4ON

Figure 174. *NAT Seen from the Non-Secure Network*

5.4.2 Translation Mechanism

For each outgoing IP packet, the source address is checked by the NAT configuration rules. If a rule matches the source address, the address is translated to an official address from the address pool. The predefined address pool contains the addresses that NAT can use for translation. For each incoming packet the destination address is checked if it is used by NAT. When this is true the address is translated to the original unofficial address. Figure 175 on page 377 shows the NAT configuration.

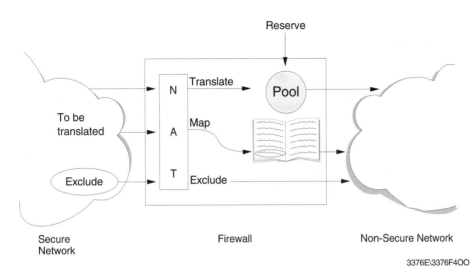

3376E\3376F4OO

Figure 175. *NAT Configuration*

If NAT translates an address for a TCP packet, the checksum is also adjusted. For FTP packets the task is even more difficult because the packets can contain addresses in the data of the packet. For example, the FTP PORT command contains an IP address in ASCII. These addresses should also be translated correctly and checksum updates and even TCP sequence and acknowledgement updates should be made accordingly.

Note that only TCP and UDP packets are translated by NAT. The ICMP protocol is not supported by NAT. For example, pinging to the NAT addresses does not work, because ping uses ICMP. (Please see 2.2, "Internet Control Message Protocol (ICMP)" on page 74 for more detail about ICMP and Ping.)

Since the TCP/IP stack that implements NAT looks like a normal IP router, there is a need to create an appropriate IP network design for connecting two or more IP networks or subnets through a router. The NAT IP addresses need to come from separate networks or subnets, and the addresses need to be unambiguous with respect to other networks or subnets in the non-secure network. If the non-secure network is the Internet, the NAT addresses need to come from a public network or subnet, in other words, the NAT addresses need to be assigned by IANA.

The non-secure addresses (official addresses) should be reserved in a pool, in order to use them when needed. If connections are established from the secure network, NAT can just pick the next free public address in the NAT pool and assign that to the requesting secure host. NAT keeps track of which secure IP addresses are mapped to which non-secure IP addresses at any given point in time, so it will be able to map a response it receives from the non-secure network into the corresponding secure IP address.

When NAT assigns IP addresses on a demand basis, it needs to know when to return the non-secure IP address to the pool of available IP addresses. There is no connection setup or tear-down at the IP level, so there is nothing in the IP protocol itself that NAT can use to determine when an association between a secure IP address and a NAT non-secure IP address is no longer needed. Since TCP is a connection-oriented protocol it is possible to obtain the connection status information from TCP header (whether connection is ended or not) whereas, UDP does not include such information. Therefore, a timeout value should be configured that instructs NAT how long to keep an association in an idle state before returning the non-secure IP address to the free NAT pool. Generally, the default value for this parameter is 15 minutes.

Network administrators also need to instruct NAT whether all the secure hosts are allowed to use NAT or not. It can be done by using corresponding configuration commands. If hosts in the non-secure network need to initiate connections to hosts in the secure network, NAT should be configured in advance as to which non-secure NAT address matches which secure IP address. Thus, a static mapping should be defined to allow connections from non-secure networks to a specific host in the internal network. The external name server may, for example, have an entry for a mail gateway that runs on a computer in the secure network. The external name server resolves the public host name of the internal mail gateway to a non-secure IP address that is in the internal NAT network, and the remote mail server sends a connection request to this IP address. When that request comes to NAT on the non-secure interface, NAT looks into its mapping rules to see if it has a static mapping between the specified non-secure public IP address and a secure IP address. If so, it translates the IP address and forwards the IP packet into the secure network to the internal mail gateway.

Please note that the non-secure NAT addresses as statically mapped to secure IP addresses should not overlap with the addresses specified as belonging to the pool of non-secure addresses NAT can use on a demand basis.

5.4.3 NAT Limitations

NAT works fine for IP addresses in the IP header. Some application protocols exchange IP address information in the application data part of an IP packet, and NAT will generally not be able to handle translation of IP addresses in the application protocol. Currently, most of the implementations handle the FTP protocol. It should be noted that implementation of NAT for specific applications that have IP information in the application data is more sophisticated than the standard NAT implementations.

Another important limitation of NAT is that NAT changes some or all of the address information in an IP packet. When end-to-end IPSec authentication is used, a packet whose address has been changed will always fail its integrity check under the AH protocol, since any change to any bit in the datagram will invalidate the integrity check value that was generated by the source. Since IPSec protocols offer some solutions to the addressing issues that were previously handled by NAT, there is no need for NAT when all hosts that compose a given virtual private network use globally unique (public) IP addresses. Address hiding can be achieved by IPSec's tunnel mode. If a company uses private addresses within its intranet, IPSec's tunnel mode can keep them from ever appearing in cleartext from in the public Internet, which eliminates the need for NAT. (Please see 5.5, "The IP Security Architecture (IPSec)" and 5.10, "Virtual Private Networks (VPN) Overview" on page 432 for details about IPSec and VPN.)

5.5 The IP Security Architecture (IPSec)

This section examines in detail the IPSec framework and its three main components, Authentication Header (AH), Encapsulating Security Payload (ESP), and Internet Key Exchange (IKE). The header formats, the specific cryptographic features and the different modes of application are discussed.

IPSec was designed for interoperability. When correctly implemented, it does not affect networks and hosts that do not support it. IPSec is independent of the current cryptographic algorithms; it can accommodate new ones as they become available. It works both with IPv4 and IPv6. Actually IPSec is a mandatory component of IPv6.

IPSec uses state-of-the-art cryptographic algorithms. The specific implementation of an algorithm for use by an IPSec protocol is often called a *transform*. For example, the DES algorithm used in ESP is called the ESP DES-CBC transform. The transforms, as the protocols, are published in RFCs and in Internet drafts.

5.5.1 Concepts

Two major IPSec concepts should be clarified before entering the details: the Security Associations and the tunneling. In fact they are not new; IPSec just makes use of them. These concepts are described in the following sections.

5.5.1.1 Security Associations

The concept of a Security Association (SA) is fundamental to IPSec. An SA is a unidirectional (simplex) logical connection between two IPSec systems, uniquely identified by the following triple:

```
<Security Parameter Index, IP Destination Address, Security Protocol>
```

The definition of the members is as follows:

Security Parameter Index (SPI)
> This is a 32-bit value used to identify different SAs with the same destination address and security protocol. The SPI is carried in the header of the security protocol (AH or ESP). The SPI has only local significance, as defined by the creator of the SA. The SPI values in the range 1 to 255 are reserved by the Internet Assigned Numbers Authority (IANA). The SPI value of 0 must be used for local implementation-specific purposes only. Generally the SPI is selected by the destination system during the SA establishment.

IP Destination Address
> This address can be a unicast, broadcast or multicast address. However, currently SA management mechanisms are defined only for unicast addresses.

Security Protocol
> This can be either AH or ESP.

An SA can be in either of two modes: transport or tunnel, depending on the mode of the protocol in that SA. You can find the explanation of these protocol modes later in this chapter.

Because SAs are simplex, for bidirectional communication between two IPSec systems, there must be two SAs defined, one in each direction.

An SA gives security services to the traffic carried by it either by using AH or ESP, but not both. In other words, for a connection that should be protected by both AH and ESP, two SAs must be defined for each direction. In this case, the set of SAs that define the connection is referred to as an *SA bundle*. The SAs in the bundle do not have to terminate at the same endpoint. For example, a mobile host could use an AH SA between itself and a firewall and a nested ESP SA that extends to a host behind the firewall.

An IPSec implementation maintains two databases related to SAs:

Security Policy Database (SPD)
> The Security Policy Database specifies what security services are to be offered to the IP traffic, depending on factors such as source, destination, whether it is

inbound, outbound, etc. It contains an ordered list of policy entries, separate for inbound and/or outbound traffic. These entries might specify that some traffic must not go through IPSec processing, some must be discarded and the rest must be processed by the IPSec module. Entries in this database are similar to the firewall rules or packet filters.

Security Association Database (SAD)

The Security Association Database contains parameter information about each SA, such as AH or ESP algorithms and keys, sequence numbers, protocol mode and SA lifetime. For outbound processing, an SPD entry points to an entry in the SAD. That is, the SPD determines which SA is to be used for a given packet. For inbound processing, the SAD is consulted to determine how the packet must be processed.

Note: The user interface of an IPSec implementation usually hides or presents in a more friendly way these databases and makes the life of the administrator easier.

5.5.1.2 Tunneling

Tunneling or encapsulation is a common technique in packet-switched networks. It consists of wrapping a packet in a new one. That is, a new header is attached to the original packet. The entire original packet becomes the payload of the new one, as it is shown in Figure 176.

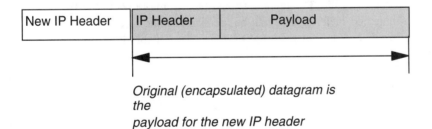

Figure 176. IP Tunneling

In general tunneling is used to carry traffic of one protocol over a network that does not support that protocol directly. For example, NetBIOS or IPX can be encapsulated in IP to carry it over a TCP/IP WAN link. In the case of IPSec, IP is tunneled through IP for a slightly different purpose: to provide total protection, including the header of the encapsulated packet. If the encapsulated packet is encrypted, an intruder cannot figure out for example the destination address of that packet. (Without tunneling he or she could.) The internal structure of a private network can be concealed in this way.

Tunneling requires intermediate processing of the original packet on its route. The destination specified in the outer header, usually an IPSec firewall or router, retrieves the original packet and sends it to the ultimate destination. The processing overhead is compensated by the extra security.

A notable advantage of IP tunneling is the possibility to exchange packets with private IP addresses between two intranets over the public Internet, which requires globally unique addresses. Since the encapsulated header is not processed by the Internet routers, only the endpoints of the tunnel (the gateways) have to have globally assigned addresses; the hosts in the intranets behind them can be assigned private addresses, for example 10.x.x.x. As globally unique IP addresses are becoming a scarce resource, this interconnection method gains importance.

Note: IPSec tunneling is modeled after RFC 2003 *IP Encapsulation within IP*. It was originally designed for Mobile IP, an architecture that allows a mobile host to keep its home IP address even if attached to remote or foreign subnets.

5.5.2 Authentication Header (AH)

AH is used to provide integrity and authentication to IP datagrams. Optional replay protection is also possible. Although its usage is optional, the replay protection service must be implemented by any IPSec-compliant system. The mentioned services are connectionless; that is they work on a per-packet basis.

AH authenticates as much of the IP datagram as possible. Some fields in the IP header change en-route and their value cannot be predicted by the receiver. These fields are called *mutable* and are not protected by AH. The mutable IPv4 fields are:

- Type of Service (TOS)
- Flags
- Fragment Offset
- Time to Live (TTL)
- Header Checksum

When protection of these fields is required, tunneling should be used. The payload of the IP packet is considered immutable and is always protected by AH.

AH is identified by protocol number 51, assigned by the IANA. The protocol header (IPv4, IPv6, or Extension) immediately preceding the AH header contains this value in its Protocol (IPv4) or Next Header (IPv6, Extension) field.

AH processing is applied only to non-fragmented IP packets. However, an IP packet with AH applied can be fragmented by intermediate routers. In this case the destination first reassembles the packet and then applies AH processing to it. If an IP packet that appears to be a fragment (offset field is non-zero, or the More Fragments bit is set) is input to AH processing, it is discarded. This prevents the so-called *overlapping fragment attack*, which misuses the fragment reassembly algorithm in order to create forged packets and force them through a firewall.

Packets that failed authentication are discarded and never delivered to upper layers. This mode of operation greatly reduces the chances of successful *denial of service* attacks, which aim to block the communication of a host or gateway by flooding it with bogus packets.

5.5.2.1 AH Header Format

The current AH header format is described in the Internet draft *draft-ietf-ipsec-auth-header-07.txt*, which contains important modifications compared to the previous AH specification, RFC 1826. The information in this section is based on the respective Internet draft.

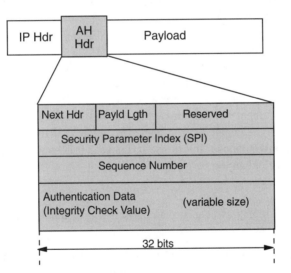

Figure 177. AH Header Format

In Figure 177 the position of the AH header in the IP packet and the header fields are shown. The explanation of the fields are as follows:

Next Header

The Next Header is an 8-bit field that identifies the type of the next payload after the Authentication Header. The value of this field is chosen from the set of IP protocol numbers defined in the most recent *Assigned Numbers* RFC from the Internet Assigned Numbers Authority (IANA).

Payload Length

This field is 8 bits long and contains the length of the AH header expressed in 32-bit words, minus 2. It does not relate to the actual payload length of the IP packet as a whole. If default options are used, the value is 4 (three 32-bit fixed words plus three 32-bit words of authentication data minus two).

Reserved

This field is reserved for future use. Its length is 16 bits and it is set to zero.

Security Parameter Index (SPI)

This field is 32 bits in length. See Security Parameter Index (SPI) on page 380 for a definition.

Sequence Number

This 32-bit field is a monotonically increasing counter which is used for replay protection. Replay protection is optional; however, this field is mandatory. The sender always includes this field and it is at the discretion of the receiver to process it or not. At the establishment of an SA the sequence number is initialized to zero. The first packet transmitted using the SA has a sequence number of 1. Sequence numbers are not allowed to repeat. Thus the maximum number of IP packets that can be transmitted on any given SA is $2^{32}-1$. After the highest sequence number is used, a new SA and consequently a new key is established. Anti-replay is enabled at the sender by default. If upon SA establishment the receiver chooses not to use it, the sender does not concern with the value in this field anymore.

Notes:

1. Typically the anti-replay mechanism is not used with manual key management.

2. The original AH specification in RFC 1826 did not discuss the concept of sequence numbers. Older IPSec implementations that are based on that RFC can therefore not provide replay protection.

Authentication Data

This is a variable-length field, also called Integrity Check Value (ICV). The ICV for the packet is calculated with the algorithm selected at the SA initialization. The authentication data length is an integral multiple of 32 bits.

As its name tells, it is used by the receiver to verify the integrity of the incoming packet.

In theory any MAC algorithm can be used to calculate the ICV. The specification requires that HMAC-MD5-96 and HMAC-SHA-1-96 must be supported. The old RFC 1826 requires Keyed MD5. In practice Keyed SHA-1 is also used. Implementations usually support two to four algorithms.

When doing the ICV calculation, the mutable fields are considered to be filled with zero.

5.5.2.2 Ways of Using AH

AH can be used in two ways: transport mode and tunnel mode.

AH in Transport Mode: In this mode the original IP datagram is taken and the AH header is inserted right after the IP header, as it is shown in Figure 178. If the datagram already has IPSec header(s), then the AH header is inserted before any of those.

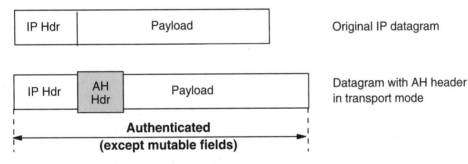

Figure 178. Authentication Header in Transport Mode

The transport mode is used by hosts, not by gateways. Gateways are not even required to support transport mode.

The advantage of the transport mode is less processing overhead. The disadvantage is that the mutable fields are not authenticated.

AH in Tunnel Mode: With this mode the tunneling concept is applied a new IP datagram is constructed and the original IP datagram is made the payload of it. Then AH in transport mode is applied to the resulting datagram. See Figure 179 on page 386 for an illustration.

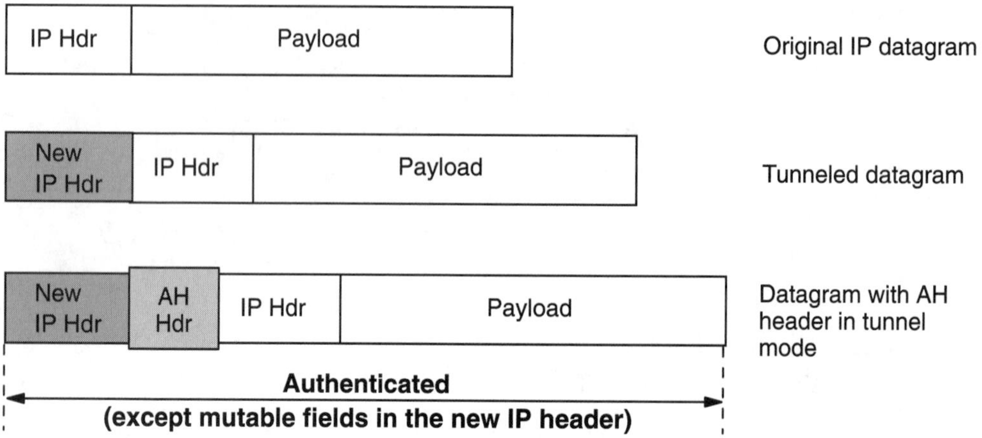

| IP Hdr | Payload | | Original IP datagram |

| New IP Hdr | IP Hdr | Payload | | Tunneled datagram |

| New IP Hdr | AH Hdr | IP Hdr | Payload | | Datagram with AH header in tunnel mode |

Authenticated
(except mutable fields in the new IP header)

Figure 179. Authentication Header in Tunnel Mode

The tunnel mode is used whenever either end of a security association is a gateway. Thus, between two firewalls the tunnel mode is always used.

Although gateways are supposed to support tunnel mode only, often they can also work in transport mode. This mode is allowed when the gateway acts as a host, that is in cases when traffic is destined to itself. Examples are SNMP commands or ICMP echo requests.

In tunnel mode the outer headers' IP addresses does not need to be the same as the inner headers' addresses. For example two security gateways can operate an AH tunnel which is used to authenticate all traffic between the networks they connect together. This is a very typical mode of operation. Hosts are not required to support tunnel mode, but often they do.

The advantages of the tunnel mode are total protection of the encapsulated IP datagram and the possibility of using private addresses. However, there is an extra processing overhead associated with this mode.

Note: The original AH specification in RFC 1825 only mentions tunnel mode in passing, not as a requirement. Because of this, there are IPSec implementations based on that RFC that do not support AH in tunnel mode.

5.5.2.3 IPv6 Considerations

AH is an integral part of IPv6 (see 6.2.2, "Extension Headers" on page 462). In an IPv6 environment, AH is considered an end-to-end payload and it appears after hop-by-hop, routing, and fragmentation extension headers. The destination options extension header(s) could appear either before or after the AH header. Figure 180 on page 387 illustrates the positioning of the AH header in transport mode for a typical IPv6 packet. The position of the extension headers marked with * is variable, if present at all.

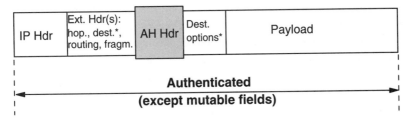

Figure 180. AH in Transport Mode for IPv6

For a detailed description of AH in IPv6 please refer to the current Internet draft.

5.5.3 Encapsulating Security Payload (ESP)

ESP is used to provide integrity check, authentication and encryption to IP datagrams. Optional replay protection is also possible. These services are connectionless; they operate on a per-packet basis. The set of desired services are selectable upon SA establishment. However, some restrictions apply:

- Integrity check and authentication go together

- Replay protection is selectable only with integrity check and authentication

- Replay protection can be selected only by the receiver

Encryption is selectable independent of the other services. It is highly recommended that if encryption is enabled, then integrity check and authentication be turned on. If only encryption is used, intruders could forge packets in order to mount cryptanalytic attacks. This is infeasible when integrity check and authentication are in place.

Although both authentication (with integrity check) and encryption are optional, at least one of them is always selected. Otherwise it really does not make sense to use ESP at all.

ESP is identified by protocol number 50, assigned by the IANA. The protocol header (IPv4, IPv6, or Extension) immediately preceding the AH header will contain this value in its Protocol (IPv4) or Next Header (IPv6, Extension) field.

ESP processing is applied only to non-fragmented IP packets. However an IP packet with ESP applied can be fragmented by intermediate routers. In this case the destination first reassembles the packet and then applies ESP processing to it. If an IP packet that appears to be a fragment (offset field is non-zero, or the More Fragments bit is set) is input to ESP processing, it is discarded. This prevents the overlapping fragment attack mentioned in 5.5.2, "Authentication Header (AH)" on page 382.

If both encryption and authentication with integrity check are selected, then the receiver first authenticates the packet and only if this step was successful proceeds with decryption. This mode of operation saves computing resources and reduces the vulnerability to denial of service attacks.

5.5.3.1 ESP Packet Format

The current ESP packet format is described in the Internet draft *draft-ietf-ipsec-esp-v2-06.txt*, dated March 1998. It contains important modifications compared to the previous ESP specification, RFC 1827. The information in this section is based on the respective Internet draft.

The format of the ESP packet is more complicated than that of the AH packet. Actually there is not only an ESP header, but also an ESP trailer and ESP authentication data (see Figure 181 on page 389). The payload is located (*encapsulated*) between the header and the trailer, hence the name of the the protocol.

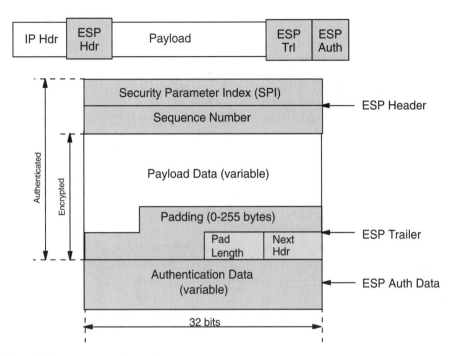

Figure 181. *ESP Header and Trailer*

The following fields are part of an ESP packet:

Security Parameter Index (SPI)
This field is 32 bits in length. See Security Parameter Index (SPI) on page 380 for the definition.

Sequence Number
This 32-bit field is a monotonically increasing counter. See Sequence Number on page 384 for the definition.

Notes:

1. Typically the anti-replay mechanism is not used with manual key management.

2. The original ESP specification in RFC 1827 did not discuss the concept of sequence numbers. Older IPSec implementations that are based on that RFC can therefore not provide replay protection.

Payload Data
The Payload Data field is mandatory. It consists of a variable number of bytes of data described by the Next Header field. This field is encrypted with the

cryptographic algorithm selected during SA establishment. If the algorithm requires initialization vectors, these are also included here.

The ESP specification require support for the DES algorithm in CBC mode (DES-CBC transform). Often other encryption algorithms are also supported, such as triple-DES and CDMF in the case of IBM products.

Padding

Most encryption algorithms require that the input data must be an integral number of blocks. Also, the resulting ciphertext (including the Padding, Pad Length and Next Header fields) must terminate on a 4-byte boundary, so that Next Header field is right-aligned. That's why this variable length field is included. It can be used to hide the length of the original messages too. However, this could adversely impact the effective bandwidth. Padding is an optional field.

Note: The encryption covers the Payload Data, Padding, Pad Length and Next Header fields.

Pad Length

This 8-bit field contains the number of the preceding padding bytes. It is always present, and the value of 0 indicates no padding.

Next Header

The Next Header is an 8-bit mandatory field that shows the data type carried in the payload, for example an upper-level protocol identifier such as TCP. The values are chosen from the set of IP protocol numbers defined by the IANA.

Authentication Data

This field is variable in length and contains the ICV calculated for the ESP packet from the SPI to the Next Header field inclusive. The Authentication Data field is optional. It is included only when integrity check and authentication have been selected at SA initialization time.

The ESP specifications require two authentication algorithms to be supported: HMAC with MD5 and HMAC with SHA-1. Often the simpler keyed versions are also supported by the IPSec implementations.

Notes:

1. The IP header is not covered by the ICV.

2. The original ESP specification in RFC 1827 discusses the concept of authentication within ESP in conjunction with the encryption transform. That is, there is no Authentication Data field and it is left to the encryption transforms to eventually provide authentication.

5.5.3.2 Ways of Using ESP

Like AH, ESP can be used in two ways: transport mode and tunnel mode.

ESP in Transport Mode: In this mode the original IP datagram is taken and the ESP header is inserted right after the IP header, as it is shown in Figure 182. If the datagram already has IPSec header(s), then the ESP header is inserted before any of those. The ESP trailer and the optional authentication data are appended to the payload.

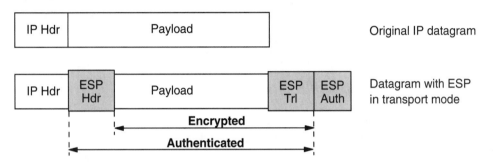

Figure 182. ESP in Transport Mode

ESP in transport mode provides neither authentication nor encryption for the IP header. This is a disadvantage, since false packets might be delivered for ESP processing. The advantage of transport mode is the lower processing overhead.

As in the case of AH, ESP in transport mode is used by hosts, not gateways. Gateways are not even required to support transport mode.

ESP in Tunnel Mode: As expected, this mode applies the tunneling principle. A new IP packet is constructed with a new IP header and then ESP in transport mode is applied, as illustrated in Figure 183 on page 392. Since the original datagram becomes the payload data for the new ESP packet, its protection is total if both encryption and authentication are selected. However, the new IP header is still not protected.

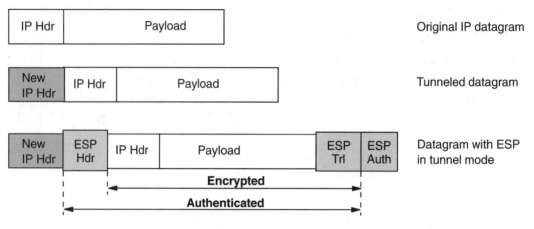

Figure 183. ESP in Tunnel Mode

The tunnel mode is used whenever either end of a security association is a gateway. Thus, between two firewalls the tunnel mode is always used.

Although gateways are supposed to support tunnel mode only, often they can also work in transport mode. This mode is allowed when the gateway acts as a host, that is in cases when traffic is destined to itself. Examples are SNMP commands or ICMP echo requests.

In tunnel mode the outer headers' IP addresses does not need to be the same as the inner headers' addresses. For example two security gateways may operate an ESP tunnel which is used to secure all traffic between the networks they connect together. Hosts are not required to support tunnel mode, but often they do.

The advantages of the tunnel mode are total protection of the encapsulated IP datagram and the possibility of using private addresses. However, there is an extra processing overhead associated with this mode.

5.5.3.3 IPv6 Considerations

Like AH, ESP is an integral part of IPv6 (see 6.2.2, "Extension Headers" on page 462). In an IPv6 environment, ESP is considered an end-to-end payload and it appears after hop-by-hop, routing, and fragmentation extension headers. The destination options extension header(s) could appear either before or after the AH header. Figure 184 on page 393 illustrates the positioning of the AH header in transport mode for a typical IPv6 packet. The position of the extension headers marked with * is variable, if present at all.

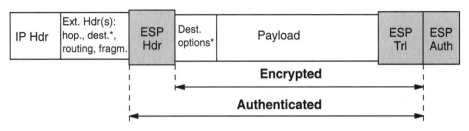

Figure 184. ESP in Transport Mode for IPv6

For more details, please refer to the respective Internet draft.

5.5.3.4 Why Two Authentication Protocols?

Knowing about the security services of ESP, one might ask if there is really a requirement for AH. Why does ESP authentication not cover the IP header as well? There is no official answer to these questions, but here are some points that justify the existence of two different IPSec authentication protocols:

- ESP requires strong cryptographic algorithms to be implemented, whether it will actually be used or not. Strong cryptography is an over-hyped and sensitive topic in some countries, with restrictive regulations in place. It might be troublesome to deploy ESP-based solutions in such areas. However, authentication is not regulated and AH can be used freely around the world.

- Often only authentication is needed. While ESP could have been specified to cover the IP header as well, AH is more performant compared to ESP with authentication only, because of the simpler format and lower processing overhead. It makes sense to use AH in these cases.

- Having two different protocols means finer-grade control over an IPSec network and more flexible security options. By nesting AH and ESP for example, one can implement IPSec tunnels that combine the strengths of both protocols.

5.5.4 Combining IPSec Protocols

The AH and ESP protocols can be applied alone or in combination. Given the two modes of each protocol, there is quite a number of possible combinations. To make things even worse, the AH and ESP SAs do not need to have identical endpoints, so the picture becomes rather complicated. Luckily, out of the many possibilities only a few make sense in real-world scenarios.

Note: The *draft-ietf-ipsec-arch-sec-07.txt* Internet draft is the current document that describes the mandatory combinations that must be supported by each IPSec implementation. Other combinations may also be supported, but this might impact interoperability.

We mentioned in 5.5.1.1, "Security Associations" on page 380 that the combinations of IPSec protocols are realized with SA bundles.

There are two approaches for an SA bundle creation:

- *Transport adjacency:* Both security protocols are applied in transport mode to the same IP datagram. This method is practical for only one level of combination.

- *Iterated (nested) tunneling:* The security protocols are applied in tunnel mode in sequence. After each application a new IP datagram is created and the next protocol is applied to it. This method has no limit in the nesting levels. However, more than three levels are impractical.

These approaches can be combined, for example an IP packet with transport adjacency IPSec headers can be sent through nested tunnels.

When designing a VPN, one should limit the IPSec processing stages applied to a certain packet to a reasonable level. In our view three applications is that limit over which further processing has no benefits. Two stages are sufficient for almost all the cases.

Note that in order to be able to create an SA bundle in which the SAs have different endpoints, at least one level of tunneling must be applied. Transport adjacency does not allow for multiple source/destination addresses, because only one IP header is present.

The practical principle of the combined usage is that upon the receipt of a packet with both protocol headers, the IPSec processing sequence should be authentication followed by decryption. It is a common sense decision not to bother with the decryption of packets of uncertain origin.

Following the above principle, the sender first applies ESP and then AH to the outbound traffic. In fact this sequence is an explicit requirement for transport mode IPSec processing. When using both ESP and AH, a new question arises: should ESP authentication be turned on? AH authenticates the packet anyway. The answer is simple. Turning ESP authentication on makes sense only when the ESP SA extends beyond the AH SA, as in the case of the supplier scenario. In this case, not only does it make sense to use ESP authentication, but it is highly recommended to do so, to avoid spoofing attacks in the intranet.

As far as the modes are concerned, the usual way is that transport mode is used between the endpoints of a connection and tunnel mode is used between two machines when at least one of them is a gateway.

Let's take a systematic look on the plausible ways of using the IPSec protocols, from the simplest to the more complicated nested setups.

5.5.4.1 Case 1: End-to-End Security

As shown in Figure 185, two hosts are connected through the Internet (or an intranet) without any IPSec gateway between them. They can use ESP, AH or both. Either transport or tunnel mode can be applied.

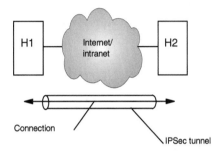

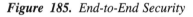

Figure 185. End-to-End Security

The combinations required to be supported by any IPSec implementation are the following:

Transport Mode
1. AH alone
2. ESP alone
3. AH applied after ESP (transport adjacency)

Tunnel Mode
1. AH alone
2. ESP alone

5.5.4.2 Case 2: Basic VPN Support

Figure 186 on page 396 illustrates the simplest VPN. The gateways G1 and G2 run the IPSec protocol stack. The hosts in the intranets are not required to support IPSec.

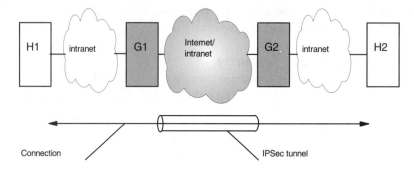

Figure 186. Basic VPN Support

In this case the gateways are required to support only tunnel mode, either with AH or ESP.

Combined Tunnels between Gateways: Although the gateways are required to support only an AH tunnel or ESP tunnel, often it is desirable to have tunnels between gateways that combine the features of both IPSec protocols.

The IBM IPSec implementations support this type of combined AH-ESP tunnels. The order of the headers is user selectable by setting the tunnel policy.

A combined tunnel between the gateways does not mean that iterated tunneling takes place. Since the SA bundle comprising the tunnel have identical endpoints, it is inefficient to do iterated tunneling. Instead, one IPSec protocol is applied in tunnel mode and the other in transport mode, which can be conceptually thought of as a combined AH-ESP tunnel. An equivalent approach is to IP tunnel the original datagram and then apply transport adjacency IPSec processing to it. The result is that we have an outer IP header followed by the IPSec headers in the order set by the tunnel policy, then the original IP packet, as it is shown in the figure below. This is the packet format in a combined AH-ESP tunnel between two IBM firewalls.

Note: The ESP authentication data is not present because the IPSec implementation in the IBM firewall does not support the new specifications yet.

Figure 187. Combined AH-ESP Tunnel

5.5.4.3 Case 3: End-to-End Security with VPN Support

This case is a combination of cases 1 and 2 and it does not raise new IPSec requirements for the machines involved (see Figure 188). The big difference from case 2 is that now the hosts are also required to support IPSec.

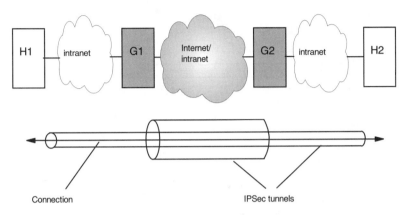

Figure 188. *End-to-End Security with VPN Support*

In a typical setup, the gateways use AH in tunnel mode, while the hosts use ESP in transport mode. An enhanced security version could use a combined AH-ESP tunnel between the gateways. In this way the ultimate destination addresses would be encrypted, the whole packet traveling the Internet would be authenticated and the carried data double encrypted. This is the only case when three stages of IPSec processing might be useful, however, at a cost; the performance impact is considerable.

5.5.4.4 Case 4: Remote Access

This case, shown in Figure 189 on page 398, applies to the remote hosts that use the Internet to reach a server in the organization protected by a firewall. The remote host commonly uses a PPP dial-in connection to an ISP.

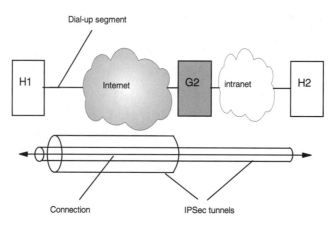

Figure 189. Remote Access

Between the remote host H1 and the firewall G2 only tunnel mode is required. The choices are the same as in case 2. Between the hosts themselves either tunnel mode or transport mode can be used, with the same choices as in case 1.

A typical setup is to use AH in tunnel mode between H1 and G2 and ESP in transport mode between H1 and H2. Older IPSec implementations that do not support AH in tunnel mode cannot implement this.

It is also common to create a combined AH-ESP tunnel between the remote host H1 and the gateway G2. In this case H1 can access the whole intranet with using just one SA bundle, whereas if it were using the setup shown in Figure 189, it only could access one host with one SA bundle.

5.5.4.5 Conclusion and an Example

While the combination of the IPSec protocols in theory leads to a large number of possibilities, in practice only a few (those presented above) are used. One very common combination is AH in tunnel mode protecting ESP traffic in transport mode. Combined AH-ESP tunnels between firewalls are also frequent.

Figure 190 on page 399 shows in detail how the first combination is realized. Consider that host H1 in Figure 188 on page 397 sends an IP packet to host H2. Here is what happens:

1. Host H1 constructs the IP packet and applies ESP transport to it. H1 then sends the datagram to gateway G1, the destination address being H2.

2. Gateway G1 realizes that this packet should be routed to G2. Upon consulting its IPSec databases (SPD and SAD) G1 concludes that AH in tunnel mode must be

applied before sending the packet out. It does the required encapsulation. Now the IP packet has the address of G2 as its destination, the ultimate destination H2 being encapsulated.

3. Gateway G2 receives the AH-tunneled packet. It is destined to itself, so it authenticates the datagram and strips off the outer header. G2 sees that the payload is yet another IP packet (that one sent by H1) with destination H2, so it forwards to H2. G2 does not care that this packet has an ESP header.

4. Finally H2 receives the packet. As this is the destination, ESP-transport processing is applied and the original payload retrieved.

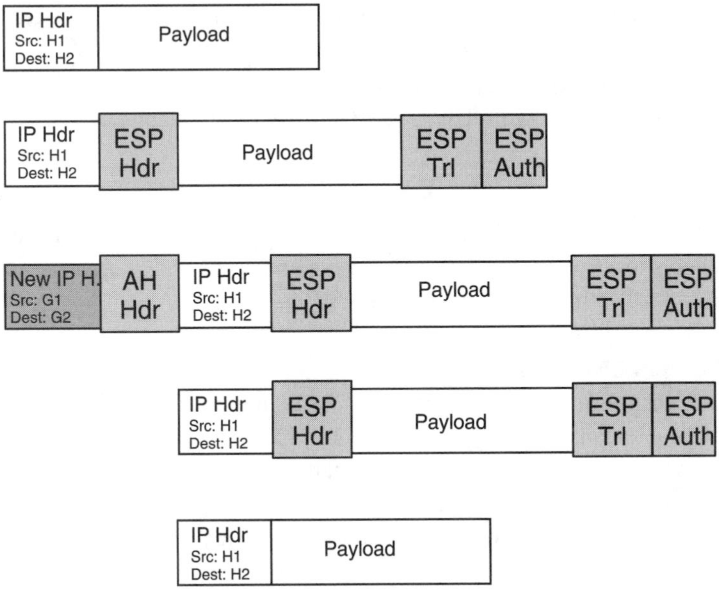

Figure 190. *Nesting of IPSec Protocols*

5.5.5 The Internet Key Exchange Protocol (IKE)

The Internet Key Exchange (IKE) framework, previously referred to as ISAKMP/Oakley, supports automated negotiation of Security Associations, and automated generation and refresh of cryptographic keys. The ability to perform these functions with little or no manual configuration of machines is a critical element to any enterprise-scale IPSec deployment.

Before describing the details of the key exchange and update messages, some explanations are due:

Internet Security Association and Key Management Protocol (ISAKMP)

A framework that defines the management of security associations (negotiate, modify, delete) and keys, and it also defines the payloads for exchanging key generation and authentication data. ISAKMP itself does not define any key exchange protocols, and the framework it provides can be applied to security mechanisms on the network, transport or application layer, and also to itself.

Oakley

A key exchange protocol that can be used with the ISAKMP framework to exchange and update keying material for security associations.

Domain of Interpretation

Definition of a set of protocols to be used with the ISAKMP framework for a particular environment, and a set of common definitions shared with those protocols regarding syntax of SA attributes and payload contents, namespace of cryptographic transforms, etc. In relation to IPSec, the DOI instantiates ISAKMP for use with IP.

Internet Key Exchange (IKE)

A protocol that uses parts of ISAKMP and parts of the Oakley and SKEME key exchange protocols to provide management of keys and security associations for the IPSec AH and ESP protocols, and for ISAKMP itself.

5.5.5.1 Protocol Overview

ISAKMP requires that all information exchanges must be both encrypted and authenticated so that no one can eavesdrop on the keying material, and the keying material will be exchanged only among authenticated parties. This is required because the ISAKMP procedures deal with initializing the keys, so they must be capable of running over links where no security can be assumed to exist. Hence, the ISAKMP protocols use the most complex and processor-intensive operations in the IPSec protocol suite.

In addition, the ISAKMP methods have been designed with the explicit goals of providing protection against several well-known exposures:

- Denial-of-Service: The messages are constructed with unique *cookies* that can be used to quickly identify and reject invalid messages without the need to execute processor-intensive cryptographic operations.

- Man-in-the-Middle: Protection is provided against the common attacks such as deletion of messages, modification of messages, reflecting messages back to the sender, replaying of old messages, and redirection of messages to unintended recipients.

- Perfect Forward Secrecy (PFS): Compromise of past keys provides no useful clues for breaking any other key, whether it occurred before or after the compromised key. That is, each refreshed key will be derived without any dependence on predecessor keys.

The following authentication methods are defined for IKE:

1. Pre-shared key

2. Digital signatures (DSS and RSA)

3. Public key encryption (RSA and revised RSA)

The robustness of any cryptography-based solution depends much more strongly on keeping the keys secret than it does on the actual details of the chosen cryptographic algorithms. Hence, the IETF IPSec Working Group has prescribed a set of extremely robust Oakley exchange protocols. It uses a 2-phase approach:

Phase 1: This set of negotiations establishes a master secret from which all cryptographic keys will subsequently be derived for protecting the users' data traffic. In the most general case, public key cryptography is used to establish an ISAKMP security association between systems, and to establish the keys that will be used to protect the ISAKMP messages that will flow in the subsequent Phase 2 negotiations. Phase 1 is concerned only with establishing the protection suite for the ISAKMP messages themselves, but it does not establish any security associations or keys for protecting user data.

In Phase 1, the cryptographic operations are the most processor-intensive but need only be done infrequently, and a single Phase 1 exchange can be used to support multiple subsequent Phase 2 exchanges. As a rule of thumb, Phase 1 negotiations are executed once a day or maybe once a week, while Phase 2 negotiations are executed once every few minutes.

Phase 2: Phase 2 exchanges are less complex, since they are used only after the security protection suite negotiated in Phase 1 has been activated. A set of communicating systems negotiate the security associations and keys that will protect user data exchanges. Phase 2 ISAKMP messages are protected by the ISAKMP security association generated in Phase 1. Phase 2 negotiations generally occur more frequently than Phase 1. For example, a typical application of a Phase 2 negotiation is to refresh the cryptographic keys once every two to three minutes.

Permanent Identifiers: The IKE protocol also offers a solution even when the remote host's IP address is not known in advance. ISAKMP allows a remote host to identify itself by a *permanent* identifier, such as a name or an e-mail address. The

ISAKMP Phase 1 exchanges will then authenticate the remote host's permanent identity using public key cryptography:

- Certificates create a binding between the permanent identifier and a public key. Therefore, ISAKMP's certificate-based Phase 1 message exchanges can authenticate the remote host's permanent identify.

- Since the ISAKMP messages themselves are carried within IP datagrams, the ISAKMP partner (for example, a firewall or destination host) can associate the remote host's dynamic IP address with its authenticated permanent identity.

5.5.5.2 Initializing Security Associations with IKE

This section outlines how ISAKMP/Oakley protocols initially establish security associations and exchange keys between two systems that wish to communicate securely.

In the remainder of this section, the parties involved are named Host-A and Host-B. Host-A will be the initiator of the ISAKMP Phase 1 exchanges, and Host-B will be the responder. If needed for clarity, subscripts A or B will be used to identify the source of various fields in the message exchanges.

Phase 1 - Setting Up the ISAKMP Security Associations: The security associations that protect the ISAKMP messages themselves are set up during the Phase 1 exchanges. Since we are starting "cold" (no previous keys or SAs have been negotiated between Host-A and Host-B), the Phase 1 exchanges will use the ISAKMP Identity Protect exchange (also known as Oakley Main Mode). Six messages are needed to complete the exchange:

- Messages 1 and 2 negotiate the characteristics of the security associations. Messages 1 and 2 flow in the clear for the initial Phase 1 exchange, and they are unauthenticated.
- Messages 3 and 4 exchange nonces (random values) and also execute a Diffie-Hellman exchange to establish a master key (SKEYID). Messages 3 and 4 flow in the clear for the initial Phase 1 exchange, and they are unauthenticated.
- Messages 5 and 6 exchange the required information for mutually authenticating the parties' identities. The payloads of Messages 5 and 6 are protected by the encryption algorithm and keying material established with messages 1 through 4.

The detailed description of the Phase 1 messages and exchanged information follows below:

1. IKE Phase 1, Message 1

Since Host-A is the initiating party, it will construct a cleartext ISAKMP message (Message 1) and send it to Host-B. The ISAKMP message itself is carried as the payload of a UDP packet, which in turn is carried as the payload of a normal IP datagram (see Figure 191 on page 403).

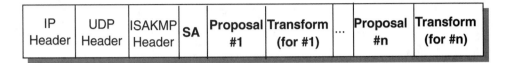

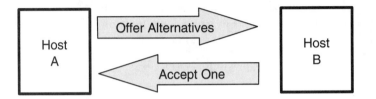

Figure 191. Message 1 of an ISAKMP Phase 1 Exchange

The source and destination addresses to be placed in the IP header are those of Host-A (initiator) and Host-B (responder), respectively. The UDP header will identify that the destination port is 500, which has been assigned for use by the ISAKMP protocol. The payload of the UDP packet carries the ISAKMP message itself.

In Message 1, Host-A, the initiator, proposes a set of one or more protection suites for consideration by Host-B, the responder. Hence, the ISAKMP Message contains at least the following fields in its payload:

ISAKMP Header
> The ISAKMP Header in Message 1 will indicate an exchange type of Main Mode, and will contain a Message ID of 0. Host-A will set the Responder Cookie field to 0, and will fill in a random value of its choice for the Initiator Cookie, denoted as Cookie-A.

Security Association
> The Security Association field identifies the Domain of Interpretation (DOI). Since the hosts plan to run IPSec protocols between themselves, the DOI is simply IP.

Proposal Payload
> Host-A's Proposal Payload will specify the protocol PROTO_ISAKMP and will set the SPI value to 0.

Note: For ISAKMP Phase 1 messages, the actual SPI field within the Proposal Payload is not used to identify the ISAKMP Security Association. During Phase 1, the ISAKMP SA is identified instead by the pair of values <Initiator Cookie, Responder Cookie>, both of which must be non-zero values. Since the Responder Cookie has not yet been generated by Host-B, the ISAKMP SA is not yet unambiguously identified.

Transform Payload

The Transform Payload will specify KEY_OAKLEY. For the KEY_OAKLEY transform, Host-A must also specify the relevant attributes: namely, the authentication method to be used, the pseudo-random function to be used, and the encryption algorithm to be used.

Note: Multiple proposals can be included in Message 1.

2. IKE Phase 1, Message 2

In Message 1, Host-A proposed one or more candidate protection suites to be used to protect the ISAKMP exchanges. Host-B uses Message 2 to indicate which one, if any, it will support. If Host-A proposed just a single option, Host-B merely needs to acknowledge that the proposal is acceptable.

The source and destination addresses to be placed in the IP header are those of Host-B (responder) and Host-A (initiator), respectively. The UDP header will identify that the destination port is 500, which has been assigned for use by the ISAKMP protocol. The payload of the UDP packet carries the ISAKMP message itself.

The message contents will be as follows:

ISAKMP Header

The ISAKMP Header in Message 2 will indicate an exchange type of Main Mode, and will contain a Message ID of 0. Host-B will set the Responder Cookie field to a random value, which we will call Cookie-B, and will copy into the Initiator Cookie field the value that was received in the Cookie-A field of Message 1. The value pair <Cookie-A, Cookie-B> will serve as the SPI for the ISAKMP Security Association.

Security Association

The Security Association field identifies the Domain of Interpretation (DOI). Since the hosts plan to run IPSec protocols between themselves, the DOI is simply IP.

Proposal Payload

Host-B's Proposal Payload will specify the protocol PROTO_ISAKMP and will set the SPI value to 0.

Transform Payload

The Transform Payload will specify KEY_OAKLEY. For the KEY_OAKLEY transform, the attributes that were accepted from the proposal offered by Host-A are copied into the appropriate fields.

At this point, the properties of the ISAKMP Security Association have been agreed to by Host-A and Host-B. The identity of the ISAKMP SA has been set equal to the pair <Cookie-A, Cookie-B>. However, the identities of the parties claiming to be Host-A and Host-B have not yet been authoritatively verified.

3. IKE Phase 1, Message 3

The third message of the Phase 1 ISAKMP exchange begins the exchange of the information from which the cryptographic keys will eventually be derived (see Figure 192 on page 406).

Important.

None of the messages themselves carry the actual cryptographic keys. Instead, they carry inputs that will be used by Host-A and Host-B to derive the keys locally.

The ISAKMP payload will be used to exchange two types of information:

Diffie-Hellman public value

The Diffie-Hellman public value g^x from the initiator. The exponent x in the public value is the private value that must be kept secret.

Nonce

The nonce N_i from the initiator. (*Nonce* is a fancy name for a value that is considered to be random according to some very strict mathematical guidelines.)

ID If authentication with RSA public key is used, the nonces are encrypted with the public key of the other party. Likewise are the IDs of either party which are then also exchanged at this stage.

If authentication with revised RSA public key is used, the KE and ID payloads are encrypted with a secret key that is derived from the nonces and the encryption algorithm agreed to in Messages 1 and 2, thus avoiding one CPU-intensive public key operation.

Certificates may optionally be exchanged in either case of public key authentication, as well as a hash value thereof.

These values are carried in the Key Exchange, and the Nonce and the ID fields, respectively.

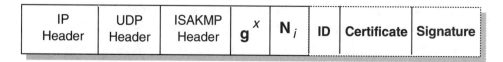

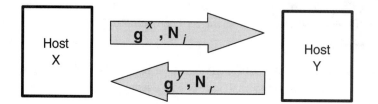

Figure 192. Message 3 of an ISAKMP Phase 1 Exchange

4. IKE Phase 1, Message 4

   After receiving a Diffie-Hellman public value and a nonce from Host-A, Host-B will respond by sending to Host-A its own Diffie-Hellman public value (g^y from the responder) and its nonce (N_r from the responder).

5. Generating the Keys (Phase 1)

   At this point, each host knows the values of the two nonces (N_i and N_r). Each host also knows its own private Diffie-Hellman value (x and y) and also knows its partner's public value (g^x or g^y). Hence each side can construct the composite value g^{xy}. And finally, each side knows the values of the initiator cookie and the responder cookie.

   Given all these bits of information, each side can then independently compute identical values for the following quantities:

   - SKEYID: This collection of bits is sometimes referred to as keying material, since it provides the raw input from which actual cryptographic keys will be derived later in the process. It is obtained by applying the agreed-to keyed pseudorandom function (prf) to the known inputs:

     a. For digital signature authentication:

     $$\text{SKEYID} = \text{prf}(N_i,\ N_r,\ g^{xy})$$

b. For authentication with public keys:

$$SKEYID = prf(hash(N_i, N_r), CookieA, CookieB)$$

c. For authentication with a pre-shared key:

$$SKEYID = prf(pre\text{-}shared\ key, N_i, N_r)$$

- Having computed the value SKEYID, each side then proceeds to generate two cryptographic keys and some additional keying material:

  - SKEYID_d is keying material that will be subsequently used in Phase 2 to derive the keys that will be used in non-ISAKMP SAs for protecting user traffic:

    $$SKEYID\_d = prf(SKEYID, g^{xy}, CookieA, CookieB, 0)$$

  - SKEYID_a is the key used for authenticating ISAKMP messages:

    $$SKEYID\_a = prf(SKEYID, SKEYID\_d, g^{xy}, CookieA, CookieB, 1)$$

  - SKEYID_e is the key used for encrypting ISAKMP exchanges:

    $$SKEYID\_e = prf(SKEYID, SKEYID\_a, g^{xy}, CookieA, CookieB, 2)$$

At this point in the protocol, both Host-A and Host-B have derived identical authentication and encryption keys that they will use to protect the ISAKMP exchanges. And they have also derived identical keying material from which they will derive keys to protect user data during Phase 2 of the ISAKMP negotiations. However, at this point, the two parties' identities still have not been authenticated to one another.

6. IKE Phase 1, Message 5

At this point in the Phase 1 flows, the two hosts will exchange identity information with each other to authenticate themselves. As shown in Figure 193 on page 408, the ISAKMP message will carry an identity payload, a signature payload, and an optional certificate payload. Host-A uses Message 5 to send information to Host-B that will allow Host-B to authenticate Host-A.

IP Header	UDP Header	ISAKMP Header	**Identity**	**Certificate**	**Signature**

Figure 193. *Message 5 of an ISAKMP Phase 1 Exchange*

When an actual certificate is present in the Certificate Payload field, the receiver can use the information directly, after verifying that it has been signed with a valid signature of a trusted certificate authority. If there is no certificate in the message, then it is the responsibility of the receiver to obtain a certificate using some implementation method. For example, it may send a query to a trusted certificate authority using a protocol such as LDAP, or it may query a secure DNS server, or it may maintain a secure local cache that maps previously used certificates to their respective ID values, or it may send an ISAKMP Certificate Request message to its peer, who must then immediately send its certificate to the requester.

Note: The method for obtaining a certificate is a local option, and is not defined as part of IKE. In particular, it is a local responsibility of the receiver to check that the certificate in question is still valid and has not been revoked.

There are several points to bear in mind:

- At this stage of the process, all ISAKMP payloads, whether in Phase 1 or Phase 2, are encrypted, using the encryption algorithm (negotiated in Messages 1 and 2) and the keys (derived from the information in Messages 3 and 4). The ISAKMP header itself, however, is still transmitted in the clear.

- In Phase 1, IPSec's ESP protocol is not used: that is, there is no ESP header. The recipient uses the Encryption Bit in the Flags field of the ISAKMP header to determine if encryption has been applied to the message. The pair of values <CookieA, CookieB>, which serve as an SPI for Phase 1 exchanges, provide a pointer to the correct algorithm and key to be used to decrypt the message.

- The Digital Signature, if used, is not applied to the ISAKMP message itself. Instead, it is applied to a hash of information that is available to both Host-A and Host-B.

- The identity carried in the identity payload does not necessarily bear any relationship to the source IP address; however, the identity carried in the identity payload must be the identity to which the certificate, if used, applies.

Host-A (the initiator) will generate the following hash function, and then place the result in the Signature Payload field:

$$\text{HASH\_I} = \text{prf}(\text{SKEYID, } g^x, g^y, \text{ CookieA, CookieB, } SA_p, ID_A)$$

If digital signatures were used for authentication, this hash will also be signed by Host-A.

ID_A is Host-A's identity information that was transmitted in the identity payload of this message, and SA_p is the entire body of the SA payload that was sent by Host-A in Message 1, including all proposals and all transforms proposed by Host-A. The cookies, public Diffie-Hellman values, and SKEYID were explicitly carried in Messages 1 through 4, or were derived from their contents.

7. IKE Phase 1, Message 6

After receiving Message 5 from Host-A, Host-B will verify the identity of Host-A by validating the hash.

If digital signatures were used for authentication, the signature of this hash will be verified by Host-B.

If this is successful, then Host-B will send Message 6 to Host-A to allow Host-A to verify the identity of Host-B.

The structure of Message 6 is the same as that of Message 5, with the obvious changes that the identity payload and the certificate payload now pertain to Host-B.

$$\text{HASH\_R} = \text{prf}(\text{SKEYID, } g^y, g^x, \text{ CookieB, CookieA, } SA_p, ID_B)$$

Notice that the order in which Diffie-Hellman public values and the cookies appear has been changed, and the final term now is the Identity Payload that Host-B has included in Message 6.

If digital signatures were used for authentication, this hash will also be signed by Host-B, which is different from the one previously signed by Host-A.

When Host-A receives Message 6 and verifies the hash or digital signature, the Phase 1 exchanges are then complete. At this point, each participant has authenticated itself to its peer. Both have agreed on the characteristics of the ISAKMP Security Associations, and both have derived the same set of keys (or keying material).

8. Miscellaneous Phase 1 Facts

There are several miscellaneous facts worth noting:

a. Regardless of the specific authentication mechanism that is used, there will be six messages exchanged for Oakley Main Mode. However, the content of the individual messages will differ, depending on the authentication method.
b. Although Oakley exchanges make use of both encryption and authentication, they do not use either IPSec's ESP or AH protocol. ISAKMP exchanges are protected with application-layer security mechanisms, not with network layer security mechanisms.
c. ISAKMP messages are sent using UDP. There is no guaranteed delivery for them.
d. The only way to identify that an ISAKMP message is part of a Phase 1 flow rather than a Phase 2 flow is to check the Message ID field in the ISAKMP Header. For Phase 1 flows, it must be 0, and (although not explicitly stated in the ISAKMP documents) for Phase 2 flows it must be non-zero.

Phase 2 - Setting Up the Protocol Security Associations: After having completed the Phase 1 negotiation process to set up the ISAKMP Security Associations, Host-A's next step is to initiate the Oakley Phase 2 message exchanges (also known as Oakley Quick Mode) to define the security associations and keys that will be used to protect IP datagrams exchanged between the pair of users. (In the Internet drafts, these are referred to somewhat obtusely as "non-ISAKMP SAs".)

Because the purpose of the Phase 1 negotiations was to agree on how to protect ISAKMP messages, all ISAKMP Phase 2 payloads, but not the ISAKMP header itself, must be encrypted using the algorithm agreed to by the Phase 1 negotiations.

When Oakley Quick Mode is used in Phase 2, authentication is achieved via the use of several cryptographically based hash functions. The input to the hash functions comes partly from Phase 1 information (SKEYID) and partly from information exchanged in Phase 2. Phase 2 authentication is based on certificates, but the Phase 2 process itself does not use certificates directly. Instead, it uses the SKEYID_a material from Phase 1, which itself was authenticated via certificates.

Oakley Quick Mode comes in two forms:

• Without a Key Exchange attribute, Quick Mode can be used to refresh the cryptographic keys, but does not provide the property of Perfect Forward Secrecy (PFS).
• With a Key Exchange attribute, Quick Mode can be used to refresh the cryptographic keys in a way that provides PFS. This is accomplished by including an exchange of public Diffie-Hellman values within messages 1 and 2.

Note: PFS apparently is a property that is very much desired by cryptography experts, but strangely enough, the specs treat PFS as optional. They mandate that a system must be capable of handling the Key Exchange field when it is present in a Quick Mode message, but do not require a system to include the field within the message.

The detailed description of the Phase 2 messages and exchanged information follows below:

1. IKE Phase 2, Message 1

   Message 1 of a Quick Mode Exchange allows Host-A to authenticate itself, to select a nonce, to propose security association(s) to Host-B, to execute an exchange of public Diffie-Hellman values, and to indicate if it is acting on its own behalf or as a proxy negotiator for another entity. An overview of the format of Message 1 is shown in Figure 194.

   Note: Inclusion of a key exchange field is optional. However, when Perfect Forward Secrecy is desired, it must be present.

IP Header	UDP Header	ISAKMP Header	Hash	SA	Prop-osal #1	Trans-form (for #1)	...	Prop-osal #n	Trans-form (for #n)	N	KE	IDs

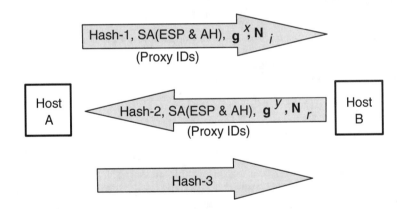

Figure 194. Message 1 of an ISAKMP Phase 2 Quick Mode Exchange

Since we have assumed that Host-A and Host-B are each acting on their own behalf, the user identity fields illustrated in Figure 194 will not be present. The message will consist of:

ISAKMP Header

The ISAKMP Header will indicate an exchange type of Quick Mode, will include a non-zero Message-ID chosen by Host-A, will include the initiator and responder cookie values chosen in Phase 1 (that is, Cookie-A and Cookie-B), and will turn on the encryption flag to indicate that the payloads of the ISAKMP message are encrypted according to the algorithm and key negotiated during Phase 1.

Hash

A Hash Payload must immediately follow the ISAKMP header. HASH_1 uses the keyed pseudo-random function that was negotiated during the Phase 1 exchanges, and is derived from the following information:

- SKEYID_a was derived from the Phase 1 exchanges.
- M-ID is the message ID of this message.
- SA is the Security Association payload carried in this message, including all proposals that were offered.
- Nonce is a new value different from the one used in Phase 1.
- KE is the public Diffie-Hellman value carried in this message. This quantity is chosen by Host-A, and is denoted as g_{qm}^x. Note that this is not the same quantity as g^x that was used in the Phase 1 exchanges.
- IDs, which can identify either the endpoints of the Phase 1 exchange or endpoints on whose behalf the protocol SA should be negotiated (proxy IDs when IKE is used in client mode). These can subsequently be different from the IDs used in Phase 1.

Note: The use of KE and ID is optional depending if PFS is desired.

```
HASH_1 = prf(SKEYID_a, M-ID, SA, N_qmi, KE, ID_qmi, ID_qmr)
```

Security Association

Indicate IP as the Domain of Interpretation.

Proposal, Transform Pairs

There can be one or more of these pairs in this message. The first proposal payload will be numbered 1, will identify an IPSec protocol to be used, and will include an SPI value that is randomly chosen by Host-A for use with that protocol. The proposal payload will be followed by a single transform payload that indicates the cryptographic algorithm to be used with that protocol. The second proposal payload will be numbered 2, etc.

Nonce Payload

This contains the nonce N_{qmi} that was chosen randomly by Host-A.

KE This is the key exchange payload that will carry the public Diffie-Hellman value chosen by Host-A, $g_{qm}{}^x$. There is also a field called Group, that indicates the prime number and generator used in the Diffie-Hellman exchange.

ID Payload

Specifies the endpoints for this SA.

2. IKE Phase 2, Message 2

After Host-B receives Message 1 from Host-A and successfully authenticates it using HASH_1, it constructs a reply, Message 2, to be sent back to Host-A. The Message ID of the reply will be the same one that Host-A used in Message 1. Host-B will choose new values for the following:

Hash

The hash payload now carries the value HASH_2, which is defined as:

$$\text{HASH\_2 = prf(SKEYID\_a, } N_{qmi}, \text{ M-ID, SA, } N_{qmr}, \text{ KE, } ID_{qmi}, \text{ } ID_{qmr})$$

Security Association

The Security Association payload only describes the single chosen proposal and its associated transforms, not all of the protection suites offered by Host-A. Host-B also chooses an SPI value for the selected protocol. Host-B's SPI does not depend in any way on the SPI that Host-A assigned to that protocol when it offered the proposal. That is, it is not necessary that SPI_A be the same as SPI_B; it is only necessary that they each be non-zero and that they each be randomly chosen.

Nonce

Nonce payload now carries N_r, a random value chosen by Host-B.

KE Key exchange payload now carries Host-B's public Diffie-Hellman value, $g_{qm}{}^y$.

At this point, Host-A and Host-B have exchanged nonces and public Diffie-Hellman values. Each one can use this in conjunction with other information to derive a pair of keys, one for each direction of transmission.

3. Generating the Keys (Phase 2)

Using the nonces, public Diffie-Hellman values, SPIs, protocol code points exchanged in Messages 1 and 2 of Phase 2, and the SKEYID value from Phase 1, each host now has enough information to derive two sets of keying material.

a. When PFS is used:

- For data generated by Host-A and received by Host-B, the keying material is:

$$KEYMAT_{AB} = prf(SKEYID\_d, g_{qm}{}^{xy}, protocol, SPI_B, N_{qmi}, N_{qmr})$$

- For data generated by Host-B and received by Host-A, the keying material is:

$$KEYMAT_{BA} = prf(SKEYID\_d, g_{qm}{}^{xy}, protocol, SPI_A, N_{qmi}, N_{qmr})$$

b. When PFS is not used:

- For data generated by Host-A and received by Host-B, the keying material is:

$$KEYMAT_{AB} = prf(SKEYID\_d, protocol, SPI_B, N_{qmi}, N_{qmr})$$

- For data generated by Host-B and received by Host-A, the keying material is:

$$KEYMAT_{BA} = prf(SKEYID\_d, protocol, SPI_A, N_{qmi}, N_{qmr})$$

Note: Depending on the particular case, Host-A may need to derive multiple keys for the following purposes:

- Generating the integrity check value for transmitted datagrams
- Validating the integrity check value of received datagrams
- Encrypting transmitted datagrams
- Decrypting received datagrams

Likewise, Host-B needs to derive the mirror image of the same keys. For example, the key that Host-B uses to encrypt its outbound messages is the same key that Host-A uses to decrypt its inbound messages, etc.

4. IKE Phase 2, Message 3

At this point, Host-A and Host-B have exchanged all the information necessary for them to derive the necessary keying material. The third message in the Quick Mode exchange is used by Host-A to prove its liveness, which it does by producing a hash function that covers the message ID and both nonces that were exchanged in Messages 1 and 2. Message 3 consists only of the ISAKMP header and a hash payload that carries:

$$\text{HASH\_3} = \text{prf}(\text{SKEYID\_a}, 0, \text{M-ID}, N_{qmi}, N_{qmr})$$

When Host-B receives this message and verifies the hash, then both systems can begin to use the negotiated security protocols to protect their user data streams.

5.5.5.3 Negotiating Multiple Security Associations

It is also possible to negotiate multiple security associations, each with its own set of keying material, within a single 3-message Quick Mode exchange.

The message formats are very similar to the previously illustrated ones, so only the differences will be highlighted below:

- Message 1 will carry multiple security association payloads, each offering a range of protection suites.

- HASH_1 will cover the entire set of all offered Security Associations carried in Message 1. That is, each Security Association and all of its offered proposals are included.

- In Message 2, for each offered SA, Host-B will select a single protection suite. That is, if n SAs are open for negotiation, then Host-B will choose n protection suites, one from each proposal.

- As was the case for HASH_1, HASH_2 will now cover the entire set of all offered security associations carried in Message 1. That is, each security association and all of its offered proposals are included.

- After Messages 1 and 2 have been exchanged, then Host-A and Host-B will be able to generate the keying material for each of the accepted protection suites, using the same formulas as in 3 on page 413, applied individually for each accepted SA. Even though the nonces and the public Diffie-Hellman values are the same for all selected suites, the keying material derived for each selected protection suite will be different because each proposal will have a different SPI.

- Because multiple security associations have been negotiated, it is a matter of local choice as to which one is used to protect a given datagram. A receiving system must be capable of processing a datagram that is protected by any SA that has been negotiated. That is, it would be legal for a given source host to send two consecutive datagrams to a destination system, where each datagram was protected by a different SA.

5.5.5.4 Using IKE with Remote Access

The critical element in the remote access scenario is the use of Oakley to identify the remote host by name, rather than by its dynamically assigned IP address. Once the remote host's identity has been authenticated and the mapping to its dynamically assigned IP address has been ascertained, the remainder of the processes are the same as we have described for the other scenarios. For example, if the corporate intranet is considered to be trusted, then the remote host needs to establish a single SA between itself and the firewall. But if the corporate intranet is considered to be untrusted, then it may be necessary for the remote host to set up two SAs: one between itself and the firewall, and a second between itself and the destination host.

Recall that a single ISAKMP Phase 1 negotiation can protect several subsequent Phase 2 negotiations. Phase 1 ISAKMP negotiations use computationally intensive public key cryptographic operations, while Phase 2 negotiations use the less computationally intensive symmetric key cryptographic operations. Hence, the heavy computational load only occurs in Phase I, which will only be executed once when the dial-up connection is first initiated.

The principal points that pertain to the remote access case are:

- The remote host's dynamically assigned address is the one that is placed in the IP header of all ISAKMP messages.

- The remote host's permanent identifier (such as an e-mail address) is the quantity that is placed in the ID field of the ISAKMP Phase 1 messages.

- The remote host's certificate used in the ISAKMP exchange must be associated with the remote host's permanent identifier.

- In traffic-bearing datagrams, the remote host's dynamically assigned IP address will be used. This is necessary since the destination IP address that appears in the datagram's IP header is used in conjunction with the SPI and protocol type to identify the relevant IPSec security association for processing the inbound datagram.

5.5.6 References

At the time of writing this book, publication of the following Internet Draft documents has been approved by the IETF as Proposed Standards but no RFC numbers have yet been assigned:

Security Architecture for the Internet Protocol
        http://www.ietf.org/internet-drafts/draft-ietf-ipsec-arch-sec-07.txt
IP Authentication Header (AH)
        http://www.ietf.org/internet-drafts/draft-ietf-ipsec-auth-header-07.txt

IP Encapsulating Security Payload (ESP)
    `http://www.ietf.org/internet-drafts/draft-ietf-ipsec-esp-v2-06.txt`
Internet Security Association and Key Management Protocol (ISAKMP)
    `http://www.ietf.org/internet-drafts/draft-ietf-ipsec-isakmp-10.txt`
Internet Key Exchange (IKE)
    `http://www.ietf.org/internet-drafts/draft-ietf-ipsec-isakmp-oakley-08.txt`
IPSec Domain of Interpretation for ISAKMP
    `http://www.ietf.org/internet-drafts/draft-ietf-ipsec-ipsec-doi-10.txt`
The Use of HMAC-MD5-96 within ESP and AH
    `http://www.ietf.org/internet-drafts/draft-ietf-ipsec-auth-hmac-md5-96-03.txt`
The Use of HMAC-SHA-1-96 within ESP and AH
    `http://www.ietf.org/internet-drafts/draft-ietf-ipsec-auth-hmac-sha196-03.txt`
The ESP DES-CBC Cipher Algorithm With Explicit IV
    `http://www.ietf.org/internet-drafts/draft-ietf-ipsec-ciph-des-expiv-02.txt`
The NULL Encryption Algorithm and Its Use With IPsec
    `http://www.ietf.org/internet-drafts/draft-ietf-ipsec-ciph-null-01.txt`

At the time of writing this book, publication of the following Internet Draft documents has been approved by the IETF as Informational RFCs but no RFC numbers have yet been assigned:

Oakley Key Determination Protocol
    `http://www.ietf.org/internet-drafts/draft-ietf-ipsec-oakley-02.txt`
IPSec Working Group to consider Security Document Roadmap
    `http://www.ietf.org/internet-drafts/draft-ietf-ipsec-doc-roadmap-02.txt`

5.6 SOCKS

SOCKS is a standard for circuit-level gateways. It does not require the overhead of a more conventional proxy server where a user has to consciously connect to the firewall first before requesting the second connection to the destination (please see Figure 195 on page 418).

The user starts a client application with the destination server IP address. Instead of directly starting a session with the destination server, the client initiates a session to the SOCKS server on the firewall. The SOCKS server then validates that the source address and user ID are permitted to establish onward connection into the nonsecure network, and then creates the second session.

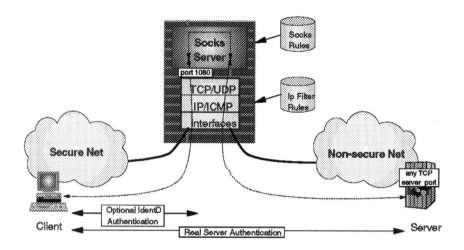

Figure 195. *SOCKS Server*

SOCKS needs to have new versions of the client code (called SOCKSified clients) and a separate set of configuration profiles on the firewall. However, the server machine does not need modification; indeed it is unaware that the session is being relayed by the SOCKS server. Both the client and the SOCKS server need to have SOCKS code. The SOCKS server acts as an application-level router between the client and the real application server. SOCKSv4 is for outbound TCP sessions only. It is simpler for the private network user, but does not have secure password delivery so it is not intended for sessions between public network users and private network applications. SOCKSv5 provides for several authentication methods and can therefore be used for inbound connections as well, though these should be used with caution. SOCKSv5 also supports UDP-based applications and protocols.

The majority of Web browsers are SOCKSified and you can get SOCKSified TCP/IP stacks for most platforms. For additional information, refer to RFC 1928, 1929, 1961 and the following URL:

http://www.socks.nec.com

5.6.1 SOCKS Version 5 (SOCKSv5)

SOCKS version 5 is a *proposed standard protocol* with a status of *elective*. It is described in RFC 1928.

Application-level gateways provide secure connections for some applications such as TELNET, FTP and SMTP. However, it is not easy to write proxy code for each new application. Generally, the proxy service becomes available after some time even if the service can be used directly and application level gateways do not allow UDP connections. SOCKSv5 satisfies all these shortcomings and requirements with a strong authentication mechanism and the hiding of addresses from a non-secure network. Although, supporting UDP might seem to be vulnerable, it can be configured to pass UDP for particular users and particular applications only.

The SOCKSv5 concept is based on SOCKSv4 with some extensions such as UDP support, new and various sophisticated authentication methods and extended addressing schemes to cover domain-name and IPv6. SOCKSv5 supports a range of authentication methods, including:

1. Username/password authentication

2. One-time password generators

3. Kerberos

4. Remote Authentication Dial-In User Services (RADIUS)

5. Password Authentication Protocol (PAP)

6. IPSEC Authentication method

SOCKSv5 also supports the following encryption standards:

1. DES

2. Triple DES

3. IPSEC

The following tunneling protocols are supported:

1. PPTP

2. L2F

3. L2TP

The following key management systems are supported:

1. SKIP

2. ISAKMP/Oakley

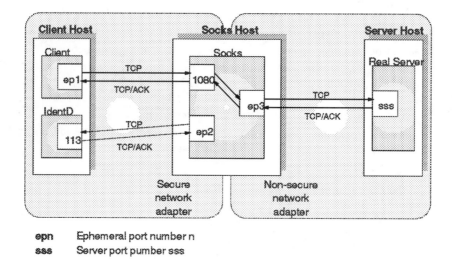

epn   Ephemeral port number n
sss   Server port pumber sss

Figure 196. Socks TCP Segment Flow

The SOCKSv5 server listens for connections on port 1080. According to the
connection type (TCP or UDP), the steps discussed in the following sections are taken
to establish a connection.

5.6.1.1 SOCKSv5 TCP Connection

To establish a connection using TCP, the client first sends a TCP packet which
contains session request information via port 1080 to the server (please see
Figure 196). If the access permissions allow this operation and the connection request
succeeds, the client enters an authentication negotiation. In this state, the
authentication type is determined, after which the client sends a relay request. The
SOCKSv5 server evaluates the request and either establishes the connection or rejects
it. The client sends the following message which contains a version identifier and
method options.

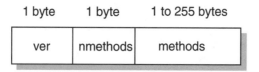

Figure 197. SOCKSv5 - Version Identifier and Method Selection Message Format

Where:

VER Indicates the version of SOCKS. For SOCKSv5, the value is hexadecimal X'05'.

NMETHODS Indicates the number of the methods appeared in the methods field.

METHODS Indicates the supported authentication and encapsulation methods

The server responds by the following message.

Figure 198. SOCKSv5 - Selected Method Message Format

The hexadecimal values for current standard METHODS are as follows;

X'00'	NO AUTHENTICATION REQUIRED
X'01'	GSSAPI
X'02'	USERNAME/PASSWORD
X'03' to X'7F'	IANA ASSIGNED
X'80' to X'FE'	RESERVED FOR PRIVATE METHODS
X'FF'	NO ACCEPTABLE METHODS

All implementations should support USERNAME/PASSWORD and GSSAPI authentication methods.

Once authentication is completed successfully, the client sends the request details. If an encapsulation method is negotiated during the method negotiation, the selected encapsulation method must be applied for the following messages. The detail request message format issued by the client is as follows:

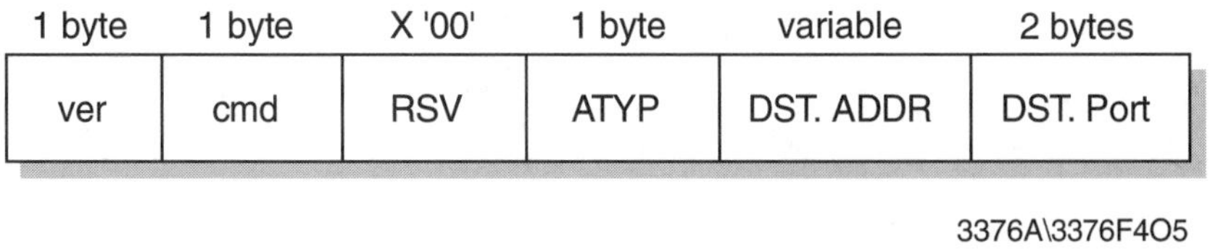

1 byte	1 byte	X '00'	1 byte	variable	2 bytes
ver	cmd	RSV	ATYP	DST. ADDR	DST. Port

3376A\3376F4O5

Figure 199. SOCKSv5 - Detail Request Message Format

Where:

VER Socks protocol version. For SOCKSv5, the value is hexadecimal X'05'.

CMD SOCKS command in octets.

X'01' CONNECT

X'02' BIND

X'03' UDP ASSOCIATE

RSV Reserved for future use.

ATYP Address types in octets.

X'01' IPv4 address

X'03' Domain-name

X'04' IPv6 address

DST.ADDR Desired destination address.

DST.PORT Desired destination port in network octet order.

The server evaluates the request detail message and replies with one or more messages. Here is the reply message format issued by the server.

1 byte	1 byte	X '00'	1 byte	variable	2 bytes
ver	rep	RSV	ATYP	BND. ADDR	BND. Port

3376A\3376F4O6

Figure 200. *SOCKSv5 - Server Reply Message Format*

Where:

VER Socks protocol version. For SOCKSv5, the value is hexadecimal X'05'.

REP Reply field:

X'00' Succeeded

X'01' General SOCKS server failure

X'02' Connection not allowed by ruleset

X'03' Network unreachable

X'04' Host unreachable

X'05' Connection refused

	X'06'	TTL expired
	X'07'	Command not supported
	X'08'	Address type not supported
	X'09' to X'FF'	Unassigned
RSV	Reserved for future use.	
ATYP	Address types in octets.	
	X'01'	IPv4 address
	X'03'	Domain name
	X'04'	IPv6 address

BND.ADDR Server bound address.

BND.PORT Server bound port in network octet order.

5.6.1.2 SOCKSv5 UDP Connection

To be able use a UDP connection over a SOCKS server, the client first issues the UDP ASSOCIATE command to the SOCKSv5 server. The SOCKSv5 server then assigns a UDP port to which the client sends all UDP datagrams. Each UDP datagram has a UDP request header. The UDP request header format is as follows:

2 bytes	1 byte	1 byte	variable	2 bytes	variable
RSV	frag	ATYP	DST. ADDR	DST. Port	data

3376A\3376F4O7

Figure 201. SOCKSv5 - UDP Datagram Request Header Format

Where:

RSV   Reserved for future use. All bytes are zero.

FRAG   Current fragment number.

ATYP   Address types in octets.

	X'01'	IPv4 address
	X'03'	Domain-name
	X'04'	IPv6 address

DST.ADDR Desired destination address.

DST.PORT   Desired destination port in network octet order.

DATA   User data.

The UDP relay server gets the IP address of the client which sends UDP datagrams to the port specified by DST.PORT. It will then discard any datagram that comes from another source.

5.7 Secure Sockets Layer (SSL)

SSL is a security protocol that was developed by Netscape Communications Corporation, along with RSA Data Security, Inc. The primary goal of the SSL protocol is to provide a private channel between communicating applications, which ensures privacy of data, authentication of the partners and integrity.

5.7.1 SSL Overview

SSL provides an alternative to the standard TCP/IP socket API that has security implemented within it. Hence, in theory it is possible to run any TCP/IP application in a secure way without changing the application. In practice, SSL is only widely implemented for HTTP connections, but Netscape Communications Corp. has stated an intention to employ it for other application types, such as NNTP and Telnet, and there are several such implementations freely available on the Internet. IBM, for example, is using SSL to enhance security for TN3270 sessions in its Host On-Demand and eNetwork Communications Server products.

SSL is composed of two layers:

- At the lower layer, a protocol for transferring data using a variety of predefined cipher and authentication combinations, called the *SSL Record Protocol*. Figure 202 on page 425 illustrates this, and contrasts it with a standard HTTP socket connection. Note that this diagram shows SSL as providing a simple socket interface, on which other applications can be layered. In reality, current implementations have the socket interface embedded within the application and do not expose an API that other applications can use.

- On the upper layer, a protocol for initial authentication and transfer of encryption keys, called the *SSL Handshake Protocol*.

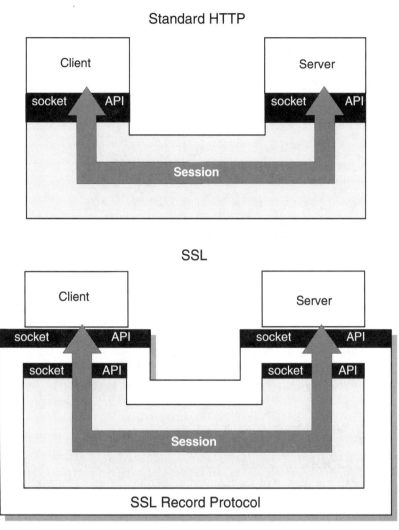

Standard HTTP

SSL

3376E\3376F4OS

Figure 202. SSL - Comparison of Standard and SSL Sessions

An SSL session is initiated as follows:

- On the client (browser) the user requests a document with a special URL that commences https: instead of http:, either by typing it into the URL input field, or by clicking on a link.

- The client code recognizes the SSL request and establishes a connection through TCP port 443 to the SSL code on the server.

- The client then initiates the SSL handshake phase, using the SSL Record Protocol as a carrier. At this point there is no encryption or integrity checking built in to the connection.

The SSL protocol addresses the following security issues:

Privacy
> After the symmetric key is established in the initial handshake, the messages are encrypted using this key.

Integrity
> Messages contain a message authentication code (MAC) ensuring the message integrity.

Authentication
> During the handshake, the client authenticates the server using an asymmetric or public key. It can also be based on certificates.

SSL requires each message to be encrypted and decrypted and therefore has a high performance and resource overhead.

5.7.1.1 Differences between SSL V2.0 and SSL V3.0

There is a backward compatibility between SSL V2.0 and SSL V3.0. An SSL V3.0 server implementation should be able accept the connection request from an SSL V2.0 client. The main differences between SSL V2.0 and SSL V3.0 are as follows:

- SSL V2.0 does not support client authentication.
- SSL V3.0 supports more ciphering types in the CipherSpec.

5.7.2 SSL Protocol

The SSL protocol is located at the top of the transport layer. SSL is also a layered protocol itself. It simply takes the data from the application layer, reformats it and transmits it to the transport layer. SSL handles a message as follows:

Sender
> Performs the following tasks:
>
> - Takes the message from upper layer
> - Fragments the data to manageable blocks
> - Optionally compresses the data
> - Applies a Message Authentication Code (MAC)
> - Encrypts the data
> - Transmits the result to the lower layer

Receiver

Performs the following tasks:

- Takes the data from lower layer
- Decrypts
- Verifies the data with the negotiated MAC key
- Decompresses the data if compression was used
- Reassembles the message
- Transmits the message to the upper layer

An SSL session works in different states. These states are *session* and *connection* states. The SSL handshake protocol (please see 5.7.2.2, "SSL Handshake Protocol" on page 428) coordinates the states of the client and the server. In addition, there are read and write states defined to coordinate the encryption according to the change cipher spec messages.

When either party sends a change cipher spec message, it changes the pending write state to current write state. Again, when either party receives a change cipher spec message, it changes the pending read state to the current read state.

The session state includes the following components:

Session identifier

An arbitrary byte sequence chosen by the server to identify an active or resumable session state.

Peer certificate

Certificate of the peer. This field is optional; it can be empty.

Compression method

The compression algorithm.

Cipher spec

Specifies data encryption algorithm (such as null, DES) and a MAC algorithm.

Master secret

48-byte shared secret between the client and the server.

Is resumable

A flag indicating whether the session can be used for new connections.

The connection state includes the following components:

Server and client random

An arbitrary byte sequence chosen by the client and server for each connection.

Server write MAC secret

The secret used for MAC operations by the server.

Client write MAC secret

The secret used for MAC operations by the client.

Server write key

The cipher key for the server to encrypt the data and the client to decrypt the data.

Client write key

The cipher key for the client to encrypt the data and the server to decrypt the data.

Initialization vectors

Initialization vectors store the encryption information.

Sequence numbers

A sequence number indicates the number of the message transmitted since the last change cipher spec message. Both the client and the server maintain sequence numbers.

5.7.2.1 Change Cipher Spec Protocol

The change cipher spec protocol is responsible for sending change cipher spec messages. At any time, the client can request to change current cryptographic parameters such as handshake key exchange. Following the change cipher spec notification, the client sends a handshake key exchange and if available, certificate verify messages, and the server sends a change cipher spec message after processing the key exchange message. After that, the newly agreed keys will be used until the next change cipher spec request. The change cipher spec message is sent after the hello messages during the negotiation.

5.7.2.2 SSL Handshake Protocol

The SSL Handshake Protocol allows the client and server to determine the required parameters for an SSL connection such as protocol version, cryptographic algorithms, optional client or server authentication, and public-key encryption methods to generate shared secrets. During this process all handshake messages are forwarded to the SSL Record Layer to be encapsulated into special SSL messages. Figure 203 on page 429 illustrates an SSL handshake process.

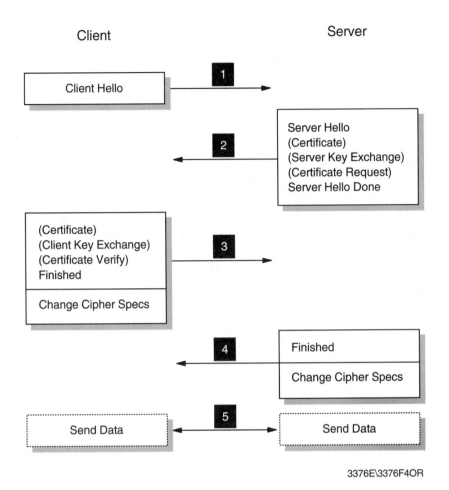

Figure 203. *SSL - Handshake Process*

1. The client sends a connection request with a client hello message. This message includes:

    - Desired version number.
    - Time information (the current time and date in standard UNIX 32-bit format).
    - Optionally session-ID. If it is not specified the server will try to resume previous sessions or return an error message
    - Cipher suites. (List of the cryptographic options supported by the client. These are authentication modes, key exchange methods, encryptions and MAC algorithms.)
    - Compression methods supported by the client.
    - A random value.

2. The server evaluates the parameters sent by the client hello message and returns a server hello message that includes the following parameters which were selected by the server to be used for the SSL session:

   - Version number
   - Time information (the current time and date in standard UNIX 32-bit format)
   - Session ID
   - Cipher suite
   - Compression method
   - A random value

   Following the server hello message the server sends the following messages:

   - Server certificate if the server is required to be authenticated
   - A server key exchange message if there is no certificate available or the certificate is for signing only
   - A certificate request if the client is required to be authenticated

   Finally, the server sends a server hello done message and begins to wait for the client response.

3. The client sends the following messages:

   - If the server has sent a certificate request, the client must send a certificate or a no certificate message.
   - If the server has sent a server key exchange message, the client sends a client key exchange message based on the public key algorithm determined with the hello messages.
   - If the client has sent a certificate, the client verifies the server certificate and sends a certificate verify message indicating the result.

   The client then sends a finished message indicating the negotiation part is completed. The client also sends a change cipher spec message to generate shared secrets. It should be noted that this is not controlled by the handshake protocol, the change cipher spec protocol manages this part of the operation.

4. The server sends a finished message indicating the negotiation part is completed. The server then sends the change cipher spec message.

5. Finally the session partners separately generate an encryption key, the master key from which they derive the keys to use in the encrypted session that follows. The Handshake protocol changes the state to the connection state. All data taken from the application layer is transmitted as special messages to the other party.

There is significant additional overhead in starting up an SSL session compared with a normal HTTP connection. The protocol avoids some of this overhead by allowing the client and server to retain session key information and to resume that session without negotiating and authenticating a second time.

Following the handshake, both session partners have generated a master key. From that key they generate other session keys, which are used in the symmetric-key encryption of the session data and in the creation of message digests. The first message encrypted in this way is the finished message from the server. If the client can interpret the finished message, it means:

- Privacy has been achieved, because the message is encrypted using a symmetric-key bulk cipher (such as DES or RC4).
- The message integrity is assured, because it contains a Message Authentication Code (MAC), which is a message digest of the message itself plus material derived from the master key.
- The server has been authenticated, because it was able to derive the master key from the pre-master key. As this was sent using the server's public key, it could only have been decrypted by the server (using its private key). Note that this relies on the integrity of the server's public key certificate.

5.7.2.3 SSL Record Protocol

Once the master key has been determined, the client and server can use it to encrypt application data. The SSL record protocol specifies a format for these messages. In general they include a message digest to ensure that they have not been altered and the whole message is encrypted using a symmetric cipher. Usually this uses the RC2 or RC4 algorithm, although DES, triple-DES and IDEA are also supported by the specification.

The U.S. National Security Agency (NSA), a department of the United States federal government imposes restrictions on the size of the encryption key that can be used in software exported outside the U.S. These rules are currently under review, but the present effect is to limit the key to an effective size of 56 bits. The RC2 and RC4 algorithms achieve this by using a key in which all but 56 bits are set to a fixed value. International (export) versions of software products have this hobbled security built into them. SSL checks for mismatches between the export and nonexport versions in the negotiation phase of the handshake. For example, if a U.S. browser tries to connect with SSL to an export server, they will agree on export-strength encryption. See 5.2.7, "Export/Import Restrictions on Cryptography" on page 358 for more information on recent changes of U.S. export regulations of cryptographic material.

5.8 Transport Layer Security (TLS)

The Transport Layer Security 1.0 protocol is based on SSL. At the time of writing, the TLS 1.0 protocol is not a standard protocol. (Please refer to current TLS draft document for more information about SSL.) There are not significant differences between SSL 3.0 and TLS 1.0. They can interoperate with some modifications on the message formats.

5.9 Secure Multipurpose Internet Mail Extension (S-MIME)

Secure Multipurpose Internet Mail Extension (S-MIME) can be thought of as a very specific SSL-like protocol. S-MIME is an application-level security construct, but its use is limited to protecting e-mail via encryption and digital signatures. It relies on public key technology, and uses X.509 certificates to establish the identities of the communicating parties. S-MIME can be implemented in the communicating end systems; it is not used by intermediate routers or firewalls.

5.10 Virtual Private Networks (VPN) Overview

The Internet has become a popular, low-cost backbone infrastructure. Its universal reach has led many companies to consider constructing a secure virtual private network (VPN) over the public Internet. The challenge in designing a VPN for today's global business environment will be to exploit the public Internet backbone for both intra-company and inter-company communication while still providing the security of the traditional private, self-administered corporate network.

In this chapter, we begin by defining a virtual private network (VPN) and explaining the benefits that customers can achieve from its implementation. After discussing the security considerations and planning aspects, we then describe the VPN solutions available in the market today.

5.10.1 VPN Introduction and Benefits

With the explosive growth of the Internet, companies are beginning to ask: "How can we best exploit the Internet for our business?". Initially, companies were using the Internet to promote their company's image, products, and services by providing World Wide Web access to corporate Web sites. Today, however, the Internet potential is limitless, and the focus has shifted to e-business, using the global reach of the Internet for easy access to key business applications and data that reside in traditional I/T systems. Companies can now securely and cost-effectively extend the reach of their applications and data across the world through the implementation of secure virtual private network (VPN) solutions.

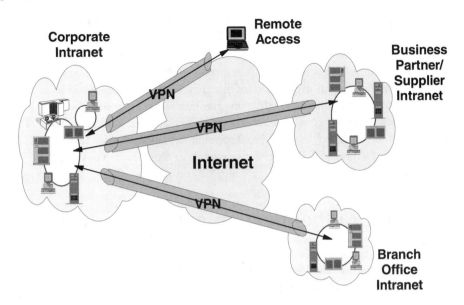

Figure 204. *Virtual Private Networks*

A virtual private network (VPN) is an extension of an enterprise's private intranet across a public network such as the Internet, creating a secure private connection, essentially through a private *tunnel*. VPNs securely convey information across the Internet connecting remote users, branch offices, and business partners into an extended corporate network, as shown in Figure 204. Internet Service Providers (ISPs) offer cost-effective access to the Internet (via direct lines or local telephone numbers), enabling companies to eliminate their current, expensive leased lines, long-distance calls, and toll-free telephone numbers.

A 1997 VPN Research Report, by Infonetics Research, Inc., estimates savings from 20% to 47% of wide area network (WAN) costs by replacing leased lines to remote sites with VPNs. And, for remote access VPNs, savings can be 60% to 80% of corporate remote access dial-up costs. Additionally, Internet access is available worldwide where other connectivity alternatives may not be available.

The technology to implement these virtual private networks, however, is just becoming standardized. Some networking vendors today are offering non-standards-based VPN solutions that make it difficult for a company to incorporate all its employees and/or business partners/suppliers into an extended corporate network. However, VPN solutions based on Internet Engineering Task Force (IETF) standards will provide support for the full range of VPN scenarios with more interoperability and expansion capabilities.

The key to maximizing the value of a VPN is the ability for companies to evolve their VPNs as their business needs change and to easily upgrade to future TCP/IP technology. Vendors who support a broad range of hardware and software VPN products provide the flexibility to meet these requirements. VPN solutions today run mainly in the IPv4 environment, but it is important that they have the capability of being upgraded to IPv6 to remain interoperable with your business partner's and/or supplier's VPN solutions. Perhaps equally critical is the ability to work with a vendor who understands the issues of deploying a VPN. The implementation of a successful VPN involves more than technology. The vendor's networking experience plays heavily into this equation.

5.11 Kerberos Authentication and Authorization System

The Kerberos Network Authentication Service Version 5 is a *proposed standard protocol*. It is status is *elective* and described in RFC 1510.

According to *The Enlarged Devil's Dictionary (Ambrose Bierce)*, Kerberos is "the watchdog of Hades, whose duty it was to guard the entrance against whom or what does not clearly appear; Kerberos is known to have had three heads."

The Kerberos Authentication and Authorization System is an encryption-based security system that provides mutual authentication between the users and the servers in a network environment. The assumed goals for this system are:

- Authentication to prevent fraudulent requests/responses between users and servers that must be confidential and on groups of at least one user and one service.

- Authorization can be implemented independently from the authentication by each service that wants to provide its own authorization system. The authorization system can assume that the authentication of a user/client is reliable.

- Permits the implementation of an accounting system that is integrated, secure and reliable, with modular attachment and support for "chargebacks" or billing purposes.

The Kerberos system is mainly used for authentication purposes, but it also provides the flexibility to add authorization information.

5.11.1 Assumptions

Kerberos assumes the following:

- The environment using this security system will include public and private workstations that can be located in areas with minimal physical security, a campus network without link encryption that can be composed of dispersed local networks connected by backbones or gateways, centrally operated servers in locked rooms with moderate physical security and centrally operated servers with considerable physical security.

- Confidential data or high-risk operations such as a bank transaction may not be part of this environment without additional security, because once you have a workstation as a terminal you can emulate certain conditions and normal data will be flowing without any encryption protection.

- One of the cryptosystems used is the Data Encryption Standard (DES), which has been developed to be modular and replaceable by the Kerberos designers.

- Kerberos assumes a loosely synchronized clock in the whole system so the workstation has to have a synchronization tool such as the time server provided.

5.11.2 Naming

A *principal identifier* is the name that identifies a client or a service for the Kerberos system.

In Version 4, the identifier consists of three components:

- The *principal* name is unique for each client and service assigned by the Kerberos Manager.

- The *instance* name used for distinct authentication is an added label for clients and services which exist in several forms. For users, an instance can provide different identifiers for different privileges. For services, an instance usually specifies the host name of the machine that provides this service.

- The *realm* name used to allow independently administered Kerberos sites. The principal name and the instance are qualified by the realm to which they belong, and are unique only within that realm. The realm is commonly the domain name.

In Version 4, each of the three components has a limit of 39 characters long. Due to conventions, the period (.) is not an acceptable character.

In Version 5, the identifier consists of two parts only, the *realm* and the *remainder*, which is a sequence of however many components are needed to name the principal. Both the realm and each component of the remainder are defined as ASN.1 (Abstract

Syntax Notation One, ISO standard 8824) GeneralStrings. This puts few restrictions on the characters available for principal identifiers.

5.11.3 Kerberos Authentication Process

In the Kerberos system, a client that wants to contact a server for its service, first has to ask for a *ticket* from a mutually trusted third party, the Kerberos Authentication Server (KAS). This ticket is obtained as a function where one of the components is a private key known only by the service and the Kerberos Authentication Server, so that the service can be confident that the information on the ticket originates from Kerberos. The client is known to the KAS as a principal name (c). The private key (K_c) is the authentication key known only to the user and the Kerberos Authentication Server (KAS).

In this chapter, the symbol {X,Y} indicates a message containing information (or data) X and Y. {X,Y}K_z indicates that a message that contains the data X and Y, has been enciphered using the key K_z.

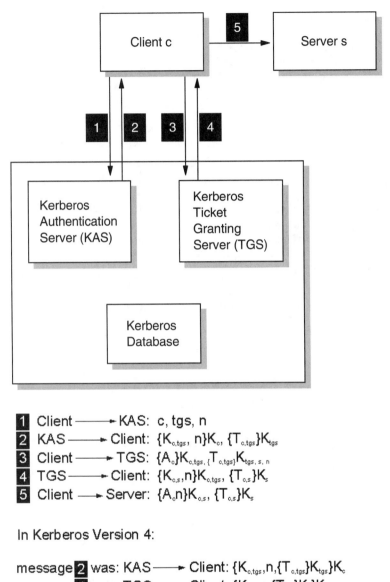

1 Client ────► KAS: c, tgs, n
2 KAS ────► Client: $\{K_{c,tgs}, n\}K_c$, $\{T_{c,tgs}\}K_{tgs}$
3 Client ────► TGS: $\{A_c\}K_{c,tgs}, \{T_{c,tgs}\}K_{tgs, s, n}$
4 TGS ────► Client: $\{K_{c,s}, n\}K_{c,tgs}$, $\{T_{c,s}\}K_s$
5 Client ────► Server: $\{A_c n\}K_{c,s}$, $\{T_{c,s}\}K_s$

In Kerberos Version 4:

message **2** was: KAS ────► Client: $\{K_{c,tgs}, n, \{T_{c,tgs}\}K_{tgs}\}K_c$
message **4** was: TGS ────► Client: $\{K_{c,s}, n, \{T_{c,s}\}K_s\}K_{c,tgs}$

3376E\3376F4OT

Figure 205. *Kerberos Authentication Scheme*

The authentication process consists of exchanging five messages (see Figure 205):

1 Client -> KAS

The client sends a message {c, tgs, n}, to the KAS, containing its identity (c), a nonce (a timestamp or other means to identify this request), and requests for a ticket for use with the ticket-granting server (TGS).

2 KAS -> Client

The authentication server looks up the client name (c) and the service name (the ticket-granting server, tgs) in the Kerberos database, and obtains an encryption key for each (K_c and K_{tgs}).

The KAS then forms a response to send back to the client. This response contains an initial ticket $T_{c,tgs}$, which grants the client access to the requested server (the ticket-granting server). $T_{c,tgs}$ contains $K_{c,tgs}$, c, tgs, nonce, lifetime and some other information. The KAS also generates a random encryption key $K_{c,tgs}$, called the session key. It then encrypts this ticket using the encryption key of the ticket-granting server (K_{tgs}). This produces what is called a *sealed ticket* $\{T_{c,tgs}\}K_{tgs}$. A message is then formed consisting of the sealed ticket and the TGS session key $K_{c,tgs}$.

Note: In Kerberos Version 4, the message is:

$$\{K_{c,tgs}, n, \{T_{c,tgs}\}K_{tgs}\}K_c$$

While in Kerberos Version 5, the message is of a simpler form:

$$\{K_{c,tgs}, n\}K_c, \{T_{c,tgs}\}K_{tgs}$$

This simplifies the (unnecessary) double encryption of the ticket.

3 Client -> TGS

Upon receiving the message, the client decrypts it using its secret key K_c which is only known to it and the KAS. It checks to see if the nonce (n) matches the specific request, and then caches the session key $K_{c,tgs}$ for future communications with the TGS.

The client then sends a message to the TGS. This message contains the initial ticket $\{T_{c,tgs}\}K_{tgs}$, the server name (s), a nonce, and a new authenticator A_c containing a timestamp. A_c is {c, nonce}. The message is:

$$\{A_c\}K_{c,tgs}, \{T_{c,tgs}\}K_{tgs}, s, n$$

4 TGS -> Client

The ticket-granting server (TGS) receives the above message from the client (c), and first deciphers the sealed ticket using its TGS encryption key. (This ticket was originally sealed by the Kerberos authentication server in step 2 using the same key.) From the deciphered ticket, the TGS obtains the TGS-session-key. It uses this TGS session key to decipher the sealed authenticator. (Validity is checked by comparing the client name both in the ticket and in the authenticator, the TGS server name in the ticket, the network address that must be equal in the ticket, in the authenticator, and in the received message.) Finally, it checks the current time in the authenticator to make certain the message is recent. This requires that all the clients and servers maintain their clocks within some prescribed tolerance. The TGS now looks up the server name from the message in the Kerberos database, and obtains the encryption key (K_s) for the specified service.

The TGS forms a new random session key $K_{c,s}$ for the benefit of the client (c) and the server (s), and then creates a new ticket $T_{c,s}$ containing:

$K_{c,s}$, n, nonce, lifetime,

It then assembles and sends a message to the client.

Note: In Kerberos Version 4, the message is:

$\{K_{c,s}, n, \{T_{c,s}\} K_s\} K_{c,tgs}$

While in Kerberos Version 5, the message is of a simpler form:

$\{K_{c,s}, n\} K_{c,tgs}, \{T_{c,s}\} K_s$

This simplifies the (unnecessary) double encryption of the ticket.

5 Client -> Server

The client receives this message and deciphers it using the TGS session key that only it and the TGS share. From this message it obtains a new session key $K_{c,s}$ that it shares with the server(s) and a sealed ticket that it cannot decipher because it is enciphered using the server's secret key K_s.

The client builds an authenticator and seals it using the new session key $K_{c,s}$. At last, it sends a message containing the sealed ticket and the authenticator to the server (s) to request its service.

The server (s) receives this message and first deciphers the sealed ticket using its encryption key, which only it and KAS know. It then uses the new session key contained in the ticket to decipher the authenticator and does the same validation process that was described in step **4** .

Once the server has validated a client, an option exists for the client to validate the server. This prevents an intruder from impersonating the server. The client requires then that the server sends back a message containing the timestamp (from the client's authenticator, with one added to the timestamp value). This message is enciphered using the session key that was passed from the client to the server.

Let us summarize some of the central points in this scheme:

- In order for the workstation to use any end server, a ticket is required. All tickets, other than the first ticket (also called the *initial ticket*) are obtained from the TGS. The first ticket is special; it is a ticket for the TGS itself and is obtained from the Kerberos authentication server.

- Every ticket is associated with a session key that is assigned every time a ticket is allocated.

- Tickets are reusable. Every ticket has a lifetime, typically eight hours. After a ticket has expired, you have to identify yourself to Kerberos again, entering your login name and password.

- Unlike a ticket, which can be reused, a new authenticator is required every time the client initiates a new connection with a server. The authenticator carries a timestamp within it, and the authenticator expires a few minutes after it is issued. (This is the reason why clocks must be synchronized between clients and servers.)

- A server should maintain a history of previous client requests for which the timestamp in the authenticator is still valid. This way a server can reject duplicate requests that could arise from a stolen ticket and authenticator.

5.11.4 Kerberos Database Management

Kerberos needs a record for each user and service in its realm and each record keeps only the needed information as follows:

- Principal identifier (c,s)
- Private key for this principal (K_c,K_s)
- Date of expiration for this identity
- Date of the last modification in this record
- Identity of the principal who last modified this record (c,s)
- Maximum lifetime of tickets to be given to this principal (Lifetime)
- Attributes (unused)
- Implementation data (not visible externally)

The private key field is enciphered using a master key so that removing the database will not cause any problem as the master key is not in it.

The entity responsible for managing this database is the Kerberos Database Manager (KDBM). There is only one KDBM in a realm, but it is possible to have more than one Kerberos Key Distribution Server (KKDS), each one having a copy of the Kerberos database. This is done to improve availability and performance so that the user can choose one in a group of KKDSs to send its request to. The KKDS performs read-only operations, leaving the actualization to the KDBM, which copies the entire database a few times a day. This is done to simplify the operation using a Kerberos protected protocol. This protocol is basically a mutual authentication between KDBM and KKDS before a file transfer operation with checkpoints and checksum.

5.11.5 Kerberos Authorization Model

The Kerberos Authentication Model permits only the service to verify the identity of the requester but it gives no information on whether the requester can use the service or not. The Kerberos Authorization Model is based on the principle that each service knows the user so that each one can maintain its own authorization information. However, the Kerberos Authentication System could be extended by information and algorithms that could be used for authorization purposes. (This is made easier in Version 5. Please see the next section.) The Kerberos could then check if a user/client is allowed to use a certain service.

Obviously, both the client and the server applications must be able to handle the Kerberos authentication process. That is, both the client and the server must be *kerberized*.

5.11.6 Kerberos Version 5 Enhancements

Kerberos Version 5 has a number of enhancements over Version 4. Some of the important ones are:

- Use of encryption has been separated into distinct program modules which allows for supporting multiple encryption systems.

- Network addresses that appear in protocol messages are now tagged with a type and length field. This allows support of multiple network protocols.

- Message encoding is now described using the ASN.1 (Abstract Syntax Notation 1) syntax in accordance with ISO standards 8824 and 8825.

- The Kerberos Version 5 ticket has an expanded format to support new features (for example, the inter-realm cooperation).

- As mentioned in 5.11.2, "Naming" on page 435, the principal identifier naming has changed.

- Inter-realm support has been enhanced.

- Authorization and accounting information can now be encrypted and transmitted inside a ticket in the authorization data field. This facilitates the extension of the authentication scheme to include an authorization scheme as well.

- A binding is provided for the Generic Security Service API (GSSAPI) to the Kerberos Version 5 implementation.

5.12 Remote Access Authentication Protocols

Remote dial-in to the corporate intranet and to the Internet has made the remote access server a very vital part of today's internetworking services. More and more mobile users are requiring access not only to central-site resources, but to information sources on the Internet. The widespread use of the Internet and the corporate intranet has fueled the growth of remote access services and devices. There is an increasing demand for simplified connection to corporate network resources from mobile computing devices such as a notebook computer, or a palmtop device for e-mail access.

The emergence of remote access has caused significant development work in the area of security. The AAA (triple A) security model has evolved in the industry to address the issues of remote access security. Authentication, authorization and accounting answers the questions who, what, and when respectively. A brief description of each of the three As in the AAA security model is listed below:

Authentication

> This is the action of determining who a user (or entity) is. Authentication can take many forms. Traditional authentication utilizes a name and a fixed password. Most computers work this way, However, fixed passwords have limitations, mainly in the area of security. Many modern authentication mechanisms utilize one-time passwords or a challenge-response query. Authentication generally takes place when the user first logs in to a machine or requests a service of it.

Authorization

> This is the action of determining what a user is allowed to do. Generally authentication precedes authorization, but again, this is not required. An authorization request may indicate that the user is not authenticated. (we don't know who they are.) In this case it is up to the authorization agent to determine if an unauthenticated user is allowed the services in question. In current remote authentication protocols authorization does not merely provide yes or no answers, but it may also customize the service for the particular user.

Accounting

This is typically the third action after authentication and authorization. But again, neither authentication or authorization are required. Accounting is the action of recording what a user is doing, and/or has done.

In the distributed client/server security database model, a number of communications servers, or clients, authenticate a dial-in user's identity through a single, central database, or authentication server. The authentication server stores all information about users, their passwords and access privileges. Distributed security provides a central location for authentication data that is more secure than scattering the user information on different devices throughout a network. A single authentication server can support hundreds of communications servers, serving up to tens of thousand of users. Communications servers can access an authentication server locally or remotely over WAN connections.

Several remote access vendors and the Internet Engineering Task Force (IETF) have been in the forefront of this remote access security effort, and the means whereby such security measures are standardized. Remote Authentication Dial In User Service (RADIUS) and Terminal Access Controller Access Control System (TACACS) are two such cooperative ventures that have evolved out of the Internet standardizing body and remote access vendors.

Remote Authentication Dial-In User Service (RADIUS) is a distributed security system developed by Livingston Enterprises. RADIUS was designed based on a previous recommendation from the IETF's Network Access Server Working Requirements Group. An IETF Working Group for RADIUS was formed in January 1996 to address the standardization of RADIUS protocol; RADIUS is now an IETF-recognized dial-in security solution (RFC 2058 and RFC 2138).

Similar to RADIUS, Terminal Access Controller Access Control System (TACACS) is an industry standard protocol specification, RFC 1492. Similar to RADIUS, TACACS receives authentication request from a NAS client and forwards the user name and password information to a centralized security server. The centralized server can either be a TACACS database or an external security database. Extended TACACS (XTACACS) is a version of TACACS with extensions that Cisco added to the basic TACACS protocol to support advanced features. TACACS+ is another Cisco extension that allows a separate access server (the TACACS+ server) to provide independent authentication, authorization, and accounting services.

Although RADIUS and TACACS Authentication Servers can be set up in a variety of ways, depending upon the security scheme of the network they are serving, the basic process for authenticating a user is essentially the same. Using a modem, a remote dial-in user connects to a remote access server, (also called the network access server or NAS) with a built-in analog or digital modem. Once the modem connection is made, the NAS prompts the user for a name and password. The NAS then creates the so-called authentication request from the supplied data packet, which consists of information identifying the specific NAS device sending the authentication request, the port that is being used for the modem connection, and the user name and password.

For protection against eavesdropping by hackers, the NAS, acting as the RADIUS or TACACS client encrypts the password before it sends it to the authentication server. If the primary security server cannot be reached, the security client or NAS device can route the request to an alternate server. When an authentication request is received, the authentication server validates the request and then decrypts the data packet to access the user name and password information. If the user name and password are correct, the server sends an Authentication Acknowledgment packet. This acknowledgement packet may include additional filters, such as information on the user's network resource requirements and authorization levels. The security server may, for instance, inform the NAS that a user needs TCP/IP and/or IPX using PPP, or that the user needs SLIP to connect to the network. It may include information on the specific network resource that the user is allowed to access.

To circumvent snooping on the network, the security server sends an authentication key, or signature, identifying itself to the security client. Once the NAS receives this information, it enables the necessary configuration to allow the user the necessary access rights to network services and resources. If at any point in this log-in process all necessary authentication conditions are not met, the security database server sends an authentication reject message to the NAS device and the user is denied access to the network.

5.13 Layer 2 Tunneling Protocol (L2TP)

L2TP permits the tunneling of PPP. Any protocol supported by PPP can be tunneled. This protocol extends the span of a PPP connection. Instead of beginning at the remote host and ending at a local ISP's point of presence (PoP), the *virtual PPP* link now extends from the remote host all the way back to the corporate gateway. L2TP tunneling is currently supported over IP/UDP. The latest specification can be found in the following Internet draft; however, it is expected that L2TP will soon be approved as a standard.

http://search.ietf.org/internet-drafts/draft-ietf-pppext-l2tp-11.txt

L2TP is a consensus standard that came from the merging of two earlier tunneling protocols: Point-to-Point Tunneling Protocol (PPTP) and Layer 2 Forwarding (L2F;

described in RFC 2341). These earlier protocols did not provide as complete a solution as the L2TP protocol; one addresses tunnels created by ISPs and the other addresses tunnels created by remote hosts. L2TP supports both host-created and ISP-created tunnels.

L2TP adds the ability to create a virtual private network where multiple protocols and privately addressed IP, IPX, and AT are allowed. In addition, L2TP will give remote users the ability to connect to a local ISP and tunnel through the internet to a home network, avoiding long distance charges. It will also provide a mechanism on which to solve the multiple box PPP multilink problem. (Calls connecting to different physical routers that are destined for the same MP bundle can be tunneled to the same endpoint where MP can be terminated for all links.)

5.13.1 Terminology

Before describing the protocol, a definition of some L2TP terminology is provided.

L2TP Access Concentrator (LAC)
> A device attached to one or more public service telephone network (PSTN) or integrated services digital network (ISDN) lines capable of handling both the PPP operation and L2TP protocol. The LAC implements the media over which L2TP operates. L2TP passes the traffic to one or more L2TP servers (LNS).

L2TP Network Server (LNS)
> An LNS operates on any platform that can be a PPP endstation. The LNS handles the server side of the L2TP protocol. Because L2TP relies only on the single media over which L2TP tunnels arrive, the LNS can have only a single LAN or WAN interface, yet is still able to terminate calls arriving from any PPP interfaces supported by an LAC, such as async, synchronous, ISDN, V.120, etc.

Network Access Servers (NAS)
> A device providing temporary, on-demand network access to users. This access is point-to-point using PSTN ir ISDN lines.

Session (Call)
> L2TP creates a session when an end-to-end PPP connection is attempted between a dial-in user and the LNS, or when an outbound call is initiated. The datagrams for the session are sent over the tunnel between the LAC and the LNS. The LNS and LAC maintain the state information for each user attached to a LAC.

Tunnel
> A tunnel is defined by an LNS-LAC pair. The tunnel carries PPP datagrams between the LAC and the LNS. A single tunnel can multiplex many sessions.

A control connection operating over the same tunnel controls the establishment, release, and maintenance of all sessions and of the tunnel itself.

Attribute Value Pair (AVP)

A uniform method of encoding message types and bodies. This method maximizes the extensibility while permitting interpretability of L2TP.

5.13.2 Protocol Overview

Since the host and the gateway share the same PPP connection, they can take advantage of PPP's ability to transport protocols other than just IP. For example, L2TP tunnels can be used to support remote LAN access as well as remote IP access. Figure 206 outlines a basic L2TP configuration:

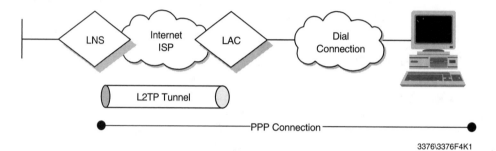

3376\3376F4K1

Figure 206. *Layer 2 Tunnel Protocol (L2TP) Scenario*

Refering to Figure 206, the following occurs:

1. The remote user initiates a PPP connection.
2. The NAS accepts the call.
3. The NAS identifies the remote user using an authorization server.
4. If the authorization is OK, the NAS/LAC initiates an L2TP tunnel to the desired LNS at the entry to the enterprise.
5. The LNS authenticates the remote user through its authentication server and accepts the tunnel.
6. The LNS confirms acceptance of the call and the L2TP tunnel.
7. The NAS logs the acceptance.
8. The LNS exchanges PPP negotiation with the remote user.
9. End-to-end data is now tunneled between the remote user and the LNS.

L2TP is actually another variation of an IP encapsulation protocol. As shown in Figure 207 on page 447, an L2TP tunnel is created by encapsulating an L2TP frame inside a UDP packet, which in turn is encapsulated inside an IP packet whose source and destination addresses define the tunnel's endpoints. Since the outer encapsulating protocol is IP, clearly IPSec protocols can be applied to this composite IP packet, thus protecting the data that flows within the L2TP tunnel. AH, ESP, and ISAKMP/Oakley protocols can all be applied in a straightforward way.

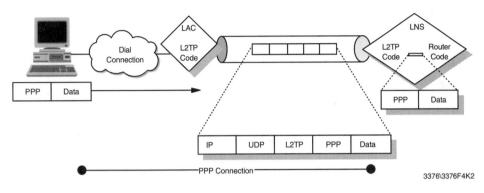

Figure 207. *L2TP Packet Changes during Transit*

L2TP can operate over UDP/IP and support the following functions:

- Tunneling of single user dial-in clients
- Tunneling of small routers, for example a router with a single static route to set up based on an authenticated user's profile
- Incoming calls to an LNS from an LAC
- Multiple calls per tunnel
- Proxy authentication for PAP and CHAP
- Proxy LCP
- LCP restart in the event that proxy LCP is not used at the LAC
- Tunnel endpoint authentication
- Hidden AVP for transmitting a proxy PAP password
- Tunneling using a local rhelm (that is user@rhelm) lookup table
- Tunneling using the PPP username lookup in the AAA subsystem (see 5.12, "Remote Access Authentication Protocols" on page 442)

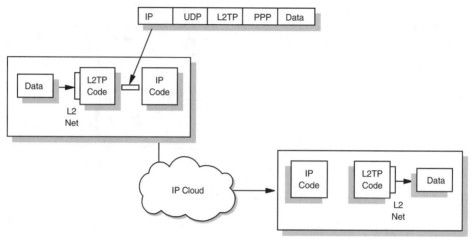

Figure 208. L2TP Packet Flow through Any IP Cloud

5.13.3 L2TP Security Issues

Although L2TP provides cost-effective access, multiprotocol transport, and remote LAN access, it does not provide cryptographically robust security features. For example:

- Authentication is provided only for the identity of tunnel endpoints, but not for each individual packet that flows inside the tunnel. This can expose the tunnel to man-in-the-middle and spoofing attacks.

- Without per-packet integrity, it is possible to mount denial-of-service attacks by generating bogus control messages that can terminate either the L2TP tunnel or the underlying PPP connection.

- L2TP itself provides no facility to encrypt user data traffic. This can lead to embarrassing exposures when data confidentiality is an issue.

- While the payload of the PPP packets can be encrypted, the PPP protocol suite does not provide mechanisms for automatic key generation or for automatic key refresh. This can lead to someone listening in on the wire to finally break that key and gain access to the data being transmitted.

Realizing these shortcomings, the PPP Extensions Working Group of the IETF considered how to remedy these shortfalls. Some members proposed to develop new IPSec-like protocols for use with PPP and L2TP. But since this work would have substantially duplicated the more mature work of the IPSec Working Group, the IETF took the position instead to support the use of the existing IPSec protocols to protect the data that flows through an L2TP tunnel.

The following reference provides additional information on how to use IPSec in conjunction with L2TP:

```
http://search.ietf.org/internet-drafts/draft-ietf-pppext-l2tp-sec-04.txt
```

In summary, layer 2 tunnel protocols are an excellent way of providing cost-effective remote access. And when used in conjunction with IPSec, they are an excellent technique for providing secure remote access. However, without complementary use of IPSec, an L2TP tunnel alone does not furnish adequate security.

5.14 Secure Electronic Transactions (SET)

SET is the outcome of an agreement by MasterCard International and Visa International to cooperate on the creation of a single electronic credit card system. Prior to SET, each organization had proposed its own protocol and each had received support from a number of networking and computing companies. Now, most of the major players are behind the SET specification (for example, IBM, Microsoft, Netscape and GTE).

The following sections describes at a high level the components and processes that make up the specification. Please refer to MasterCard and Visa home pages for more information about SET.

5.14.1 SET Roles

The SET specification defines several roles involved in the payment process:

The merchant
> This is any seller of goods, services or information.

The acquirer
> This is the organization that provides the credit card service and keeps the money flowing. The most widely known acquirers are MasterCard and Visa.

The issuer
> This is the organization that issued the card to the purchaser in the first place. Usually this is a bank or some other financial institution who should know better.

The cardholder

This is the Web surfer, who has been given a credit card by the issuer and now wants to exercise his or her purchasing power on the Web.

The acquirer payment gateway

This provides an interface between the merchant and the bankcard network used by the acquirer and the issuer. It is important to remember that the bankcard network already exists. The acquirer payment gateway provides a well-defined, secure interface to that established network from the Internet. Acquirer payment gateways will be operated on behalf of the acquirers, but they may be provided by third-party organizations, such as Internet services providers (ISPs).

The certificate authority

SET processing uses public key cryptography, so each element of the system need one or more public key certificates. Several layers of CA are described in the specification. (SET certificates are discussed in 5.14.3, "The SET Certificate Scheme" on page 453.)

5.14.2 SET Transactions

The SET specification describes a number of transaction flows for purchasing, authentication, payment reversal, etc. Figure 209 on page 451 shows the transactions involved in a typical online purchase.

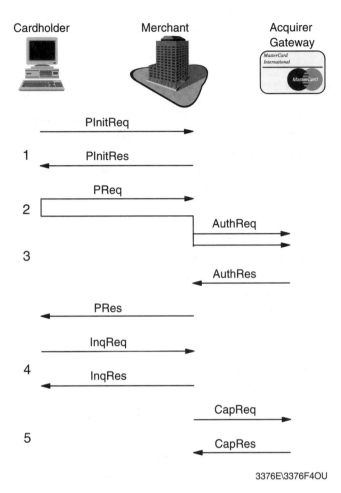

Figure 209. *Typical SET Transaction Sequence*

The diagram shows the following transactions (each transaction consists of a request/response pair):

1. PInit

This initializes the system, including details such as the brand of card being used and the certificates held by the cardholder. SET does not insist that cardholders have signing certificates, but it does recommend them. A cardholder certificate binds the credit card account number to the owner of a public key. If the acquirer receives a request for a given card number signed with the cardholder's public key, it knows that the request came from the real cardholder. To be precise, it knows that the request came from a computer where the cardholder's keyring was installed and available. It *could* still be a thief who had stolen the computer and cracked the keyring password.

2. Purchase Order

This is the actual request from the cardholder to buy something. The request message is in fact two messages combined, the order instruction (OI), which is sent in the clear to the merchant and the purchase instruction (PI), which the merchant passes on to the acquirer payment gateway. The PI is encrypted in the public key of the acquirer, so the merchant cannot read it. The merchant stores the message for later transmission to the acquirer. The PI also includes a hash of the OI, so the two messages can only be handled as a pair. Note that the card number is only placed in the PI portion of the request. This means that the merchant never has access to it, thereby preventing a fraudulent user from setting up a false store front to collect credit card information.

The purchase order has a response, which is usually sent (as shown here) after acquirer approval has been granted. However, the merchant can complete the transaction with the cardholder before authorization, in which case the cardholder would see a message that the request was accepted pending authorization.

3. Authorization

In this request the merchant asks the acquirer, via the acquirer payment gateway, to authorize the request. The message includes a description of the purchase and the cost. It also includes the PI from the purchase order that the cardholder sent. In this way the acquirer knows that the merchant and the cardholder both agree on what is being purchased and the amount.

When the acquirer receives the request it uses the existing bank card network to authorize the request and sends back an appropriate response.

4. Inquiry

The cardholder may want to know how his or her request is getting on. The SET specification provides an inquiry transaction for that purpose.

5. Capture

Up to this point, no money has changed hands. The capture request from the merchant tells the acquirer to transfer the previously authorized amount to its account.

In fact, capture can be incorporated as part of the authorization request/response (see above). However there are situations in which the merchant may want to capture the funds later. For example, most mail order operations do not debit the credit card account until the goods have actually been shipped.

There are several other transactions within the SET specification, but the summary above shows the principles on which it is based.

5.14.3 The SET Certificate Scheme

The SET specification envisions hundreds of thousands of participants worldwide. Potentially, each of these would have at least one public key certificate. In fact the protocol calls for an entity to have multiple certificates in some cases. For example, the acquirer payment gateways need one for signing messages and another for encryption purposes.

Key management on such a large scale requires something beyond a simple, flat certification structure. The organization of certifying authorities proposed for SET is shown in Figure 210.

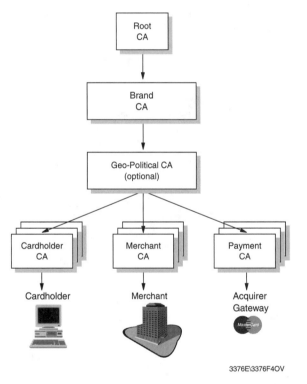

3376E\3376F4OV

Figure 210. SET Certifying Authorities

At the top of the certificate chain, the root certifying authority is to be kept offline under extremely tight arrangements. It will only be accessed when a new credit card brand joins the SET consortium. At the next level in the hierarchy, the brand level

CAs are also very secure. They are administered independently by each credit card brand.

Under each brand there is some flexibility permitted for different operating policies. It would be possible to set up CAs based on region or country for example. At the base of the CA hierarchy are the CAs that provide certificates for merchants, cardholders and acquirer payment gateways. The SET specification provides protocols for merchants and cardholders to request certificates online. It is important to have a simple process because SET aims to encourage cardholders to have their own certificates. It envisions the cardholder surfing to the CA Web site, choosing a Request Certificate option to invoke the certificate request application on the browser and then filling in a form to send and receive the certificate request.

Of course, if the system allows certificates to be created easily it must also be able to revoke them easily, in the event of a theft or other security breach. The SET specification includes some certificate update and revocation protocols for this purpose. Although the mechanism for requesting a certificate may be simple, there is still a need for user education. For example, it is obvious that a cardholder should notify the credit card company if his or her wallet is stolen, but less obvious that he or she should also notify them if his or her computer is stolen. However, if the computer includes his keyring file containing the private key and certificate, it could allow the thief to go shopping at the cardholder's expense.

5.15 References

The following RFCs provide detailed information on the TCP/IP security solutions presented in this chapter:

- *RFC 1492 — An Access Control Protocol, Sometimes Called TACACS*
- *RFC 1510 — The Kerberos Network Authentication Service (V5)*
- *RFC 1579 — Firewall-Friendly FTP*
- *RFC 1631 — The IP Network Address Translator (NAT)*
- *RFC 1928 — SOCKS Protocol Version 5*
- *RFC 1929 — Username/Password Authentication for SOCKS V5*
- *RFC 1961 — GSS-API Authentication Method for SOCKS Version 5*
- *RFC 2003 — IP Encapsulation within IP*
- *RFC 2104 — HMAC: Keyed-Hashing for Message Authentication*
- *RFC 2138 — Remote Authentication Dial In User Service (RADIUS)*

- *RFC 2313 — PKCS 1: RSA Encryption Version 1-5*
- *RFC 2314 — PKCS 10: Certification Request Syntax Version 1-5*
- *RFC 2315 — PKCS 7: Cryptographic Message Syntax Version 1-5*

Chapter 6. IP Version 6

The Internet is growing extremely rapidly. The latest Internet Domain Survey, conducted in January 1998, counted over 29.5 million hosts in more than 190 countries. The IPv4 addressing scheme, with a 32-bit address field, provides for over 4 billion possible addresses, so it might seem more than adequate to the task of addressing all of the hosts on the Internet, since there appears to be room for a thousand-fold increase before it is completely filled. Unfortunately, this is not the case, for a number of reasons, including the following:

- The IP address is divided into a network number and a local part which is administered separately. Although the address space within a network may be very sparsely filled, as far as the effective IP address space is concerned, if a network number has been allocated, then all addresses within that network are unavailable for allocation elsewhere.

- The address space for networks is structured into Class A, B and C networks of differing sizes, and the space within each needs to be considered separately.

- The IP addressing model requires that unique network numbers be assigned to all IP networks whether or not they are actually connected to the Internet.

- It is anticipated that growth of TCP/IP usage into new areas outside the traditional connected PC will shortly result in a rapid explosion of demand for IP addresses. For example, widespread use of TCP/IP for interconnecting hand-held devices, electronic point-of-sale terminals or for Web-enabled television receivers, all devices that are now available, will enormously increase the number of IP hosts.

These factors mean that the address space is much more constrained than our simple analysis would indicate. This problem is called *IP Address Exhaustion*. Methods of relieving this problem are already being employed (see Chapter 7, "Dynamic IP, Mobile IP and Network Computers" on page 511) but eventually, the present IP address space will be exhausted. The Internet Engineering Task Force (IETF) set up a working group on *Address Lifetime Expectations (ALE)* with the express purpose of providing estimates of when exhaustion of the IP will become an intractable problem. Their final estimates (reported in the ALE working group minutes for December 1994) were that the IP address space would be exhausted at some point between 2005 and 2011. Since then the position may have changed somewhat in that the use of CIDR (Classless Inter Domain Routing - see 2.1.7, "Classless Inter-Domain Routing (CIDR)" on page 58) and the increased use of DHCP may have relieved pressure on the address space, but on the other hand, current growth rates are probably exceeding expectation at that time.

Apart from address exhaustion, other restrictions in IPv4 also called for the definition of a new IP protocol:

1. Even with the use of CIDR, routing tables, primarily in the IP backbone routers, are growing too large to be manageable.

2. Traffic priority, or class of service, is vaguely defined, scarcely used and not at all enforced in IPv4, but highly desirable for modern real-time applications.

In view of these issues, the IETF established an IPng (IP next generation) working group and published *RFC 1752 —The Recommendation for the IP Next Generation Protocol*. Eventually, the specification for *Internet Protocol, Version 6 (IPv6)* was produced in *RFC 1883*.

6.1 IPv6 Overview

IPv6 offers the following significant features:

- A dramatically larger address space, said to be sufficient for the next 30 years

- Globally unique and hierarchical addressing, based on prefixes rather than address classes, to keep routing tables small and backbone routing efficient

- A mechanism for the autoconfiguration of network interfaces

- Support for encapsulation of itself and other protocols

- Class of service to distinguish types of data

- Improved multicast routing support (in preference to broadcasting)

- Built-in authentication and encryption

- Transition methods to migrate from IPv4

- Compatibility methods to coexist and communicate with IPv4

Note: IPv6 uses the term *packet* rather than *datagram*. The meaning is the same, although the formats are different.

IPv6 uses the term *node* for any system running IPv6, that is, a host or a router. An IPv6 host is a node that does not forward IPv6 packets that are not explicitly addressed to it. A router is a node that does forward IP packets not addressed to it.

6.2 The IPv6 Header Format

The format of the IPv6 packet header has been simplified from its counterpart in IPv4. The length of the IPv6 header is increased to 40 bytes (from 20 bytes), and contains two 16-byte addresses (source and destination) preceded by 8 bytes of control information as shown in Figure 211. The IPv4 header (see Figure 20 on page 63) has two 4-byte addresses preceded by 12 bytes of control information and possibly followed by option data. The reduction of the control information and the elimination of options in the header for most IP packets are intended to optimize the processing time per packet in a router. The infrequently used fields that have been removed from the header are moved to optional extension headers when they are required.

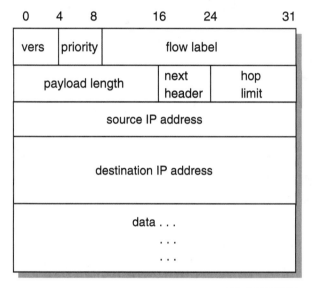

3376\3376F3D1

Figure 211. IPv6 Header

Vers

> 4-bit Internet Protocol version number: 6.

Priority

> 4-bit priority value. See 6.2.4, "Priority" on page 475.

Flow Label

> 28-bit field. See 6.2.5, "Flow Labels" on page 476 below.

Payload Length

The length of the packet in bytes (excluding this header) encoded as a 16-bit unsigned integer. If length is greater than 64 KB, this field is 0 and an option header (Jumbo Payload) gives the true length.

Next Header

Indicates the type of header immediately following the basic IP header. It may indicate an IP option header or an upper layer protocol. Protocol numbers used are the same as those used in IPv4 (see the list in 2.1, "Internet Protocol (IP)" on page 35). The next header field is also used to indicate the presence of extension headers, which provide the mechanism for appending optional information to the IPv6 packet. The following values will appear in IPv6 packets, in addition to those mentioned for IPv4.

41 IPv6 Header
45 Interdomain Routing Protocol
46 Resource Reservation Protocol
58 IPv6 ICMP Packet

The following values are all extension headers:

0 Hop-by-Hop Options Header
43 IPv6 Routing Header
44 IPv6 Fragment Header
50 Encapsulating Security Payload
51 IPv6 Authentication Header
59 No Next Header
60 Destination Options Header

The different types of extension header are discussed in 6.2.2, "Extension Headers" on page 462.

Hop Limit

This is the IPv4 TTL field but now it is measured in hops and not seconds. It was changed for two reasons:

- IP normally forwards datagrams at faster than one hop per second and the TTL field is always decremented on each hop, so in practice it is measured in hops and not seconds.

- Many IP implementations do not expire outstanding datagrams on the basis of elapsed time.

The packet is discarded once the hop limit is decremented to zero.

Source Address

A 128-bit address. IPv6 addresses are discussed in 6.2.3, "IPv6 Addressing" on page 469.

Destination Address

A 128-bit address. IPv6 addresses are discussed in 6.2.3, "IPv6 Addressing" on page 469.

A comparison between the IPv4 and IPv6 header formats will show that a number of IPv4 header fields have no direct equivalents in the IPv6 header.

Type of Service

Type of service issues in IPv6 will be handled using the *flow* concept, described in 6.2.5, "Flow Labels" on page 476.

Identification, Fragmentation Flags and Fragment Offset

Fragmented packets have an extension header rather than fragmentation information in the IPv6 header. This reduces the size of the basic IPv6 header. Since higher level protocols, particularly TCP, tend to avoid fragmentation of datagrams, this reduces the IPv6 header overhead for the normal case. As noted below, IPv6 does not fragment packets en route to their destinations, only at the source.

Header Checksum

Because transport protocols implement checksums, and because IPv6 includes an optional authentication header that can also be used to ensure integrity, IPv6 does *not* provide checksum monitoring of IP packets.

Both TCP and UDP include a pseudo IP header in the checksums they use, so in these cases, the IP header in IPv4 is being checked twice.

TCP and UDP, and any other protocols using the same checksum mechanisms running over IPv6 will continue to use a pseudo IP header although, obviously, the format of the pseudo IPv6 header will be different from the pseudo IPv4 header. ICMP and IGMP and any other protocols that do not use a pseudo IP header over IPv4 will use a pseudo IPv6 header in their checksums.

Options

All optional values associated with IPv6 packets are contained in extension headers ensuring that the basic IP header is always the same size.

At time of writing an Internet draft exists which proposes a change to the IPv6 header format. The draft specifies the replacement of the 4-bit priority field and 24-bit flow label with an 8-bit traffic class field followed by a 20-bit flow label. The 8-bit Traffic Class field in the IPv6 header is intended for use by originating nodes and/or forwarding routers to identify and distinguish between different classes or priorities of IPv6 packets. Currently, there are a number of experiments underway in the use of the IPv4 Type of Service and/or Precedence bits to provide various forms of *differentiated service* for IP packets (see 10.3, "Differentiated Services" on page 665), other than through the use of explicit flow setup. The Traffic Class field in the IPv6 header is intended to allow similar functionality to be supported in IPv6.

For the latest information, please refer to the Internet draft at:

```
http://search.ietf.org/internet-drafts/draft-ietf-ipngwg-ipv6-sp
ec-v2-02.txt
```

6.2.1 Packet Sizes

All IPv6 nodes are expected to dynamically determine the maximum transmission unit (MTU) supported by all links along a path (as described in *RFC 1191 — Path MTU Discovery*) and source nodes will only send packets that do not exceed the Path MTU. IPv6 routers will therefore not have to fragment packets in the middle of multihop routes and allow much more efficient use of paths that traverse diverse physical transmission media. IPv6 requires that every link supports an MTU of 576 bytes or greater.

6.2.2 Extension Headers

Every IPv6 packet starts with the basic header. In most cases this will be the only header necessary to deliver the packet. Sometimes, however, it is necessary for additional information to be conveyed along with the packet to the destination or to intermediate systems on route (information that would previously have been carried in the Options field in an IPv4 datagram). Extension headers are used for this purpose.

Extension headers are placed immediately after the IPv6 basic packet header and are counted as part of the payload length. Each extension header (with the exception of 59) has its own 8-bit *Next Header field* as the first byte of the header that identifies the type of the following header. This structure allows IPv6 to chain multiple extension headers together. Figure 212 on page 463 shows an example packet with multiple extension headers.

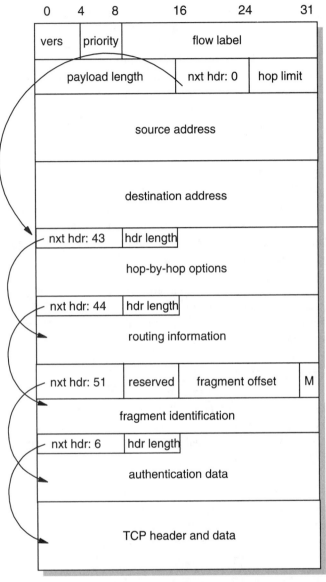

3376\3376F3D2

Figure 212. IPv6 Packet Containing Multiple Extension Headers

The length of each header varies, depending on type, but is always a multiple of 8 bytes. There are a limited number of IPv6 extension headers, any one of which may be present once only in the IPv6 packet (with the exception of the Destination Options

Header - 60, which may appear more than once). IPv6 nodes that originate packets are required to place extension headers in a specific order (numeric order with exception of 60), although IPv6 nodes that receive packets are not required to verify that this is the case. The order is important for efficient processing at intermediate routers. Routers will generally only be interested in the hop-by-hop options and the routing header. Once the router has read this far, it does not need to read further in the packet and can forward immediately. When the Next Header field contains a value other than one for an extension header, this indicates the end of the IPv6 headers and the start of the higher level protocol data.

IPv6 allows for encapsulation of IPv6 within IPv6 ("tunneling"). This is done with a Next Header value of 41 (IPv6). The encapsulated IPv6 packet may have its own extension headers. Because the size of a packet is calculated by the originating node to match the path MTU, IPv6 routers should not add extension headers to a packet but instead should encapsulate the received packet within an IPv6 packet of their own making (which may be fragmented if necessary).

With the exception of the Hop-by-Hop header (which must immediately follow the IP header if present) and sometimes the Destination Options header (see 6.2.2.6, "Destination Options Header" on page 469), extension headers are not processed by any router on the packet's path except the final one.

6.2.2.1 Hop-by-Hop Header

A Hop-by-Hop header contains options that must be examined by every node the packet traverses as well as the destination node. It must immediately follow the IPv6 header if present and is identified by the special value 0 in the Next Header field of the IPv6 basic header. (This value is not actually a protocol number but a special case to identify this unique type of extension header).

Hop-by-hop headers contain variable length options of the following format (commonly known as the *Type-Length-Value (TLV)* format):

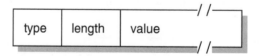

Figure 213. IPv6 Type-Length-Value (TLV) Option Format

Type   The type of the option. The option types all have a common format:

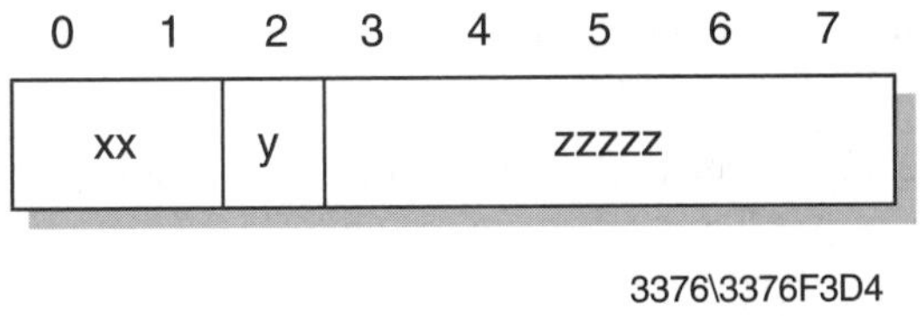

```
  0   1   2   3   4   5   6   7
┌───────┬───┬───────────────────┐
│  xx   │ y │      zzzzz         │
└───────┴───┴───────────────────┘
```

3376\3376F3D4

Figure 214. IPv6 Type-Length-Value (TLV) Option Type Format

xx   A 2-bit number indicating how an IPv6 node that does not recognize the option should treat it.

0   Skip the option and continue.

1   Discard the packet quietly.

2   Discard the packet and inform the sender with an ICMP Unrecognized Type message.

3   Discard the packet and inform the sender with an ICMP Unrecognized Type message unless the destination address is a multicast address.

y   If set, this bit indicates that the value of the option may change en route. If this bit is set, the entire Option Data field is excluded from any integrity calculations performed on the packet.

zzzzz   The remaining bits define the option:

0	Pad1
1	PadN
194	Jumbo Payload Length

Length   The length of the option value field in bytes.

Value   The value of the option. This is dependent on the type.

Hop-by-Hop Header Option Types: You may have noticed that each extension header is an integer multiple of 8 bytes long, in order to retain 8-byte alignment for subsequent headers. This is done, not purely for "neatness," but because processing is much more efficient if multibyte values are positioned on natural boundaries in memory (and today's processors have natural word sizes of 32 or 64 bits).

In the same way, individual options are also aligned so that multibyte values are positioned on their natural boundaries. In many cases, this will result in the option headers being longer than otherwise necessary, but still allows nodes to process packets more quickly. To allow this alignment, two padding options are used in Hop-by-Hop headers.

Pad1   A X'00' byte used for padding a single byte. Longer padding sequences
          should be done with the PadN option.

PadN   An option in the TLV format described above. The length byte gives the
          number of bytes of padding after the minimum two that are required.

The third option type in a Hop-by-Hop header is the *Jumbo Payload Length*. This
option is used to indicate a packet with a payload size in excess of 65,535 bytes
(which is the maximum size that can be specified by the 16-bit Payload Length field in
the IPv6 basic header). When this option is used, the Payload Length in the basic
header must be set to zero and this option carries the total packet size, less the 40 byte
basic header.

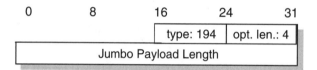

Figure 215. *Jumbo Payload Length Option*

6.2.2.2 Routing Header

The path that a packet takes through the network is normally determined by the
network itself. Sometimes, however, the source may wish to have more control over
the route taken by the packet. It may wish, for example, for certain data to take a
slower, but more secure route than would normally be taken. The routing header
allows a path through the network to be predefined. The routing header is identified
by the value 43 in the preceding Next Header field. It has its next header field as the
first byte and a single byte routing type as the second. The only type defined initially
is type 0 - Strict/Loose Source Routing, which operates in a similar way to source
routing in IPv4 (see 2.1.8.3, "IP Datagram Routing Options" on page 70).

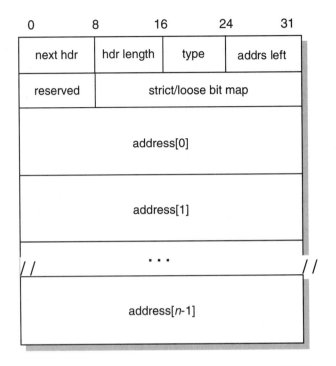

3376\3376F3D6

Figure 216. IPv6 Routing Header

Next Hdr   The type of header after this one.

Hdr Length

Length of this routing header, not including the first 8 bytes.

Type   Type of routing header. Currently this can only have the value 0, meaning Strict/Loose Source Routing.

Addresses Left

Number of intermediate nodes still to be visited on route to the final destination. Maximum allowed value is 23.

Reserved   Initialized to zero for transmission and ignored on reception.

Strict/Loose bit map

This is 24-bit series of bits indicating for each segment of the route whether the next address must be a neighbor of the preceding address (1, strict) or whether the packet is allowed to pass through intermediate routers on the way to the next destination address (2, loose).

Address n   A series of 16-byte IPv6 addresses that comprise the source route.

The first hop on the required path of the packet is indicated by the destination address in the basic header of the packet. When the packet arrives at this address, the router swaps the next address from the router extension header with the destination address in the basic header. The router also decrements the addresses left field by one, then forwards the packet.

6.2.2.3 Fragment Header

As discussed in 6.2.1, "Packet Sizes" on page 462, the source node determines the MTU for a path before sending a packet. If the packet to be sent is larger than the MTU, the packet is divided into pieces, each of which is a multiple of 8 bytes and carries a fragment header. The fragment header is identified by the value 44 in the preceding Next Header field and has the following format:

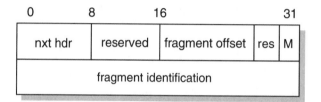

3376\3376F3D7

Figure 217. IPv6 Fragment Header

Nxt Hdr   The type of next header after this one.

reserved   8-bit reserved field - initialized to zero for transmission and ignored on reception.

Fragment Offset
A 13-bit unsigned integer giving the offset, in 8-byte units, of the following data relative to the start of the original data before it was fragmented.

Res   2-bit reserved field - initialized to zero for transmission and ignored on reception.

M   More flag. If set it indicates that this is not the last fragment.

Fragment Identification
This is an unambiguous identifier used to identify fragments of the same datagram. This is very similar to the IPv4 Identifier field, but it is twice as wide.

6.2.2.4 Authentication Header

The authentication header is used to ensure that a received packet has not been altered in transit and that it really came from the claimed sender. The authentication header is identified by the value 51 in the preceding Next Header field. The format of the authentication header and further details on authentication can be found in 5.5.2, "Authentication Header (AH)" on page 382.

6.2.2.5 Encapsulating Security Payload

The Encapsulated Security Payload (ESP) is a special extension header, in that it can appear anywhere in a packet between the basic header and the upper layer protocol. All data following the ESP header is encrypted. For further details, please see 5.5.3, "Encapsulating Security Payload (ESP)" on page 387.

6.2.2.6 Destination Options Header

This has the same format as the Hop-by-Hop header, but it is only examined by the destination node(s). Normally the destination options are only intended for the final destination only and the destination options header will be immediately before the upper layer header. However, destination options can also be intended for intermediate nodes, in which case they must precede a routing header. A single packet may therefore include two destination options headers. Currently, only the Pad1 and PadN types of options are specified for this header (see 6.2.2.1, "Hop-by-Hop Header" on page 464). The value for the preceding Next Header field is 60.

6.2.3 IPv6 Addressing

The IPv6 address model is specified in *RFC 2373 — IP Version 6 Addressing Architecture*. IPv6 uses a 128-bit address instead of the 32-bit address of IPv4. That theoretically allows for as many as 340,282,366,920,938,463,463,374,607,431,768,211,456 addresses. Even when used with the same efficiency as today's IPv4 address space, that would still allow for 50,000 addresses per square meter of land on Earth.

IPv6 addresses are represented in the form of eight hexadecimal numbers divided by colons, for example:

```
FE80:0000:0000:0000:0001:0800:23e7
:f5db
```

To shorten the notation of addresses, leading zeroes in any of the groups can be omitted, for example:

```
FE80:0:0:0:1:800:23e7:f5db
```

Finally, a group of all zeroes, or consecutive groups of all zeroes, can be substituted by a double colon, for example:

FE80::1:800:23e7:f5db

Note: The double colon shortcut can be 0sed only once in the notation of an IPv6 address. If there are more groups of all zeroes that are not consecutive, only one may be substituted by the double colon; the others would have to be noted as 0.

The IPv6 address space is organized using format prefixes, similar to telephone country and area codes, that logically divide it in the form of a tree so that a route from one network to another can easily be found. The following prefixes have been assigned so far:

Table 12. IPv6 - Format Prefix Allocation

Allocation	Prefix (bin)	Start of Address Range (hex)	Mask Length (bits)	Fraction of Address Space
Reserved	0000 0000	0:: /8	8	1/256
Reserved for NSAP	0000 001	200:: /7	7	1/128
Reserved for IPX	0000 010	400:: /7	7	1/128
Aggregatable Global Unicast Addresses	001	2000:: /3	3	1/8
Link-local Unicast	1111 1110 10	FE80:: /10	10	1/1024
Site-local Unicast	1111 1110 11	FEC0:: /10	10	1/1024
Multicast	1111 1111	FF00:: /8	8	1/256
Total Allocation				15%

IPv6 defines the following types of addresses:

Unicast Address

A unicast address is an identifier assigned to a single interface. Packets sent to that address will only be delivered to that interface. Special purpose unicast addresses are defined as follows:

Loopback address (::1) This address is assigned to a virtual interface over which a host can send packets only to itself. It is equivalent to the IPv4 loopback address 127.0.0.1.

Unspecified address (::) This address is used as a source address by hosts while performing autoconfiguration. It is equivalent to the IPv4 unspecified address 0.0.0.0.

IPv4-compatible address (::<IPv4_address>) Addresses of this kind are used when IPv6 traffic needs to be tunneled across existing IPv4 networks. The endpoint of such tunnels can be either hosts (automatic tunneling) or routers (configured tunneling). IPv4-compatible addresses are formed by placing 96 bits of zero in front of a valid 32-bit IPv4 address. For example, the address 1.2.3.4 (hex 01.02.03.04) becomes ::0102:0304

IPv4-mapped address (::FFFF:<IPv4_address>) Addresses of this kind are used when an IPv6 host needs to communicate with an IPv4 host. This requires a dual stack host or router for header translations. For example, if an IPv6 node wishes to send data to host with an IPv4 address of 1.2.3.4, it uses a destination address of ::FFFF:0102:0304.

Link-local address Addresses of this kind can be used only on the physical network that a host's interface is attached to.

Site-local address Addresses of this kind cannot be routed into the Internet. They are the equivalent of IPv4 networks for private use (10.0.0.0, 176.16.0.0-176.31.0.0, 192.168.0.0-192.168.255.0).

Global Unicast Address Format

The Global Unicast address format, as specified in *RFC 2374 — An IPv6 Aggregatable Global Unicast Address Format* is expected to become the predominant format used for IPv6 nodes connected to the Internet. The aggregatable address can be split into three sections that relate to the three-level hierarchy of the Internet, namely:

Public Topology Providers and exchanges that provide public Internet transit services.

Site Topology Local to an organization that does not provide public transit service to nodes outside of the site.

Interface Identifiers Identify interfaces on links.

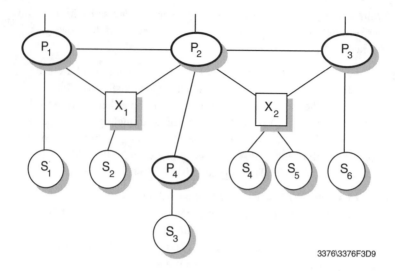

3376\3376F3D9

Figure 218. Global Unicast Address Format - Three-Level Hierarchy

The Global Unicast Address Format is designed for the infrastructure shown in Figure 218. P1, P2 and P3 are long-haul providers. P4 is a smaller provider that obtains services from P2. Exchanges (X1 and X2), which are analagous to exchanges in a telephone network, will allocate addresses. Subscribers (S1-S6) have the choice of connecting directly to a provider or to an exchange (in which case they must also subscribe to a provider for long-haul service). Organizations connecting via an exchange have the flexibility to be able to change their long-haul provider without having to change their IP addresses.

The format of the aggregatable global unicast address is shown in Figure 219.

3376\3376F3DA

Figure 219. Global Unicast Address Format

FP   Format Prefix (001).

TLA ID   Top-Level Aggregation Identifier. These are the top level in the
            routing hierarchy. Internet top-level routers will need a routing table
            entry for every active TLA ID. This will be a maximum of 8,192
            entries, which compares with around 50,000 entries in today's IPv4
            top-level routers.

RES   Reserved for future use. This will allow growth in the number of
            either TLA IDs or NLA IDs in the future if this becomes necessary.

NLA ID   Next-Level Aggregation Identifier. Used by organizations assigned
            a TLA ID (who may be providers) to create their own addressing
            hierarchy and to identify sites. The 24-bit NLA ID space allows
            each organization to provide service to as many sites as the current
            total number of networks supported by IPv4.

SLA ID   Site-Level Aggregation Identifier. This field is used by an
            individual organization to create its own local addressing hierarchy.
            The 16-bit field allows for up to 65,535 individual subnets.

Multicast Address

A multicast address is an identifier assigned to a set of interfaces on multiple
hosts. Packets sent to that address will be delivered to all interfaces
corresponding to that address. (See 9.2, "Internet Group Management Protocol
(IGMP)" on page 596 for more information on IP multicasting.) There are no
broadcast addresses in IPv6, their function being superceded by multicast
addresses. Figure 220 shows the format of an IPv6 multicast address:

```
0        8   12   16                                             127
+--------+-----+-----+---------------------------------------------+
|        |     |     |                                             |
|   FP   |Flags|Scope|                 Group ID                    |
|        |     |     |                                             |
+--------+-----+-----+---------------------------------------------+
```

3376\3376F3DB

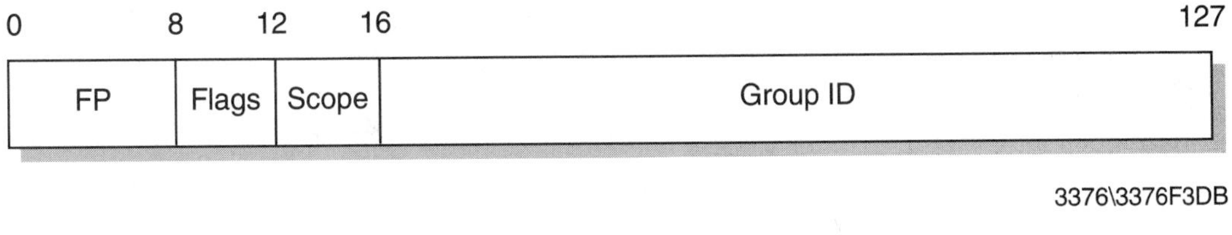

Figure 220. IPv6 Multicast Address Format

FP   Format Prefix - 1111 1111.

Flags   Set of four flag bits. Only the low order bit currently has any
            meaning, as follows:

            0000   Permanent address assigned by a numbering authority

0001   Transient address. Addresses of this kind can be established by applications as required. When the application ends, the address will be released by the application and can be reused.

Scope   4-bit value indicating the scope of the multicast. Possible values are:

0	Reserved
1	Confined to interfaces on the local node (node-local)
2	Confined to nodes on the local link (link-local)
5	Confined to the local site
8	Confined to the organization
E	Global scope
F	Reserved

Group ID   Identifies the multicast group.

For example if the NTP servers group is assigned a permanent multicast address, with a group ID of X'101, then:

FF02::101 means all NTP servers on the same link as the sender.

FF05::101 means all NTP servers on the same site as the sender.

Certain special purpose multicast addresses are pre-defined as follows:

FF01::1	All interfaces node-local - Defines all interfaces on the host itself.
FF02::1	All nodes link-local - Defines all systems on the local network.
FF01::2	All routers node-local - Defines all routers local to the host itself.
FF02::2	All routers link-local - Defines all routers on the same link as the host.
FF05::2	All routers site-local - Defines all routers on the same site as the host.
FF02::B	Mobile agents link-local.
FF02::1:2	All DHCP agents link-local.
FF05::1:3	All DHCP servers site-local.

A more complete listing of reserved multicast addresses may be found in *RFC 2375 — IPv6 Multicast Address Assignments*

This RFC also defines a special multicast address known as the *solicited node address*, which has the format FF02::1:FFxx:xxxx, where xx xxxx is taken from the last 24-bits of a nodes unicast address. For example, the node with the IPv6 address of 4025::01:800:100F:7B5B belongs to the multicast group FF02::1:FF 0F:7B5B. The solicited node address is used by ICMP for neighbour discovery and to detect duplicate addresses. Please see 6.3, "Internet Control Message Protocol Version 6 (ICMPv6)" on page 476 for further details.

Anycast Address

An anycast address is a special type of unicast address that is assigned to interfaces on multiple hosts. Packets sent to such an address will be delivered to the nearest interface with that address. Routers determine the nearest interface based upon their definition of distance, for example hops in case of RIP or link state in case of OSPF.

Anycast addresses use the same format as unicast addresses and are indistinguishable from them. However, a node that has been assigned an anycast address must be configured to be aware of this fact.

RFC 2373 currently specifies the following restrictions on anycast addresses:

- An anycast address must not be used as the source address of a packet.

- Any anycast address may only be assigned to a router

A special anycast address, the *subnet-router address*, is predefined. This address consists of the subnet prefix for a particular subnet followed by trailing zeroes. This address may be used when a node needs to contact a router on a particular subnet and it does not matter which router is reached (for example, when a mobile node needs to communicate with one of the mobile agents on its "home" subnet),

6.2.4 Priority

The 4-bit priority field allows applications to specify a certain priority for the traffic they generate thus introducing the concept of *Class of Service*.

IPv4-based routers normally treat all traffic equal, whereas IPv6-based routers now must act on such prioritized packets in the following way:

1. For priorities 0 to 7, start dropping packets when the network becomes congested (congestion-controlled).
2. For priorities 8 to 15, try to forward packets even when the network is becoming congested by dropping packets with lower priority (noncongestion-controlled). Real-time applications would opt for this range of priority. For a comparison of how priority traffic may be handled in an IPv4 network, please see 10.1, "Why QoS?" on page 643.

6.2.5 Flow Labels

IPv6 introduces the concept of a *flow*, which is a series of related packets from a source to a destination that requires a particular type of handling by the intervening routers, for example real-time service. The nature of that handling can either be conveyed by options attached to the datagrams (that is, by using the IPv6 Hop-by-Hop options header) or by a separate protocol (such as resource reservation protocol - see 10.2.2, "The Reservation Protocol (RSVP)" on page 651). The handling requirement for a particular flow label is known as the *state information*; this is cached at the router. When packets with a known flow label arrive at the router, the router can efficiently decide how to route and forward the packets without having to examine the rest of the header for each packet.

There may be multiple active flows between a source and a destination, as well as traffic that is not associated with any flow. Each flow is distinctly labelled by the 24-bit flow label field in the IPv6 packet. See RFC 1883 and RFC 1809 for further details on the use of the flow label.

6.3 Internet Control Message Protocol Version 6 (ICMPv6)

The IP protocol concerns itself with moving data from one node to another. However, in order for IP to perform this task successfully, there are many other functions that need to be carried out: error reporting, route discovery and diagnostics to name but a few. All these tasks are carried out by the Internet Control Message Protocol (see 2.2, "Internet Control Message Protocol (ICMP)" on page 74). ICMPv6, in addition, carries out ICMPv6 the tasks of conveying multicast group membership information, a function that was previously performed by the IGMP protocol in IPv4 ICMPv6 (see 9.2, "Internet Group Management Protocol (IGMP)" on page 596) and address resolution, previously performed by ARP (see 2.4, "Address Resolution Protocol (ARP)" on page 87).

ICMPv6 messages, and their use, are specified in *RFC 1885 — Internet Control Message Protocol (ICMPv6) for the Internet Protocol Version 6 (IPv6) Specification* and *RFC 1970 — Neighbor Discovery for IP Version 6 (IPv6)*. Both RFCs are proposed standards with a status of elective.

Every ICMPv6 message is preceded by an IPv6 header (and possibly some IP extension headers). The ICMPv6 header is identified by a Next Header value of 58 in the immediately preceding header.

ICMPv6 messages all have a similar format, shown in Figure 221 on page 477.

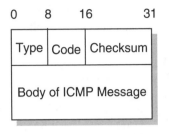

3376\3376F3DC

Figure 221. ICMPv6 General Message Format

Type   There are two classes of ICMPv6 messages. Error messages have a Type
        from 0 to 127. Informational messages have a Type from 128 to 255.

1	Destination Unreachable
2	Packet Too Big
3	Time (Hop Count) Exceeded
4	Parameter Problem
128	Echo Request
129	Echo Reply
130	Group Membership Query
131	Group Membership Report
132	Group Membership Reduction
133	Router Solicitation
134	Router Advertisement
135	Neighbor Solicitation
136	Neighbor Advertisement
137	Redirect Message

Code   Varies according to message type.

Checksum   Used to detect data corruption in the ICMPv6 message and parts of the
            IPv6 header.

Body of Message
        Varies according to message type.

For full details of ICMPv6 messages for all Types please refer to RFC 1885 and RFC
1970.

6.3.1 Neighbor Discovery

Neighbor discovery is an ICMPv6 function that enables a node to neighbor discovery
identify other hosts and routers on its links. The node needs to know of at least one
router, so that it knows where to forward packets if a target node is not on its local

link. Neighbor discovery also allows a router to redirect a node to use a more appropriate router if the node has initially made an incorrect choice.

6.3.1.1 Address Resolution
Figure 222 shows a simple Ethernet LAN segment with four IPv6 workstations.

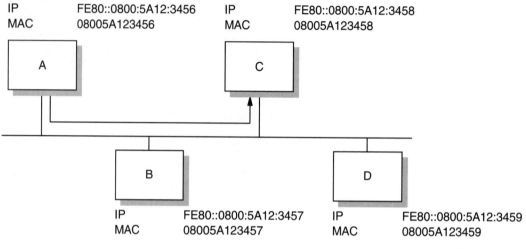

Figure 222. *IPv6 Address Resolution*

Workstation A needs to send data to workstation B. It knows the IPv6 address of workstation B, but it does not know how to send a packet because it does not know its MAC address. To find this information, it sends a *neighbor solicitation* message, of the format shown in Figure 223 on page 479.

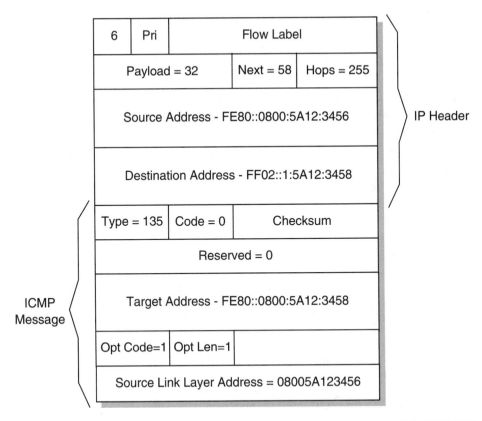

6	Pri	Flow Label		
Payload = 32			Next = 58	Hops = 255

Source Address - FE80::0800:5A12:3456

Destination Address - FF02::1:5A12:3458

IP Header

Type = 135	Code = 0	Checksum

Reserved = 0

Target Address - FE80::0800:5A12:3458

Opt Code=1	Opt Len=1	

Source Link Layer Address = 08005A123456

ICMP Message

3376\3376F3DE

Figure 223. *Neighbor Solicitation Message Format*

Notice the following important fields in the IP header of this packet:

Next   58 (for the following ICMP message header).

Hops   Any solicitation packet that does *not* have hops set to 255 is discarded; this ensures that the solicitation has not crossed a router.

Destination address

This address is the *solicited node address* for the target workstation (a special type of multicast - see 474). Every workstation *must* respond to its own solicited node address but other workstations will simply ignore it. This is an improvement over ARP in IPv4, which uses broadcast frames that have to be processed by every node on the link.

In the ICMP message itself, notice:

Type   135 (Neighbor Solicitation).

Target address
>   This is the known IP address of the target workstation.

Source link layer address
>   This is useful to the target workstation and saves it having to initiate a neighbor discovery process of its own when it sends a packet back to the source workstation.

The response to the neighbor solicitation message is a *neighbor advertisement,* which has the following format:

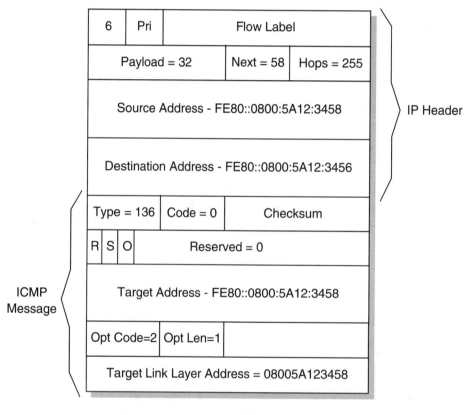

3376\3376F3DF

Figure 224. *Neighbor Advertisement Message*

The neighbor advertisement is addressed directly back to Workstation A. The ICMP message option contains the target IP address together with the target's link layer (MAC) address. Note also the following flags in the advertisement message:

R   Router Flag. This bit is set on if the sender of the advertisement is a router.

S   Solicited Flag. This bit is set on if the advertisement is in response to a solicitation.

O   Override Flag. When this bit is set on, the receiving node must update an existing cached link layer entry in its neighbor cache.

Once Workstation A receives this packet, it commits the information to memory in its neighbor cache, then forwards the data packet that it wanted to send to Workstation C originally.

Neighbor advertisement messages may also be sent by a node to force updates to neighbor caches if it becomes aware that its link layer address has changed.

6.3.1.2 Router and Prefix Discovery
router discovery prefix discovery

Figure 222 on page 478 shows a very simple network example. In a larger network, particularly one connected to the Internet, the neighbor discovery process is used to find nodes on the same link in exactly the same way. However, it is more than likely that a node will need to communicate, not just with other nodes on the same link, but with nodes on other network segments that may be anywhere in the world. In this case there are two important pieces of information that a node needs to know:

1. The address of a router that the node can use to reach the rest of the world

2. The Prefix (or prefixes) that define the range of IP addresses on the same link as the node and which can be reached without going through a router.

Routers use ICMP to convey this information to hosts, by means of *router advertisements*. The format of the router advertisement message is shown in Figure 225 on page 482. The message will generally have one or more attached options; all three possible options are shown in this example:

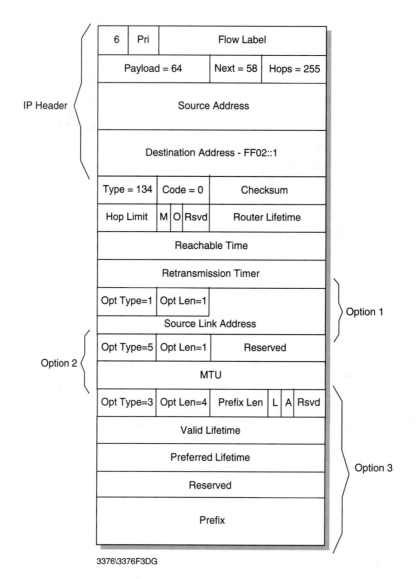

3376\3376F3DG

Figure 225. *Router Advertisement Message Format*

Notice the following important fields in the IP header of this packet:

Next   58 (for the following ICMP message header).

Hops   Any advertisement packet that does *not* have hops set to 255 is discarded.
           This ensures that the packet has not crossed a router.

Destination address

> This address is the special multicast address defining all systems on the local link.

In the ICMP message itself:

Type   134 (Router Advertisement).

Hop Limit   The default value that a node should place in the Hop Count field of its outgoing IP packets.

M   1-bit Managed Address Configuration Flag (see 6.3.2, "Stateless Address Autoconfiguration" on page 488).

O   1-bit Other Stateful Configuration Flag (see 6.3.2, "Stateless Address Autoconfiguration" on page 488).

Router Lifetime

> How long the node should consider this router to be available. If this time period is exceeded and the node has not received another router advertisement message, the node should consider this router to be unavailable.

Reachable Time

> This sets a parameter for all nodes on the local link. It is the time in milliseconds that the node should assume a neighbor is still reachable after having received a response to a neighbor solicitation.

Retransmission Timer

> This sets the time, in milliseconds, that nodes should allow between retransmitting neighbor solicitation messages if no initial response is received.

The three possible options in a router advertisement message are:

Option 1 (source link address)

> Allows a receiving node to respond directly to the router without having to do a neighbor solicitation.

Option 5 (MTU)

> Specifies the maximum transmission unit size for the link. For some media, such as Ethernet, this value is fixed so this option is not necessary.

Option 3 (Prefix)

> Defines the address prefix for the link. Nodes use this information to determine when they do, and do not, need to use a router. Prefix options used for this purpose have the L (link) bit set on. Prefix options are also used as part of address configuration, in which case the A bit is set on.

Please see 6.3.2, "Stateless Address Autoconfiguration" on page 488 for further details.

A router constantly sends unsolicited advertisements at a frequency defined in the router configuration. A node may, however, wish to obtain information about the nearest router without having to wait for the next scheduled advertisement (a new workstation that has just attached to the network, for example). In this case, the node can send a *router solicitation message*. The format of the router solicitation message is shown in Figure 226:

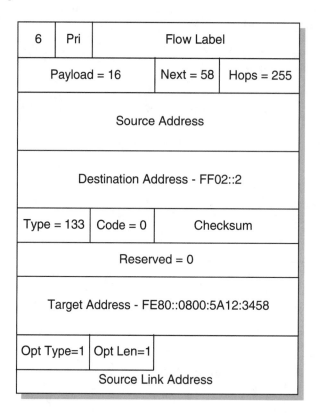

3376\3376F3DH

Figure 226. Router Solicitation Message Format

Notice the following important fields in the IP header of this packet:

Next   58 (for the following ICMP message header).

Hops   Any advertisement packet that does *not* have hops set to 255 is discarded. This ensures that the packet has not crossed a router.

Destination address
This address is the special multicast address defining all routers on the local link.

In the ICMP message itself:

Type   133 (Router Solicitation)

Option 1 (source link address)
Allows the receiving router to respond directly to the node without having to do a neighbor solicitation.

Each router that receives the solicitation message responds with a router advertisement sent *directly* to the node that sent the solicitation (not to the all systems link-local multicast address).

6.3.1.3 Redirection

The router advertisement mechanism ensures that a node will always be aware of one or more routers through which it is able to connect to devices outside of its local links. However, in a situation where a node is aware of more than one router, it is likely that the default router selected when sending data will not always be the most suitable router to select for every packet. In this case, ICMPv6 allows for *redirection* to a more efficient path for a particular destination.

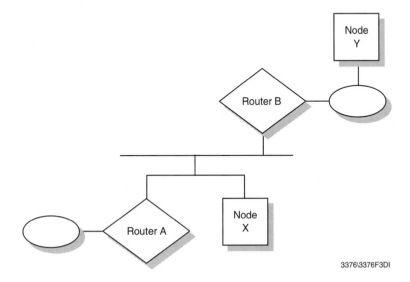

3376\3376F3DI

Figure 227. Redirection

Consider the simple example shown in Figure 227. Node X is aware of routers A and B, having received router advertisement messages from both. Node X wishes to send data to Node Y. By a comparison of Node Y's IP address against the local link prefix, Node X knows that Node Y is not on the local link, and that it must therefore use a router. Node X selects router A from its list of default routers and forwards the packet. Obviously, this is not the most efficient path to Node Y. As soon as router A has forwarded the packet to Node Y (via router B), router A sends a *redirect* message to Node X. The format of the redirect message (complete with IP header) is shown in Figure 228 on page 487.

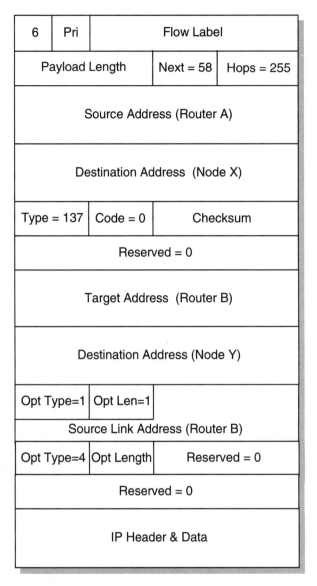

6	Pri	Flow Label	
Payload Length		Next = 58	Hops = 255

Source Address (Router A)

Destination Address (Node X)

Type = 137	Code = 0	Checksum

Reserved = 0

Target Address (Router B)

Destination Address (Node Y)

Opt Type=1	Opt Len=1

Source Link Address (Router B)

Opt Type=4	Opt Length	Reserved = 0

Reserved = 0

IP Header & Data

3376\3376F3DJ

Figure 228. *Redirect Message Format*

The fields to note in the message are:

Type   137 (Redirect).

Target Address
> This is address of the router that should be used when trying to reach Node Y.

Destination Address
> Node Y's IP address.

Option 2 (target link layer address)
> Gives link address of router B so that Node X can reach it without a neighbor solicitation.

Option 4 (redirected header)
> Includes the original packet sent by node X, full IP header and as much of the data that will fit, such that the total size of the redirect message does not exceed 576 bytes.

6.3.1.4 Neighbor Unreachability Detection

An additional responsibility of the neighbor discovery function of ICMPv6 is *neighbor unreachability detection* (NUD).

A node actively tracks the reachability state of the neighbors to which it is sending packets. It may do this in two ways: either by monitoring the upper layer protocols to see if a connection is making forward progress (for example, TCP acknowledgments are being received), or it may issue specific neighbor solicitations to check that the path to a target host is still available. When a path to a neighbor appears to be failing, then appropriate action is taken to try and recover the link. This may include restarting the address resolution process or deletion of a neighbor cache entry so that a new router may be tried in order to find a working path to the target.

NUD is used for all paths between nodes, including host-to-host, host-to-router and router-to-host. NUD may also be used for router-to-router communication, if the routing protocol being used does not already include a similar mechanism. For further information on neighbor unreachability detection, please refer to RFC 1970.

6.3.2 Stateless Address Autoconfiguration

Although the 128-bit address field of IPv6 solves a number of problems inherent in IPv4, the size of the address itself represents a potential problem to the TCP/IP administrator. Because of this, IPv6 has been designed with the capability to automatically assign an address to an interface at initialization time, with the intention that a network can become operational with minimal to no action on the part of the TCP/IP administrator. IPv6 nodes will generally always use autoconfiguration to obtain their autoconfiguration IPv6 address. This may be achieved using DHCP (see

6.5, "DHCP in IPv6" on page 497), which is known as *stateful* autoconfiguration, or by *stateless* autoconfiguration, which is a new feature of IPv6 and relies on ICMPv6.

The stateless autoconfiguration process is defined in *RFC 1971 — IPv6 Stateless Address Autoconfiguration*. It consists of the following steps:

1. During system startup, the node begins the autoconfiguration by obtaining an interface token from the interface hardware, for instance, a 48-bit MAC address on token-ring or Ethernet networks.

2. The node creates a tentative link-local unicast address. This is done by combining the well-known link-local prefix (FE80::/10) with the interface token.

3. The node attempts to verify that this tentative address is unique by issuing a neighbor solicitation message with the tentative address as the target. If the address is already in use, the node will receive a neighbor advertisement in response, in which case the autoconfiguration process stops. (Manual configuration of the node is then required.)

4. If no response is received, the node assigns the link-level address to its interface. The host then sends one or more router solicitations to the all-routers multicast group. If there are any routers present, they will respond with a router advertisement. If no router advertisement is received, the node should attempt to use DHCP to obtain an address and configuration information. If no DHCP server responds, the node continues using the link-level address and can communicate with other nodes on the same link only.

5. If a router advertisement *is* received in response to the router solicitation, then this message contains several pieces of information that tells the node how to proceed with the autoconfiguration process (see Figure 225 on page 482).

   M flag   Managed address configuration

                If this bit is set, the node should use DHCP to obtain its IP address.

   O flag   Other stateful configuration.

                If this bit is set then the node uses DHCP to obtain other configuration parameters.

   Prefix Option

                If the router advertisement has a prefix option with the A bit (autonomous address configuration flag) set on, then the prefix is used for stateless address autoconfiguration.

6. If stateless address configuration is to be used, the prefix is taken from the router advertisement and added to the interface token to form the global unicast IP address, which is assigned to the network interface.

7. The working node will continue to receive periodic router advertisements. If the information in the advertisement changes, the node must take appropriate action.

Note that it is possible to use both stateless and stateful configuration simultaneously. It is quite likely that stateless configuration will be used to obtain the IP address, but DHCP will then be used to obtain further configuration information. However, plug-and-play configuration is possible in both small and large networks without the requirement for DHCP servers.

The stateless address configuration process, together with the fact that more than one address can be allocated to the same interface, also allows for the graceful renumbering of all the nodes on a site (for example, if a switch to a new network provider necessitates new addressing) without disruption to the network. For further details, please refer to RFC 1971.

6.3.3 Multicast Listener Discovery (MLD)

The process used by a router to discover the members of a particular multicast group is known as *Multicast Listener Discovery* (MLD). MLD is a subset of ICMPv6 and provides the equivalent function of IGMP for IPv4 (see 9.2, "Internet Group Management Protocol (IGMP)" on page 596). This information is then provided by the router to whichever multicast routing protocol is being used, so that multicast packets are correctly delivered to all links where there are nodes listening for the appropriate multicast address.

MLD uses ICMPv6 messages of the format shown in Figure 229 on page 491.

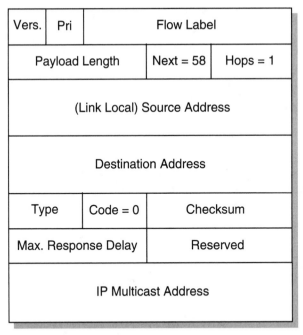

Vers.	Pri	Flow Label	
Payload Length		Next = 58	Hops = 1
(Link Local) Source Address			
Destination Address			
Type	Code = 0	Checksum	
Max. Response Delay		Reserved	
IP Multicast Address			

3376A\3376F3DR

Figure 229. *MLD Message Format*

Note the following fields in the IPv6 header of the message:

Next 58 (for the following ICMPv6 message header).

Hops Always set to 1.

Source Address
  A link-local source address is used.

In the MLD message itself, notice:

Type There are three types of MLD message:

   130   Multicast Listener Query

       There are two types of queries:
       General query
          Used to find which multicast addresses are being
          listened for on a link.
       Multicast-address-specific query
          Used to find if any nodes are listening for a
          specific multicast address on a link.

131   Multicast listener report

Used by a node to report that it is listening to a multicast address.

132   Multicast listener done

Used by a node to report that it is ceasing to listen to a multicast address.

Code   Set to 0 by sender and ignored by receivers.

Max Response Delay

This sets the maximum allowed delay before a responding report must be sent. This parameter is only valid in query messages. Increasing this parameter can prevent sudden bursts of high traffic if there a lot of responders on a network.

Multicast Address

In a query message, this field is set to zero for a general query, or set to the specific IPv6 multicast address for a multicast-address-specific query.

In a response or done message, this field contains the multicast address being listened for.

A router users MLD to learn which multicast addresses are being listened for on each of its attached links. The router only needs to know that nodes listening for a particular address are present on a link; it does not need to know the unicast address of those listening nodes, or how many listening nodes are present.

A router periodically sends a General Query on each of its links to the all nodes link-local address (FF02::1). When a node listening for any multicast addresses receives this query, it sets a delay timer (which may be anything between 0 and maximum response delay) for each multicast address for which it is listening. As each timer expires, the node sends a *multicast listener report* message containing the appropriate multicast address. If a node receives another node's report for a multicast address while it has a timer still running for that address, then it stops its timer and does not send a report for that address. This prevents duplicate reports being sent and, together with the timer mechanism, prevents excess, or bursty traffic being generated.

The router manages a list of, and sets a timer for, each multicast address it is aware of on each of its links. If one of these timers expires without a report being received for that address, the router assumes that no nodes are still listening for that address, and the address is removed from the list. Whenever a report *is* received, the router resets the timer for that particular address.

When a node has finished listening to a multicast address, if it was the last node on a link to send a report to the router (that is, its timer delay was not interrupted by the receipt of another node's report), then it sends a *multicast listener done* message to the router. If the node *was* interrupted by another node before its timer expired, then it assumes that other nodes are still listening to the multicast address on the link and therefore does not send a done message.

When a router receives a done message, it sends a multicast-address-specific message on the link. If no report is received in response to this message, the router assumes that there are no nodes still listening to this multicast address and removes the address from its list.

MLD is not currently specified in an RFC, but is the subject of an Internet draft, *Multicast Listener Discovery for IPv6*. For further information, please refer to the latest draft at:

```
http://www.ietf.org/internet-drafts/draft-ietf-ipngwg-mld-00.txt
```

6.4 DNS in IPv6

With the introduction of 128-bit addresses, IPv6 makes it even more difficult for the network user to be able to identify another network user by means of the IP address of his or her network device. The use of the Domain Name Service, therefore, becomes even more of a necessity (please see 4.2, "Domain Name System (DNS)" on page 194).

A number of extensions to DNS are specified to support the storage and retrieval of IPv6 addresses. These are defined in *RFC 1886 — DNS Extensions to Support IP Version 6*, which is a proposed standard with elective status. However, there is also work in progress on useability enhancements to this RFC, described in an Internet draft of the same name.

The following extensions are specified:

- A new resource record type, AAAA, which maps the domain name to the IPv6 address

- A new domain, which is used to support address-to-domain name lookups

- A change to the definition of existing queries, so that they will perform correct processing on both A and AAAA record types

6.4.1 Format of IPv6 Resource Records

RFC 1886 defines the format of the AAAA record as similar to an A resource record, but with the 128-bit IPv6 address encoded in the data section, and a Type value of 28 (decimal).

A special domain, IP6.INT, is defined for inverse (address-to-host name) lookups (similar to the *in-addr.arpa* domain used in IPv4). As in IPv4, the address must be entered in reverse order, but hexadecimal digits are used rather than decimal notation.

For example, the inverse domain name entry for the IPv6 address

```
2222:0:1:2:3:4:5678:9abc
```

is:

```
c.b.a.9.8.7.6.5.4.0.0.0.3.0.0.0.2.0.0.0.1.0.0.0.0.0.0.0.2.2.2.2.IP6.INT.
```

So, if the above address relates to the node ND1.test.com, we might expect to see the following entries in the name server zone data:

```
$origin test.com.

ND1     99999 IN AAAA 2222:0:1:2:3:4:5678:9abc

cba9876540003000200010000000002222.IP6.INT. IN  PTR ND1  ▌1▐
```

▌1▐ All characters making up the reversed IPv6 address in this PTR entry should be separated by a period(.). These have been omitted in this example for clarity.

6.4.1.1 Proposed Changes to Resource Records

The IPv6 addressing system has been designed to allow for multiple addresses on a single interface and to facilitate address renumbering (for example, when company changes one of its service providers). Using the AAAA resource record format specified in RFC 1886 would require a major administrative effort in the event of a renumbering change. The work in progress in the current Internet draft *DNS Extensions to Support IP Version 6* proposes changes to the format of the AAAA resource record to simplify network renumbering.

The proposed format of the data section of the AAAA record is as shown in Figure 230 on page 495

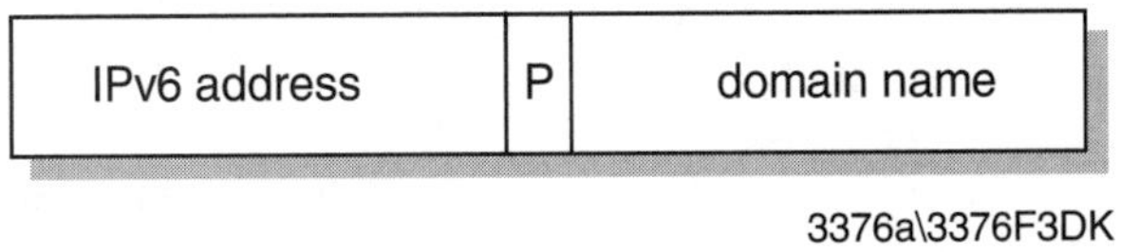

IPv6 address	P	domain name

3376a\3376F3DK

Figure 230. *AAAA Resource Record - Proposed Data Format*

IPv6 Address
> 128-bit address (contains only the lower bits of the address)

P   Prefix Length (0-128)

Domain Name
> The domain name of the prefix

To see how this format works, consider the example shown in Figure 231.

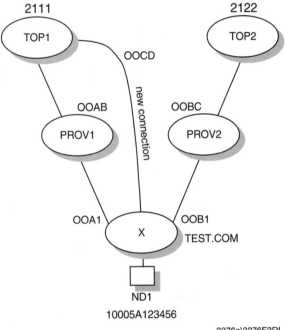

3376a\3376F3DL

Figure 231. *Prefix Numbering Example*

Site X is multihomed to two providers, PROV1 and PROV2. PROV1 gets its transit services from top-level provider TOP1. PROV2 gets its service from TOP2. TOP1 has the top-level aggregate (TLA ID + format prefix) of 2111 (see Figure 219 on page 472). TOP2 has the TLA of 2222.

TOP1 has assigned the next-level aggregate (NLA) of 00AB to PROV1. PROV2 has been assigned the NLA of 00BC by TOP2.

PROV1 has assigned the subscriber identifier 00A1 to site X. PROV2 has assigned the subscriber identifier 00B1 to site X.

Node ND1, at site X, which has the interface token of 10005A123456, is therefore configured with the following two IP addresses:

```
2111:00AB:00A1::1000:5A12:3456
2222:00BC:00B1::1000:5A12:3456
```

Site X is represented by the domain name test.com. Each provider has their own domain, top1.com, top2.com, prov1.com and prov2.com. In each of these domains is created an IP6 subdomain that is used to hold prefixes. The node ND1 can now be represented by the following entries in the DNS:

```
ND1.TEST.COM AAAA ::1000:5A12:3456 80
IP6.TEST.COM

IP6.TEST.COM AAAA 0:0:00A1:: 32 IP6.PROV1.COM
IP6.TEST.COM AAAA 0:0:00B1:: 32 IP6.PROV2.COM

IP6.PROV1.COM AAAA 0:00AB:: 16 IP6.TOP1.COM

IP6.PROV2.COM AAAA 0:00BC:: 16 IP6.TOP2.COM

IP6.TOP1.COM AAAA 2111::

IP6.TOP2.COM AAAA 2222::
```

This format simplifies the job of the DNS administrator considerably and makes renumbering changes much easier to implement. Say, for example, site X decides to stop using links from providers PROV1 and PROV2 and invests in a connection direct from the top-level service provider TOP1 (who allocates the next-level aggregate 00CD to site X). The only change necessary in the DNS would be for the two IP6.TEST.COM entries to be replaced with a single entry as follows:

```
IP6.TEST.COM AAAA 0:00CD:: 16 IP6.TOP1.COM
```

Note: Note that the proposed AAAA resource record format is currently work in progress only. Please refer to the latest Internet draft at :

```
http://www.ietf.org/internet-drafts/draft-ietf-ipngwg-aaaa-03.txt
```

6.5 DHCP in IPv6

Although IPv6 introduces stateless address autoconfiguration, DHCP DHCPv6 retains its importance as the stateful alternative for those sites that wish to have more control over their addressing scheme. Used together with stateless autoconfiguration, DHCP provides a means of passing additional configuration options to nodes once they have obtained their addresses. (See 7.2, "Dynamic Host Configuration Protocol (DHCP)" on page 516 for a detailed description of DHCP.)

There is currently no RFC covering DHCP in IPv6, although there is work in progress described in two Internet drafts, *Dynamic Host Configuration Protocol for IPv6 (DHCPv6)* and *Extensions for the Dynamic Host Configuration Protocol for IPv6*.

6.5.1 Differences between DHCPv6 and DHCPv4

DHCPv6 has some significant differences to DHCPv4, as it takes advantage of some of the inherent enhancements of the IPv6 protocol. Some of the principal differences are as follows:

- As soon as a client boots it already has a link-local IP address, which it can use to communicate with a DHCP server or a relay agent.

- The client uses multicast addresses to contact the server, rather than broadcasts.

- IPv6 allows the use of multiple IP addresses per interface and DHCPv6 can provide more than one address when requested.

- Some DHCP options are now unnecessary. Default routers, for example, are now obtained by a client using IPv6 neighbor discovery.

- DHCP messages (including address allocations) appear in IPv6 message extensions, rather than in the IP header as in IPv4.

- There is no requirement for BOOTP compatibility.

- There is a new reconfigure message, which is used by the server to send configuration changes to clients (for example, the reduction in an address lifetime). Clients must continue to listen for reconfigure messages once they have received their initial configuration.

6.5.2 DHCPv6 Messages

The following DHCPv6 messages are currently defined:

DHCP Solicit

       This is an IP multicast message. The DHCP client forwards the message to FF02::1:2, the well-known multicast address for all DHCP agents (relays and servers). If received by a relay, the relay forwards the message to FF05::1:3, the well-known multicast address for all DHCP servers.

DHCP Advertise

This is a unicast message sent in response to a DHCP Solicit. A DHCP server will respond directly to the soliciting client, if on the same link, or via the relay agent, if the DHCP Solicit was forwarded by a relay. The advertise message may contain one or more extensions (DHCP options).

DHCP Request

Once the client has located the DHCP server, the DHCP request (unicast message) is sent to request an address and/or configuration parameters. The request must be forwarded by a relay if the server is not on the same link as the client. The request may contain extensions (options specified by the client) that may be a subset of all the options available on the server.

DHCP Reply

An IP unicast message sent in response to a DHCP request (may be sent directly to the client or via a relay). Extensions contain the address and/or parameters committed to the client.

DHCP Release

An IP unicast sent by the client to the server, informing of resources that are being released.

DHCP Reconfigure

An IP unicast or multicast message, sent by the server to one or more clients, to inform them that there is new configuration information available. The client must respond to this message with a DHCP request, to request these new changes from the server.

For further details of DHCPv6, please refer to the latest Internet drafts. Note that exact numbering of the drafts is subject to change.

```
http://www.ietf.org/internet-drafts/draft-ietf-dhc-dhcpv6-13.txt
http://www.ietf.org/internet-drafts/draft-ietf-dhc-v6exts-10.txt
```

6.6 Mobility Support in IPv6

At time of writing, there is no RFC covering mobility support in IPv6, although there is work in progress on the subject, described in a current Internet draft, *Mobility Support in IPv6*.

Certain enhancements in the IPv6 protocol lend themselves particularly to the mobile environment. For example, unlike Mobile IPv4, there is no requirement for routers to act as "foreign agents" on behalf of the mobile node (see 7.4, "Mobile IP" on page 541), as neighbor discovery and address autoconfiguration allow the node to operate away from home without any special support from a local router. Also, most packets sent to a mobile node while it is away from its home location can be tunneled by using IPv6 routing (extension) headers, rather than a complete encapsulation, as used in Mobile IPv4, which reduces the overhead of delivering packets to mobile nodes.

For further information on mobility support in IPv6, please refer to the latest Internet draft at:

`http://www.ietf.org/internet-drafts/draft-ietf-mobileip-ipv6-06.txt`

6.7 Internet Transition - Migrating from IPv4 to IPv6

If the Internet is to realize the benefits of IPv6, then a period of transition will be necessary when new IPv6 hosts and routers will need to be deployed alongside existing IPv4 systems. *RFC1933 — Transition Mechanisms for IPv6 Hosts and Routers* and *RFC2185 — Routing Aspects of IPv6 Transition* define a number of mechanisms to be employed to ensure both compatibility between old and new systems and a gradual transition that does not impact the functionality of the Internet. These techniques are sometimes collectively termed *Simple Internet Transition (SIT)*. The transition employs the following techniques:

- Dual-stack IP implementations for hosts and routers that must interoperate between IPv4 and IPv6.

- Imbedding of IPv4 addresses in IPv6 addresses.

  IPv6 hosts will be assigned addresses that are interoperable with IPv4, and IPv4 host addresses will be mapped to IPv6.

- IPv6-over-IPv4 tunneling mechanisms for carrying IPv6 packets across IPv4 router networks

- IPv4/IPv6 header translation.

  This technique is intended for use when implementation of IPv6 is well advanced and only a few IPv4-only systems remain.

The techniques are also adaptable to other protocols, notably Novell IPX, which has similar internetwork layer semantics and an addressing scheme which can be mapped easily to a part of the IPv6 address space.

6.7.1 Dual IP Stack Implementation - The IPv6/IPv4 Node

The simplest way to ensure that a new IPv6 node maintains compatibility with existing IPv4 systems is to provide a dual IP stack implementation. An IPv6/IPv4 node can send and receive either IPv6 packets or IPv4 datagrams, depending on the type of system with which it is communicating. The node will have both a 128-bit IPv6 address and a 32-bit IPv4 address, which do not necessarily need to be related. Figure 232 shows a dual stack IPv6/IPv4 system communicating with both IPv6 and IPv4 systems on the same link.

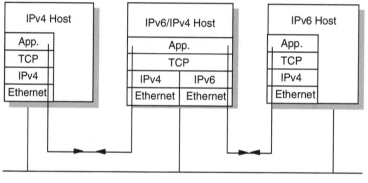

3376a\3376F3DM

Figure 232. IPv6/IPv4 Dual Stack System

The IPv6/IPv4 node may use stateless or stateful autoconfiguration to obtain its IPv6 address. It may also use any method to obtain its IPv4 address, such as DHCP, BOOTP or manual configuration. However, if the node is to perform automatic tunneling, then the IPv6 address must be an IPv4-compatible address, with the low order 32-bits of the address serving as the IPv4 address. (See 6.2.3, "IPv6 Addressing" on page 469)

Conceptually, the dual stack model envisages a doubling-up of the protocols in the internetwork layer only. However, related changes are obviously needed in all transport-layer protocols to operate using either stack, and possibly in applications if they are to exploit IPv6 capabilities, such as longer addresses.

When an IPv6/IPv4 node wishes to communicate with another system, it needs to know the capabilities of that system and which type of packet it should send. The

DNS plays a key role here. As described in 6.4, "DNS in IPv6" on page 493, a new resource record type, AAAA, is defined for mapping hostnames to IPv6 addresses. The results of a name server lookup determine how a node will attempt to communicate with that system. The records found in the DNS for a node depend on which protocols it is running.

- IPv4-only nodes have only A records containing IPv4 addresses in the DNS.

- IPv6/IPv4 nodes that can interoperate with IPv4-only nodes have AAAA records containing IPv4-compatible IPv6 addresses and A records containing the equivalent IPv4 addresses.

- IPv6-only nodes that cannot interoperate with IPv4-only nodes have only AAAA records containing IPv6 addresses.

Because IPv6/IPv4 nodes make decisions about which protocols to use based on the information returned by the DNS, the incorporation of AAAA records in the DNS is a prerequisite to interoperability between IPv6 and IPv4 systems. Note that name servers do not necessarily need to use an IPv6-capable protocol stack, but they must support the additional record type.

6.7.2 Tunneling

When IPv6 or IPv6/IPv4 systems are separated from other similar systems, with which they wish to communicate, by older IPv4 networks, then IPv6 packets must be tunneled through the IPv4 network.

IPv6 packets are tunnelled over IPv4 very simply; the IPv6 packet is encapsulated in an IPv4 datagram, or in other words, a complete IPv4 header is added to the IPv6 packet. The presence of the IPv6 packet within the IPv4 datagram is indicated by a Protocol value of 41 in the IPv4 header.

There are two kinds of tunneling of IPv6 packets over IPv4 networks: *automatic* and *configured*.

6.7.2.1 Automatic Tunneling

Automatic tunneling relies on IPv4-compatible addresses. The decision on when to tunnel is made by an IPv6/IPv4 host that has a packet to send across an IPv4-routed network area, and it follows the following rules:

- If the destination is an IPv4 or an IPv4-mapped address, send the packet using IPv4 because the recipient is not IPv6-capable.

Otherwise:

- If the destination is on the same subnet, send it using IPv6 because the recipient is IPv6-capable.

- If the destination is not on the same subnet but there is at least one default router on the subnet that is IPv6-capable, or there is a route configured to an IPv6 router for that destination, then send it to that router using IPv6.

Otherwise:

- If the address is an IPv4-compatible address, send the packet using automatic IPv6-over-IPv4 tunneling.

Otherwise:

- The destination is a node with an IPv6-only address that is connected via an IPv4-routed area, which is not also IPv6-routed. Therefore, the destination is unreachable.

Note: The IP address must be IPv4-compatible for tunneling to be used. Automatic tunneling cannot be used to reach IPv6-only addresses because they cannot be addressed using IPv4. Packets from IPv6/IPv4 nodes to IPv4-mapped addresses are not tunnelled to because they refer to IPv4-only nodes.

The rules listed above emphasize the use of an IPv6 router in preference to a tunnel for three reasons:

- There is less overhead because there is no encapsulating IPv4 header.

- IPv6-only features are available.

- The IPv6 routing topology will be used when it is deployed in preference to the pre-existing IPv4 topology.

A node does not need to know whether it is attached to an IPv6-routed or an IPv4-routed area; it will always use an IPv6 router if one is configured on its subnet and will use tunneling if one is not (in which case it can infer that it is attached to an IPv4-routed area).

Automatic tunneling may be either host-to-host, or it may be router-to-host. A source host will send an IPv6 packet to an IPv6 router if possible, but that router may not be able to do the same, and will have to perform automatic tunneling to the destination host itself. Because of the preference for the use of IPv6 routers rather than tunneling, the tunnel will always be as "short" as possible. However, the tunnel will always extend all of the way to the destination host; because IPv6 uses the same hop-by-hop routing paradigm, a host cannot determine if the packet will eventually emerge into an IPv6-complete area before it reaches the destination host. In order to use a tunnel that does not extend all of the way to the recipient, configured tunneling must be used.

The mechanism used for automatic tunneling is very simple.

- The encapsulating IPv4 datagram uses the low-order 32 bits of the IPv6 source and destination addresses to create the equivalent IPv4 addresses and sets the protocol number to 41 (IPv6).

- The receiving node's network interface layer identifies the incoming packets (or packets if the IPv4 datagram was fragmented) as belonging to IPv4 and passes them upwards to the IPv4 part of the dual IPv6/IPv4 internetwork layer.

- The IPv4 layer then receives the datagram in the normal way, re-assembling fragments if necessary, notes the protocol number of 41, then removes the IPv4 header and passes the original IPv6 packet "sideways" to the IPv6 part of the internetwork layer.

- The IPv6 code then processes the original packet as normal. Since the destination IPv6 address in the packet is the IPv6 address of the node (an IPv4-compatible address matching the IPv4 address used in the encapsulating IPv4 datagram) the packet is at its final destination. IPv6 then processes any extension headers as normal and then passes the packet's remaining payload to the next protocol listed in the last IPv6 header.

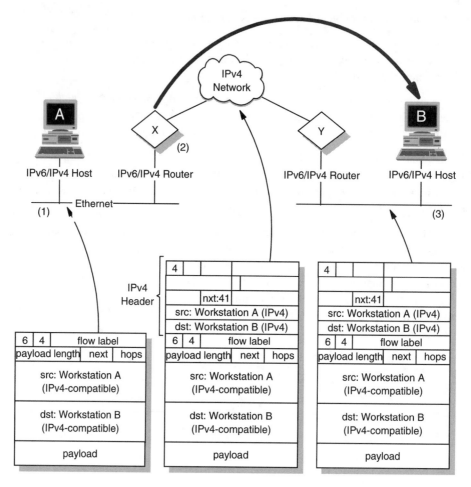

3376a\3376F3DN

Figure 233. *Router-to-Host Automatic Tunneling*

Figure 233 shows two IPv6/IPv4 nodes separated by an IPv4 network. Both
workstations have IPv4-compatible IPv6 addresses. Workstation A sends a packet to
workstation B, as follows:

1. Workstation A has received router solicitation messages from an IPv6-capable
   router (X) on its local link. It forwards the packet to this router.

2. Router X adds an IPv4 header to the packet, using IPv4 source and destination
   addresses derived from the IPv4-compatible addresses. The packet is then
   forwarded across the IPv4 network, all the way to workstation B. This is
   router-to-host automatic tunneling.

3. The IPv4 datagram is received by the IPv4 stack of workstation B. As the
   Protocol field shows that the next header is 41 (IPv6), the IPv4 header is stripped
   from the datagram and the remaining IPv6 packet is then handled by the IPv6
   stack.

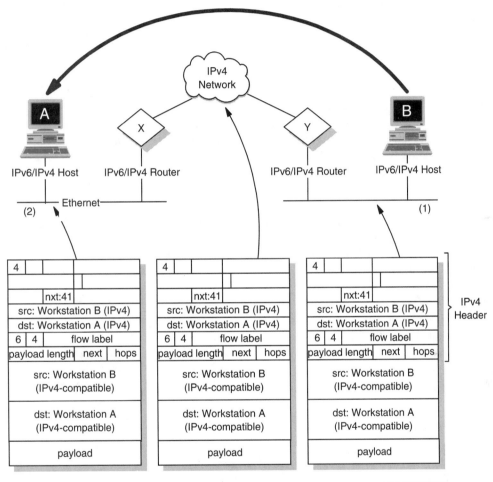

3376a\3376F3DN

Figure 234. Host-to-Host Automatic Tunneling

In Figure 234, workstation B responds as follows:

1. Workstation B has no IPv6-capable router on its local link. It therefore adds an
   IPv4 header to its own IPv6 frame and forwards the resulting IPv4 datagram

directly to the IPv4 address of workstation A via the IPv4 network. This is *host-to-host* automatic tunneling.

2. The IPv4 datagram is received by the IPv4 stack of workstation A. As the Protocol field shows that the next header is 41 (IPv6), the IPv4 header is stripped from the datagram and the remaining IPv6 packet is then handled by the IPv6 stack.

6.7.2.2 Configured Tunneling

Configured tunneling is used for host-router or router-router tunneling of IPv6-over-IPv4. The sending host or the forwarding router is configured so that the route, as well as having a next hop, also has a *tunnel end* address (which is always an IPv4-compatible address). The process of encapsulation is the same as for automatic tunneling except that the IPv4 destination address is not derived from the low-order 32 bits of the IPv6 destination address, but from the low-order 32 bits of the tunnel end. The IPv6 destination and source addresses *do not* need to be IPv4-compatible addresses in this case.

When the router at the end of the tunnel receives the IPv4 datagram, it processes it in exactly the same way as a node at the end of an automatic tunnel. When the original IPv6 packet is passed to the IPv6 layer in the router, it recognizes that it is not the destination, and the router forwards the packet on to the final destination as it would for any other IPv6 packet.

It is, of course, possible that after emerging from the tunnel, the IPv6 packet is tunnelled again by another router.

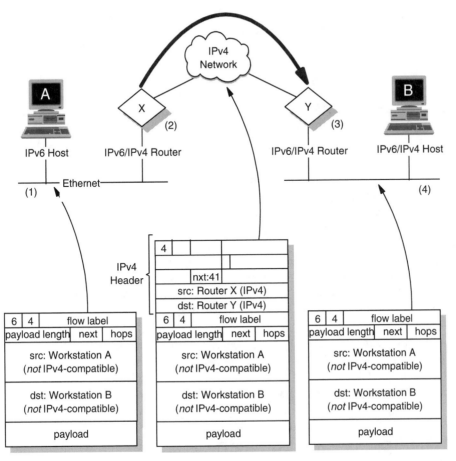

Figure 235. Router-to-Router Configured Tunnel

Figure 235 shows two IPv6-only nodes separated by an IPv4 network. A router-to-router tunnel is configured between the two IPv6/IPv4 routers X and Y.

1. Workstation A constructs an IPv6 packet to send to workstation B. It forwards the packet to the IPv6 router advertising on its local link (X).

2. Router X receives the packet, but has no direct IPv6 connection to the destination subnet. However, a tunnel has been configured for this subnet. The router therefore adds an IPv4 header to the packet, with a destination address of the tunnel-end (router Y) and forwards the datagram over the IPv4 network.

3. The IPv4 stack of router Y receives the frame. Seeing the Protocol field value of 41, it removes the IPv4 header, and passes the remaining IPv6 packet to its IPv6 stack. The IPv6 stack reads the destination IPv6 address, and forwards the packet.

4. Workstation B receives the IP6 packet.

6.7.3 Header Translation

Installing IPv6/IPv4 nodes allows for backward compatibility with existing IPv4 systems. However, when migration of networks to IPv6 reaches an advanced stage, it is likely that new systems being installed will be IPv6 only. There will therefore be a requirement for IPv6-only systems to communicate with the remaining IPv4-only systems. Header translation is required for IPv6-only nodes to interoperate with IPv4-only nodes. Header translation is performed by IPv6/IPv4 routers on the boundaries between IPv6 routed areas and IPv4 routed areas.

The translating router strips the header completely from IPv6 packets and replaces it with an equivalent IPv4 header (or the reverse). In addition to correctly mapping between the fields in the two headers, the router must convert source and destination addresses from IPv4-mapped addresses to real IPv4 addresses (by taking the low-order 32 bits of the IP address). In the reverse direction, the router adds the ::FFFF /96 prefix to the IPv4 address to form the IPv4-mapped address. If either the source or the destination IPv6 address is IPv6 only, the header cannot be translated.

Note that for a site with even just one IPv4 host, every IPv6 node with which it needs to communicate must have an IPv4-mapped address.

6.7.4 Interoperability Summary

Whether two nodes can interoperate depends upon their capabilities and their addresses.

An IPv4 node can communicate with:

- Any IPv4 node on the local link

- Any IPv4 node via an IPv4 router

- Any IPv6 node with IPv4-mapped address via a header translator

An IPv6 node (IPv6-only address) can communicate with:

- Any IPv6 node on the local link

- Any IPv6 node via an IPv6 router on the local link (may require tunneling through IPv4 network from the router)

An IPv6 node (IPv4-mapped address) can communicate with:

- Any IPv6 node on the local link

- Any IPv6 node via an IPv6 router on the local link (may require tunneling through IPv4 network from the router)

- Any IPv4 node via a header translator

An IPv6/IPv4 node (IPv4-compatible address) can communicate with:

- Any IPv4 node on the local link

- Any IPv4 node via an IPv4 router on the local link

- Any IPv6 node on the local link

- Any IPv6 node via an IPv6 router on the local link (may require tunneling through IPv4 network from the router)

- Any IPv6/IPv4 node (IPv4-compatible address) via host-to-host tunnel

6.8 The Drive Towards IPv6

The drivers for the introduction of IPv6 networks are likely to be requirements for new facilities that require IPv6, or exhaustion of the IPv4 address space. Which of these is seen as more important will vary between organizations. For example, commercial organizations with large, long-established internal IPv4 networks are unlikely to be keen to upgrade thousands of working IPv4 hosts and routers, unless they have a problem with the address space within their own networks. They will, however, be likely to invest in IPv6 deployment if new business-critical applications require facilities that are only available on IPv6 or if they require connectivity to other organizations that are using IPv6-only addresses.

Businesses that are implementing IP networks for the first time, however, may be interested in some of the capabilities of IPv6, such as the address autoconfiguration. However, anyone thinking of implementing IPv6 today needs to be aware that the protocol is still, as of today, very much under development. It may be said that IPv4 is also still under development, as new RFCs and Internet drafts are constantly being produced, but for IPv6, certain key protocols, such as DHCP, at time of writing are still at Internet draft stage only. The Internet backbone today consists of IPv4 routers and, until such time as the IPv6 protocols have been widely used and tested, the owners of these production routers are unlikely to put them at risk by upgrading them to IPv6.

One off-shoot of the IETF IPng (next generation) project was the development of the 6Bone, which is an Internet-wide IPv6 virtual network, layered on top of the physical IPv4 Internet. The 6Bone consists of many islands supporting IPv6 packets, linked by tunnels across the existing IPv4 backbone. The 6Bone is widely used for testing of IPv6 protocols and products. It is expected that, as confidence grows in IPv6 and more products with IPv6 capability become available, the 6Bone will eventually be replaced by a production backbone of ISP and user network IPv6 capable routers.

6.9 References

The following RFCs contain detailed information on IPv6:

- *RFC 1752 —The Recommendation for the IP Next Generation Protocol*
- *RFC 1883 — Internet Protocol, Version 6 (IPv6)*
- *RFC 1191 — Path MTU Discovery*
- *RFC 2373 — IP Version 6 Addressing Architecture*
- *RFC 2374 — An IPv6 Aggregatable Global Unicast Address Format*
- *RFC 2375 — IPv6 Multicast Address Assignments*
- *RFC 1885 — Internet Control Message Protocol (ICMPv6) for the Internet Protocol Version 6 (IPv6) Specification*
- *RFC 1970 — Neighbor Discovery for IP Version 6 (IPv6)*
- *RFC 1971 — IPv6 Stateless Address Autoconfiguration*
- *RFC 1886 — DNS Extensions to Support IP Version 6*
- *RFC 1933 — Transition Mechanisms for IPv6 Hosts and Routers*
- *RFC 2185 — Routing Aspects of IPv6 Transition*

Chapter 7. Dynamic IP, Mobile IP and Network Computers

There are generally three pieces of information needed by a system in order to be able to communicate on a TCP/IP network: an IP address (to uniquely identify the system on the network), a subnet mask (to determine the network and subnet parts of the address) and the address of at least one router (if the system is to be able to communicate with other devices outside of its immediate subnet). These three values represent the bare minimum of information that must be programmed into each and every device that is to participate in the TCP/IP world. Often the number of necessary parameters will be much higher. With the exponential growth rate of networking today, it is easy to see that manual programming of these values into every device that is to attach to the network represents a major administrative workload.

The increasingly mobile nature of the workforce also presents problems with regard to configuration of network devices. It is possible to allocate multiple sets of configuration parameters to a device, but this obviously means even more workload for the administrator, puts the or she onus on the or she user to ensure that he or she is using the appropriate configuration for his or her current location, and perhaps most importantly, is wasteful with respect to the number of IP addresses allocated.

This chapter looks at several components of TCP/IP that help automate device configuration, reduce the number of IP addresses allocated, and/or cope with the demands of the mobile user.

7.1 Bootstrap Protocol (BOOTP)

BOOTP is a *draft standard protocol*. Its status is *recommended*. The BOOTP specifications can be found in *RFC 951 — Bootstrap Protocol*.

There are also updates to BOOTP, some relating to interoperability with DHCP (see 7.2, "Dynamic Host Configuration Protocol (DHCP)" on page 516), described in *RFC 1542 — Clarifications and Extensions for the Bootstrap Protocol*, which updates RFC 951 and *RFC 2132 — DHCP Options and BOOTP Vendor Extensions*. These updates to BOOTP are *draft standards* with a status of *elective* and *recommended* respectively.

The BOOTP protocol was originally developed as a mechanism to enable diskless hosts to be remotely booted over a network as workstations, routers, terminal concentrators and so on. It allows a minimum IP protocol stack with no configuration information to obtain enough information to begin the process of downloading the necessary boot code. BOOTP does not define how the downloading is done, but this process typically uses TFTP (see also 4.5, "Trivial File Transfer Protocol (TFTP)" on page 233) as described in *RFC 906 — Bootstrap Loading Using TFTP*. Although still widely for this purpose by diskless hosts, BOOTP is also commonly used solely as a mechanism to deliver configuration information to a client that has not been manually configured.

The BOOTP process involves the following steps:

1. The client determines its own hardware address; this is normally in a ROM on the hardware.

2. A BOOTP client sends its hardware address in a UDP datagram to the server. The full contents of this datagram are shown in Figure 236 on page 513. If the client knows its IP address and/or the address of the server, it should use them, but in general BOOTP clients have no IP configuration data at all. If the client does not know its own IP address, it uses 0.0.0.0. If the client does not know the server's IP address, it uses the limited broadcast address (255.255.255.255). The UDP port number is 67.

3. The server receives the datagram and looks up the hardware address of the client in its configuration file, which contains the client's IP address. The server fills in the remaining fields in the UDP datagram and returns it to the client using UDP port 68. One of three methods may be used to do this:

   - If the client knows its own IP address (it was included in the BOOTP request), then the server returns the datagram directly to this address. It is likely that the ARP cache in the server's protocol stack will not know the hardware address matching the IP address. ARP will be used to determine it as normal.

   - If the client does not know its own IP address (it was 0.0.0.0 in the BOOTP request), then the server must concern itself with its own ARP cache.

   - ARP on the server cannot be used to find the hardware address of the client because the client does not know its IP address and so cannot reply to an ARP request. This is called the "chicken and egg" problem. There are two possible solutions:

     - If the server has a mechanism for directly updating its own ARP cache without using ARP itself, it does so and then sends the datagram directly.

     - If the server cannot update its own ARP cache, it must send a broadcast reply.

4. When it receives the reply, the BOOTP client will record its own IP address (allowing it to respond to ARP requests) and begin the bootstrap process.

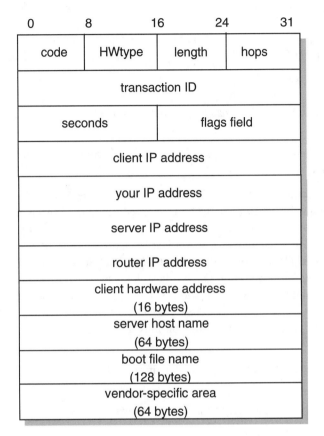

3376\3376F5D1

Figure 236. BOOTP Message Format

code   Indicates a request or a reply.

  1   Request
  2   Reply

HWtype   The type of hardware, for example:

  1   Ethernet
  6   IEEE 802 Networks :

  Refer to *STD 2 — Assigned Internet Numbers* for a complete list.

length   Hardware address length in bytes. Ethernet and token-ring both use 6, for example.

hops   The client sets this to 0.

It is incremented by a router that relays the request to another server and is used to identify loops. RFC 951 suggests that a value of 3 indicates a loop.

Transaction ID

A random number used to match this boot request with the response it generates.

Seconds   Set by the client. It is the elapsed time in seconds since the client started its boot process.

Flags field   The most significant bit of the flags field is used as a broadcast flag. All other bits must be set to zero; they are reserved for future use. Normally, BOOTP servers attempt to deliver BOOTREPLY messages directly to a client using unicast delivery. The destination address in the IP header is set to the BOOTP *your IP address* and the MAC address is set to the BOOTP *client hardware address*. If a host is unable to receive a unicast IP datagram until it knows its IP address, then this broadcast bit must be set to indicate to the server that the BOOTREPLY must be sent as an IP and MAC broadcast. Otherwise this bit must be set to zero.

Client IP address

Set by the client. Either its known IP address, or 0.0.0.0.

Your IP address

Set by the server if the client IP address field was 0.0.0.0.

Server IP address

Set by the server.

Router IP address

This is the address of a BOOTP relay agent, *not* a general IP router to be used by the client. It is set by the forwarding agent when BOOTP forwarding is being used (see 7.1.1, "BOOTP Forwarding" on page 515).

Client hardware address

Set by the client and used by the server to identify which registered client is booting.

Server host name

Optional server host name terminated by X'00'.

Boot file name

> The client either leaves this null or specifies a generic name, such as router indicating the type of boot file to be used. The server returns the fully qualified filename of a boot file suitable for the client. The value is terminated by X'00'.

Vendor-specific area

> Optional vendor-specific area. It is recommended that clients always fill the first four bytes with a "magic cookie." If a vendor-specific magic cookie is not used the client should use 99.130.83.99 followed by an end tag (255) and set the remaining bytes to zero. The vendor-specific area can also contain *BOOTP Vendor extensions*. These are options that can be passed to the client at boot time along with its IP address. For example, the client could also receive the address of a default router, the address of a domain name server and a subnet mask. BOOTP shares the same options as DHCP, with the exception of several DHCP-specific options. Please see RFC 2132 for full details.

Once the BOOTP client has processed the reply, it may proceed with the transfer of the boot file and execute the full boot process. See RFC 906 for the specification of how this is done with TFTP. In the case of a diskless host, the full boot process will normally replace the minimal IP protocol stack, loaded from ROM, and used by BOOTP and TFTP, with a normal IP protocol stack transferred as part of the boot file and containing the correct customization for the client.

7.1.1 BOOTP Forwarding

The BOOTP client uses the limited broadcast address for BOOTP requests, which requires the BOOTP server to be on the same subnet as the client. BOOTP forwarding is a mechanism for routers to forward BOOTP requests across subnets. It is a configuration option available on most routers. The router configured to forward BOOTP requests is known as a *BOOTP relay agent*.

A router will normally discard any datagrams containing illegal source addresses, such as 0.0.0.0, which is used by a BOOTP client. A router will also generally discard datagrams with the limited broadcast destination address. However, a BOOTP relay agent will accept such datagrams from BOOTP clients on port 67. The process carried out by a BOOTP relay agent on receiving a BOOTPREQUEST is as follows:

1. When the BOOTP relay agent receives a BOOTPREQUEST, it first checks the hops field to check the number of hops already completed, in order to decide whether to forward the request. The threshold for allowable number of hops is normally configurable.

2. If the relay agent decides to relay the request, it checks the contents of the router IP address field. If this field is zero, it fills this field with the IP address of the interface on which the BOOTPREQUEST was received. If this field already has an IP address of another relay agent, it is not touched.

3. The value of the hops field is incremented.

4. The relay agent then forwards the BOOTPREQUEST to one or more BOOTP servers. The address of the BOOTP server(s) is preconfigured at the relay agent. The BOOTPREQUEST is normally forwarded as a unicast frame, although some implementations use broadcast forwarding.

5. When the BOOTP server receives the BOOTPREQUEST with the non-zero router IP address field, it sends an IP unicast BOOTREPLY to the BOOTP relay agent at the address in this field on port 67.

6. When the BOOTP relay agent receives the BOOTREPLY, the HWtype, length and client hardware address fields in the message supply sufficient link-layer information to return the reply to the client. The relay agent checks the broadcast flag. If this flag is set, the agent forwards the BOOTPREPLY to the client as a broadcast. If the broadcast flag is not set, the relay agent sends a reply as a unicast to the address specified in your IP address.

When a router is configured as a BOOTP relay agent, the BOOTP forwarding task is considerably different to the task of switching datagrams between subnets normally carried out by a router. Forwarding of BOOTP messages can be considered to be receiving BOOTP messages as a final destination, then generating new BOOTP messages to be forwarded to another destination.

7.1.2 BOOTP Considerations

The use of BOOTP allows centralized configuration of multiple clients. However, it requires a static table to be maintained with an IP address preallocated for every client that is likely to attach to the BOOTP server, even if the client is seldom active. This means that there is no relief on the number of IP addresses required. There is a measure of security in an environment utilizing BOOTP, because a client will only be allocated an IP address by the server if it has a valid MAC address.

7.2 Dynamic Host Configuration Protocol (DHCP)

DHCP is a *draft standard protocol*. Its status is *elective*. The current DHCP specifications can be found in *RFC 2131 — Dynamic Host Configuration Protocol* and *RFC 2132 — DHCP Options and BOOTP Vendor Extensions*.

The Dynamic Host Configuration Protocol (DHCP) provides a framework for passing configuration information to hosts on a TCP/IP network. DHCP is based on the BOOTP protocol, adding the capability of automatic allocation of reusable network addresses and additional configuration options. For information according to BOOTP please refer to 7.1, "Bootstrap Protocol (BOOTP)" on page 511. DHCP messages use UDP port 67, the BOOTP server's well-known port and UDP port 68, the BOOTP client's well-known port. DHCP participants can interoperate with BOOTP participants. See 7.2.8, "BOOTP and DHCP Interoperability" on page 526 for further details.

DHCP consists of two components:

1. A protocol that delivers host-specific configuration parameters from a DHCP server to a host.
2. A mechanism for the allocation of temporary or permanent network addresses to hosts.

IP requires the setting of many parameters within the protocol implementation software. Because IP can be used on many dissimilar kinds of network hardware, values for those parameters cannot be guessed at or assumed to have correct defaults. The use of a distributed address allocation scheme based on a polling/defense mechanism, for discovery of network addresses already in use, cannot guarantee unique network addresses because hosts may not always be able to defend their network addresses.

DHCP supports three mechanisms for IP address allocation: address allocation

1. Automatic allocation

   DHCP assigns a permanent IP address to the host.

2. Dynamic allocation

   DHCP assigns an IP address for a limited period of time. Such a network address is called a *lease*. This is the only mechanism that allows automatic reuse of addresses that are no longer needed by the host to which it was assigned.

3. Manual allocation

   The host's address is assigned by a network administrator.

7.2.1 The DHCP Message Format

The format of a DHCP message is shown in Figure 237 on page 518:

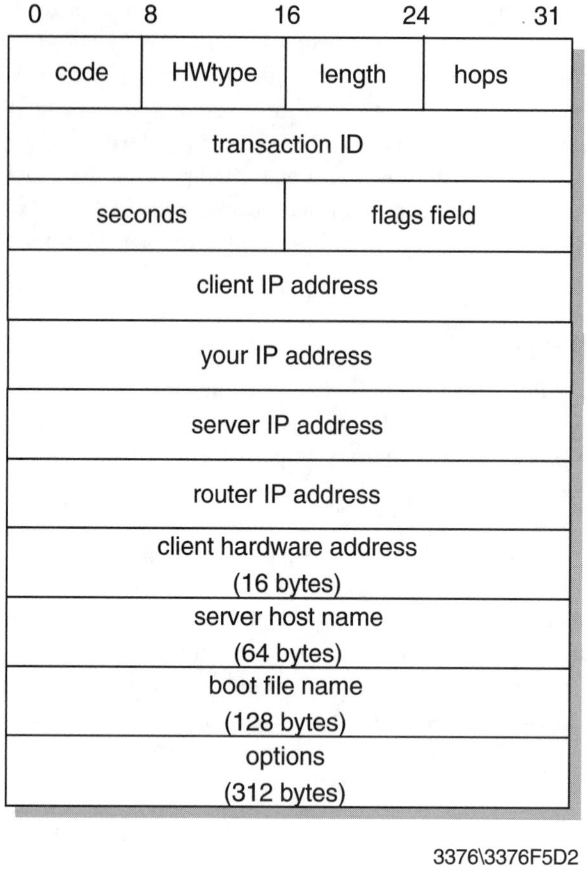

```
         0        8        16        24      . 31
      ┌────────┬────────┬────────┬────────┐
      │  code  │ HWtype │ length │  hops  │
      ├────────┴────────┴────────┴────────┤
      │          transaction ID           │
      ├─────────────────┬─────────────────┤
      │     seconds     │   flags field   │
      ├─────────────────┴─────────────────┤
      │         client IP address         │
      ├───────────────────────────────────┤
      │          your IP address          │
      ├───────────────────────────────────┤
      │         server IP address         │
      ├───────────────────────────────────┤
      │         router IP address         │
      ├───────────────────────────────────┤
      │      client hardware address      │
      │            (16 bytes)             │
      ├───────────────────────────────────┤
      │         server host name          │
      │            (64 bytes)             │
      ├───────────────────────────────────┤
      │          boot file name           │
      │           (128 bytes)            │
      ├───────────────────────────────────┤
      │             options               │
      │           (312 bytes)            │
      └───────────────────────────────────┘
```

3376\3376F5D2

Figure 237. *DHCP Message Format*

code   Indicates a request or a reply

           1   Request
           2   Reply

HWtype   The type of hardware, for example:

           1   Ethernet
           6   IEEE 802 Networks

           Refer to *STD 2 — Assigned Internet Numbers* for a complete list.

length   Hardware address length in bytes. Ethernet and token-ring both use 6, for example.

hops   The client sets this to 0. It is incremented by a router that relays the request to another server and is used to identify loops. RFC 951 suggests that a value of 3 indicates a loop.

Transaction ID
A random number used to match this boot request with the response it generates.

Seconds   Set by the client. It is the elapsed time in seconds since the client started its boot process.

Flags field   The most significant bit of the flags field is used as a broadcast flag. All other bits must be set to zero, and are reserved for future use. Normally, DHCP servers attempt to deliver DHCP messages directly to a client using unicast delivery. The destination address in the IP header is set to the DHCP *your IP address* and the MAC address is set to the DHCP *client hardware address*. If a host is unable to receive a unicast IP datagram until it knows its IP address, then this broadcast bit must be set to indicate to the server that the DHCP reply must be sent as an IP and MAC broadcast. Otherwise this bit must be set to zero.

Client IP address
Set by the client. Either its known IP address, or 0.0.0.0.

Your IP address
Set by the server if the client IP address field was 0.0.0.0.

Server IP address
Set by the server.

Router IP address
This is the address of a BOOTP relay agent, *not* a general IP router to be used by the client. It is set by the forwarding agent when BOOTP forwarding is being used (see 7.1.1, "BOOTP Forwarding" on page 515).

Client hardware address
Set by the client. DHCP defines a client identifier option that is used for client identification. If this option is not used the client is identified by its MAC address.

Server host name
Optional server host name terminated by X'00'.

Boot file name
The client either leaves this null or specifies a generic name, such as router, indicating the type of boot file to be used. In a DHCPDISCOVER

request this is set to null. The server returns a fully qualified directory path name in a DHCPOFFER request. The value is terminated by X'00'.

Options   The first four bytes of the options field of the DHCP message contain the magic cookie (99.130.83.99). The remainder of the options field consists of tagged parameters that are called *options*. Please see RFC 2132 for details.

7.2.2 DHCP Message Types

DHCP messages fall into one of the following categories:

Message	Use
DHCPDISCOVER	Broadcast by a client to find available DHCP servers.
DHCPOFFER	Response from a server to a DHCPDISCOVER and offering IP address and other parameters.
DHCPREQUEST	Message from a client to servers that does one of the following: • Requests the parameters offered by one of the servers and declines all other offers • Verifies a previously allocated address after a system or network change (a reboot for example) • Requests the extension of a lease on a particular address
DHCPACK	Acknowledgement from server to client with parameters, including IP address.
DHCPNACK	Negative acknowledgement from server to client, indicating that the client's lease has expired or that a requested IP address is incorrect.
DHCPDECLINE	Message from client to server indicating that the offered address is already in use.
DHCPRELEASE	Message from client to server cancelling remainder of a lease and relinquishing network address.
DHCPINFORM	Message from a client that already has an IP address (manually configured for example), requesting further configuration parameters from the DHCP server.

7.2.3 Allocating a New Network Address

This section describes the client/server interaction if the client does not know its network address. Assume that the DHCP server has a block of network addresses from which it can satisfy requests for new addresses. Each server also maintains a database of allocated addresses and leases in permanent local storage.

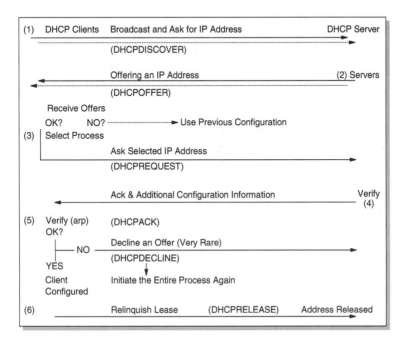

Figure 238. DHCP Client and DHCP Server Interaction

The following is a description of the DHCP client/server interaction steps illustrated in Figure 238:

1. The client broadcasts a DHCPDISCOVER message on its local physical subnet. At this point, the client is in the INIT state. The DHCPDISCOVER message may include some options such as network address suggestion or lease duration.

2. Each server may respond with a DHCPOFFER message that includes an available network address (your IP address) and other configuration options. The servers may record the address as offered to the client to prevent the same address being offered to other clients in the event of further DHCPDISCOVER messages being received before the first client has completed its configuration.

3. The client receives one or more DHCPOFFER messages from one or more servers. The client chooses one based on the configuration parameters offered and

broadcasts a DHCPREQUEST message that includes the server identifier option to indicate which message it has selected and the requested IP address option, taken from Your IP Address in the selected offer.

In the event that no offers are received, if the client has knowledge of a previous network address, the client may reuse that address if its lease is still valid, until the lease expires.

4. The servers receive the DHCPREQUEST broadcast from the client. Those servers not selected by the DHCPREQUEST message use the message as notification that the client has declined that server's offer. The server selected in the DHCPREQUEST message commits the binding for the client to persistent storage and responds with a DHCPACK message containing the configuration parameters for the requesting client. The combination of client hardware and assigned network address constitute a unique identifier for the client's lease and are used by both the client and server to identify a lease referred to in any DHCP messages. The Your IP Address field in the DHCPACK messages is filled in with the selected network address.

5. The client receives the DHCPACK message with configuration parameters. The client performs a final check on the parameters, for example with ARP for allocated network address, and notes the duration of the lease and the lease identification cookie specified in the DHCPACK message. At this point, the client is configured.

If the client detects a problem with the parameters in the DHCPACK message (the address is already in use on the network for example), the client sends a DHCPDECLINE message to the server and restarts the configuration process. The client should wait a minimum of ten seconds before restarting the configuration process to avoid excessive network traffic in case of looping. On receipt of a DHCPDECLINE, the server must mark the offered address as unavailable (and possibly inform the system administrator that there is a configuration problem).

If the client receives a DHCPNAK message, the client restarts the configuration process.

6. The client may choose to relinquish its lease on a network address by sending a DHCPRELEASE message to the server. The client identifies the lease to be released by including its network address and its hardware address.

Note: Responses from the DHCP server to the DHCP client may be broadcast or unicast, depending on whether the client is able to receive a unicast message before the TCP/IP stack is fully configured; this varies between implementations. (See Flags field on page 519.)

7.2.4 DHCP Lease Renewal Process

This section describes the interaction between DHCP servers and clients that have already been configured and the process that ensures lease expiry and renewal.

1. When a server sends the DHCPACK to a client with IP address and configuration parameters, it also registers the start of the lease time for that address. This lease time is passed to the client as one of the options in the DHCPACK message, together with two timer values, T1 and T2. The client is rightfully entitled to use the given address for the duration of the lease time. On applying the received configuration, the client also starts the timers T1 and T2. At this time the client is in the BOUND state. Times T1 and T2 are options configurable by the server but T1 must be less than T2, and T2 must be less than the lease time. According to RFC 2132, T1 defaults to (0.5 * lease time) and T2 defaults to (0.875 * lease time).

2. When timer T1 expires, the client will send a DHCPREQUEST (unicast) to the server that offered the address, asking to extend the lease for the given configuration. The client is now in the RENEWING state. The server would usually respond with a DHCPACK message indicating the new lease time, and timers T1 and T2 are reset at the client accordingly. The server also resets its record of the lease time. In normal circumstances, an active client would continually renew its lease in this way indefinitely, without the lease ever expiring.

3. If no DHCPACK is received until timer T2 expires, the client enters the REBINDING state. It now broadcasts a DHCPREQUEST message to extend its lease. This request can be confirmed by a DHCPACK message from any DHCP server on the network.

4. If the client does not receive a DHCPACK message after its lease has expired, it has to stop using its current TCP/IP configuration. The client may then return to the INIT state, issuing a DHCPDISCOVER broadcast to try and obtain any valid address.

Figure 239 on page 524 shows the DHCP process and changing client state during that process.

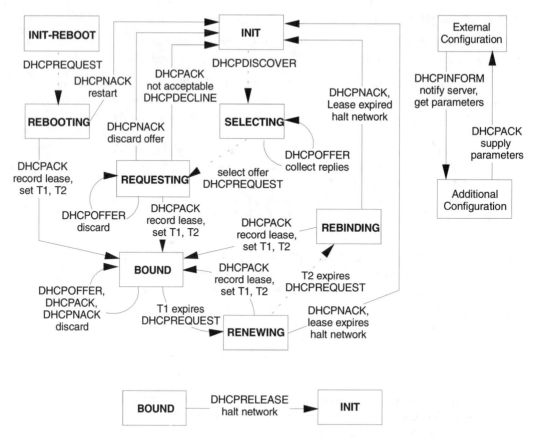

Figure 239. *DHCP Client State and DHCP Process*

7.2.5 Reusing a Previously Allocated Network Address

If the client remembers and wishes to reuse a previously allocated network address then the following steps are carried out:

1. The client broadcasts a DHCPREQUEST message on its local subnet. The DHCPREQUEST message includes the client's network address.

2. A server with knowledge of the client's configuration parameters responds with a DHCPACK message to the client (provided the lease is still current), renewing the lease at the same time.

   If the client's lease has expired, the server with knowledge of the client responds with DHCPNACK.

3. The client receives the DHCPACK message with configuration parameters. The client performs a final check on the parameters and notes the duration of the lease and the lease identification cookie specified in the DHCPACK message. At this point, the client is configured and its T1 and T2 timers are reset.

If the client detects a problem with the parameters in the DHCPACK message, the client sends a DHCPDECLINE message to the server and restarts the configuration process by requesting a new network address. If the client receives a DHCPNAK message, it cannot reuse its remembered network address. It must instead request a new address by restarting the configuration process as described in 7.2.3, "Allocating a New Network Address" on page 521.

Note: A host should use DHCP to reacquire or verify its IP address and network parameters whenever the local network parameters have changed, for example at system boot time or after a disconnection from the local network, as the local network configuration may change without the host's or user's knowledge. If a client has multiple IP interfaces, each of them must be configured by DHCP separately.

For further information please refer to the above-mentioned RFCs.

7.2.6 Configuration Parameters Repository

DHCP provides persistent storage of network parameters for network clients. A DHCP server stores a key-value entry for each client, the key being some unique identifier, for example an IP subnet number and a unique identifier within the subnet (normally a hardware address), and the value contains the configuration parameters last allocated to this particular client.

One effect of this is that a DHCP client will tend to always be allocated the same IP address by the server, provided the pool of addresses is not over-subscribed and the previous address has not already been allocated to another client.

7.2.7 DHCP Considerations

DHCP dynamic allocation of IP addresses and configuration parameters relieves the network administrator of great deal of manual configuration work. The ability for a device to be moved from network to network and to automatically obtain valid configuration parameters for the current network can be of great benefit to mobile users. Also, because IP addresses are only allocated when clients are actually active, it is possible, by the use of reasonably short lease times and the fact that mobile clients do not need to be allocated more than one address, to reduce the total number of addresses in use in an organization. However, the following should be considered when DHCP is being implemented:

- DHCP is built on UDP, which is, as yet, inherently insecure. In normal operation, an unauthorized client could connect to a network and obtain a valid IP address and configuration. To prevent this, it is possible to preallocate IP addresses to particular MAC addresses (similar to BOOTP), but this increases the administration workload and removes the benefit of recycling of addresses. Unauthorized DHCP servers could also be set up, sending false and potentially disruptive information to clients.

- In a DHCP environment where automatic or dynamic address allocation is used, it is generally not possible to predetermine the IP address of a client at any particular point in time. In this case, if static DNS servers are also used, the DNS servers will not likely contain valid host name to IP address mappings for the clients. If having client entries in the DNS is important for the network, one may use DHCP to manually assign IP addresses to those clients and then administer the client mappings in the DNS accordingly.

7.2.8 BOOTP and DHCP Interoperability

The format of DHCP messages is based on the format of BOOTP messages, which enables BOOTP and DHCP clients to interoperate in certain circumstances. Every DHCP message contains a DHCP message type (51) option. Any message without this option is assumed to be from a BOOTP client.

Support for BOOTP clients at a DHCP server must be configured by a system administrator, if required. The DHCP Server responds to BOOTPREQUEST messages with BOOTPREPLY, rather than DHCPOFFER. Any DHCP server that is not configured in this way will discard any BOOTPREQUEST frames sent to it. A DHCP server may offer static addresses, or automatic addresses (from its pool of unassigned addresses) to a BOOTP client (although not all BOOTP implementations will understand automatic addresses). If an automatic address *is* offered to a BOOTP client, then that address must have an infinite lease time, as the client will not understand the DHCP lease mechanism.

DHCP messages may be forwarded by routers configured as BOOTP relay agents.

7.3 Dynamic Domain Name System

The Domain Name System described in 4.2, "Domain Name System (DNS)" on page 194is a static implementation without recommendations with regard to security. In order to take advantage of DHCP, yet still to be able to locate any specific host by means of a meaningful label, such as its host name, the following extensions to DNS are required:

- A method for the host name to address mapping entry for a client in the domain name server to be updated, once the client has obtained an address from a DHCP server

- A method for the reverse address to hostname mapping to take place once the client obtains its address

- Updates to the DNS to take effect immediately, without the need for intervention by an administrator

- Updates to the DNS to be authenticated to prevent unauthorized hosts from accessing the network and to stop imposters from using an existing host name and remapping the address entry for the unsuspecting host to that of its own

- A method for primary and secondary DNS servers to quickly forward and receive changes as entries are being updated dynamically by clients

In short, a secure Dynamic Domain Name System (DDNS) is necessary.

Several RFCs relate to DDNS. These are:

RFC 2065 — DNS Security Extensions
>   The extensions described in this RFC provide for the storage of digital signatures and authenticated public keys in secured zones in the DNS. KEY and SIG (signature) resource record types are introduced. Three distinct services are provided:
>
>   - Distribution of keys
>
>   - Data origin authentication (by associating digital signatures with the resource records in the DNS)
>
>   - Transaction and request authentication
>
>   The RFC makes provision for any type of key and security algorithm, but by default assumes the MD5/RSA algorithm (see 5.2, "A Short Introduction to Cryptography" on page 342).

RFC 2136 — Dynamic Updates in the Domain Name System
>   This RFC introduces the UPDATE DNS message format, which is used to add or delete resource records in the DNS. The ability for updates to take effect without the DNS having to be reloaded is also described.

RFC 1995 —Incremental Zone Transfer in DNS
>   This RFC introduces the IXFR DNS message type, which allows incremental transfers of DNS zone data between primary and secondary DNS servers. In other words, when an update has been made to the zone data, only the change has to be copied to other DNS servers who maintain

a copy of the zone data, rather than the whole DNS database (as is the case with the AXFR DNS message type).

RFC 1996 — Prompt Notification of Zone Transfer
This RFC introduces the NOTIFY DNS message type, which is used by a master server to inform slave servers that an update has taken place and that they should initiate a query to discover the new data.

RFC 2137 —Secure DNS Dynamic Updates
This RFC extends recommendations from both RFC 2065 and RFC 2136 to provide a detailed description for secure dynamic DNS updates.

The above RFCs are all proposed standard protocols with elective status.

7.3.1 The UPDATE DNS Message Format

The DNS message format (shown in Figure 110 on page 206) was designed for the querying of a static DNS database. RFC 2136 defines a modified DNS message for updates, shown in Figure 240.

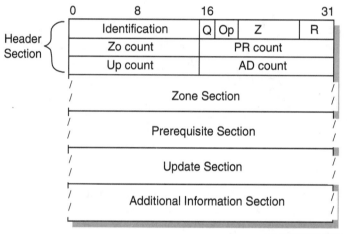

Figure 240. DDNS UPDATE Message Format

The header section is always present and has a fixed length of 12 bytes. The other sections are of variable length.

Identification
A 16-bit identifier assigned by the program. This identifier is copied in the corresponding reply from the name server and can be used for differentiation when multiple queries/updates are outstanding at the same time.

Q	Flag identifying an update request (0) or a response (1).
Op	Opcode - The value 5 indicates an UPDATE message.
z	7-bit field set to 0 and reserved for future use.
R	Response code (undefined in update requests). Possible values are:

	0	No error.
	1	Format error. The server was unable to interpret the message.
	2	Server failure. The message was not processed due to a problem with the server.
	3	Name error. A name specified does not exist.
	4	Not implemented. The type of message specified in Opcode is not supported by this server.
	5	Refused. The server refuses to perform the UPDATE requested for security or policy reasons.
	6	Name error. A name exists when it should not.
	7	RRset error. A resource record set exists when it should not.
	8	RRset error. A resource record set specified does not exist.
	9	Zone Authority error. The server is not authoritative for the Zone specified.
	10	Zone error. A name specified in the Prerequisite or Update sections is not in the Zone specified.

$ZOcount$	The number of RRs in the Zone section.
$PRcount$	The number of RRs in the Prerequisite section.
$UPcount$	The number of RRs in the Update section.
$ADcount$	The number of RRs in the Additional Information section.

Zone section

This section is used to indicate the zone of the records that are to be updated. As all records to be updated must belong to the same zone, the zone section has a single entry specifying the zone name, zone type (which must be SOA) and zone class.

Prerequisite section

This section contains RRs or RRsets that either must, or must not, exist, depending on the type of update.

Update section
> This section contains the RRs and/or RRsets that are to be added to, or deleted from the zone.

Additional information section
> This section can be used to pass additional RRs that relate to the update operation in process.

For further information on the UPDATE message format, please refer to RFC 2136.

Note: The IBM implementation of DDNS uses a different UPDATE message format. Please see 7.3.2.5, "IBM DDNS UPDATE Message Format" on page 538.

7.3.2 IBM's Implementation of DDNS

IBM's Dynamic Domain Name System (DDNS) is based on, and is a superset of, the Internet Software Consortium's publicly available implementation of the Berkeley Internet Name Domain (BIND) level 4.9.3 (which did not include any security functions). The IBM implementation supports both static and dynamic DNS domains. In dynamic domains, only authorized clients can update their own data. RSA public-key digital signature technology is used for client authentication.

Using IBM's DHCP Server, an administrator configures (at the server) host configuration parameters, including IP address, to automate the configuration of IP hosts. The DDNS provides dynamic host name-to-IP address (and IP address-to-host name) mapping for dynamic IP clients. Using DDNS, when the client receives its new address from the DHCP server, it automatically updates its A record on the DNS server with the new address. The IBM DHCP server automatically updates the PTR record on behalf of the client.

7.3.2.1 DDNS Mechanism

The DDNS client program, NSUPDATE, is used to update information in a DDNS server. Dynamic updates are performed by any of the following:

Network client
> A host that has DHCP and DDNS client software and can update its A and TXT records with the current IP address information

DHCP server
> Updates PTR records with the current host name information for the address it has just allocated. In certain circumstances it can also perform updates to A records for clients that either cannot, or do not, update the A records themselves (see 7.3.3, "Proxy A Record Update (ProxyArec)" on page 540).

DDNS system administrator

A system administrator can make manual changes to all resource record types in the DDNS database, or can use the NSUPDATE command from a command line to make the changes. All changes take effect immediately.

The interaction between the DDNS client, DDNS server and DHCP server is shown in Figure 241:

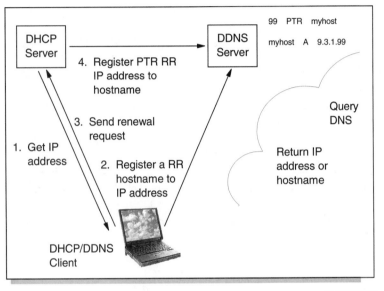

3376\3376F5D5

***Figure 241.** DDNS-to-DHCP Client Interaction*

Note: For ease of explanation, the DHCP and DDNS servers are shown as separate devices in Figure 241. In practice, it is common for these two servers to be on the same machine.

1. The DHCP makes the normal exchanges with the DHCP server to obtain configuration data (see 7.2.3, "Allocating a New Network Address" on page 521).

2. The DDNS client then sends an update request, including its newly obtained IP address, to the DDNS server for the resource records that are associated with the client's hostname. The client also sends its public key and signs all resource records with a digital signature. The combination of the key and the signature verifies that this client is indeed entitled to use the hostname and that the information contained in the client's record is valid.

If the client's updates have been successful, the server commits the changes to its database. The client is now reachable by its hostname.

3. The DHCP client sends a lease renewal request message to the DHCP server. This message includes the hostname being used by the client. The DHCP server updates the PTR record (IP address-to-hostname mapping) for the client on the DDNS server. An inverse query on the client's IP address to the DDNS server will now return the client's host name.

7.3.2.2 DDNS Security

Having a DHCP and DDNS server in your network allows a client to automatically obtain a valid, working configuration from the network and to register its presence automatically with the DDNS server. However, this means that without authentication of the DDNS client, an unauthorized host might impersonate an unsuspecting host by copying the hostname of that client. It could then update the DDNS server with its own IP address and could then intercept data (for example, logon passwords) intended for the unsuspecting host.

IBM implements RSA digital signature technology in its DDNS server and client code to authenticate the owner of the DNS records and to secure the DNS database updates. See 5.2, "A Short Introduction to Cryptography" on page 342 for more information on RSA digital signature technology. DDNS supports two modes of securing updates for a dynamic domain, dynamic secured mode and dynamic presecured mode. Both modes protect A records in the database from unauthorized updates.

Dynamic Secured Mode: When a DDNS client registers its host name for the first time, it generates an RSA key pair. A public key is sent to the DDNS server and registered for that particular host name.

The DDNS client stores the RSA key pair (with the private key encrypted) in a client key file. When the DDNS client updates the resource records on the DDNS server, the digital signature is generated by using the private key and is sent to the server with the update data. On receiving the update request, the DDNS server uses the client's public key (in the KEY resource record) to:

- Authenticate the owner of the update request to verify that the update request was signed with the corresponding private key

- Verify that the data was not changed since it was signed (to verify that no one intercepted and changed the data on the way to the name server)

In this way, only the owners of the original records, who possess the correct private key necessary to generate the correct digital signature, can update resource records that are protected by an existing KEY resource record.

In addition, a DDNS administrator can create and use a zone key for each dynamic domain. The zone key is the administrator's RSA key pair for a particular domain. This key enables the administrator to create, modify or delete any host's record in the domain, regardless of who created the records. The private key is used to generate the signature when the administrator carries out update requests and the server examines the signature to verify that update requests are from the administrator. The public key is registered in the domain data file as a KEY resource record for the domain. The private and public keys are stored in the administrator's key file on the server.

The dynamic secured mode ensures that impersonation of hosts cannot occur in a domain, but it does not prevent any DDNS client with a new hostname from obtaining a working and valid configuration for the domain. The dynamic secured domain requires a minimal amount of configuration on the part of the administrator.

Dynamic Presecured Mode: In the presecured dynamic domain, DDNS clients must be pre-authorized by a DDNS administrator before they can create their name record. The DDNS administrator must preregister hosts and generate RSA keys for each client. This means that in presecured mode, the KEY resource record for a client must be already defined in the domain before an update from that client is accepted. The DDNS administrator must also distribute the correct, corresponding key information to each host before they create the resource records.

The presecured domain represents the most secure DNS name space available. In addition to preventing updates to A and PTR records from unknown or unauthenticated hosts, the DDNS server is able to log attempts at invalid updates and the administrator can identify MAC addresses of offending clients and can take appropriate action.

The DDNS administrator obviously has a higher workload establishing a presecured domain, but the other benefits of the dynamic domain, namely support for mobile clients and address space conservation, are still realized.

7.3.2.3 DDNS Resource Records

The information that composes a DNS server database is represented in the form of resource records (RRs). The RR format is shown 4.2.9, "Domain Name System Resource Records" on page 203. The security mechanism introduced with DDNS introduces two new types of resource records, KEY and SIG.

1. The KEY resource record (type 25)

This record represents a public encryption key for a name in the DDNS database. This can be a key for a zone, a host or a user. A KEY RR is authenticated by a SIG RR. KEY RRs contain the public exponent and modulus of an encryption key.

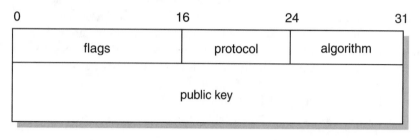

3376a\3376F5D7

Figure 242. *KEY Resource Record Rdata Format*

All resource records have the format shown in Figure 109 on page 204. Figure 242 shows the fields used within the Rdata section of a KEY resource record.

flags

This field indicates the type of resource record for which this KEY RR is provided.

protocol

This field indicates the protocols (in addition to DDNS) that are to be secured for authentication by this KEY RR.

algorithm

This field indicates which encryption algorithm should be used with this key; in the case of IBM Dynamic IP, this field has a value of 1, which means that the RSA/MD5 algorithm is being used.

public key

The actual public key to be used for authentication. This field is structured in a public exponent length field, the public key exponent portion, and the public key modulus portion.

An example of a KEY resource record is shown below:

```
client1 IN   KEY   0x0000   0   1 AQO3P+UqipNXsuijeL3yyfJLw9PagI+NZg9oXrgYI1cSKOAo
                                   +WwPOxpEqUsj0hFsKNo4V0q6LH1LKl7XcytwAI01    ;Cr=auth
```

2. The SIG resource record (type 24)

This record represents a digital signature to authenticate any resource records in a DDNS database. SIG RRs contain, within the digital signature itself, the type of resource record they are signing, the time until the signature will be valid, the time when the RR was signed, and the original time to live (TTL) value for the RR being signed.

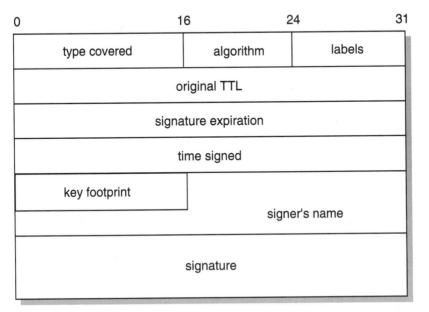

3376a\3376F5D8

Figure 243. SIG Resource Record Rdata Format

Figure 243 shows the fields used within the Rdata section of a SIG resource record.

type covered
> This field indicates the type of RR covered by this signature.

algorithm
> This field indicates which encryption algorithm should be used with this key; in the case of IBM Dynamic IP, this field has a value of 1, which means that the RSA/MD5 algorithm is being used.

labels
> This field indicates the number of labels (host and domain name strings separated by dots) in the SIG owner name.

original TTL

> The original time to live for the signed resource record is included in order to avoid caching name servers to decrement this value. This value is protected by the signature, and it is different from the TTL of the SIG record itself.

signature expiration

> The time until which this signature is valid. This value is represented in a number of seconds starting from 1 January 1970, GMT (ignoring leap seconds).

time signed

> The time when this signature was actually signed, represented in the same format as mentioned above.

key footprint

> This field determines, depending on the applicable encryption algorithm, how to decode the signature.

signer's name

> The fully qualified domain name of the signer generating this SIG RR.

signature

> The actual digital signature that authenticates an RR of the type indicated in the type covered field.

An example of a SIG resource record is shown below:

```
4660   IN   SIG   KEY 1 4 4660 820470267 817356268 0x8d00 client1.test.itsc.austin.ibm.com
                  ecK2L1zhtyVnNrI24/Viitl41reduDy7TU8dxSCoGoc9zc4IIGEy4E4uVPu
                  d4fjessH8XS+H2UVjLXhr66y6Gg==     ;Cr=auth
```

To keep data traffic and memory requirements in the DDNS server as small as possible, public encryption keys and digital signatures are converted to strings using a hash function, and they are then represented in so-called base-64 format.

Note: KEY and SIG resource records always use a single line. We have indented the examples for illustration purposes only.

7.3.2.4 IBM Implementation in Relation to Current Standards

IBM implemented Dynamic DNS in 1995. This implementation was done by IBM research based on an Internet draft being discussed in the IETF at that time. In their opinion, the protocol was going to become a standard in a very short time. It is important to note that the IETF only standardizes protocol on the wire. The key management policies and the integration of DHCP & DDNS are IBM design, which is what differentiates an integrated product from a pure technology (such as an RFC-proposed standard).

The IETF did not standardize the draft from which IBM research worked. That standard evolved into the current *RFC 2137 (Secure Dynamic Updates)*. Its resource records in the DNS are almost identical to IBM's implementation. However, the protocol on the wire is different. Also, it deals with the issue of integrating dynamic updates into secure DNS resolving (RFC 2065) and describes two modes of operation, Mode A and Mode B. In Mode A, the client-signed RRs are stored as part of the DNS data, whereas in Mode B, the server signs all the records. The IBM implementation of DDNS is actually very close to Mode A (although does not yet support the secure resolving described in RFC 2065).

The current version of BIND (8.1.1.) includes DDNS function based on RFC 2136 and includes no security for dynamic updates.

There is also another Internet draft that proposes a secure method of dynamic updates - *Secret Key Transaction Signatures for DNS (TSIG)*. This draft may be found at:

```
http://www.ietf.org/internet-drafts/draft-ietf-dnsind-tsig-05.txt
```

TSIG uses shared secrets rather than public key cryptography to secure communication between the name server and a client. It seeks to be a simpler alternative to both RFC 2065 for secure resolving and RFC 2137 for dynamic updates, in those situations where the client and the server can establish a trust relationship. This is the mechanism Microsoft will use in Windows NT 5.0.

The following summary describes how IBM's implementation of Dynamic IP is different from the RFCs and also explains the reasons for that:

IBM DDNS versus RFC 2137

> The logical evolution of IBM's implementation would be to move towards the RFC 2137 mechanism. This would not gain IBM any additional functionality but would ensure that IBM's DDNS clients and servers would maintain compatibility with software from other vendors complying with RFC 2137. This would become important if other vendors were developing clients or servers with this capability. At the current time, to our knowledge, no other vendor has a DDNS client or server that complies with RFC 2137, so making this change at this time would not be of any practical advantage to IBM.

IBM DDNS versus RFC 2136

> RFC 2136 was not designed for any authentication or expiration of resource records. It was also not designed for clients updating the DNS records. Its main design point was to allow administrators to update certain records without having to recycle the DNS. Thus it does not have the following capabilities that are essential for the IBM integrated product:

1. No real security mechanism. It is possible to configure a list of IP addresses from where update requests to any record in the system can originate (per zone). Not only is this mechanism unsecure (that is, anyone who has update capability can update anyone else's record), it is not scalable.

2. No mechanism of expiration. Thus if a DHCP client was allocated an address and then moved away from the network, the DHCP server's IP address lease would expire after a period of time and the address would get reused, but the DNS entry would have to be manually removed.

3. No mechanism to detect out-of order update requests or prevent replay attacks. (No time stamp is associated with the update request.)

IBM DDNS verus T-Sig

T-Sig accomplishes the goal of providing an authentication mechanism for updates from clients. But it still does not provide an expiration mechanism. This means that if a client created its A-RR, and moved away from the network for some period of time. The PTR record created by the DHCP server could be deleted by it but the A-RR (the hostname to IP address mapping) would remain in the DNS. This has a security implication, because data intended for the old hostname would be forwarded to the new holder of the IP address.

T-Sig also has scalability issues, since the shared secret keys are theoretically unique between every client-name server pair and must be predefined in each.

T-Sig does have a time stamp associated with its update requests, but since these time stamps are not stored with the data updated, it is questionable how out-of-order update requests or replay attacks could be effectively detected/prevented.

7.3.2.5 IBM DDNS UPDATE Message Format

The IBM implementation of DDNS uses the UPDATE message format shown in Figure 244 on page 539.

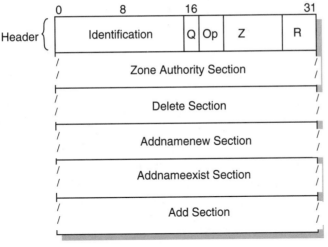

Figure 244. IBM DDNS UPDATE Message Format

The IBM message has a 32-bit header, which is identical to the first 32 bits of the RFC 2136 format header (see Figure 240 on page 528). However, there are no "count" sections in the header. A response consists of the header only.

The body of an UPDATE message contains one or more of the following sections. Each section consists of a 1-byte type code, followed by a 1-byte count field (in units of RRs), followed by the RRs themselves.

ZONEAUTHORITY

This contains the SOA RR of the zone that is to be updated. There may only be one ZONEAUTHORITY section and it is always the first section in the body of the message.

DELETE   Used to specify RRs that are to be deleted.

ADDNAMENEW

Used to add an RR with a new name.

ADDNAMEEXIST

Used to update RRs with existing names.

ADD   Used for adding records with either new or existing names.

With the exception of the ZONEAUTHORITY section, sections in the body of the message may appear multiple times and in any order.

7.3.3 Proxy A Record Update (ProxyArec)

In a DDNS environment, the client workstation requires DDNS client code to be able to update its A record on the DDNS server. The DHCP Server updates the PTR record at the DDNS server on behalf of the client.

An alternative approach is for the DHCP server to update both the PTR record *and* the A record at the DDNS server. This process is known as Proxy A Record Update (ProxyArec) and ProxyArec can be utilized in a situation where clients support DHCP but do not have DDNS client code. ProxyArec is discussed in the Internet draft *Interaction between DHCP and DNS*, which may be found at:

```
http://www.ietf.org/internet-drafts/draft-ietf-dhc-dhcp-dns-08.txt
```

When using ProxyArec, the DDNS server cannot carry out an RSA authentication check on the client for which an update is being made; there is no interaction between the client and the DDNS server.

ProxyArec can be used in a situation where:

- Hosts are not mobile, or at least do not move from one domain to another.

- If mobile hosts have to be accommodated, then all the DHCP servers across which ProxyArec mobile hosts roam must be configured with the same RSA public/private key pair, otherwise the digital signature verification would fail.

- The client host's DHCP program is capable of sending its fully qualified domain name (FQDN) to the DHCP server, using DHCP options 12 and 15 or 81.

- Hostname hijacking is not a security concern.

The Internet draft specifies the new DHCP option 81 for use with ProxyArec. Option 81 has the following format:

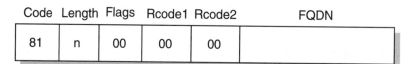

3376\3376F5D6

Figure 245. DHCP Option 81 Format

Flags

        Has the following values:

0	Client wants to retain responsibility for updating A record on DDNS server
1	Client wants DHCP server to update A records
3	DHCP server informs client that server assumes responsibility for A record updates (even if client wants to be responsible for update)

The default value is 1.

Rcode1 and Rcode2
Used by DHCP server to inform a DHCP client of the response code(s) from DDNS update.

FQDN
Fully qualified domain name of client.

A DHCP client does not necessarily need to support option 81 in order to take advantage of ProxyArec, provided it uses options 12 and/or 15 to pass the hostname to the DHCP server.

7.3.3.1 Using DDNS and ProxyArec Together

In a mixed environment with both DDNS clients and clients that support DHCP only, if the DHCP server is configured for ProxyArec, the DDNS clients must be manually configured with option 81 and with Flags=0 if you wish the DDNS clients to carry out their own (secure) updates, otherwise the DHCP server will carry out all A record updates.

7.3.3.2 IBM Implementation of ProxyArec

IBM have implemented an enhancement of ProxyArec that introduces a level of security. The DHCP server can be configured as being in "ProxyArec Protected" mode. In this mode, the DHCP server maintains a record of the MAC address of the client for which it created an A record initially. In a subsequent request for an update to the A record, the DHCP server checks the MAC address of the client before making the update. This gives some security against hostname impersonation.

7.4 Mobile IP

In the DHCP and DDNS environment, DHCP provides a device with a valid IP address for the point at which it is attached to the network. DDNS provides a method of locating that device by its host name, no matter where that device happens to be attached to a network and what IP address it has been allocated. An alternative approach to the problem of dealing with mobile devices is provided in *RFC 2002 — IP*

Mobility Support. IP Mobility Support, commonly referred to as Mobile IP, is a *proposed standard*, with a status of *elective*.

7.4.1 Mobile IP Overview

Mobile IP allows a device to maintain the same IP address (its *home address*) wherever it attaches to the network. (Obviously, a device with an IP address plugged into the wrong subnet will normally be unreachable.) However, the mobile device also has a *care-of* address, which relates to the subnet where it is currently located. The care-of address is managed by a *home agent*, which is a device on the home subnet of the mobile device. Any packet addressed to the IP address of the mobile device is intercepted by the home agent and then forwarded on to the care-of address through a tunnel. Once it arrives at the end of the tunnel, the datagram is delivered to the mobile device. The mobile node generally uses its home address as the source address of all datagrams that it sends.

Mobile IP can help resolve address shortage problems and reduce administrative workload, because each device that needs to attach to the network at multiple locations requires a single IP address only.

The following terminology is used in a mobile IP network configuration:

Home Address

> The static IP address allocated to a mobile node. It does not change no matter where the node attaches to the network.

Home Network

> A subnet with a network prefix matching the home address of the mobile node. Datagrams intended for the home address of the mobile node will always be routed to this network.

Tunnel

> The path followed by an encapsulated datagram.

Visited Network

> A network to which the mobile node is connected, other than the node's home network.

Home Agent

> A router on the home network of the mobile node that maintains current location information for the node and tunnels datagrams for delivery to the node when it is away from home.

Foreign Agent

A router on a visited network that registers the presence of a mobile node and detunnels and forwards datagrams to the node that have been tunneled by the mobile node's home agent.

7.4.2 Mobile IP Operation

Mobility agents (home agents and foreign agents) advertise their presence on the network by means of *agent advertisement* messages, which are ICMP router advertisement messages with extensions (see 7.4.3, "Mobility Agent Advertisement Extensions" on page 544). A mobile node may also explicitly request one of these messages with an agent solicitation message. When a mobile node connects to the network and receives one of these messages, it is able to determine whether it is on its home network or a foreign network. If the mobile node detects that it is on its home network, it will operate normally, without the use of mobility services. In addition, if it has just returned to the home network, having previously been working elsewhere, it will deregister itself with the home agent. This is done through the exchange of a registration request and registration reply.

f, however, the mobile node detects from an agent advertisement that it has moved to a foreign network, then it obtains a care-of address for the foreign network. This address may be obtained from the foreign agent (a foreign agent care-of address, which is the address of the foreign agent itself), or it may be obtained by some other mechanism such as DHCP (in which case it is known as a co-located care-of address). The use of co-located care-of addresses has the advantage that the mobile node does not need a foreign agent to be present at every network that it visits, but it does require that a pool of IP addresses is made available for visiting mobile nodes by the DHCP server.

Note that communication between a mobile node and a foreign agent takes place at the link layer level. It cannot use the normal IP routing mechanism, because the mobile node's IP address does not belong to the subnet in which it is currently located.

Once the mobile node has received its care-of address, it needs to register itself with its home agent. This may be done through the foreign agent, which forwards the request to the home agent, or directly with the home agent (see 7.4.4, "Mobile IP Registration Process" on page 546).

Once the home agent has registered the care-of address for the mobile node in its new position, any datagram intended for the home address of the mobile node is intercepted by the home agent and tunneled to the care-of address. The tunnel endpoint may be at a foreign agent if the mobile node has a foreign agent care-of address), or at the mobile node itself (if it has a co-located care-of address). Here the original datagram is removed from the tunnel and delivered to the mobile node.

The mobile node will generally respond to the received datagram using standard IP routing mechanisms.

Mobile IP operation is shown in Figure 246

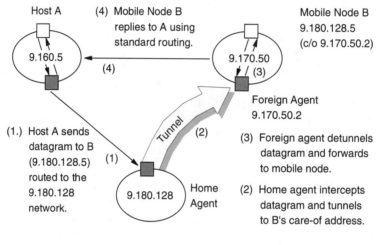

3376\3376F5D4

Figure 246. Mobile IP Operation

7.4.3 Mobility Agent Advertisement Extensions

p. The mobility agent advertisement consists of an ICMP router Advertisement with one or more of the following extensions.

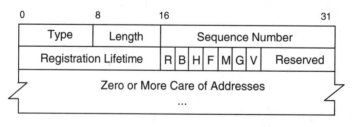

3376D\3376F5DP

Figure 247. Mobility Agent Advertisement Extension

Type 16

Length (6+[4*N]), where N is the number of care-of addresses advertised.

Sequence Number
The number of advertisements sent by this agent since it was initialized.

Registration Lifetime
The longest lifetime, in seconds, that this agent will accept in a Registration Request. A value of 0xffff indicates infinity. This field bears no relationship with the lifetime field in the router advertisement itself.

R Registration required - Mobile node must register with this agent rather than use a co-located care-of address.

B Busy - Foreign agent cannot accept additional registrations.

H Home Agent - This agent offers service as a home agent on this link.

F Foreign Agent - This agent offers service as a foreign agent on this link.

M Minimal encapsulation - This agent receives tunneled datagrams that use minimal encapsulation.

G GRE encapsulation - This agent receives tunneled datagrams that use GRE encapsulation.

V Van Jacobson header compression - This agent supports use of Van Jacobson header compression over the link with any registered mobile node.

Reserved This area ignored.

Care-of Address(es)
The care-of address(es) advertised by this agent. At least one must be included if the F bit is set.

Note that a foreign agent may be too busy to service additional mobile nodes at certain times. However, it must continue to send agent advertisements (with the B bit set) so that mobile nodes that are already registered will know that the agent has not failed or that they are still in range of the foreign agent.

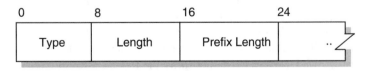

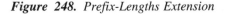

Figure 248. Prefix-Lengths Extension

Type

> 19

Length

> The number of router address entries in the router advertisement portion of the agent advertisement.

Prefix Length(s)

> The number of leading bits that make up the network prefix for each of the router addresses in the router advertisement portion of the agent advertisement. Each prefix length is a separate byte, in the order that the router addresses are listed.

The prefix lengths extension may follow the mobility agent advertisement extension. It is used to indicate the number of bits that should be applied to each router address (in the ICMP router advertisement portion of the message), when network prefixes are being used for move detection (see 7.4.7, "Move Detection" on page 550).

7.4.4 Mobile IP Registration Process

RFC 2002 defines two different procedures for mobile IP registration. The mobile node may register via a foreign agent, which relays the registration to the mobile node's home agent, or it may register directly with its home agent. The following rules are used to determine which of these registration processes is used:

- If the mobile node has obtained its care-of address from a foreign agent, it must register via that foreign agent.

- If the mobile node is using a co-located care-of address, but has received an agent advertisement from a foreign agent on this subnet, which has the R bit (registration required) set in that advertisement, then it should register via the agent. This mechanism allows for accounting to take place on foreign subnets, even if DHCP and co-located care-of address is the preferred method of address allocation.

- If the mobile node is using a co-located care-of address but has not received such an advertisement, it must register directly with its home agent.

- If the mobile node returns to its home network, it must (de)register directly with its home agent.

The registration process involves the exchange of registration request and registration reply messages, which are UDP datagrams. The registration request is sent to port 434. The request consists of a UDP header, followed by the fields shown in Figure 249 on page 547:

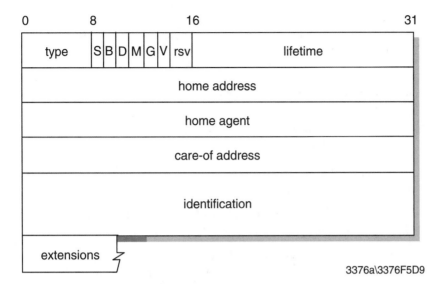

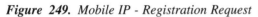

3376a\3376F5D9

Figure 249. Mobile IP - Registration Request

Type   1

S   Simultaneous bindings - If this bit is set, the home agent should keep any previous bindings for this node as well as adding the new binding. The home agent will then forward any datagrams for the node to multiple care-of addresses. This capability is intended particularly for wireless mobile nodes.

B   Broadcast datagrams - If this bit is set, the home agent should tunnel any broadcast datagrams on the home network to the mobile node.

D   Decapsulation by mobile node - The mobile node is using a co-located care-of address and will, itself, decapsulate the datagrams sent to it.

M   Minimal encapsulation should be used for datagrams tunneled to the mobile node.

G   GRE encapsulation should be used for datagrams tunneled to the mobile node.

V   Van Jacobson compression should be used over the link between agent and mobile node.

rsv   Reserved bits - Sent as zero.

Lifetime   The number of seconds remaining before the registration will be considered expired. A value of zero indicates a request for deregistration. 0xffff indicates infinity.

Home Address
The home IP address of the mobile node.

Home Agent
The IP address of the mobile node's home agent.

Care-of Address
The IP address for the end of the tunnel.

Identification
64-bit identification number constructed by the mobile node and used for matching registration requests with replies.

Extensions   A number of extensions are defined, all relating to authentication of the registration process. Please see RFC 2002 for full details.

The mobility agent responds to a registration request with a registration reply, with a destination port copied from the source port of the registration request. The registration reply is of the format shown in Figure 250:

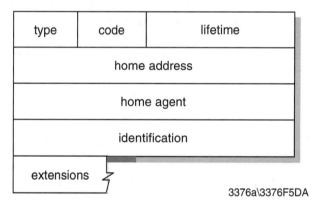

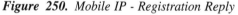

3376a\3376F5DA

Figure 250. *Mobile IP - Registration Reply*

Type   3

Code   Indicates the result of the registration request.

0	Registration accepted.
1	Registration accepted, but simultaneous bindings unsupported.
64-88	Registration denied by foreign agent.
128-136	Registration denied by home agent.

Lifetime　　The number of seconds remaining before the registration is considered expired. (Code field must be 0 or 1.)

Home Address
　　　　　Home IP address of the mobile node.

Home Agent
　　　　　IP address of the mobile node's home agent.

Identification
　　　　　64-bit identification number used for matching registration requests with replies.

Extensions　A number of extensions are defined, all relating to authentication of the registration process.

For full details of these messages, please refer to RFC 2002.

7.4.5 Tunneling

The home agent examines the destination IP address of all datagrams arriving on the home network. If the address matches with any of the mobile nodes currently registered as being away from home, then the home agent tunnels (using IP in IP encapsulation) the datagram to the care-of address for that mobile node. It is likely that the home agent will also be a router on the home network. In this case it is likely that it will receive datagrams addressed for a mobile node that is *not* currently registered as being away from home. In this case, the home agent assumes that the mobile node is at home, and forwards the datagram to the home network.

When a foreign agent receives a datagram sent to its advertised care-of address, it compares the inner destination address with its list of registered visitors. If it finds a match, the foreign agent forwards the decapsulated datagram to the appropriate mobile node. If there is no match, the datagram is discarded. (The foreign agent must not forward such a datagram to the original IP header, otherwise a routing loop will occur.)

If the mobile node is using a co-located care-of address, then the end of the tunnel lies at the mobile node itself. The mobile node is responsible for decapsulating the datagrams received from the home agent.

7.4.6 Broadcast Datagrams

If the home agent receives a broadcast datagram, it should not forward it to mobile nodes unless the mobile node specifically requested forwarding of broadcasts in its registration request. In this case, it will forward the datagram in one of the following manners:

- If the mobile node has a co-located care-of address, the home agent simply encapsulates the datagram and tunnels it directly to the care-of address.

- If the mobile node has a foreign agent care-of address, the home agent first encapsulates the broadcast in a unicast datagram addressed to the home address of the node. It then encapsulates and tunnels this datagram to the care-of address. In this way the foreign agent, when it decapsulates the datagram, knows to which of its registered mobile nodes it should forward the broadcast.

7.4.7 Move Detection

Mobile IP is designed not just for mobile users who regularly move from one site to another and attach their laptops to different subnets each time, but also for truly dynamic mobile users (for example, users of a wireless connection from an aircraft). Two mechanisms are defined that allow the mobile node to detect when it has moved from one subnet to another. When the mobile node detects that it has moved, it must re-register with a care-of address on the new foreign network. The two methods of move detection are as follows:

1. Foreign agents are consistently advertising their presence on the network by means of agent advertisements. When the mobile node receives an agent advertisement from its foreign agent, it starts a timer based on the lifetime field in the advertisement. If the mobile node has not received another advertisement from the same foreign agent by the time the lifetime has expired, then the mobile node assumes that it has lost contact with that agent. If in the meantime it has received an advertisement from *another* foreign agent, it may immediately attempt registration with the new agent. If it has not received any further agent advertisements, it should use Agent solicitation to try and locate a new foreign agent with which to register.

2. The mobile node checks whether any newly received agent advertisement is on the same subnet as its current care-of address. If the network prefix is different, the mobile node assumes that it has moved. On expiry of its current care-of address, the mobile node registers with the foreign agent that sent the new agent advertisement.

7.4.7.1 Returning Home

When the mobile node receives an agent advertisement from its own home agent, it knows that it has returned to its home network. Before deregistering with the home agent, the mobile node must configure its routing table for operation on the home subnet.

7.4.8 ARP Considerations

Mobile IP requires two extensions to ARP to cope with the movement of mobile nodes. These are:

Proxy ARP
> An ARP reply sent by one node on behalf of another that is either unable or unwilling to answer ARP request on its own behalf.

Gratuitous ARP
> An ARP packet sent as a local broadcast packet by one node that causes all receiving nodes to update an entry in their ARP cache.

When a mobile node is registered as being on a foreign network, its home agent will use proxy ARP in response to any ARP request seeking the mobile node's MAC address. The home agent responds to the request giving its own MAC address.

When a mobile node moves from its home network and registers itself with a foreign network, the home agent does a gratuitous ARP broadcast to update the ARP caches of all local nodes on the network. The MAC address used is again the MAC address of the home agent.

When a mobile node returns to its home network, having been previously registered at a foreign network, gratuitous ARP is again used to update ARP caches of all local nodes, this time with the real MAC address of the mobile node.

7.4.9 Mobile IP Security Considerations

The mobile computing environment has many potential vulnerabilities with regard to security, particularly if wireless links are in use, which are particularly exposed to eavesdropping. The tunnel between a home agent and the care-of address of a mobile node could also be susceptible to interception, unless a strong authentication mechanism is implemented as part of the registration process. RFC 2002 specifies implementation of keyed MD5 for the authentication protocol and advocates the use of additional mechanisms (such as encryption) for environments where total privacy is required.

7.5 IP Masquerading

One way to combat an IP address shortage is to avoid assigning addresses in the first place. Yet without an IP address, no system can communicate on a TCP/IP network.

IP masquerading allows you to effectively share one IP address among several different systems while still providing reliable, full function TCP/IP connections to every host. This technique can be used to provide Internet service to more than one computer using a single dial-up connection from an Internet Service Provider (ISP) for example. Or, you may wish to link branch office systems to your company's network without assigning IP addresses from your company's main address pool.

In practice, an IP address *is* assigned to each host that needs to communicate on the TCP/IP network, but the addresses are from a private network pool, such as the Class A network 10. A masquerading gateway accepts connection requests from these private hosts and translates them into requests originating from the IP address of the gateway itself. Responses from the TCP/IP network are then routed by the gateway back to the correct host on the private network. As a result, a single IP address on a network can effectively serve several different hosts without requiring additional IP address assignments on that same network.

There are currently no RFCs or IETF drafts that cover IP masquerading. However, IP masquerading is implemented in certain routers and is available for several software platforms.

7.6 The Network Computer

An alternative approach to solving the problem of a mobile workforce is not to try and cope with the addressing issues of users' machines being moved around the organization, but to provide fixed workstations around the organization that allow any user to access their own data and applications from anywhere. This is the principle of the *network computer*.

In general terms, a network computer is usually a microprocessor-based system with:

- Local memory (NVRAM)
- No disk (neither hard drive nor diskette)
- Some form of network connection
- Terminal emulation capabilities
- IP-based protocols, such as:
  - TCP
  - FTP
  - Telnet
  - NFS
- A Web browser

- A Java Virtual Machine (see 8.5, "Java" on page 569)

In short, a network computer can be thought of as a smart terminal.

All of the software required by a network computer, including the operating system, is stored on a server in the network and downloaded on demand when the network computer is powered on or when the user activates new functions.

The network computer stores only sufficient code in its own local NVRAM (the boot monitor program) to be able to make a BOOTP or DHCP connection to a server, in order to be able to download its operating system kernel. Download of the remainder of the operating system is then carried out using TFTP or NFS, depending upon implementation and configuration.

Typically, having powered on a network computer, a user is presented with a logon panel. On completion of a successful logon, the user is presented with a personalized desktop with his or her own set of application icons. Selection of any of those icons causes an application to be downloaded from a server. (Several different servers may be accessed.)

The network computer relies on TCP/IP protocols for all of its connectivity. As well as using NFS or TFTP to download applications, the applications themselves, if they require communication, will use TCP/IP. SNA emulators, for example, use TN3270 or TN5250 as appropriate.

Although the network computer is not, typically, based on an Intel processor, it is able to access Windows applications on a Windows Terminal Server or Citrix Systems Metaframe, by loading an ICA (independent console architecture) client. In this case, processing of the Windows application is carried out on the NT server itself and only screen changes are delivered to the client. The network computer may run applications remotely on a UNIX system, in a similar manner, by downloading an X Window server.

Having all the network computer software stored on a server allows for centralized management and simplified updates of operating system and application code.

IBM's implementation of the network computer, the IBM Network Station, may be booted, and managed from, Windows NT, AIX, OS/400, OS/390 and OS/2 servers. For further information on the IBM Network Station, please refer to the following IBM Redbooks:

SG24-4954 S/390 IBM Network Station - Getting Started

SG24-2153 AS/400 IBM Network Station - Getting Started

SG24-2127 IBM Network Station and the Windows NT Platform

SG24-2016 IBM Network Station - RS/6000 Notebook

You may also refer to the IBM Network Station home page at:
`http://www.pc.ibm.com/networkstation/`

7.7 References

The following RFCs contain detailed information on dynamic and mobile IP:

- *RFC 951 — Bootstrap Protocol*
- *RFC 1542 — Clarifications and Extensions for the Bootstrap Protocol*
- *RFC 2131 — Dynamic Host Configuration Protocol*
- *RFC 2132 — DHCP Options and BOOTP Vendor Extensions*
- *RFC 1995 —Incremental Zone Transfer in DNS*
- *RFC 1996 — Prompt Notification of Zone Transfer*
- *RFC 2065 — DNS Security Extensions*
- *RFC 2136 — Dynamic Updates in the Domain Name System*
- *RFC 2137 —Secure DNS Dynamic Updates*
- *RFC 2002 — IP Mobility Support*

Chapter 8. Internet Protocols and Applications

This chapter introduces some of the protocols and applications that have made the task of using the Internet both easier and very popular over the past couple of years. In fact, World Wide Web traffic, which is mostly HTTP, has outrun FTP as using the most bandwidth of all protocols across the Internet. Modern computer operating systems provide Web browser applications by default, some even provide Web servers, thus making it ever easier for end users and businesses to explore and exploit the vast capabilities of worldwide networked computing.

8.1 The World Wide Web (WWW)

The World Wide Web is a global hypertext system that was initially developed in 1989 by Tim Berners Lee at the European Laboratory for Particle Physics, CERN in Switzerland to facilitate an easy way of sharing and editing research documents among a geographically dispersed group of scientists.

In 1993 the Web started to grow rapidly which was mainly due to the National Center for Supercomputing Applications (NCSA) developing a Web browser program called Mosaic, an X Windows-based application. This application provided the first graphical user interface to the Web and made browsing more convenient.

Today there are Web browsers and servers available for nearly all platforms. You can get them either from an FTP site for free or buy a licensed copy. The rapid growth in popularity of the Web is due to the flexible way people can navigate through worldwide resources in the Internet and retrieve them.

The number of Web servers is also increasing rapidly and the traffic over port 80, which is the well-known port for HTTP Web servers, on the NSF backbone has had a phenomenal rate of growth too. The NSFNET, however, was converted back to a private research network in 1995; therefore comprehensive statistics of backbone traffic are not as easily available anymore, if they are at all.

8.1.1 Web Browsers

Generally, a browser is referred to as an application that provides access to a Web server. Depending on the implementation, browser capabilities and hence structures may vary. A Web browser, at a minimum, consists of an HTML interpreter and HTTP client which is used to access HTML Web pages. Besides this basic requirement, many browsers also support FTP, NNTP, e-mail (POP and SMTP clients), among other features, with an easy-to-manage graphical interface. Figure 251 on page 556 illustrates a basic Web browser structure.

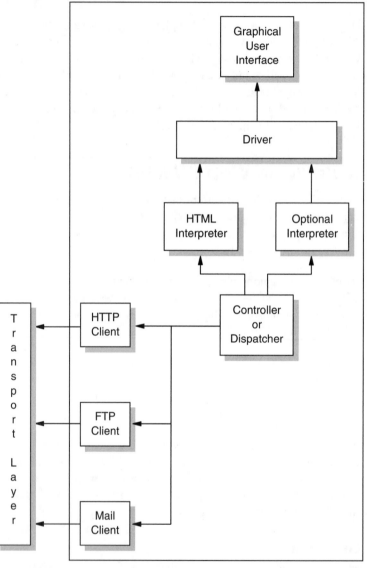

3376E\3376F8O7

Figure 251. Structure of a Web Browser

As with many other Internet facilities, the Web uses a client/server processing model. The Web browser is the client component. Examples of Web browsers include Mosaic, Netscape Navigator, Microsoft Internet Explorer, or Sun HotJava browser. Web browsers are responsible for formatting and displaying information, interacting with the user, and invoking external functions, such as telnet, or external viewers for data types that Web browsers do not directly support. Web browsers have become the "universal client" for the GUI workstation environment, in much the same way that the ability to emulate popular terminals such as the DEC VT100 or IBM 3270 allows connectivity and access to character-based applications on a wide variety of computers. Web browsers are widely available for all popular GUI workstation platforms and are inexpensive.

8.1.2 Web Servers

Web servers are responsible for servicing requests for information from Web browsers. The information can be a file retrieved from the server's local disk, or it can be generated by a program called by the server to perform a specific application function.

There are a number of public-domain Web servers available for a variety of platforms including most UNIX variants, as well as personal computer environments such as OS/2 Warp and Windows NT. Some well-known public domain servers are CERN, NCSA httpd, and Apache servers.

IBM has released the Domino Go Webserver, a scalable, high-performance Web server that is available on OS/390 as Version 5 (including WebSphere Application Server as described in 8.6.4.2, "IBM Web Application Servers" on page 582). Domino Go Webserver V4.6.2.5 is available on many workstation platforms (AIX, Solaris, HP-UX, OS/2 Warp, Windows NT, and Windows 95). Both versions provide state-of-the-art security, site indexing capabilities, advanced server statistics reporting, PICS support, and relational database connectivity with Net.Data (see 8.6.4.1, "IBM Web Connectors" on page 581). Domino Go Webserver is the successor to IBM's well-known Internet Connection Secure Server (ICSS), and it is a Java-enabled Web server that supports the development and running of servlets (see 8.5, "Java" on page 569).

8.1.3 Web Server Application Technologies

As mentioned earlier, Web server can serve static (mere HTML pages) or dynamic (generated by a program upon invocation) content. This section discusses some commonly used technologies used to provide dynamic content and to facilitate interaction between a Web server and an application server that is not directly accessible to a client (Web browser).

8.1.3.1 Common Gateway Interface (CGI)

The Common Gateway Interface (CGI) is a means of allowing a Web server to execute a program that is provided by the Web server administrator, rather than retrieving a file. CGI programs allow a Web server to generate a dynamic response, usually based on the client's input. A number of popular Web servers support the CGI, and a variety of programming languages can be used to develop programs that interface with CGI. Unless using PERL, however, CGI programs are not easily portable across platforms.

8.1.3.2 Server-Specific APIs

Some Web servers offer specific APIs that allow developers to create programs that can be invoked for special purposes upon certain events. Those APIs are usually quite powerful but offer no portability across Web server platforms. The most popular server-specific APIs are Netscape Server API (NSAPI) and Microsoft Internet Information Server API (ISAPI).

8.1.3.3 Servlets

Based on Java, this technology allows the invocation of a Java program in the server's memory. This method is usually very portable across platforms and incurs little processing overhead. See 8.5, "Java" on page 569 for more details.

8.1.3.4 Server-Side Includes (SSI)

This is a technology that a Java-enabled Web server (meaning, a Web server with a servlet engine) can use to convert a section of an HTML file into an alternative dynamic portion each time the document is sent to the client's browser. This dynamic portion invokes an appropriate servlet and passes to it the parameters it needs. The replacement is performed at the server and it is completely transparent to the client. Pages that use this technology have the extension .shtml instead of .html (or .htm).

8.1.3.5 Java Server Pages (JSP)

This is an easy-to-use solution for generating HTML pages with dynamic content. A JSP file contains combinations of HTML tags, NCSA tags (special tags that were the first method of implementing server-side includes), <SERVLET> tags, and JSP syntax. JSP files have the extension .jsp. One of the many advantages of JSP is that it enables programmers to effectively separate the HTML coding from the business logic in Web pages. JSP can be used to access reusable components, such as servlets, JavaBeans, and Java-based Web applications. JSP also supports embedding inline Java code within Web pages.

8.2 Hypertext Transfer Protocol (HTTP)

HTTP 1.1 is a *proposed standard protocol*. Its status is *elective*. It is described in RFC 2068. The older HTTP 1.0 is an *informational protocol* and described in RFC 1945.

The hypertext transfer protocol is a protocol designed to allow the transfer of hypertext markup language (HTML) documents (please see 8.3, "Hypertext Markup Language (HTML)" on page 569). HTML is a tag language used to create hypertext documents. Hypertext documents include links to other documents that contain additional information about the highlighted term or subject. Such documents may contain other elements apart from text, such as graphic images, audio and video clips, Java applets, and even virtual reality worlds (which are described in VRML, a scripting language for that kind of elements). See 8.3, "Hypertext Markup Language (HTML)" on page 569 for more information on HTML.

8.2.1 Overview of HTTP

HTTP is based on request-response activity. A client, running an application called a browser, establishes a connection with a server and sends a request to the server in the form of a request method. The server responds with a status line, including the message's protocol version and a success or error code, followed by a message containing server information, entity information and possible body content.

An HTTP transaction is divided into four steps:

1. The browser opens a connection.
2. The browser sends a request to the server.
3. The server sends a response to the browser.
4. The connection is closed.

On the Internet, HTTP communication generally takes place over TCP connections. The default port is TCP 80, but other ports can be used. This does not preclude HTTP from being implemented on top of any other protocol on the Internet, or on other networks. HTTP only presumes a reliable transport; any protocol that provides such guarantees can be used.

Except for experimental applications, current practice requires that the connection be established by the client prior to each request and closed by the server after sending the response. Both clients and servers should be aware that either party may close the connection prematurely, due to user action, automated timeout, or program failure, and should handle such closing in a predictable fashion. In any case, the closing of the connection by either or both parties always terminates the current request, regardless of its status.

In simple terms, HTTP is a stateless protocol because it keeps no track of the connections. To load a page including two graphics for example, a graphic-enabled browser will open three TCP connections: one for the page, and two for the graphics. Most browsers, however, are able to handle several of these connections simultaneously.

This behavior can be rather resource-intensive if one page consists of a lot of elements as quite a number of Web pages nowadays do. HTTP 1.1, as defined in RFC 2068, alleviates this problem to the extent that one TCP connection will be established per type of element on a page, and all elements of that kind will be transferred over the same connection respectively.

However, if a request depends on the information exchanged during a previous connection, then this information has to be kept outside the protocol. One way of tracking such persistent information is the use of cookies. A cookie is a set of information that is exchanged between a client Web browser and a Web server during an HTTP transaction. The maximum size of a cookie is 4 KB. All these pieces of information, or cookies, are then stored in one single file and placed in the directory of the Web browser. If cookies are disabled, that file is automatically deleted. A cookie can be retrieved and checked by the server at any subsequent connection. Because cookies are regarded as a potential privacy exposure, a Web browser should allow the user to decide whether to accept cookies or not and from which servers. While cookies merely serve the purpose of keeping some kind of state for HTTP connections, secure client and server authentication is provided by the Secure Sockets Layer (SSL) which is described in 5.7, "Secure Sockets Layer (SSL)" on page 424.

8.2.2 HTTP Operation

In most cases, the HTTP communication is initiated by the user agent requesting a resource on the origin server. In simplest case, the connection is established via a single connection between the user agent and the origin server as shown in Figure 252 on page 561.

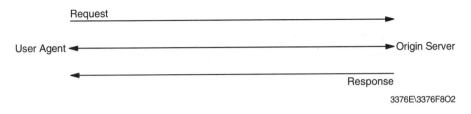

Figure 252. HTTP - Single Client/Server Connection

In some cases, there is no direct connection between the user agent and the origin server. There are one or more intermediaries between the user agent and origin server such as a proxy, gateway, or tunnel. Requests and responses are evaluated by the intermediaries and forwarded to the destination or another intermediary in the request-response chain as shown in Figure 253.

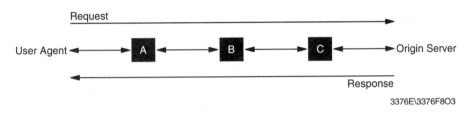

Figure 253. HTTP - Client/Server Connection with Intermediaries Between

As described in 5.3.4, "Application Level Gateway (Proxy)" on page 363, a proxy can handle the content of the data and therefore modify the data accordingly. When a request comes to a proxy, it rewrites all or part of the message and forwards the message to the next destination. A gateway receives the message and sends the message to the underlying protocols with an appropriate format. A tunnel does not deal with the content of the message, therefore it simply forwards the message as it is.

Proxies and gateways in general can handle caching of HTTP messages. This can dramatically reduce the response time and IP traffic on the network. Since tunnels cannot understand the message content they cannot store cached data of HTTP messages. In the previous figure (Figure 253), if one of the intermediaries (A,B and C) employs an internal cache for HTTP messages, the user agent can get response from the intermediary if it is previously cached from the origin server in the response chain. The following figure (Figure 254 on page 562) illustrates that A has a cached copy of an earlier response from the origin server in the response chain. Hence, if the server response for the request is not already cached in the user agent's internal cache, it can directly be obtained from A.

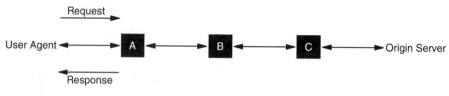

Figure 254. *HTTP - Cached Server Response*

Caching is not applicable to all server responses. Caching behavior can be modified by special requests to determine which server responses can or cannot be cached. For this purpose, server responses can be marked as non-cachable, public or private (cannot be cached in a public cache). Cache behavior and cachable responses are discussed in 8.2.2.11, "HTTP Caching" on page 568.

8.2.2.1 Protocol Parameters

Some of the HTTP protocol parameters are given below. Please refer to RFC 2068 for the full list and details:

HTTP Version

HTTP uses a <major>.<minor> numbering scheme to indicate the versions of the protocol. The further connection will be performed according to the protocol versioning policy. The <major> number is incremented when there are significant changes in protocol such as changing a message format. The <minor> number is incremented when the changes does not effect the message format.

The version of HTTP messages is sent by an HTTP-Version field in the first line of the message. The HTTP-Version field is in the following format. (Please refer to RFC 822 for augmented Backus-Naur Form.)

```
HTTP-Version   =   "HTTP" "/" 1*DIGIT "." 1*DIGIT
```

Uniform Resource Identifiers (URI)

Uniform Resource Identifiers are generally refer to as WWW addresses and combination of Uniform Resource Locators (URL) and Uniform Resource Names (URN). In fact, URIs are strings that indicate the location and name of the source on the server. Please see RFC 2068 and 2396 for more detail about the URI and URL syntax.

HTTP URL

The HTTP URL scheme allows you to locate network resources via HTTP protocol. It is based on the URI Generic Syntax and described in RFC 2396. The general syntax of a URL scheme is shown below:

```
HTTP_URL  =  "http" "//" host  [ ":" port ]  [ abs_path ]
```

The port number is optional. If it is not specified, the default value is 80.

8.2.2.2 HTTP Message

HTTP messages consist of the following fields:

Message Types

A HTTP message can be either a client request or a server response. The
following string indicates the HTTP message type:

```
HTTP-message  =  Request | Response
```

Message Headers

HTTP message header field can be one of the following:

- General header
- Request header
- Response header
- Entity header

Message Body

Message body can be referred to as entity body if there is no transfer coding has
been applied. Message body simply carries the entity body of the relevant
request or response.

Message Length

Message length indicates the length of the message body if it is included. The
message length is determined according to the criteria that is described in RFC
2068 in detail.

General Header Fields

General header fields can apply both request and response messages. Currently
defined general header field options are as follows:

- Cache-Control
- Connection
- Date
- Pragma
- Transfer-Encoding
- Upgrade
- Via

8.2.2.3 Request

A request messages from a client to a server includes the method to be applied to the resource, the identifier of the source, and the protocol version in use. A request message field is as follows:

```
Request  =  Request-Line
            *( general-header | request-header | entity-header )
            CRLF
            [ message-body ]
```

Please refer to RFC 2068 for detailed information.

8.2.2.4 Response

HTTP server returns a response after evaluating the client request. A response message field is as follows:

```
Request  =  Request-Line
            *( general-header | request-header | entity-header )
            CRLF
            [ message-body ]
```

Please refer to RFC 2068 for detailed information.

8.2.2.5 Entity

Either the client or server might send Entity in the request message or response message unless otherwise indicated. Entity consists of the following:

- Entity header fields
- Entity body

8.2.2.6 Connections

A significant difference between HTTP 1.1 and earlier versions of HTTP is that HTTP 1.1 uses persistent connection as default. In other words, the server maintains a persistent connection. In earlier version implementations, a separate TCP connection is established for each URL and clients have to make multiple requests for images and associated data on the same URL. This approach was causing congestion and performance problems on the network. Persistent HTTP connections have a number of advantages.

8.2.2.7 Method Definitions

Currently defined methods are as follows:

Safe and Idempotent Methods

Methods considered not to cause side effects are referred to as *safe.*. Idempotent methods are GET, HEAD, PUT and DELETE.

OPTIONS

This method allows the client to determine the options or requirements associated with a source or capabilities of a server, without any resource retrieval.

GET This method allows the client to retrieve the data which was determined by the request URI.

HEAD

This method allows the client to retrieve metainformation about the entity which does not require you to transfer the entity body.

POST

The post function is determined by the server.

PUT This method is similar to the post method with one important difference which is the URI in post request identifies the resource that will handle enclosed entity.

DELETE

This methods requests that the server delete the source determined by the request URI.

TRACE

Trace method allows the client to see how the message was retrieved at the other side for testing and diagnostic purposes.

8.2.2.8 Status Code Definitions

The status code definitions are as follows:

Informational (1xx)

Informational status codes indicate a provisional response. Currently defined codes are as follows:

- 100 Continue
- 101 Switching Protocols

Successful (2xx)

This class of codes indicates that a particular request was successfully received, understood and accepted. Currently defined codes are as follows:

- 200 OK
- 201 Created
- 202 Accepted
- 203 Non-Authoritative Information
- 204 No Content
- 205 Reset Content
- 206 Partial Content

Redirection (3xx)

This class of codes indicates that an action is required from the user agent in order to complete the request. Currently defined codes are as follows:

- 300 Multiple Choices
- 301 Moved Permanently
- 302 Moved Temporarily
- 303 See Other
- 304 Not Modified
- 305 Use Proxy

Client Error (4xx)

This class of codes indicates client errors. Currently defined codes are as follows:

- 400 Bad Request
- 401 Unauthorized
- 402 Payment Required
- 403 Forbidden
- 404 Not Found
- 405 Method Not Allowed
- 406 Not Acceptable
- 407 Proxy Authentication Required
- 408 Request Timeout
- 409 Conflict
- 410 Gone
- 411 Length Required
- 412 Precondition Failed
- 413 Request Entity Too Large
- 414 Request-URI Too Long
- 415 Unsupported Media Type

Server Error (5xx)

This class of codes indicate client errors. Currently defined codes are as follows:

- 500 Internal Server Error
- 501 Not Implemented
- 502 Bad Gateway
- 503 Service Unavailable
- 504 Gateway Timeout
- 505 HTTP Version Not Supported

8.2.2.9 Access Authentication

HTTP provides an authentication mechanism to allow servers to define access permissions on resources and clients to use these resources. The authentication method can be one of the following:

Basic Authentication Scheme

 Basic authentication is based on user IDs and passwords. In this authentication scheme, the server will permit the connection if only the user ID and password are validated. In basic authentication, user IDs and passwords are not encrypted. They are encoded in base64 format (see 4.8.3.5, "Base64 Encoding" on page 264).

Digest Authentication Scheme

 Digest authentication scheme is an extension to HTTP and described in RFC 2069. In this authentication scheme, the user ID and a digest containing an encrypted form of the password are sent to the server. The server computes a similar digest and grants access to the protected resources if the two digests are equal. Notice that if the digest authentication is enabled, what is sent over the network is not simply an encrypted form of the password, which could be decrypted if one had the correct key, but is a one-hash value of the password, which cannot be decrypted. So digest authentication provides a higher level of security than the base-64 encoded password. Unfortunately, digest authentication is not yet supported by all browsers.

8.2.2.10 Content Negotiation

In order to find the best handling for different types of data, the correct representation for a particular entity body should be negotiated. Actually, the user might handle this by himself or herself but this sometimes is not the best way of representation. There are three types of negotiation:

Server-Driven Negotiation

 The representation for a response is determined according to the algorithms located at the server.

Agent-Driven Negotiation

 If the representation for a response is determined according to the algorithms located.

Transparent Negotiation

 This is a combination of both server-driven and agent-driven negotiation. It is accomplished by a cache that includes a list of all available representations.

8.2.2.11 HTTP Caching

One of the most important features of HTTP is caching capability. Since HTTP is distributed information-based protocol, caching can improve the performance significantly. There are number of functions that came with the HTTP 1.1 protocol to use caching efficiently and properly.

In most cases, client requests and server responses can be stored in a cache within a reasonable amount of time, to handle the corresponding future requests. If the response is in the cache and accurate, there is no need to request another response from the server. This approach not only reduces the network bandwidth requirement but also increases the speed. There is a mechanism that the server estimates a minimum time in which the response message will be valid. That means, an *expiration* time is determined by the server for that particular response message. Therefore, within this time the message can be used without referring to the server.

Consider that this time is exceeded and there is a need for that response message. The data inside the message might have been changed or not after the expiration date. To be able to ensure whether the data is changed or not, a *validation* mechanism is defined as follows:

Expiration Mechanism

In order to decide whether the data is fresh or not, an expiration time should be determined. In most cases, the origin server explicitly defines the expiration time for a particular response message within that message. If this is the case, the cached data can be used to send from cache for subsequent requests within the expiration time.

If the origin server did not define any expiration time, there are some methods to estimate/calculate a reasonable expiration time (such as the Last-Modified time). Since this is not originated from the server, they should be used cautiously.

Validation Mechanism

When the expiration time is exceeded, there is a possibility that the data is stale. In order to ensure the validation of the response message, the cache has to check with the origin server (or possibly an intermediate cache with a fresh response) whether the response message is still usable. HTTP 1.1 provides conditional methods for this purpose.

When an origin server sends a full response, it attaches some sort of validator to the message. This will then be used as a *cache validator* by the user agent or the proxy cache. The client (user agent or the proxy cache) generates a conditional request with a cache validator attached to it. The server then evaluates the message and responds with a special code (usually, 304 (Not Modified)) and no entity body. Otherwise, the server sends the full response

(including the entity body). This approach avoids an extra round-trip if the
validator does not match and also avoids sending the full response if the
validator matches.

Please refer to RFC 2068 for more details about HTTP caching.

8.3 Hypertext Markup Language (HTML)

HTML is one of the major attractions of the Web. It has an architected set of tags that
should be understood by all Web browsers and Web servers, although as new features
are added to HTML, they may not be supported by older Web browsers. These tags
are device independent. The same document can be sent from a personal computer, an
AIX or UNIX machine, or a mainframe, and the Web browser on any client machine
can understand the HTML tags and build the data stream to display it on the target
device. HTML tags describe basic elements of a Web document, such as headers,
paragraphs, text styles, and lists. There are also more sophisticated tags to create
tables and to include interactive elements, such as forms, scripts or Java applets.

Once document writers and programmers have mastered HTML, those skills are
applicable to any operating system on any machine, provided that it has a Web
browser.

Since HTML supports hypertext, it allows document writers to include links to other
HTML documents. Those documents might be on the same machine as the original,
or they might be on a machine on another network on the other side of the world; such
is the power of HTML links.

8.4 The Extensible Markup Language (XML)

The Extensible Markup Language (XML) describes a class of data objects called XML
documents which are stored on computers, and partially describes the behavior of
programs that process these objects. XML is an application profile or restricted form
of SGML. The goal of XML is to enable generic SGML to be served, received, and
processed on the Web in the way that is now possible with HTML. XML has been
designed for ease of implementation and for interoperability with both SGML and
HTML.

8.5 Java

Java is an important new technology in the world of the Internet. In Java summary, it
is a simple, robust, object-oriented, platform-independent, multithreaded, dynamic

general-purpose programming environment for creating applications for the Internet and intranet.

8.5.1 Java Components Overview

Java itself is a programming language, developed by Sun Microsystems. It is object-oriented, and was designed to be a close cousin of C and C++, but easier to program, more portable and more robust. The authors have done an excellent job of removing the features in C++ that give programmers sleepless nights, yet retaining good functionality.

The features of Java that are especially important in the Web environment are:

Portability

Java is a compiled language, but unlike other languages it does not compile into machine instructions, but into architecture-neutral *byte codes*. This means that the same program will run on any system that has the Java run-time environment, regardless of the operating system or hardware type.

Thread Support

Java has multithread support built in to it, making it very effective for dynamic applications and multimedia.

Memory Management

Java does not require the programmer to perform any memory allocation; it handles it automatically. It also does not provide any pointer data types, so it is impossible for a program to attempt to read or write from unallocated memory. These are probably the two most pervasive causes of program failures in conventional languages. Apart from the fact that this makes the language more robust, it also removes a potential security exposure. A favorite attack technique in conventional languages is to find code errors that allow sensitive data to be overridden.

Code Verification

In a more conventional programming language, it is possible for the program to alter execution and data address pointers at run time. In Java this is not allowed; all references are made by name. This means that it is possible to verify in advance whether a program is doing anything you do not want it to.

Java includes the components discussed in the following sections.

8.5.1.1 Java Language

Java is a programming language developed by Sun Microsystems, which is object-oriented, distributed, interpreted, architecture-neutral, and portable. Java can be used to create downloadable program fragments, so-called applets, that augment the functionality of a Java-capable browser such as HotJava or Netscape Navigator. To develop applications in Java, a Java Development Kit (JDK) is required. To run Java programs, either a Web browser that supports Java, or a Java Run-time Environment (JRE) is required, which is the smallest subset of the Java Development Kit.

8.5.1.2 Java Virtual Machine

The Java Virtual Machine (JVM) is an abstract computer that runs compiled Java programs (or precisely, interprets Java byte-code that has been produced by a Java compiler). JVM is virtual because it is generally implemented in software on top of a real hardware platform and operating system. In this way, it is architecture-neutral and platform-independent. All Java programs should be compiled to run in a JVM.

The following diagram describes in simple terms how Java is implemented:

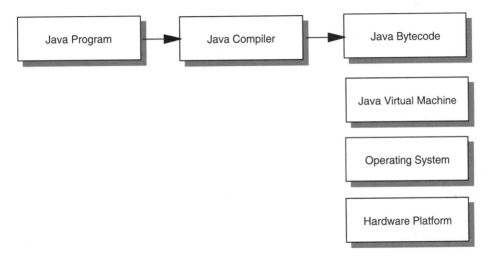

Figure 255. Java - Implementation of Java

8.5.1.3 Programs, Applets and Servlets

When a Java program is started from inside an HTML (Web) page, it is called a Java applet as opposed to a Java program that is executed from the command line or otherwise on the local system. Applets are downloaded via the Web browser from a server and, by definition, are somewhat limited in the way they can use resources of the local system.

Originally, no Java applet was supposed to touch anything locally outside of its JVM and could only communicate back to the server it was downloaded from. With Java

1.1, applets can be signed with security keys and certificates and can therefore be authenticated. Thus, an applet can be authorized to access local resources, such as file systems, and it may communicate with other systems.

In order to spare resources on clients and networks, Java applets can be executed on the server rather than downloaded and started at the client. Such programs are then referred to as servlets. Though that method requires a significantly more powerful server, it is highly suitable for environments with medialess systems, such as network computers (see 7.6, "The Network Computer" on page 552).

8.5.1.4 HotJava

HotJava is the Java-enabled Web browser, developed by Sun Microsystems. It comes with fully enabled Java support, which lets you run Java applets.

8.5.1.5 JavaOS

JavaOS is a highly compact operating system, developed by JavaSoft, which is designed to run Java applications directly on microprocessors in anything from personal computers to pagers. JavaOS will run equally well on a network computer, a PDA, a printer, a game machine, or countless other devices that require a very compact OS and the ability to run Java applications.

8.5.1.6 JavaBeans

An initiative called JavaBeans is brewing a similar set of APIs that will make it easy to create Java applications from reusable components. JavaBeans will be used in a wide range of applications, from simple widgets to full-scale, mission-critical applications. Many software vendors including IBM have announced plans to support it.

8.5.2 JavaScript

JavaScript is an HTML extension and programming language, developed by Netscape, which is a simple object-based language compatible with Java. JavaScript programs are embedded as a source directly in an HTML document. They can control the behavior of forms, buttons and text elements. It is used to create dynamic behavior in elements of the Web page. In addition, it can be used to create forms whose fields have built-in error checking routines.

8.5.3 Java in the World Wide Web

Java on its own would be just another, rather interesting, programming language. It is when it is combined with the HotJava Web browser that it really comes into its own. HotJava is Sun Microsystems' browser that contains the Java run-time environment combined with conventional Web browser functions. The Java code has been licensed by several other browser manufacturers, including IBM, Netscape and Microsoft. (Note that Netscape also provides another client-side execution language named JavaScript, which despite its name is not directly related to Java.)

Special new HTML tags allow you to specify in a document a small Java program, called an applet to be sent to the browser and executed. The HotJava run-time environment provides access to the client machine's facilities, such as graphics, sound and network access. The Java language itself provides class libraries that allow you to write simple programs that exploit these resources. The end result is greatly enhanced Web document content, for example animation and dialogs with local response times.

8.5.4 Java Security

Java has a powerful programming language available on browsers for any server to use sounds like a recipe for disaster. Fortunately, the designers were alert to the potential for security problems when they created Java. It has built-in facilities to prevent an applet from damaging or accessing private parts of the file system, memory or network of a browser machine. The programming language itself is also designed to prevent an unscrupulous programmer from extending its capabilities and circumventing the security limitations. The main point of control lies in the code verification capability that we described above.

1. The compilation step can take place at any time before the applet is requested. It results in a byte-code program, suitable for any Java environment. Note that at this point there are no restrictions to what the programmer can code. He or she can use any of the Java object classes or derive his or her own subclasses if he or she wishes.

2. The browser invokes an HTML page containing an applet tag, causing the byte-code program to be transmitted.

3. The byte-code is checked to ensure that it does not violate any of the restrictions imposed by the browser. Because of the way the language is designed there is no way for a programmer to disguise a dangerous action as legitimate code.

4. Only when the verification has succeeded is the program passed to the Java run time for execution.

The limitations imposed by the verification step are browser-specific, but they always include:

- Writing to files is forbidden.

- Reading from files is heavily restricted.

- Executing operating system commands and invoking dynamic load libraries are forbidden.

- Network access is restricted. Java includes class libraries for retrieving image data, defined as URLs. Usually the browser will restrict these to URLs on the applet host itself (that is, the server from which the applet was originally loaded).

Java has a well thought-out security structure. Nonetheless, Java should still be treated with suspicion from a security standpoint, for the following reasons:

- The Java process itself may be totally secure, but it relies on the browser configuration to provide such things as access controls. It is therefore imperative that Java is properly integrated into the browser.

- It is important to ensure that there are no situations in which other client facilities can inadvertently provide Java with access to restricted resources.

- The Java run-time code is a relatively large set of programs. In any program of that complexity, there will certainly be bugs and security holes that an attacker could exploit.

At the time of writing, several flaws had been found in the Java applet security mechanisms. One example is a weakness against IP address spoofing. Figure 256 on page 575 illustrates the problem. It relies on an attacker machine being able to send subverted DNS updates that identify its real IP name as an alias for an IP address of a server inside the firewall. The Java applet then specifies a URL on the subverted address, and so gains access to data on the internal server.

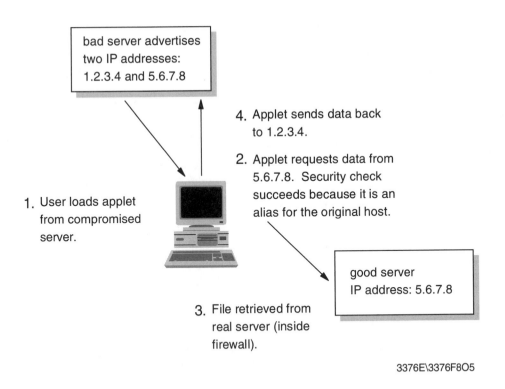

bad server advertises
two IP addresses:
1.2.3.4 and 5.6.7.8

4. Applet sends data back
   to 1.2.3.4.

2. Applet requests data from
   5.6.7.8. Security check
   succeeds because it is an
   alias for the original host.

1. User loads applet
   from compromised
   server.

good server
IP address: 5.6.7.8

3. File retrieved from
   real server (inside
   firewall).

3376E\3376F8O5

Figure 256. Java - A Java Security Exposure

This particular problem was fixed very rapidly in Netscape Navigator and Sun
HotJava, but you can expect many more similar exploits to be discovered, as people
start to scrutinize Java's defenses. Java has also suffered by association, as a result of
some well-publicized security loopholes in Netscape's JavaScript support.

For more information about Java, check out the following URLs:

```
http://ncc.hursley.ibm.com/javainfo/
http://java.sun.com/
```

8.5.5 Distributed Objects

An application is enabled to use distributed objects by using the Object Request
Broker (ORB). The ORB transparently forwards remote object requests (for example,
a method invocation) to the appropriate server objects, dispatches the requests and
returns the results (for example, a method return value).

The Internet Inter-ORB Protocol (IIOP) is a communications protocol based on the
Common Object Request Broker Architecture (CORBA) specifications provided by the

Object Management Group (OMG). Further information about the Object Management Group can be found at the OMG home page at the following URL:

http://www.omg.org/

IIOP is the standard protocol supported by the IBM Network Computing Framework for remote method call support. It allows client communication with Business Object Framework objects on a remote server. By using the CORBA/IIOP protocol, a Java applet running in a client machine can communicate with a servlet running in the Web server and supporting IIOP as well. IIOP is much more efficient than communicating over HTTP, since IIOP may reuse a single connection for multiple requests. That is the reason why the applet and the servlet can exchange method calls in both directions, along the same connection.

The IBM Network Computing Framework provides two possibilities to add distribution to Java and Web-centric applications using the IIOP protocol:

1. A standard IIOP mode, which ensures inter-operability between different ORBs through the Internet distributing objects to remote servers. This is accomplished by passing objects by reference.

2. An enhanced IIOP mode, which ensures that a client can use a local copy of a remote object. This is accomplished by passing objects by value rather than by reference. In this way the overhead of object interactions involving remote method invocations is no longer incurred.

The communication between server and client in the CORBA support of IBM WebSphere Application Server can use two connection methods:

1. Direct IIOP connection (independent on the Web server)

2. IIOP over HTTP (through the Web server)

The flow of both methods is described in the following list:

1. The applet is downloaded from a Web server machine to a Java-enabled Web browser of a client machine by using a typical HTML page.

2. The applet automatically activates a client ORB within itself.

3. The applet sends an HTTP request to the Web server in order to load and run the servlet.

4. The servlet will then activate the server ORB inside itself.

5. The client ORB controls IIOP communication with the server.

a. IIOP communication between client and server uses a long-running socket connection directly from the client to the object server port if WebSphere Application Server CORBA Support can successfully activate a direct IIOP connection. This socket is used for the entire period that the client is connected to the server.

b. IIOP communication between client and server uses short-running socket connections to the Web server port (usually port 80) if WebSphere Application Server CORBA Support uses IIOP over HTTP. In this mode, a new connection is used for each IIOP request encoded over HTTP, and that connection is closed at the end of each reply from the server.

Once the IIOP communication is established, object activations and method calls on those objects may occur back and forth using either a direct IIOP connection or IIOP over HTTP, depending on what type of connection has been activated. Notice that it is the client ORB that decides whether to use a direct IIOP connection or revert to IIOP over HTTP. The client will use the best quality of service available. It tries to establish a direct IIOP connection first and, if that doesn't work, it uses IIOP over HTTP.

8.6 Accessing Legacy Applications from the Web

About 70% of corporate data today still resides on legacy systems, most of them mainframes, that are, at best, not directly connected to the World Wide Web. Such data in many cases is only accessible using proprietary protocols and applications and is embedded in hierarchical processes and system architectures. On the other hand, it may be desirable, if not a matter of survival, to make this data accessible to the outside. The area where classic I/T meets the Web is one of the hot spots of contemporary computer research and application development because it is seen to be the key to business computing in the years to come.

8.6.1 Business Requirements

Since the Internet is virtually everywhere and is growing at a phenomenal rate, it offers consumers and businesses an effective way to communicate directly with suppliers, vendors, customers and other members of the community and beyond. Many companies today are already using the Web to allow customers to purchase products online. This is expected to grow as security technologies become more widely implemented and provide both customers and vendors with confidence in a secured environment.

- Access to corporate legacy data from the Web must be provided on-demand and regardless of time and location.

- Web users are opportunistic (they browse and shop at sites that are most appealing, most attractive, or fast and easy to access), whereas corporate users are deterministic. (They use the same information, access method and user interfaces every day.) This different behavior must be accounted for in order to attract business on the Web.

- Access to corporate legacy data from the Web should be provided without changing existing applications wherever possible.

- Access to corporate data from the Web should be seamless to both the users and the back-end servers.

There are many possible scenarios for a connection between Web-based clients and legacy applications. The scenario should be determined according to the business needs and security issues. Figure 257 illustrates a few examples.

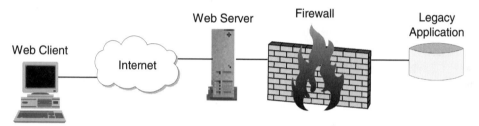

3376E\3376F8O8

Figure 257. *A Web-to-Legacy Scenario*

8.6.2 Technical Issues

There are, of course, also technical requirements to fulfill before a connection can be established between the Web and legacy back-end systems. The main issue here is combining the hierarchical structure of legacy systems with the peer structure of the Web.

- If non-IP protocols are used to access the legacy system, a gateway can be installed on the Web server or elsewhere to map the IP traffic from the Web to the non-IP network.

- Regardless of the network protocol, an application connector has to be developed to translate and/or propagate transaction requests and results between the Web server or gateway and the back-end legacy system.

- A user interface has to be developed to retrieve input from, and to represent the legacy data to, the Web client.

Some of the technologies that can be used to develop application connectors and Web user interfaces are Java, JavaScript, CGI and ActiveX.

8.6.3 Security Issues

Because the data that is at the heart of this discussion is also at the very heart of an enterprise, security has always been an issue even in times of proprietary protocols, in-house access applications and corporate owned and controlled networks. The more open access to legacy data becomes, the higher the potential security risks involved in having data stolen, compromised or in any other way abused.

- A firewall or gateway should be installed between the Web server and the back-end system to protect the data on the internal network.

- An advanced authentication mechanism should be used to deny unauthorized users to access and invoke the application connector on the Web server or gateway.

- Running a protocol other than IP between the Web server or gateway and the back-end system can be seen as an additional security advantage. Hackers may not be able to analyze that other protocol, or they may not be able to penetrate the gateway, or the other protocol is more secure than IP. In any case, the more effort for a malicious attacker to get to a company's data, the better for that company.

Possible configurations resulting from the discussion of technical and security issues for a Web-to-legacy scenario are illustrated in Figure 258 on page 580.

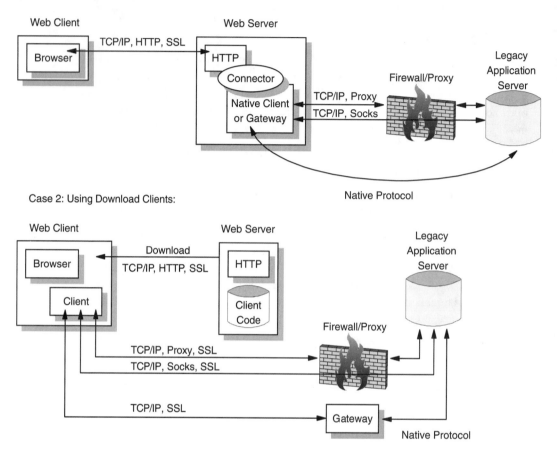

Figure 258. Web-to-Legacy Configuration Examples

8.6.4 IBM e-business Solutions

IBM has always been very active in this area because it has both the expertise on the back-end legacy side as well as the innovative knowledge and technology on the Web server, application connector and overall security side of this complex equation. IBM has made this the theme of its e-business initiative.

8.6.4.1 IBM Web Connectors

To allow seamless access from the Web to legacy applications, IBM offers, among others, the following connectors and enablers on many operating system platforms:

Net.Data
> Allows Web application developers to build macros that embed dynamic SQL statements into HTML documents to access relational databases.

DB2 Connect
> Allows end users to directly access DB2 databases and incorporate that information into business documents and spread sheets.

MQSeries Client for Java
> Allows Web application developers to manage transactions from within Java programs, thus bringing more flexibility to end users without the requirement of locally installed clients.

MQSeries Internet Gateway
> Allows translation of Web requests to MQSeries transactions at a Web server.

CICS Internet Gateway
> Allows access to CICS applications from Web clients and translation between 3270 data streams and HTML formats at a Web server.

CICS Gateway for Java and CICS Client
> Allows seamless access to CICS applications from within Java programs.

IMS Connectors
> Allow Web access to IMS and DB2 databases via a Web server through IMS transactions.

Lotus Domino Enterprise Integration tools
> Allows access from Domino environments to back-end legacy applications running CICS, MQSeries, DB2 or other relational database systems, and SAP R/3.

eNetwork Host On-Demand
> Allows host application access from a Web browser by providing a variety of terminal emulation capabilities (3270, 5250 and VT100/220) implemented as Java applets. Signed applets and SSL security are provided so that both gateway and direct access configurations are possible for TN3270, TN5250 and ASCII telnet access.

DCE Encina Lightweight Client
> Allows Web access to DCE and Encina-based applications.

More information on e-business Web connectors from IBM can be found at the following URL:

```
http://www.software.ibm.com/webservers/connectors
```

8.6.4.2 IBM Web Application Servers

To develop powerful Web application servers and solutions, IBM offers, among others, the following products on a variety of server platforms:

WebSpere Application Server

> An application server environment based on Java servlets and open standards such as XML, CORBA and JDBC. WebSphere application server allows the development and object component distribution from simple Web publishing to enterprise transaction processing. WebSphere application server leverages the power of existing Web servers, such as Lotus Domino Go, Domino, Apache, Netscape Enterprise Server and Microsoft Internet Information Server.

WebSphere Performance Pack

> Provides enhanced caching, filtering, server monitoring, proxy, scalability and high availability functions to Web servers, based on technologies that have successfully handled some of the most heavily loaded Web sites ever, such as the 1996 and 1998 Olympic Games, the Wimbledon, U.S. Open and French Open tennis tournaments, and the Garry Kasparov versus Deep Blue chess match. This solution is also described in 11.3.11, "ISP Configuration" on page 705.

Lotus Domino

> Domino is a messaging and collaboration, Web application and workflow server platform. It offers a rich set of server (Notes, HTTP, NNTP, SMTP, POP, IMAP, LDAP), client and security (SSL, hierarchical certificate-based authentication, multi-level access control list authorization) functions and a consistent user and development interface for corporate applications.

Net.Commerce

> Allows businesses to create online stores and electronic catalogs to get ready for doing business over the Web. Net.Commerce is scalable across platforms, it ties into back-end relational database systems, and it provides an interface to the SET environment for secure credit card transactions.

eNetwork Communications Server

> Enable secure access to back-end applications, regardless of platform or network environment, by providing the necessary gateway and communications functions between SNA/APPN/HPR, TCP/IP and IPX-based networks.

More information on IBM's e-business Web servers can be found at the following URLs:

```
http://www.software.ibm.com/webservers
http://www.software.ibm.com/commerce
http://www.software.ibm.com/enetwork
http://www.lotus.com/home.nsf/welcome/domino
```

8.6.4.3 Security, Management and Application Development Solutions

To complete the picture, IBM also offers solutions in the following areas:

Security

Firewalls, certification authority and public key infrastructure environments, security development toolkits, authentication servers, and more, on various platforms, to provide the necessary security components as well as granularity of access control for networks and applications.

Management

The Tivoli Enterprise management framework provides cross-platform solutions for systems and network management. NetObjects Fusion and Domino Designer provide page composition and component assembly, Web site authoring and construction, hyperlink management and scripting support. The DSSeries offers LDAP and X.500 directories.

Web Application Development

VisualAge for Java and Lotus Bean Machine provide Web developers with powerful platforms for creating applets, servlets, Java beans and other objects and components, and to turn them into highly portable, enterprise strength applications. VisualAge is also available for other programming languages, such as C++ and SmallTalk.

More information on e-business security, management and application development solutions from IBM can be found at the following URLs:

```
http://www.ibm.com/security
http://www.software.ibm.com/enetwork
http://www.tivoli.com
http://www.software.ibm.com/ad
http://www.lotus.com/home.nsf/welcome/domino
```

8.7 Network News Transfer Protocol (NNTP)

One application that is particularly popular on the Internet is Network News, also known as Usenet News. Based on the Network News Transfer Protocol (NNTP), users on the Internet can view and contribute to news groups covering topics such as science, education, computers, business, politics, recreation, sports, and many more. News groups are stored on news servers. NNTP is used for both server-to-server and client-to-server communication.

Clients use a news agent application, such as the IBM NewsReader/2, to retrieve articles from one or more news groups, and to post articles to one or more news groups. For more information about NNTP, see RFC 977.

8.8 Gopher

In short, the Internet Gopher is a distributed document search and retrieval system. It combines the best features of browsing through collections of information and fully indexed databases. The protocol and software follow a client/server model and permit users on a heterogeneous mix of desktop systems to browse, search, and retrieve documents residing on multiple distributed server machines.

The Gopher protocol was developed at the University of Minnesota and is available under RFC 1436. Its state is *informational*.

The reason for developing Gopher was the need for a campus-wide information system which enables anybody to be able to publish documents or information even with a small desktop computer. Gopher client software presents users with a hierarchy of items and directories much like a file system. In fact, the Gopher interface is designed to resemble a file system since a file system is a good model for locating documents and services. So if you are connected to a Gopher server you get a list of different items, similar to the display of a root directory from a PC. After selecting a menu item for example you get all the items included, similar to a subdirectory and so forth. If you select a file item for example the file is automatically transmitted and displayed at the client. It is not necessary for the file to reside on the same Gopher server where you got the information. A Gopher menu can include items from different Gopher servers and the user gets automatically connected to the server where the selected item points to and so on. The user does not know or care that the items up for selection may reside on many different machines anywhere on the Internet.

A simple example:

You would like to have a look at the menu of your cafeteria.

1. Start your Gopher client and connect to the main Gopher server.

2. Find an item which could include the menu and select it, for example Facilities.

3. The sub-items of Facilities are displayed.

4. One of the items may be Today's Menu which is a file residing on the canteen's Gopher server.

5. If you select it, your Gopher client automatically establishes a connection to the server pointed to in the item, retrieves and displays the file.

The path to the file could be very complex and Gopher servers around the world could be involved.

To implement the above-mentioned hierarchy the Gopher client needs some information of the object type in order to display a file or a directory icon for example. The Gopher type is coded as a single digit at the beginning of each line. Following is a list of known Gopher types included in the RFC:

- 0 - Item is a file.
- 1 - Item is a directory.
- 2 - Item is a CSO (qi) phone-book server.
- 3 - Error.
- 4 - Item is a BinHexed Macintosh file.
- 5 - Item is a DOS binary archive of some sort.
- 6 - Item is a UNIX uuencoded file.
- 7 - Item is an Index-Search server.
- 8 - Item points to a text-based telnet session.
- 9 - Item is a binary file.
- T - TN3270 connection.
- s - Sound type. Data stream is a mulaw sound.
- g - GIF type.
- M - Item contains MIME data.
- h - html type.
- I - Image type.
- i - "inline" text type.

The following paragraphs describe the basic functionality of the Gopher protocol.

In essence, the Gopher protocol consists of a client connecting to a server and sending the server a selector (a line of text, which may be empty) via a TCP connection. The server responds with a block of text terminated with a period on a line by itself, and closes the connection. No state is retained by the server between transactions with a client. Let's assume a Gopher server listens to port 70. The only configuration information the client software retains is this server's name and port number. (In this example that machine is rawBits.micro.umn.edu and the port 70.) In the example below the F character denotes the tab character.

```
Client: {Opens connection to rawBits.micro.umn.edu at port 70}
Server: {Accepts connection but says nothing}

Client: <CR><LF> {Sends an empty line: Meaning "list what you have"}
Server: {Sends a series of lines, each ending with CR LF}
0About internet GopherFStuff:About usFrawBits.micro.umn.eduF70
1Around University of MinnesotaFZ,5692,AUMFunderdog.micro.umn.eduF70
1Microcomputer News & PricesFPrices/Fpserver.bookstore.umn.eduF70
1Courses, Schedules, CalendarsFFevents.ais.umn.eduF9120
1Student-Staff DirectoriesFFuinfo.ais.umn.eduF70
1Departmental PublicationsFStuff:DP:FrawBits.micro.umn.eduF70
                    {.....etc.....}
   .                {Period on a line by itself}
                    {Server closes connection}
```

The first character on each line describes the Gopher type as shown above. The succeeding characters up to the tab build the display string to be shown to the user for making a selection. The characters following the tab, up to the next tab form a selector string that the client software must send to the server to retrieve the document (or directory listing). In practice, the selector string is often a path name or other file selector used by the server to locate the item desired. The next two tab delimited fields denote the domain name of the host that has this document (or directory), and the port at which to connect. A CR/LF denotes the end of the item. The client may present the above data stream as follows:

```
About Internet Gopher
Around the University of Minnesota...
Microcomputer News & Prices...
Courses, Schedules, Calendars...
Student-Staff Directories...
Departmental Publications...
```

In this case, directories are displayed with an ellipsis and files are displayed without any. However, depending on the platform the client is written for and the author's taste, item types could be denoted by other text tags or by icons.

In the example, line 1 describes a document the user will see as *About Internet Gopher*. To retrieve this document, the client software must send the retrieval string: Stuff:About us to rawBits.micro.umn.edu at port 70. If the client does this, the server will respond with the contents of the document, terminated by a period on a line by itself. As you can see in this example the user does not know or care that the items up for selection may reside on many different machines anywhere on the Internet. The connection between server and client only exists while the information is transferred. After this the client can connect to a different server in order to get the contents of a displayed directory.

For further information about the Gopher protocol please refer to the RFC 1436. For a list of frequently asked questions including the anonymous FTP sites for retrieving the Gopher client and server code please get the following file from anonymous FTP:

`ftp://rtfm.mit.edu/pub/usenet/news.answers/gopher-faq.`

8.9 Internet2

Internet2 has 130 participating universities across the United States. Affiliate organizations provide the project with valuable input. All participants in the Internet2 project are members of the University Corporation for Advanced Internet Development (UCAID).

8.9.1 Mission

Internet2 mission is to facilitate and coordinate the development, operation and technology transfer of advanced, network-based applications and network services to further U.S. leadership in research and higher education and accelerate the availability of new services and applications on the Internet.

The goals of Internet2 are the following:

- Demonstrate new applications that can dramatically enhance researchers' ability to collaborate and conduct experiments.

- Demonstrate enhanced delivery of education and other services (for instance, health care, environmental monitoring, etc.) by taking advantage of *virtual proximity* created by an advanced communications infrastructure.

- Support development and adoption of advanced applications by providing middleware and development tools.

- Facilitate development, deployment, and operation of an affordable communications infrastructure, capable of supporting differentiated Quality of Service (QoS) based on applications requirements of the research and education community.

- Promote experimentation with the next generation of communications technologies.

- Coordinate adoption of agreed working standards and common practices among participating institutions to ensure end-to-end quality of service and interoperability.

- Catalyze partnerships with governmental and private sector organizations.

- Encourage transfer of technology from Internet2 to the rest of the Internet.

- Study impact of new infrastructure, services and applications on higher education and the Internet community in general.

8.9.2 Project Description

Building on the tremendous success of the last ten years in generalizing and adapting research Internet technology to academic needs, the university community has joined together with government and industry partners to accelerate the next stage of Internet development in academia. The Internet2 project, as it is known, is bringing focus, energy and resources to the development of a new family of advanced applications to meet emerging academic requirements in research, teaching and learning. Internet2 addresses major challenges facing the next generation of university networks by:

1. First and most importantly, creating and sustaining a leading edge network capability for the national research community. For a number of years beginning in 1987, the network services of NSFnet were unequaled anywhere in the world. But the privitization of that network and the frequent congestion of its commercial replacement have deprived many faculty of the network capability needed to support world class research. This unintended result has had a significant negative impact on the university research community.

2. Second, directing network development efforts to enable a new generation of applications to fully exploit the capabilities of broadband networks media integration, interactivity and real-time collaboration to name a few. This work is essential if new priorities within higher education for support of national research objectives, distance education, lifelong learning, and related efforts are to be fulfilled.

3. Third, integrating the work of Internet2 with ongoing efforts to improve production Internet services for all members of the academic community. A major goal of the project is to rapidly transfer new network services and applications to all levels of educational use and to the broader Internet community, both nationally and internationally.

The project will be conducted in phases over the next three to five years, with initial participation expected from leading research universities, a number of federal agencies, and many of the leading computer and telecommunications companies. In the initial project phase, end-to-end broadband network services will be established among the participating universities. On a parallel basis, teams of university faculty, researchers, technical staff and industry experts will begin designing applications. It is expected that within eighteen months, "beta" versions of a number of applications will be in operation among the Internet2 Project universities.

8.9.2.1 University Participation in Internet2

At a meeting in Chicago in October, 1996, representatives of thirty-four universities agreed unanimously to endorse the goals of the project, committed their institutions to finding the resources necessary to participate in the project, and pledged initial funding to enable planning efforts to proceed without delay. Support for the project from the academic community has grown quickly. To date, over one hundred universities have become members of Internet2. Each member university has pledged substantial staff resources and financial support for the duration of the project.

8.9.2.2 Internet2 Partnerships

Soon after the announcement in October, 1996, the project's central goals were adopted as part of the White House's Next Generation Internet (NGI) initiative. In his State of the Union message on February 4, 1997, President Clinton committed his Administration to supporting a "second generation of the Internet so that our leading universities and national laboratories can communicate in speeds 1,000 times faster than today." By extending the partnership between academia, government, and industry that created today's commercial Internet, Internet2 will accelerate the development of next generation Internet technologies and contribute to continued U.S. leadership in this emerging industry.

In most respects, the partnership and funding arrangements for Internet2 will parallel those of previous joint networking efforts of academia and government, of which the NSFnet project is a very successful example. The federal government will participate in Internet2 through the NGI initiative and related programs.

Internet2 will also join with corporate leaders to create the advanced network services necessary to meet the requirements of broadband, networked applications. Industry partners will work primarily with campus-based and regional university teams to provide the services and products needed to implement the applications developed by the project. Major corporations such as Ameritech, Cisco Systems, Digital Equipment Corporation, IBM, MCI, Sprint and Sun Microsystems have already pledged their support for Internet2.

Additional support for Internet2 will come from collaboration with non-profit organizations working in research and educational networking. Affiliate organizations already committed to the project include: MCNC, National Center for Supercomputing Applications, Northwest Academic Computing Consortium, NYSERNET, OARnet,

SURA, PeachNet, Merit, CiCNet, and the State University System of Florida. By promoting cooperation among these organizations, government agencies and private industry, Internet2 will effectively leverage research funding, accelerate the development of campus networks, and create new standards and technologies urgently needed for advanced research, and eventually, by all Internet users.

8.9.3 Internet2 and NGI

The Next Generation Internet (NGI) initiative is a multi-agency Federal research and development program that is developing advanced networking technologies, developing revolutionary applications that require advanced networking, and demonstrating these capabilities on testbeds that are 100 to 1,000 times faster end-to-end than today's Internet.

Specific ways in which the Federal NGI initiative and the university-led Internet2 work together include:

- The NSF has made more that 70 High-Performance Connections awards to Internet2 universities. These merit-based awards allow universities to connect to NSF's very high-performance Backbone Network Service (vBNS). vBNS connectivity is a key part of NSF's NGI program.

- Internet2 universities are establishing gigaPoPs (Gigabit per second Points of Presence) that provide regional connectivity among universities and other organizations. Through the gigaPoPs, universities will connect to NGI networks and other advanced Federal networks, including the vBNS, NASA's Research and Education Network (NREN), DoD's Defense Research and Education Network (DREN), and the Department of Energy's Energy Sciences network (ESnet). The NGI and Internet2 will help ensure that advanced networking services are available on interoperable backbone, regional, and local networks that are competitively provided by multiple vendors.

- Researchers at Internet2 universities are developing a wide range of applications that require advanced networking. Many of these applications are funded by Federal initiatives including the NGI.

For more information on Internet2 see their Web page at:

`http://www.internet2.edu`

8.10 References

Please see the following RFCs for more information on Internet protocols and applications:

- *RFC 822 — Standard for the Format of ARPA Internet Text Messages.* (Updated by RFC 1123, RFC 1138, RFC 1148, RFC 1327, RFC 2156.)

- *RFC 977 — Network News Transfer Protocol*

- *RFC 1436 — The Internet Gopher Protocol (A Distributed Document Search and Retrieval Protocol)*

- *RFC 1945 — Hypertext Transfer Protocol -- HTTP/1.0*

- *RFC 2068 — Hypertext Transfer Protocol -- HTTP/1.1*

- *RFC 2069 — An Extension to HTTP: Digest Access Authentication*

- *RFC 2109 — HTTP State Management Mechanism*

- *RFC 2396 — Uniform Resource Identifiers (URI): Generic Syntax*

Chapter 9. Multicast and Multimedia

In early IP networks, a packet could be sent either to one receiver (unicast) or to all receivers (broadcast). A single transmission, which could reach a specific group of receivers, was not possible. The idea of IP multicasting was developed in 1988 by Steve Deering at Stanford University, promoted by the wish to provide audio and video transmissions in real-time from the Internet Engineering Task Forces (IETF) meetings through the Internet. The audio and video data should be transmitted only to one multicast IP address but should be received by any user that wanted to see the transmission.

The first multicast multimedia transmission that worked in this case was realized in 1992. To synchronize audio and video packets in the transmission the newly developed real-time transport protocol (RTP) was used. The following chapter describes how IP multicasting, the Internet Group Management Protocol (IGMP), the multicast routing protocols and RTP work and gives an overview of the applications that use multicasting.

9.1 Multicasting

As described in 2.1.4, "Methods of Delivery - Unicast, Broadcast, Multicast and Anycast" on page 51, multicast uses Class D IP addresses, which means that they are in a range from 224.0.0.0 to 239.255.255.255. For each multicast address there is a set of zero or more hosts that are listening to it. This set is called the *host group*. A host that sends to a group must not be a member of this group. There are two kinds of host groups:

permanent
> The IP address is permanently assigned by IANA. The membership of a host group is not permanent; a host can leave or join the group at will. The list of IP addresses assigned to permanent host groups is included in *STD 2 — Assigned Internet Numbers* (RFC 1700). Important ones are:

224.0.0.0	Reserved base address
224.0.0.1	All systems on this subnet
224.0.0.2	All routers on this subnet
224.0.0.9	All RIP2 routers

> Some other examples used by the OSPF routing protocol (see 3.3.4, "Open Shortest Path First (OSPF)" on page 146) are:

224.0.0.5	All OSPF routers

224.0.0.6   OSPF designated routers

An application can also retrieve a permanent host group's IP address from the
domain name system (see 4.2, "Domain Name System (DNS)" on page 194)
using the domain mcast.net, or determine the permanent group from an address
by using a pointer query (see 4.2.6, "Mapping IP Addresses to Domain Names
— Pointer Queries" on page 198) in the domain 224.in-addr.arpa. A permanent
group exists even if it has no members.

transient

Any group that is not permanent is transient and is available for dynamic
assignment as needed. Transient groups cease to exist when their membership
drops to zero.

Multicasting on a single physical network that supports the use of multicasting is
simple. To join a group, a process running on a host must somehow inform its
network device drivers that it wishes to be a member of the specified group. The
device driver software itself must map the multicast IP address to a physical multicast
address and enable the reception of packets for that address. The device driver must
also ensure that the receiving process does not receive any spurious datagrams by
checking the destination address in the IP header before passing it to the IP layer.

For example, Ethernet supports multicasting if the high-order byte of the 48-byte
address is X'01' and IANA owns an Ethernet address block, which consists of the
addresses between X'01005E000000' and X'01005EFFFFFF'. The lower half of this
range has been assigned by IANA for multicast addresses, so on an Ethernet LAN
there is a range of physical addresses between X'01005E000000' and
X'01005E7FFFFF', which is used for IP multicasting. This range has 23 usable bits.
The 32-bit multicast IP addresses are mapped to the Ethernet addresses by placing the
low-order 23 bits of the Class D address into the low order 23 bits of IANA's reserved
address block. Figure 259 on page 595 shows the mapping of a multicast group
address to an Ethernet multicast address.

Class D Address: 224.11.9.7

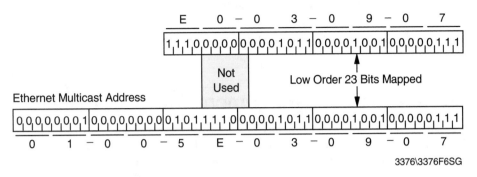

Figure 259. Mapping of Class D IP Addresses to IEEE-802.3 Ethernet Addresses

Since the upper five bits of the IP multicast group ID are ignored, this type of mapping places all 32 different multicast groups into the same Ethernet address. Because of this non-unique mapping, filtering by the device driver is required. There are two other reasons why filtering might still be needed:

- Some LAN adapters are limited to a finite number of concurrent multicast addresses and if this is exceeded they must receive all multicasts.

- Other LAN adapters tend to filter according to a hash table value rather than the whole address, which means that there is a chance that two multicast addresses with the same hash value might be in use at the same time and the filter might "leak."

Despite this requirement for software filtering of multicast packets, multicasting still causes much less overhead for hosts that are not interested. In particular, those hosts that are not in any host group are not listening to any multicast addresses and all multicast messages are filtered by the network interface hardware.

Multicasting is not limited to a single physical network. There are two aspects to multicasting across physical networks:

- A mechanism for deciding how widespread the multicast is. (Remember that, unlike unicast addresses and broadcast addresses, multicast addresses cover the entire Internet.)

- A mechanism for deciding whether a multicast datagram needs to be forwarded to a particular network.

The first problem is easily solved: the multicast datagram has a Time To Live (TTL) value like any other datagram, which is decremented with each hop to a new network.

When the Time to Live field is decremented to zero, the datagram can go no further. The mechanism for deciding whether a router should forward a multicast datagram is called *Internet Group Management Protocol (IGMP)* or *Internet Group Multicast Protocol*. IGMP and multicasting are defined in *RFC 1112 — Host Extensions for IP Multicasting*.

9.2 Internet Group Management Protocol (IGMP)

The Internet Group Management Protocol is used by hosts that want to join or leave a multicast host group. Group membership requests are reported from a host directly to the nearest multicast router. The status of IGMP is *recommended* and it is described in RFC 1112.

IGMP is best regarded as an extension to ICMP and occupies the same place in the IP protocol stack. In IPv6 (see 6.3, "Internet Control Message Protocol Version 6 (ICMPv6)" on page 476) IGMP is integrated into ICMPv6 since all IPv6 hosts will be required to support multicasting. In IPv4, multicasting support is optional, so unlike IP and ICMP, IGMP is not required.

9.2.1 IGMP Messages

IGMP messages are encapsulated in IP datagrams. The IP header will always have a protocol number of 2 (see RFC 1700 for more information about IP protocol numbers), indicating IGMP and a Type of Service of zero (routine). The IP data field will contain the 8-byte IGMP message in the format shown in Figure 260.

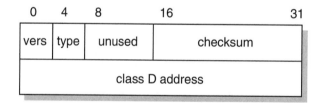

3376\3376F6S1

Figure 260. IGMP Message Format

Where:

Vers

> 4-bit IP version. Always 1.

Type

> Specifies a query or a report.

1 Specifies a query sent by a multicast router.

2 Specifies a report sent by a host.

Checksum

A 16-bit checksum calculated as for ICMP.

Class D Address

This is zero for a request, and is a valid multicast group address for a report.

9.2.2 IGMP Operation

Systems participating in IGMP fall into two types: hosts and multicast routers. To receive multicast datagrams a host must join a host group. When a host is multi-homed, it can join any group on one or more of its interfaces (attached subnets). The multicast messages that the host receives from the same group on two different subnets may be different. For example 244.0.0.1 is the group for "all hosts on this subnet," so the messages received on one subnet will always be different for this group from those on another subnet. Multiple processes on a single host may be listening for messages for a multicast group on a subnet. If this is the case, the host joins the group once only, and keeps track internally of which processes are interested in that group.

To join a group, the host sends a report on an interface. The report is addressed to the multicast group of interest. Multicast routers on the same subnet receive the report and set a flag to indicate that at least one host on that subnet is a member of that group. No host has to join the all hosts group (224.0.0.1) because the membership is automatic. Multicast routers have to listen to all multicast addresses (that is, all groups) in order to detect such reports. The alternatives would be to use broadcasts for reports or to configure hosts with unicast addresses for multicast routers.

Multicast routers regularly, but infrequently (RFC 1112 mentions one-minute intervals), send out a query to the all-hosts multicast address. Each host that still wishes to be a member of one or more groups replies once for each group of interest (but never the all hosts group, since membership is automatic). Each reply is sent after a random delay to ensure that IGMP does not cause bursts of traffic on the subnet. Since routers do not care how many hosts are members of a group and since all hosts that are members of this group can hear each other replying, any host that hears another host claim membership of a group will cancel any reply that it is due to send in order to avoid wasting resources. If no hosts claim membership of a group within a specified interval, the multicast router decides that no host is a member of this group.

Since IGMP only performs the communication between the receiving hosts and the last multicast router in the delivery tree, routing of the packets between multicast routers must be managed by a multicast routing protocol. There are several algorithms for packet routing between multicast routers, which are described in detail in 9.3, "Multicast Routing Protocols" on page 600. Figure 261 on page 599 shows that a multicast routing protocol and the group membership protocol work in different sections of the multicast delivery tree during a multicast transmission.

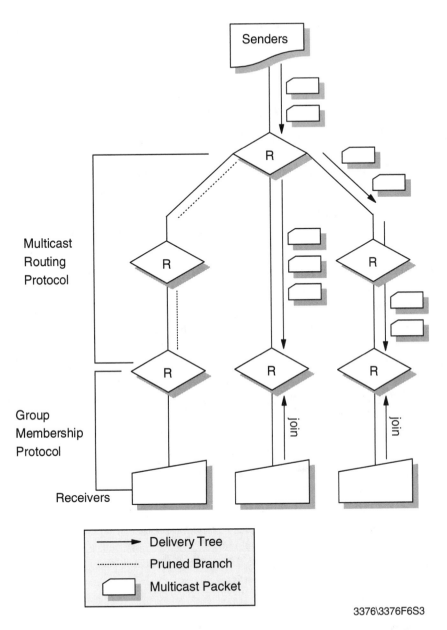

Figure 261. *IP Multicast Routing*

The figure shows that multicast packets are transmitted from a sender through a delivery tree to the receivers. If none of the hosts connected directly to a multicast router has joined this specific multicast group, no packets are delivered on the branch which leads to those hosts. The branch is *pruned*.

When a host or a multicast router receives a multicast datagram, its action is dependent upon the TTL value and the destination IP address.

0   A datagram sent with a TTL value of zero is restricted to the source host.

1   A datagram with a TTL value of one reaches all hosts on the subnet that are members of the group. Multicast routers decrement the value to zero, but unlike unicast datagrams, they do not report this with an ICMP Time Exceeded message. Expiration of a multicast datagram is a normal occurrence.

2+ All hosts that are members of the group and all multicast routers receive the datagram. The action of the routers depends on the multicast group address.

> *224.0.0.0 - 224.0.0.255*
>
> This range is intended for single-hop multicasting applications only. Multicast routers will not forward datagrams with destination IP addresses in this range.
>
> It may seem at first as though a host need not bother reporting its membership of a group in this range since multicast routers will not forward datagrams from other subnets. However, the report also informs other hosts on the subnet that the reporting host is a member of the group. The only group that is never reported is 224.0.0.1 because all hosts know that the group consists of all hosts on that subnet.
>
> *other*
>
> Datagrams with other values for the destination address are forwarded as normal by the multicast router; it decrements the TTL value by one at each hop.
>
> This allows a host to locate the nearest server that is listening on a multicast address using what is called an *expanding ring search*. The host sends out a datagram with a TTL value of 1 (same subnet) and waits for a reply. If none is received, it tries a TTL value of 2, then 3, and so on. Eventually it will find the closest server.

9.3 Multicast Routing Protocols

The following standard multicast routing protocols are described in the sections below:

1. Distance Vector Multicast Routing Protocol (DVMRP)

2. Multicast OSPF (MOSPF)

3. Protocol Independent Multicast (PIM)

9.3.1 Distance Vector Multicast Routing Protocol (DVMRP)

DVMRP is a rather old multicast routing protocol originally defined in RFC 1075 in 1988. It has since been enhanced to support Reverse Path Multicasting (RPM). DVMRP is an IGP (see IGP in 3.3, "Interior Gateway Protocols (IGP)" on page 137) in order to build per-source-group multicast delivery trees suitable for use within an AS (see 3.1.2, "Autonomous Systems" on page 126), but not between different ASs. DVMRP is not currently developed for use in routing non-multicast datagrams, so a router that routes both multicast and unicast datagrams must run two separate routing processes. DVMRP has the following two advantages compared with MOSPF (see MOSPF in 9.3.2, "Multicast OSPF (MOSPF)" on page 607).

1. Tunnel encapsulation

2. Widespread use on the Internet and well-understood

9.3.1.1 DVMRP Terminology

Before giving a protocol overview of DVMRP, we define some terms used in DVMRP.

Reverse Path Multicasting (RPM)

Datagrams follow multicast delivery trees from a source to all members of a multicast group, replicating the packet only at necessary branches in the delivery tree (see Figure 262 on page 602).

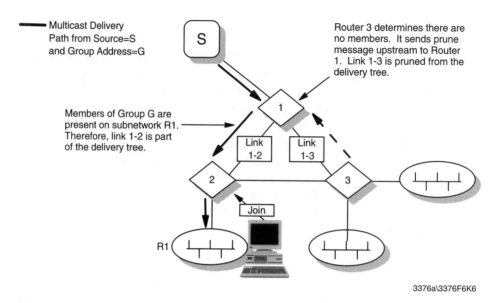

Figure 262. *Reverse Path Multicasting (RPM)*

The trees are calculated and updated dynamically to track the membership of individual groups. When a datagram arrives at an interface, the reverse path to the source of the datagram is determined by examining a DVMRP routing table of known source networks. If the datagram arrives at an interface that would be used to transmit datagrams back to the source, then it is forwarded to the appropriate list of downstream interfaces. Otherwise, it is not on the optimal delivery tree and should be discarded. In this way duplicate packets can be filtered when loops exist in the network topology. The source-specific delivery trees are automatically pruned back as group membership changes or leaf routers determine that no group members are present. This keeps the delivery trees to the minimum branches necessary to reach all of the group members. New sections of the tree can also be added dynamically as new members join the multicast group by grafting the new sections onto the delivery trees.

DVMRP Tunnel Encapsulation

Because not all IP routers support native multicast routing, DVMRP includes direct support for tunneling IP Multicast datagrams through routers. The IP Multicast datagrams are encapsulated in unicast IP packets and addressed to the routers that do support native multicast routing. DVMRP treats tunnel interfaces in an identical manner to physical network interfaces as in Figure 263 on page 603.

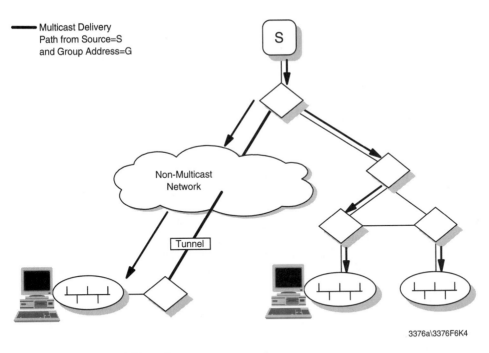

Multicast Delivery
Path from Source=S
and Group Address=G

S

Non-Multicast
Network

Tunnel

3376a\3376F6K4

Figure 263. DVMRP Tunnel

9.3.1.2 Protocol Overview

DVMRP can be summarized as a *broadcast and prune* multicast routing protocol. It builds per-source broadcast trees based upon routing exchanges, then dynamically creates per-source-group multicast delivery trees by pruning (removing branches from) the source's truncated broadcast tree. It performs reverse path forwarding checks to determine when multicast traffic should be forwarded to downstream interfaces. In this way, source-rooted shortest path trees can be formed to reach all group members from each source network of multicast traffic.

Neighbor Discovery: Neighbor DVMRP routers are discovered dynamically by sending neighbor probe messages on local multicast-capable network interfaces and tunnel pseudo interfaces. These messages are sent periodically to the All-DVMRP-Routers IP multicast addresses. Each neighbor probe message contains the list of neighbor DVMRP routers for which Neighbor Probe messages have been received on that interface. In this way, neighbor DVMRP routers can ensure that they are seen by each other. Once a router has received a probe from a neighbor that contains a router address in the neighbor list, the router establishes a two-way neighbor adjacency with this router.

Source Location: When an IP Multicast datagram is received by a router running DVMRP, it first looks up the source network in the DVMRP routing table. The interface on which the best route to the source of the datagram was received is called the upstream (also called RPF) interface. If the datagram arrived on the correct upstream interface, then it is a candidate for forwarding to one or more downstream interfaces. If the datagram did not arrive on the anticipated upstream interface, it is discarded. This check is known as a reverse path forwarding check and must be performed by all DVMRP routers.

In order to ensure that all DVMRP routers have a consistent view of the path back to a source, a routing table is propagated to all DVMRP routers as an integral part of the protocol. Each router advertises the network number and mask of the interfaces it is directly connected to as well as relaying the routes received from neighbor routers. DVMRP requires an interface metric to be configured on all physical and tunnel interfaces. When a route is received, the metric of the interface over which the datagram was received must be added to the metric of the route being advertised in the route report message. This adjusted metric should be used when comparing metrics to determine the best upstream neighbor.

Dependent Downstream Routers: In addition to providing a consistent view of source networks, the exchange of routes in DVMRP provides one other important feature. DVMRP uses the route exchange as a mechanism for upstream routers to determine if any downstream routers depend on them for forwarding from particular source networks. DVMRP accomplishes this by using a technique called *poison reverse* (see 3.2.2.3, "Split Horizon with Poison Reverse" on page 134). If a downstream router selects an upstream router as the best next hop to a particular source network, this is indicated by echoing back the route on the upstream interface with a metric equal to the original metric plus infinity. When the upstream router receives the report and sees a metric that lies between infinity and twice infinity, it can then add the downstream router from which it received the report to a list of dependent routers for this source. This list of dependent routers per source network built by the poison reverse technique will provide the foundation necessary to determine when it is appropriate to prune back the IP source specific multicast trees.

Designated Forwarder: When two or more multicast routers are connected to a multi-access network, it could be possible for duplicate packets to be forwarded on the network (one copy from each router). DVMRP prevents this possibility by electing a forwarder for each source as a side effect of its route exchange. When two routers on a multi-access network exchange source networks, each of the routers will know the others metric back to each source network. Therefore, of all the DVMRP routers on a shared network, the router with the lowest metric to a source network is responsible for forwarding data on to the shared network. If two or more routers have an equally low metric, the router with the lowest IP address becomes the designated forwarder for the network. In this way, DVMRP performs an implicit designated forwarder election for each source network on each downstream interface.

9.3.1.3 Building Multicast Trees

As previously mentioned, when an IP multicast datagram arrives, the upstream interface is determined by looking up the interface on which the best route to the source of the datagram was received. If the upstream interface is correct, then a DVMRP router will forward the datagram to a list of downstream interfaces.

Adding Leaf Networks: Initially, the DVMRP router must consider all of the remaining IP multicast capable interfaces (including tunnels) on the router. If the downstream interface under consideration is a leaf network (has no dependent downstream neighbors for the source network), then the IGMP local group database must be consulted. The IGMP local group database is maintained by all IP multicast routers on each physical, multicast-capable network. If the destination group address is listed in the local group database, and the router is the designated forwarder for the source, then the interface is included in the list of downstream interfaces. If there are no group members on the interface, then the interface is removed from the outgoing interface list.

Adding Non-Leaf Networks: Initially, all non-leaf networks should be included in the downstream interface list when a forwarding cache entry is first being created. This allows all downstream routers to be aware of traffic destined for a particular [source network, group] pair. The downstream routers will then have the option to send prunes and grafts for this [source network, group] pair as requirements change from their respective downstream routers and local group members.

9.3.1.4 Pruning Multicast Trees

As mentioned above, routers at the edges with leaf networks will remove their leaf interfaces that have no group members associated with an IP Multicast datagram. If a router removes all of its downstream interfaces, it notifies the upstream router that it no longer wants traffic destined for a particular [source network, group] pair. This is accomplished by sending a DVMRP prune message upstream to the router it expects to forward datagrams from a particular source.

Recall that a downstream router will inform an upstream router that it depends on the upstream router to receive datagrams from particular source networks by using the poison reverse technique during the exchange of DVMRP routes. This method allows the upstream router to build a list of downstream routers on each interface that are dependent upon it for datagrams from a particular source network. If the upstream router receives prune messages from each one of the dependent downstream routers on an interface, then the upstream router can in turn remove this interface from its downstream interface list. If the upstream router is able to remove all of its downstream interfaces in this way, it can then send a DVMRP prune message to its upstream router. This continues until the unnecessary branches are removed from the delivery tree.

In order to remove old prune state information for [source network, group] pairs that are no longer active, it is necessary to limit the life of a prune and periodically resume the broadcasting procedure. The prune message contains a prune lifetime, indicating the length of time that the prune should remain in effect. When the prune lifetime expires, if the interface is still a non-leaf, the interface is joined back onto the multicast delivery tree. If unwanted multicast datagrams continue to arrive, the prune mechanism will be reinitiated and the cycle will continue. If all of the downstream interfaces are removed from a multicast delivery tree causing a DVMRP prune message to be sent upstream, the lifetime of the prune sent must be equal to the minimum of the remaining lifetimes of the received prunes.

9.3.1.5 Grafting Multicast Trees

Once a tree branch has been pruned from a multicast delivery tree, packets from the corresponding [source network, group] pair will no longer be forwarded. However, since IP Multicast supports dynamic group membership, hosts may join a multicast group at any time. In this case, DVMRP routers use Grafts to cancel the prunes that are in place from the host back on to the multicast delivery tree. A router will send a Graft message to its upstream neighbor if a group join occurs for a group that the router has previously sent a prune. Separate graft messages must be sent to the appropriate upstream neighbor for each source network that has been pruned.

Since there would be no way to tell if a Graft message sent upstream was lost or the source simply quit sending traffic, it is necessary to acknowledge each Graft message with a DVMRP Graft Ack message. If an acknowledgment is not received within a Graft Time-out period, the Graft message should be retransmitted using binary exponential back-off between retransmissions. Duplicate Graft Ack messages should simply be ignored. The purpose of the Graft Ack message is to simply acknowledge the receipt of a Graft message. It does not imply that any action was taken as a result of receiving the Graft message. Therefore, all Graft messages received from a neighbor with whom a two-way neighbor relationship has been formed should be acknowledged whether or not they cause an action on the receiving router.

9.3.1.6 Current DVMRP Internet Drafts

At the time this book was published, the current Internet draft specifications for the core components of DVMRP were the following:

Distance Vector Multicast Routing Protocol
  http://www.ietf.org/internet-drafts/draft-ietf-idmr-dvmrp-v3-07.txt

9.3.2 Multicast OSPF (MOSPF)

MOSPF is the multicast extension that is built on top of OSPF Version 2 (see OSPF in 3.3.4, "Open Shortest Path First (OSPF)" on page 146) and defined in RFC 1584. MOSPF is not actually a separate multicast routing protocol like DVMRP. MOSPF The multicast extensions have been implemented to leverage an already existing OSPF topology database to compute source-rooted shortest path delivery tree. The following two main MOSPF characteristics are described here to understand MOSPF in comparison to OSPF and DVMRP.

1. MOSPF adds a new type of LSA on the top of OSPF.

2. MOSPF does not support tunnel function, whereas DVMRP does.

9.3.2.1 New Type of LSA

MOSPF forwards a multicast datagram on the basis of both the datagram's source and destination . The OSPF link state database provides a complete description of the AS's topology. By adding a new type of LSA (see "Link State Advertisements" on page 155), the group-membership-LSA, the location of all multicast group members is pinpointed in the database. The path of a multicast datagram can then be calculated by building a shortest-path tree (SPT) rooted at the datagram's source (see 3.2.3.1, "Shortest-Path First (SPF)" on page 137). All branches not containing multicast members are pruned from the tree. These pruned shortest-path trees are initially built when the first datagram is received on demand. The results of the shortest path calculation are then cached for use by subsequent datagrams having the same source and destination.

OSPF allows an AS to be split into areas. However, when this is done complete knowledge of the AS's topology is lost. When forwarding multicasts between areas, only incomplete shortest-path trees can be built. This may lead to some inefficiency in routing. An analogous situation exists when the source of the multicast datagram lies in another autonomous system. In both cases the neighborhood immediately surrounding the source is unknown. In these cases the source's neighborhood is approximated by OSPF summary link advertisements or by OSPF AS external link advertisements respectively.

Note: For a given multicast datagram, all routers calculate an identical shortest-path tree. There is a single path between the datagram's source and any particular destination group member. This means that, unlike OSPF's treatment of regular (unicast) IP data traffic, there is no provision for equal-cost multipath.

9.3.2.2 No Tunnel Function

Routers running MOSPF can be intermixed with non-multicast OSPF routers. Both types of routers can interoperate when forwarding unicast IP data traffic. Obviously, the forwarding extent of IP multicasts is limited by the number of MOSPF routers present in the AS. An ability to tunnel (see tunnel in 9.3.1.1, "DVMRP Terminology" on page 601) multicast datagrams through non-multicast routers is not provided. In MOSPF, just as in the base OSPF protocol, datagrams (multicast or unicast) are routed "as is", they are not further encapsulated or decapsulated as they transit the AS.

9.3.3 Protocol Independent Multicast (PIM)

PIM is new multicast routing protocol developed by the IETF IDMR working group. PIM is independent of any underlying unicast routing protocol like DVMRP (see DVMRP in 9.3.1, "Distance Vector Multicast Routing Protocol (DVMRP)" on page 601).

There are two modes defined:

- Dense mode (PIM-DM)

- Sparse mode (PIM-SM), specified in RFC 2362

9.3.3.1 PIM Terminology

Here are some definitions that are necessary to understand the protocol overview.

Reverse Path Forwarding (RPF) / RPF interface / RPF lookup
> RPF is a multicast forwarding mode where a data packet is accepted for forwarding if it is received on an interface used to reach the source in unicast. The interface passing this check is called the RPF interface. An RPF lookup for a source returns the RPF interface and the next-hop information, as if a route lookup is done for the source on a unicast routing table.

Rendezvous Point (RP)
> RP is the point in network where senders meet receivers. Receivers must join the RP-rooted tree and senders must register their existence with RP.

9.3.3.2 PIM-DM Protocol Overview

PIM-DM is designed for dense multicast regions; group membership is dense, such as with DVMRP and MOSPF. PIM-DM assumes that when a source starts sending, all downstream systems want to receive multicast datagrams. Initially, multicast datagrams are flooded to all areas of the network. If some areas of the network do not have group members, PIM-DM will prune off the forwarding branch by setting up prune state. The prune state has an associated timer, which on expiration will turn into forward state, allowing data to go down the branch previously in prune state (see Figure 264 on page 609).

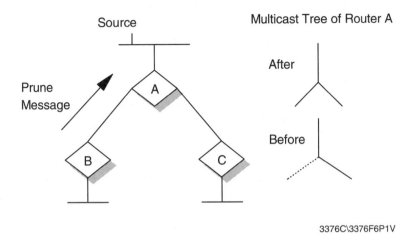

3376C\3376F6P1V

Figure 264. PIM-DM Flood and Prune Message Example

The prune state contains source and group address information. When a new member appears in a pruned area, a router can graft toward the source for the group, turning the pruned branch into forward state. The forwarding branches form a tree rooted at the source leading to all members of the group. This tree is called a source-rooted tree.

9.3.3.3 PIM-DM and DVMRP
In order to understand PIM-DM, comparing it with DVMRP is helpful. PIM-DM differs from DVMRP in the following ways:

- PIM-DM forwards out all interfaces until explicit pruning occurs; DVMRP uses the parent-child relationship, and split-horizon to recognize downstream routers.

- PIM-DM is independent of specific unicast routing technology; DVMRP uses distance vectors such as RIP (see 3.2.2, "Distance Vector Routing" on page 129).

- PIM-DM does not support tunnels; DVMRP does (see tunnels in 9.3.1.1, "DVMRP Terminology" on page 601).

9.3.3.4 PIM-SM Protocol Overview
PIM-SM is designed for sparse multicast regions. The basic concept is that multicast data is blocked unless a downstream router explicitly asks for it in order to control the amounts of the traffic that traverse the network.

A router receives explicit join/prune messages from those neighboring routers that have downstream group members. The router then forwards data packets addressed to a multicast group, G, only onto those interfaces on which explicit joins have been received. The basic PIM-SM operation is described below.

Note: All routers mentioned in this document are assumed to be PIM-SM capable, unless otherwise specified.

1. A designated router (DR) sends periodic join/prune messages toward a group-specific rendezvous point (RP) for each group for which it has active members. The DR is responsible for sending triggered join/prune and register messages toward the RP.

2. Each router along the path toward the RP builds and sends join/prune messages on toward the RP. Routers with local members join the group-specific multicast tree rooted at the RP (see Figure 265).

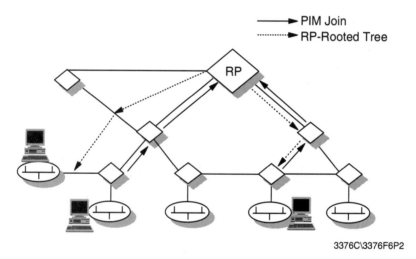

Figure 265. PIM-SM Join and RP-Rooted Tree Example

The RP's route entry may include such fields as the source address, the group address, the incoming interface from which packets are accepted, the list of outgoing interfaces to which packets are sent, timers, flag bits, etc.

3. The sender's DR initially encapsulates multicast packets in the resister message and unicast it to the RP for the group (see Figure 266 on page 611).

PIM Register

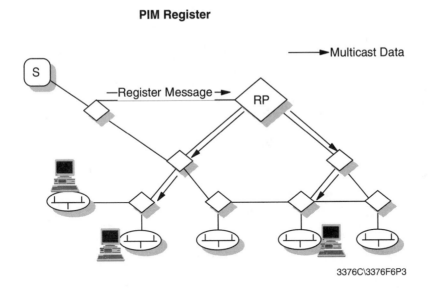

Figure 266. PIM-SM Resister Message Example

The RP decapsulates each register message and forwards the data packet natively to downstream routers on the shared RP tree.

4. A router with directly connected members first joins the shared RP tree. The router can initiate a source's SPT based on a threshold (see Figure 267 on page 612).

PIM Join - SPT

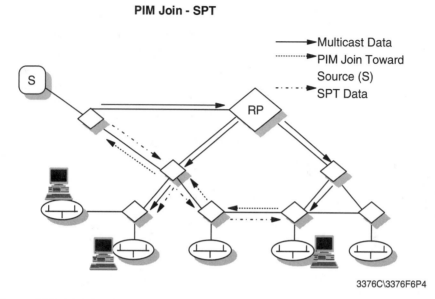

3376C\3376F6P4

Figure 267. PIM-SM SPT

5. After the router receives multicast packets from both the source's SPT and RP tree, PIM prune messages are sent upstream towards the RP to prune the RP tree. Now multicast data from the source will only flow over the source's SPT towards group members (see Figure 268).

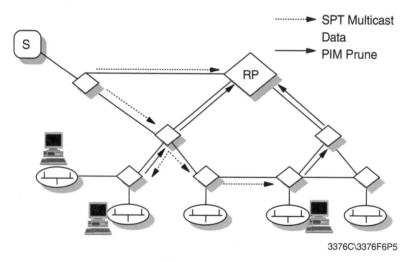

3376C\3376F6P5

Figure 268. PIM-SM RP Tree to Source's SPT Switch Example

The recommended policy is to initiate the switch to the SP tree after receiving a significant number of data packets during a specified time interval from a particular source. To realize this policy the router can monitor data packets from sources for which it has no source-specific multicast route entry and initiate such an entry when the data rate exceeds the configured threshold.

9.3.3.5 PIM-DM and PIM-SM

In relation to PIM-DM, PIM-SM differs in two essential ways:

1. There are no periodic joins transmitted, only explicit triggered grafts/prunes in PIM-DM.

2. There is no rendezvous point (RP) in PIM-DM.

9.3.3.6 Current PIM Internet Drafts

By the time this book was published, the current Internet draft specifications for the core components of PIM were the following:

Protocol Independent Multicast Routing in the Internet Protocol Version 6 (IPv6)
    http://www.ietf.org/internet-drafts/draft-ietf-pim-ipv6-00.txt
Protocol Independent Multicast Version 2 Dense Mode Specification
    http://www.ietf.org/internet-drafts/draft-ietf-pim-v2-dm-00.txt

9.4 The Multicast Backbone

The Multicast Backbone (MBONE) was started in March 1992, to provide a real-time audio transmission from the Internet Engineering Task Force (IETF) meeting in San Diego via multicasting on the Internet. At that time, 20 sites were listening to the audio transmission. Two years later, the IETF meeting in Seattle was broadcast to 567 hosts in 15 countries on two parallel channels (audio and video) on the MBONE. Since then, the MBONE was used for video and audio conferencing, video broadcasts from international technical conferences and NASA Space Shuttle missions.

The multicast backbone is a virtual overlay network that uses the physical infrastructure of the existing Internet. Since not many routers in the Internet support multicasting the MBONE is layered on top of the existing Internet protocols.

Networks that are connected to the MBONE must comply with special requirements for the available bandwidth. For video transmissions, a minimum bandwidth of 128 kbps is required. Audio transmissions require a minimum of 9-16 kbps. The IETF multicast traffic has average transmission rates of 100 to 300 kbps, with spikes up to 500 kbps.

9.4.1 MBONE Routing

The MBONE consists of many network islands that support IP multicasting. These islands are connected by virtual point-to-point links (tunnels) which bridges the areas in the Internet that don't support multicasting. Most routers in todays Internet are unicast routers that normally can't handle multicast packets.

A multicast router (mrouter) that wants to send multicast packets to another multicast router through a tunnel hides the multicast packets in normal unicast packets that can be transmitted through normal Internet routers. The multicast packets are encapsulated in IP packets with the destination address of the endpoint of the tunnel. The receiving mrouter at the end of the tunnel strips off the encapsulating IP header and forwards the enclosed multicast packet. This technique is called tunneling.

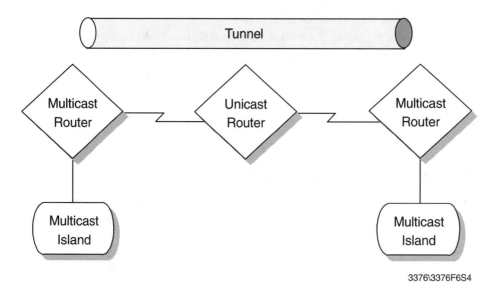

3376\3376F6S4

Figure 269. MBONE Tunnel

Mrouters are either commercial multicast routers or special workstations running a multicast routing daemon (mrouted). The mrouted implementation uses the Distance Vector Multicast Routing Protocol (DVMRP) for the routing of the multicast packets.

The MBONE tunnels are established with a metric and a threshold. The metric parameter is used for multicast routing. It specifies the routing cost for the tunnel which is used in DVMRP to choose the cheapest path for the packets through the routers. The lower the metric the lower the costs for routing the packets through a tunnel. Figure 270 on page 615 shows an example for tunnels between MBONE multicast routers which have different metric values.

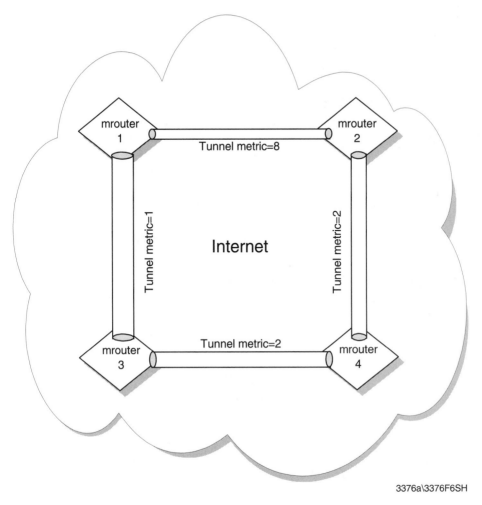

Internet

mrouter 1

mrouter 2

Tunnel metric=8

Tunnel metric=1

Tunnel metric=2

mrouter 3

mrouter 4

Tunnel metric=2

3376a\3376F6SH

Figure 270. MBONE Tunnel Metric

If a multicast packet should be sent from mrouter 1 to all other routers, the tunnel 1-2 is never used, because the sum of the tunnel metrics 1-3, 3-4, and 4-2 (1+2+2=5) is lower than the metric of tunnel 1-2. This means that the cheapest way to send packets from mrouter 1 to mrouter 2 is to send them through routers 3 and 4.

The threshold limits the distribution of multicast packets. It specifies the minimum TTL for a multicast packet to be forwarded into an established tunnel. The TTL is decremented by 1 at each multicast router.

In the future, most routers will support IP multicast directly which will make tunneling dispensable. This makes clear that the MBONE is only a temporary utility that will eventually become obsolete when multicasting is supported as standard in all Internet routers.

9.4.2 MBONE Applications

The first multiparty conferencing tools that used the MBONE were developed by the Network Research Group at Lawrence Berkeley National Laboratory (LBNL). The videoconferencing tool vic in conjunction with the audio tool vat allows videoconferences between multiple hosts connected to the MBONE. The tool WB (White Board) provides a shared drawing space that can be used by the participants of a videoconference to work on one document commonly.

The following list contains some popular MBONE applications that are available today:

- SDR Session Directory. SDR is used to announce MBONE sessions.
- NV Netvideo. A videoconferencing tool.
- VIC Videoconferencing System.
- IVS Inria Videoconferencing System.
- VAT Visual Audio Tool. An audio conferencing tool.
- RAT Robust Audio Tool. An audio conferencing tool.
- WB Whiteboard.

Most of the MBONE tools use the User Datagram Protocol (UDP) instead of the usual Transport Control Protocol (TCP) because the reliability and flow control mechanisms of TCP are not practical for real-time broadcasting of multimedia data. The loss of an audio or video packet is acceptable rather than transmission delays because of TCP retransmissions. On top of UDP, most of the MBONE applications use the Real-Time Transport Protocol (RTP) which is described in 9.5, "The Real-Time Protocols RTP and RTCP." Mostly, the RTP protocol is implemented directly in the MBONE application. It provides mechanisms to transmit multimedia data streams continuously and without delays through the Internet.

9.5 The Real-Time Protocols RTP and RTCP

The Real-Time Transport Protocol (RTP) was developed by the Audio/Video Transport Working Group from the Internet Engineering Task Force (IETF). It is specified in RFCs 1889 and 1890. RTP is used in real-time applications such as videoconferencing, audio broadcasting or Internet telephony, and is usually implemented directly in those applications. Most of the MBONE tools use the RTP protocol for the delivery of real-time data. Therefore, RTP is mostly used together with UDP. RTP itself is not aware of a connection. It operates over connection-oriented or connectionless lower layer protocols. Because RTP provides no reliability mechanisms and does not guarantee delivery the application must decide if packet loss is acceptable or if it needs its own reliability routines. RTP also does not provide functions to ensure timely delivery or provide other quality-of-service guarantees.

To use real-time services in an application, two protocols must be implemented:

- The Real-Time Transport Protocol (RTP), which is responsible for the transport of real-time data packets.

- The RTP Control Protocol (RTCP), which controls and monitors the RTP session.

9.5.1 The Real-Time Transport Protocol (RTP)

The RTP protocol provides transport mechanisms that allow the synchronization of multimedia data streams from different applications.

If a user works with a video tool to provide a video stream and an audio tool to provide an audio stream on the Internet, RTP marks the packets from the different applications with a specific payload type and time stamps so that audio and video data can be synchronized on the receiving host. Figure 271 shows the operation of RTP in a multimedia transmission. Audio and video data are encapsulated in RTP packets and transmitted from the sender to the receiver.

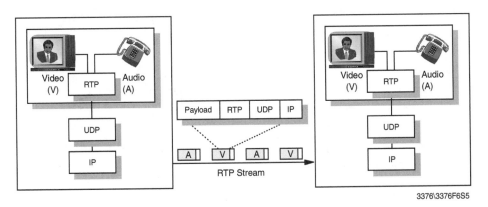

3376\3376F6S5

Figure 271. RTP Operation

Without using RTP, the video and audio data, which eventually doesn't arrive at the same time at the receiving host because of delays in the network, are displayed unsynchronized. A videoconference doesn't work very well if the audio and video have different delays.

The header of an RTP packet has the following format:

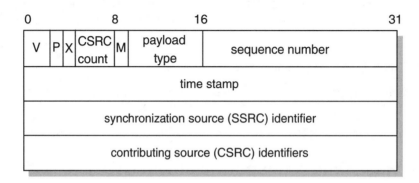

3376\3376F6S2

Figure 272. *RTP Header Fields*

Where:

V

2-bit RTP version.

P

Padding bit. If this is set, there are one or more additional padding octets at the end of the packet that are not part of the payload. This function is used for some encryption algorithms.

X

Extension bit. If this is set, there is exactly one header extension that follows the fixed header.

CSRC count

4-bit count, that contains the number of the contributing source identifiers that follow the fixed header.

M

Marker bit. For special use.

Payload type.

7-bit payload type. Specifies the format of the payload in the RTP packet.

16-bit Sequence number

Each RTP packet gets a sequence number that is used from the receiver to restore the packet sequence and detect packet loss.

timestamp

The timestamp field contains a value that represents the time when the data in the RTP packet was sampled. The initial value of the timestamp is random.

SSRC identifier

The Synchronization Source (SSRC) field is a randomly chosen identification for the source of a stream of RTP packets, identified by a 32-bit number. All packets from a synchronization source contain an unique SSRC identifier so that a receiver can group the packets by synchronization source for playback. All synchronization sources in an RTP session must have a different SSRC identifier.

CSRC list

The CSRC list contains the contributing sources for the payload in the current packet. This field is used if a mixer (see 9.5.3, "RTP Translators and Mixers" on page 630) has combined different streams of RTP packets with the same payload type (audio) from different senders. The mixer inserts a list of the different SSRC identifiers of the sources that contributed to the generation of the new RTP packet into the header of this packet. This list makes sure that a receiver that gets a packet which was modified by a mixer, still gets all SSRC identifiers of the senders, because the modified RTP packet contains the SSRC identifier of the mixer.

The main functions of the RTP protocol are:

- Payload type identification

- Sequence numbering

- Time stamping

The payload of an RTP packet can be either an audio or a video format. The sending application writes the code for the payload type in the RTP header so that the receiving application knows which audio or video format must be decoded. The following payload types are defined today (RFC 1890):

Table 13. *RTP Payload Types*

Audio		Video	
Payload Type	**Encoding Name**	**Payload Type**	**Encoding Name**
0	PCMU	24	HDCC
1	1016	25	CellB
2	G.721	26	JPEG
3	GSM	27	CUSM
4	G.723	28	NV
5	DVI4 (8 KHz)	29	PicW
6	DVI4 (16 KHz)	30	CPV
7	LPC	31	H.261
8	PCMA	32	MPV
9	G.722	33	MP2T
10	L16 Stereo	34	H.263
11	L16 Mono	35-71	Unassigned
12	TPSO	72-76	Reserved
13	VSC	77-95	Unassigned
14	MPA	96-127	Dynamic
15	G.728		
16	DVI4		
17	DVI4		
18	G.725		
19	CN		
20	Unassigned		
21	Unassigned		
22	Unassigned		
23	Unassigned		

This list may be enhanced in the future with new audio and video formats. Although RTP was primarily designed to transport multimedia data it is not limited to that particular use. All applications that produce continuous data streams can use RTP.

Sequence numbering is used in RTP to restore the order of the packets on the receiving host and to detect packet loss. Sequence numbers are also used to determine the original location of a packet, for example in video decoding, without necessarily decoding packets in sequence. The initial value of the sequence number is random (unpredictable).

Time stamps are used in RTP to synchronize the packets from different sources. The time stamp represents the sampling (creation) time of the first byte in the RTP data packet and it must be derived from a timer instance that increments monotonically and linearly. The resolution of the timer depends on the desired synchronization accuracy for the application data. The clock frequency depends on the payload format and is defined statically in the payload format specifications.

The initial value of the time stamp is random, as for the sequence number. It is possible that several consecutive RTP packets may have the same time stamp. This happens if a videoframe is transmitted in different RTP packets so that the payload of those packets was logically generated at the same time. Figure 273 on page 622 shows an example for the generation of RTP packets in a video application:

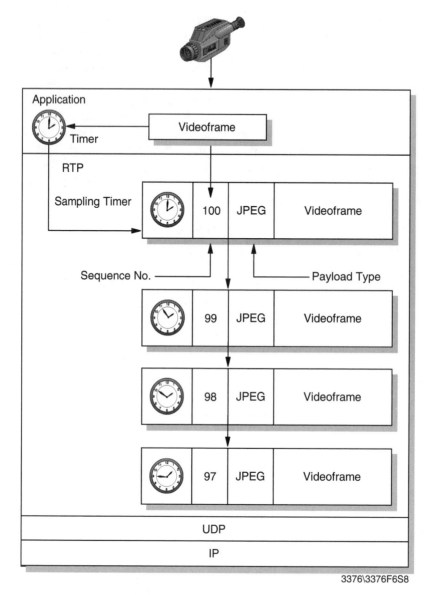

Figure 273. RTP Packet Generation in a Video Application

9.5.2 The Real-Time Control Protocol

The RTP protocol itself provides only one message format, the RTP data packet. But many real-time applications need a feedback for the provided packets in order to guarantee real-time delivery. This function is provided by the Real-Time Control Protocol (RTCP).

The primary function of RTCP is to provide feedback about the quality of the RTP data distribution. This is comparable to the flow and congestion control functions of other transport protocols. Feedback from the receivers is necessary for diagnosing distribution faults. RTCP produces sender and receiver reports, such as stream statistics and packet counts. It uses a separate UDP port from the RTP protocol (RTP-port+1). Figure 274 shows the cooperation of the RTP and the RTCP protocol.

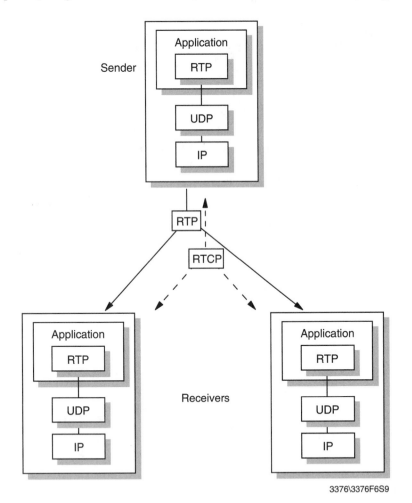

3376\3376F6S9

Figure 274. RTCP and RTP Packet Delivery

Because RTCP packets can have different functions, there are different formats defined:

- SR   Sender report
- RR   Receiver report
- SDES   Source description items
- BYE   Indicates end of participation
- APP   Application-specific functions

9.5.2.1 RTCP Sender Report

An RTCP sender report will be sent by the sources of an RTP data stream to inform the receivers what they should have received. It is a multicast packet that reaches all receivers.

The sender report packet can be grouped in three parts. First the header, which specifies the RTCP packet type, packet length and the sender identification. The second part contains the sender information and the third part the receiver report blocks. Most times, the RTCP sender packet contains more than one receiver report block. They allow the sender to report feedback for received RTP packets from other senders. The following figure shows the format of an RTCP sender report packet.

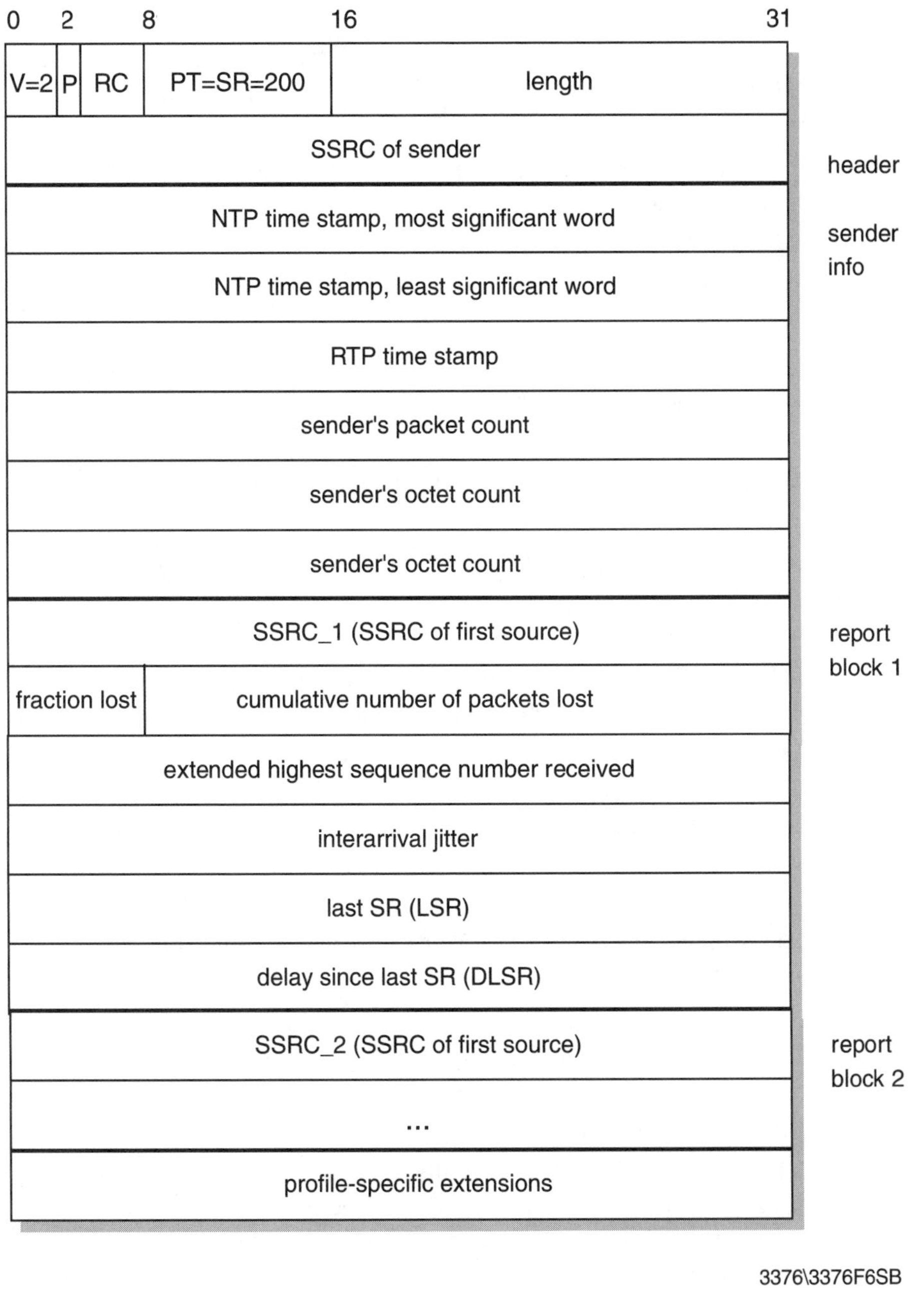

0	2	8	16	31	

```
 0   2   8              16                              31
┌───┬─┬────┬─────────────┬──────────────────────────────┐
│V=2│P│ RC │ PT=SR=200   │            length            │
├───┴─┴────┴─────────────┴──────────────────────────────┤  header
│                   SSRC of sender                       │
├────────────────────────────────────────────────────────┤  sender
│            NTP time stamp, most significant word        │  info
├────────────────────────────────────────────────────────┤
│            NTP time stamp, least significant word       │
├────────────────────────────────────────────────────────┤
│                    RTP time stamp                       │
├────────────────────────────────────────────────────────┤
│                 sender's packet count                   │
├────────────────────────────────────────────────────────┤
│                  sender's octet count                   │
├────────────────────────────────────────────────────────┤
│                  sender's octet count                   │
├────────────────────────────────────────────────────────┤
│             SSRC_1 (SSRC of first source)               │  report
├──────────────┬─────────────────────────────────────────┤  block 1
│ fraction lost│   cumulative number of packets lost      │
├──────────────┴─────────────────────────────────────────┤
│        extended highest sequence number received        │
├────────────────────────────────────────────────────────┤
│                  interarrival jitter                    │
├────────────────────────────────────────────────────────┤
│                    last SR (LSR)                        │
├────────────────────────────────────────────────────────┤
│              delay since last SR (DLSR)                 │
├────────────────────────────────────────────────────────┤
│             SSRC_2 (SSRC of first source)               │  report
├────────────────────────────────────────────────────────┤  block 2
│                        ...                              │
├────────────────────────────────────────────────────────┤
│               profile-specific extensions               │
└────────────────────────────────────────────────────────┘
```

3376\3376F6SB

Figure 275. RTCP Sender Report Packet Format

Where:

V

> 2-bit version field which is set to 1.

P

> Padding bit. If this is set, there are one or more additional padding bytes at the end of the packet.

RC

> 5-bit reception report count. Contains the number of reception report blocks in this packet.

PT

> 8-bit packet type field. For sender reports the value is 200.

length

> 16-bit packet length in bytes (including any added padding).

SSRC of Sender

> 32-bit field that contains the SSRC identifier of the host sending this packet.

NTP time stamp

> Two 32-bit fields containing the absolute time in the Network Time Protocol (NTP) format. This timer counts the number of seconds since January 1, 1900.

RTP timestamp

> 32-bit field that contains the time stamp from the RTP packets according to the sender.

sender's packet count

> 32-bit field with the total number of RTP data packets transmitted by the sender since the start of the transmission.

sender's octet count

> 32-bit field with the total number of payload bytes transmitted by the sender since the start of the transmission.

SSRC_n (source identifier):

> 32-bit field that contains the SSRC identifier of another RTP sender from which this sender has received packets. The number of report blocks with different sender SSRCs depends on the number of other sources that were heard by this sender since the last report.

fraction lost

8-bit field that represents the fraction of RTP data packets that was lost since the previous SR or RR packet was sent from the source SSRC_n.

cumulative number of packets lost

24-bit field that represents the total number of lost RTP data packets from source SSRC_n.

extended highest sequence number received

32-bit field. It contains the highest sequence number that was received in an RTP data packet from the source SSRC_n.

interarrival jitter

32-bit field that contains the estimated variance of the interarrival times from the appropriate source. If the packets arrive regularly, the jitter value is zero. If the packets arrive irregularly, the jitter value is high.

last SR timestamp (LSR)

32-bit field that contains the middle 32 bits from the 64-bit NTP timestamp received with the last RTCP sender report packet from the source SSRC_n.

delay since last SR (DLSR)

32-bit field. It contains the delay between receiving the last SR packet from the source SSRC_n and the sending of the current exception report block in units of 1/65536 seconds.

9.5.2.2 RTCP Receiver Report

The RTCP Receiver Report (RR) packet is similar to the sender report packet. The packet type field contains the constant 201 and the sender information section (NTP and RTP timestamps/sender's packet and octet counts) is not included in the packet. The other fields in the receiver report have the same function as in the SR packet.

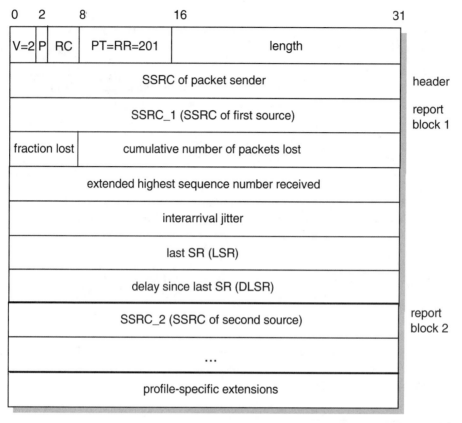

0 2	8	16	31

V=2	P	RC	PT=RR=201	length	
SSRC of packet sender					header
SSRC_1 (SSRC of first source)					report block 1
fraction lost	cumulative number of packets lost				
extended highest sequence number received					
interarrival jitter					
last SR (LSR)					
delay since last SR (DLSR)					
SSRC_2 (SSRC of second source)					report block 2
...					
profile-specific extensions					

3376\3376F6SB

Figure 276. RTCP Receiver Report Packet Format

9.5.2.3 RTCP Source Description Packet

A source description packet (SDES) has the packet type 202 and is used from the RTP packet sources to provide more information about themselves. The currently defined source description items are:

CNAME	Unique name for the source
NAME	The real user name of the source
EMAIL	The e-mail address of the user
PHONE	Phone number of the user
LOC	Geographic user location
TOOL	User's application or tool name
NOTE	Note about the source
PRIV	Private extensions

The SDES packet consists of the basic RTCP header and a series of source identifiers and description items.

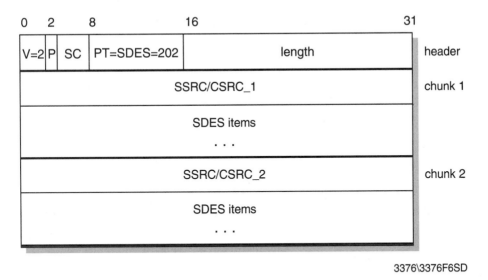

Figure 277. RTCP SDES Packet Format

9.5.2.4 RTCP BYE Message

The RTCP bye message has the packet type 203 and is used by a source if it leaves a conference. The bye message is especially helpful for mixers. If a mixer shuts down, it can send a bye message containing all contributing sources.

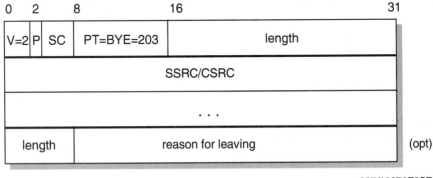

Figure 278. RTCP BYE Packet Format

9.5.2.5 RTCP APP Messages

RTCP application-specific messages have the packet type 204 and are reserved for application-specific features. APP packets are for experimental use to develop new features and applications.

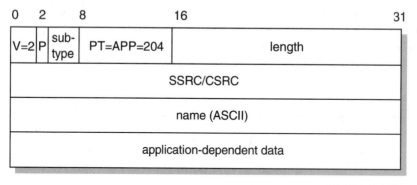

3376\3376F6SF

Figure 279. RTCP APP Packet Format

9.5.3 RTP Translators and Mixers

The RTP protocol supports the use of translators and mixers to modify the RTP packet stream. RTP translators are used to change the payload type in an RTP packet.

For example, three workstations connected to a high-speed network are used for a videoconference and exchange MPEG data with 1.5 Mbps. If another workstation that is connected only through a 1 Mbps route to the high-speed network wishes to participate on the videoconference, the problem appears that this bandwidth is insufficient for even one video stream. One solution for this problem is that the workstations change to another video format (maybe h.261 with 256 kbps). But lower bandwidth reduces the quality of the video.

The idea of RTP translation is that the RTP packets that contain the MPEG data from the workstations are converted to another format that needs less bandwidth. This means that the three 1.5 Mbps streams from the workstations are converted to three 256 kbps streams that can be transmitted through a 1 Mbps route. The three workstations connected to the high-speed network can use the high quality MPEG format for the communication among each other.

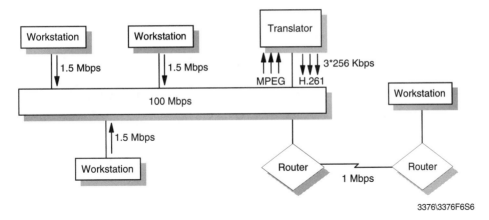

Figure 280. RTP Translator

The translated RTP packets are forwarded with their synchronization source identifier intact. Only the payload type is changed by the translator. Therefore, receivers of the RTP packets can still identify the different sources even though packets from all the sources pass through the translator and carry the same network source address. This means that a receiver can't detect the presence of a translator unless he or she knows which payload type or transport address was used by the original source.

With an RTP mixer, different RTP data streams can be mixed to one RTP stream. This makes sense only for audio transmissions. For example, there are three participants of an audio conference connected to a 1 Mbps medium. Each of them produces a PCM audio stream with 64 kbps. If another station wants to join the conference, a bandwidth of 192 Kbit/s is necessary to receive all senders. But if the joining station only has a connection with 64 kbps, an RTP mixer can merge the three sender streams to one stream with 64 kbps, and the new station can join the conference.

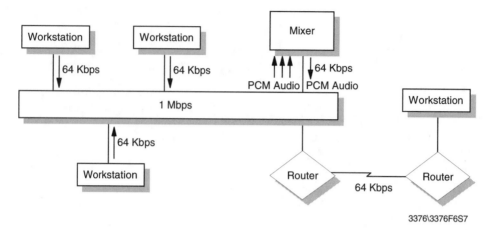

Figure 281. RTP Mixer

In the mixing process, it is not necessary to change the data format of the output stream. The payload type of the incoming and outgoing packets can be the same. But if in our example, the new user only has a 28kbps modem connection to the other conference members, the payload format of the outgoing stream can be changed to GSM audio which only needs 8-16 kbps. This example makes clear that mixing can only be used for audio transmissions. Video streams cannot be mixed to each other.

In a general description, an RTP mixer is an intermediate system that receives RTP packets from one or more (audio) sources, possibly changes the data format, combines the packets in some manner and then forwards a new RTP packet. Possibly, the timing of the different input sources will not generally be synchronized. Therefore, the mixer will adjust the timing of the different streams and generate a new timing for the combined stream. But this means that the mixer is the new synchronization source and the SSRC identifier of the new RTP packets will be marked with the mixer's own SSRC identifier. To preserve the identity of the original sources that contributed to the new mixed packets, the mixer must insert their SSRC identifiers into the CSRC identifier list.

9.5.4 Real-Time Applications

Most of the applications that use RTP are multimedia applications, such as videoconferencing systems or Internet phone software. As mentioned in 9.4.2, "MBONE Applications" on page 616 most of the MBONE tools use RTP to guarantee real-time delivery of multimedia data. The following list contains RTP multimedia applications that are available today:

BambaPhone

BambaPhone is a video phone for two-way, real-time communication over the Internet or any LAN using the TCP/IP protocol. BambaPhone automatically negotiates the compression technique appropriate to a connection bandwidth making videoconferencing possible over dial-up 28.8 kbps modem links and LAN-based connections to the Internet or an intranet. BambaPhone code conforms to H.323 multimedia conferencing recommendations for LANs and the Internet. However, the current implementation is not fully compliant with H.323 and will not interoperate with any other video phones. BambaPhone includes modular components for call setup, multimedia control, and video and audio support. The BambaPhone was written to the high-level APIs of these components.

BambaPhone will automatically detect the systems audio and video capabilities and adapt itself accordingly. The BambaPhone call control starts a session between two users. End-to-end call signaling is achieved through a reliable TCP/IP connection. A call is made using the destination IP address or host name. BambaPhone will ring when an incoming call arrives and allow the user to see who is calling from the IP address. The call will continue to ring until the user answers or the caller hangs up, exactly as a standard telephone operates. BambaPhone can also be put into automatic answer mode such that any incoming call is immediately answered and accepted.

BambaPhone is part of the Bamba suite of research technology demonstrations that includes Web browser plug-ins for audio and video streaming. Because of the experimental character, BambaPhone has not been released as a product. The experimental version of BambaPhone is available at

`http://www.alphaWorks.ibm.com/formula/BambaPhone`

Cu-SeeMe

CU-SeeMe is an Internet video chat software that supports video, audio, text and whiteboard communications. It uses RTP for real-time transmissions, but it doesn't use multicasting.

Intel Internet Video Phone

A video phone software that allows one-to-one video and audio connections through the Internet. The software uses RTP but doesn't support multicast connections.

IP/TV

IP/TV is a client/server video application from Precept Software that supports different high quality video and audio standards (MPEG, H.261

and Video for Windows). With fast network connections it is possible to provide video and audio in TV quality. IP/TV supports multicasting.

Rendez-Vous

Rendez-Vous is a videoconferencing tool developed by the French National Institute for Research in Computer Science and Control (INRIA). It supports RTP over multicast or unicast IP and different high-quality audio standards for videoconferences with multiple participants.

Free Phone

Free Phone is an Internet audio tool that is also developed at INRIA. It allows audio conferences with multiple participants. Free Phone uses special RTP payload types, GSM for example, to reduce the bandwidth for an Internet phone connection. Furthermore, it includes special redundancy mechanisms to allow reconstruction of lost packets which improves the audio quality especially during high packet loss situations. Free Phone is compatible with some of the MBONE tools like vat and rat.

9.6 Voice over IP

The possibility of running voice over IP networks is extremely attractive because IP technology is very low in cost and also that "bandwidth is free" on the Internet. This can reduce dramatically the costs for long distance phone calls. If the Internet can be used successfully for voice, then a range of interesting applications become possible. Some of these applications have been described in 9.5.4, "Real-Time Applications" on page 632. The disadvantage of these applications is, that they all use their own protocols and compression algorithms to transport the voice over IP networks. Therefore, most of today's Internet telephone programs are incompatible to each other. Additionally, a PC or a workstation is required to run the voice software.

To provide Voice over IP, or better yet Voice over Internet, to a larger group of people, it is necessary to define a standard for the protocols and the voice compression algorithms. Furthermore, constitutions are required to use a normal phone for Voice over IP connections instead of a computer.

A standard that realizes this feature is currently being developed by the Voice over IP Forum which consists of members from different telecommunications companies.

The VoIP forum operates as a working group in the International Multimedia Teleconferencing Consortium. They have published the *VoIP Forum Service Interoperability Implementation Agreement* (the VoIP IA), which seeks to complete, and extend existing standards into a specification to provide a complete Internet telephony interoperability protocol. The VoIP forum came into being to define a framework within which existing standards could be used in a way that enabled equipment made by different manufacturers to interoperate. The VoIP IA includes specifications for Internet telephony client software and the gateways to the public telephone network.

The basic standard recommended by the VoIP Forum is the International Telecommunication Union (ITU) standard H.323. It is a standard for multimedia communication over packet networks that references many other standards including definitions for the transport of voice, data and video as well as establishing standards for audio and video compression and decompression. The Forum Interoperability Implementation Agreement is:

1. A clarification (and interpretation) of the H.323 series of recommendations.

2. A specification as to how H.323 should be used.

3. An extension of H.323 to cover areas (such as Directory Services) that are absent from the standard.

The key elements of the VoIP IA are:

1. H.323 is used for call establishment and capability negotiation.

2. Call signaling between service elements is performed using ITU-T recommendation Q.931 (part of H.323). Each service element provides the necessary conversion from its local endpoint signaling to the H.323/Q.931 backbone protocol.

3. Other telephony specific requirements such as the transfer and reproduction of DTMF data have been added to provide a high level of connectivity with the traditional telephone infrastructure.

4. Directory services are not covered in the base H.323 recommendation. The VoIP IA defines dynamic IP address resolution mechanisms via H.323 RAS.

The main goal of the VoIP IA is to help ensure interoperability between equipment from different vendors. In order to achieve this, the VoIP Forum has specified strict conformance requirements. Currently, the VoIP IA includes support for two-party voice and similar audio communications over IP networks in a manner similar and compatible (via gateways) with existing *Public Switched Telephone Network (PSTN)* telephone calls. However, it is expected that the IA will be extended to include multipoint communications in the future. Such multipoint function would be added in such a way that conforming networks were backward-compatible with the existing VoIP IA. Compatibility with existing (non-IP) multipoint circuit mode conferencing standards is also considered highly desirable.

Whenever possible the VoIP IA uses existing IETF and ITU-T protocols and services. Interworking between the VoIP connections and the PSTN is provided through the use of H.323 gateways.

9.6.1 ITU-T Recommendation H.323

H.323 is an ITU-T standard for multimedia videoconferencing on packet-switched networks. Its formal title is *Visual Telephone Systems and Equipment for Local Area Networks Which Provide a Non-Guaranteed Quality of Service*. Since voice is one part of multimedia the standard covers most of the things you have to do to handle voice in:

- LANs

- Corporate intranets

- The Internet

H.323 has been developed very rapidly, much more rapidly than has been customary in the past. Work commenced in the ITU-T in May 1995 and was completed by June of 1996. In January 1998, Version 2 of H.323 with added function will be under development.

The components of an H.323 network are:

- Terminals

- Gateways

- Gatekeepers

- Multipoint Control Units (MCUs). An MCU consists of a Multipoint Controller (MC) and a Multipoint Processor (MP)

Figure 282 on page 637 shows a possible VoIP configuration realized using the H.323 standard. The IP network is connected to public telephone networks through an H.323 to PSTN gateway. Therefore, users of the IP network that have an H.323 terminal (PC with LAN or modem access) can communicate with standard phones in a PSTN. Also two users of standard telephones can use the IP network for communications.

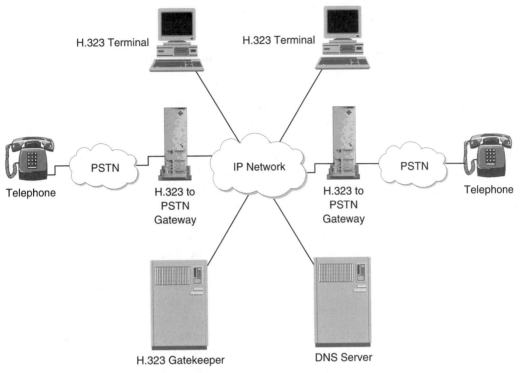

Figure 282. *Voice over IP Network Elements*

This example configuration shows that is is not necessary to use H.323 native mode terminals to use H.323. It is perfectly possible to use regular telephones and similar devices connected through gateways. The H.323 terminal specification is *not* a specification for a particular terminal type. Instead it specifies the protocols necessary to support multimedia terminal function. That is, it doesn't prescribe the design or functions of any particular device. It specifies protocols needed to support certain kinds of functions and leaves the physical realization and structure of these to the equipment designer.

There are two versions of the H.323 terminal specification which are intended for use in two different environments:

- Corporate network terminal

  This is envisaged as a high-quality, high-function device which may perform multiway videoconferencing or just point-to-point voice connection.

- Internet terminal

In this the specification is optimized to use the minimum bandwidth.

H.323 terminals have built-in multipoint capability for ad-hoc conferences and a multicast feature which allows 3-4 people in a call without centralized mixing or switching.

H.323 gateways provide interoperability between IP-connected H.323 terminals and other audio devices (such as regular telephones), either directly connected to the gateway or connected through a network that is not IP. These could be multimedia devices such as H.320 videoconference terminals or ordinary telephones connected through the public telephone network. The functions performed by the gateway include the mapping of the call signaling protocols, the control protocols and media mapping (multiplexing, rate matching and audio transcoding).

The H.323 gatekeeper provides the functions of directory server and system supervisor. The network of H.323 terminals and gateways under the control of a particular gatekeeper forms an integrated sub-network within the wider TCP/IP network environment. The gatekeeper's detailed functions are as follows:

- Directory Server (Address Translation) Function

  This function translates an H.323 alias address to an IP (transport) address using information obtained at terminal registration. This allows the user to have meaningful, unchanging names with which to refer to other users in the system. These names are arbitrary. You can use addresses similar to those used in TCP/IP e-mail systems. Alternatively you can use "phone number like" names or another completely different system.

- Supervisory Functions (for example, Call Admission Control)

  The gatekeeper can grant or deny permission to make the call. In doing this it can apply bandwidth limits to manage the network traffic and so prevent congestion occurring. This function is particularly relevant in a LAN environment.

  The gatekeeper also manages gateways and provides necessary address translation between external addresses and IP addresses by which external resources are known within the H.323 network.

- Call Signaling

  The gatekeeper may route calls in order to provide supplementary services or to provide Multipoint Controller functionality for calls with a large number of parties.

- Call Management

Because the gatekeeper controls network access it is also the logical place to perform call accounting and management.

The Multipoint Controller and Multipoint Processor form the Multipoint Control Unit (MCU). This H.323 component provides conference management, media processing and the multipoint conference model. The MCU supports media distribution for unicast and multicast data.

9.6.2 Voice Compression (G.723.1 and G.729)

The ITU recommendations G.723.1, G.729 and G.729A specify the operation of Codecs in low-quality networking environments similar to that found in the current public Internet.

G.723.1 offers a relatively high degree of compression with an output bit rate of either 5.3 or 6.4 kbps. Using a data length in the packet of 20 or 24 bytes this means that each packet carries 30 ms of the real-time voice signal.

The coder typically causes a one-way processing delay of 30 ms, a lookahead delay (to the next packet) of 7.5 ms and of course the packet assembly time of 30 ms (because 30 ms of voice is carried in a single packet). This imposes a one-way delay at each end of the connection of 67.5 ms, that is, 135 ms end-to-end one-way.

G.729 comes in two flavors: G.729 and G.729A. The key difference is in the amount of processing required to implement the algorithm. In both cases the compressed bit rate is 8 kbps and the amount of real-time voice encoded is 10 ms. This gives a data packet size of 10 bytes.

The algorithm used is called Conjugate Structured Algebraic Code Excited Linear Predictive (CS-ACELP). As input, CS-ACELP takes 80 samples of standard or linear PCM (64 kbps Pulse Code Modulation). This algorithm was designed for implementation by advanced Fixed Point Digital Signal Processors (DSPs) and is noted for delivering an exceptionally high level of voice quality with minimal delay.

In terms of delay both of these protocols are the same, requiring 10 ms for packet assembly, 10 ms for processing and 5 ms for lookahead. This means a 50 ms end-to-end delay due to the Codecs.

GSM The Group Special Mobile (GSM) audio compression is an algorithm originally defined for use with digital mobile telephones. It is a European standard not one of the ITU set. GSM is an allowed alternative for VoIP. A frame of 160 samples (each sample consists of 16 bits signed word) is used which is then compressed it into a smaller frame of 260 bits. These 260 bits are made up of different variables, each variable requiring a different number of bits. The VoIP forum selected the use of the RTP basic packaging type which enables the packaging of even or odd number of GSM frames within a single packet of RTP.

G.729 speech frames can be made into packets consuming approximately 9 kbps on a private leased line and 10.6 kbps on a frame relay link, including overhead. If silence suppression is used, the bandwidth required is reduced to an average of approximately 4 kbps.

It seems obvious that it is not very efficient to add a TCP/IP header to a packet that has a data payload of only 10 bytes. Thus G.723.1 is much more efficient in use of bandwidth than G.729 but G.729 has a significantly lower delays.

9.6.3 The VoIP Protocol Stack

The VoIP IA consists of a number of protocols interworking with one another to perform the overall function. These protocols operate in a hierarchical fashion and may be represented as a stack in the same way as most other communications systems are described. The VoIP protocol stack is shown in Figure 283.

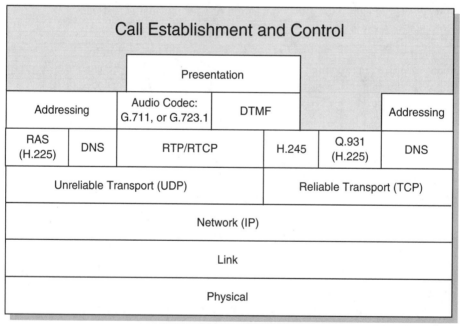

3376a\3376F6SJ

Figure 283. The VoIP Protocol Stack

Each protocol is defined according to what its purpose is, and what relevant standard (or draft) defines it. The VoIP stack is very similar to the H.323 stack. However, there are several additional functions that are not present in H.323.

Call Establishment and Control The call establishment and control protocols determine the sequence and timing of:

1. Call establishment

2. Call disconnection

3. Control of the H.323 session after it is established

Presentation The presentation function interprets the syntax of all transferred audio and "in-band" control information such as dual tone multiple frequency (DTMF) dialing signals.

Addressing Because IP networks are dynamic addressing environments, it can happen that the IP address that identified an H.323 terminal in a past telephone connection is different from the IP address in a later connection. Even if addresses were stable, it would be a big problem for every end user to know every IP address that was needed. Therefore, a very dynamic "telephone book" is needed to allow the end user to look up the IP address of an H.323 terminal dynamically.

In fact there are two methods available for constructing such a "telephone book". The first method is a protocol called RAS which allows H.323 endpoints to locate other H.323 endpoints via an H.323 gatekeeper. Alternatively an H.323 endpoint can be allowed to initially locate an H.323 gatekeeper via DNS.

RAS Registration, Admission, Status (RAS) is a protocol that specifies how H.323 entities can access gatekeepers to realize address translation.

Audio Codec Audio Coder/Decoder (Codec) are used to convert analog audio to/from digital signals. Please see 9.6.2, "Voice Compression (G.723.1 and G.729)" on page 639 for the audio codecs used in the VoIP specifications.

H.245 In general, H.245 defines a control protocol for multimedia communications. In the VoIP stack H.245 specifies how the channels inside of telephone calls are established and controlled. It also includes methods for sending and receiving DTMF dial tones.

H.225.0 H.225.0 is entitled *Media Stream Packetisation and Synchronization on Non-Guaranteed Quality of Service LANs*.

It defines the method of how audio packets, control packets and DTMF dial information are transmitted over IP networks.

Q.931 Q.931 is a signaling protocol that is used to set up, tear down, and control H.323 communication sessions. The protocol originated as the signaling specification for ISDN. The way in which it is used in VoIP is defined in H.225.0.

RTP/RTCP RTP/RTCP and the G.723.1 RTP audio packetisation was originally standardized by the IETF. Please see 9.5, "The Real-Time Protocols RTP and RTCP" on page 616 for a detailed description of the RTP protocol. RTP is a real-time protocol that is used in VoIP control and monitors the packet delivery. The G.723.1 RTP audio packetisation defines how the G.723.1 audio frames are transmitted in the RTP payload.

On the transport layer, VoIP uses UDP for RAS, DNS and RTP/RTCP and TCP for H.245, Q.931 and sometimes for DNS.

9.7 References

The following RFCs contain more information on IP multicasting:

- *RFC 1075 — Distance Vector Multicast Routing Protocol*
- *RFC 1112 — Host Extensions for IP Multicasting*
- *RFC 1584 — Multicast Extensions to OSPF*
- *RFC 1700 — Assigned Numbers*
- *RFC 1889 — RTP: A Transport Protocol for Real-Time Applications*
- *RFC 1890 — RTP Profile for Audio and Videoconferences with Minimal Control*
- *RFC 2029 — RTP Payload Format of Sun's CellB Video Encoding*
- *RFC 2032 — RTP Payload Format for H.261 Video Streams*
- *RFC 2035 — RTP Payload Format for JPEG-Compressed Video*
- *RFC 2190 — RTP Payload Format for H.263 Video Streams*
- *RFC 2198 — RTP Payload for Redundant Audio Data*
- *RFC 2250 — RTP Payload Format for MPEG1/MPEG2 Video*
- *RFC 2343 — RTP Payload Format for Bundled MPEG*
- *RFC 2362 — Protocol-Independent Multicast-Sparse Mode (PIM-SM): Protocol Specification*

Chapter 10. Quality of Service

This chapter discusses the topic of traffic priority, or quality of service, QoS. It explains why QoS may be desireable in an intranet as well as in the Internet, and it presents two approaches to implement QoS in TCP/IP networks:

- Integrated Services
- Differentiated Services

10.1 Why QoS?

In the Internet and intranets of today, bandwidth is an important subject. More and more people are using the Internet for private and business reasons. The amount of data that must be transmitted through the Internet increases exponential. New applications such as RealAudio, RealVideo, Internet Phone software and videoconferencing systems need a lot more bandwidth than the applications that were used in the early years of the Internet. Whereas traditional Internet applications, such as WWW, FTP or telnet, cannot tolerate packet loss but are less sensitive to variable delays, most real-time applications show just the opposite behavior, meaning they can compensate for a reasonable amount of packet loss but are usually very critical towards high variable delays.

This means that without any bandwidth control, the quality of these real-time streams depends on the bandwidth that is just available. Low bandwidth, or better unstable bandwidth, causes bad quality in real-time transmissions, for instance dropouts and hangs. Even the quality of a transmission using the real-time protocol RTP depends on the utilization of the underlying IP delivery service.

Therefore, new concepts are necessary to guarantee a specific Quality of Service (QoS) for real-time applications in the Internet. A QoS can be described as a set of parameters that describe the quality (for example, bandwidth, buffer usage, priority, CPU usage, etc.) of a specific stream of data. The basic IP protocol stack provides only one QoS which is called *best-effort*. The packets are transmitted from point to point without any guarantee for a special bandwidth or minimum time delay. With the best-effort traffic model, Internet requests are handled with the *first come, first serve* strategy. This means that all requests have the same priority and are handled one after the other. There is no possibility to make bandwidth reservations for specific connections or to raise the priority for special request. Therefore, new strategies were developed to provide predictable services for the Internet.

Today, there are two main rudiments to bring QoS to the Internet:

- Integrated Services
- Differentiated Services

Integrated Services bring enhancements to the IP Network Model to support real-time transmissions and guaranteed bandwidth for specific flows. In this case, we define a *flow* as a distinguishable stream of related datagrams from a unique sender to a unique receiver that results from a single user activity and requires the same QoS.

For example, a flow might consist of one video stream between a given host pair. To establish the video connection in both directions, two flows are necessary. Each application that initiates data flows can specify which QoS are required for this flow. If the videoconferencing tool needs a minimum bandwidth of 128 kbps and a minimum packet delay of 100 ms to assure a continuous video display, such a QoSs can be reserved for this connection.

Differentiated Services mechanism do not use per-flow signaling. Different service levels can be allocated to different groups of Internet users, which means that the whole traffic is split into groups with different QoS parameters. This reduces the maintenance overhead in comparison to Integrated Services. The following sections describe Integrated Services and Differentiated Services in more detail.

10.2 Integrated Services

The Integrated Services (IS) model was defined by an IETF working group to be the keystone of the planned IS Internet. This Internet architecture model includes the currently used best-effort service and a new real-time service that provides functions to reserve bandwidth on the Internet.

IS was developed to optimize network and resource utilization for new applications, such as real-time multimedia, which requires QoS guarantees. Because of routing delays and congestion losses, real-time applications do not work very well on the current best-effort Internet. Videoconferencing, video broadcast and audio conferencing software needs a guaranteed bandwidth to provide video and audio in acceptable quality. Integrated Services makes it possible to divide the Internet traffic into the standard best-effort traffic for traditional uses and application data flows with guaranteed QoS.

To support the Integrated Services model, an Internet router must be able to provide an appropriate QoS for each flow, in accordance with the service model. The router function that provides different qualities of service is called *traffic control*. It consists of the following components:

Packet scheduler

The packet scheduler manages the forwarding of different packet streams in hosts and routers, based on their service class, using queue management and various scheduling algorithms. The packet scheduler must ensure that the packet delivery corresponds to the QoS parameter for each flow. A scheduler can also police or shape the traffic to conform to a certain level of service. The packet scheduler must be implemented at the point where packets are queued. This is typically the output driver level of an operating system and corresponds to the link layer protocol.

Packet classifier

The packet classifier identifies packets of an IP flow in hosts and routers that will receive a certain level of service. To realize effective traffic control, each incoming packet is mapped by the classifier into a specific class. All packets that are classified in the same class get the same treatment from the packet scheduler. The choice of a class is based upon the source and destination IP address and port number in the existing packet header or an additional classification number which must be added to each packet. A class can correspond to a broad category of flows.

For example, all video flows from a videoconferencing with several participants can belong to one service class. But it is also possible that only one flow belongs to a specific service class.

Admission control

The admission control contains the decision algorithm that a router uses to determine if there are enough routing resources to accept the requested QoS for a new flow. If there are not enough free routing resources, accepting a new flow would impact earlier guarantees and the new flow must be rejected. If the new flow is accepted, the reservation instance in the router assigns the packet classifier and the packet scheduler to reserve the requested QoS for this flow. Admission control is invoked at each router along a reservation path, to make a local accept/reject decision at the time a host requests a real-time service. The admission control algorithm must be consistent with the service model.

Please note that admission control is sometimes confused with policy control, which is a packet-by-packet function, processed by the packet scheduler. It ensures that a host does not violate its promised traffic characteristics. Nevertheless, to ensure that QoS guarantees are honored, the admission control will be concerned with enforcing administrative policies on resource reservations. Some policies will be used to check the user authentification for a requested reservation. Unauthorized reservation requests can be rejected. Admission control will play an important role in accounting costs for Internet resources in the future.

Figure 284 shows the operation of the Integrated Service model into a host and a router.

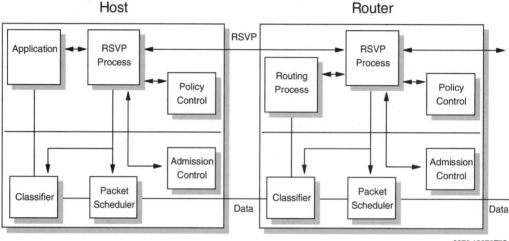

Figure 284. *Integrated Services Model*

Integrated Services use the Reservation Protocol (RSVP) for the signalling of the reservation messages. The IS instances communicate via RSVP to create and maintain flow-specific states in the endpoint hosts and in routers along the path of a flow. Please see 10.2.2, "The Reservation Protocol (RSVP)" on page 651 for a detailed description of the RSVP protocol.

As shown in Figure 284, the application that wants to send data packets in a reserved flow, communicates with the reservation instance RSVP. The RSVP protocol tries to set up a flow reservation with the requested QoS, which will be accepted if the application fulfilled the policy restrictions and the routers can handle the requested QoS. RSVP advises the packet classifier and packet scheduler in each node to process the packets for this flow adequately. If the application now delivers the data packets to the classifier in the first node, which has mapped this flow into a specific service class complying the requested QoS, the flow is recognized with the sender IP address and is transmitted to the packet scheduler. The packet scheduler forwards the packets, dependent on their service class, to the next router or, finally, to the receiving host.

Because RSVP is a simplex protocol, QoS reservations are only made in one direction, from the sending node to the receiving node. If the application in our example wants to cancel the reservation for the data flow, it sends a message to the reservation instance which frees the reserved QoS resources in all routers along the path, and the resources can be used for other flows. The IS specifications are defined in RFC 1633.

10.2.1 Service Classes

The Integrated Services model uses different classes of service that are defined by the integrated services IETF working group. Depending on the application, those service classes provide tighter or looser bounds on QoS controls. The current IS model includes the *Guaranteed Service* which is defined in RFC 2212 and the *Controlled Load Service* which is defined in RFC 2211. To understand these service classes, some terms need to be explained.

Because the IS model provides per-flow reservations, each flow has assigned a flow descriptor. The flow descriptor defines the traffic and QoS characteristics for a specific flow of data packets. In the IS specifications, the flow descriptor consist of a filter specification (filterspec) and a flow specification (flowspec).

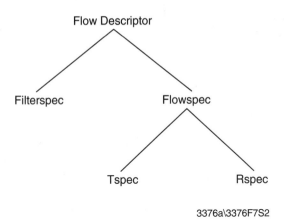

Figure 285. Flow Descriptor

The filterspec is used to identify the packets that belong to a specific flow with the sender IP address and source port. The information from the filterspec is used in the packet classifier. The flowspec contains a set of parameters that are called the *invocation information*. It is possible to assort the invocation information in two groups:

- Traffic Specification (Tspec)
- Servive Request Specification (Rspec)

The Tspec describes the traffic characteristics of the requested service. In the IS model, this Tspec is represented with a *token bucket filter*. This principle defines a data-flow control mechanism that adds characters (token) in periodical time intervals into a buffer (bucket) and allows a data packet to leave the sender only if there are at least as many tokens in the bucket as the packet length of the data packet. This strategy allows a precise control of the time interval between two data packets on the network. The token bucket system is specified by two parameters: the *token rate r*, which represents the rate at which tokens are placed into the bucket and the *bucket capacity* b. Both r and b must be positive.

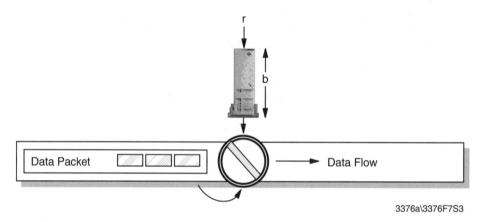

3376a\3376F7S3

Figure 286. *Token Bucket Filter*

The parameter r specifies the long term data rate and is measured in bytes of IP datagrams per second. The value of this parameter can range from 1 byte per second to 40 terabytes per second. The parameter b specifies the burst data rate allowed by the system and is measured in bytes. The value of this parameter can range from 1 byte to 250 gigabytes. The range of values allowed for these parameters is intentionally large to be prepared for future network technologies. The network elements are not expected to support the full range of the values. Traffic that passes the token bucket filter must obey the rule that over all time periods T, the amount of data sent does not exceed rT+b, where r and b are the token bucket parameters.

Two other token bucket parameters are also part of the Tspec. The *minimum policed unit* m and the *maximum packet size* M. The parameter m specifies the minimum IP datagram size in bytes. Smaller packets are counted against the token bucket filter as being of size m. The parameter M specifies the maximum packet size in bytes that conforms to the Tspec. Network elements must reject a service request if the requested maximum packet size is larger than the MTU size of the link. Summarizing, the token bucket filter is a policing function that isolates the packets that conform to the traffic specifications from the ones that do not conform.

The Service Request Specification (Rspec) specifies the Quality of Service the application wants to request for a specific flow. This information depends on the type of service and the needs of the QoS requesting application. It may consist of a specific bandwidth, a maximum packet delay or a maximum packet loss rate. In the IS implementation, the information from Tspec and Rspec is used in the packet scheduler.

10.2.1.1 Controlled Load Service

The Controlled Load Service is intended to support the class of applications that are highly sensitive to overloaded conditions in the Internet, such as real-time applications. These applications are working well on unloaded networks but degrade quickly under overloaded conditions. If an application uses the Controlled Load Service, the performance of a specific data flow does not degrade if the network load increases.

The Controlled Load Service offers only one service level which is intentionally minimal. There are no optional features or capabilities in the specification. The service offers only a single function. It approximates best-effort service over lightly loaded networks. This means that applications that make QoS reservations using Controlled Load Services are provided with service closely equivalent to the service provided to uncontrolled (best-effort) traffic under lightly loaded conditions. In this context, *lightly loaded conditions* means that a very high percentage of transmitted packets will be successfully delivered to the destination, and the transit delay for a very high percentage of the delivered packets will not greatly exceed the minimum transit delay.

Each router in a network that accepts requests for Controlled Load Services must ensure that adequate bandwidth and packet processing resources are available to handle QoS reservation requests. This can be realized with active admission control. Before a router accepts a new QoS reservation, represented by the Tspec, it must consider all important resources, such as link bandwidth, router or switch port buffer space and computational capacity of the packet forwarding.

The Controlled Load Service class does not accept or make use of specific target values for control parameters such as bandwidth, delay or loss. Applications that use Controlled Load Services must be proof against small amounts of packet loss and packet delays.

QoS reservations using Controlled Load Services need to provide a Tspec that consists of the token bucket parameters r and b as well as the minimum policed unit m and the maximum packet size M. An Rspec is not necessary because Controlled Load Services doesn't provide functions to reserve a fixed bandwidth or guarantee minimum packet delays. Controlled Load Service provides QoS control only for traffic that conforms to the Tspec that was provided at setup time. This means that the service guarantees only apply for packets that respect the token bucket rule that over all time periods T, the amount of data sent can not exceed rT+b.

Controlled Load Service is designed for applications that can tolerate reasonable amount of packet loss and delay, such as audio and videoconferencing software.

10.2.1.2 Guaranteed Service

The Guaranteed Service model provides functions that assure that datagrams will arrive within a guaranteed delivery time. This means that every packet of a flow that conforms to the traffic specifications will arrive at least at the maximum delay time that is specified in the flow descriptor. Guaranteed Service is used for applications that need a guarantee that a datagram will arrive at the receiver not later than a certain time after it was transmitted by its source.

For example, real-time multimedia applications, such as video and audio broadcasting systems that use streaming technologies, cannot use datagrams that arrive after their proper play-back time. Applications that have hard real-time requirements, such as real-time distribution of financial data (share prices), will also require guaranteed service. Guaranteed Service does not minimize the jitter (the difference between the minimal and maximal datagram delays), but it controls the maximum queueing delay.

The Guaranteed Service model represents the extreme end of delay control for networks. Other service models providing delay control have much weaker delay restrictions. Therefore, Guaranteed Service is only useful if it is provided by every router along the reservation path.

Guaranteed Service gives applications considerable control over their delay. It is important to understand that the delay in an IP network has two parts: a fixed transmission delay and a variable queueing delay. The fixed delay depends on the chosen path, which is determined not by guaranteed service but by the setup mechanism. All data packets in an IP network have a minimum delay that is limited by the speed of light and the turnaround time of the data packets in all routers on the routing path. The queueing delay is determined by Guaranteed Service and it is controlled by two parameters: the token bucket (in particular, the bucket size b) and the bandwidth R that is requested for the reservation. These parameters are used to construct the *fluid model* for the end-to-end behavior of a flow that uses Guaranteed Services.

The fluid model specifies the service that would be provided by a dedicated link between sender and receiver that provides the bandwidth R. In the fluid model, the flow's service is completely independent from the service for other flows. The definition of guaranteed service relies on the result that the fluid delay of a flow obeying a token bucket (r,b) and being served by a line with bandwidth R is bounded by b/R as long as R is not less than r. Guaranteed Service approximates this behavior with the service rate R, where now R is a share of bandwidth through the routing path and not the bandwidth of a dedicated line.

In the Guaranteed Service model, Tspec and Rspec are used to set up a flow reservation. The Tspec is represented by the token bucket parameters. The Rspec contains the parameter R that specifies the bandwidth for the flow reservation. The Guaranteed Service model is defined in RFC 2212.

10.2.2 The Reservation Protocol (RSVP)

The Integrated Services model uses the Reservation Protocol (RSVP) to set up and control QoS reservations. RSVP is defined in RFC 2205 and has the status of a proposed standard. Because RSVP is an Internet control protocol and not a routing protocol, it requires an existing routing protocol to operate. The RSVP protocol runs on top of IP and UDP and must be implemented in all routers on the reservation path. The key concepts of RSVP are flows and reservations.

An RSVP reservation applies for a specific flow of data packets on a specific path through the routers. As described in 10.1, "Why QoS?" on page 643, a flow is defined as a distinguishable stream of related datagrams from a unique sender to a unique receiver. If the receiver is a multicast address, a flow can reach multiple receivers. RSVP provides the same service for unicast and multicast flows. Each flow is identified from RSVP by its destination IP address and destination port. All flows have dedicated a flow descriptor which contains the QoS that a specific flow requires. The RSVP protocol does not understand the contents of the flow descriptor. It is carried as an opaque object by RSVP and is delivered to the router's traffic control functions (packet classifier and scheduler) for processing.

Because RSVP is a simplex protocol, reservations are only done in one direction. For duplex connections, such as video and audio conferences where each sender is also a receiver, it is necessary to set up two RSVP sessions for each station.

The RSVP protocol is receiver-initiated. Using RSVP signalling messages, the sender provides a specific QoS to the receiver which sends an RSVP reservation message back with the QoS that should be reserved for the flow from the sender to the receiver. This behavior considers the different QoS requirements for heterogeneous receivers in large multicast groups. The sender doesn't need to know the characteristics of all possible receivers to structure the reservations.

To establish a reservation with RSVP the receivers send reservation requests to the senders depending on their system capabilities. For example, a fast workstation and a slow PC want to receive a high-quality MPEG video stream with 30 frames per second which has a data rate of 1.5 Mbps. The workstation has enough CPU performance to decode the video stream, but the PC can only decode 10 frames per second. If the video server sends the messages to the two receivers that it can provide the 1.5 Mbps video stream, the workstation can return a reservation request for the full 1.5 Mbps. But the PC doesn't need the full bandwidth for its flow because it cannot decode all frames. So the PC may send a reservation request for a flow with 10 frames per second and 500 kbps.

10.2.2.1 RSVP Operation

A basic part of a resource reservation is the path. The path is the way of a packet flow through the different routers from the sender to the receiver. All packets that belong to a specific flow will use the same path. The path gets determined if a sender generates RSVP path messages that travel in the same direction as the flow. Each sender host periodically sends a path message for each data flow it originates. The path message contains traffic information that describes the QoS for a specific flow. Because RSVP doesn't handle routing by itself, it uses the information from the routing tables in each router to forward the RSVP messages.

If the path message reaches the first RSVP router, the router stores the IP address from the *last hop* field in the message, which is the address of the sender. Then the router inserts its own IP address into the last hop field, sends the path message to the next router and the process repeats until the message has reached the receiver. At the end of this process, each router will know the address from the previous router and the path can be accessed backwards. Figure 287 on page 653 shows the process of the path definition.

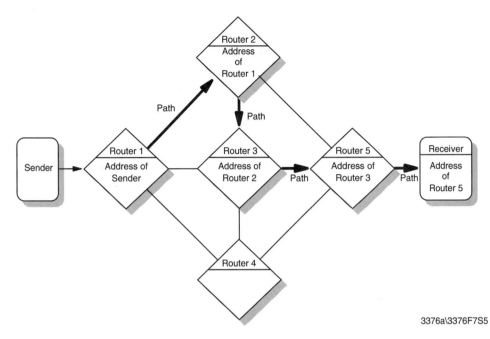

Figure 287. RSVP Path Definition Process

Routers that have received a path message are prepared to process resource reservations for a flow. All packets that belongs to this flow will take the same way through the routers; the way that was defined with the path messages.

The status in a system after sending the path messages is the following: All receivers know that a sender can provide a special QoS for a flow and all routers know about the possible resource reservation for this flow.

Now if a receiver wants to reserve QoS for this flow, it sends a reservation (resv) message. The reservation message contains the QoS requested from this receiver for a specific flow and is represented by the filterspec and flowspec that form the flow descriptor. The receiver sends the resv message to the last router in the path with the address it received from the path message. Because every RSVP-capable device knows the address of the previous device on the path, reservation messages travel the path in reverse direction towards the sender and establish the resource reservation in every router. Figure 288 on page 654 shows the flow of the reservation messages trough the routers.

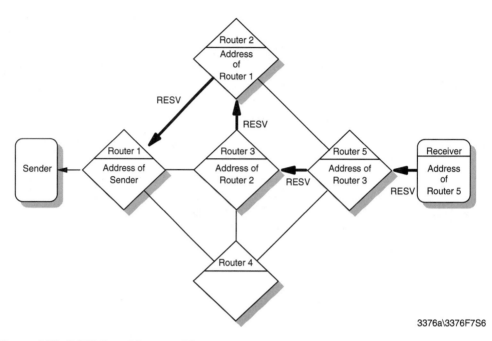

3376a\3376F7S6

Figure 288. *RSVP Resv Messages Flow*

At each node, a reservation request initiates two actions:

1. QoS reservation on this link

   The RSVP process passes the request to the admission control and policy control
   instance on the node. The admission control checks if the router has the necessary
   resources to establish the new QoS reservation and the policy control checks if the
   application has the authorization to make QoS requests. If one of these tests fails,
   the reservation is rejected and the RSVP process returns a *ResvErr* error message
   to the appropriate receiver. If both checks succeed, the node uses the filterspec
   information in the resv message to set the packet classifier and the flowspec
   information to set the packet scheduler. After this, the packet classifier will
   recognize the packets that belong to this flow and the packet scheduler will obtain
   the desired QoS defined by the flowspec.

   Figure 289 on page 655 shows the reservation process in an RSVP router.

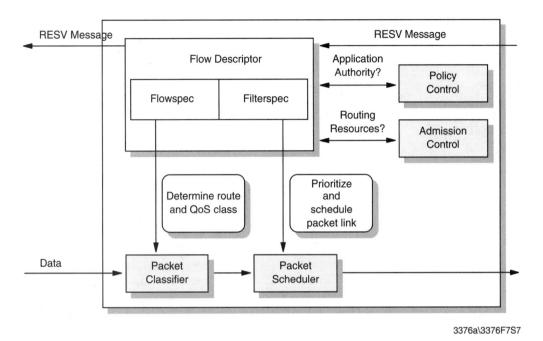

RESV Message   RESV Message

Flow Descriptor   Application
                                 Authority?   Policy
                                                       Control
Flowspec   Filterspec
                                 Routing
                                 Resources?   Admission
                                                       Control

Determine route   Prioritize
and QoS class   and
                             schedule
                             packet link

Data   Packet   Packet
              Classifier   Scheduler

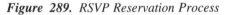

3376a\3376F7S7

Figure 289. RSVP Reservation Process

2. Forwarding of the reservation request

   After a successful admission and policy check, a reservation request is propagated upstream towards the sender. In a multicast environment, a receiver can get data from multiple senders. The set of sender hosts to which a given reservation request is propagated is called the *scope* of that request. The reservation request that is forwarded by a node after a successful reservation can differ from the request that was received from the previous hop downstream. One possible reason for this is that the traffic control mechanism may modify the flowspec hop-by-hop. Another, more important reason is that in a multicast environment, reservations from different downstream branches but for the same sender are *merged* together as they travel across the upstream path. This merging is necessary to conserve resources in the routers.

   A successful reservation request propagates upstream along the multicast tree until it reaches a point where an existing reservation is equal or greater than that being requested. At this point, the arriving request is merged with the reservation in place and need not be forwarded further.

   Figure 290 on page 656 shows the reservation merging for a multicast flow.

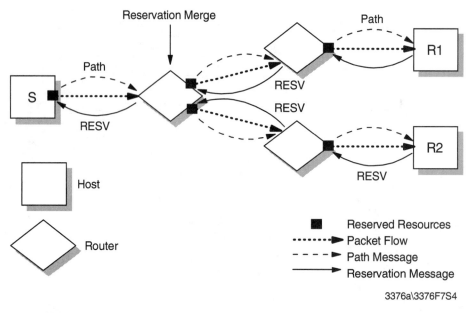

Figure 290. RSVP Reservation Merging for Multicast Flows

If the reservation request reaches the sender, the QoS reservation was established in every router on the path and the application can start to send packets downstream to the receivers. The packet classifier and the packet scheduler in each router make sure that the packets are forwarded according to the requested QoS.

This type of reservation is only reasonable if all routers on the path support RSVP. If only one router doesn't support resource reservation, the service cannot be guaranteed for the whole path because of the "best effort" restrictions that apply for normal routers. A router on the path that doesn't support RSVP would be a bottleneck for the flow.

A receiver that originates a reservation request can also request a confirmation message that indicates that the request was installed in the network. The receiver includes a confirmation request in the Resv message and gets a ResvConf message if the reservation was established successfully.

RSVP resource reservations maintain soft-state in routers and hosts, which means that a reservation is canceled if RSVP doesn't send refresh messages along the path for an existing reservation. This allows route changes without resulting in protocol overhead. Path messages must also be resent because the path state fields in the routers will be reset after a time-out period.

Path and reservation states can also be deleted with RSVP *teardown* messages. There are two types of teardown messages:

- PathTear messages

  PathTear messages travel downstream from the point of initiation to all receivers, deleting the path state as well as all dependent reservation states in each RSVP-capable device.

- ResvTear messages

  ResvTear messages travel upstream from the point of initiation to all senders, deleting reservation states in all routers and hosts.

Teardown request can be initiated by senders, receivers or routers that notice a state timeout. Because of the soft-state principle of RSVP reservations, it is not really necessary to explicitly tear down an old reservation. Nevertheless, it is recommended that all end hosts send a teardown request if a consisting reservation is no longer needed.

10.2.2.2 RSVP Reservation Styles

Users of multicast multimedia applications often receive flows from different senders. In the reservation process described in 10.2.2.1, "RSVP Operation" on page 652, a receiver must initiate a separate reservation request for each flow it wants to receive. But RSVP provides a more flexible way to reserve QoS for flows from different senders. A reservation request includes a set of options that are called the *reservation style*. One of these options deals with the treatment of reservations for different senders within the same session. The receiver can establish a *distinct* reservation for each sender or make a single *shared* reservation for all packets from the senders in one session.

Another option defines how the senders for a reservation request are selected. It is possible to specify an *explicit* list or a *wildcard* that selects the senders belonging to one session. In an explicit sender-selection reservation, a filterspec must identify exactly one sender. In a wildcard sender-selection the filterspec is not needed. Figure 291 on page 658 shows the reservation styles that are defined with this reservation option:

Sender Selection	**Distinct** Reservation	**Shared** Reservation
Explicit	Fixed-Filter (FF) Style	Shared-Explicit (SE)Style
Wildcard	(Not Defined)	Wildcard-Filter (WF) Style

3376A\3376F7S8

Figure 291. RSVP Reservation Styles

Wildcard-Filter (WF)

The Wildcard-Filter style uses the options shared reservation and wildcard sender selection. This reservation style establishes a single reservation for all senders in a session. Reservations from different senders are merged together along the path so that only the biggest reservation request reaches the senders.

A wildcard reservation is forwarded upstream to all sender hosts. If new senders appear in the session, for example, new members enter a videoconferencing, the reservation is extended to this new senders.

Fixed-Filter (FF)

The Fixed-Filter style uses the option's distinct reservations and explicit sender selection. This means that a distinct reservation is created for data packets from a particular sender. Packets from different senders that are in the the same session do not share reservations.

Shared-Explicit (SE)

The Shared-Explicit style uses the option's shared reservation and explicit sender selection. This means that a single reservation covers flows from a specified subset of senders. Therefore a sender list must be included into the reservation request from the receiver.

Reservations established in shared style (WF and SE) are mostly used for multicast applications. For this type of application, it is unlikely that several data sources transmits data simultaneously so that it is not necessary to reserve QoS for each sender.

For example, in an audio conference that consists of five participants, every station sends a data stream with 64 kbps. With a Fixed-Filter style reservation, all members of the conference must establish four separate 64 kbps reservations for the flows from the other senders. But in an audio conference most times only one or two people speak at the same time. Therefore it would be sufficient to reserve a bandwidth of 128 kbps for all senders, because most audio conferencing software uses silence suppression which means that if a person doesn't speak, no packets are sent. This can be realized if every receiver makes one shared reservation of 128 kbps for all senders.

Using the Shared-Explicit style, all receivers must explicitly identify all other senders in the conference. With Wildcard-Filter style the reservation counts for every sender that matches the reservation specifications. If, for example the audio conferencing tool sends the data packets to a special TCP/IP port, the receivers can make a Wildcard-Filter reservation for all packets with this destination port.

10.2.2.3 RSVP Messages Format

Basically an RSVP message consists of a common header, followed by a body consisting of a variable number of *objects*. The number and the content of these objects depends on the message type. The message objects contain the information that is necessary to realize resource reservations, for example the flow descriptor or the reservation style. In most cases, the order of the objects in an RSVP message makes no logical difference. RFC 2205 recommends that an RSVP implementation should use the object order defined in the RFC but accept the objects in any permissible order. Figure 292 shows the common header of a RSVP message:

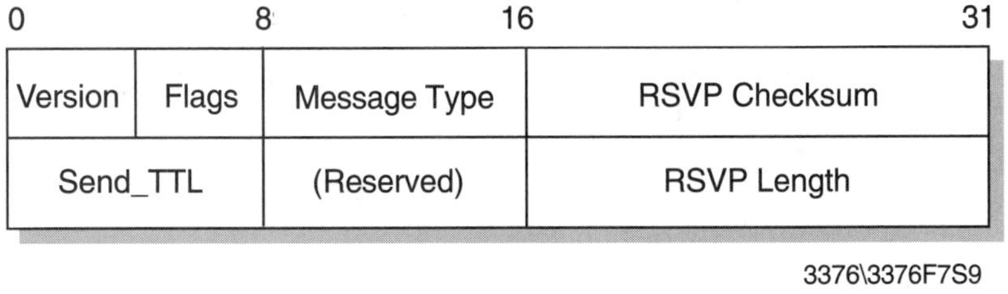

0	8	16	31
Version	Flags	Message Type	RSVP Checksum
Send_TTL		(Reserved)	RSVP Length

3376\3376F7S9

Figure 292. RSVP Common Header

Where:

Version

4-bit RSVP protocol number. The current version is 1.

Flags

4-bit field that is reserved for flags. No flags are defined yet.

Message Type

8-bit field that specifies the message type:

1. Path

2. Resv

3. PathErr

4. ResvErr

5. PathTear

6. ResvTear

7. ResvConf

RSVP Checksum

16-bit field. The Checksum can be used by receivers of an RSVP message to detect errors in the transmission of this message.

Send_TTL

8-bit field, which contains the IP TTL value the message was sent with.

RSVP Length

16-bit field that contains the total length of the RSVP message including the common header and all objects that follow. The length is counted in bytes.

The RSVP objects that follow the common header consist of a 32-bit header and one or more 32-bit words. Figure 293 shows the RSVP object header:

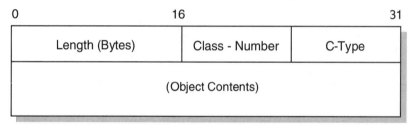

```
0                          16                        31
┌──────────────────────┬──────────────┬──────────────┐
│    Length (Bytes)    │ Class - Number │    C-Type    │
├──────────────────────┴──────────────┴──────────────┤
│                 (Object Contents)                   │
└─────────────────────────────────────────────────────┘
```

3376\3376F7SA

Figure 293. *RSVP Object Header*

Where:

Length

16-bit field that contains the object length in bytes. This must be a multiple of 4. The minimum length is 4 bytes.

Class-Number

Identifies the object class. The following classes are defined:

- Null

  The NULL object has a Class-Number of zero. The length of this object must be at least 4, but can be any multiple of 4. The NULL object can appear anywhere in the object sequence of an RSVP message. The content is ignored by the receiver.

- Session

  The session object contains the IP destination address, the IP protocol ID and the destination port, to define a specific session for the other objects that follow. The session object is required in every RSVP message.

- RSVP_HOP

  The RSVP_HOP object contains the IP address of the node that sent this message and a logical outgoing interface handle. For downstream messages (for example, path messages) the RSVP_HOP object represents a PHOP (previous hop) object and for upstream messages (for example, resv messages) it represents an NHOP (next hop) object.

- Time_Values

  The Time_Values object contains the refresh period for path and reservation messages. If these messages are not refreshed within the specified time period, the path or reservation state is canceled.

- Style

  The style object defines the reservation style and some style-specific information that is not in Flowspec or Fiterspec. The style object is required in every resv message.

- Flowspec

  This object specifies the required QoS in reservation messages.

- Filterspec

  The Filterspec object defines which data packets receive the QoS specified in the Flowspec.

- Sender_Template

  This object contains the sender IP address and additional demultiplexing information, which is used to identify a sender. The Sender_Template is required in every Path message.

- Sender_Tspec

  This object defines the traffic characteristics of a data flow from a sender. The Sender_Tspec is required in all path messages.

- Adspec

The adspec object is used to provide advertising information to the traffic control modules in the RSVP nodes along the path.

- Error_Spec

  This object specifies an error in a PathErr, ResvErr, or a confirmation in a ResvConf message.

- Policy_Data

  This object contains information that allows a policy module to decide whether an associated reservation is administratively permitted or not. It can be used in Path, Resv, PathErr, or ResvErr messages.

- Integrity

  The integrity object contains cryptographic data to authenticate the originating node and to verify the contents of an RSVP message.

- Scope

  The Scope object contains an explicit list of sender hosts to which the information in the message are sent. The object can appear in a Resv, ResvErr, or ResvTear messages.

- Resv_Confirm

  This object contains the IP address of a receiver that requests confirmation for its reservation. It can be used in a Resv or ResvConf message.

C-Type

The C-Type specifies the object type within the class number. Different object types are used for IPv4 and IPv6.

Object contents

The object content depend on the object type and has a maximum length of 65528 bytes.

All RSVP messages are built of a variable number of objects. The recommended object order for the most important RSVP messages, the path and the resv message are shown in the following. Figure 294 on page 663 gives an overview about the format of the RSVP path message. Objects that can appear in a path message but that are not required are parenthesized.

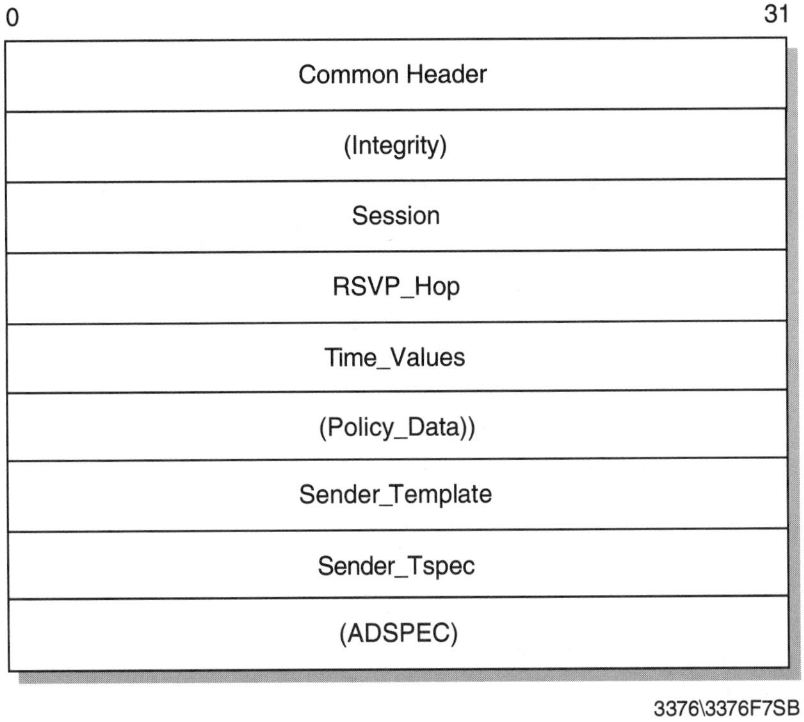

```
       0                                                        31
      ┌──────────────────────────────────────────────────────┐
      │                   Common Header                       │
      ├──────────────────────────────────────────────────────┤
      │                    (Integrity)                        │
      ├──────────────────────────────────────────────────────┤
      │                     Session                           │
      ├──────────────────────────────────────────────────────┤
      │                    RSVP_Hop                           │
      ├──────────────────────────────────────────────────────┤
      │                   Time_Values                         │
      ├──────────────────────────────────────────────────────┤
      │                  (Policy_Data))                       │
      ├──────────────────────────────────────────────────────┤
      │                 Sender_Template                       │
      ├──────────────────────────────────────────────────────┤
      │                  Sender_Tspec                         │
      ├──────────────────────────────────────────────────────┤
      │                    (ADSPEC)                           │
      └──────────────────────────────────────────────────────┘
```

3376\3376F7SB

Figure 294. RSVP Path Message Format

If the Integrity object is used in the path message, it must immediately follow the common header. The order of the other objects may differ in different RSVP implementations, but the one shown above is recommended by the RFC.

The RSVP Resv messages looks similar to the path message. Figure 295 on page 664 shows the objects used for reservation messages:

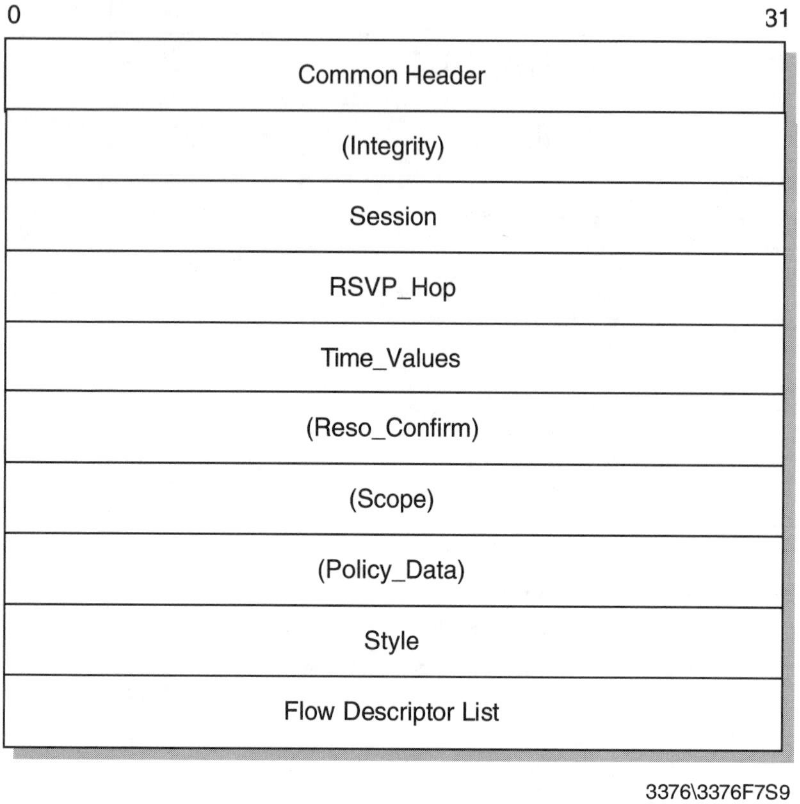

Common Header
(Integrity)
Session
RSVP_Hop
Time_Values
(Reso_Confirm)
(Scope)
(Policy_Data)
Style
Flow Descriptor List

3376\3376F7S9

Figure 295. *RSVP Resv Message Format*

As in the path message, the Integrity object must follow the common header if it is used. Another restriction applies for the Style object and the following flow descriptor list. They must occur at the end of the message. The order of the other objects follows the recommendation from the RFC.

For a detailed description of the RSVP message structure and the handling of the different reservation styles in reservation messages, please consult RFC 2205.

10.2.3 The Future of Integrated Services

At the moment it is not known if the integrated services model will win recognition in the future Internet. More and more router manufacturers support RSVP in their routers. But to provide IS for a larger group of users, many Internet routers should support RSVP.

An important point that should be monitored by the router manufacturers is the traffic control overhead in RSVP-capable routers that may decrease the routing performance. The more data flows are passing a router, the more RSVP sessions must be handled by the RSVP daemon inside of the router. Router manufacturers must make sure that in high traffic situations a router is not blocked with managing RSVP sessions instead of routing data packets and keeping up with routing table updates.

Future extensions of the policy control module may implement a priority mechanism that allows users to send reservation requests with higher priority than others. If the routers on the path run out of routing capacity, the high-priority requests will be favored. This may be coupled with a billing system that charges the user for high-priority reservation requests. If IS is supported in the Internet, it must be assured that the normal best-effort traffic is still served. It must not happen that some routers are blocked with RSVP reservations and can't handle any best-effort traffic. This may even be an economic policy decision for ISPs to make. A conceivable scenario is that one half of the routing capacity is used for RSVP flow reservations and the other half for the classic best-effort traffic.

It may be some time, if ever, that RSVP end-to-end services are deployed on the Internet. At the moment, IS is preferably used in corporate intranets to provide multimedia and other real-time data to the end users. For example, if all routers in an intranet support RSVP, a video transmission can be broadcasted, for informational or educational reasons, to all workstations in a company.

10.3 Differentiated Services

The Differentiated Services (DS) concept is currently under development at the IETF DS working group. The DS specifications are defined in some IETF Internet drafts and there is no RFC available yet. This paragraph gives an overview about the rudiments and ideas to provide service differentiation in the Internet. Because the concept is still under development, some of the specifications mentioned in this book may be changed in the final definition of differentiated services.

The goal of the DS development is to get a possibility to provide differentiated classes of service for Internet traffic, to support various types of applications, and specific business requirements. DS offers predictable performance (delay, thruput, packet loss, etc.) for a given load at a given time. The difference between Integrated Services, described in 10.2, "Integrated Services" on page 644, and Differentiated Services is, that DS provides scalable service discrimination in the Internet without the need for per-flow state and signaling at every hop. It is not necessary to perform a unique QoS reservation for each flow. With DS, the Internet traffic is split into different classes with different QoS requirements.

A central component of DS is the Service Level Agreement (SLA). The SLA is a service contract between a customer and a service provider that specifies the details of the traffic classifying and the corresponding forwarding service a customer should receive. A customer may be a user organization or another DS domain. The service provider must assure that the traffic of a customer, with whom it has an SLA, gets the contracted QoS. Therefore the service provider's network administration must set up the appropriate service policies and measure the network performance to guarantee the agreed traffic performance.

To distinguish the data packets from different customers in DS-capable network devices, the IP packets are modified in a specific field. A small bit-pattern, called the *DS byte*, in each IP packet is used to mark the packets that receive a particular forwarding treatment at each network node. The DS byte uses the space of the TOS octet in the IPv4 IP header 2.1.8.1, "IP Datagram Format" on page 62 and the traffic class octet in the IPv6 header. All network traffic inside of a domain receives a service that depends on the traffic class that is specified in the DS byte.

To provide SLA conform services, the following mechanisms must be combined in a network:

- Setting bits in the DS byte (TOS octet) at network edges and administrative boundaries.

- Using those bits to determine how packets are treated by the routers inside the network.

- Conditioning the marked packets at network boundaries in accordance with the QoS requirements of each service.

The currently defined DS architecture only provides service differentiation in one direction and is therefore asymmetric. Development of a complementary symmetric architecture is a topic of current research. The following paragraph describes the DS architecture in more detail.

10.3.1 Differentiated Services Architecture

Unlike Integrated Services, QoS guarantees with Differentiated Services are static and stay long-term in routers. This means that applications using DS don't need to set up QoS reservations for specific data packets. All traffic that passes DS-capable networks can receive a specific QoS. The data packets must be marked with the DS byte which is interpreted by the routers in the network.

10.3.1.1 The Per-Hop Behavior

As mentioned before, the IETF DS working group has proposed to redefine the structure of the IPv4 TOS byte and the IPv6 traffic class field and re-label this field as the DS byte. The DS byte specifications supersede the IPv4 TOS octet definitions of RFC 1349.Figure 296 shows the structure of the newly defined DS byte.

3376X\3376F7SG

Figure 296. DS Byte

Six bits of the DS field are used as a Differentiated Services CodePoint (DSCP) to select the traffic class a packet experiences at each node. A two-bit currently unused (CU) field is reserved and can be assigned later.

Each DS-capable network device must have information on how packets with different DS bytes should be handled. In the DS specifications this information is called the *Per-Hop Behavior (PHB)*. It is a description of the forwarding treatment a packet receives at a given network node. The DSCP value in the DS byte is used to select the PHB a packet experiences at each node. To provide predictable services, per-hop behaviors need to be available in all routers in a Differentiated Services-capable network. The PHB can be described as a set of parameters inside of a router that can be used to control how packets are scheduled onto an output interface. This can be a number of separate queues with settable priorities, parameters for queue lengths or drop algorithms and drop preference weights for packets.

DS requires routers that support queue scheduling and management to prioritize outbound packets and control the queue depth to minimize congestion on the network. The traditional FIFO queuing in common Internet routers provides no service differentiation and can lead to network performance problems. The packet treatment inside of a router depends on the router's capabilities and its particular configuration and it is selected by the DS byte in the IP packet. For example, if a IP packet reaches a router with eight different queues that all have different priorities, the DS byte can be used to select which queue is liable for the routing of this packet. The scale reaches from zero, for lowest priority to seven for highest priority.

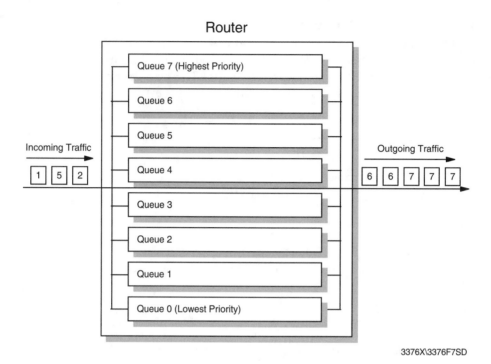

Figure 297. *DS Routing Example*

Another example is a router that has a single queue with multiple drop priorities for data packets. It uses the DS byte to select the drop preference for the packets in the queue. A value of zero means "it is most likely to drop this packet", and seven means "it is least likely to drop this packet". Another possible constellation are four queues with two levels of drop preference in each.

To make sure that the per-hop behaviors in each router are functionally equivalent, certain common PHBs must be defined in future DS specifications to avoid that the same DS byte value causes different forwarding behaviors in different routers of one DS domain. This means that in future DS specifications some unique PHB values must be defined that represent specific service classes. All routers in one DS domain must know which service a packet with a specific PHB should receive. The DiffServ Working Group will propose PHBs that should be used to provide differentiated services. Some of these proposed PHBs will be standardized, others may have widespread use and still others may remain experimental.

PHBs will be defined in groups. A PHB group is a a set of one or more PHBs that can only be specified and implemented simultaneously, because of queue servicing or queue management policies that apply to all PHBs in one group. A default PHB must be available in all DS-compliant nodes. It represents the standard best-effort forwarding behavior available in existing routers. When no other agreements are in place, it is assumed that packets belong to this service level. The IETF working group recommends to use the DSCP value 000000 in the DS byte to define the default PHB.

Another PHB that is proposed for standardization is the *Expedited Forwarding* (EF) PHB. It is a high priority behavior that is typically used for network control traffic such as routing updates. The value 101100 in the DSCP field of the DS byte is recommended for the EF PHB.

10.3.1.2 Differentiated Services Domains

The setup of QoS guarantees is not made for specific end-to-end connections but for well-defined Differentiated Services domains. The IETF working group defines a Differentiated Services domain as a contiguous portion of the Internet over which a consistent set of Differentiated Services policies are administered in a coordinated fashion. It can represent different administrative domains or autonomous systems, different trust regions, different network technologies, such as cell or frame-based techniques, hosts and routers. A DS domain consists of boundary components that are used to connect different DS domains to each other and interior components that are only used inside of the domains. Figure 298 shows the use of boundary and interior components for two DS domains.

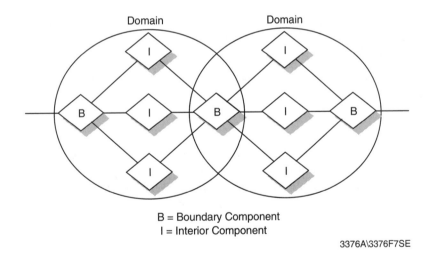

B = Boundary Component
I = Interior Component

3376A\3376F7SE

Figure 298. DS Domain

A DS domain normally consists of one or more networks under the same administration. This can be, for example, a corporate intranet or an Internet Service Provider (ISP). The administration of the DS domain is responsible for ensuring that adequate resources are provisioned and reserved to support the SLAs offered by the domain. Network administrators must use appropriate measurement techniques to monitor if the network resources in a DS domain are sufficient to satisfy all authorized QoS requests.

10.3.1.3 DS Boundary Nodes

All data packets that travel from one DS domain to another must pass a boundary node which can be a router, a host or a firewall. A DS boundary node that handles traffic leaving a DS domain is called an *egress node* and a boundary node that handles traffic entering a DS domain is called an *ingress node*. Normally, DS boundary nodes act both as ingress node and egress node depending on the traffic direction. The ingress node must make sure, that the packets entering a domain receives the same QoS as in the domain the packets traveled before. A DS egress node performs conditioning functions on traffic that is forwarded to a directly connected peering domain. The traffic conditioning is done inside of a boundary node by a *traffic conditioner*. It classifies, marks and possibly conditions packets that enter or leave the DS domain. A traffic conditioner consists of the following components:

Classifier

> A classifier selects packets based on their packet header and forwards the packets that match the classifier rules for further processing. The DS model specifies two types of packet classifiers:
>
> 1. Multi-field (MF) classifiers which can classify on the DS byte as well as on any other IP header field, for example the IP address and the port number like an RSVP classifier.
>
> 2. Behavior Aggregate (BA) classifiers which classify only on the bits in the DS byte.

Meter

> Traffic meters measure if the forwarding of the packets that are selected by the classifier correspond to the traffic profile that describes the QoS for the SLA between customer and service provider. A meter passes state information to other conditioning functions to trigger a particular action for each packet which either does or does not comply with the requested QoS requirements.

Marker

> DS markers set the DS byte of the incoming IP packets to a particular bit pattern. The PHB is set in the first 6 bits of the DS byte so that the marked packets are forwarded inside of the DS domain accordingly to the SLA between service provider and customer.

Shaper/Dropper

Packet shapers and droppers cause conformance to some configured traffic properties, for example a token bucket filter as described in 10.2.1, "Service Classes" on page 647. They use different methods to bring the stream into compliance with a traffic profile. Shapers delay some or all of the packets. A shaper usually has a finite-size buffer, and packets may be discarded if there is not sufficient buffer space to hold the delayed packets. Droppers discard some or all of the packets. This process is know as *policing* the stream. A dropper can be implemented as a special case of a shaper by setting the shaper buffer size to zero packets.

The traffic conditioner is mainly used in DS boundary components but it can also be implemented in an interior component. Figure 299 shows the cooperation of the traffic conditioner components.

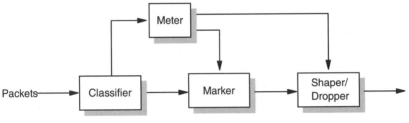

3376A\3376F7SH

Figure 299. DS Traffic Conditioner

The traffic conditioner in a boundary component makes sure that packets that transit the domain are correctly marked to select a PHB from one of the PHB groups supported within the domain. This is necessary because different DS domains can have different groups of PHBs, which means that the same entry in the DS byte can be interpreted variably in different domains.

For example, in the first domain a packet traverses, all routers have four queues with different queue priorities (0-3). Packets with a PHB value of three are routed with the highest priority. But in the next domain the packet travels through, all routers have eight different queues and all packets with the PHB value of seven are routed with the highest priority. The packet that was forwarded in the first domain with high priority has only medium priority in the second domain. This may violate the SLA contract between customer and service provider. Therefore, the traffic conditioner in the boundary router that connects the two domains, must assure that the PHB value is remarked from three to seven if the packet travels from the first to the second domain.

Figure 300 on page 672 shows an example for the remarking of data packets that travel trough two different domains.

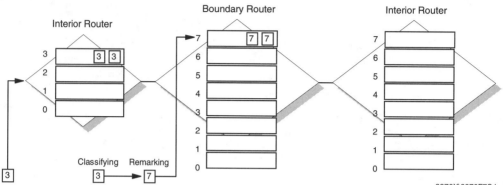

Figure 300. *Remarking of Data Packets*

If a data packet travels through multiple domains, the DS byte can be remarked at every boundary component to guarantee the QoS that was contracted in the SLA. The SLA contains the details of the *Traffic Conditioning Agreement (TCA)* that specifies classifier rules and temporal properties of a traffic stream. The TCA contains information how metering, marking, discarding and shaping of packets must be done in the traffic conditioner to fulfill the SLA. The TCA information must be available in all boundary components of a DS network to guarantee that packets passing different DS domains receives the same service in each domain.

10.3.1.4 DS Interior Components

The interior components inside of a DS domain select the forwarding behavior for packets based on their DS byte. The interior component is usually a router that contains a traffic prioritization algorithm. Because the value of the DS byte normally doesn't change inside of a DS domain, all interior routers must use the same traffic forwarding policies to comply with the QoS agreement. Data packets with different PHB values in the DS byte receive different QoSs according to the QoS definitions for this PHB. Because all interior routers in a domain use the same policy functions for incoming traffic, the traffic conditioning inside of an interior node is done only by a packet classifier. It selects packets based on their PHB value or other IP header fields and forwards the packets to the queue management and scheduling instance of the node. Figure 301 on page 673 shows the traffic conditioning in an interior node.

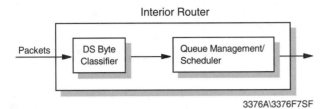

Figure 301. DS Interior Component

Traffic classifying and prioritized routing is done in every interior component of a DS domain. After a data packet has crossed a domain, it reaches the boundary router of the next domain and gets possibly remarked to cross this domain with the requested QoS.

10.3.1.5 Source Domains

The IETF DS working group defines a source domain as the domain that contains one or more nodes which originate the traffic that receives a particular service. Traffic sources and intermediate nodes within a source domain can perform traffic classification and conditioning functions. The traffic that is sent from a source domain may be marked by the traffic sources directly or by intermediate nodes before leaving the source domain.

In this context it is important to understand that the first PHB marking of the data packets is not done by the sending application itself. Applications do not notice the availability of Differentiated Services in a network. Therefore, applications using DS networks must not be rewritten to support DS. This is an important difference to Integrated Services, where most applications support the RSVP protocol directly whereby some code changes are necessary.

The first PHB marking of packets that are sent from an application can be done in the source host or the first router the packet passes. The packets are identified with their IP address and source port. For example, a customer has an SLA with a service provider that guarantees a higher priority for the packets sent by an audio application. The audio application sends the data packets through a specific port and can be recognized in multi-field classifiers. This classifier type recognizes the IP address and port number of a packet and can distinguish the packets from different applications. If the host contains a traffic conditioner with an MF classifier, the IP packet can be marked with the appropriate PHB value and consequently receives the QoSs that are requested by the customer. If the host doesn't contain a traffic conditioner, the initial marking of the packets is done by the first router in the source domain that supports traffic conditioning. Figure 302 on page 674 shows the initial marking of a packet inside of a host and a router.

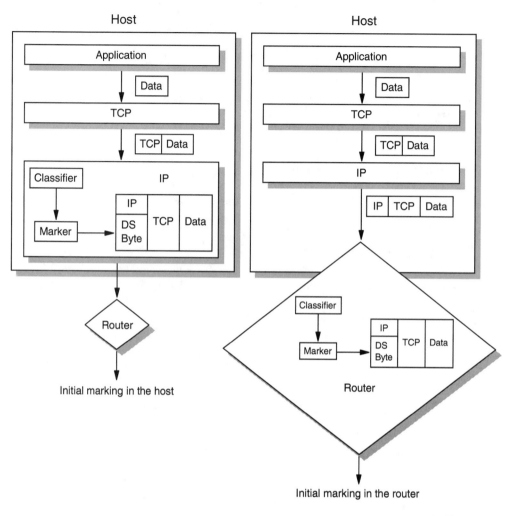

Figure 302. *Initial Marking of Data Packets*

In our example, the DS network has the policy that the packets from the audio
application should have higher priority than other packets. The sender host can mark
the DS field of all outgoing packets with a DS codepoint that indicates higher priority.
Alternatively, the first-hop router directly connected to the sender's host may classify
the traffic and mark the packets with the correct DS codepoint. The source DS
domain is responsible for ensuring that the aggregated traffic towards its provider DS
domain conforms to the SLA between customer and service provider. The boundary

node of the source domain should also monitor that the provided service conforms to the requested service and may police, shape, or re-mark packets as necessary.

10.3.2 Using RSVP with Differentiated Services

The RSVP protocol, which is described in 10.2.2, "The Reservation Protocol (RSVP)" on page 651, enables applications to signal per-flow requirements to a network. Integrated services parameters are used to quantify these requirements for the purpose of admission control. But RSVP and integrated services have some basic limitations that impede deployment of these mechanisms in the Internet at large:

1. The reliance of RSVP on per-flow state and per-flow processing raises scalability concerns in large networks.

2. Today, only a small number of hosts generate RSVP signaling. Although this number is expected to grow dramatically, many applications may never generate RSVP signaling.

3. Many applications require a form of QoS, but are unable to express these requirements using the IS model.

These disadvantages can be circumvented if Integrated Services is implemented only in intranets and it uses Differentiated Services 10.3, "Differentiated Services" on page 665 in the Internet as a backbone. Figure 303 shows an imaginable network structure:

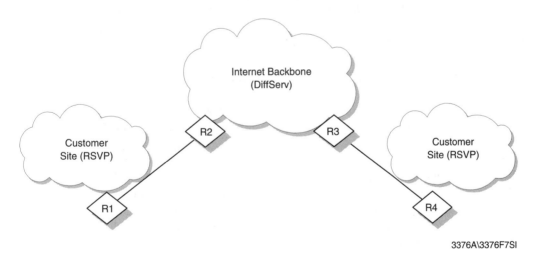

3376A\3376F7SI

Figure 303. Using RSVP with Differentiated Services

Two RSVP-capable customer intranets are connected to the DS Internet backbone. The routers R2 and R3 are boundary routers that can condition incoming and outgoing traffic at the interfaces of the DS network to the IS networks. In our example, the boundary routers are not required to run RSVP. They are expected to implement the policing functions of the DS ingress router. There must be a set of end-to-end services defined in the DS network that allows the mapping of RSVP flow reservations to an appropriate DS service class. The routers in the DS network must provide a set of per-hop behaviors (see 10.3.1.1, "The Per-Hop Behavior" on page 667), which provide the service of a true end-to-end connection. It must be possible for RSVP applications to invoke specific end-to-end service levels for their traffic flows in the DS network. In this model, the IS intranets are customers of the DS Internet.

The edge routers R1 and R4 are special routers that work both in the RSVP/IS region of the network and the DS region of the network. These routers can be visualized as split in two halves. One half supports standard RSVP and it interfaces to the intranets. The other half supports DS and interfaces to the DS Internet. The RSVP half must be at least partially RSVP-capable. The router must be able to process PATH and RESV messages but it is not required to support packet classification and storing of RSVP states. The DS half of the router provides the interface to the Admission Control function for the DS network. If the service agreement between the IS intranets and the DS Internet is static, the Admission Control Service can be a simple table which specifies the QoS at each service level. If the service agreement is dynamic, Admission Control Service communicates with counterparts within the DS network to make admission control decisions based on the capacity of the network.

In our model, RSVP signaling is used to provide admission control to specific service levels in the DS and the IS network. RSVP signaling messages carry an IS QoS description that specifies the type of service that should be provided in the IS regions of the network. At the boundary between the IS network and a DS network the edge routers map the requested IS QoS to an appropriate DS service level. After this, the edge router can provide admission control to the DS network by accepting or rejecting the QoS request based on the capacity available at the requested DS service level. If an RSVP reservation message from the IS network arrives at an edge router, the RSVP flow descriptor will be mapped to a PHB that represents the corresponding service level in the DS network. The edge router appends the PHB value to the RSVP reservation message which is carried to the sending host. The sending host then marks all outgoing packets with this PHB value. This approach allows end-to-end QoS guarantees for RSVP applications in different intranets that use the DS Internet as backbone.

10.3.3 Configuration and Administration of DS Components with LDAP

In a differentiated services network, the service level information must be provided to all network elements to ensure correct administrative control of bandwidth, delay or dropping preferences for a given customer flow. All DS boundary components must have the same policy information for the defined service levels. This makes sure that the packets marked with the DS byte receive the same service in all DS domains. If only one domain in the DS network has different policy information, it can happen that the data packets passing this domain don't receive the service that was contracted in the SLA between customer and service provider.

Network administrators can define different service levels for different customers and provide this information manually to all boundary components. This policy information remains statically in the network components until the next manual change.

But in dynamic network environments it is necessary to enable flexible definitions of class-based packet handling behaviors and class-based policy control. Administrative policies can change in a running environment whereby it is necessary to store the policies in a directory-based repository. The policy information from the directory can be distributed across multiple physical servers, but the administration is done for a a single entity by the network administrator. The directory information must be propagated on all network elements, such as hosts, proxies and routers, that use the policy information for traffic conditioning in the DS network.

In today's heterogeneous environments, it is likely that network devices and administrative tools are developed by different vendors. Therefore, it is necessary to use a standardized format to store the administrative policies in the directory server function and a standardized mechanism to provide the directory information to the DS boundary components which act as directory clients. These functions are provided by the *Lightweight Directory Access Protocol (LDAP)* which is a commonly used industry standard for directory accessing (see 12.3, "Lightweight Directory Access Protocol (LDAP)" on page 734). LDAP is a widely deployed and simple protocol for directory access. Policy rules for different service levels are stored in directories as LDAP schema and can be downloaded to devices that implement the policies, such as hosts, routers, policy servers or proxies. Figure 304 on page 678 shows the cooperation of the DS network elements with the LDAP server.

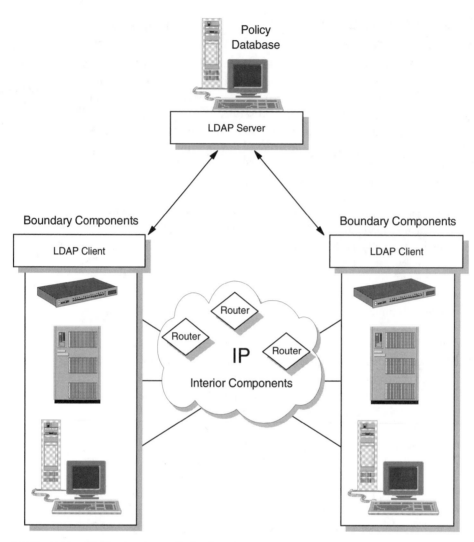

Policy
Database

LDAP Server

Boundary Components

LDAP Client

Boundary Components

LDAP Client

Router

Router

IP

Router

Interior Components

LDAP = Lightweight Directory Access Protocol

3376X\3376F7SK

Figure 304. Administration of DS Components with LDAP

10.3.4 Using Differentiated Services with IPSec

The IPsec protocol that is described in 5.5, "The IP Security Architecture (IPSec)" on page 379 does not use the DS field in an IP header for its cryptographic calculations. Therefore, modification of the DS field by a network node has no effect on IPsec's end-to-end security, because it cannot cause any IPsec integrity check to fail. This makes it possible to use IPsec-secured packets in DS networks.

IPsec's tunnel mode provides security for the encapsulated IP header's DS field. A tunnel mode IPsec packet contains an outer header that is supplied by the tunnel start point, and an encapsulated inner header that is supplied by the host that has originally sent the packet.

Processing of the DS field in the presence of IPSec tunnels would then work as follows:

1. The node where the IPsec tunnel begins encapsulates the incoming IP packets with an outer IP header and sets the DS byte of the outer header accordingly to the SLA in the local DS domain.

2. The secured packet travels through the DS network and intermediate nodes modify the DS field in the outer IP header as appropriate.

3. If a packet reaches the end of an IPSec tunnel, the outer IP header is stripped off by the tunnel end node and the packet is forwarded using the information contained in the inner (original) IP header.

4. If the DS domain of the original datagram is different from the DS domain where the IPSec tunnel ends, the tunnel end node must modify the DS byte of the inner header to match the SLA in its domain. The tunnel end node would then effectively act as a DS ingress node.

5. As the packet travels onwards in the DS network on the other side of the IPSec tunnel, intermediate nodes use the original IP header to modify the DS byte.

10.3.5 Internet Drafts on Differentiated Services

The following Internet drafts were available on Differentiated Services at the time of writing:

```
http://www.ietf.org/internet-drafts/draft-ietf-diffserv-arch-01.txt
http://www.ietf.org/internet-drafts/draft-nichols-dsopdef-00.txt
http://www.ietf.org/internet-drafts/draft-ietf-diffserv-header-02.txt
http://www.ietf.org/internet-drafts/draft-ietf-diffserv-framework-00.txt
http://www.ietf.org/internet-drafts/draft-ietf-diffserv-rsvp-00.txt
http://www.ietf.org/internet-drafts/draft-ietf-diffserv-phb-ef-00.txt
```

10.4 References

Please refer to the following RFCs for more information on QoS in the Internet:

- *RFC 1349 — Type of Service in the Internet Protocol Suite*

- *RFC 1633 — Integrated Services in the Internet Architecture: An Overview*

- *RFC 2205 — Resource Reservation Protocol (RSVP) -- Version 1 Functional Specification*

- *RFC 2206 — RSVP Management Information Base Using SMIv2*

- *RFC 2207 — RSVP Extensions for IPSEC Data Flows*

- *RFC 2208 — Resource Reservation Protocol (RSVP) -- Version 1 Applicability Statement*

- *RFC 2209 — Resource Reservation Protocol (RSVP) -- Version 1 Message Processing Rules*

- *RFC 2210 — The Use of RSVP with IETF Integrated Services*

- *RFC 2211 — Specification of the Controlled Load Network Element Service*

- *RFC 2212 — Specification of Guaranteed Quality of Service*

Chapter 11. Availability, Scalability and Load Balancing

The Internet has grown so rapidly over the last few years that many companies are looking for effective ways of dealing with the ever increasing amount of network traffic and server load. If this growth is not handled properly, users experience slow response times or refused connections. Internet sites become unstable or even fail under critical load conditions, which are sometimes referred to as hot spots. Users are unhappy and often complain. What is needed is a solution that provides scalability, load balancing and availability. Before we take a look at some solutions that provide those desired capabilities, we think it is appropriate to explain the terms and applicabilities of balancing, scaling and availability:

Scaling

> Refers to adding more devices to a server or a network, or both, to seamlessly accommodate growth, that is, without interrupting or rebuilding an existing environment and without adversely affecting existing applications.

Balancing

> Refers to sharing, or distributing, a load among multiple devices within a server or network, or both, to facilitate low response times and continuous traffic flows. Balancing can also be used to better accommodate peak traffic and to forestall the development of bottlenecks.

Availability

> Refers to providing alternative server or network resources, or both, to seamlessly compensate system or component failures that would otherwise cause down time and/or delay. Depending on the nature of a business, down time can amount to millions of dollars per minute and become the most costly problem to occur in a company's network. It is therefore highly desirable to have mechanisms in place that avoid down time and delay by providing an automatic and instant take-over of failing components without disrupting existing connections.

This chapter describes the following TCP/IP-related scalability, balancing and availability protocols, applications and techniques:

- Virtual Router Redundancy Protocol (VRRP)

- Round-robin DNS

- IBM eNetwork Dispatcher (also known as Interactive Network Dispatcher or IND)

- NAT-based techniques

- TCP/IP for OS/390 using Workload Manager (WLM)

- OSPF Equal-cost multipath

- OS/390 VIPA connection recovery

The concepts of scaling, balancing and availability can be applied to servers, to networks, or both. In the server context, they can be grouped by techniques that apply those concepts to name resolution, and by techniques that apply them to application connections. In the network context, we can distinguish between techniques for traffic and techniques for component failure. Some of those techniques provide several of these capabilities, which are summarized in the table below:

Table 14. Server: Name Resolution Level			
	Scalability	**Balancing**	**Availability**
Server - Name Resolution			
Round-Robin DNS	X	X	
TCP/IP for OS/390 using Workload Manager (WLM)	X	X	X
Server - Connection			
IND	X	X	X
NAT-Based Techniques	X	X	
Network - Traffic and Component Failure			
Dynamic Routing Protocol	X		X
VRRP		X	X
Equal-Cost Multipath		X	
Network - Component Failure			
OS/390 VIPA Connection Recovery			X

11.1 Virtual Router Redundancy Protocol (VRRP)

VRRP was issued to the IETF by IBM, Ascend Communications, Microsoft and Digital Equipment Corp. in April 1998 and is documented in RFC number 2338. Its status is proposed standard.

11.1.1 Introduction

The use of a statically configured default route is quite popular for host IP configurations. It minimizes configuration and processing overhead on the end host and is supported by virtually every IP implementation. This mode of operation is likely where dynamic host configuration protocols such as DHCP (see DHCP in 7.2, "Dynamic Host Configuration Protocol (DHCP)" on page 516) are deployed, which typically provide configuration for an end-host IP address and default gateway. However, this creates a single point of failure. Loss of the default router results in a catastrophic event, isolating all end hosts that are unable to detect any alternate path that may be available.

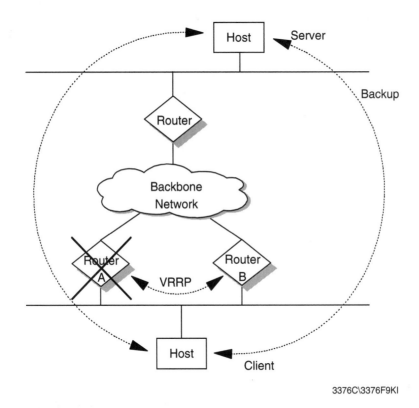

Figure 305. *What Is VRRP? - An Illustration*

VRRP is designed to eliminate the single point of failure inherent in the static default routed environment. VRRP specifies an election protocol that dynamically assigns responsibility for a virtual router to one of the VRRP routers on a LAN. The VRRP router controlling the IP address(es) associated with a virtual router is called the master, and forwards packets sent to these IP addresses. The election process provides dynamic fail-over in the forwarding responsibility should the master become unavailable. Any of the virtual router's IP addresses on a LAN can then be used as the default first hop router by end hosts. The advantage gained from using VRRP is a higher availability default path without requiring configuration of dynamic routing or router discovery protocols on every end host (see router discovery protocols in 2.2, "Internet Control Message Protocol (ICMP)" on page 74).

11.1.2 VRRP Definitions

Before giving an overview of VRRP, some terms used in VRRP need to be defined.

VRRP Router
>A router running the Virtual Router Redundancy Protocol. It may participate in one or more virtual routers.

Virtual Router
>An abstract object managed by VRRP that acts as a default router for hosts on a shared LAN. It consists of a virtual router identifier and a set of associated IP address(es) across a common LAN. A VRRP Router may back up one or more virtual routers.

IP Address Owner
>The VRRP router that has the virtual router's IP address(es) as real interface address(es). This is the router that, when up, will respond to packets addressed to one of these IP addresses for ICMP pings, TCP connections, etc.

Primary IP Address
>An IP address selected from the set of real interface addresses. One possible selection algorithm is to always select the first address. VRRP advertisements are always sent using the primary IP address as the source of the IP packet.

Virtual Router Master
>The VRRP router that is assuming the responsibility of forwarding packets sent to the IP address(es) associated with the virtual router, and answering ARP requests for these IP addresses. Note that if the IP address owner is available, then it will always become the master.

Virtual Router Backup
>The set of VRRP routers available to assume forwarding responsibility for a virtual router should the current master fail.

11.1.3 VRRP Overview

VRRP specifies an election protocol to provide the virtual router function described earlier. All protocol messaging is performed using IP multicast datagrams (see multicast in 9.1, "Multicasting" on page 593), thus the protocol can operate over a variety of multiaccess LAN technologies supporting IP multicast. Each VRRP virtual router has a single well-known MAC address allocated to it. The virtual router MAC address is used as the source in all periodic VRRP messages sent by the master router to enable bridge learning in an extended LAN.

A virtual router is defined by its virtual router identifier (VRID) and a set of IP addresses. A VRRP router can associate a virtual router with its real addresses on an interface, and can also be configured with additional virtual router mappings and priority for virtual routers it is willing to back up. The mapping between VRID and addresses must be coordinated among all VRRP routers on a LAN. However, there is no restriction against reusing a VRID with a different address mapping on different LANs.

The scope of each virtual router is restricted to a single LAN. To minimize network traffic, only the master for each virtual router sends periodic VRRP advertisement messages. A backup router will not attempt to pre-empt the master unless it has higher priority. This eliminates service disruption unless a more preferred path becomes available. It's also possible to administratively prohibit all pre-emption attempts. The only exception is that a VRRP router will always become master of any virtual router associated with addresses it owns. If the master becomes unavailable then the highest priority backup will transition to master after a short delay, providing a controlled transition of the virtual router responsibility with minimal service interruption.

The VRRP protocol design provides rapid transition from master to backup to minimize service interruption, and incorporates optimizations that reduce protocol complexity while guaranteeing controlled master transition for typical operational scenarios. The optimizations result in an election protocol with minimal runtime state requirements, minimal active protocol states, and a single message type and sender. The typical operational scenarios are defined to be two redundant routers and/or distinct path preferences among each router. A side effect when these assumptions are violated (for example, more than two redundant paths all with equal preference) is that duplicate packets can be forwarded for a brief period during master election. However, the typical scenario assumptions are likely to cover the vast majority of deployments, loss of the master router is infrequent, and the expected duration in master election convergence is quite small (<< 1 second). Thus the VRRP optimizations represent significant simplifications in the protocol design while incurring an insignificant probability of brief network degradation.

11.1.4 Sample Configuration

The following figure shows a simple example network with two VRRP routers implementing one virtual router.

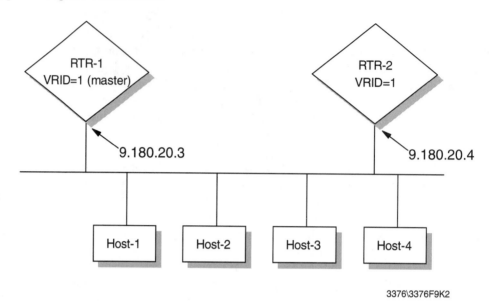

3376\3376F9K2

Figure 306. VRRP Simple Configuration Example

The above configuration shows a very simple VRRP scenario. In this configuration, the end hosts install a default route to the IP address of virtual router #1 (IP address 9.180.20.3) and both routers run VRRP. The router on the left becomes the master for virtual router #1 (VRID=1) and the router on the right is the backup for virtual router #1. If the router on the left should fail, the other router will take over virtual router #1 and its IP addresses, and provide uninterrupted service for the hosts. Note that in this example, IP address 9.180.20.4 is not backed up by the router on the left. IP address 9.180.20.4 is only used by the router on the right as its interface address. In order to back up IP address 9.180.20.4, a second virtual router would have to be configured. This is shown in following example.

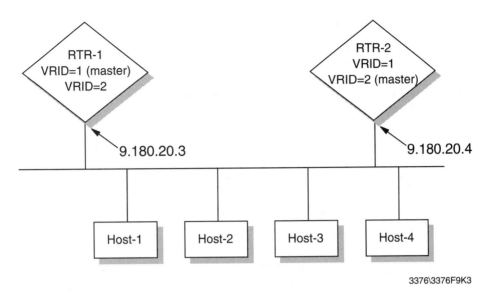

3376\3376F9K3

Figure 307. VRRP Simple Load-Splitting Configuration Example

The following figure shows a configuration with two virtual routers with the hosts splitting their traffic between them. This example is expected to be very common in actual practice. In the above configuration, half of the hosts install a default route to virtual router #1's (IP address 9.180.20.3), and the other half of the hosts install a default route to virtual router #2's (IP address 9.180.20.4). This has the effect of load balancing the traffic from the hosts through the routers, while also providing full redundancy.

11.1.5 VRRP Packet Format

The purpose of the VRRP packet is to communicate to all VRRP routers the priority and the state of the master router associated with the virtual router ID. VRRP packets are sent encapsulated in IP packets. They are sent to the IPv4 multicast address assigned to VRRP (see multicast in 9.1, "Multicasting" on page 593). The IP address as assigned by the IANA for VRRP is 224.0.0.18. This is a link local scope multicast address. Routers must not forward a datagram with this destination address regardless of its TTL (see TTL in 2.1, "Internet Protocol (IP)" on page 35). The TTL must be set to 255. A VRRP router receiving a packet with the TTL not equal to 255 must discard the packet.

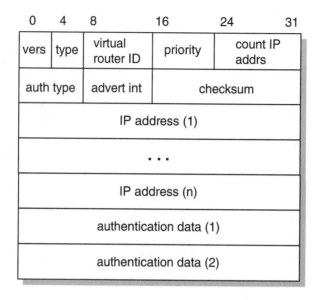

Figure 308. VRRP Packet Format

The fields of the VRRP header are defined as follows:

Version

The version field specifies the VRRP protocol version of this packet. (In RFC 2338 the version is 2.)

Type The type field specifies the type of this VRRP packet. The only packet type defined in this version of the protocol is 1.

Virtual Router ID (VRID)

The virtual router identifier (VRID) field identifies the virtual router this packet is reporting status for.

Priority

The priority field specifies the sending VRRP router's priority for the virtual router. Higher values equal higher priority. The priority value for the VRRP router that owns the IP address(es) associated with the virtual router must be 255. VRRP routers backing up a virtual router must use priority values between 1-254. The default priority value for VRRP routers backing up a virtual router is 100. The priority value zero (0) has special meaning indicating that the current master has stopped participating in VRRP. This is used to trigger backup routers to quickly transition to master without having to wait for the current master to time out.

Count IP Addrs

> The number of IP addresses contained in this VRRP advertisement.

Auth Type

> The authentication type field identifies the authentication method being utilized. Authentication type is unique on a per interface basis. The authentication type field is an 8-bit unsigned integer. A packet with unknown authentication type or that does not match the locally configured authentication method must be discarded. The authentication methods currently defined are:
>
> - 0 - No Authentication
>
> - 1 - Simple text password
>
> - 2 - IP Authentication Header

Advertisement Interval (Adver Int)

> The default is 1 second. This field may be used for troubleshooting misconfigured routers.

Checksum

> It is used to detect data corruption in the VRRP message.

IP Address(es)

> One or more IP addresses that are associated with the virtual router.

Authentication Data

> The authentication string is currently only utilized for simple text authentication.

11.2 Round-Robin DNS

Early solutions to address load balancing were often located at the point where host names are translated into actual IP addresses: the Domain Name System (see DNS in 4.2, "Domain Name System (DNS)" on page 194). By rotating through a table of alternate IP addresses for a specific service, some degree of load balancing is achieved. This approach is often called round-robin DNS. The advantages of this approach are that it is protocol-compliant and transparent both to the client and the destination host. Also it is performed only once at the start of the transaction.

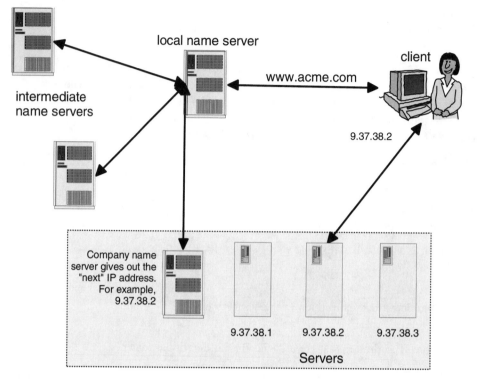

Figure 309. *Round-Robin DNS*

Unfortunately, this approach is sometimes defeated by the fact that intermediate name servers and client software (including some of the most popular browsers) cache the IP address returned by the DNS service, and ignore an expressly specified time-to-live (TTL) value (see TTL in 2.1, "Internet Protocol (IP)" on page 35), particularly if the TTL is short or zero. As a result, the balancing function provided by the DNS is bypassed, because the client continues to use a cached IP address instead of resolving again. Even if a client does not cache the IP address, basic round-robin DNS still has limitations:

- It does not provide the ability to differentiate by port.

- It has no awareness of the availability of the servers.

- It does not take into account the workload on the servers.

11.3 IBM eNetwork Dispatcher

eNetwork Dispatcher, formerly known as Interactive Network Dispatcher (IND), is a fundamentally new approach to load balancing. It is described and compared to other solutions in the following sections.

11.3.1 eNetwork Dispatcher Components

IBM eNetwork Dispatcher has been developed to address these limitations and provide customers with advanced functions to meet their site's scaleability and availability needs. It consists of two components:

Interactive Session Support[14]

> Can address the above limitations of round-robin DNS while still providing the same DNS interface as before for the clients. It provides a least-disruptive migration path for applications that are already deployed using round-robin DNS.

Dispatcher

> Provides an advanced IP level load balancing mechanism that can be installed instead of round-robin DNS. Once installed, the Dispatcher remains completely invisible to clients, but can deliver superior load balancing, management and availability function.

These two components can be deployed separately or together in various configurations to suit a wide variety of customer application requirements.

11.3.1.1 Interactive Session Support

Interactive Session Support (ISS) is the DNS-based component. It provides a load-monitoring daemon that can be installed on each of the servers that form part of your installation. This group of daemons is referred to as a cell. One of the members of the cell becomes the "spokesman" for the load-monitoring service.

Standard memory or processor utilization figures can be used to measure load with the ISS daemon, or alternatively a custom set of criteria can be provided, for example with an application-aware executable module, or a simple shell script, and tell ISS to use it. This is referred to as a custom metric.

---

[14] Functions such as Interactive Session Support, Dispatcher, Executor, Manager, Advisor, ISS Load Monitor, and Configurator referenced with capital letters are not specific products but have been capitalized to indicate a specific eNetwork Dispatcher functional component.

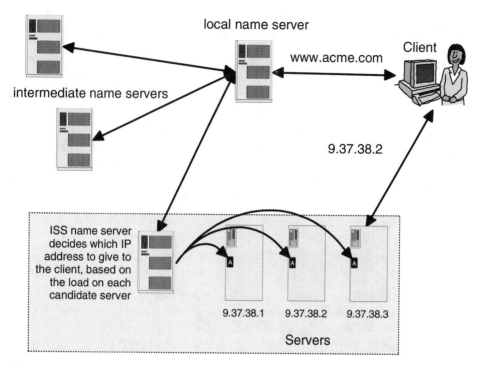

Figure 310. *Interactive Session Support*

ISS provides an *observer* interface to enable other applications to use the load-monitoring service. Observers watch the cell and initiate actions based on the load. The observer applications provided in eNetwork Dispatcher are of two kinds: name server observer and dispatcher observer.

1. As shown in Figure 310, the name server observer allows the load monitoring service to provide an intelligent DNS name resolution service that returns IP addresses to your clients (in response to a gethostbyname() call) based on feedback from the ISS daemons running on each server machine, rather than the strict rotation of round-robin. Also, if a server is down, its IP address will not be returned.

2. The dispatcher observer is used in conjunction with the Dispatcher component, and is described later.

ISS can also be configured in *ping triangulation* mode where the ISS daemons respond based on the ping time from each of them to the client. This allows load balancing based on network topology

11.3.1.2 The Dispatcher

The Dispatcher is an IP-level load balancer. It uses a fundamentally different approach to load balancing based on patented technology from IBM's Research Division. Dispatcher does not use DNS in any way, although normal static DNS will still usually be used in front of the Dispatcher. Once installed and configured, the Dispatcher actually becomes the site IP address to which clients send all packets. This externally advertised address is referred to as the cluster address. As many cluster addresses as needed can be defined. Then, the ports that should be supported inside each cluster can be configured, and then the actual servers that will provide the service on each of those ports. Optionally, the real IP addresses of the servers in the cluster can be concealed from the clients, by filtering them at the gateway router. This object-oriented cluster-port-server structure provides a simple configuration interface that can be created and modified dynamically, permitting true 24 x 7 operation.

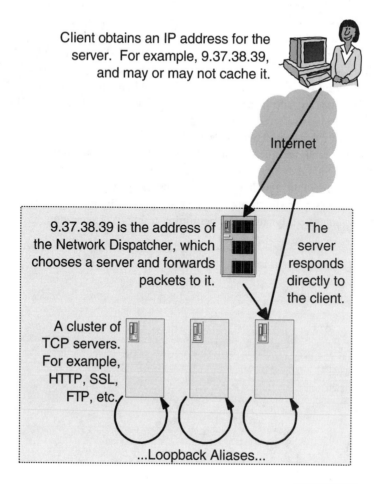

Figure 311. Dispatcher

The core function of the Dispatcher is the Executor. It is a kernel-level function (or device driver) which examines only the header of each packet and decides whether the packet belongs to an existing connection, or represents a new connection request. It uses a simple connection table stored in memory to achieve this. Note that the connection is never actually set up on the Dispatcher machine (it is between the client and the server, just as it would be if the Dispatcher were not installed) but the connection table records its existence and the address of the server to which the connection was sent.

If the connection already exists, which means it has an existing entry in the in-memory connection table, then without further processing, the packet is rapidly forwarded to the same server chosen on the initial connection request. Since most of the packets that flow are of this type, the overhead of the whole load balancing process is kept to a minimum. This is one of the reasons why the Dispatcher is so superior to its competition in performance and scaleability.

If the packet is a new connection request, the Executor will look at the configuration to see which servers can support a request on the port requested by the client on the requested cluster address. Then it uses stored weights for each such server to determine the right server to which the connection will be forwarded. An entry mentioning this server is made in the connection table, ensuring that subsequent packets for this connection are correctly forwarded to the chosen server.

Note that the right server is not always the best server, since it is desirable for all eligible servers to process their share of the load. Even the worst server needs to shoulder some of the burden. If traffic is only ever forwarded to the best server, it can be guaranteed that it will rapidly cease to be the best. As a result, load allocation experiences swings that prevent optimal balance from being achieved. Dispatcher's patented algorithm for choosing the right server and its advanced smoothing techniques achieve optimal balance in the shortest possible time.

The Executor does not modify the client's IP packet when forwarding it. Because the Dispatcher is on the same subnet as its clustered servers, it simply forwards the packet explicitly to the IP address of the chosen server, just like any ordinary IP packet. The Dispatcher's TCP/IP stack modifies only the packet's MAC address in the operating system approved manner and sends the packet to the chosen server.

To allow the TCP/IP stack on that server to accept the unmodified packet from the Dispatcher and pass it to the chosen port for normal application processing, the IP address of the Dispatcher machine is also installed as a non-advertising alias on each of the clustered servers. This is achieved by configuring the alias on the loopback adapter.

The server's TCP then establishes the server-to-client half of the connection according to standard TCP semantics, by simply swapping the source and target addresses as supplied by the client, rather than determining them from its own basic configuration. This means that it replies to the client with the IP address of the Dispatcher. As a direct result, the balancing function is invisible both to the client and the clustered servers. This invisibility means that the Dispatcher is not dependent upon server platforms, provided they implement standard TCP/IP protocols.

Another key performance and scaleability benefit of the Dispatcher is that the application server returns the response to the client's request directly to the client without passing back through the Dispatcher. Indeed there is no need even to return using the original physical path; a separate high-bandwidth connection can be used. In many cases, the volume of outbound server-to-client traffic is substantially greater than the inbound traffic. For example, Web page HTML and imbedded images sent from the server are typically at least 10 times the size of the client URLs that request them. This capability was important to address the scaling requirements of the Web site for the 1998 Nagano Winter Olympic Games.

Because the Dispatcher is a truly generic TCP/IP application, its functions can be applied not only to HTTP or FTP traffic, but also to other standards-compliant types of TCP and UDP traffic.

11.3.2 Load Balancing with Weights

The Dispatcher has a Manager function, which sets the weights that the Executor obeys. The Manager uses four metrics to set these weights:

- Active connection counts for each server on each port. This count is held inside the Executor.

- New connection counts for each server on each port. This count is held inside the Executor.

- A check that each server is up-and-running. The Advisor performs this function.

- A check that each server has *displaceable capacity* which means that it can realistically process the work. The ISS Load Monitor performs this function.

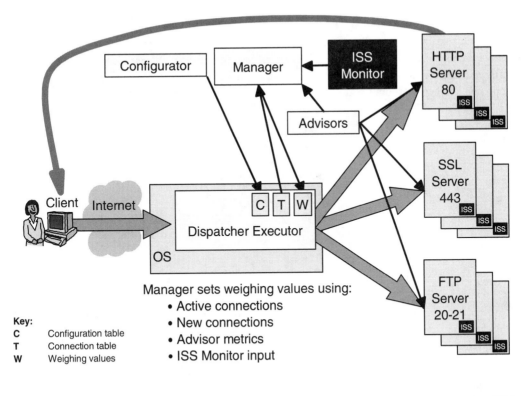

Key:
C   Configuration table
T   Connection table
W   Weighing values

Manager sets weighing values using:
- Active connections
- New connections
- Advisor metrics
- ISS Monitor input

3376\3376F9K6

Figure 312. Dispatcher Components

The Advisor is a lightweight client that runs as a part of the Dispatcher but actually passes real commands to each application server. It only executes a trivial command, but it needs to be more than a ping which will only verify that the TCP/IP protocol stack is up. If this request is successful, the server is deemed to be up. If it fails, the Advisor informs the Manager, and the Manager sets the weight of that server to zero, until the server responds again.

If the application server has the ISS Load Monitor daemon installed (with or without a custom metric), periodic load reports can be passed to the Dispatcher via the Dispatcher observer. The results of these reports can be factored into the process of setting the individual server weights for the Dispatcher.

11.3.3 High Availability

The Dispatcher already provides high availability, because one of its basic functions is to avoid choosing a failed server clustered behind it. The Dispatcher can also be configured to eliminate the load balancer itself as a single point of failure, as part of a comprehensive hardware and software implementation of high availability.

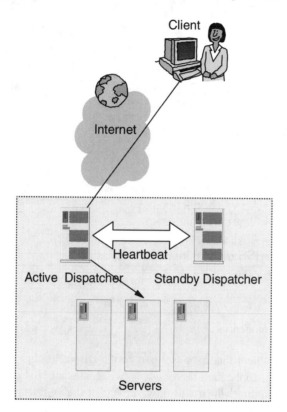

Figure 313. *High Availability*

As shown in Figure 313, the Dispatcher can optionally be configured with a secondary/standby machine on the same subnet that synchronizes its state, including that of its connection table, with that of the primary/active machine, and listens for a heartbeat from the primary/active machine.

Various additional customer-defined *reachability* criteria can also be specified, such as access to gateway routers across duplicated adapters and networks, etc. If the heartbeat fails, or defined reachability criteria are not met, the primary machine is deemed to be down, and the standby machine takes over the role of forwarding packets. Typically the failover process will take less than five seconds, minimizing the number of connection failures that might occur. Other failover approaches that rely on the age-out of ARP entries can take as much as a minute to complete.

In the event of a failure, the connection table on the standby machine is closely synchronized with that of the now failed primary machine, so the great majority of the existing connections in flight will survive the failure. The newly active machine still knows where to send all packets that it receives, and TCP automatically resends any individual packets that were lost during the actual failover. The most likely connections to fail are those that are just in the process of either opening or closing. In the case of opening requests, the client TCP/IP stack or the application may be able to retry and be successful without the client being aware of the failure. In the case of closing requests, it is likely that there will be no loss of data.

11.3.4 Server Affinity

This function is sometimes referred to as the *sticky* option. It is provided to allow load balancing for those applications which preserve some kind of persistent state in between connections on behalf of clients, without losing the state when the client reconnects.

When a client originally contacts the site, it is associated with a chosen server in the normal way. When the sticky option is configured, the difference is that any subsequent connections sent in by the client will be dispatched to the same server until a configurable time-out value expires. The Dispatcher allows configuration of this sticky capability on a per-port basis.

11.3.5 Rules-Based Balancing

Rules-based balancing introduces the concept of rules and a set of servers among which to load balance if the rule is obeyed. The following rules are available:

- Client IP address

- Client port

- Time of day

- Connections per second for a port

- Active connections for a port

This allows the site to take account of its traffic and the identity of the clients that access it when setting up the load balancing policy. A range can be specified where required, so for example all client IP addresses in a particular subnet can be forwarded to a particular set of servers, or "between the hours of 8 a.m. to 5 p.m., use this set of ten servers, otherwise use that set of five servers". This provides a simple method of implementing quality of service for individuals, groups of clients or time-of-day, without imposing unique or proprietary additional semantics or protocols on the client/server relationship.

11.3.6 Wide Area Network Dispatcher

Previous releases of the Dispatcher required that all clustered servers be on the same subnet as the Dispatcher. With Version 2 of the Dispatcher, there is no distance limitation to remote servers, either inside a private network or even across the Internet, to provide a site that is geographically distributed over a few miles or across the globe. Another Dispatcher must be installed at the remote location.

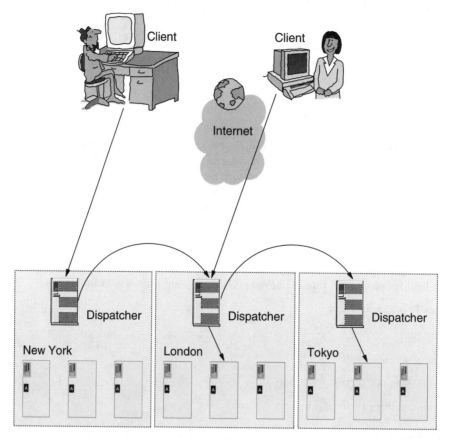

3376F9\3376F9M1

Figure 314. Wide Area Network Dispatcher

As shown in Figure 314, using this option, a truly distributed wide area network site can be configured. Any client data can be forwarded to any of the configured servers at any location. The choice can be based on server load, or rules, or a combination of the two. The choice of which site should receive the client's packets first can be achieved in several ways, including the "which site is closest" mode provided by ISS running in ping triangulation mode (see below under ISS and Dispatcher together).

The transmission of packets to remote sites is achieved by encapsulating the unmodified client packets at the originating Dispatcher, and then un-encapsulating them at the receiving Dispatcher. The server to client data flow goes direct, as it does with the local area network Dispatcher, thus keeping the overhead to a minimum.

11.3.7 Combining ISS and Dispatcher

The two components of the eNetwork Dispatcher product can be usefully deployed together to support a geographically distributed site.

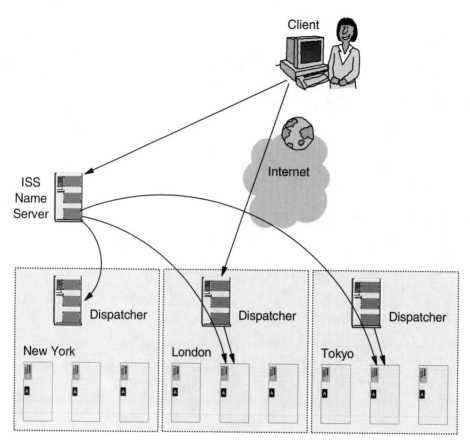

Figure 315. *ISS and Dispatcher Together*

As shown in Figure 315, in response to a standard name resolution request from an application program, the ISS name server returns to the client the IP address of the chosen site, based on feedback from the ISS daemons running on the Dispatcher machines running at the individual sites. The ISS daemons can be configured to return results in one of two ways:

1. Based on system load, which will direct the client to the least loaded site. The ISS daemon can use a custom metric if needed.

2. Based on ping triangulation that will direct the client to the closest site from a network topology point of view.

The client then sends its connection request to the selected Dispatcher machine at the chosen location, which will in turn select the individual server from the cluster at that site, based on its own set of weights. Note that this configuration can also include the wide area network Dispatcher support described above.

11.3.8 Advisors and Custom Advisors

The Dispatcher supplies standard advisors for HTTP, HTTPS (SSL), FTP, NNTP, SMTP, POP3 and Telnet. A customer may wish to use other standard or private protocols with the Dispatcher or to implement specific extensions to the standard advisors. For this purpose a Custom Advisor facility has been provided, with well-documented sample source code. Custom advisors must be written in Java at Release 1.1.2 or higher of the Java Development Kit, which is not provided with Dispatcher.

This powerful extension capability can be coupled with custom code written to run on the application server machine to provide a high degree of synergy between the Dispatcher and the applications it balances. One example of this use would be a link between a custom advisor and a Java servlet running inside a Web server. The servlet could be coded to extract in-depth performance data from each server and return it to the Dispatcher, thus allowing the Dispatcher to benefit from results more precisely tailored to the customer's real application environment.

11.3.9 SNMP Support

A simple network management protocol (SNMP) management information base (MIB) for Dispatcher data is provided. This MIB contains a comprehensive set of values associated with the state and current performance of the Dispatcher. An SNMP-enabled management tool such as Tivoli TME 10 NetView, or any other similarly equipped tool can access this MIB. In addition, SNMP traps are also generated if a clustered server fails or if the Dispatcher itself fails over to its standby.

11.3.10 Co-Location Option

If a company is starting from a small site, but has plans to grow rapidly, it has some simple options to keep costs down in the early stages of its growth, while still benefiting from the high availability and scaleability options of eNetwork Dispatcher, and positioning itself for that growth when it occurs.

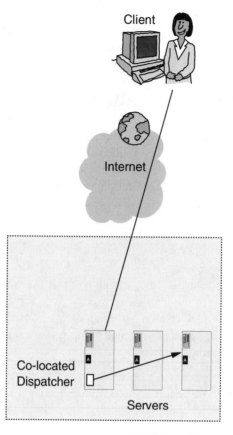

Co-located
Dispatcher

Servers

3376F9\3376F9M3

Figure 316. *Co-Location Option*

As shown in Figure 316, as the site's load increases to the point where it needs more than one server to handle the traffic, the company can add the Dispatcher to its existing network infrastructure with a minimum of hardware and software investment by installing the Dispatcher software on one of the machines where the application servers reside. It will not have to change its existing network configuration in any way. In the simplest case, all that needs to be done is configuring the Dispatcher and either replicating the application server content on to another server, or sharing it with a shared file system.

The co-location option of the Dispatcher lets a company start quickly with minimum cost and evolve to a stand-alone Dispatcher or to a high-availability configuration when the volume of traffic requires it. Even when a dedicated Dispatcher has been deployed, one can still choose to co-locate a standby Dispatcher with one of the application servers.

11.3.11 ISP Configuration

Internet Service Providers (ISPs) with a large backbone network, or hosting a busy search engine, can address their scaling and availability requirements by coupling eNetwork Dispatcher in high availability mode with high-capacity caching proxy servers and an enterprise shared file system. These components have been combined into the IBM WebSphere Performance Pack, as shown in Figure 317 on page 706.

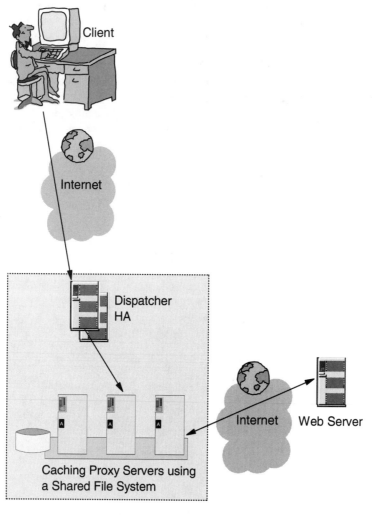

Client

Internet

Dispatcher
HA

A
A
A

Internet   Web Server

Caching Proxy Servers using
a Shared File System

3376F9\3376F9M4

Figure 317. IBM WebSphere Performance Pack

An efficiently managed cache can significantly reduce backbone network congestion, which provides delivery of faster response times to the clients and better customer service, while reducing traffic costs. The additional components in the IBM WebSphere Performance Pack are IBM Web Traffic Express caching proxy server and Transarc AFS enterprise shared file system.

11.3.12 OS/390 Parallel Sysplex Support

Companies with enterprise application servers on the OS/390 parallel sysplex can use information from OS/390's Workload Manager (WLM) as input to the load balancing process of the Dispatcher feature on the IBM 2210 or 2216 Nways routers.

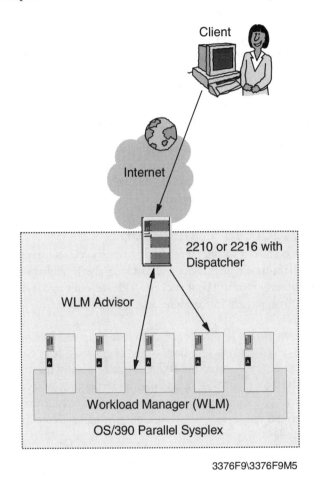

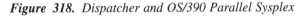

3376F9\3376F9M5

Figure 318. Dispatcher and OS/390 Parallel Sysplex

These versions of the Dispatcher have an additional advisor called the WLM Advisor. As shown in Figure 318, it interacts with the OS/390 Workload Manager and feeds tailored results to the Dispatcher's Manager in the same format as the ISS Dispatcher observer. The WLM Advisor metric measures the following for each configured server:

- The server is available.

- The server has displaceable capacity.

- The server is currently doing work deemed less important.

- The speed of the processor.

- No shortage conditions exist.

Please refer to 11.5, "TCP/IP for OS/390 Using Workload Manager (WLM)" on page 712 for more information on WLM, and to 14.2.1, "The IBM Nways Router Family" on page 841 for more information on the IBM Nways routers.

11.4 Alternative Solutions to Load Balancing

There are many vendors currently offering load balancing hardware or software products. The techniques used vary widely, and have advantages and disadvantages. What follows is a consideration of some of these alternative approaches in comparison to the approach used by IBM eNetwork Dispatcher.

11.4.1 Network Address Translation

Network Address Translation (NAT) works by modifying the source and target IP addresses in the inbound client-to-server packets and restoring the IP address to the original values in the outbound server-to-client packets. (Please refer to 5.4, "Network Address Translation (NAT)" on page 375 for more details on NAT.)

Note that if NAT is to be transparent to the server, eliminating the need for specialized agent code on the server, then all packets sent back to the client must pass back through the load balancer in order to restore the IP addresses originally used by the client, as shown in Figure 319 on page 709, in comparison to the previously discussed mode of the Dispatcher. This is a significant overhead which will have a varying impact on the load balancer and the servers whose resources it manages

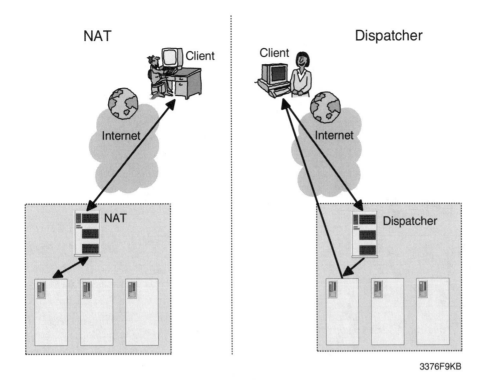

NAT

Client

Internet

NAT

Dispatcher

Client

Internet

Dispatcher

3376F9KB

Figure 319. Network Address Translation versus eNetwork Dispatcher - 1

This added overhead and latency can mean network delay, and queuing delay in the load balancer itself. This in turn drastically limits the potential scaleability of NAT solutions. To overcome such delays, the capacity of the load balancer must not only be sufficient to handle both inbound and outbound packets, but also be able to cope with the disproportionately higher volume of the outbound traffic.

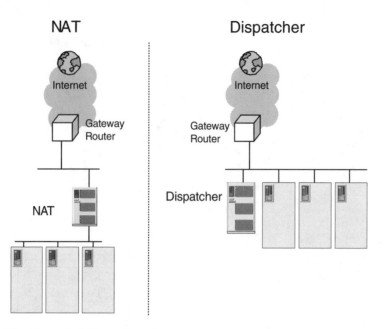

Figure 320. Network Address Translation versus eNetwork Dispatcher - 2

As shown in Figure 320, NAT offerings sometimes enforce the need to see both inbound and outbound requests by obliging the NAT device to be installed as a bridge (without permitting bridges of any other kind) thus forcing the servers on to what is essentially a private segment. This can complicate installation since it requires significant physical change to existing networks. All traffic for those servers must pass through the load balancer whether the traffic is to be load balanced or not.

Conversely the Dispatcher can be quickly and easily installed without disruption to the existing network infrastructure. Also the flexibility of configuration offered by the Dispatcher allows an asymmetric network to be configured to handle very high bandwidth.

The one advantage of NAT as originally conceived (the ability to forward packets to remote destinations across a wide area network) cannot be usefully deployed since the wide area network connection is behind the bridge, and therefore can only be within the site's private network, and the same NAT device must still be the only exit from the wide area network link. Dispatcher's wide area network support does not suffer from this limitation.

To attempt to overcome these limitations, some NAT solutions add to the overhead that is fundamental to NAT by providing unnecessary add-ons, for example, the capability to map one port address to another. This is implicitly at odds with the standards for well-known ports. This is often touted as an advantage for NAT-based solutions, but in fact the so-called advantages of port mapping are of marginal value, and the same functionality can be deployed in other ways that are more standards-compliant.

To check if a server is up, NAT-based load balancing solutions need to sacrifice an actual client request, and so a server outage is typically perceived only as a result of a timeout of one of these real client requests. Dispatcher's use of specialized advisors is less disruptive and reacts more quickly to a failure.

NAT Devices often only map affinity or *stickiness* based on the client's IP address, and not at the port level. This means that once a client has contacted a server, then all traffic from that client that is intended for other applications is forwarded to the same server. This drastically restricts configuration flexibility, in many cases rendering the sticky capability unusable in the real world.

11.4.2 Encapsulation

Other approaches to load balancing are proxies that encapsulate packets rather than modifying them, and then pass them to the server. This approach has some merit, particularly as, unlike the bridging NAT solutions, it does permit the load balancer to forward traffic across a wide area network; indeed this is how the Dispatcher's wide area network support works. But other implementations use encapsulation for all traffic, and in turn this requires an agent of the load balancer to be installed on each server. This agent reverses the encapsulation process. As a result the choice of server platform is by definition restricted to the platforms for which the server agent is available. Also, like NAT, it entails further processing of the packet, which increases the likelihood that it will not be scaleable to the levels required for major sites.

Dispatcher, on the other hand, does not require any code to be installed on the servers clustered behind it. Indeed it has no knowledge of the hardware or operating system platform on which the servers are running.

11.4.3 HTTP Redirection

Some load balancing offerings use HTTP redirection. It has the advantage of being simple to implement and it is transparent. However, it is restricted to HTTP (Web) traffic only. Redirection forces the client to make two interactions (even though the client may not be aware that two interactions are occurring) imposes unnecessary overhead on the server that does the redirecting, and generates unnecessary network traffic in a world where excessive network traffic is already seen to be the cause of many problems. In addition, if the user bookmarks the site URL returned by the redirect, then the load balancing function that the customer is trying to deploy is immediately defeated and bypassed by the client. This is in some ways akin to some of the original problems of round-robin DNS.

11.5 TCP/IP for OS/390 Using Workload Manager (WLM)

Sysplex, WLM and TCP/IP consist of an entirely new way of implementing a network on the OS/390 platform.

11.5.1 Related Terminology and Products

Before the overview TCP/IP for OS/390 using Workload Manager (WLM), we describe the related terminology.

11.5.1.1 Sysplex

In the context of this chapter, we use the term Sysplex to refer to a group of loosely coupled S/390 (MVS) images. For example, a Sysplex could be multiple physical hosts connected via channels and S/390 Coupling Facility technology. These OS/390 hosts in a Sysplex are able to cooperate with each other to share DASD, provide back up capabilities and distribute workload.

See *The OS/390 V2R4.0 Parallel Sysplex Overview*, GC28-1860, for more details.

11.5.1.2 Work Load Manager (WLM)

WLM is a component of OS/390 used for the control of work scheduling, load balancing, and performance management. TCP/IP for OS/390 V2R5 uses its own interface to WLM that provides the DNS (see 4.2, "Domain Name System (DNS)" on page 194) server with information allowing it to load balance. Periodic updates received from WLM tell the server which hosts in the Sysplex have the most processing resources available.

See *OS/390 V2R5.0 MVS Planning: Workload Management*, GC28-1761, for more details.

11.5.1.3 OS/390 eNetwork Communications Server V2R5 IP

OS/390 eNetwork Communications Server V2R5 is the communications engine of OS/390 V2R5. It is composed of TCP/IP, VTAM and AnyNet. Connection optimization provides intelligent Sysplex distribution of requests through cooperation between WLM and the Domain Name System (DNS) server. For customers that elect to place a name server in an OS/390 Sysplex, the DNS server can utilize WLM

Sysplex load balancing services to determine the best system to service a given client request. Note that the best system is evaluated only at connection setup time. Once the connection is made, the system being used cannot be changed without reinitiating the connection.

For a complete list of changes between OS/390 eNetwork Communications Server V2R5 and previous releases of TCP/IP, see the OS/390 eNetwork *Communications Server: IP Planning and Migration Guide V2R5*, SC31-8512, for more details.

11.5.2 Overview of WLM

WLM provides various workload-related services: performance administration, performance management and workload balancing, for example. OS/390 V2R5 IP takes advantage of WLM's workload balancing capabilities. WLM is capable of dynamically assessing resource utilization on all participating hosts within a Sysplex.

An IP V2R5 DNS server running on a host in the Sysplex can take advantage of WLM's knowledge and use it to control how often an address for a particular host in the Sysplex is returned on a DNS query. When a Sysplex name server queries the WLM for information, it is provided with a weight corresponding to the relative resource availability of each participating host in the Sysplex. These weights are used by the name server to control the frequency with which an address will be returned for a given host. If a host in the Sysplex is relatively busy, its address will not be returned by the server as often as a less busy host's address. As you might have guessed, this means that you must use host names when accessing an application on the Sysplex. The name server is the only place where address selection based upon resource availability can occur. If you use an IP address directly, no workload balancing can occur.

Here is a general outline of how WLM and DNS work together in a Sysplex. Refer to Figure 321 on page 714 for a schematic diagram.

1. When each application becomes active in the Sysplex, it registers with WLM as well as interface IP addresses.

2. The Sysplex-enabled name server will query WLM for a list of available applications.

3. Resource records representing the application's information are dynamically (and not permanently) added to the name server's data files.

4. When a request to resolve the name of a dynamically registered applications occurs, the DNS will choose an address to return based upon the weighting factor provided from WLM.

5. The next request for the same information within the Sysplex will be given the next address according to the weighting. Depending on the relative resource utilization of the hosts in the Sysplex, this could be the same address as retrieved in the previous query, it could be a different address for the same host, or it could be an address for another host in the Sysplex.

6. WLM is queried by the name server every 60 seconds (by default) for a new set of addresses and host weightings.

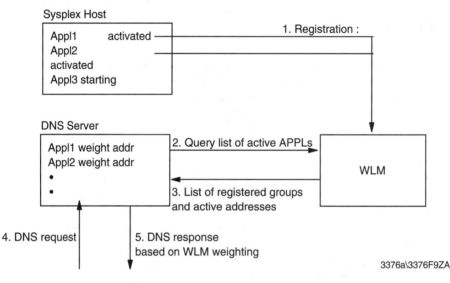

Figure 321. WLM and Name Server Working Together

11.6 OSPF Equal-Cost Multipath

OSPF has a function called equal-cost multipath (see ospf 3.3.4, "Open Shortest Path First (OSPF)" on page 146). With equal-cost multipath, a router potentially has several available next hops towards any given destination.

Actually, it is pretty simple, but the implementation of equal-cost multipath is different depending on the platform such as router. The IBM 2210 implementation is described here as an example.

When OSPF computes an equal-cost multipath routes there is more than one next hop corresponding to the route, IBM 2210 allows you to use two case of equal-cost multicast function.

A TCP session on the same path

If most of traffic is forwarded to different hosts in same subnet for example, we want to keep packets associated with a TCP session. Each time a packet is forwarded and there is not a cached route to the destination, a different next hop is cached for the destination host. This has the effect of keeping packets associated with a TCP session on the same path, which is desirable.

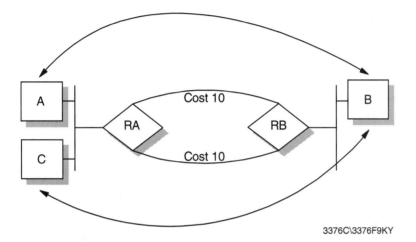

3376C\3376F9KY

Figure 322. OSPF Equal Cost Multipath and IBM 2210 Per-Packet-Multipath Disable Example

A TCP session on the different path based on round-robin fashion

If most of the traffic is with a single host, for example, the per-packet multipath IP option can be configured and a different next hop will be selected round-robin each time a packet matching the route is forwarded (see Figure 323 on page 716).

Note: The per-packet-multipath is the IBM 2210 enable command parameter. Enable command is used to activate IP features and the default for this feature is disable.

Example: enable per-packet-multipath

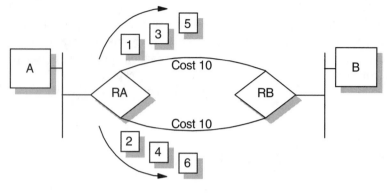

3376C\3376F9KZ

Figure 323. *OSPF Equal Cost Multipath and IBM 2210 Per-Packet-Multipath Example*

11.7 OS/390 VIPA Connection Recovery

The purpose of VIPA is to eliminate host dependency on particular network attachments to OS/390 V2R5. VIPA provides an IP address that selects a TCP/IP image without selecting a specific network attachment. Other hosts that connect to OS/390 V2R5 applications can send data via paths selected by routing protocols. VIPA provides tolerance of failures of network attachment hardware. VIPA uses a virtual device and a virtual IP address. The virtual device will always remain active and never see a failure. The virtual IP address will be the virtual address for the device, with no physical devices associated with it. Failure of a physical interface is handled by routing traffic to another interface. Similarly outbound traffic can be routed around failing interfaces provided alternate interfaces exist.

Chapter 12. Directory Protocols and Distributed Computing

The TCP/IP protocol suite contains many applications, but these generally take the form of network utilities. Although these are obviously important to a company using a network, they are not, in themselves, the reason why a company invests in a network in the first place. The network exists to provide access for users, who may be both local and remote, to a company's business applications, data and resources, which may be distributed across many servers throughout a building, city, or even the world. Those servers may be running on hardware from many different vendors and on several different operating systems. This chapter looks at methods of accessing resources and applications in a distributed network.

12.1 Introduction to the Distributed Computing Environment (DCE)

Distributed Computing Environment (DCE) is an architecture, a set of open standard services and associated APIs used to support the development and administration of distributed applications in a multiplatform, multivendor environment.

DCE is the result of work from the Open Systems Foundation (now called the Open Group), a collaboration of many hardware vendors, software vendors, customers, and consulting firms. The OSF began in 1988 with the purpose of supporting the research, development and delivery of vendor-neutral technology and industry standards. One such standard developed was DCE. DCE Version 1.0 was released in January 1992.

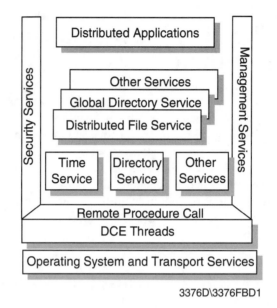

3376D\3376FBD1

Figure 324. *DCE Architectural Components*

As shown in Figure 324, DCE includes the following major services:

- Directory Service

- Security Service

- Distributed Time Service

- Distributed File Service

- Threads

- Remote Procedure Call

All the services above have Application Program Interfaces (APIs) that allow the programmer to use these functions. These services are described in more detail in the following pages.

The DCE architecture does not specifically require that TCP/IP should be used for Transport Services, but few other protocols today meet the open and multivendor requirements of the DCE design goals. In practice, the vast majority, if not all, implementations of DCE are based on TCP/IP networks.

12.1.1 DCE Directory Service

When working in a large, complex network environment, it is important to keep track of the locations, names and services (and many other details) of the participants and resources in that network. It is also important to be able to access this information easily. To enable this, information should be stored in a logical, central location and should have standard interfaces for accessing the information. The DCE Cell Directory Service does exactly this.

The DCE Directory Service has the following major components:

- Cell Directory Service (CDS)

- Global Directory Service (GDS)

- Global Directory Agent (GDA)

- Application Program Interface (API)

12.1.1.1 Cell Directory Service

The Cell Directory Service manages a database of information about the resources in a group of closely cooperating hosts, which is called a cell. A DCE cell is very scaleable and may contain many thousands of entities. Typically even fairly large corporate companies will be organized within a single cell, which may cover several countries. The Directory Service database contains a hierarchical set of names which represent a logical view of the machines, applications, users and resources within the cell. These names are usually directory entries within a directory unit. Often, this hierarchical set of names is also called the namespace. Every cell requires at least one DCE server configured with the Cell Directory Service (a directory server).

The CDS has two very important characteristics: it can be distributed, and it can be replicated. Distributed means that the entire database does not have to reside on one physical machine in the cell. The database can logically be partitioned into multiple sections (called replicas), and each replica can reside on a separate machine. The first instance of that replica is the master replica, which has read/write access. The ability of the cell directory to be split into several master replicas allows the option of distributing the management responsibility for resources in different parts of the cell. This might be particularly important if the cell covers, say, several countries.

Each master replica can be replicated. That is, a copy of this replica can be made on a different machine (which is also a directory server). This is called a read-only replica. Read-only replicas provide both resilience and performance enhancement by allowing a host machine to perform lookups to the nearest available replica.

Replicas are stored in a clearinghouse. A clearinghouse is a collection of directory replicas at a particular server. All directory replicas must be part of a clearinghouse (although not necessarily the same one).

The Cell Directory Service makes use of the DCE Security Service. When the CDS initializes, it must authenticate itself to the DCE Security Service. This prevents a fraudulent CDS from participating in the existing cell.

Figure 325 shows the directory structure of the CDS namespace. As you can see, the namespace is organized in a hierarchical manner.

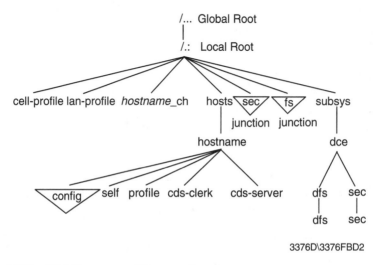

Figure 325. DCE - CDS Namespace Directory Structure

Not all DCE names are stored directly in the DCE directory service. Resource entries managed by some services, such as the Security Service (sec) and the Distributed File System (fs), connect into the namespace by means of specialized CDS entries, called junctions. A junction entry contains binding information that enables a client to connect to a directory server outside of the directory service.

The security namespace is managed by the registry service of the DCE security component, and the DFS namespace is managed by the Fileset Location Database (FLDB) service of DFS.

12.1.1.2 Global Directory Service and Agent
The Cell Directory Service is responsible for knowing where resources are within the cell. However, in a multi-cell network, each cell is part of a larger hierarchical namespace, called the Global Directory namespace. The Global Directory Service

(GDS) allows us to resolve the location of resources in foreign cells. This is the case when a company wants to connect their cells together, or to the Internet.

In order to find a resource in another cell, a communication path needs to exist between the two cells. This communication path can currently be one of two types:

- CCITT X.500 (see 1.1.8.1, "X.500: The Directory Service Standard" on page 13)

- Internet Domain Name Services (DNS)

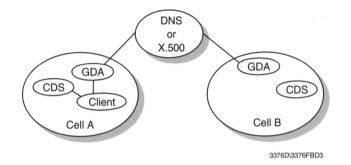

Figure 326. DCE - Global Directory Agent

In order for intercell communications to be accomplished, another component, the global directory agent, is required. The global directory agent (GDA) is the intermediary between the local cell and the Global Directory Service. In Figure 326, if the CDS does not know the location of a resource, it tells the client to ask the GDA for assistance. The GDA knows to which global namespace it is connected and queries the GDS (either DNS or X.500) for the name of the foreign cell directory server with which to communicate. Once in direct communication with the foreign cell directory server, the network name of the resource requested can be found. The global directory agent is the component that provides communications support for either DNS or X.500 environments.

12.1.2 DCE Security Service

Security is always a concern in a networked environment. In a large, distributed environment, it is even more crucial to ensure that all participants are valid users who access only the data with which they are permitted to work. The two primary concerns are authentication and authorization. Authentication is the process of proving or confirming the identity of a user or service. Authorization is the process of checking a user's level of authority when an access attempt is made. For example, if a user tries to make a change when read-only access has been granted, then the update attempt will fail.

The DCE Security Service ensures secure communications and controlled access to resources in this distributed environment. It is based on the Massachusetts Institute of Technology's Project Athena, which produced Kerberos. Kerberos is an authentication service that validates a user or service. The current DCE Security Service (DCE 1.2.2) is based on Kerberos Version 5.

Since the DCE Security Service must be able to validate users and services, it must also have a database to hold this information. This is indeed the case. The DCE Security Service maintains a database of principals, accounts, groups, organizations, policies, properties, and attributes. This database is called the registry. Figure 327 shows a pictorial representation of the registry tree. The registry is actually part of the cell directory namespace, although it is stored on a separate server.

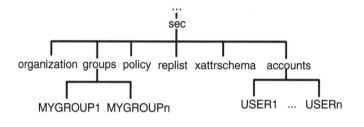

3376D\3376FBD4

Figure 327. DCE - Registry Directory Structure

The DCE Security Service consists of several components:

Authentication Service
> Handles the process of verifying that principals are correctly identified. This also contains a Ticket Granting Service, which allows the engagement of secure communications.

Privilege Service
> Supplies a user's privilege attributes to enable them to be forwarded to DCE servers.

Registry Service
> Maintains the registry database, which contains accounts, groups, principals, organizations, and policies.

Access Control List Facility
> Provides a mechanism to match a principal's access request against the access controls for the resource.

Login Facility
> Provides the environment for a user to log in and initialize the security
> environment and credentials.

These services allow for user authentication, secure communication, authorized access
to resources, and proper enforcement of security.

The DCE Security Service communicates with the Cell Directory Service to advertise
its existence to the other systems that are part of the cell. The DCE Security Service
also uses the Distributed Time Service to obtain timestamps for use in many of its
processes.

12.1.2.1 Authentication Service

The role of the authentication service is to allow principals to positively identify
themselves and participate in a DCE network. Both users and servers authenticate
themselves in a DCE environment, unlike security in most other client/server systems
where only users are authenticated. There are two distinct steps to authentication. At
initial logon time, the Kerberos third-party protocol is used within DCE to verify the
identity of a client requesting to participate in a DSS network. This process results in
the client obtaining credentials which form the basis for setting up secure sessions with
DCE servers when the user tries to access resources.

In DCE Version 1.1, the idea of preauthentication was introduced, which is not present
in the Kerberos authentication protocols. Preauthentication protects the security server
from a rogue client trying to guess valid user IDs in order to hack into the system. In
DCE 1.1 there are three protocols for preauthentication:

No preauthentication
> This is provided to support DCE clients earlier than Version 1.1.

Timestamps
> This is used by DCE Version 1.1 clients that are unable to use the
> third-party protocol. An encrypted timestamp is sent to the security server.
> The timestamp is decrypted and if the time is within 5 minutes, the user is
> considered preauthenticated. This option should be specified for cell
> administrators and non-interactive principals.

Third-party
> This is the default used by DCE Version 1.1 (and later) clients. It is
> similar to the timestamps protocol, but additional information about the
> client is also encrypted in various keys.

The login and authentication process using the third-party preauthentication protocol is shown in Figure 328 on page 724.

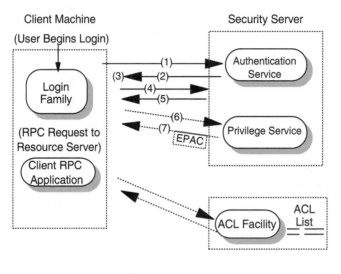

3376D\3376FBD5

Figure 328. *DCE - Authentication and Login Using Third-Party Protocol*

This process is described in detail below:

1. The user issues a request to log into the cell. However, the user must first be authenticated. The client creates two random conversation keys, one of them based on the machine session key. The Login Facility on the client then uses these keys and the supplied password to encrypt a request for an authentication ticket (ticket granting ticket, or TGT) from the security server.

2. The Authentication Service (AS) on a security server receives the request. The AS looks up the machine session key from the registry to decrypt the request. (Note that by knowing the machine session key the security server proves to be valid for the cell. A false server would not know the machine session key.) If the decryption is successful and the timestamp is within five minutes, the AS encrypts a TGT using one of the client conversation keys provided. When successful, this encrypted TGT is returned to the client.

3. The client receives the TGT envelope and decrypts it using one of the client conversation keys it provided. Also included is a conversation key for the AS. Note that the TGT itself is encrypted with a conversation key of the AS. This valid TGT is proof that the user is now authenticated.

4. Now the user needs its authorization credentials, known as Extended Privilege Attribute Certificate (EPAC), from the Privilege Service (PS). Therefore, it must construct a Privilege Ticket Granting Ticket (PTGT) request to retrieve this from the PS. To communicate with the PS, the client sends a request to the AS to contact the PS. This request is encrypted with the conversation key of the AS.

5. The AS receives this request. Using the secret key of the PS, the AS generates a conversation key for the client to use when contacting the PS. This is returned to the client and encrypted again with the AS conversation key. The client receives the envelope and decrypts it (using the conversation key) and discovers the conversation key for the PS. The client can now send a Privilege Service ticket to the PS.

6. The PS receives the request and decrypts it with its secret key successfully. This proves that the service ticket is legitimate, which also implies that the AS involved is also legitimate. From this, the PS knows that the client and the AS are valid. The PS constructs the EPAC, which lists the user's standard and extended registry attributes, including group membership. The PS creates more conversation keys and sends the EPAC and other information in an encrypted PTGT envelope to the client.

7. The client decrypts the PTGT envelope using the PS conversation key. Also, the client has the conversation key information and an encrypted PTGT (which the client cannot decrypt, since it is encrypted using the AS secret key).

8. Now, the client wants to contact an application server. To do so, it sends the PTGT to the AS and requests a service ticket for the application server. The AS receives the PTGT and decrypts it to obtain the EPAC information. It encrypts the EPAC information with the secret key of the application server and also provides a conversation key for the application server. This information is encrypted with the conversation key of the AS (which the client knows) and is returned to the client.

9. The client decrypts the envelope and discovers the application server's secret conversation key. Using this key, it can now contact the application server. By correctly decrypting the request from the client, the application server is able to determine that the client has been authenticated and by responding to the client, the client knows that it was, indeed, the real application server that it has contacted. The two will then establish a *mutually authenticated* session.

In addition to the extensive use of secret keys during logon, third-party authentication makes use of timestamps to ensure that the conversation is protected against intruders and eavesdropping. Timestamps make impersonation techniques, such as record and playback, ineffective. Also, the actual user password entered at logon time does not flow to the server as such. Instead, it is used as an encryption key for the initial logon messages which are then decrypted by the security server using its own copy of the password stored in the registry database.

If the security server is not able to authenticate the client for some reason, such as the entering an invalid password, an error is returned and the logon is terminated. However, if the exchange completes with the client being successfully authenticated, the security server returns credentials which are then used by the client to establish sessions with other DCE servers, such as resource and directory servers. These credentials contain information in the form of a Privilege Ticket Granting Ticket (PTGT) and Extended Privilege Attribute Certificate (EPAC):

EPAC   This is a validated list supplied by the security server containing the client's name, groups the client belongs to, and the extended registry attributes for the authenticated client (if any were defined and associated with their account). A client must present its EPAC (acquired during third-party authentication) to any server the client wishes to connect to in order to access its resources.

PTGT   A PTGT is a Privilege Ticket Granting Ticket. It contains the EPAC, which has all the relevant information about a user (UUID, group membership, ERAs, and so on). The PTGT is what is actually passed from a DCE client to a DCE server when it needs to access resources.

Public Key Support: The latest version of DCE (DCE Version 1.2.2) introduces the option of using public key technology (such as that from RSA or smart cards) to support login. Using this technology, the long-term key (or password) for a user (or other DCE object) does not need to be stored at the security server, providing enhanced security in the event of compromise of the security server. Administrators can specify that some principals may use the pre-DCE 1.2 mechanisms while others have access to the public key mechanism. DCE 1.2.2 retains full interoperability with previous DCE releases. At login, public key users receive credentials that allow them to use the current (Kerberos-based) DCE authentication mechanism. A new pre-authentication protocol is used. The login client does not have to determine whether a given user is public key-capable prior to requesting credentials.

12.1.3 DCE Threads

Traditional applications (written in languages such as C, COBOL, etc.) have many lines of programming code which usually execute in a sequential manner. At any time, there is one point in the program that is executing. This can be defined as single threading. A thread is a single unit of execution flow within a process. Better application performance can often be obtained when a program is structured so that several areas can be executed concurrently. This is called multithreading. The capability of executing multiple threads is also dependent on the operating system.

In a distributed computing environment based on the client/server model, threads provide the ability to perform many procedures at the same time. Work can continue in another thread while the thread waiting for a specific response is blocked (waiting for response from the network, for example). A server may issue concurrent procedure call processing. While one server thread is waiting for an I/O operation to finish, another server thread can continue working on a different request.

To function well, thread support needs to be integrated into the operating system. If threads are implemented at the application software level instead of within the operating system, performance of multithreaded applications may seem slow.

The DCE Threads APIs are either user-level (in operating systems that don't support threads, such as Windows 3.x) or kernel threads (such as AIX and OS/2). They are based on the POSIX 1003.4a Draft 4 standard. Since OS/2 also has threads, the programmer can use DCE threads or OS/2 threads.

DCE threads can be *mapped* onto OS/2 threads through special programming constructs. However, in order to write portable applications that can run on different platforms, only DCE threads should be used. In many cases, there is little performance difference resulting from this mapping.

12.1.4 DCE Remote Procedure Call

The DCE Remote Procedure Call (RPC) architecture is the foundation of communication between the client and server within the DCE environment.

Note: The DCE RPC is conceptually similar to the ONC RPC (see 4.19.2, "Remote Procedure Call (RPC)" on page 323), but the protocol used on the wire is not compatible.

RPCs provide the ability for an application program's code to be distributed across multiple systems, which can be anywhere in the network.

An application written using DCE RPCs has a client portion, which usually issues RPC requests, and a server portion, which receives RPC requests, processes them, and returns the results to the client. RPCs have three main components:

- The Interface Definition Language (IDL) and its associated compiler. From the specification file, it generates the header file, the client stub and the server stub. This allows an application to issue a remote procedure call in the same manner that it would issue a local procedure call.

- The network data representation, which defines the format for passing data such as input and output parameters. This ensures that the bit-ordering and platform-specific data representation can be converted properly once it arrives at the target system. This process of preparing data for an RPC call is called marshalling.

- The run-time library, which shields the application from the details of network communications between client and server nodes.

The application programmer may choose to use multiple threads when making RPC calls. This is because an RPC is synchronous; that is, when an RPC call is made, the thread that issued the call is blocked from further processing until a response is received.

Remote procedure calls can be used to build applications that make use of other DCE facilities, such as the Cell Directory Service (CDS) and the Security Service. The CDS may be used to find servers or to advertise a server's address for client access. The Security Service might be used to make authenticated RPCs which enable various levels of data integrity and encryption using the Commercial Data Masking Facility (CDMF), Data Encryption Standard (DES), and other functions such as authorization.

12.1.5 Distributed Time Service

Keeping the clocks on different hosts synchronized is a difficult task as the hardware clocks do not typically run at the same rates. This presents problems for distributed applications that depend on the ordering of events that happen during their execution. For example, let's say that a programmer is compiling some code on a workstation, and some files are also located on a server. If the workstation and the server don't have their time synchronized, it is possible that the compiler may not process a file because the date is older than an existing one on the server. In reality, the file is newer, but the clock on the workstation is slow. As a result, the compiled code will not reflect the latest source code changes. This problem becomes more acute in a large cell where servers are distributed across multiple time zones.

The DCE Distributed Time Service (DTS) provides standard software mechanisms to synchronize clocks on the different hosts in a distributed environment. It also provides a way of keeping a host's time close to the absolute time. DTS is optional. It is not a required core service for the DCE cell. However, if DTS is not implemented, the administrator must use some other means of keeping clocks synchronized for all the systems in the cell.

The Distributed Time Service has several components. They are:

- Local time server

- Global time server

- Courier and backup courier time server

12.1.5.1 Local Time Server

The local time server is responsible for answering time queries from time clerks on the LAN. Local time servers also query each other to maintain synchronization on the LAN. If a time clerk cannot contact the required number of local time servers (as specified by the minservers attribute), it must contact global time servers through a CDS lookup.

It is recommended that there are at least three local time servers per LAN. This ensures that the time on the LAN is synchronized. The task of synchronization across multiple LANs in the cell is performed by global and courier time servers.

12.1.5.2 Global Time Server

A global time server (GTS) advertises itself in the Cell Directory Service namespace so that all systems can find it easily. A GTS participates in the local LAN in the same way that local time servers do, but it has an additional responsibility. It also gives its time to a courier time server, which is located in a different LAN.

12.1.5.3 Courier Roles

Local and global time servers can also have a courier role; they can be couriers, backup couriers or non-couriers. The courier behaves similar to other local time servers, participating in the time synchronization process. However, the courier does not look at its own clock. It requests the time from a global time server located in another LAN or in another part of the cell. Because the time is imported from another part of the network, this enables many remote LAN segments in all parts of the cell to have a very closely synchronized time value.

The backup courier role provides support in the event that the primary courier for that LAN is not available. The backup couriers will negotiate to elect a new courier and thus maintain the proper time synchronization with the global time servers. Note that even if a courier time server is not defined, local time servers and clerks will try to contact a global time server if they cannot contact the minimum number of servers from the local segment.

The default for time servers is the non-courier role. As long as enough local time servers can be contacted, they will not contact a global time server.

In a large or distributed network, local time servers, global time servers and courier time servers make the process of time synchronization function automatically and accurately.

12.1.6 Distributed File Service (DFS)

The Distributed File Service is not really a core component of DCE but an application that is integrated with, and uses, the other DCE services. DFS provides global file sharing. Access to files located anywhere in interconnected DCE cells is transparent to the user. To the user, it appears as if the files were located on a local drive. DFS servers and clients may be heterogeneous computers running different operating systems.

The origin of DFS is Transarc Corporation's implementation of the Andrew File System (AFS) from Carnegie-Mellon University (see 12.2, "The Andrew File System (AFS)" on page 733). DFS conforms to POSIX 1003.1 for file system semantics and POSIX 1003.6 for access control security. DFS is built onto, and integrated with, all of the other DCE services and was developed to address identified distributed file system needs, such as:

- Location transparency
- Uniform naming
- Good performance
- Security
- High availability
- File consistency control
- NFS interoperability

DFS follows the client/server model, and it extends the concept of DCE cells by providing DFS administrative domains, which are an administratively independent collection of DFS server and client systems within a DCE cell.

There may be many DFS file servers in a cell. Each DFS file server runs the file exporter service which makes files available to DFS clients. The file exporter is also known as the protocol exporter. DFS clients run the cache manager, an intermediary between applications that request files from DFS servers. The cache manager translates file requests into RPCs to the file exporter on the file server system and stores (caches) file data on disk or in memory to minimize server accesses. It also ensures that the client always has an up-to-date copy of a file.

The DFS file server can serve two different types of file systems:

- Local File System (LFS), also known as the Episode File System
- Some other file system, such as the UNIX File System (UFS)

Full DFS functionality is only available with LFS and includes:

- High performance

- Log-based, fast restarting file sets for quick recovery from failure

- High availability with replication, automatic updates and automatic bypassing of failed file server

- Strong security with integration to the DCE security service providing ACL authorization control

12.1.6.1 File Naming

DFS uses the Cell Directory Service (CDS) name /.:/fs as a junction to its self-administered namespace (see Figure 325 on page 720). DFS objects of a cell (files and directories) build a file system tree rooted in /.:/fs of every cell. Directories and files can be accessed by users anywhere on the network, using the same file or directory names, no matter where they are physically located, since all DCE resources are part of a global namespace.

As an example of DFS file naming, to access a particular file from within a cell, a user might use the following name:

```
/.:/fs/usr/woodd/games/tictactoe.exe
```

From outside the cell, using GDS (X.500) format, the following name would be used:

```
/.../C=US/O=IBM/OU=ITSC/fs/usr/woodd/games/tictactoe.exe
```

or in DNS format:

```
/.../itsc.ibm.com/usr/woodd/games/tictactoe.exe
```

12.1.6.2 DFS Performance

Performance is one of the main goals of DFS, and it achieves it by including features, such as:

Cache manager

Files requested from the server are stored in cache at the client so that the client does not need to send requests for data across the network every time the user needs a file. This reduces load on the server file systems and minimizes network traffic, thereby improving performance.

Multithreaded servers

DFS servers make use of DCE threads support to efficiently handle multiple file requests from clients.

RPC pipes The RPC pipe facility is extensively used to transport large amounts of data efficiently.

Replication

Replication support allows efficient load-balancing by spreading out the requests for files across multiple servers.

12.1.6.3 File Consistency

Using copies of files cached in memory at the client side could potentially cause problems when the file is being used by multiple clients in different locations. DFS uses a token mechanism to synchronize concurrent file accesses by multiple users and ensure that each user is always working with the latest version of a file. The whole process is transparent to the user.

12.1.6.4 Availability

LFS file sets can be replicated on multiple servers for better availability. Every file set has a single read/write version and multiple read-only replicas. The read/write version is the only one that can be modified. Every change in the read/write file set is reflected in the replicated file sets. If there is a crash of a server system housing a replicated file set, the work is not interrupted, and the client is automatically switched to another replica.

12.1.6.5 DFS Security

DCE security provides DFS with authentication of user identities, verification of user privileges and authorization control. Using the DCE security's ACL mechanism, DFS provides more flexible and powerful access control than that typically provided by an operating system (UNIX read, write and execute permissions, for example).

12.1.6.6 DFS/NFS Interoperability

DFS files can be exported to NFS so that NFS clients can access them as unauthenticated users. This requires an NFS/DFS Authenticating Gateway facility, which may not be available in every implementation.

12.1.7 References

For additional information on DCE, please refer to one of the following IBM redbooks:

Understanding OSF DCE 1.1 for AIX and OS/2, SG24-4616

DCE Cell Design Considerations, SG24-4746

Administering DCE and DFS 2.1 for AIX (and OS/2 Clients), SG24-4714

Security on the Web Using DCE Technology, SG24-4949

For information on the most current release of DCE (Version 1.2.2) view the Open Group Web site at :

`http://www.opengroup.org`

12.2 The Andrew File System (AFS)

The Andrew File System (AFS) is a distributed file system used in non-DCE environments. DCE DFS was based upon AFS, and the two file systems are similar in architecture.

The latest version (AFS 3) has the following attributes:

Single logical shared namespace
> Every AFS user shares the same uniform name space. File names are independent of both the user's and the file's physical locations. Groups of client and server machines are known as cells.

Client caching
> Data is cached on client machines to reduce subsequent data requests directed at file servers, which reduces network and server loads. Servers keep track of client caches through callbacks, guaranteeing cache consistency without constant queries to the server to see if the file has changed.

RPCs   AFS uses its remote procedure call (RPC) reads and writes for efficient data transfer across the network.

Security   Kerberos-based authentication requires that users prove their identities before accessing network services. Once authenticated, AFS access control lists (ACLs) give individual users or groups of users varying levels of authority to perform operations on the files in a directory.

Replication
> Replication techniques are used for file system reliability. Multiple copies of applications and data may be replicated on multiple file servers within a cell. When accessing this information, a client will choose among the available servers. Replication also reduces the load on any particular server by placing frequently accessed information on multiple servers.

Management Utilities
> Backup, reconfiguration and routine maintenance are all done without any system down time, files remain available to users during these operations. This is done by creating online clones of volumes (subsets of related files).

AFS commands are RPC-based. Administrative commands can be issued by any authenticated administrator from any client workstation. System databases track file locations, authentication information and access control lists. These databases are replicated on multiple servers, and are dynamically updated as information changes.

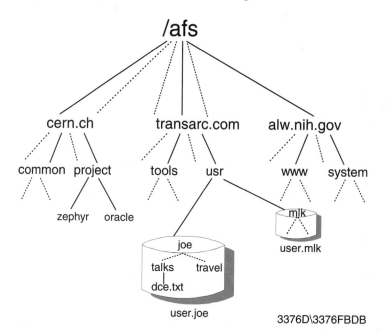

Figure 329. *AFS 3 Name Space*

Figure 329 shows an example of an AFS namespace. user.joe is a *volume*, which is a group of files managed as a single unit. Any user, situated anywhere in the network, can access Joe's dce.txt file by using the filename:

`/afs/transarc.com/usr/joe/talks/dce.txt`

Further information on AFS can be found at the Transarc Web site at:

`http://www.transarc.com/`

12.3 Lightweight Directory Access Protocol (LDAP)

The DCE architecture includes its own directory services. However, DCE, although widely implemented is not a practical solution for every company. DCE is an "all-or-nothing" implementation. That is, in order for a company to gain the most benefit from its sophisticated security and directory services, every workstation must have a DCE client installed, every application and data server must be a DCE server, and the additional security and directory servers which make up the DCE infrastructure must also be in place. However, every company that has any kind of network has a requirement for at least some of the type of services provided by DCE.

Many network-based applications exist today that rely on their own directories (or databases) containing information describing various users, applications, files and other resources accessible from the network. For example, a company may have one directory containing information on all users and resources for their file servers and another directory containing information on all users and departments for their e-mail system. Much of the information in the two directories is common, but the two are most probably totally incompatible with each other. As the number of different networks and applications has grown, the number of specialized directories of information has also grown, resulting in islands of information that cannot be shared and are difficult to maintain. If all of this information could be maintained and accessed in a consistent and controlled manner, it would provide a focal point for integrating a distributed environment into a consistent and seamless system.

The Lightweight Directory Access Protocol (LDAP) is an open industry standard that has evolved to meet these needs. LDAP defines a standard method for accessing and updating information in a directory. LDAP is gaining wide acceptance as the directory access method of the Internet and is therefore also becoming strategic within corporate intranets. It is being supported by a growing number of software vendors and is being incorporated into a growing number of applications.

Further information on LDAP can be found in the IBM Redbook *SG24-4986 Understanding LDAP*.

12.3.1 LDAP - Lightweight Access to X.500

The OSI directory standard, X.500 (see 1.1.8.1, "X.500: The Directory Service Standard" on page 13), specifies that communication between the directory client and the directory server uses the Directory Access Protocol (DAP). However, as an application layer protocol, DAP requires the entire OSI protocol stack to operate. Supporting the OSI protocol stack requires more resources than are available in many small environments. Therefore, an interface to an X.500 directory server using a less resource-intensive or lightweight protocol was desired.

LDAP was developed as a lightweight alternative to DAP. LDAP requires the lighter weight and more popular TCP/IP protocol stack rather than the OSI protocol stack. LDAP also simplifies some X.500 operations and omits some esoteric features. Two precursors to LDAP appeared as RFCs issued by the IETF, RFC 1202 *Directory Assistance Service* and RFC 1249 *DIXIE Protocol Specification*. These were both informational RFCs which were not proposed as standards. The directory assistance service (DAS) defined a method by which a directory client could communicate to a proxy on an OSI-capable host which issued X.500 requests on the client's behalf. DIXIE is similar to DAS, but provides a more direct translation of the DAP. The first version of LDAP was defined in RFC 1487 *X.500 Lightweight Access*, which was replaced by RFC 1777 *Lightweight Directory Access Protocol*. LDAP further refines the ideas and protocols of DAS and DIXIE. It is more implementation-neutral and reduces the complexity of clients to encourage the deployment of directory-enabled applications. Much of the work on DIXIE and LDAP was carried out at the University of Michigan, which provides reference implementations of LDAP and maintains LDAP-related Web pages and mailing lists (see 12.3.9, "References" on page 752).

RFC 1777 defines the LDAP protocol itself. RFC 1777, together with the following RFCs, defines LDAP Version 2:

- *RFC 1778 — The String Representation of Standard Attribute Syntaxes*

- *RFC 1779 — A String Representation of Distinguished Names*

- *RFC 1959 — An LDAP URL Format*

- *RFC 1960 — A String Representation of LDAP Search Filters*

LDAP Version 2 has reached the status of draft standard in the IETF standardization process. Many vendors have implemented products that support LDAP Version 2. Some vendors are also implementing products that support all or parts of LDAP Version 3.

LDAP Version 3 is defined by RFC 2251 *Lightweight Directory Access Protocol (v3)*, which is a proposed standard. Related RFCs that are new or updated for LDAP Version 3 are:

- *RFC 2252 — Lightweight Directory Access Protocol (v3) :Attribute Syntax Definitions*

- *RFC 2253 — Lightweight Directory Access Protocol (v3) :UTF-8 String Representation of Distinguished Names*

- *RFC 2254 — The String Representation of LDAP Search Filters*

- *RFC 2255 — The LDAP URL Format*

- *A Summary of the X.500 (96) User Schema for use with LDAPv3*

LDAP defines the communication protocol between the directory client and server, but does not define a programming interface for the client. *RFC 1823 — The LDAP Application Program Interface* defines a C language API to access a directory using LDAP Version 2. This is an informational RFC only, but it has become a de-facto standard. A standardized protocol and the availability of a common API on different platforms are the major reasons for the wide acceptance of LDAP. At the time of writing this book, RFC 1823 is in the process of being updated to support LDAP Version 3, but a new RFC number has not yet been assigned. This work in progress is the subject of an Internet draft *The C LDAP Application Program Interface* (see 12.3.9, "References" on page 752).

12.3.2 The LDAP Directory Server

LDAP defines a communication protocol. That is, it defines the transport and format of messages used by a client to access data in an X.500-like directory. LDAP does not define the directory service itself. An application client program initiates an LDAP message by calling an LDAP API. But an X.500 directory server does not understand LDAP messages. In fact, the LDAP client and X.500 server even use different communication protocols (TCP/IP vs. OSI). The LDAP client actually communicates with a gateway process (also called a proxy or front end) that forwards requests to the X.500 directory server (see Figure 330). This gateway is known as an LDAP server. It services requests from the LDAP client. It does this by becoming a client of the X.500 server. The LDAP server must communicate using both TCP/IP and OSI.

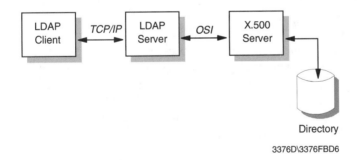

3376D\3376FBD6

Figure 330. LDAP Server Acting as a Gateway to an X.500 Directory Server

As the use of LDAP grew and its benefits became apparent, people who did not have X.500 servers or the environments to support them wanted to build directories that could be accessed by LDAP clients. This requires that the LDAP server must store and access the directory itself instead of only acting as a gateway to X.500 servers (see Figure 331 on page 738). This eliminates any need for the OSI protocol stack but, of course, makes the LDAP server much more complicated since it must store and retrieve directory entries. These LDAP servers are often called stand-alone LDAP servers because they do not depend on an X.500 directory server. Since LDAP does not support all X.500 capabilities, a stand-alone LDAP server only needs to support the capabilities required by LDAP.

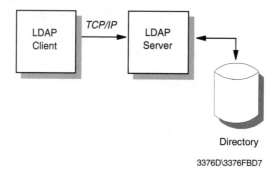

Figure 331. Stand-Alone LDAP Server

The concept of the LDAP server being able to provide access to local directories supporting the X.500 model, rather than acting only as a gateway to an X.500 server is introduced in RFC 2251 (LDAP Version 3). From the client's point of view, any server that implements the LDAP protocol is an LDAP directory server, whether the server actually implements the directory or is a gateway to an X.500 server. The directory that is accessed can be called an LDAP directory, whether the directory is implemented by a stand-alone LDAP server or by an X.500 server.

12.3.3 Overview of LDAP Architecture

LDAP defines the content of messages exchanged between an LDAP client and an LDAP server. The messages specify the operations requested by the client (search, modify, delete, and so on), the responses from the server, and the format of data carried in the messages. LDAP messages are carried over TCP/IP, a connection-oriented protocol; so there are also operations to establish and disconnect a session between the client and server.

The general interaction between an LDAP client and an LDAP server takes the following form:

- The client establishes a session with an LDAP server. This is known as binding to the server. The client specifies the host name or IP address and TCP/IP port number where the LDAP server is listening. The client can provide a user name and a password to properly authenticate with the server, or the client can establish an anonymous session with default access rights. The client and server can also establish a session that uses stronger security methods such as encryption of data (see 12.3.5, "LDAP Security" on page 746).

- The client then performs operations on directory data. LDAP offers both read and update capabilities. This allows directory information to be managed as well as queried. LDAP supports searching the directory for data meeting arbitrary user-specified criteria. Searching is the most common operation in LDAP. A user can specify what part of the directory to search and what information to return. A search filter that uses Boolean conditions specifies which directory data matches the search.

- When the client has finished making requests, it closes the session with the server. This is also known as unbinding.

Because LDAP was originally intended as a lightweight alternative to DAP for accessing X.500 directories, the LDAP server follows an X.500 model. The directory stores and organizes data structures known as entries. A directory entry usually describes an object such as a person, a printer, a server, and so on. Each entry has a name called a distinguished name (DN) that uniquely identifies it. The DN consists of a sequence of parts called relative distinguished names (RDNs), much like a file name consists of a path of directory names in many operating systems such as UNIX and OS/2. The entries can be arranged into a hierarchical tree-like structure based on their distinguished names. This tree of directory entries is called the directory information tree (DIT).

LDAP defines operations for accessing and modifying directory entries such as:

- Searching for entries meeting user-specified criteria

- Adding an entry

- Deleting an entry

- Modifying an entry

- Modifying the distinguished name or relative distinguished name of an entry (move)

- Comparing an entry

12.3.4 LDAP Models

LDAP can be better understood by considering the four models upon which it is based:

Information
> Describes the structure of information stored in an LDAP directory.

Naming   Describes how information in an LDAP directory is organized and identified.

Functional Describes the operations that can be performed on the information stored in an LDAP directory.

Security Describes how the information in an LDAP directory can be protected from unauthorized access.

The following sections discuss the first three LDAP models. LDAP security is covered in 12.3.5, "LDAP Security" on page 746.

12.3.4.1 The Information Model

The basic unit of information stored in the directory is an entry, which represents an object of interest in the real world such as a person, server or organization. Each entry contains one or more attributes that describe the entry. Each attribute has a type and one or more values. For example, the directory entry for a person might have an attribute called telephoneNumber. The syntax of the telephoneNumber attribute would specify that a telephone number must be a string of numbers that can contain spaces and hyphens. The value of the attribute would be the person's telephone number, such as 919-555-1212. (A person might have multiple telephone numbers, in which case this attribute would have multiple values.)

In addition to defining what data can be stored as the value of an attribute, an attribute syntax also defines how those values behave during searches and other directory operations. The attribute telephoneNumber, for example, has a syntax that specifies:

- Lexicographic ordering.

- Case, spaces and dashes are ignored during the comparisons.

- Values must be character strings.

For example, using the correct definitions, the telephone numbers 512-838-6008, 512838-6008 and 5128386008 are considered to be the same. A few of the syntaxes that have been defined for LDAP are listed in the following table.

Table 15 (Page 1 of 2). Common LDAP Attribute Syntaxes

Syntax	Description
bin	Binary information.
ces	Case exact string, also known as a directory string. Case is significant during comparisons.
cis	Case ignore string. Case is not significant during comparisons.
tel	Telephone number. The numbers are treated as text, but all blanks and dashes are ignored.
dn	Distinguished name.

Table 15 (Page 2 of 2). Common LDAP Attribute Syntaxes

Syntax	Description
Generalized Time	Year, month, day, and time represented as a printable string.
Postal Address	Postal address with lines separated by "$" characters.

Table 16 lists some common attributes. Some attributes have alias names that can be used wherever the full attribute name is used.

Table 16. Common LDAP Attributes

Attribute, Alias	Syntax	Description	Example
commonName, cn	cis	Common name of an entry	John Smith
surname, sn	cis	Surname (last name) of a person	Smith
telephoneNumber	tel	Telephone number	512-838-6008

An object class is a general description, sometimes called a template, of an object as opposed to the description of a particular object. For instance, the object class person has a surname attribute, whereas the object describing John Smith has a surname attribute with the value Smith. The object classes that a directory server can store and the attributes they contain are described by *schema*. Schema define which object classes are allowed where in the directory, which attributes they must contain, which attributes are optional, and the syntax of each attribute. For example, a schema could define a person object class. The person schema might require that a person has a surname attribute that is a character string, specify that a person entry can optionally have a telephoneNumber attribute that is a string of numbers with spaces and hyphens, and so on.

Schema-checking ensures that all required attributes for an entry are present before an entry is stored. Schema also define the inheritance and subclassing of objects and where in the DIT structure (hierarchy) objects may appear. Table 17 lists a few of the common schema (object classes and their required attributes). In many cases, an entry can consist of more than one object class:

Table 17 (Page 1 of 2). Object Classes and Required Attributes

Object Class	Description	Required Attributes
InetOrgPerson	Defines entries for a person	commonName (cn) surname (sn) objectClass

Table 17 (Page 2 of 2). Object Classes and Required Attributes

Object Class	Description	Required Attributes
organizationalUnit	Defines entries for organizational units	ou objectClass
organization	Defines entries for organizations	o objectClass

Though each server can define its own schema, for interoperability it is expected that many common schema will be standardized. There are times when new schema will be needed at a particular server or within an organization. In LDAP Version 3, a server is required to return information about itself, including the schema that it uses. A program can therefore query a server to determine the contents of the schema.

12.3.4.2 The Naming Model

The LDAP naming model defines how entries are identified and organized. Entries are organized in a tree-like structure called the directory information tree (DIT). Entries are arranged within the DIT based on their distinguished name (DN). A DN is a unique name that unambiguously identifies a single entry. DNs are made up of a sequence of relative distinguished names (RDNs). Each RDN in a DN corresponds to a branch in the DIT leading from the root of the DIT to the directory entry.

Each RDN is derived from the attributes of the directory entry. In the simple and common case, an RDN has the form <attribute-name>=<value>. A DN is composed of a sequence of RDNs separated by commas.

An example of a DIT is shown in Figure 332 on page 743. The example is very simple, but can be used to illustrate some basic concepts. Each box represents a directory entry. The root directory entry is conceptual and does not actually exist. Attributes are listed inside each entry. The list of attributes shown is not complete. For example, the entry for the country UK (c=UK) could have an attribute called description with the value United Kingdom.

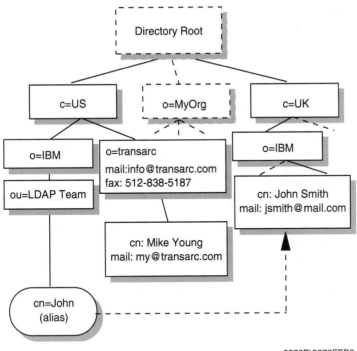

3376D\3376FBD8

Figure 332. *Example Directory Information Tree (DIT)*

It is usual to follow either a geographical or an organizational scheme to position entries in the DIT. For example, entries that represent countries would be at the top of the DIT. Below the countries would be national organizations, states, and provinces, and so on. Below this level, entries might represent people within those organizations or further subdivisions of the organization. The lowest layers of the DIT entries could represent any object, such as people, printers, application servers, and so on. The depth or breadth of the DIT is not restricted and can be designed to suit application requirements.

Entries are named according to their position in the DIT. The directory entry in the lower-right corner of Figure 332 has the DN cn=John Smith,o=IBM,c=DE.

Note: DNs read from leaf to root as opposed to names in a file system directory which usually read from root to leaf. DCE directory entries are also named starting from the root.

The DN is made up of a sequence of RDNs. Each RDN is constructed from an attribute (or attributes) of the entry it names. For example, the DN cn=John

Smith,o=IBM,c=DE is constructed by adding the RDN cn=John Smith to the DN of the ancestor entry o=IBM,c=DE.

The DIT is described as being tree-like, implying it is not a tree. This is because of aliases. Aliases allow the tree structure to be circumvented. This can be useful if an entry belongs to more than one organization or if a commonly used DN is too complex. Another common use of aliases is when entries are moved within the DIT and you want access to continue to work as before. In Figure 332 on page 743, cn=John,ou=LDAP Team,o=IBM,c=US is an alias for cn=John Smith,o=IBM,c=UK.

DNs in LDAP Version 3 are more restrictive than in LDAP V2. For example, in LDAP V2, semicolons could also be used to separate RDNs. LDAP V3 must accept the older syntax, but must not generate DNs that do not conform to the newer syntax.

As an LDAP directory can be distributed, an individual LDAP server might not store the entire DIT. A server might store the entries for a particular department and not the entries for the ancestors of the department. For example, a server might store the entries for the ITSO department at IBM. The highest node in the DIT stored by the server would be ou=ITSO,o=IBM,c=US. The server would not store entries for c=US or for o=IBM,c=US. The highest entry stored by a server is called a suffix. Each entry stored by the server ends with this suffix.

A single server can support multiple suffixes. For example, in addition to storing information about the ITSO department, the same server could store information about the sales department at Transarc. The server would then have the suffixes ou=ITSO,o=IBM,c=US and ou=sales,o=Transarc,c=US. Since a server might not store the entire DIT, servers need to be linked together in some way in order to form a distributed directory that contains the entire DIT. This is accomplished with *referrals*. A referral acts as a pointer to an entry on another LDAP server where requested information is stored. A referral is an entry of objectClass referral. It has an attribute, ref, whose value is the LDAP URL of the referred entry on another LDAP server. See 12.3.6, "LDAP URLs" on page 749, for further information.

The referral is a new feature in LDAP Version 3. Referrals allow a DIT to be partitioned and distributed across multiple servers. Portions of the DIT can also be replicated. This can improve performance and availability.

Note: When an application uses LDAP to request directory information from a server, but the server only has a referral for that information, the LDAP URL for that information is passed to the client, and it is then the responsibility of that client to contact the new server to obtain the information. This is unlike the standard mechanisms of both DCE and X.500, where a directory server, if it does not contain the requested information locally, will always obtain the information from another server and pass it back to the client.

12.3.4.3 The Functional Model

LDAP defines operations for accessing and modifying directory entries. LDAP operations can be divided into the following three categories:

Query   Includes the search and compare operations used to retrieve information from a directory

Update   Includes the add, delete, modify, and modify RDN operations used to update stored information in a directory. These operations will normally be carried out by an administrator.

Authentication

    Includes the bind, unbind, and abandon operations used to connect and disconnect to and from an LDAP server, establish access rights and protect information. For further information, please see 12.3.5, "LDAP Security" on page 746.

The Search Operation: The most common operation is the search. This operation is very flexible and has some of the most complex options. The search operation allows a client to request that an LDAP server search through some portion of the DIT for information meeting user-specified criteria in order to read and list the result(s).

The search can be very general or very specific. The search operation allows the specification of the starting point within the DIT, how deep within the DIT to search, the attributes an entry must have to be considered a match, and the attributes to return for matched entries.

Some example searches expressed informally in English are:

* Find the postal address for `cn=John Smith,o=IBM,c=DE`.

* Find all the entries that are children of the entry `ou=ITSO,o=IBM,c=US`.

* Find the e-mail address and phone number of anyone in an organization whose last name contains the characters "miller" and who also has a fax number.

To perform a search, the following parameters must be specified:

Base   A DN that defines the starting point, called the base object, of the search. The base object is a node within the DIT.

Scope   Specifies how deep within the DIT to search from the base object. There are three choices:

baseObject	Only the base object is examined.
singleLevel	Only the immediate children of the base object are examined; the base object itself is not examined.
wholeSubtree	The base object and all of its descendants are examined.

Search Filter

> Specifies the criteria an entry must match to be returned from a search. The search filter is a Boolean combination of attribute value assertions. An attribute value assertion tests the value of an attribute for equality, less than or equal, and so on.

Attributes to Return

> Specifies which attributes to retrieve from entries that match the search criteria. Since an entry may have many attributes, this allows the user to only see the attributes they are interested in. Normally, the user is interested in the value of the attributes. However, it is possible to return only the attribute types and not their values.

Alias Dereferencing

> Specifies if aliases are dereferenced. That is, the actual object of interest, pointed to by an alias entry, is examined. Not dereferencing aliases allows the alias entries themselves to be examined.

Limits   Searches can be very general, examining large subtrees and causing many entries to be returned. The user, (or the server), can specify time and size limits to prevent wayward searching from consuming too many resources. The size limit restricts the number of entries returned from the search. The time limit limits the total time of the search.

12.3.5 LDAP Security

Security is of great importance in the networked world of computers, and this is true for LDAP as well. When sending data over insecure networks. Internally or externally, sensitive information may need to be protected during transportation. There is also a need to know who is requesting the information and who is sending it. This is especially important when it comes to the update operations on a directory. The term security may be considered to cover the following four aspects:

Authentication Assurance that the opposite party (machine or person) really is who he/she/it claims to be.

Integrity Assurance that the information that arrives is really the same as what was sent.

Confidentiality Protection of information disclosure by means of data encryption to those who are not intended to receive it.

Authorization Assurance that a party is really allowed to do what it is requesting to do. This is usually checked after user authentication. In LDAP Version 3, this is currently not part of the protocol specification and is therefore implementation- (or vendor-) specific. Authorization is achieved by assigning access controls, such as read, write, or delete, for user IDs or common names to the resources being accessed. There is an Internet draft that proposes access control for LDAP (see 12.3.9, "References" on page 752).

The following sections focus on the first three aspects (since authorization is not contained in the LDAP Version 3 standard): authentication, integrity and confidentiality. There are several mechanisms that can be used for this purpose; the most important ones are discussed here. These are:

- No authentication

- Basic authentication

- Simple Authentication and Security Layer (SASL)

The security mechanism to be used in LDAP is negotiated when the connection between the client and the server is established.

12.3.5.1 No Authentication

No authentication should only be used when data security is not an issue and when no special access control permissions are involved. This could be the case, for example, when your directory is an address book browsable by anybody. No authentication is assumed when you leave the password and DN field empty in the bind API call. The LDAP server then automatically assumes an anonymous user session and grants access with the appropriate access controls defined for this kind of access (not to be confused with the SASL anonymous user as discussed in 12.3.5.3, "Simple Authentication and Security Layer (SASL)" on page 748).

12.3.5.2 Basic Authentication

Basic authentication is also used in several other Web-related protocols, such as HTTP. When using basic authentication with LDAP, the client identifies itself to the server by means of a DN and a password which are sent in the clear over the network (some implementation may use Base64 encoding instead). The server considers the client authenticated if the DN and password sent by the client matches the password for that DN stored in the directory. Base64 encoding is defined in the Multipurpose Internet Mail Extensions (MIME - see 4.8, "Multipurpose Internet Mail Extensions (MIME)" on page 250). Base64 is a relatively simple encryption, and therefore it is not hard to break once the data has been captured on the network.

12.3.5.3 Simple Authentication and Security Layer (SASL)

SASL is a framework for adding additional authentication mechanisms to connection-oriented protocols. It has been added to LDAP Version 3 to overcome the authentication shortcomings of Version 2. SASL was originally devised to add stronger authentication to the IMAP protocol. SASL has since evolved into a more general system for mediating between protocols and authentication systems. It is a proposed Internet standard defined in RFC 2222 *Simple Authentication and Security Layer (SASL)*.

In SASL, connection protocols, such as LDAP, IMAP, and so on, are represented by profiles; each profile is considered a protocol extension that allows the protocol and SASL to work together. A complete list of SASL profiles can be obtained from the Information Sciences Institute (ISI) (see 12.3.9, "References" on page 752). Among these are IMAP4, SMTP, POP3, and LDAP. Each protocol that intends to use SASL needs to be extended with a command to identify an authentication mechanism and to carry out an authentication exchange. Optionally, a security layer can be negotiated to encrypt the data after authentication and so ensure confidentiality. LDAP Version 3 includes such a command (ldap_sasl_bind()). The key parameters that influence the security method used are:

dn   This is the distinguished name of the entry which is to bind. This can be thought of as the user ID in a normal user ID and password authentication.

mechanism This is the name of the security method that should be used. Valid security mechanisms are currently Kerberos Version 4, S/Key, GSSAPI, CRAM-MD5 and EXTERNAL. There is also an ANONYMOUS mechanism available which enables an authentication as user anonymous. In LDAP, the most common mechanism used is SSL (or its successor, TLS), which is provided as an EXTERNAL mechanism.

credentials This contains the arbitrary data that identifies the DN. The format and content of the parameter depends on the mechanism chosen. If it is, for example, the ANONYMOUS mechanism, it can be an arbitrary string or an e-mail address that identifies the user.

SASL provides a high-level framework that lets the involved parties decide on the particular security mechanism to use. The SASL security mechanism negotiation between client and server is done in the clear. Once the client and the server have agreed on a common mechanism, the connection is secure against modifying the authentication identities. However, an attacker could try to eavesdrop the mechanism negotiation and cause a party to use the least secure mechanism. In order to prevent this from happening, clients and servers should be configured to use a minimum security mechanism, provided they support such a configuration option. As stated earlier, SSL and its successor, TLS, are the mechanisms commonly used in SASL for LDAP. For details on these protocols, please refer to 5.7, "Secure Sockets Layer (SSL)" on page 424.

As no data encryption method was specified in LDAP Version 2, some vendors, for example Netscape and IBM, added their own SSL calls to the LDAP API. A potential drawback of such an approach is that the API calls might not be compatible among different vendor implementations. The use of SASL, as specified in LDAP Version 3 should assure compatibility, although it is likely that vendor products will support only a subset of the possible range of mechanisms (maybe only SSL).

12.3.6 LDAP URLs

Since LDAP has become an important protocol on the Internet, a URL format for LDAP resources has been defined. RFC 2255 *The LDAP URL Format* describes the format of the LDAP URL. LDAP URLs begin with ldap:// or ldaps:// if the LDAP server communicates using SSL. LDAP URLs can simply name an LDAP server, or can specify a complex directory search.

Some examples will help make the format of LDAP URLs clear. The following refers to the LDAP server on the host saturn.itso.austin.ibm.com, (using the default port 389):

`ldap://saturn.itso.austin.ibm.com/`

The following retrieves all the attributes for the DN `o=Transarc,c=US` from the LDAP server on host saturn.itso.austin.ibm.com. Note that the port 389 is explicitly specified here as an example. Since 389 is the default port, it would not have been necessary to specify it in the URL.

`ldap://saturn.itso.austin.ibm.com:389/o=Transarc,c=US`

The following retrieves all the attributes for the DN `cn=JohnSmith,ou=Austin,o=IBM,c=US`. Note that some characters are considered unsafe in URLs because they can be removed or treated as delimiters by some programs. Unsafe characters such as space, comma, brackets, and so forth should be represented by their hexadecimal value preceded by the percent sign.

`ldap://saturn.itso.austin.ibm.com/cn=John%20Smith,ou=Austin,o=IBM,c=US`

In this example, %20 is a space. More information about unsafe characters and URLs in general can be found in RFC 1738 *Uniform Resource Locators (URL)*.

12.3.7 LDAP and DCE

DCE has its own cell directory service (CDS - see 12.1.1.1, "Cell Directory Service" on page 719). If applications never access resources outside of their DCE cell, only CDS is required. However, if an application needs to communicate with resources in other DCE cells, the Global Directory Agent (GDA) is required. The GDA accesses a global (that is, non-CDS) directory where the names of DCE cells can be registered. This global directory (GDS) can be either a Domain Name System (DNS) directory or an X.500 directory. The GDA retrieves the address of a CDS server in the remote cell. The remote CDS can then be contacted to find DCE resources in that cell. Using the GDA enables an organization to link multiple DCE cells together using either a private directory on an intranet or a public directory on the Internet.

In view of LDAP's strong presence in the Internet, two LDAP projects have been sponsored by The Open Group to investigate LDAP integration with DCE technology.

12.3.7.1 LDAP Interface for the GDA

One way LDAP is being integrated into DCE is to allow DCE cells to be registered in LDAP directories. The GDA in a cell that wants to connect to remote cells is configured to enable access to the LDAP directory (see Figure 333).

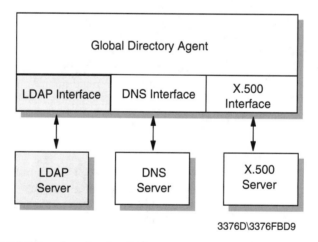

Figure 333. LDAP Interface for the GDA

DCE originally supports only X.500 and DNS name syntax for cell names. LDAP and X.500 names both follow the same hierarchical naming model, but their syntax is slightly different. X.500 names are written in reverse order and use a slash (/) rather than a comma (,) to separated relative distinguished names. When the GDA is configured to use LDAP, it converts cell names in X.500 format to LDAP format to look them up in an LDAP directory.

12.3.7.2 LDAP Interface for the CDS

DCE provides two programming interfaces to the Directory Service; Name Service Interface (NSI) and the X/Open Directory Service (XDS). XDS is an X.500 compatible interface used to access information in the GDS, and it can also be used to access information in the CDS. However, the use of NSI is much more common in DCE applications. The NSI API provides functionality that is specifically tailored for use with DCE client and server programs that use RPC. NSI allows servers to register their address and the type of RPC interface they support. This address/interface information is called an RPC binding and is needed by clients that want to contact the server. NSI allows clients to search the CDS for RPC binding information.

NSI was designed to be independent of the directory where the RPC bindings are stored. However, the only supported directory to date has been CDS. NSI will be extended to also support adding and retrieving RPC bindings from an LDAP directory. This will allow servers to advertise their RPC binding information in either CDS or an LDAP directory. Application programs could use either the NSI or the LDAP API when an LDAP directory is used (see Figure 334).

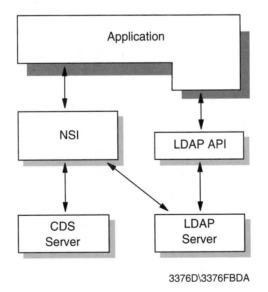

3376D\3376FBDA

Figure 334. LDAP Interface for NSI

An LDAP schema to represent RPC binding information is in the draft stage of development within the IETF.

12.3.8 The Directory-Enabled Networks Initiative (DEN)

In September 1997, Cisco Systems Inc. and Microsoft Corp. announced the so-called Directory-Enabled Networks Initiative (DEN) as a result of a collaborative work. Many companies, such as IBM, either support this initiative or even actively participate in ad hoc working groups (ADWGs). DEN represents an information model specification for an integrated directory that stores information about people, network devices and applications. The DEN schema defines the object classes and their related attributes for those objects. In such, DEN is a key piece to building intelligent networks, where products from multiple vendors can store and retrieve topology and configuration-related data. Since DEN is a relatively new specification, products supporting it cannot be expected until about one to two years after its first draft was published late in 1997.

Of special interest is that the DEN specification defines LDAP Version 3 as the core protocol for accessing DEN information, which makes information available to LDAP-enabled clients and/or network devices.

More information about the DEN initiative can be found on the founders Web sites or at:

`http://murchiso.com/den/`

12.3.9 References

Please refer to the following documents for more information about LDAP.

RFCs

> RFC 1487 — *X.500 Lightweight Access*
>
> RFC 1777 — *Lightweight Directory Access Protocol*
>
> RFC 1778 — *The String Representation of Standard Attribute Syntaxes*
>
> RFC 1779 — *A String Representation of Distinguished Names*
>
> RFC 1959 — *An LDAP URL Format*
>
> RFC 1960 — *A String Representation of LDAP Search Filters*
>
> RFC 2251 — *Lightweight Directory Access Protocol (v3)*
>
> RFC 2252 — *Lightweight Directory Access Protocol (v3): Attribute Syntax Definitions*
>
> RFC 2253 — *Lightweight Directory Access Protocol (v3): UTF-8 String Representation of Distinguished Names*
>
> RFC 2254 — *The String Representation of LDAP Search Filters*

RFC 2255 — The LDAP URL Format

RFC 2256 — A Summary of the X.500(96) User Schema for use with LDAPv3

RFC 1823 — The LDAP Application Program Interface

RFC 2222 — Simple Authentication and Security Layer (SASL)

Internet Drafts

The C LDAP Application Program Interface:

`http://search.ietf.org/internet-drafts/draft-ietf-ldapext-ldap-c-api-01.txt`

Access Control Requirements for LDAP:

`http://search.ietf.org/internet-drafts/draft-ietf-ldapext-acl-reqts-01.txt`

Other Resources

SASL Mechanisms:

`ftp://ftp.isi.edu/in-notes/iana/assignments/sasl-mechanisms`

The Unversity of Michigan was, and still is, an important contributor to the development of LDAP and can be considered a reliable, neutral source for extensive information.

`http://www.umich.edu/~dirsvcs/ldap/`

Part 3. Connection Protocols and Platform Implementations

Chapter 13. Connection Protocols

This chapter provides an overview of protocols and interfaces that allow TCP/IP traffic to flow over various kinds of physical networks as well as over logical multiprotocol connections.

13.1 Ethernet and IEEE 802.x Local Area Networks (LANs)

Two frame formats can be used on the Ethernet coaxial cable:

1. The standard issued in 1978 by Xerox Corporation, Intel Corporation and Digital Equipment Corporation, usually called *Ethernet* (or *DIX* Ethernet).

2. The international IEEE 802.3 standard, a more recently defined standard.

The difference between the two standards is in the use of one of the header fields, which contains a protocol-type number for Ethernet and the length of the data in the frame for IEEE 802.3.

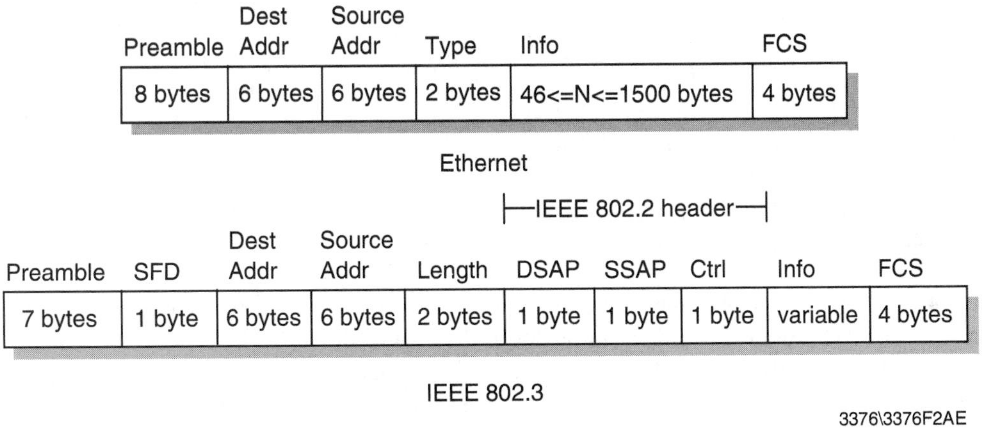

Figure 335. ARP - Frame Formats for Ethernet and IEEE 802.3

- The type field in Ethernet is used to distinguish between different protocols running on the coaxial cable, and allows their coexistence on the same physical cable.

- The maximum length of an Ethernet frame is 1526 bytes. This means a data field length of up to 1500 bytes. The length of the 802.3 data field is also limited to 1500 bytes for 10 Mbps networks, but is different for other transmission speeds.

- In the 802.3 MAC frame, the length of the data field is indicated in the 802.3 header. The type of protocol it carries is then indicated in the 802.2 header (higher protocol level, see Figure 335 on page 757).

- In practice however, both frame formats can coexist on the same physical coax. This is done by using protocol type numbers (type field) greater than 1500 in the Ethernet frame. However, different device drivers are needed to handle each of these formats.

Thus, for all practical purposes, the Ethernet physical layer and the IEEE 802.3 physical layer are compatible. However, the Ethernet data link layer and the IEEE 802.3/802.2 data link layer are incompatible.

The 802.2 Logical Link Control (LLC) layer above IEEE 802.3 uses a concept known as *link service access point* (LSAP) which uses a 3-byte header, where DSAP and SSAP stand for destination and source service:

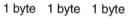
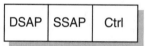

Figure 336. ARP - IEEE 802.2 LSAP Header

Access Point respectively. Numbers for these fields are assigned by an IEEE committee.

Due to a growing number of applications using IEEE 802 as lower protocol layers, an extension was made to the IEEE 802.2 protocol in the form of the Sub-Network Access Protocol (SNAP). It is an extension to the LSAP header above, and its use is indicated by the value 170 in both the SSAP and DSAP fields of the LSAP frame above.

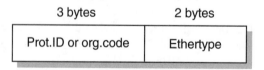

Figure 337. ARP - IEEE 802.2 SNAP Header

In the evolution of TCP/IP, three standards were established that describe the encapsulation of IP and ARP frames on these networks:

1. 1984: *RFC 894 — Standard for the Transmission of IP Datagrams over Ethernet Networks* specifies only the use of Ethernet type of networks. The values assigned to the type field are:

   2048 (hex 0800)   for IP datagrams
   2054 (hex 0806)   for ARP datagrams

2. 1985: *RFC 948 — Two Methods for the Transmission of IP Datagrams over IEEE 802.3 Networks* specifies two possibilities:

   a. The Ethernet compatible method: The frames are sent on a real IEEE 802.3 network in the same fashion as on an Ethernet network, that is, using the IEEE 802.3 data-length field as the Ethernet type field, thereby violating the IEEE 802.3 rules, but compatible with an Ethernet network.
   b. IEEE 802.2/802.3 LLC type 1 format: Using 802.2 LSAP header with IP using the value 6 for the SSAP and DSAP fields.

   The RFC indicates clearly that the IEEE 802.2/802.3 method is the preferred method. That is, that all future IP implementations on IEEE 802.3 networks are supposed to use the second method.

3. 1987: *RFC 1010 - Assigned Numbers* (now obsoleted by RFC 1700 dated 1994) notes that as a result of IEEE 802.2 evolution and the need for more Internet protocol numbers, a new approach was developed based on practical experiences exchanged during the August 1986 TCP Vendors Workshop. It states in an almost completely overlooked part of this RFC that from now on all IEEE 802.3, 802.4 and 802.5 implementations should use the Sub-Network Access Protocol (SNAP) form of the IEEE 802.2 LLC: DSAP and SSAP fields set to 170 (indicating the use of SNAP) and then SNAP assigned as follows:

   - 0 (zero) as organization code.
   - EtherType field:
     2048 (hex 0800)   for IP datagrams
     2054 (hex 0806)   for ARP datagrams
     32821 (hex 8035)   for RARP datagrams
     These are the same values as used in the Ethernet type field.

4. 1988: *RFC 1042 — Standard for the Transmission of IP Datagrams over IEEE 802 Networks*.

   As this new approach (very important for implementations) passed almost unnoticed in a little note of an unrelated RFC, it became quite confusing, and finally, in February 1988, it was repeated in an RFC on its own: *RFC 1042*, which obsoletes *RFC 948*.

The relevant IBM TCP/IP products implement RFC 894 for DIX Ethernet and RFC 1700 for IEEE 802.3 networks.

However, in practical situations, there are still TCP/IP implementations that use the older LSAP method (RFC 948 or 1042). Such implementations will not communicate with the more recent implementations (such as IBM's).

Note also that the last method covers not only the IEEE 802.3 networks, but also the IEEE 802.4 and 802.5 networks such as the IBM Token-Ring LAN.

13.2 Fiber Distributed Data Interface (FDDI)

The FDDI specifications define a family of standards for 100 Mbps fiber optic LANs that provides the physical layer and media access control sublayer of the data link layer as defined by the ISO/OSI Model.

IP-FDDI is a *draft-standard protocol*. Its status is *elective*. It defines the encapsulating of IP datagrams and ARP requests and replies in FDDI frames. Figure 338 on page 761 shows the related protocol layers.

It is defined in *RFC 1188 - A Proposed Standard for the Transmission of IP Datagrams over FDDI Networks* for single MAC stations. Operation on dual MAC stations will be described in a forthcoming RFC.

RFC 1188 states that all frames are transmitted in standard IEEE 802.2 LLC Type 1 Unnumbered Information format, with the DSAP and SSAP fields of the 802.2 header set to the assigned global SAP value for SNAP (decimal 170). The 24-bit Organization Code in the SNAP header is set to zero, and the remaining 16 bits are the EtherType from Assigned Numbers (see RFC 1700), that is:

- 2048 for IP
- 2054 for ARP

The mapping of 32-bit Internet addresses to 48-bit FDDI addresses is done via the ARP dynamic discovery procedure. The broadcast Internet addresses (whose <host address> is set to all ones) are mapped to the broadcast FDDI address (all ones).

IP datagrams are transmitted as series of 8-bit bytes using the usual TCP/IP transmission order called *big-endian* or *network byte order*.

The FDDI MAC specification (*ISO 9314-2 - ISO, Fiber Distributed Data Interface - Media Access Control*) defines a maximum frame size of 4500 bytes for all frame fields. After taking the LLC/SNAP header into account, and to allow future extensions to the MAC header and frame status fields, the MTU of FDDI networks is set to 4352 bytes.

Please refer to *LAN Concepts and Products,* SG24-4753 for more details on the FDDI architecture.

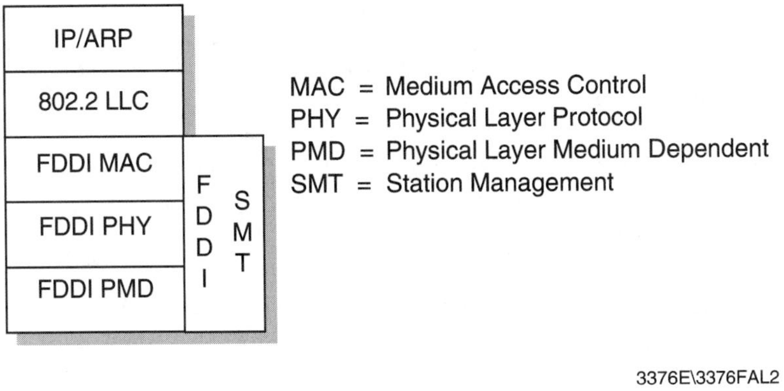

```
+-----------+
|  IP/ARP   |
+-----------+----+           MAC = Medium Access Control
| 802.2 LLC |    |           PHY = Physical Layer Protocol
+-----------+--+ |           PMD = Physical Layer Medium Dependent
| FDDI MAC  |F | |           SMT = Station Management
+-----------+D |S|
| FDDI PHY  |D |M|
+-----------+D |T|
| FDDI PMD  |I | |
+-----------+--+-+
```

3376E\3376FAL2

Figure 338. IP and ARP over FDDI

13.3 Asynchronous Transfer Mode (ATM)

ATM-based networks are of increasing interest for both local and wide area applications. There are already some products available to build your physical ATM network. The ATM architecture is new and therefore different from the standard LAN architectures. For this reason, changes are required so that traditional LAN products will work in the ATM environment. In the case of TCP/IP the main change required is in the network interface to provide support for ATM.

There are several approaches already available, two of which are important to the transport of TCP/IP traffic. They are described in 13.3.2, "Classical IP over ATM" on page 765 and 13.3.3, "ATM LAN Emulation" on page 770. They are also compared in 13.3.4, "Classical IP over ATM versus LAN Emulation" on page 773.

13.3.1 Address Resolution (ATMARP and InATMARP)

The address resolution in an ATM logical IP subnet is done by the ATM Address Resolution Protocol (ATMARP) based on RFC 826 and the Inverse ATM Address Resolution Protocol (InATMARP) based on RFC 1293 (which is updated in RFC 2390). ATMARP is the same protocol as the ARP protocol with extensions needed to support ARP in a unicast server ATM environment. InATMARP is the same protocol as the original InARP protocol but applied to ATM networks. Use of these protocols differs depending on whether permanent virtual connections (PVCs) or switched virtual connections (SVCs) are used.

Both ATMARP and InATMARP are defined in RFC 2225 (updating RFC 1577), which is a proposed standard with a state of elective.

The encapsulation of ATMARP and InATMARP requests/replies is described in 13.3.2, "Classical IP over ATM" on page 765.

13.3.1.1 InATMARP

The ARP protocol is used to resolve a host's hardware address for a known IP address. The InATMARP protocol is used to resolve a host's IP address for a known hardware address. In a switched environment you first establish a virtual connection (VC) of either a permanent virtual connection (PVC) or switched virtual connection (SVC) in order to communicate with another station. Therefore you know the exact hardware address of the partner by administration but the IP address is unknown. InATMARP provides dynamic address resolution. InARP uses the same frame format as the standard ARP but defines two new operation codes:

- InARP request=8

- InARP reply=9

Please see 2.4.2.1, "ARP Packet Generation" on page 88 for more details.

Basic InATMARP operates essentially the same as ARP with the exception that InATMARP does not broadcast requests. This is because the hardware address of the destination station is already known. A requesting station simply formats a request by inserting its source hardware and IP address and the known target hardware address. It then zero fills the target protocol address field and sends it directly to the target station. For every InATMARP request, the receiving station formats a reply using the source address from the request as the target address of the reply. Both sides update their ARP tables. The hardware type value for ATM is 19 decimal and the EtherType field is set to 0x806, which indicates ARP according to RFC 1700.

13.3.1.2 Address Resolution in a PVC Environment

In a PVC environment each station uses the InATMARP protocol to determine the IP addresses of all other connected stations. The resolution is done for those PVCs that are configured for LLC/SNAP encapsulation. It is the responsibility of each IP station supporting PVCs to revalidate ARP table entries as part of the aging process.

13.3.1.3 Address Resolution in an SVC Environment

SVCs require support for ATMARP in the non-broadcast environment of ATM. To meet this need, a single ATMARP server must be located within the Logical IP Subnetwork (LIS) (see 13.3.2.1, "The Logical IP Subnetwork (LIS)" on page 767). This server has authoritative responsibility for resolving the ATMARP requests of all IP members within the LIS. For an explanation of ATM terms please refer to 13.3.2, "Classical IP over ATM" on page 765.

The server itself does not actively establish connections. It depends on the clients in the LIS to initiate the ATMARP registration procedure. An individual client connects to the ATMARP server using a point-to-point VC. The server, upon the completion of an ATM call/connection of a new VC specifying LLC/SNAP encapsulation, will transmit an InATMARP request to determine the IP address of the client. The InATMARP reply from the client contains the information necessary for the ATMARP server to build its ATMARP table cache. This table consists of:

- IP address
- ATM address
- Timestamp
- Associated VC

This information is used to generate replies to the ATMARP requests it receives.

Note: The ATMARP server mechanism requires that each client be administratively configured with the ATM address of the ATMARP server.

ARP Table Add/Update Algorithm:

- If the ATMARP server receives a new IP address in an InATMARP reply the IP address is added to the ATMARP table.

- If the InATMARP IP address duplicates a table entry IP address and the InATMARP ATM address does not match the table entry ATM address and there is an open VC associated with that table entry, the InATMARP information is discarded and no modifications to the table are made.

- When the server receives an ATMARP request over a VC, where the source IP and ATM address match the association already in the ATMARP table and the ATM address matches that associated with the VC, the server updates the timeout on the source ATMARP table entry. For example, if the client is sending ATMARP requests to the server over the same VC that it used to register its ATMARP entry, the server notes that the client is still "alive" and updates the timeout on the client's ATMARP table entry.

- When the server receives an ARP_REQUEST over a VC, it examines the source information. If there is no IP address associated with the VC over which the ATMARP request was received and if the source IP address is not associated with any other connection, then the server adds this station to its ATMARP table. This is not the normal way because, as mentioned above, it is the responsibility of the client to register at the ATMARP server.

ATMARP Table Aging: ATMARP table entries are valid:

- In clients for a maximum time of 15 minutes

- In servers for a minimum time of 20 minutes

Prior to aging an ATMARP table entry, the ATMARP server generates an InARP_REQUEST on any open VC associated with that entry and decides what to do according to the following rules:

- If an InARP_REPLY is received, that table entry is updated and not deleted.

- If there is no open VC associated with the table entry, the entry is deleted.

Therefore, if the client does not maintain an open VC to the server, the client must refresh its ATMARP information with the server at least once every 20 minutes. This is done by opening a VC to the server and exchanging the initial InATMARP packets.

The client handles the table updates according to the following:

- When an ATMARP table entry ages, the ATMARP client invalidates this table entry.

- If there is no open VC associated with the invalidated entry, that entry is deleted.

- In the case of an invalidated entry and an open VC, the ATMARP client revalidates the entry prior to transmitting any non-address resolution traffic on that VC. There are two possibilities:

  - In the case of a PVC, the client validates the entry by transmitting an InARP_REQUEST and updating the entry on receipt of an InARP_REPLY.

  - In the case of an SVC, the client validates the entry by transmitting an ARP_REQUEST to the ATMARP server and updating the entry on receipt of an ARP_REPLY.

- If a VC with an associated invalidated ATMARP table entry is closed, that table entry is removed.

As mentioned above, every ATM IP client that uses SVCs must know its ATMARP server's ATM address for the particular LIS. This address must be named at every client during customization. There is at present no well-known ATMARP server address defined.

13.3.2 Classical IP over ATM

The definitions for implementations of classical IP over Asynchronous Transfer Mode (ATM) are described in RFC 2225 which is a proposed standard with a status of elective according to RFC 2400 (STD 1). This RFC considers only the application of ATM as a direct replacement for the "wires", local LAN segments connecting IP endstations (members) and routers operating in the classical LAN-based paradigm. Issues raised by MAC level bridging and LAN emulation are not covered.

For ATM Forum's method of providing ATM migration please see 13.3.3, "ATM LAN Emulation" on page 770.

Initial deployment of ATM provides a LAN segment replacement for:

- Ethernets, token-rings or FDDI networks
- Local area backbones between existing (non-ATM) LANs
- Dedicated circuits of frame relay PVCs between IP routers

This RFC also describes extensions to the ARP protocol (RFC 826) in order to work over ATM. This is discussed separately in 13.3.1, "Address Resolution (ATMARP and InATMARP)" on page 762.

First some ATM basics:

Cells   All information (voice, image, video, data , etc.) is transported through the network in very short (48 data bytes plus a 5-byte header) blocks called *cells*.

Routing   Information flow is along paths (called *virtual channels*) set up as a series of pointers through the network. The cell header contains an identifier that links the cell to the correct path that it will take towards its destination.

            Cells on a particular virtual channel always follow the same path through the network and are delivered to the destination in the same order in which they were received.

Hardware-Based Switching

ATM is designed so that simple hardware-based logic elements may be employed at each node to perform the switching. On a link of 1 Gbps a new cell arrives and a cell is transmitted every .43 microseconds. There is not a lot of time to decide what to do with an arriving packet.

Virtual Connection VC

ATM provides a virtual connection switched environment. VC setup can be done on either a permanent virtual connection (PVC) or a dynamic switched virtual connection (SVC) basis. SVC call management is performed via implementations of the Q.93B protocol.

End-User Interface

The only way for a higher layer protocol to communicate across an ATM network is over the ATM Adaptation Layer (AAL). The function of this layer is to perform the mapping of protocol data units (PDUs) into the information field of the ATM cell and vice versa. There are four different AAL types defined: AAL1, AAL2, AAL3/4 and AAL5. These AALs offer different services for higher layer protocols. Here are the characteristics of AAL5, which is used for TCP/IP:

- Message mode and streaming mode
- Assured delivery
- Non-assured delivery (used by TCP/IP)
- Blocking and segmentation of data
- Multipoint operation

AAL5 provides the same functions as a LAN at the Medium Access Control (MAC) layer. The AAL type is known by the VC endpoints via the cell setup mechanism and is not carried in the ATM cell header. For PVCs the AAL type is administratively configured at the endpoints when the connection (circuit) is set up. For SVCs, the AAL type is communicated along the VC path via Q.93B as part of call setup establishment and the endpoints use the signaled information for configuration. ATM switches generally do not care about the AAL type of VCs. The AAL5 format specifies a packet format with a maximum size of 64KB - 1 byte of user data. The *primitives*, which the higher layer protocol has to use in order to interface with the AAL layer (at the AAL service access point - SAP), are rigorously defined. When a high-layer protocol sends data, that data is processed first by the adaptation layer, then by the ATM layer and then the physical layer takes over to send the data to the ATM network. The cells are transported by the network and then received on the other side first by the physical layer, then processed by the ATM layer and then by the receiving AAL. When all this is complete, the information (data) is passed to the receiving higher layer protocol. The total function performed by the ATM network has been the non-assured transport (it might have lost some) of information from one side to the other. Looked at from a traditional data processing viewpoint all the ATM network has done is to replace a physical link connection with another kind of physical connection. All the higher layer network functions must still be performed (for example IEEE 802.2).

Addressing An ATM Forum endpoint address is either encoded as a 20-byte OSI NSAP-based address (used for private network addressing, three formats possible) or is an E.164 Public UNI address (telephone number style address used for public ATM networks).[15]

Broadcast, Multicast

There are currently no broadcast functions similar to LANs provided. But there is a multicast function available. The ATM term for multicast is *point-to-multipoint connection.*

13.3.2.1 The Logical IP Subnetwork (LIS)

The term LIS was introduced to map the logical IP structure to the ATM network. In the LIS scenario, each separate administrative entity configures its hosts and routers within a closed logical IP subnetwork (same IP network/subnet number and address mask). Each LIS operates and communicates independently of other LISs on the same ATM network. Hosts that are connected to an ATM network communicate directly to other hosts within the same LIS. This implies that all members of a LIS are able to communicate via ATM with all other members in the same LIS. (VC topology is fully meshed.) Communication to hosts outside of the local LIS is provided via an IP router. This router is an ATM endpoint attached to the ATM network that is configured as a member of one or more LISs. This configuration may result in a number of separate LISs operating over the same ATM network. Hosts of differing IP subnets must communicate via an intermediate IP router even though it may be possible to open a direct VC between the two IP members over the ATM network.

13.3.2.2 Multiprotocol Encapsulation

If you want to use more than one type of network protocol (IP, IPX, etc.) concurrently over a physical network, you need a method of multiplexing the different protocols. This can be done in the case of ATM either by VC-based multiplexing or LLC

---

15 The ATM Forum is a worldwide organization, aimed at promoting ATM within the industry and the end-user community. The membership includes more than 500 companies representing all sectors of the communications and computer industries as well as a number of government agencies, research organizations and users.

encapsulation. If you choose VC-based multiplexing you have to have a VC for each different protocol between the two hosts. The LLC encapsulation provides the multiplexing function at the LLC layer and therefore needs only one VC. TCP/IP uses, according to RFC 2225 and 1483, the second method because this kind of multiplexing was already defined in RFC 1042 for all other LAN types such as Ethernet, token-ring and FDDI. With this definition IP uses ATM simply as a LAN replacement. All the other benefits ATM has to offer, such as transportation of isochronous traffic etc., are not used. There is an IETF working group with the mission of improving the IP implementation and to interface with the ATM Forum in order to represent the interests of the Internet community for future standards.

To be exact, the TCP/IP PDU is encapsulated in an IEEE 802.2 LLC header followed by an IEEE 802.1a SubNetwork Attachment Point (SNAP) header and carried within the payload field of an AAL5 CPCS-PDU (Common Part Convergence Sublayer). The AAL5 CPCS-PDU format is shown in Figure 339.

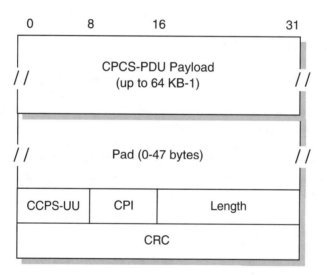

3376E\3376FAL3

Figure 339. AAL5 CPCS-PDU Format

Where:

CPCS-PDU Payload

> The CPCS-PDU payload is shown in Figure 340.

Pad

> The Pad field pads out the CDCS-PDU to fit exactly into the the ATM cells.

CPCS-UU

> The CPCS-UU (User-to-User identification) field is used to transparently transfer CPCS user-to-user information. This field has no function for the encapsulation and can be set to any value.

CPI

> The Common Part Indicator (CPI) field aligns the CPCS-PDU trailer with 64 bits.

Length

> The Length field indicates the length, in bytes, of the Payload field. The maximum value is 65535 which is 64KB - 1.

CRC

> The CRC field protects the entire CPCS-PDU except the CRC field itself.

The payload format for routed IP PDUs is shown in Figure 340.

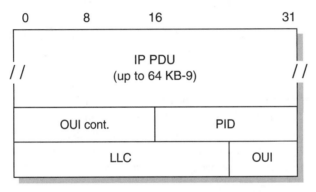

3376E\3376FAL4

Figure 340. *CPCS-PDU Payload Format for IP PDUs*

Where:

IP PDU

> Normal IP datagram starting with the IP header.

LLC

> 3-byte LLC header with the format DSAP-SSAP-Ctrl. For IP data it is set to 0xAA-AA-03 to indicate the presence of a SNAP header. The Ctrl field always has the value 0x03 specifying Unnumbered Information Command PDU.

OUI

> The 3-byte Organizationally Unique Identifier (OUI) identifies an organization which administers the meaning of the following 2-byte Protocol Identifier (PID). To specify an EtherType in PID the OUI has to be set to 0x00-00-00.

PID

> The Protocol Identifier (PID) field specifies the protocol type of the following PDU. For IP datagrams the assigned EtherType or PID is 0x08-00.

The default MTU size for IP members in an ATM network is discussed in RFC 1626 and defined to be 9180 bytes. The LLC/SNAP header is 8 bytes; therefore, the default ATM AAL5 PDU size is 9188 bytes. The possible values can be between zero and 65535. You are allowed to change the MTU size but then all members of a LIS must be changed as well in order to have the same value. RFC 1755 recommends that all implementations should support MTU sizes up to and including 64 KB.

The address resolution in an ATM network is defined as an extension of the ARP protocol and is described in 13.3.1, "Address Resolution (ATMARP and InATMARP)" on page 762.

There is no mapping from IP broadcast or multicast addresses to ATM *broadcast* or multicast addresses available. But there are no restrictions for transmitting or receiving IP datagrams specifying any of the four standard IP broadcast address forms as described in RFC 1122. Members, upon receiving an IP broadcast or IP subnet broadcast for their LIS, must process the packet as if addressed to that station.

13.3.3 ATM LAN Emulation

Another approach to provide a migration path to a native ATM network is ATM LAN emulation. ATM LAN emulation is still under construction by ATM Forum working groups. For the IETF approach please see 13.3.2, "Classical IP over ATM" on page 765. There is no ATM Forum implementation agreement available covering virtual LANs over ATM but there are some basic agreements on the different proposals made to the ATM Forum. The descriptions below are based on the IBM proposals.

The concept of ATM LAN emulation is to construct a system such that the workstation application software "thinks" it is a member of a real shared medium LAN, such as a token-ring. This method maximizes the reuse of existing LAN software and significantly reduces the cost of migration to ATM. In PC LAN environments, for example, the LAN emulation layer could be implemented under the

NDIS/ODI-type interface. With such an implementation all the higher layer protocols, such as IP, IPX, NetBIOS and SNA, could be run over ATM networks without any change.

Refer to Figure 341 for the implementation of token-ring and Ethernet.

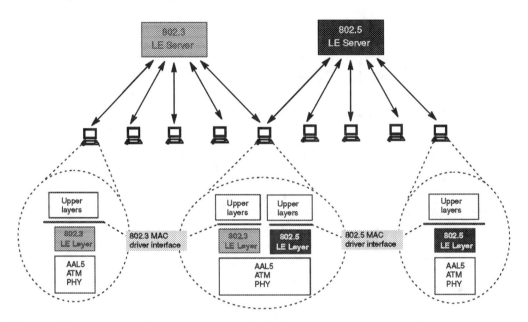

Figure 341. Ethernet and Token-Ring LAN Emulation

13.3.3.1 LAN Emulation Layer (Workstation Software)

Each workstation that performs the LE function needs to have software to provide the LE service. This software is called the LAN emulation layer (LE layer). It provides the interface to existing protocol support (such as IP, IPX, IEEE 802.2 LLC, NetBIOS, etc.) and emulates the functions of a real shared medium LAN. This means that no changes are needed to existing LAN application software to use ATM services. The LE layer interfaces to the ATM network through a hardware ATM adapter.

The primary function of the LE layer is to transfer encapsulated LAN frames (arriving from higher layers) to their destination either directly (over a direct VC) or through the LE server. This is done by using AAL5 services provided by ATM.

Each LE layer has one or more LAN addresses as well as an ATM address.

A separate instance (logical copy or LE client) of the LE layer is needed in each workstation for each different LAN or type of LAN to be supported. For example, if both token-ring and Ethernet LAN types are to be emulated, then you need two LE layers. In fact they will probably just be different threads within the same copy of the same code but they are logically separate LE layers. Separate LE layers would also be used if one workstation needed to be part of two different emulated token-ring LANs. Each separate LE layer needs a different MAC address but can share the same physical ATM connection (adapter).

13.3.3.2 LAN Emulation Server

The basic function of the LE server is to provide directory, multicast and address resolution services to the LE layers in the workstations. It also provides a connectionless data transfer service to the LE layers in the workstations if needed.

Each emulated LAN must have an LE server. It would be possible to have multiple LE servers sharing the same hardware and code (via multithreading) but the LE servers are logically separate entities. As for the LE layers, an emulated token-ring LAN cannot have members that are emulating an Ethernet LAN. Thus an instance of an LE server is dedicated to a single type of LAN emulation. The LE server can be physically internal to the ATM network or provided in an external device, but logically it is always an external function that simply uses the services provided by ATM to do its job.

13.3.3.3 Default VCs

A default VC is a connection between an LE layer in a workstation and the LE server. These connections can be permanent or switched.

All LE control messages are carried between the LE layer and the LE server on the default VC. Encapsulated data frames can also be sent on the default VC.

The presence of the LE server and the default VCs is necessary for the LE function to be performed.

13.3.3.4 Direct VCs

Direct VCs are connections between LE layers in the end systems. They are always switched and set up on demand. If the ATM network does not support switched connections then you cannot have direct VCs and all the data must be sent through the LE server on default VCs. If there is no direct VC available for any reason then data transfer must take place through the LE server. (There is no other way.)

Direct VCs are set up on request by an LE layer. (The server cannot set them up as there is no third party call setup function in ATM.) The ATM address of a destination

LE layer is provided to a requesting LE layer by the LE server. Direct VCs stay in place until one of the partner LE layers decides to end the connection (because there is no more data).

13.3.3.5 Initialization
During initialization the LE layer (workstation) establishes the default VC with the LE server. It also discovers its own ATM address, which is needed if it is to later set up direct VCs.

13.3.3.6 Registration
In this phase the LE layer (workstation) registers its MAC addresses with the LE server. Other things such as filtering requirements (optional) may be provided.

13.3.3.7 Management and Resolution
This is the method used by ATM endstations to set up direct VCs with other endstations (LE layers). This function includes mechanisms for learning the ATM address of a target station, mapping the MAC address to an ATM address, storing the mapping in a table and managing the table.

For the server this function provides the means for supporting the use of direct VCs by endstations. This includes a mechanism for mapping the MAC address of an end system to its ATM address, storing the information and providing it to a requesting endstation.

This structure maintains full LAN function and can support most higher layer LAN protocols. Reliance on the server for data transfer is minimized by using switched VCs for the transport of most bulk data.

13.3.4 Classical IP over ATM versus LAN Emulation
These two approaches to providing an easier way to migrate to ATM were made with different goals in mind.

Classical IP over ATM defines an encapsulation and address resolution method. The definitions are made for IP only and not for use with other protocols. So if you have applications requiring other protocol stacks (such as IPX or SNA) then IP over ATM will not provide a complete solution. On the other hand if you only have TCP or UDP-based applications then this might be the better solution, since this specialized adaptation of the IP protocol to the ATM architecture is likely to produce less overhead than a more global solution and therefore be more efficient. Another advantage of this implementation is the use of some ATM-specific functions, such as large MTU sizes, etc.

The major goal of the ATM Forum's approach is to run layer 3 and higher protocols unchanged over the ATM network. This means that existing protocols, such as TCP/IP, IPX, NetBIOS and SNA for example, and their applications can use the benefits of the fast ATM network without any changes. The mapping for all protocols is already defined. The LAN emulation layer provides all the services of a classic LAN; thus, the upper layer does not know of the existence of ATM. This is both an advantage and a disadvantage because the knowledge of the underlying network could be used to provide a more effective implementation.

In the near future both approaches will be used depending on the particular requirements. Over time, when the mapping of applications to ATM is fully defined and implemented, the scheme of a dedicated ATM implementation may be used.

13.4 Data Link Switching: Switch-to-Switch Protocol

Data Link Switching (DLSw) was issued by IBM in March 1993 and is documented in RFC number 1795. Its state is informational.

13.4.1 Introduction

Data Link Switching is a forwarding mechanism for the IBM SNA and IBM NetBIOS protocols. It does not provide full routing, but instead provides switching at the data link layer and encapsulation in TCP/IP for transport over the Internet. This Switch-to-Switch Protocol (SSP) is used between IBM 2216 Nways Multiaccess Connector and/or IBM 2210 Nways Multiprotocol Routers. Routers of other vendors can participate if they comply to the above RFC or without DLSw capability as intermediate routers because the DLSw connection exists only between the two end routers.

13.4.2 Functional Description

DLSw was developed to provide support for SNA and NetBIOS in multiprotocol routers. Since SNA and NetBIOS are basically connection-oriented protocols, the data link control procedure that they use on the LAN is IEEE 802.2 Logical Link Control (LLC) Type 2. DLSw also accommodates SNA protocols over WAN links via the SDLC protocol.

IEEE 802.2 LLC Type 2 was designed with the assumption that the network transit delay would be small and predictable (for example, a local LAN). Therefore LLC uses a fixed timer for detecting lost frames. When bridging is used over wide area lines (especially at lower speeds), the network delay is larger and can vary greatly based upon congestion. When the delay exceeds the timeout value LLC attempts to retransmit. If the frame is not actually lost, only delayed, it is possible for the LLC Type 2 procedures to become confused, and as a result, the link is eventually taken down.

Given the use of LLC Type 2 services, DLSw addresses the following bridging problems:

- DLC timeouts
- DLC acknowledgments over the WAN
- Flow and congestion control
- Broadcast control of search packets
- Source-route bridging hop count limits

NetBIOS also makes extensive use of datagram services that use LLC Type 1. In this case, DLSw addresses the last two problems in the above list. The principal difference between DLSw and bridging is that DLS terminates the data link control whereas bridging does not. Figure 342 on page 776 illustrates this difference based upon two end systems operating with LLC Type 2 services.

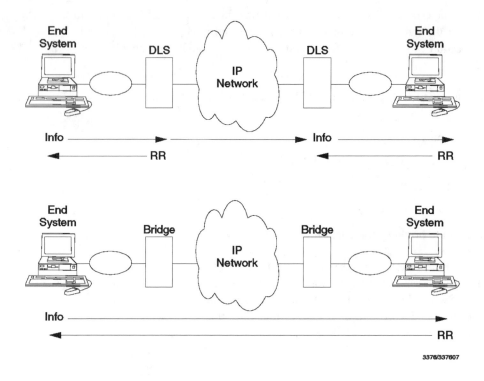

Figure 342. DLSw Compared to Bridging

In traditional bridging, the data link control is end-to-end. DLSw terminates the LLC Type 2 connection at the switch. This means that the LLC Type 2 connections do not cross the wide area network. The DLS multiplexes LLC connections onto a TCP connection to another DLS. Therefore, the LLC connections at each end are totally independent of each other. It is the responsibility of the data link switch to deliver frames that it has received from an LLC connection to the other end. TCP is used between the data link switches to guarantee delivery of frames.

As a result of this design, LLC timeouts are limited to the local LAN. (For example they do not traverse the wide area.) Also, the LLC Type 2 acknowledgments (RRs) do not traverse the WAN, thereby reducing traffic across the wide area links. For SDLC links, polling and poll response occurs locally, not over the WAN. Broadcast of search frames is controlled by the data link switches once the location of a target system is discovered. Finally, the switches can now apply back pressure to the end systems to provide flow and congestion control.

DLSw uses LAN addressing to set up connections between SNA systems. SDLC-attached devices are defined with MAC addresses to enable them to communicate with LAN-attached devices. For NetBIOS systems, DLSw uses the NetBIOS name to forward datagrams and to set up connections for NetBIOS sessions. For circuit establishment, SNA systems send TEST (or in some cases, XID) frames to the null (x'00') SAP. NetBIOS systems have an address resolution procedure, based upon the name query and name recognized frames, that is used to establish an end-to-end circuit.

Since DLSw can be implemented in multiprotocol routers, there may be situations where both bridging and switching are enabled. SNA frames can be identified by their link SAP. Typical SAP values for SNA are x'04', x'08', and x'0C'. NetBIOS always uses a link SAP value of x'F0'.

For further details please refer to *RFC 1795*.

13.5 Serial Line IP (SLIP)

The TCP/IP protocol family runs over a variety of network media: IEEE 802.3 and 802.5 LANs, X.25 lines, satellite links, and serial lines. Standards for the encapsulation of IP packets have been defined for many of these networks, but there is no standard for serial lines. SLIP is currently a *de facto* standard, commonly used for point-to-point serial connections running TCP/IP. Even though SLIP is not an Internet standard, it is documented by RFC 1055.

SLIP is just a very simple protocol designed quite a long time ago and is merely a packet framing protocol. It defines a sequence of characters that frame IP packets on a serial line, and nothing more. It does not provide any of the following:

- Addressing: Both computers on a SLIP link need to know each other's IP address for routing purposes. SLIP defines only the encapsulation protocol, not any form of handshaking or link control. Links are manually connected and configured, including the specification of the IP address.

- Packet type identification: SLIP cannot support multiple protocols across a single link; thus, only one protocol can be run over a SLIP connection.

- Error detection/correction: SLIP does no form of frame error detection. The higher level protocols should detect corrupted packets caused by errors on noisy lines. (IP header and UDP/TCP checksums should be sufficient.) Because it takes so long to retransmit a packet that was altered, it would be efficient if SLIP could provide some sort of simple error correction mechanism of its own.

- Compression: SLIP provides no mechanism for compressing frequently used IP header fields. Many applications over slow serial links tend to be single-user interactive TCP traffic such as TELNET. This frequently involves small packet sizes and therefore a relatively large overhead in TCP and IP headers which do not change much between datagrams, but which can have a noticeably detrimental effect on interactive response times.

  However, many SLIP implementations now use *Van Jacobsen Header Compression*. This is used to reduce the size of the combined IP and TCP headers from 40 bytes to 8 bytes by recording the states of a set of TCP connections at each end of the link and replacing the full headers with encoded updates for the normal case where many of the fields are unchanged or are incremented by small amounts between successive IP datagrams for a session. This compression is described in RFC 1144.

The SLIP protocol is expected to be replaced by the Point-to-Point Protocol (PPP). Please see 13.6, "Point-to-Point Protocol (PPP)."

13.6 Point-to-Point Protocol (PPP)

PPP is a *network-specific standard protocol* with STD number 51. Its status is *elective*. It is described in RFC 1661 and RFC 1662.

There are a large number of *proposed standard protocols*, which specify the operation of PPP over different kinds of point-to-point link. Each has a status of *elective*. The reader is advised to consult *STD 1 — Internet Official Protocol Standards* for a list of PPP-related RFCs which are on the Standards Track.

Point-to-point circuits in the form of asynchronous and synchronous lines have long been the mainstay for data communications. In the TCP/IP world, the de facto standard SLIP protocol has served admirably in this area, and is still in widespread use for dial-up TCP/IP connections. However, SLIP has a number of drawbacks that are addressed by the point-to-point protocol.

PPP has three main components:

1. A method for encapsulating datagrams over serial links.

2. A *Link Control Protocol (LCP)* for establishing, configuring, and testing the data-link connection.

3. A family of *Network Control Protocols (NCPs)* for establishing and configuring different network-layer protocols. PPP is designed to allow the simultaneous use of multiple network-layer protocols.

Before a link is considered to be ready for use by network-layer protocols, a specific sequence of events must happen. The LCP provides a method of establishing, configuring, maintaining and terminating the connection. LCP goes through the following phases:

1. Link establishment and configuration negotiation:

   In this phase, link control packets are exchanged and link configuration options are negotiated. Once options are agreed upon, the link is *open*, but not necessarily *ready* for network-layer protocols to be started.

2. Link quality determination:

   This phase is optional. PPP does not specify the policy for determining quality, but does provide low-level tools, such as echo request and reply.

3. Authentication:

   This phase is optional. Each end of the link authenticates itself with the remote end using authentication methods agreed to during phase 1.

4. Network-layer protocol configuration negotiation:

   Once LCP has finished the previous phase, network-layer protocols may be separately configured by the appropriate NCP.

5. Link termination:

   LCP may terminate the link at any time. This will usually be done at the request of a human user, but may happen because of a physical event.

13.6.1 Point-to-Point Encapsulation

A summary of the PPP encapsulation is shown below.

Protocol 8/16 bits	Information *	Padding *

3376E\3376FAL1

Figure 343. PPP Encapsulation Frame

Protocol Field - The protocol field is one or two octets, and its value identifies the datagram encapsulated in the Information field of the packet. Up-to-date values of the Protocol field are specified in the most recent *Assigned Numbers* RFC (RFC 1700).

Information Field - The Information field is zero or more octets. The Information field contains the datagram for the protocol specified in the Protocol field. The maximum length for the information field, including padding, but not including the Protocol field, is termed the Maximum Receive Unit (MRU), which defaults to 1500 octets. By negotiation, other values can be used for the MRU.

Padding - On transmission, the information field may be padded with an arbitrary number of octets up to the MRU. It is the responsibility of each protocol to distinguish padding octets from real information.

The *IP Control Protocol (IPCP)* is the NCP for IP and is responsible for configuring, enabling and disabling the IP protocol on both ends of the point-to-point link. The IPCP options negotiation sequence is the same as for LCP, thus allowing the possibility of reusing the code.

One important option used with IPCP is *Van Jacobson Header Compression* which is used to reduce the size of the combined IP and TCP headers from 40 bytes to approximately 4 by recording the states of a set of TCP connections at each end of the link and replacing the full headers with encoded updates for the normal case where many of the fields are unchanged or are incremented by small amounts between successive IP datagrams for a session. This compression is described in RFC 1144.

13.7 Integrated Services Digital Network (ISDN)

This section describes how to use the PPP encapsulation over ISDN point-to-point links. PPP over ISDN is documented by RFC 1618. Its status is elective. Since the ISDN B-channel is by definition a point-to-point circuit, PPP is well suited for use over these links.

The ISDN Basic Rate Interface (BRI) usually supports two B-channels with a capacity of 64 kbps each, and a 16 kbps D-channel for control information. B-channels can be used for voice or data or just for data in a combined way.

The ISDN Primary Rate Interface (PRI) may support many concurrent B-channel links (usually 30) and one 64 Kbps D-channel. The PPP LCP and NCP mechanisms are particularly useful in this situation in reducing or eliminating manual configuration, and facilitating ease of communication between diverse implementations. The ISDN D-channel can also be used for sending PPP packets when suitably framed, but is limited in bandwidth and often restricts communication links to a local switch.

PPP treats ISDN channels as bit or octet-oriented synchronous links. These links must be full-duplex, but may be either dedicated or circuit-switched. PPP presents an octet interface to the physical layer. There is no provision for sub-octets to be supplied or accepted. PPP does not impose any restrictions regarding transmission rate other than that of the particular ISDN channel interface. PPP does not require the use of control signals. When available, using such signals can allow greater functionality and performance.

The definition of various encodings and scrambling is the responsibility of the DTE/DCE equipment in use. While PPP will operate without regard to the underlying representation of the bit stream, lack of standards for transmission will hinder interoperability as surely as lack of data link standards. The D-channel interface requires NRZ encoding. Therefore it is recommended that NRZ be used over the B-channel interface. This will allow frames to be easily exchanged between the B and D channels. However, when configuration of the encoding is allowed, NRZI is recommended as an alternative in order to ensure a minimum ones density where required over the clear B-channel. Implementations that want to interoperate with multiple encodings may choose to detect those encodings automatically. Automatic encoding detection is particularly important for primary rate interfaces, to avoid extensive pre-configuration.

Terminal adapters conforming to V.120 [16] can be used as a simple interface to workstations. The terminal adapter provides async-to-sync conversion. Multiple B-channels can be used in parallel. V.120 is not interoperable with bit-synchronous links, since V.120 does not provide octet stuffing to bit stuffing conversion. Despite the fact that HDLC, LAPB, LAPD, and LAPF are nominally distinguishable, multiple methods of framing should not be used concurrently on the same ISDN channel. There is no requirement that PPP recognize alternative framing techniques, or switch between framing techniques without specific configuration. Experience has shown that the LLC Information Element is not reliably transmitted end to end. Therefore, transmission of the LLC-IE should not be relied upon for framing or encoding determination. No LLC-IE values that pertain to PPP have been assigned. Any other values that are received are not valid for PPP links, and can be ignored for PPP service. The LCP recommended sync configuration options apply to ISDN links. The standard LCP sync configuration defaults apply to ISDN links. The typical network connected to the link is likely to have an MRU size of either 1500 or 2048 bytes or greater. To avoid fragmentation, the maximum transmission unit (MTU) at the network layer should not exceed 1500, unless a peer MRU of 2048 or greater is specifically negotiated.

---

[16] CCITT Recommendations I.465 and V.120, "Data Terminal Equipment Communications over the Telephone Network with Provision for Statistical Multiplexing," CCITT Blue Book, Volume VIII, Fascicle VIII.1, 1988.

13.8 TCP/IP and X.25

This topic describes the encapsulation of IP over X.25 networks, in accordance with ISO/IEC and CCITT standards. IP over X.25 networks is documented by RFC 1356 which obsoletes RFC 877. RFC 1356 is a Draft Standard with a status of elective. The substantive change to the IP encapsulation over X.25 is an increase in the IP datagram MTU size, the X.25 maximum data packet size, the virtual circuit management, and the interoperable encapsulation over X.25 of protocols other than IP between multiprotocol routers and bridges.

One or more X.25 virtual circuits are opened on demand when datagrams arrive at the network interface for transmission. Protocol data units (PDUs) are sent as X.25 *complete packet sequences*. That is PDUs begin on X.25 data packet boundaries and the M bit (more data) is used to fragment PDUs that are larger than one X.25 data packet in length. In the IP encapsulation the PDU is the IP datagram. The first octet in the call user data (CUD) field (the first data octet in the Call Request packet) is used for protocol demultiplexing, in accordance with the Subsequent Protocol Identifier (SPI) in ISO/IEC TR 9577. This field contains a one octet Network Layer Protocol Identifier (NLPID), which identifies the network layer protocol encapsulated over the X.25 virtual circuit. For the Internet community, the NLPID has four relevant values:

1. The value hex CC (binary 11001100, decimal 204) is IP.

2. The value hex 81 (binary 10000001, decimal 129) identifies ISO/IEC 8473 (CLNP).

3. The value hex 82 (binary 10000010, decimal 130) is used specifically for ISO/IEC 9542 (ES-IS). If there is already a circuit open to carry CLNP, then it is not necessary to open a second circuit to carry ES-IS.

4. The value hex 80 (binary 10000000, decimal 128) identifies the use of the IEEE Subnetwork Access Protocol (SNAP) to further encapsulate and identify a single network-layer protocol. The SNAP-encapsulated protocol is identified by including a five-octet SNAP header in the Call Request CUD field immediately following the hex 80 octet. SNAP headers are not included in the subsequent X.25 data packets. Only one SNAP-encapsulated protocol can be carried over a virtual circuit opened using this encoding.

The value hex 00 identifies the null encapsulation used to multiplex multiple network layer protocols over the same circuit. The *Assigned Numbers* RFC (RFC 1700) contains one other non-CCITT and non-ISO/IEC value that has been used for Internet X.25 encapsulation identification, namely hex C5 (binary 11000101, decimal 197) for Blacker X.25. This value may continue to be used but only by prior preconfiguration of the sending and receiving X.25 interfaces to support this value. The hex CD (binary

11001101, decimal 205), listed in *Assigned Numbers* for ISO-IP is also used by Blacker and also can only be used by prior preconfiguration of the sending and receiving X.25 interfaces.

Each system must only accept calls for protocols it can process. Every Internet system must be able to accept the CC encapsulation for IP datagrams. Systems that support NLPIDs other than hex CC (for IP) should allow their use to be configured on a per-peer address basis. The Null encapsulation, identified by a NLPID encoding of hex 00, is used in order to multiplex multiple network layer protocols over one circuit. When the Null encapsulation is used each X.25 complete packet sequence sent on the circuit begins with a one-octet NLPID which identifies the network layer protocol data unit contained only in that particular complete packet sequence. Further, if the SNAP NLPID (hex 80) is used, then the NLPID octet is immediately followed by the five-octet SNAP header which is then immediately followed by the encapsulated PDU. The encapsulated network layer protocol may differ from one complete packet sequence to the next over the same circuit.

Use of the single network layer protocol circuits is more efficient in terms of bandwidth if only a limited number of protocols are supported by a system. It also allows each system to determine exactly which protocols are supported by its communicating partner. Other advantages include being able to use X.25 accounting to detail each protocol and different quality of service or flow control windows for different protocols. The Null encapsulation, for multiplexing, is useful when a system for any reason (such as implementation restrictions or network cost considerations), may only open a limited number of virtual circuits simultaneously. This is the method most likely to be used by a multiprotocol router to avoid using an unreasonable number of virtual circuits. If performing IEEE 802.1d bridging across X.25 is required, then the Null encapsulation must be used.

IP datagrams must by default be encapsulated on a virtual circuit opened with the CC CUD. Implementations may also support up to three other possible encapsulations of IP:

- IP datagrams may be contained in multiplexed data packets on a circuit using the Null encapsulation. Such data packets are identified by a NLPID of hex CC.

- IP may be incapsulated within the SNAP encapsulation on a circuit. This encapsulation is identified by containing in the 5-octet SNAP header an Organizationally Unique Identifier (OUI) of hex 00-00-00 and Protocol Identifier (PID) of hex 08-00.

- On a circuit using the Null encapsulation, IP may be contained within the SNAP encapsulation of IP in multiplexed data packets.

13.9 Frame Relay

The frame relay network provides a number of virtual circuits that form the basis for connections between stations attached to the same frame relay network. The resulting set of interconnected devices forms a private frame relay group, which may be either fully interconnected with a complete *mesh* of virtual circuits, or only partially interconnected. In either case, each virtual circuit is uniquely identified at each frame relay interface by a data link connection identifier (DLCI). In most circumstances, DLCIs have strictly local significance at each frame relay interface. Frame relay is documented in RFC 2427.

13.9.1 Frame Format

All protocols must encapsulate their packets within a Q.922 Annex A frame{1}. Additionally, frames contain information necessary to identify the protocol carried within the protocol data unit (PDU), thus allowing the receiver to properly process the incoming packet (refer to Figure 344 on page 785). The format will be as follows:

The control field is the Q.922 control field. The UI (0x03) value is used unless it is negotiated otherwise. The use of XID (0xAF or 0xBF) is permitted.

The pad field is used to align the data portion (beyond the encapsulation header) of the frame to a two octet boundary. If present, the pad is a single octet and must have a value of zero.

The Network Level Protocol ID (NLPID) field is administered by ISO and the ITU. It contains values for many different protocols including IP, CLNP, and IEEE Subnetwork Access Protocol (SNAP). This field tells the receiver what encapsulation or what protocol follows. Values for this field are defined in ISO/IEC TR 9577 {2}. An NLPID value of 0x00 is defined within ISO/IEC TR 9577 as the null network layer or inactive set. Since it cannot be distinguished from a pad field, and because it has no significance within the context of this encapsulation scheme, an NLPID value of 0x00 is invalid under the frame relay encapsulation.

There is no commonly implemented minimum or maximum frame size for frame relay. A network must, however, support at least a 262-octet maximum. Generally, the maximum will be greater than or equal to 1600 octets, but each frame relay provider will specify an appropriate value for its network. A frame relay data terminal equipment (DTE), therefore must allow the maximum acceptable frame size to be configurable.

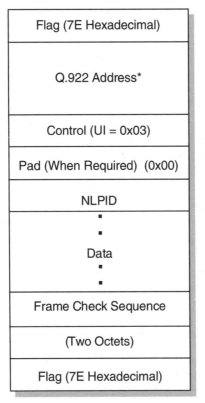

| Flag (7E Hexadecimal) |
| Q.922 Address* |
| Control (UI = 0x03) |
| Pad (When Required) (0x00) |
| NLPID |
| Data |
| Frame Check Sequence |
| (Two Octets) |
| Flag (7E Hexadecimal) |

3376\3376FALG

Figure 344. Frame Relay Packet Format

13.9.2 Interconnect Issues

There are two basic types of data packets that travel within the frame relay network: routed packets and bridged packets. These packets have distinct formats and therefore, must contain an indicator that the destination can use to correctly interpret the contents of the frame. This indicator is embedded within the NLPID and SNAP header information.

13.9.3 Data Link Layer Parameter Negotiation

Frame relay stations may choose to support the Exchange Identification (XID) specified in Appendix III of Q.922 {1}. This XID exchange allows the following parameters to be negotiated at the initialization of a frame relay circuit: maximum frame size, retransmission timer, and the maximum number of outstanding information (I) frames.

If this exchange is not used, these values must be statically configured by mutual agreement of data link connection (DLC) endpoints, or must be defaulted to the values specified in Section 5.9 of Q.922 {1}.

There are situations in which a frame relay station may wish to dynamically resolve a protocol address over permanent virtual circuits (PVCs). This may be accomplished using the standard Address Resolution Protocol (ARP) encapsulated within a SNAP-encoded frame relay packet.

Because of the inefficiencies of emulating broadcasting in a frame relay environment, a new address resolution variation was developed. It is called Inverse ARP and describes a method for resolving a protocol address when the hardware address is already known. In a frame relay network, the known hardware address is the DLCI. Support for Inverse ARP is not required to implement this specification, but it has proven useful for frame relay interface autoconfiguration.

Stations must be able to map more than one IP address in the same IP subnet to a particular DLCI on a frame relay interface. This need arises from applications such as remote access, where servers must act as ARP proxies for many dial-in clients, each assigned a unique IP address while sharing bandwidth on the same DLC. The dynamic nature of such applications results in frequent address association changes with no affect on the DLC's status.

As with any other interface that utilizes ARP, stations may learn the associations between IP addresses and DLCIs by processing unsolicited (*gratuitous*) ARP requests that arrive on the DLC. If one station wishes to inform its peer station on the other end of a frame relay DLC of a new association between an IP address and that PVC, it should send an unsolicited ARP request with the source IP address equal to the destination IP address, and both set to the new IP address being used on the DLC. This allows a station to "announce" new client connections on a particular DLCI. The receiving station must store the new association, and remove any old existing association, if necessary, from any other DLCI on the interface.

13.9.4 IP over Frame Relay

Internet Protocol (IP) datagrams sent over a frame relay network conform to the encapsulation described previously. Within this context, IP could be encapsulated in two different ways: NLPID value indicating IP or NLPID value indicating SNAP.

Although both of these encapsulations are supported under the given definitions, it is advantageous to select only one method as the appropriate mechanism for encapsulating IP data. Therefore, IP data should be encapsulated using the NLPID value of 0xcc indicating an IP packet. This option is more efficient because it transmits 48 fewer bits without the SNAP header and is consistent with the encapsulation of IP in an X.25 network.

13.10 PPP over SONET and SDH Circuits

This discussion describes the use of the PPP encapsulation over Synchronous Optical Network (SONET) and Synchronous Digital Hierarchy (SDH) links which is documented by RFC 1619. Since SONET and SDH are by definition point-to-point circuits, PPP is well suited to use over these links. SONET is an octet-synchronous multiplex scheme that defines a family of standard rates and formats. Despite the name it is not limited to optical links. Electrical specifications have been defined for single-mode fiber, multimode fiber, and CATV 75 ohm coaxial cable. The transmission rates are integral multiples of 51.840 Mbps, which may be used to carry T3/E3 bit-synchronous signals. The allowed multiples are currently specified as:

Table 18. SONET Speed Hierarchy

Signal Level	Bit Rate	DS-0s	DS-1s	DS-3s
STS-1 and OC-1	51.84 Mbps	672	28	1
STS-3 and OC-3 (STM-1)	155.52 Mbps	2,016	84	3
STS-9 and OC-9	466.56 Mbps	6,048	252	9
STS-12 and OC-12 (STM-4)	622.08 Mbps	8,064	336	12
STS-18 and OC-18	933.12 Mbps	12,096	504	18
STS-24 and OC-24	1,244.16 Mbps	16,128	672	24
STS-36 and OC-36	1,866.24 Mbps	24,192	1,008	36
STS-48 and OC-48 (STM-16)	2,488.32 Mbps	32,256	1,344	48
STS-n and OC-n (STM-n/3)	n x 51.84 Mbps	n x 672	n x 28	n

The CCITT Synchronous Digital Hierarchy defines a subset of SONET transmission rates beginning at 155.52 Mbps, as shown in the table above.

13.10.1 Physical Layer

PPP presents an octet interface to the physical layer. There is no provision for sub-octets to be supplied or accepted. SONET and SDH links are full-duplex by definition. The octet stream is mapped into the SONET/SDH Synchronous Payload Envelope (SPE) with the octet boundaries aligned with the SPE octet boundaries. No scrambling is needed during insertion into the SPE. The path signal label is intended to indicate the contents of the SPE. The experimental value of 207 (hex CF) is used to indicate PPP. The multiframe indicator is currently unused and must be zero.

The basic rate for PPP over SONET/SDH is that of STS-3c/STM-1 at 155.52 Mbps. The available information bandwidth is 149.76 Mbps which is the STS-3c/STM-1 SPE with section, line and path overhead removed. This is the same upper layer mapping that is used for ATM and FDDI. Lower signal rates must use the Virtual Tributary (VT) mechanism of SONET/SDH. This maps existing signals up to T3/E3 rates asynchronously into the SPE or uses available clocks for bit-synchronous and byte-synchronous mapping. Higher signal rates should conform to the SDH STM series rather than the SONET STS series as equipment becomes available. The STM series progresses in powers of 4 instead of 3 and employs fewer steps which is likely to simplify multiplexing and integration.

13.11 Multiprotocol Label Switching (MPLS)

MPLS is documented by an Internet draft. Internet drafts are working documents of the IETF. The primary goal of the MPLS working group is to standardize a base technology that integrates the label swapping forwarding paradigm with network layer routing. The initial MPLS effort will be focused on IPv4 and IPv6. However the core technology will be extendible to multiple network layer protocols. MPLS is not confined to any specific link layer technology. It can work with any media over which network layer packets can be passed between network layer entities.

13.11.1 Forwarding Methods

MPLS makes use of a routing approach whereby the normal mode of operation is that L3 routing (for example, existing IP routing protocols and/or new IP routing protocols) is used by all nodes to determine the routed path.

13.11.1.1 Peer Model

This model has the following characteristics:

- Routing information is mapped to labels

- Switch's label-swap tables are updated with the new labels

- Use specialized control protocol to distribute routing to label mappings among participating devices along routed path

- L3 processing replaced with L2 switching at intermediate nodes

- Packets/cells are switched from network ingress to egress

- Forwarding reduced to label lookup, label swap and output port selection

13.11.1.2 Flow-Driven

This model has the following characteristics:

- Arrival of flow triggers exchange of flow setup messages between adjacent devices. Cells of a flow are then re-labeled (new VCI) along each segment

- Ingress-to-egress switch path is formed when switch/routers splice together adjacent VCs.

Using flow-driven switching individual flows (host/host or appl/appl) are switched through the network. Some but not all flows may be switched.

13.11.1.3 Topology-Driven

This model has the following characteristics:

- Routing table entries are mapped to labels (VPI/VCI) and distributed among participating devices.

- Ingress-to-egress switch path is established. It carries *all* traffic with destination of NET X.

Using topology-driven IP switching all traffic going to a common destination will be switched. A destination can be a network or collection of networks.

13.11.2 MPLS Usefulness

The following should be considered when a possible MPLS deployment is discussed:

- Growth of the Internet is exceeding the L3 processing capacity of traditional routers.

- Enables routing to leverage the price, performance and maturity of layer-2 switching.

- ATM switches can be augmented with IP routing.

- MPLS forwarding is independent of current and future enhancements to network layer protocols.

- Works over any layer-2 datalink technology (for example, ATM, frame relay, Ethernet, SONET, etc.)

- More efficient traffic engineering capabilities:

  - Use label stacks rather than IP-OVER-IP encapsulation for tunnels

  - Explicit routes

- ISP's need to support and deliver special services.

13.12 Enterprise Extender

The Enterprise Extender network connection is a simple set of extensions to the existing open high performance routing (HPR) technology. It performs an efficient integration of the HPR frames using UDP/IP packets. To the HPR network, the IP backbone is a logical link. To the IP network, the SNA traffic is UDP datagrams that are routed without any hardware or software changes to the IP backbone. Unlike gateways there is no protocol transformation and unlike common tunneling mechanisms the integration is performed at the routing layers without the overhead of additional transport functions. The advanced technology enables efficient use of the intranet infrastructure for support of IP-based client accessing SNA-based data (for example, TN2370 emulators or Web browsers using services such as IBM's Host On-Demand) as well as SNA clients using any of the SNA LU types.

Enterprise Extender seamlessly routes packets through the network protocol "edges" eliminating the need to perform costly protocol translation and the store-and-forward associated with transport-layer functions. Unlike Data Link Switching (DLSw), for example, there are no TCP retransmit buffers and timers and no congestion control logic in the router because it uses connectionless UDP and the congestion control is provided end system to end system. Because of these savings, the "edge" routers have less work to do and can perform the job they do best which is forwarding packets instead of incurring protocol translation overhead and maintaining many TCP connections. This technology, then, allows the data center routers to handle larger networks and larger volumes of network traffic, thus providing more capacity for the money.

13.12.1 Performance and Recovery

The Enterprise Extender also provides many of the traffic control features that SNA users have come to expect. Using Class of Service (COS), SNA applications specify the nature of the services they require from the network (for example, interactive or batch). Included in this specification is the required traffic priority. Most routers support some form of prioritized queuing. In IBM routers this function is called the

Bandwidth Reservation System (BRS). Enterprise Extender exploits this existing function by mapping the SNA priority to the UDP port numbers that routers can easily use to determine the appropriate priority. Defaults for these port numbers have been registered with the Internet Assigned Numbers Authority (IANA).

Network failures, even in a network of combined technologies, can be handled successfully. Unlike other technologies such as Data Link Switching, Enterprise Extender can switch around failures that occur at the edges of the SNA and IP protocols. Since HPR can switch between routes as required and Enterprise Extender provides the flexibility for those routes to include an IP backbone, Enterprise Extender makes it possible for SNA networks to use the IP attachment as alternate and backup routes for the SNA network.

13.13 Multiprotocol Transport Network (MPTN)

Multiprotocol transport networking (MPTN), developed by IBM, is an open architecture for:

- Mixed-protocol networking: running applications associated with one network protocol over different network protocols

- Network concatenation: connection matching applications across networks of different protocols through gateways

13.13.1 Requirements for Mixed-Protocol Networking

With the growth of networking in general and local area networks in particular, many large customer networks have become confederations of individual networks running different networking protocols. This heterogeneity has arisen for a number of reasons. Some of these include:

- Shift of customer interest away from selecting a particular networking architecture in favor of finding solutions to business problems, regardless of the specific network protocol required

- Inter-enterprise information exchange requirement, for example, direct manufacturing, order placement, or billing systems

- Company mergers requiring interconnection

13.13.2 MPTN Architecture

Networking protocols generally provide three types of functions:

- Transport

- Naming and addressing

- Higher level functions

Transport functions are those that provide the basic facility for two partners to communicate, either through connections or in a connectionless manner through datagrams. Naming and addressing conventions define how entities are known and how they are to be found. The higher level functions include allocation of the connections to users and control of their use. Not all networking protocols support higher level functions. SNA and OSI do; TCP/IP and NetBIOS do not.

MPTN separates transport functions from higher level functions and from the address formats as seen by the users of the protocol. Its goal is to allow any higher level protocol using the corresponding address structure to run over any transport function. The division of functions between transport and higher level was chosen because the transport level is the highest level at which there are common functions that can be reasonably mapped across protocols. At other levels the number of services is either too large or too small to provide a practical division.

13.13.3 MPTN Methodology

MPTN architecture solves the above requirements by defining a new canonical interface to a set of transport services that concatenate connections across multiple networking protocols. When an application is written for a particular transport service, it may be written so that it makes assumptions about the particular transport service. Thus it may appear to be transport-specific in the services that it uses. For example, applications written to the NetBEUI interface may request a message be broadcast. In environments where a particular service is not natively supported over the underlying transport network, MPTN provides compensation. In essence though, MPTN frees up applications so that they are able to operate over different transport networks.

Another way of thinking about this is that (in the OSI model) functions from the session layer up are users of transport services or transport users. These services are in turn provided by functions from the transport layer down. MPTN defines a boundary interface, called the transport-layer protocol boundary (TLPB), which clearly delineates this distinction between transport user and transport provider. This is shown graphically in Figure 345 on page 793.

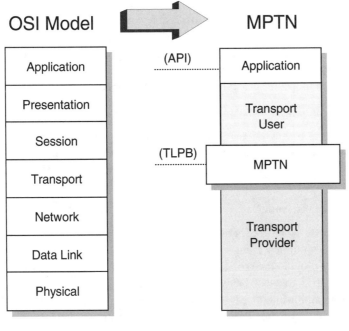

Figure 345. *Transport-Layer Protocol Boundary*

13.13.4 MPTN Major Components

MPTN functions appear in four types of nodes:

- **MPTN Access Node**

  An MPTN access node contains the transport-layer protocol boundary (TLPB), which provides a semantic interface so that higher level protocols or application interfaces written for a particular transport protocol can be transported over another protocol with no apparent change. Such a node can run application programs independent of the underlying transport network and can run application programs on different underlying transport networks.

  The applications in the MPTN access node are generally written to an existing application programming interface (API). The API uses the functions of the native communications protocol. When transport-level MPTN functions are accessed, the API will be converted to access these functions instead of the native communication protocol, while keeping the same interface to the application program. For example, the NetBEUI application interface is written to use the

NetBIOS communications protocol. To use another protocol stack below the transport layer, the NetBEUI API must be made to invoke the MPTN functions. After this is done, all programs using NetBEUI on this MPTN access node can communicate via, for example, SNA, TCP/IP, OSI and other protocols, with another NetBEUI application within the MPTN network. All this is possible without the original application program requiring any change.

- **MPTN Address Mapping Server Node**

    An address mapping server node is an MPTN node with a special function that provides a general address mapping service to the address mapping client component of other MPTN nodes, access or gateway, connected to the same transport provider network.

- **MPTN Multicast Server Node**

    A multicast server node is an MPTN node with a special function, the multicast server, which manages multicast and broadcast distribution of datagrams in networks that do not provide the service as a natural consequence of their design. For example, a NetBIOS transport network is designed to support multicast distribution of datagrams while an SNA network is not. The multicast server operates in cooperation with the address mapping server to provide a multicast service where this capability does not exist within the services offered by the transport network.

- **MPTN Gateway Node**

    An MPTN gateway connects two transport networks to provide an end-to-end service over both of them for one or more transport user protocols. There are two types of gateways, nonnative-to-nonnative, with respect to the supported transport user protocol, and native-to-nonnative, with respect to the supported transport user protocol.

    In the case of nonnative-to-native one of the transport providers connected to the gateway node is native to the transport user. This type of gateway allows access to an end node that has no MPTN function. When one side is native, the MPTN protocol (of the nonnative side) terminates in the gateway (refer to Figure 346 on page 795).

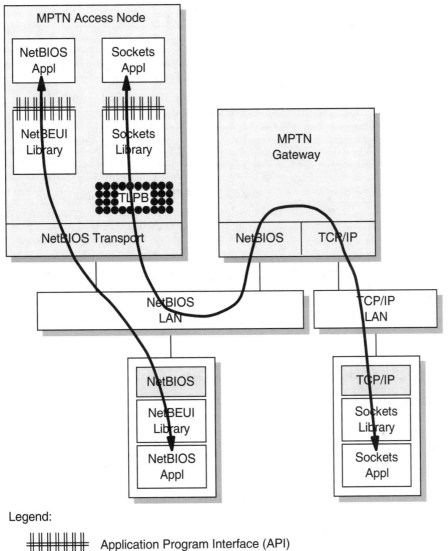

Legend:

┼┼┼┼┼┼┼ Application Program Interface (API)

●●●●●● Transport Layer Protocol Boundary (TLPB)

3376E\3376FAL6

Figure 346. An MPTN Network - Nonnative-to-Native Gateway

13.14 Multi-Path Channel+ (MPC+)

The MPC support is a protocol layer that allows multiple read and write subchannels to be treated as a single transmission group between the host and channel-attached devices. One level of MPC support, high performance data transfer (HPDT), also referred to as MPC+, provides more efficient transfer of data than non-HPDT MPC connections. Multi-Path Channel+ (MPC+) connections allow you to define a single transmission group (TG) that uses multiple write-direction and read-direction subchannels. Because each subchannel operates in only one direction, the half-duplex turnaround time that occurs with other channel-to-channel connections is reduced.

If at least one read and one write path is allocated successfully, the MPC+ channel connection is activated. Additional paths (defined but not online) in an MPC+ group can later be dynamically added to the active group using the MVS VARY device ONLINE command.

For example, if there is a need for an increase in capacity to allow for extra traffic over a channel, additional paths can be added to the active group without disruption. Similarly, paths can be deleted from the active group when no longer needed using the MVS VARY device OFFLINE command.

13.15 S/390 Open Systems Adapter 2

Open Systems Adapter 2 is an integrated hardware feature that has been implemented as a channel type on the S/390 Parallel Enterprise Server R2 and R3 models. It appears to the application software as a channel-attached control unit. The small size of the package allows the feature to be plugged into an I/O slot in a CEC or I/O expansion cage.

The OSA is defined to the hardware as a new type of S/390 channel. As such, it is highly integrated into the hardware configuration to take advantage of the availability characteristics of the 9672 S/390 Parallel Enterprise Server.

The OSA-2 has an Ethernet/Token-Ring (ENTR) feature that has two independent ports. The ports can be configured in either non-full duplex or full duplex, as:

- Two Ethernets
- Two token-rings
- One Ethernet and one token-ring

This provides maximum flexibility.

The OSA-2 FDDI feature has one port that supports dual-ring or single-ring attachment, as well as attachment to an optical bypass switch.

The OSA-2 ATM feature has one physical port and two logical ports that provide access to Token Ring or Ethernet LANs attached to a high-speed ATM network. Each logical port is configured independently as token-ring or Ethernet and they support TCP/IP, or SNA/APPN, or both.

13.15.1 OSA-2 Modes

The OSA-2 can be configured into several mode combinations depending on your requirements. There are up to six possible combinations.

- TCP/IP Passthru Mode (Non-Shared Port)

  In this mode, an OSA-2 port is capable of transferring TCP/IP LAN traffic to and from just one TCP/IP host or logical partition (refer to Figure 347 on page 798).

- TCP/IP Passthru Mode (Shared Port)

  In this mode, an OSA-2 port is capable of transferring TCP/IP LAN traffic to and from more than one TCP/IP host within multiple logical partitions.

- SNA Mode (Non-Shared Port)

  In this mode, an OSA-2 port is capable of transferring SNA LAN traffic to and from just one SNA host or logical partition.

- SNA Mode (Shared Port)

  In this mode, an OSA-2 port is capable of transferring TCP/IP and SNA LAN traffic to and from more than one TCP/IP and SNA logical partition.

- TCP/IP and SNA Mixed Mode for OSA-2 ATM (Shared Port)

  In this mode, one physical ATM port may be configured into two logical ports. Each logical port may then be configured to support TCP/IP, or SNA traffic, or both. Each logical port is capable of transferring TCP/IP and SNA LAN traffic to and from one or multiple TCP/IP and SNA logical partitions.

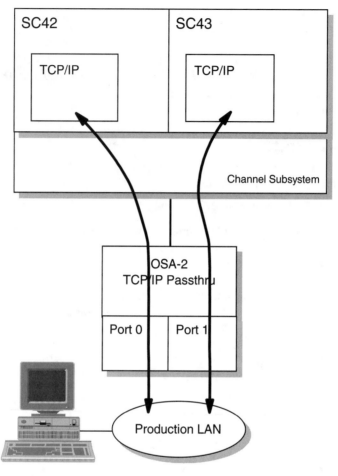

Figure 347. TCP/IP Passthru Mode - (Non-Shared Port)

13.15.2 S/390 Unit Addresses Correlate with OSA-2 LAN Port Numbers

One function of the OSA-2 adapters is to correlate the S/390 devices that are connected to its channel path with its LAN port or ports through which data will be transferred. Device numbers are assigned to OSA port unit addresses through definitions made using the Hardware Configuration Definition (HCD), provided in MVS/ESA or OS/390.

The OSA port default unit addresses are:

- **Port 0**   00-01

- **Port 1**   02-03

In LPAR mode these unit addresses are made available within the OSA adapter to every logical partition. The OSA adapter default mode is TCP/IP Passthru. The default unit addresses and modes can only be changed through the use of the Open Systems Adapter/Support Facility (OSA/SF) (see 13.15.3, "Open Systems Adapter/Support Facility (OSA/SF)").

13.15.2.1 TCP/IP Addressing

Each port on an OSA-2 is a LAN channel station (LCS) device through which LAN data passes. As a passthru agent, OSA can transfer data to and from any TCP/IP host program that is running in any of the logical partitions to which the OSA has been properly defined.

A pair of devices must be defined for each OSA port being used for every logical partition that is accessing the OSA. One device is used for reading and the other for writing.

13.15.2.2 ATM Addressing

LAN clients that use the Asynchronous Transfer Mode to communicate with host applications may do so through either TCP/IP or ACF/VTAM on the host.

An OSA-2 ATM has only one physical port, but two logical LAN emulation ports. The OSA-2 ATM must have one pair of device addresses per accessing logical partition per port when configured for TCP/IP. The OSA-2 ATM must have one device address per accessing logical partition per port when configured for SNA. The OSA-2 ATM can correlate one device address to one or both of its logical ports when configured for SNA.

13.15.3 Open Systems Adapter/Support Facility (OSA/SF)

OSA/SF is an MVS/ESA program product (5655-104) that allows you to customize the OSA hardware to run in different modes. In some cases OSA/SF is optional and in others it s required.

OSA/SF for MVS/ESA runs in an MVS address space. It includes software that can be installed to run on a personal computer that communicates with OSA/SF on the host and the OSA hardware feature. This tool delivers a simple means to configure and manage the OSA-2 and to download software updates for supported applications.

OSA/SF is used to implement the TCP/IP, SNA/APPN, or ATM function onto the appropriate OSA-2 adapter.

When the S/390 server is running in LPAR (logically partitioned) mode, it is possible to configure the OSA so that any or all LPARs may share the same LAN connection. This is called port sharing. Port sharing support is provided by OSA/SF.

13.16 Multiprotocol over ATM (MPOA)

The objectives of MPOA are to:

- Provide end-to-end layer 3 internetworking connectivity across an ATM network. This is for hosts that are attached either:

  - Directly to the ATM network
  - Indirectly to the ATM network on a legacy LAN

- Support the distribution of the internetwork layer (for example, an IP subnet) across legacy and ATM-attached devices.

  - Removes the port to layer 3 network restriction of routers to enable the building of protocol-based virtual LANs (VLANs).

- Ensure interoperability among the distributed routing components while allowing flexibility in implementations.

- Address how internetwork layer protocols use the services of an ATM network.

Although the name is multiprotocol over ATM, the actual work being done at the moment in the MPOA subworking group is entirely focused on IP.

13.16.1 Benefits of MPOA

MPOA represents the transition from LAN emulation to direct exploitation of ATM by the internetwork layer protocols. The advantages are:

- Protocols would see ATM as more than just another link.
  - Hence we are able to exploit the facilities of ATM.
- Eliminates the need for the overhead of the legacy LAN frame structure.

The MPOA solution has the following benefits over both Classical IP (RFC 1577) and LAN emulation solutions:

- Lower latency by allowing direct connectivity between end systems that can cut across subnet boundaries. This is achieved by minimizing the need for multiple hops through ATM routers for communication between end systems on different virtual LANs.

- Higher aggregate layer 3 forwarding capacity by distributing processing functions to the edge of the network.
- Allows mapping of specific flows to specific QOS characteristics.
- Allows a layer 3 subnet to be distributed across a physical network.

13.16.2 MPOA Logical Components

The MPOA solution consists of a number of logical components and information flows between those components. The logical components are of two kinds:

MPOA Server

MPOA servers maintain *complete* knowledge of the MAC and internetworking layer topologies for the IASGs they serve. To accomplish this, they exchange information among themselves and with MPOA clients.

MPOA Client

MPOA clients maintain local caches of mappings (from packet prefix to ATM information). These caches are populated by requesting the information from the appropriate MPOA server on an as-needed basis.

The layer 3 addresses associated with an MPOA client would represent either the layer 3 address of the client itself, or the layer 3 addresses reachable through the client. (The client has an edge device or router.)

An MPOA client will connect to its MPOA server to register the client's ATM address and the layer 3 addresses reachable via the client.

13.16.3 MPOA Functional Components

Figure 348 on page 802 shows the mapping between the logical and physical components, which are split between the following layers:

- MPOA Functional Group Layer
- LAN Emulation Layer
- Physical Layer

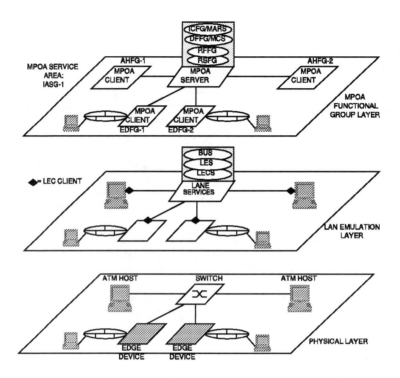

Figure 348. *MPOA Functional Components*

The MPOA solution will be implemented into various functional groups that include:

Internetwork Address Sub-Group (IASG)

> A range of internetwork layer addresses (for example, an IPv4 subnet).
> Hence, if a host operates two internetwork layer protocols, it will be a
> member of, at least, two IASGs.

Edge Device Functional Group (EDFG)

> EDFG is the group of functions performed by a device that provides
> internetworking level connections between a legacy subnetwork and ATM.

> - An EDFG implements layer 3 packet forwarding, but does not execute
>   any routing protocols (executed in the RSFG).
> - Two types of EDFG are allowed: *simple* and *smart*.
>   - Smart EDFGs request resolution of internetwork addresses (that is, it
>   will send a query ARP type frame if it doesn't have an entry for the
>   destination).

- Simple EDFGs will send a frame via a default class to a default destination if no entry exists.
- A coresident proxy LEC function is required.

ATM-Attached Host Functional Group (AHFG)

AHFG is the group of functions performed by an ATM-attached host that is participating in the MPOA network.

- A coresident proxy LEC function is optional.

  Within an IASG, LAN emulation is used as a transport mechanism to either legacy devices or LAN emulation devices, in which case access to a LEC is required. If the AHFG will not be communicating with LANE or legacy devices, then a coresident LEC is not required.

IASG Coordination Functional Group (ICFG)[17]

ICFG is the group of functions performed to coordinate the distribution of a single IASG across multiple legacy LAN ports on one or more EDFG and/or ATM device. The ICFG tracks the location of the functional components so that it is able to respond to queries for layer 3 addresses.

Default Forwarder Function Group (DFFG)[17]

In the absence of direct client-to-client connectivity, the DFFG provides default forwarding for traffic destined either within or outside the IASG.

- Provides internetwork layer multicast forwarding in an IASG; that is, the DFFG acts as the multicast server (MCS) in an MPOA-based MARS implementation.
- Provides *proxy* LAN emulation function for AHFGs (that is, for AHFGs that don't have a LANE client) to enable AHFGs to send/receive traffic with legacy-attached systems.

Route Server Functional Group (RSFG)[18]

RSFG performs internetworking level functions in an MPOA network. This includes:

- Running conventional internetworking routing protocols (for example, OSPF, RIP and BGP)
- Providing address resolution between IASGs, handling requests and building responses

---

[17] ICFG/DFFG functional groups are coresident hence no protocol exists, or needs to be defined between the two.

Remote Forwarder Functional Group (RFFG)[18]

> RFFG is the group of functions performed in association with forwarding traffic from a source to a destination, where these can be either an IASG or an MPOA client. An RFFG is synonymous with the *default router* function of a typical IPv4 subnet.

Note: One or more of these functional groups may coreside in the same physical entity. MPOA allows arbitrary physical locations of these groups.

13.16.4 MPOA Operation

The MPOA system operates as a set of functional groups that exchange information in order to exhibit the desired behavior. To provide an overview of the MPOA system, the behavior of the components is described in a sequence order by *significant events*:

Configuration:

> Ensures that all functional groups have the appropriate set of administrative information.

Registration and Discovery:

> Includes the functional groups informing each other of their existence and of the identities of attached devices and EDFGs informing the ICFG of legacy devices.

Destination Resolution:

> The action of determining the route description given a destination internetwork layer address and possibly other information (for example, QOS). This is the part of the MPOA system that allows it to perform cut-through (with respect to IASG boundaries).

Data Transfer:

> To get internetworking layer data from one MPOA client to another.

Intra-IASG Coordination:

> The function that enables IASGs to be spread across multiple physical interfaces.

Routing Protocol Support:

> Enables the MPOA system to interact with traditional internetworks.

Spanning Tree Support:

> Enables the MPOA system to interact with existing extended LANs.

---

[18] RSFG/RFFG functional groups are coresident hence no protocol exists, or needs to be defined between the two.

Replication Support:
>   Provides for replication of key components for reasons of capacity or
>   resilience.

13.17 Private Network-to-Network Interface (PNNI)

In the layered routing model, layer-3 packets are forwarded by routers on a
hop-by-hop basis based on the contents of the destination network address. A dynamic
routing protocol such as OSPF is used to distribute network topology and reachability
information among the routers in the network. In ATM networks a similar mechanism
is required to forward SVC requests through a network of switches based on the called
or destination ATM address. Likewise a dynamic routing protocol can be used to
distribute ATM network topology and reachability information among the switches in
the network. This will enable ATM switches to compute an accurate path through the
network to the destination.

Due to the unique scaling and QoS features of ATM as well as the connection-oriented
nature of SVCs, the ATM routing protocol must address several important
requirements:

- Must be stable and reflect the current topology and capacity of the network.

- Must scale from a network of several switches to one containing hundreds and
  perhaps thousands.

- Must support efficient and loop-free routing of SVC requests over a path that will
  meet the QoS objectives of the SVC.

- Must support a heterogeneous mix of ATM switches.

- Must be extensible. That is it should be simple to add and enhance new function
  as requirements arise.

The ATM forum is currently working on the Private Network-to-Network Interface
Specification Version 1.0 (PNNI Phase I) which is designed to meet the above
requirements.

The ATM Forum is also examining ways to leverage and exploit the PNNI Phase I
protocol as a means to support layer-3 internetworking over ATM. Two other
specifications are under development:

PNNI Augmented Routing (PAR)
>   PAR allows IP routers directly connected to ATM switches to participate in
>   PNNI and use the information gained from PNNI for establishing SVCs with
>   other routers attached to the same ATM network.

Integrated PNNI (I-PNNI)

> I-PNNI is an extension to PNNI Phase I in which a network of routers and switches run a single routing protocol that supports both SVC and packet routing. This single protocol is I-PNNI.

13.17.1 PNNI Overview

The PNNI protocol is intended for use between ATM switches in a private ATM network. The abbreviation PNNI stands for either Private Network Node Interface or Private Network-to-Network Interface and to some degree reflects the duality of its capability based on its recursive behavior as described below. The PNNI Phase I specification defines two distinct protocols:

PNNI Routing Protocol

> This protocol is responsible for distributing topology information between switches in an ATM network. This information is used to compute a path through the network for the SVC that will satisfy the requested QoS. A hierarchy mechanism ensures that this protocol scales well for large ATM networks.

PNNI Signalling Protocol

> This protocol defines the signalling flows used to establish point-to-point and multipoint connections across the ATM network. The protocol is based on standard ATM UNI signalling (3.1 and 4.0). PNNI signalling employs source routing and a crankback mechanism to route SVC requests around failed network components at call setup.

13.17.2 PNNI Routing

The PNNI routing protocol is responsible for distributing topology information between switches in an ATM network. The following sections explain how the PNNI routing protocol works.

13.17.2.1 Addressing

The fundamental purpose of PNNI is to compute a route from a source to a destination based on a called ATM address. The called ATM address is an information element contained in the SETUP message that is sent over the UNI from the device to a switch. Presumably a switch running PNNI Phase I will have in its topology database an entry that will match a portion or prefix of the 20-byte ATM address that is contained in the SETUP message. The switch will then be able to compute a path through the network to the destination switch.

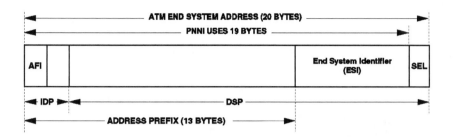

Figure 349. ATM End System Address

To best understand PNNI routing, it would be helpful to review ATM addressing from PNNI's perspective. Addressing and identification of components of the PNNI routing hierarchy are based on the use of ATM end system addresses. An ATM end system address is 20 bytes long and is shown in Figure 349. PNNI routing works off of the first 19 bytes of this address or some prefix of this address. The 20th byte is the selector field which only has local significance to the endstation and is ignored by PNNI routing. A prefix is the first "p" bits of an ATM address with "p" being a value between 0 and 152. Generally speaking PNNI will advertise reachability to ATM end systems using an address prefix rather than advertise each unique ATM end system address. This is analogous to routers advertising reachability to IP subnets rather than to each individual IP host.

Nodes in a peer group have the same prefix address bits in common. This is illustrated in Figure 350 on page 808.

- At the highest level illustrated, the LGNs that make up the high-order LGN have their left x high-order bits the same.

- At the next lower level, the three LGNs shown have their left $x+y$ high-order bits the same.

- At the lowest level illustrated, the LGNs have their left $x+y+z$ high-order bits the same. (At this level, they are real physical switches.)

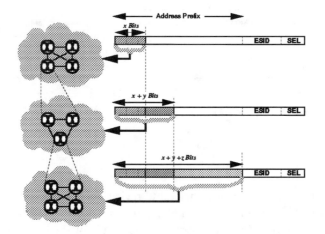

Figure 350. Addressing Hierarchy

Two identifiers are used in PNNI to define the hierarchy and a nodes placement in the hierarchy. The first is the peer group identifier. This is a 14-byte value and is illustrated in Figure 351. The first byte is a level indicator which defines which of the next 104 leftmost bits are shared by switches in the peer group. Peer group identifiers must be prefixes of ATM addresses.

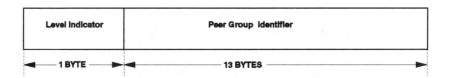

Figure 351. Peer Group Identifier

A peer group is identified by its peer group identifier. Peer group IDs are specified at configuration time. Neighboring nodes exchange peer group IDs in hello packets. If they have the same peer group ID, then they belong to the same peer group. If the exchanged peer group IDs are different, then the nodes belong to different peer groups.

The node identifier is 22 bytes in length and consists of a 1-byte level indicator and a unique 21-byte value. The node identifier is unique for each PNNI node in the routing domain. A PNNI node that advertises topology information in PNNI topology state packets will include the node identifier and the peer group identifier to indicate the originator of the information and the scope (on which level of the hierarchy it is directed to).

13.17.2.2 PNNI Information Exchange

A PNNI node will advertise its own direct knowledge of the ATM network. The scope of this advertisement is the peer group. The information is encoded in TLVs called PNNI Topology State Elements (PTSE). Multiple PTSEs can be carried in a single PNNI Topology State Packet (PTSP). The PTSP is the packet used to send topology information to a neighbor node in the peer group. Each switch advertises the following:

Nodal Information

> This includes the switch's ATM address, peer group identifier, leadership priority and other aspects about the switch itself.

Topology State Information

> This covers outbound link and switch resources.

Reachability

> ATM addresses and ATM address prefixes that the switch has learned about or is configured with.

It was mentioned that PNNI is a topology state protocol. This means that logical nodes will advertise link state and nodal state parameters. A link state parameter describes the characteristics of a specific link and a nodal state parameter describes the characteristics of a node. Together these can form topology state parameters that are advertised by PNNI nodes within their own peer group.

Topology state parameters are either metrics or attributes. A topology state metric is a parameter whose values must be combined for all links and nodes in the SVC request path to determine if the path is acceptable. A topology state attribute is a parameter that is considered individually to determine if a path is acceptable for an SVC request. Topology state attributes can be further subdivided into two categories: performance-related and policy-related. Performance-related attributes measure the performance of a particular link or node. Policy-related attributes provide a measure of conformance level to a specific policy by a node or link in the topology.

13.17.3 PNNI Signalling

PNNI signaling is based on a subset of UNI 4.0 signalling. It does not support some of the UNI Signalling 4.0 signalling features such as proxy signalling, leaf initiated join capability or user-to-user supplementary, but does support new capabilities such as specific QoS parameters, ATM anycast addressing and scoping and ABR. In addition, PNNI signalling differs from UNI 4.0 signalling in that it is symmetric. This makes sense because this is a switch-to-switch signalling protocol rather than an end user-to-switch protocol.

PNNI signalling utilizes information gathered by PNNI routing. Specifically, it uses the route calculations derived from reachability, connectivity, and resource information dynamically maintained by PNNI routing. These routes are calculated as needed from the node's view of the current topology.

The unique capabilities that PNNI signalling defines are designated transit lists and crankback and alternate routing. DTLs are used to carry hierarchically complete source routes. Crankback and alternate routing allows for an SVC request to be rerouted around a failed component as it makes its way to the destination switch. Additionally associated signalling is used for PNNI operation over virtual path connections and soft permanent VPCs/VCCs are supported.

13.18 References

The following RFCs provide detailed information on the connection protocols and architectures presented throughout this chapter:

- *RFC 826 — Ethernet Address Resolution Protocol*
- *RFC 894 — Standard for the Transmission of IP Datagrams over Ethernet Networks*
- *RFC 1042 — Standard for the Transmission of IP Datagrams over IEEE 802 Networks*
- *RFC 1055 — Nonstandard for Transmission of IP Datagrams over Serial Lines: SLIP*
- *RFC 1144 — Compressing TCP/IP Headers for Low-Speed Serial Links*
- *RFC 1188 — Proposed Standard for the Transmission of IP Datagrams over FDDI Networks*
- *RFC 1356 — Multiprotocol Interconnect on X.25 and ISDN in the Packet Mode*
- *RFC 1483 — Multiprotocol Encapsulation over ATM Adaptation Layer 5*
- *RFC 1618 — PPP over ISDN*
- *RFC 1619 — PPP over SONET/SDH*
- *RFC 1661 — The Point-to-Point Protocol (PPP)*
- *RFC 1662 — PPP in HDLC-Like Framing*

- *RFC 1700 — Assigned Numbers*
- *RFC 1755 — ATM Signaling Support for IP over ATM*
- *RFC 1795 — Data Link Switching: Switch-to-Switch Protocol AIW DLSw RIG: DLSw Closed Pages, DLSw Standard Version 1*
- *RFC 2225 — Classical IP and ARP over ATM*
- *RFC 2390 — Inverse Address Resolution Protocol*
- *RFC 2400 — Internet Official Protocol Standards*
- *RFC 2427 — Multiprotocol Interconnect over Frame Relay*

Chapter 14. Platform Implementations

This chapter presents an overview of the main TCP/IP functions, protocols and applications that can be found in IBM operating systems and hardware platforms.

14.1 Software Operating System Implementations

IBM operating systems have been equipped with TCP/IP functionality for the past 15 years and have constantly increased and improved their coverage of TCP/IP. The following sections provide an overview of the TCP/IP capabilities of the respective system platforms, followed by a set of tables that offer a comprehensive summary and cross-platform comparison.

14.1.1 IBM OS/390 V2R6

IBM enterprise servers running OS/390, the S/390 flagship operating system, provide customers with the necessary power, scalability, security and availability to help them run their mission-critical workloads. IBM will enrich its server platform offerings even further with new releases of OS/390.

14.1.1.1 eNetwork Communications Server for OS/390

IBM significantly redesigned the TCP/IP services within the OS/390 Version 2 Release 5 eNetwork Communications Server to provide customers with world-class networking support for multiple e-business applications. These TCP/IP services enabled UNIX, Web serving and traditional applications to benefit from improved performance, function and increased connectivity bandwidth with native ATM and Fast Ethernet.

Laying the foundation for the next steps in TCP/IP performance, TCP/IP High Speed Web Access (HSWA) servers also were integrated into OS/390 V. 2 Rel. 5 and provided a robust, high performance Internet Protocol (IP) environment for those customers with intense Web-serving needs. As announced in May 1998, internal IBM performance tests on a 10-way S/390 G4 Server, with the enhanced TCP/IP HSWA services of OS/390 V. 2 Rel. 5, could handle up to 400 million Internet hits per day. With the S/390 G5 Server providing more than double the power of the S/390 G4 Server, OS/390 Release 5's TCP/IP HSWA servers are capable of handling substantially more than 400 million Internet hits per day.

The OS/390 V.2 Rel. 6 eNetwork Communications Server TCP/IP services leverage the significant enhancements in the prior release and provide a single, highly scalable, high-performance IP stack capable of satisfying all customer and TCP/IP communications requirements. In addition to providing the same levels of performance for intense Web-serving, internal IBM performance tests on a 10-way S/390 G4 Server comparing MVS TCP/IP Version 3 Release 2 (TCP/IP 3.2 was integrated with OS/390 Version 2 Release 4) with the enhanced TCP/IP services of OS/390 V. 2 Rel. 6 have shown up to 15 times improved performance for a full range of applications — whether they be file transfer, telnet, UNIX or any ISV application using the TCP/IP sockets interface. Alternative modes of operation, such as offloading TCP/IP workload to the network router, have been made obsolete with these levels of integrated performance.

14.1.1.2 OS/390 Network Computing Services

IBM continues to enhance S/390's Web-serving capabilities with each new release of OS/390. IBM announced in May 1998 the e-business Series for S/390, an e-business product solution which gives customers scalable and secure e-business tools focusing on groupware, e-commerce and Web-serving. The latest functionality integrated into Release 6 includes WebSphere Application Server for OS/390 and increased performance and security for Web data access with the improved TCP/IP Services in the eNetwork Communications Server.

WebSphere Application Server for OS/390, a rebranded and enhanced Lotus Domino Go Webserver for OS/390, integrated into OS/390 V. 2 Rel. 6. It can help customers build a secure Internet presence. New features in WebSphere Application Server for OS/390 include automated support of digital certificates and enhanced Java servlet support. The new Java servlet engine, previously code-named ServletExpress, helps to improve Java performance. Digital certificate support in OS/390 is also enhanced as OS/390 now can act as the local Certificate Authority to locally issue and manage certificates. The OS/390 Security Server will accept authenticated digital certificates from WebSphere Application Server for OS/390 and associate the certificate with a user, without requiring a user to enter an ID or password before accessing critical data. Also available in WebSphere Application Server for OS/390 is enhanced support for Workload Manager, whereby customers can dynamically prioritize all Web requests from the Secure Sockets Layer (SSL) to be handled according to business requirements. SSL provides encryption for the transmission of private information over the Internet. Workload Manager now can manage secure Web requests, as well as non-SSL Web requests, providing secure systems management and better scalability for both workloads.

14.1.1.3 OS/390 Security Server

OS/390 Version 2 Release 6 provides enhancements to many critical e-business security capabilities. An essential part of these enhancements is contained in OS/390 Security Server, which provides support for digital certificates, Resource Access

Control Facility (RACF), Lightweight Directory Access Protocol (LDAP) Server, Firewall Technologies and Distributed Computing Environment (DCE) Security Server.

Network security protects data while it is in transit over public backbones and also denies access by unauthorized parties to private networks and machines and the data stored on them. System security uses hardware security facilities, user authentication and resource access control to help protect a system and its files, programs and data from unauthorized activity. Transaction security works to ensure that an electronic transaction takes place securely, privately and is authenticated. IBM's S/390 platform provides integrated support of these three forms of security to offer industry-leading security solutions to customers. Together, they help provide the critical levels of network, system and transaction security needed for safe e-business applications.

OS/390 V.2 Rel. 6, together with S/390 hardware and OS/390 Security Server, extends support for OS/390 V.2 e-business security technologies such as digital certificates, public key infrastructure, OS/390 Firewall Technologies and cryptography. OS/390 V.2 Rel. 6 also offers enhancements to Web server security management.

Transaction Security: IBM has enhanced OS/390 V. 2 Rel. 6 to support the security of transactions through WebSphere Application Server, including enhancements in performance, configuration and flexibility to areas that are necessary for secure transactions. These include:

Multiple Internet Protocol (IP) address Secure Sockets Layer (SSL) support
> This feature provides SSL support for multiple IP addresses hosted by the same server and for individual certificates associated with each distinct IP address. A single server will sometimes support multiple Universal Resource Locators (URL) and IP addresses. This support extends the SSL security protocols from a single, server-wide certificate to better allow certificates that are IP-specific.

SSL workload management
> This enhanced support allows OS/390 Workload Manager (WLM) to dynamically prioritize SSL requests, improving the overall throughput of this critical secure transaction protocol. SSL provides encryption for the transmission of private data over the Internet. WLM can manage servers for secure Web requests, as well as non-SSL Web requests, providing better scalability for business-critical applications.

Lightweight Directory Access Protocol (LDAP) support
> This feature provides centralized access and administration of authentication information, such as user names or passwords, stored in an LDAP directory. A system administrator can now add a user account once and any LDAP-enabled application such as the Web server will automatically recognize the new user.

Also, multiple Web servers can share the same configuration via a new LDAP directive.

Crypto keysize selection

A WebSphere Application Server system administrator can specify maximum and minimum levels of encryption to be used by the server when communicating with a requester. Normally the server and requester programs select the highest level of encryption that is supported by both. This enhanced feature allows the server administrator to better control security.

128-bit encryption support

This function enables export browsers (outside of North America) with 128-bit encryption capability to use this level of encryption when communicating with financial institution servers worldwide that also are authorized to use 128-bit encryption.

Digital Certificates and Public Key Infrastructure: One of the fastest growing aspects of e-business security is the use of digital certificates for user authentication. This entire process of issuing and managing certificates is commonly referred to as a Public Key Infrastructure. OS/390 Version 2 and the OS/390 Security Server, together with S/390 hardware, provide enhanced support for this capability, including:

Digital Certificate Authentication

WebSphere Application Server can now accept and authenticate digital certificates presented by many popular Web browsers. The user can then be given access to Web server pages and functions.

Accessing OS/390 resources

Beginning with OS/390 Version 2 Release 4, OS/390 Security Server will accept authenticated digital certificates from WebSphere Application Server and associate that certificate with an OS/390 Security Server user, providing authorization based on the user's RACF identity associated with the authenticated digital certificate.

Mapping a certificate to a user ID

A user's digital certificate can be mapped to an OS/390 Security Server RACF user ID by an administrator or by the user. The latter case, provided by recent enhancements included in OS/390 V. 2 Rel. 6 Security Server, allows the user to self-register a digital certificate to the user's existing Security Server RACF user ID directly from a Web browser through a Secure Sockets Layer (SSL) protected Web page.

Issuing digital certificates locally

Companies may wish to issue their own digital certificates for use within the company and act as their own trusted "local" Certificate Authority. WebSphere

Application Server provides a new function, the IBM HTTP Server Certificate Authority, which can be used to issue and manage locally issued certificates. Digital certificates can be requested by a user, routed for approval, issued and registered. If the user is using a Netscape browser, the certificate can be automatically transmitted and installed in the browser's user certificate list over the network.

Working with other Certificate Authorities

WebSphere Application Server can process digital certificates from any Certificate Authority. This might be from specialized Certificate Authority applications owned by the customer, or from a third-party digital certificate provider. In OS/390 V. 2 Rel. 6, WebSphere Application Server can process Certificate Revocation Lists (CRL) "published" by the IBM Registry certificate authority product. This is a key prerequisite in implementing a standards-based Public Key Infrastructure that can handle the revoking of certificates that have expired or been compromised.

Network Security: OS/390 V. 2 Rel. 6 now supports secure, encrypted communications across unsecured networks between the OS/390 TN3270 server and SSL-enabled clients such as Host On-Demand Version 2. Host On-Demand uses Java applet technology to provide host terminal emulation windows within a Web browser. With the new SSL support in OS/390 TN3270, Host On-Demand can provide Web browser-based 3270 ("green screen") host terminal emulation with privacy across the Internet or other unsecured networks.

OS/390 Firewall Technologies

Firewall Technologies, integrated into OS/390 beginning with Version 2 Release 5, builds upon existing S/390 security capabilities to offer customers higher levels of protection for network applications by helping to control user access to separate servers inside and outside a secured network.

Delivered by a combination of the eNetwork Communication Server for OS/390 and OS/390 Security Server functions, OS/390 Firewall Technologies provides customers with high network security to transact e-business across both secured and unsecured networks.

OS/390 Firewall Technologies also contains a *Virtual Private Network* (VPN) function which works with the S/390 cryptographic coprocessor to help enable data to flow securely across a network or between networks.

- The Internet Protocol Security (IPSec) function for VPNs will be upgraded to help provide support for the "transport mode" option of IPSec allowing customers to protect data along the entire end-to-end path from client to server. VPN will continue to support "tunnel mode" for cases when protection is needed selectively along portions of an end-to-end path, such as between a client and an OS/390 server or between two OS/390 systems acting as firewalls. This broadens the VPN support to include more flexible configurations of servers, clients and gateway (firewall) functions.

- IBM is also enhancing OS/390 Security Server's File Transfer Protocol (FTP) proxy performance by adding multithread support. Performance improvements are also being made to other portions of the OS/390 Security Server's Firewall Technologies.

System Security/Cryptography: Cryptography is an essential part of e-business applications. It is the underlying technology of all security and privacy on the Internet today. S/390 Parallel Enterprise Servers and OS/390 provide hardware-based cryptography support.

The cryptographic coprocessor is a hardware-embedded chip that is standard with the S/390 G4 and G5 Enterprise Servers. OS/390 software exploits the cryptographic coprocessor to provide customers with higher levels of security protection than what is available with software cryptography alone. The S/390 G5 Server will provide a dual processor chip path that enhances the overall availability of cryptographic processing.

IBM also received US government approval to export Triple DES on both the S/390 G4 and S/390 G5 servers to banks worldwide, in accordance with US government export laws and regulations. Triple DES, critical for financial institutions, is based on DES, a reliable standard for network and information security for the past 20 years. Triple DES provides customers with exponentially stronger encryption protection than standard DES. IBM also increased the cryptographic coprocessor Triple DES performance on S/390 G5 servers by replacing its microcode implementation with an all-hardware implementation.

OS/390 V. 2 Rel. 6 also includes enhancements to Integrated Cryptographic Services Facility (ICSF) to work in conjunction with the S/390 G5 server cryptographic coprocessor enhancements:

Enhanced ICSF Support for Double-Key MAC
> IBM enhanced S/390 support for the Key-MAC security protocol by allowing use of a double-length key for message authentication (MAC) processing. This support helps enable enhanced message authentication between sender and receiver. Emerging VISA International and MasterCard protocols in Europe support this important security standard, known as the ANSI X9.19 Optional Double-MAC Procedure.

RSA key generation

Keys can be generated in the TKE (Trusted Key Element) workstation and transmitted to the host where they are imported and used by the S/390 cryptographic coprocessor. This support, available with ICSF in OS/390 V. 2 Rel. 6, conforms to the VISA and MasterCard requirements for RSA key generation for SET protocol-based Payment Gateways.

14.1.2 IBM TCP/IP V2R4 for VM

A TCP/IP built for business IBM TCP/IP for VM, Version 2 Release 4, brings the power and resources of your System/390 computer to the Internet. Using the TCP/IP for VM TCP/IP protocol suite, you can reach open multivendor networking environments from your VM system. With TCP/IP for VM, VM systems can act as peers of other central computers in TCP/IP open networks. Applications can be shared transparently across VM, UNIX, VAX, and other environments. VM users can send messages, transfer files, share printers, and access remote resources across a broad range of systems from multiple vendors.

IBM TCP/IP for VM is the first choice for VM TCP/IP connectivity. Designed to meet the needs of enterprises with complex networking requirements, TCP/IP for VM applies IBM's experience in the design and development of large systems to the implementation of TCP/IP on large computers. TCP/IP for VM, Version 2 Release 4 offers a wide range of client/server applications, programming interfaces, and connectivity options, plus the data integrity and performance that network users have come to expect from IBM.

High-speed file transfer

TCP/IP for VM includes File Transfer Protocol (FTP), CMS shared file system (SFS), and byte file system (BFS) support. FTP clients running either on VM or other systems can access enterprise data residing anywhere in the VM hierarchical file system-BFS, SFS, or on CMS minidisks.

With FTP access capability, TCP/IP for VM lets you continue to use VM SFS or BFS for storing large amounts of enterprise data, while expanding your VM environment and moving you toward a TCP/IP future.

Access control

New configuration statements provide the TCP/IP administrator added capabilities regarding the use of TCP/IP services. The eligible administrator can specify a list of users authorized to use TCP/IP services with the new PERMIT statement, or, the administrator can prevent this usage with a new RESTRICT statement.

Internet services

TCP/IP for VM provides Internet mail services through a Simple Mail Transfer
Protocol (SMTP) server. This server receives mail over a TCP/IP network
connection or from its virtual reader. It sends mail through TCP/IP or Remote
Spooling Communications Subsystem (RSCS) networks, according to the mail's
destination.

TCP/IP for VM also enables the deployment of VM Web servers currently
available from IBM Business Partners. Utilizing the TCP/IP interfaces, the Web
servers give easy access to VM applications and central computer data, such as
mail, calendars, and notelogs of OfficeVision/VM and relational data of
DATABASE 2 (DB2) for VSE & VM (formerly SQL/DS).

Application development

With TCP/IP for VM, you get a variety of application programming interfaces
(APIs) and services to help you develop new and better applications for network
connectivity. You can work with remote procedure call (RPC) libraries and the
Network Computing System (NCS) programming interface to build distributing
applications and allow for distributed processing. With an enhanced sockets
library from TCP/IP for VM, you can easily move UNIX applications to the
System/390 computer. TCP/IP for VM also allows you to invoke high-quality
graphics with the Motif/X toolkit and provides better security with Kerberos
client and server services.

Remote printing

TCP/IP for VM gives you the added advantage of printing data from your VM
system on remote printers in your TCP/IP network. With support for line printer
router (LPR) and line printer daemon (LPD), TCP/IP for VM delivers
enterprise-wide network printing support.

Network management

You can use the Tivoli Enterprise family of products with TCP/IP for VM
through the Simple Network Management Protocol (SNMP). You can manage
TCP/IP for VM with any management product that supports SNMP, including
Tivoli Enterprise for AIX and equivalent vendor programs. TCP/IP for VM also
supports Routing Information Protocol (RIP), which helps automate the
administration of routing tables.

With an optional offload feature, you can reduce central computer processor
usage by processing TCP/IP protocols in an attached 3172 Interconnect
Controller Model 3. You can also manage your 3172 controllers through the
3172 Simple Network Management Protocol (SNMP) agent support provided by
TCP/IP for VM.

Terminal access

A new Telnet session-connection user exit feature lets clients directly connect to VTAM, PVM, VSE, or any other second-level system when the VM/ESA CP DIAL command is specified in the user exit. This exit can be used to control system access based on the client's foreign Internet protocol or local port addresses, or both.

If you need access to 3270-based applications from UNIX and other systems, you can get it easily with the Telnet TN3270 support provided by TCP/IP for VM. Telnet features include full-screen and ASCII line-mode support.

Expanded capacity

In TCP/IP for VM, Version 2 Release 4, the limit of 2000 sockets per TCP/IP client has been removed. Now, the only limit to the number of sockets is the amount of available virtual storage. This enhancement enables applications, such as Telnet, to support more than 2000 clients.

Network interfaces

TCP/IP for VM provides broad support for local area network (LAN) connectivity, channel attachment interfaces, and wide area network (WAN) support. Supported LAN interfaces include Ethernet, token-ring, PC Network, and Fiber Distributed Data Interface (FDDI). Channel attachment support includes channel-to-channel (CTC) 3088 support, Open Systems Adapter, ESCON, HYPERchannel, and Continuously Executing Transfer Interface (CETI). TCP/IP for VM includes SNAlink and X.25 support for WANs.

Reduced cost of computing

TCP/IP for VM, Version 2 Release 4, has been recompiled using IBM C for VM/ESA, Version 3 Release 1. This recompilation eliminates the requirement for the C/370 run-time libraries on VM/ESA, Version 2, systems. It also supports the run-time execution environment provided by IBM Language Environment for MVS and VM.

14.1.2.1 TCP/IP in the Latest Release of VM/ESA

Transmission Control Protocol/Internet Protocol (TCP/IP) support in VM/ESA is now provided by the optional TCP/IP Feature for VM/ESA (Function Level 310), which contains the functions available in IBM TCP/IP Version 2 Release 4 for VM plus the following enhancements:

NFS Support of Byte File and Shared File Systems (BFS, SFS)

In addition to minidisk files, the Network File System (NFS) allows a client to access the CMS Byte File (BFS) and Shared File Systems (SFS) as if they were local to the client. Clients can now access these files using the enhanced MOUNT and MOUNTPW commands.

Expanded CMS/Internet Mail Capability

This support lets CMS end users send mail and file objects through a TCP/IP network using enhanced CMS utilities. While a similar capability exists today through separate, TCP/IP-provided utilities, this support incorporates the capability in existing CMS facilities (EXECUTE, NOTE, PEEK, RDRLIST, RECEIVE, SENDFILE, and TELL).

Line Printer Client

The current Line Printer Client (LPR) operations have been enhanced to allow the end user to have print data processed by the RSCS server. Specifically, this enhancement allows users to select either asynchronous printing through RSCS or the currently supported synchronous delivery. Additional flexibility is provided with support for the specification of user-defined nicknames.

Configuration of Servers

A new server definition methodology provides a way to easily define, or change the attributes of the set of server virtual machines used by TCP/IP. This implementation focuses on a standard method of server configuration and consolidates that configuration into a single file. The ability to simplify the replication of TCP/IP servers is further complemented by the ability to add new application protocols by simply defining them in a CMS NAMES file.

SMTP Performance Enhancement

SMTP (Simple Mail Transfer Protocol) performance has been improved by increasing the throughput of the server. The throughput gains are realized by reducing synchronous minidisk I/O, converting to asynchronous spool services, and improved use of data-in-memory techniques. All current SMTP server functions are still supported with these enhancements. Robust debugging support through extensive tracing capability is also provided in the server.

Base Improvements

Many new functions improve the usability, function, performance and serviceability of TCP/IP in the VM environment. These include multiple logical hosts, selective trace, performance monitoring, TN3270E printing, multiport Telnet server, and improved server inactivity detection.

14.1.3 IBM OS/400 V4R3

This section provides an overview of the capabilities of an AS/400 system in TCP/IP environments as an Internet application platform and as a security server.

14.1.3.1 TCP/IP

An extension to OS/400 called AS/400 TCP/IP Communications Utilities (#5738-TC1) allows AS/400 systems to participate in communications networks that use the

Transmission Control Protocol/Internet Protocol (TCP/IP). The IBM TCP/IP Server Support/400 product (#5798-RWY) gives clients access to AS/400 database files and folder files via Sun Microsystems' Network File System (NFS), which is commonly used in TCP/IP environments. The TCP/IP protocol has become increasingly significant as the client/server environment has moved into a networked environment including both intranets and the Internet.

Standards supported by AS/400 TCP/IP include Dynamic Host Configuration Protocol (DHCP) and Domain Name Server (DNS). Dynamic Host Configuration Protocol support allows the AS/400 to dynamically assign Internet Protocol (IP) addresses when new hosts are added to the network, such as when a network station or PC is turned on in an intranet. Domain Name Server converts the text names as used in URLs to the 32-bit codes used for network routing. As an example it converts www.as400.ibm.com to 205.217.130.11. Other functions supported are TCP/IP dial-in via PPP (Point to Point) and ISDN as well as full TCP/IP routing. Operations Navigator provides a Windows-like graphical interface to the TCP/IP configuration function.

The network integration characteristics of TCP/IP have been enhanced through the addition of Graphical User Interface (GUI) support of all TCP/IP configuration and administrative tasks.

14.1.3.2 Load Balancing

Virtual IP Addressing (VIPA) provides network load balancing and fault tolerance between multiple IP interfaces (adapters). Outgoing balancing and incoming balancing work differently. Outgoing balancing is done through the routing configuration. Incoming balancing needs an external router which is capable of distributing IP packets to multiple interfaces. The distribution information is provided to the routers by the RIP protocol. The load balancing using routers enables multiple redundant paths from the server to the network, providing horizontal bandwidth growth and high availability tolerance for link or router failures.

14.1.3.3 NFS

The AS/400's Integrated File System includes support for the Network File System - a popular protocol used in UNIX-based client/server computing environments. The NFS Server and NFS Client communicate using Remote Program Calls. The NFS Client is a physical file system that implements the AS/400 Virtual File System architecture. The NFS Client provides seamless access to remote files for local applications. The remote files could be on a remote UNIX machine, the AIX IOP, or any machine that is running an NFS Server.

14.1.3.4 Internet

The AS/400 is well equipped to be an Internet server. Many programs (IBM and non-IBM) are available that allow an AS/400 to be a Web server on the Internet or intranet (a private network built using Internet standards). IBM's Web server for the AS/400 is the Internet Connection Secure Server.

With the AS/400's support for the Internet and the appropriate set of identifiers and passwords, it is possible to access the Web through the AS/400 to obtain information, but as an Internet user, the AS/400 can also be used to develop a program, download that program to your system from a remote site, download the information to execute against that program, and execute the program at a local system. A user has the option of accessing information in any of the files on the AS/400 and having that information HTML formatted on its way to the user's system. The user can have the AS/400 execute the program and present the output in HTML format to the Web browser, and can develop an application on the AS/400 using CGI/WGS or Net.Data and have that application downloaded to the browser.

Finally, to make this all work, the Internet connection server requires that the system administrator grant object access to the user profiles under which the server runs and then grant permission to the server to serve specific objects. If the server is on a system with multiple network addresses, it can be configured to serve different files based on the IP address that comes in on a request. Multiple server instances can also be configured by using either a different IP address or a single IP address and different ports for each server instance. Internet Connection Secure Server (ICSS) uses Secure Sockets Layer (SSL) defined protocols to provide encryption and other security functions to ICSS.

14.1.3.5 Java

AS/400 has a Java virtual machine residing below the Technology Independent Machine Interface for fast interpretation and execution. In addition to supporting Sun's javac compiler, there is also a direct-execution static compiler, called the Java Transformer, to generate AS/400-dependent machine code. The Java Transformer is IBM's solution to improve Java runtime performance which replaces the use of a just-in-time compiler. The static compiler provides AS/400-dependent object code. The AS/400 Toolbox for Java includes a set of enablers that support an Internet programming model. Provided is a set of client/server programming interfaces for use by Java applets and applications plus a set of applets that can be integrated into HTML documents. Client support required is Java virtual machine and AS/400 Developer Kit for Java.

Since graphical user interfaces cannot be displayed by an AS/400 green screen, AS/400 implements Remote AWT. Java on AS/400 intercepts GUI requests coming from a Java program and reroutes the requests to an attached workstation running its own JVM, which will interpret and display the JAVA.AWT graphical components. Other Java packages are being integrated with OS/400 to improve ease-of-use and performance. Java objects on AS/400 are full-fledged AS/400 objects that can be persistent, shared, secure, backed up, and restored, something not available in two-level-store operating systems.

Also included is a standardized set of Class Libraries (packages) that support creating Graphical User Interfaces (GUIs), controlling multimedia data, communicating over networks, and accessing data in stream files and relational databases.

The AS/400 Developer Kit for Java, available with OS/400 V4R2, is a no-cost tool designed to produce Java applets and full-scale applications. Included are a collection of development tools, help files, and documentation for Java programmers. The Developer Kit is compliant with Sun's Java 1.1.6 specifications and provides improved performance either through improved transaction rates or through lower CPU utilization on applications that use the database.

The AS/400 Toolbox for Java, available on AS/400 and other Java-compliant platforms, enables Java applets and applications to access AS/400 data and resources, by providing a collection of classes that represent AS/400 data and providing AS/400 client/server program interfaces for Java programs.

The AS/400 Toolbox for Java also includes a set of enablers that support an Internet programming model. Provided is a set of client/server programming interfaces for use by Java applets and applications.

The AS/400 Toolbox for Java requires that both the TC1 Licensed Program (TCP/IP Connectivity Utilities for AS/400) and the Host Server option of OS/400 to be installed and configured on the AS/400. Client machines and Web browsers must contain a Java virtual machine that fully supports Java Version 1.1.2. The AS/400 Toolbox for Java Classes can access data and resources on V3R2, V3R7, V4R1 and above.

14.1.3.6 Firewall
The AS/400 firewall is implemented using the Integrated PC Server (IPCS) internal to the AS/400 server system. This allows processor separation without requiring an additional system. Security functions running on the IPCS are separate from applications running on the AS/400 processor. The software used by the firewall is on a read-only disk, eliminating the possibility of a virus being introduced and preventing modification of programs that carry out the communications security functions. Communication between the main processor and the firewall is over an internal system bus immune from sniffing programs on local area networks. The firewall can be

disabled by the main processor when it detects tampering, independent of the state of the firewall. Installation of firewall software is the same as for any other AS/400 software. The administrator is guided through the initial installation and configuration. The firewall is administered by a Web browser on the internal (secure) network. The Secure Sockets Layer (SSL) protocol can be used to protect the administration session. Authentication of the administrator is done with OS/400 security support.

IBM Firewall for AS/400 (#5769-FW1) is an application gateway firewall using Internet Protocol (IP) packet filtering to prevent undesirable traffic from reaching the internal network. The packets may be filtered by source IP address, protocol, port number, direction, and network interface. RealAudio is supported through dynamic packet filtering technology. A proxy server provides Web access to servers on the Internet without revealing the name or address on the browser, and can cache Web pages for better response time. All internal users have a single mail domain with hidden internal e-mail addresses. Various levels of logging are supported, ranging from logging all traffic to logging only exceptions.

Network Address Translation (NAT) and filtering activities can be journaled. The entries will be added each time IP packets are examined, IP addresses are translated or rules are updated. The user can choose to start the journal or not. Users have the opportunity to change IP addresses of IP packets going out from the network, so the internal address is not known by the external hosts. This secures the internal network.

Using the AS/400 SOCKS Client program, AS/400 TCP/IP client programs such as FTP client can communicate with server programs running on systems outside the IBM Firewall for AS/400 program. SOCKS proxy support on the IBM Firewall for AS/400 program is used by the client programs to safely transmit data packets to external servers. Funneling these requests through the firewall proxy protects the customer's secure internal network from data packets coming from an unsecured network. The AS/400 SOCKS Client program is transparent to TCP/IP client programs and works for all client programs written to the sockets interface. The IBM TCP/IP clients programs, including Telnet and FTP, can be enabled to use a SOCKS proxy. The sockets API also supports TCP/IP multicast.

The IPCS uses Network Address Translation (NAT) to conceal internal network address while allowing direct access from secure clients to the external network without proxies. This simplifies exposing secure hosts, protected by the firewall to the Internet community without exposing internal network addresses. A virtual private network is enabled by the establishment of encrypted connections between firewalls to safeguard data transported through the network. Database tables are created from firewall log files, allowing SQL queries to tailor reports on usage or identify potential attacks. Log files can be deleted when they are no longer needed.

14.1.3.7 Digital Certificate Manager

The AS/400 is able to serve as a Digital Certificate Manager at V4R2. This means that the AS/400 can set up an intranet certificate authority, sign client and server certificates, distribute client certificates via a Web browser, and provide support for MD5 and SHA-1 hash algorithms. Although the AS/400 can set up a certificate authority, it cannot act as a certificate authority at this time.

The AS/400 accepts digital certificates for authentication. Both the HTTP and LDAP servers support digital certificates. The certificates are used for identification only. A digital certificate is associated with a user profile and with a user in a validation list.

14.1.3.8 Cryptographic Processor

The Cryptographic Processor (#2620) helps improve the security of an AS/400 system by encoding information using cryptographic techniques (ANSI Data Encryption Standard DES). That is, AS/400-resident information is scrambled via encryption keys (special codes), making it meaningless to anyone except those who have the key. This capability is particularly beneficial when AS/400 information might be exposed to unauthorized access via a communications network such as the Internet.

The Security Interface Unit (SIU) (#4754) is an optional device that attaches to the cryptographic processor and allows the user to enter cryptography keys by swiping a personal security card through a reader.

Supported cryptography standards include 40-bit, 56-bit, and 128-bit encryption. Digital certificates are also accepted as a Web server sign-on.

14.1.4 IBM AIX 4.3

IBM's award-winning UNIX operating system, AIX 4.3, has been enhanced to deliver even more in scalability, security, connectivity, performance, interoperability, and usability.

AIX 4.3 is an integrated operating environment that supports both existing 32-bit and new 64-bit RS/6000 systems in their full range of scalability while providing improved software features for both environments. On 64-bit systems, AIX 4.3 provides full interoperability and coexistence between 32- and 64-bit applications with processes that may run concurrently or cooperatively, sharing access to files, memory, and other system services.

14.1.4.1 Internet and e-business Ready

AIX 4.3 technology enables systems to perform as robust Internet servers. While maintaining binary compatibility, AIX 4.3 offers 64-bit scalability for Web serving through increased system capacity via large memories and the mapping of large files into memory.

AIX 4.3 helps support the security requirements of Internet servers. It includes the next generation of Internet Protocol (IPv6) and an Lightweight Directory Access Protocol (LDAP) compliant directory. The IP security (IPSec) supports unlimited filter rules to control network traffic by characteristics such as source and destination address, interface, type of TCP/IP, subnet mask, specific protocol, and port (FTP, mail, etc.).

14.1.4.2 Features and Benefits

AIX 4.3 offers the following features and benefits:

64-bit support

- Delivers new dimensions in scalability and capacity (32,786 threads/process)
- Supports concurrent execution of 32- and 64-bit applications on 64-bit hardware
- Implements LP64 (32-bit integers, 64-bit long and pointer types)
- Supports up to 16GB real memory on 64-bit hardware

Binary Compatibility

- Helps assure continuing application availability across AIX Version 4 releases

Web-based system management

- Allows managing AIX from any Java 1.1- and Abstract Windows Toolkit (AWT) 1.1-enabled browser
- Configuration Assistant automatically launches TaskGuide after base AIX installation to help simplify the remaining installation configuration tasks

Java Development Kit (JDK) V1.1.4

- Includes a full range of development tools, such as source and run-time interpreters, with Just-In-Time (JIT) 2.01 compiler class compiler, source-level debugger, HTML document generator, runtime libraries for Java multimedia links, and a set of Java class APIs (JDBC, JavaBeans, RMI, and Java security)
- Compiles Java byte code to native machine code at run-time to boost Java performance
- Accommodates multiple Java versions to enhance flexibility in developing Java applications

Internet Protocol Version 6 (IPv6)

- Increases IP addressability, security and integrity through redundant routing, dynamic rerouting, and tunneling (supports IPv6 to IPv6 tunnels through IPv4)
- Provides IPsec authentication and security for IPv4 and IPv6
- Provides Triple DES (3DES) encapsulation (U.S. & Canada only)

Internet Protocol Version 4 (IPv4)

- Includes DHCP updates to support classless interdomain routing (CIDR)
- Enhances password protection with secure TCP/IP commands (rsh, rcp, rlogin, telnet, ftp) eNetwork Lightweight Directory
- Supports up to 4 million directory entries with sub-second search response time

Lightweight Directory Access Protocol (LDAP) V1.1.1

- Supports replication of directories across multiple systems
- Provides Secure Sockets Layer (SSL) Version 3 for data encryption and authentication using X.509v3 public-key certificates
- Provides Triple DES (3DES) encapsulation (U.S. and Canada only)

HTML-based documentation

- Offers easy access to system documentation via a Web browser, delivered on separate CDs

Print spooler enhancements

- Provide robust network support and increased capacity for up to 1000 print jobs

X11R6

- Enhances X Windows functions with thread-safe 64-bit client libraries for graphics application development

3D Graphics

- OpenGL and graphics APIs are included at no additional charge
- Virtual Frame Buffer (VFB) is the enabling software technology for creating 3D rendering server applications (for example, CATweb Navigator) without a graphics adapter. This environment supports viewing 3D graphics on multiple thin client platforms.

Performance analysis/control tools

- Supports more complex statistical analysis for local AIX system performance

AutoFS, CacheFS from ONC+ suite

- AutoFS provides network file system mounts automatically
- CacheFS provides faster file access when using Network File System mounts

Direct I/O

- Allows higher bandwidth I/O for performance critical applications

Sendmail 8.8.8

- Notifies senders when mail is delivered successfully

Telnet performance enhancements

- Provide 40% to 60% Telnet performance improvement over prior AIX releases

Multilingual support

- Enables UCS-based application development via Unicode 2.0
- Provides localization support for Thai, Vietnamese, Byelorussian, and Ukranian

C2 security

- Designed to meet US DoD C2 specifications; formal certification for AIX 4.3.1 is in process
- AIX 4.2 is certified for European ITSEC F-C2/E3 specifications; AIX 4.3.1 certification is in process

The Open Group

- Maintains conformance to previous UNIX brandings and certifications

UNIX 98

- Implements IEEE POSIX 1003-1996 (.1c) threads including M:N thread support

Bonus Pack Version 4.3

- Provides users with options, tools and products including:
  - Ultimedia Services Version 2.2
  - LDAP-SSL Version 3 128/40 bit encryption
  - Lotus Domino Go Webserver 4.6.1
  - Novell Network Services Version 2.2. with Novell Directory Services
  - Netscape FastTrack Server 2.0.1
  - Netscape Navigator 3.0.4
  - Syntax TotalNET Advanced Server Version 5.2 Evaluation Copy

- Netscape Navigator 4.0.4 (browser only)
- IP Security triple or 40/56 bit DES
- Network Station Manager (NSM) Version 1.2
- DCE Client Version 2.1
- Adobe Acrobat Version 3.01

Note: Contents may change within each release; products with data encryption may be subject to import/export restrictions outside the United States and may be slightly different in or not offered with the Bonus Pack.

14.1.5 IBM TCP/IP 4.1 for OS/2

IBM TCP/IP Version 4.1 for OS/2 and corequisite MPTS Version 5.3 represent a significant upgrade of the TCP/IP stack and applications previously included in OS/2 Warp. Functional changes include:

Multi-Platform Capability

TCP/IP Version 4.1 can be installed on:

- OS/2 Warp 4
- OS/2 Warp Server
- OS/2 Warp Server SMP

Now, all three platforms can use the latest version of TCP/IP.

32-Bit, BSD 4.4-Compliant TCP/IP Stack

You may notice substantial performance improvements over the previous 16-bit BSD 4.3-compliant stack. Also, INETCFG.EXE is enhanced to allow you to tune TCP/IP by setting many new protocol parameters.

Dynamic IP - DHCP Server Enhancements

- Proxy dynamic DNS update: This allows Dynamic DNS updates to be done by the DHCP Server on behalf of clients that do not support Dynamic DNS.
- Multiple logical subnets on the same wire: The DHCP server can allocate addresses for multiple logical subnets on the same physical wire.
- BOOTP server functionality: The DHCP server can act as a BOOTP server, including giving appropriate information for remote booting of machines including the Network Station.
- Server statistics: The DHCP server can provide complete statistics for its DHCP/BOOTP activity on the network.

Dynamic IP - DDNS Server Enhancements

- Incremental Zone Transfer: The Dynamic DNS server can perform Incremental Zone Transfer as defined in IETF RFC 1995.

- Notify: The Dynamic DNS Server can perform Notify function for prompt notification of zone changes as defined in IETF RFC 1996.
- Dynamic Zone Performance Enhancements: This includes the capability to separate dynamic and static zone files.
- Time Zone Reconciliation: The DDNS Server can now reconcile time zone time differences between the server and client for dynamic updates.
- Crash Recovery: The DDNS Server can checkpoint files to facilitate crash recovery.
- Java 1.1 Configuration Programs: New graphical user interfaces (GUIs) allow local and remote configuration of DHCP and DDNS servers. A Java 1.1 GUI to manage a DHCP server is also included.

Dynamic IP Client Enhancements

- Detecting a laptop that was relocated while in hibernation mode.
- Releasing the DHCP address when shutting down (optional).
- Reusing old lease information if a DHCP server cannot be found on the network (optional).

Remote Configuration

TCP/IP configuration and Dynamic-IP server configuration (DHCP and DDNS) are written in the Java language. A Java 1.1-capable browser can be used to configure a server remotely.

CID Support for all TCP/IP Configuration Parameters

All configuration parameters can now be set during CID (Configuration, Installation and Distribution) installation. Configuration settings that would normally be done through the new Java GUI after installation can now be done during a local or remote CID installation.

Web-based Installation

Installation has been enhanced to provide for downloading and installing TCP/IP from the Web. Using the latest Netscape plug-ins, either the guided or advanced installation paths can be performed.

Virtual Private Network and IP Security

TCP/IP 4.1 for OS/2 uses the IBM Secure Remote IP Client program, together with the standards-based IP-Security protocol, to configure a virtual private network (VPN). A VPN provides a secure communications channel from a remote computer across the Internet to an intranet protected by an IBM Firewall Version 3.1 (or subsequent releases).

RSVP Daemon and API

Resource Reservation Protocol (RSVP) allows applications to control the bandwidth, data rate, and transmission latency capabilities that are being implemented in routers and operating systems. The API and daemon provide this control to OS/2 applications that are written to use it. The library and header files used to access this API are available in the TCP/IP Version 4.1 Programmer's Toolkit in the IBM Developer Connection.

Application Enhancements

- SyslogD: Enhanced to read from the configuration file (syslog.cnf) which resides in the ETC directory. The configuration file allows the user to specify different options including the log file size and the number of backup log files to maintain.
- RSHD: A command line timeout parameter has been added (like the REXECD timeout parameter). RSHD has also been updated to record certain events in the system log when SyslogD is running.
- REXECD: Acquires and validates a client's user ID and password using the new TCP/IP configuration. The user ID and password are no longer stored in environment variables. REXECD has also been updated to record certain events in the system log when SyslogD is running.
- TelnetD: Acquires and validates a client's user ID and password using the new TCP/IP configuration. A user ID is now required and the password is no longer stored in an environment variable. The telnet shell program is also obtained from the configuration and is customizable by user ID. TelnetD has also been updated to record certain events in the system log when SyslogD is running.
- FTPD: Acquires and validates a client's user ID, password, and other customized user information from the new TCP/IP configuration. The TRUSERS file is no longer used.
- LPR, LPRMON, LPQ, LPRM: The print server name and print queue name can now default to names received from a DHCP server (or use values entered in the Configuration Notebook, entered as environment variables, or entered on the command line with the -s and -p options).
- LPR: Has a -cp command line option (similar to the -cp option for LPD and LPRMON) to convert text files using the specified code page before sending the files to an LPD server.
- LPRPORTD Performance Enhancements: LPRPORTD now processes print files faster.

Year-2000 Support

TCP/IP Version 4.1 is year-2000 ready.

14.1.6 Functional Comparisons

The tables below list the major TCP/IP protocols and applications as they are implemented and supported by the aforementioned software platforms. To provide a better and more comprehensive overview, we have grouped the tables into blocks that follow in sequence the previous chapters of this book.

Because of their significance in the PC market, from corporate to end user, and because of IBM's dedication to provide a comprehensive suite of applications and middleware in that area, we have also included the latest versions of the Windows operating systems from Microsoft.

Table 19 (Page 1 of 2). Operating Systems - Protocol Support

	OS/390	MVS	VM	OS/400	AIX	OS/2	Windows NT 4.0	Windows 98
Base Protocols								
IP	X	X	X	X	X	X	X	X
TCP	X	X	X	X	X	X	X	X
UDP	X	X	X	X	X	X	X	X
ARP	X	X	X	X	X	X	X	X
RARP	X	X			X			
ICMP	X	X	X	X	X	X	X	X
PING	X	X	X	X	X	X	X	X
TRACEROUTE	X	X	X		X	X	X	X
IPv6	X[8]				X			
Application Protocols								
DNS	X	X	X	X	X	X	X	C
NSLOOKUP	X	X	X		X	X	X	
HOST	X	X			X	X		
FINGER	X[9]				X	C	C	
FTP	X	X	X	X	X	X	X[1]	C
IMAP					X	IBM[2]	IBM[2]	C
LPR/LPD	X	X	X	X	X	X	X	
MIME	X	X	X	X	X	X	X	X

Legend:
X=Implemented C=Client Implementation only S=Server Implementation n/a=Not Applicable
OEM=requires additional non-IBM software IBM=requires additional IBM software

Table 19 (Page 2 of 2). Operating Systems - Protocol Support

	OS/390	MVS	VM	OS/400	AIX	OS/2	Windows NT 4.0	Windows 98
NETSTAT	X	X	X	X	X	X	X	X
NIS					X			
ONC-RPC	X	X	X	X	X	IBM[7]		
POP	S			X	X	IBM[2]	IBM[2]	C
REXEC/RSH	X	X	X	S	X	X	C	
SMTP	X	X	X	X	X	X	IBM[2]	C
SNMP	X	X	X	X	X	X	X	X
TALK					X	X		
TELNET	X	X	X	X	X	X	C	C
TFTP	X	X	X	X	X	X	C	
TimeD	X		X		X			
TN3270	X	X	S	S	IBM[4]	IBM[3]	IBM[4,5]	C(IBM)[5]
TN3270E	S		S		IBM[4]	IBM[3]	IBM[4,5]	C(IBM)[5]
TN5250				S		C	C(IBM)[5]	C(IBM)[5]
X Windows	C	C	C		X	OEM		
Routing Protocols								
Static Routing	X	X	X	X	X	X	X	X
RIP-1	X	X	X	X	X	X	X[6]	Passive Only
RIP-2	X	X		X	X	X	X	
OSPF	X				X			
BGP-4					X			
CIDR	X	X			X	X	X	

Legend:
X=Implemented C=Client Implementation only S=Server Implementation n/a=Not Applicable
OEM=requires additional non-IBM software IBM=requires additional IBM software

Notes:

1. Server function provided by Microsoft Internet Information Server (Windows NT Server) or Personal Web Server (Windows NT Workstation)

2. Server function provided by Lotus Domino, client included in Web browser

3. Server function provided by IBM eNetwork Communications Server, client included in operating system

4. Server function provided by IBM eNetwork Communications Server

5. Client function provided by IBM eNetwork Personal Communications

6. Active RIP provided by Windows NT Server, passive RIP provided by Windows NT Workstation

7. Function provided by IBM TCP/IP for OS/2 NFS Kit

8. Prototype

9. Via NSLOOKUP

Table 20 (Page 1 of 3). Operating Systems - Special Protocols and Services

	OS/390	MVS	VM	OS/400	AIX	OS/2	Windows NT 4.0	Windows 98
Dynamic IP								
BOOTP	S		S	S	X	X	S[1]	
BOOTP/DHCP Forwarding	X			X	X	X	X	
DHCP	S		S	S	X	X	X	C
DDNS (secure update)	X				X	X	C(IBM)[26]	C(IBM)[26]
DDNS Incremental Zone Transfer	X				X	X		
ProxyArec	X				X	X		
Directory & File Services								
DCE	IBM[2]	IBM[2]	IBM[2]	C(IBM)[2]	IBM[2]	IBM[2]	IBM[2]	
NFS	X	X	S	S	X	IBM[3]		
Legend: X=Implemented C=Client Implementation only S=Server Implementation n/a=Not Applicable OEM=requires additional non-IBM software IBM=requires additional IBM software								

Table 20 (Page 2 of 3). *Operating Systems - Special Protocols and Services*

	OS/390	MVS	VM	OS/400	AIX	OS/2	Windows NT 4.0	Windows 98
AFS					Transarc		Transarc	
LDAP	X				X	IBM[4,25]	S(IBM)[4]	
NetBIOS Services								
NetBIOS over TCP	OEM				OEM	X	X	X
NBNS					OEM		X[5]	
NBDD					OEM			
Security								
IP filtering	X			X	X	X	X[6]	
Firewall[7]	X			X	IBM[8]		IBM[8]	
SOCKS	S			X	S(IBM)[9]	C[10]	S(IBM)[9]	C
Telnet Proxy				X	IBM[8]		IBM[8]	
FTP Proxy	X			X	IBM[11]	IBM[12]	IBM[11]	
HTTP Proxy	X			X	IBM[11]	IBM[12]	IBM[11]	
NAT	X			X	IBM[8]		IBM[8]	
SSL	X			X	X	X	X	X
S-MIME							X	X
IPSec	X			X	X	X		
Kerberos	X	X	X	IBM[2]	IBM[2]	IBM[2]	IBM[2]	
Internet Protocols								
HTTP	S	S(IBM)[13]	OEM	S	X	S(IBM)[14]	X[15]	X[15]
Java	S[16]			X	X[17]	X[17]	X[18]	C
IIOP	IBM[19]				IBM[19]	IBM[19]	IBM[19]	
NNTP	S(IBM)[4]				S(IBM)[20]	S(IBM)[20]	S(IBM)[20]	C
Gopher			X		C	C	X[21]	C
Multicasting and Multimedia								
IGMP	X			X	X	X	X	X
QoS								
RSVP	X				X	X	X[27]	X[27]

Legend:
X=Implemented C=Client Implementation only S=Server Implementation n/a=Not Applicable
OEM=requires additional non-IBM software IBM=requires additional IBM software

	OS/390	MVS	VM	OS/400	AIX	OS/2	Windows NT 4.0	Windows 98
Table 20 (Page 3 of 3). Operating Systems - Special Protocols and Services								
Differentiated Services	X						X[27]	X[27]
Load Balancing								
Round robin DNS	X				X	X		
IND	C[22]				IBM[23]		IBM[23]	
WLM	X	X						
VIPA	X	X		X	X[24]	X[24]	X[24]	

Legend:
X=Implemented C=Client Implementation only S=Server Implementation n/a=Not Applicable
OEM=requires additional non-IBM software IBM=requires additional IBM software

Notes:

1. DHCP server can provide fixed addresses to BOOTP clients

2. Function provided by IBM DCE

3. Function provided by IBM TCP/IP for OS/2 NFS Kit

4. Server function provided by Lotus Domino

5. Using Windows Internet Name Service (WINS)

6. Only on ports and protocols, not on IP addresses

7. Refers to a combined set of security features, including IP filtering, NAT, application proxies, SOCKS, special DNS and mail

8. Function provided by IBM eNetwork Firewall

9. Server function provided by IBM eNetwork Firewall, client included in Web browser

10. Socksified TCP/IP stack

11. Function provided by IBM WebTraffic Express or IBM eNetwork Firewall

12. Function provided by IBM WebTraffic Express

13. Server function provided by Lotus Domino or Lotus Domino Go Webserver

14. Server function provided by Lotus Domino or Lotus Domino Go Webserver, client included in operating system

15. Server function provided by Lotus Domino Go Webserver (IBM), or by Microsoft Internet Information Server (Windows NT Server) or Personal Web Server (Windows NT Server and Windows 98); client included in operating system

16. Servlet support provided by IBM WebSphere Application Server or Host On-Demand Server

17. Servlet support provided by IBM WebSphere Application Server, client included in operating system

18. Servlet support provided by IBM WebSphere Application Server or Microsoft Internet Information Server, client (local JVM) included in Web browser

19. Function provided by IBM WebSphere Application Server

20. Server function provided by Lotus Domino, client included in Web browser

21. Server function provided by Microsoft Internet Information Server (Windows NT Server) or Personal Web Server (Windows NT Workstation)

22. WLM Advisor for eNetwork Dispatcher

23. Function provided by IBM eNetwork Dispatcher

24. Similar concept provided using IP alias addresses

25. Function available through IBM OS/2 LDAP Client Toolkit for C and Java

26. Function provided by IBM Dynamic IP Client for Windows 95 and Windows NT

27. Similar concept provided using Winsock V2.0 APIs

Table 21 (Page 1 of 2). Operating Systems - Connection Support

	OS/390	MVS	VM	OS/400	AIX	OS/2	Windows NT 4.0	Windows 98
Token-Ring	X	X	X	X	X	X	X	X
Ethernet v2	X	X	X	X	X	X	X	X
Ethernet 802.3	X	X	X	X	X	X		
Fast Ethernet	X	X	X		X	X	X	X
FDDI	X	X	X	X	X	X	X	X
ATM Classic IP	X			X	X		X	
Legend: X=Implemented C=Client Implementation only s=Server Implementation n/a=Not Applicable OEM=requires additional non-IBM software IBM=requires additional IBM software								

Table 21 (Page 2 of 2). *Operating Systems - Connection Support*

	OS/390	MVS	VM	OS/400	AIX	OS/2	Windows NT 4.0	Windows 98
ATM LAN Emulation	X	X	X			X		X
X.25	IBM[1]	IBM[1]	IBM[1]	X	X	IBM[2]		
Frame Relay	IBM[3]	IBM[3]	IBM[3]	X	X	X[6]		
ISDN	IBM[3]	IBM[3]	IBM[3]	X	X	X	X	X
PPP	IBM[3]	IBM[3]	IBM[3]	X	X	X	X	X
SLIP	IBM[3]	IBM[3]	IBM[3]	X	X	X	X	X
Sonet	IBM[3]	IBM[3]	IBM[3]	X	X			
Enterprise Extender	X						IBM[4]	
MPTN	X	X		X	IBM[4]	IBM[4]	IBM[4,5]	IBM[5]
MPC+	X							
SNALink	X	X	X			IBM[2]		
CTC	X	X	X					

Legend:
X=Implemented C=Client Implementation only s=Server Implementation n/a=Not Applicable
OEM=requires additional non-IBM software IBM=requires additional IBM software

Notes:

1. Function provided by NCP and NPSI

2. Function provided by IBM TCP/IP for OS/2 Extended Networking Kit

3. Function provided by channel-attached IBM 2216 router

4. Function provided by IBM eNetwork Communications Server

5. Function provided by IBM eNetwork Personal Communications

6. Function provided by IBM RouteXpander/2 in conjunction with IBM WAC adapter

14.2 IBM Hardware Platform Implementations

Networking hardware from IBM has been used in the TCP/IP world ever since the establishment of the second NSF backbone (see 1.1.4, "NSFNET" on page 6). Today, IBM routers provide state-of-the-art TCP/IP functionality, and routers, switches and hubs alike provide management capabilities for TCP/IP-based networks. The following sections provide an overview of the TCP/IP capabilities of the respective system platforms, followed by a set of tables that offer a comprehensive summary and cross-platform comparison.

14.2.1 The IBM Nways Router Family

IBM offers three different multiprotocol routers:

- IBM 2210 Nways Multiprotocol Router
- IBM Nways Access Utility
- IBM 2216 Nways Multiaccess Connector
- IBM Nways Network Utility

All IBM routers use the following common set of software functions:

- The Nways Multiprotocol Routing Services (Nways MRS) for the 2210
- The Nways Access Integration Services (Nways AIS) for the Access Utility
- The Nways Multiprotocol Access Services (Nways MAS) for the 2216
- The Nways Multiaccess Connector and the Nways Multiprotocol Switched Services (Nways MSS) for the 8210, Nways MSS Server and the IBM 8260 Nways Multiprotocol Switching Hub MSS Module.

The following is a brief description of routers and their major functions.

14.2.1.1 IBM 2210 Nways Multiprotocol Router

This router provides an extensive range of connectivity, protocols and price granularity to enable you to cost-effectively implement network computing across a broad range of remote locations, branch offices and regional sites.

The most affordable models, the 1S4, 1S8, 1U4, and 1U8, are well-suited to the demands of small-business networking. They offer one Ethernet port for LAN architectures and either one serial WAN port or one ISDN BRI port (or allow concurrent serial WAN with a single ISDN B+D channel).

The midrange models the 12T, 12E, 127, and 128 offer one Ethernet or token-ring LAN port and two serial WAN ports to support medium-sized businesses and larger branch offices.

Some midrange models also provide a single ISDN BRI port. The most sophisticated models, the 14T, 24T, 24E, and 24M, double the connectivity and performance of other 2210 models. They can be configured with up to two LAN ports and four serial WAN ports to provide connectivity for large branch offices and regional locations. The 2210 most sophisticated models also include one open adapter slot that supports the following adapters: 4- or 8-port Dial Access Adapter, ISDN BRI, ISDN Quad BRI (S/T or U interfaces), ISDN PRI, channelized T1/E1/J1, 25 Mbps ATM, or 4- or 8-port WAN concentration.

14.2.1.2 IBM Nways Access Utility

This is a mid-size router between IBM 2210 and IBM 2216. One of the big features of this router is Voice/FAX support.

There are two models:

- Model 40F: 48M flash and No Hard-drive

- Model 40H: Hard-drive and No flash

Both models contain:

- System board with four WAN serial ports and one LAN Adapter

- 64 MB (max 128 MB) DRAM

- Four adapter slots -both WAN and LAN adapters available

- Power supply and fans

14.2.1.3 IBM 2216 Nways Multiaccess Connector

The IBM 2216 features an Nways Multiaccess Connector and two models of the Network Utility. The Network Utility offers scalable capacity by allowing users to cost-effectively add additional network utilities. The Network Dispatcher function in the Network Utility Transport, the 2216 Multiaccess Connector, the 2210 Nways Multiprotocol Router, or the 3746 Multiaccess Enclosure can be used to balance the load among Network Utility TN3270E Servers. The Network Utility includes a Network Dispatcher Advisor for TN3270 to maximize the efficiency of multiple Network Utility TN3270E Servers.

IBM 2216 Model 400: The IBM 2216 Model 400 is supported by IBM's open, standards-based Multiprotocol Access Services software. The 2216 Multiaccess Connector Model 400 features eight adapter slots for superior scalability facilitating cost-effective device concentration; high system availability with load-sharing hot-pluggable dual power supplies, individually powered adapter slots, hot-plugging of adapters, fast boot time, environmental monitoring, and redundant cooling with a hot-pluggable fan tray; superior serviceability built around IBM's on-site service combined with easy, front-side access to all critical components, intuitive status LEDs, and an integrated modem (where homologated); and broad network connectivity options:

- LANs - Token-ring, Ethernet, Fast Ethernet and FDDI
- WANs - V.35, EIA-232, X.21, V.36, worldwide ISDN Primary, HSSI, and Channelized T1/J1/E1
- Channel - ESCON and Parallel
- ATM - 155Mbps multimode and 155Mbps single-mode

IBM Network Utility Model: Network Utility models offer:

- Two adapter slots for LANs, ATM, channels, and WANs
- Support for high numbers of user connections
- Customized configurations
- Integrated Network Dispatcher for TCP/IP load balancing

The Network Utility TN3270E Server offers:

- Support for 8,000 TN3270E sessions at a low cost per session while handling more than 300 transactions per second
- Code tailored to TN3270 to get you up and running quickly and easily
- Exploitation of the Network Dispatcher Advisor for TN3270 to optimize the efficiency of balancing traffic among multiple TN3270's servers

The Network Utility Transport offers:

- Support for up to 500 DLSw partners and up to 10,000 circuits while handling more than 1,500 transactions per second
- Support for over 10,000 LU sessions with APPN DLUR
- A single channel gateway to S/390 servers
- Low-cost and high-capacity (10,000 connections/second) load balancing
- Code tailored to IP and SNA Transport to get you up and running quickly and easily

14.2.2 The IBM Multiprotocol Switch Hub Family

IBM offers the following multiprotocol hubs:

- IBM 8210 Multiprotocol Switched Services Server

- IBM 8260 Nways Multiprotocol Switching Hub

- IBM 8265 Nways ATM Switch

- IBM 8274 Nways LAN RouteSwitch

The following is a brief description of the latest multiprotocol switching hubs and their major functions.

14.2.2.1 IBM 8210 Multiprotocol Switched Services Server

The 8210 provides a smooth migration path to ATM by enabling legacy networking software and hardware to take advantage of high-speed ATM backbones with Multiprotocol Switched Services (MSS).

14.2.2.2 IBM 8260 Nways Multiprotocol Switching Hub

The IBM 8260 Nways Multiprotocol Switching Hub delivers flexibility, reliability and manageability in a single, high-capacity multiprotocol hub. Designed for multi-workgroup and campus backbone applications, the 8260 delivers the functions you need to build high-speed ATM networks while you continue to connect existing Ethernet, token-ring and FDDI networks.

With more than 70 modules available, the 8260 combines the functions of a shared-media, modular, intelligent hub with LAN and ATM switches in a single unit, providing a smooth migration path from shared-media to high-speed switched networks. The 8260 accepts a wide range of Ethernet, token-ring, FDDI, ATM and unique features such as MPEG-2 Video Distribution Modules and can also accept any module from IBM's mid-range 8250 Multiprotocol Intelligent Hub.

The 8260 eliminates the need for multiple devices, reducing cost and network complexity. With its fault-tolerant features, such as hot-swappability, intelligent power management and a distributed management system, the 8260 can improve overall network availability and reduce the cost of operation and ownership.

14.2.2.3 IBM 8265 Nways ATM Switch

IBM 8265 Nways ATM Switch is IBM's next-generation ATM switch offering the following highlights:

- Priority queues per Quality of Service (QoS)

- Early- and partial-packet discard

- Policing per virtual circuit (VC)

- Traffic shaping per virtual path (VP)

- Statistics per VCs

- Buffering

- Port-mirroring

Superior ATM Control Point:

- High call setup capacity

- Exclusive PNNI extensions

Port capacities of:

- 56 155-Mbps OC3

- 14 622-Mbps OC12

- WAN interfaces from T1/E1 to OC3 speeds

Support for these existing 8260 ATM features:

- Multiprotocol Switched Services (MSS)

- LAN switching

- WAN interface modules

- Video Distribution Module

- ATM Circuit Emulation Module

High-availability features for mission-critical operations

Compatibility with current 8260 ATM

14.2.2.4 IBM 8274 Nways LAN RouteSwitch

The 8274 is a chassis-based switch available in three sizes: 3-slot, 5-slot and 9-slot. In all models, one slot is occupied by the Management Processor Module (MPM), which must be ordered as a feature for all models. Model W33 contains three slots (one for the MPM and up to two wide switching-module slots); Model W53 contains five slots (one for the MPM and up to four wide switching-module slots); and Model W93 contains nine slots (one for the MPM and up to eight wide switching-module slots). The wide switching-module slots offer the potential for greater port density and lower port cost. Two earlier models are available: Model 513 with five slots (one for the MPM and four for the switching modules) and Model 913 with nine slots (one for the MPM and eight for the switching modules).

The 8274 features an intelligent hardware design that supports high data rates and a sophisticated feature set, yet is priced to serve as a basic network building block. The 8274 provides powerful and complete LAN switching with ATM speed for the desktop and the backbone. It integrates the most complete, flexible VLAN architecture on the market today. To build the most comprehensive, scalable networking solution, begin with an IBM 8260 Nways Multiprotocol Switching Hub or an IBM 8265 Nways ATM Switch.

Install an IBM Multiprotocol Switched Services (MSS) backbone to work with the LAN Emulation (LANE) clients in your 8274s. Your network can now route local traffic across ATM for maximum speed and reliability. All 8274 models provide policy-based VLANs, IP and IPX routing, FDDI trunking, ATM private virtual circuits, ATM LANE, Multiprotocol Encapsulation over ATM, Classical IP over ATM and graphical network management on a broad set of standard management platforms.

14.2.3 The IBM Workgroup Hubs and Workgroup Switches

IBM offers the following workgroup hubs and workgroup switches:

Workgroup hubs for fast Ethernet/Ethernet

- IBM Ethernet Desktop Hub (8242) Models 008 and 016
- IBM 8245 10/100 Stackable Ethernet Hub
- IBM 8222 Nways Ethernet Workgroup Hubs
- IBM 8223 Fast Ethernet Workgroup Hub
- IBM 8224 Ethernet Stackable Hub
- IBM 8225 Fast Ethernet Stackable Hub
- IBM 8237 Stackable Ethernet Hub 10BASE-T
- IBM 8276 Nways Ethernet RoutePort

Workgroup hubs for token-ring

- IBM 8239 Token-Ring Stackable Hub
- IBM 8226 Token-Ring RJ-45 Connection Model 100
- IBM 8228 Multistation Access Unit
- IBM 8230 Controlled Access Unit
- IBM 8238 Nways Token-Ring Stackable Hub

Workgroup switches for fast Ethernet/Ethernet

- IBM 8275 Ethernet Desktop Switch Model 113
- IBM 8277 Nways Ethernet RouteSwitch
- IBM 8271 Nways Ethernet LAN Switch
- IBM 8271 Series
- IBM 8273 Nways Ethernet Route Switch

Workgroup switches for token-ring

- IBM 8270 Nways LAN Switch Model 800
- IBM 8272 Nways Token-Ring LAN Switch Models 108 and 216

Workgroup switches for ATM

- IBM 8285 Nways ATM Workgroup Switch

The following is a brief description of the latest IBM workgroup hub and switch products and their major functions.

14.2.3.1 IBM Ethernet Desktop Hub (8242) Models 008 and 016

The IBM Ethernet Desktop Hub (8242) Models 008 and 016 are high-availability 10BASE-T Ethernet Hubs for small business and home networking. These hubs have been designed and tested to be qualified as high-availability hubs and, when combined with their silent operation, they can be used in any environment. Two models support 8 and 16 ports respectively. Both models can be cascaded to support larger networks via the MDI (uplink) port.

14.2.3.2 IBM 8245 10/100 Stackable Ethernet Hub

The IBM 8245 10/100 Ethernet Stackable Hub is a dual-speed (10BASE-T and 100BASE-TX), dual-backplane stackable hub. As a Class II repeater, it can be used to cascade to other hubs through its MDI and MDI-X ports. There are four models available. Models 012 and 024 are 12- and 24-port manageable slave repeaters. Models 112 and 124 are 12- and 24-port managed master hubs that can manage Models 012 and 024 in a stacked configuration. A maximum of six hubs can be in one stack, providing up to 144 ports.

14.2.3.3 IBM 8237 Stackable Ethernet Hub 10BASE-T

IBM 8237 Ethernet Stackable Hub is the simple, reliable, high-performance Ethernet solution with the following highlights:

Model 001:

- 17-port 10BASE-T stackable hub/170 ports per stack

- A full range of migration solutions

- Management using the 8237 Model 002 or Model 003

- Support for redundant port links

- Jabber/excessive collision control featuring automatic partition and reconnection

- Optional Fast Ethernet connectivity

- Comprehensive EtherWatch LED display

- Only one IP address required for each stack

- Intrusion and eavesdropping security with automatic address learning mode

Model 002 has all the features of Model 001 plus:

- SNMP agent that provides in-band and out-of-band management for a full 10-unit stack

- EIA 232-C management port

- Easily installed upgrade to RMON management

Model 003 has all the features of Model 002 plus:

- RMON agents (full 9 groups)

- Hub stack

- Maximum 10 hubs per stack (170 ports)

- Hot-swappable design

- 3 backplanes (3 segments per stack)

- Redundant management capability

- Manage Model 001s using Model 002 or Model 003

14.2.3.4 IBM 8239 Token-Ring Stackable Hub

IBM 8239 Token-Ring Stackable Hub has the following highlights:

- Offers two models allowing you a choice of device and network management Provides event-driven token-ring fault isolation through token-ring media management

- Uses RMON and RMON 2 in the Model 001 to provide analysis and trending for superior network management, plus beacon recovery and address-to-port mapping

- Allows up to eight hubs in a single stack - all in one place or in a number of locations

- Integrates with non-8239 token-ring hubs and concentrators using copper or fiber RI/RO connections (Model 001 only)

- Provides 16 ports on each hub, plus a slot for an additional 16 ports when you need them

- Supports fan-out devices, such as the IBM 8228 or 8226, to allow a port to serve up to eight attaching devices over a single cable

- Works well in a variety of SNMP-based network management products from IBM and other vendors.

14.2.3.5 IBM 8271 Nways Ethernet LAN Switch Models 524, 612, 624 and 712

The new IBM 8271 Nways Ethernet LAN Switch Models 524, 612, 624 and 712 are the latest additions to the popular family of Ethernet switches available from IBM. These new switches, based on ASIC technology, are the most cost-effective means available for extending the benefits of LAN switching to the user's desktop. Any size business can upgrade its workgroup or campus LANs to relieve existing Ethernet LAN congestion. With the integrated Fast Ethernet and optional ATM modules that provide connections to high-speed backbones, the new switches offer an extremely attractive, cost-effective, scalable enhancement to Ethernet networks of any size.

Model 524 is the most economical way to deliver a full 10 Mbps of bandwidth to the user's desktop. Each of its 24 Ethernet ports supports one workstation. Models 612 and 624 provide 12 and 24 10-Mbps Ethernet ports, respectively. Each of these ports can connect to a dedicated workstation or hub. In addition to the fixed 10-Mbps ports, Models 524, 612 and 624 provide one integrated 100BASE-TX port. All of the models provide an additional, optional high-speed port that can be either Fast Ethernet (100BASE-TX or 100BASE-FX) or 155-Mbps ATM OC3c.

14.2.3.6 IBM 8270 Nways LAN Switch

IBM 8270 Nways LAN Switch is a fully configurable token-ring LAN switch at a competitive cost and with the following highlights:

- Layer 3 switching

- Multiprotocol support

- Full-duplex (bidirectional) communication

- ATM uplinks

- Three new MSS Universal Feature Cards

14.2.3.7 IBM 8272 Nways Token-Ring LAN Switch

IBM 8272 Nways Token-Ring LAN Switch is an evolutionary step to improved token-ring performance and with the following highlights:

- New Multiprotocol Switched Services (MSS) Universal Feature Card (UFC)

- Additional network configuration options for increased flexibility and fewer network performance problems

- Automatic configuration to the optimum operating level

- Increased network capacity with minimal disruption to an existing infrastructure

- Source-route switching and internal source-route bridging to maximize the benefits in source-routing environments

- Adaptive cut-through, token-ring switching at an industry-leading price per port

- Full-duplex

14.2.4 The IBM High Performance Controllers

IBM offers two different performance controllers:

- IBM 3745 Communication Controller

- IBM 3746 Nways Multiprotocol Controller Models 900 and 950

The following is a brief description of IBM 3746 Nways Multiprotocol Controller Models 900 and 950 and their major functions.

14.2.4.1 IBM 3746 Nways Multiprotocol Controller Models 900 and 950

The IBM 3746 Nways Multiprotocol Controllers are a high-performance solution for supporting distributed multiprotocol networks. They're designed to provide high connectivity and high throughput as APPN/HPR and IP routing nodes. Model 950 operates in stand-alone mode, without the need for a Network Control Program (NCP), whereas Model 900 attaches to a 3745 Communication Controller, enabling the transport of SNA subarea traffic as well as supporting all the advanced functions of Model 950.

IBM continues to improve the performance of the 3746 and add new functions. Recent additions include new processors for ESCON, LAN and WAN connectivity. Built with improved technology, these processors improve performance by up to 70 percent. And by doubling the memory size, connectivity can be increased by as much as 100 percent. The addition of the Multiaccess Enclosure (MAE) with its PowerPC technology and common code support not only increases the breadth of connectivity, but also makes available important new functions such as TN3270e, Network Dispatcher, and Enterprise Extender.

The IP function operates without a requirement for Advanced Communications Functions (ACF)/NCP support. The Network Dispatcher function provides a powerful solution when clustering Web servers. It allows multiple S/390 servers to be viewed from the network as a single system image and provides load-balancing among different servers.

Enterprise Extender technology uses HPR to carry SNA applications across an IP backbone, allowing users to exploit SNA Class of Service (COS) benefits.

14.2.5 The IBM Nways Wide Area Switches

IBM offers the following wide area switch:

- IBM 2220 Nways BroadBand Switch

The following is a brief description of IBM the 2220 Nways BroadBand Switch and its major functions.

14.2.5.1 IBM 2220 Nways BroadBand Switch

IBM 2220 Nways BroadBand Switch is designed for building cost-effective multiservice broadband networks and has the following highlights:

- Optimized bandwidth for cost efficiency using Networking BroadBand Services (NBBS)

- Integration of applications with different quality-of-service requirements (voice, video, data and image) to consolidate networks

- Existing and new wide area link support ranging from low to very high speeds

- Efficient voice server with compression (GSM, ADPCM), echo cancellation and Group 3 Fax transport

- ATM Bearer Services function for the support of several logical NBBS trunks over one physical ATM interface

- ISDN support for cost-effective connection of remote establishments and transport of voice, video and data

- Euro-ISDN trunk backup support through the new LIC 563 for more flexibility and reliability to the NBBS network

- Frame relay over ISDN to establish a backup link for frame relay devices through ISDN

- Flexible PBX interworking in multivendor environments using Q.SIG

- Real-time frame relay support, a complementary solution for the deployment of voice Frame Relay Access Devices (FRADs) in small branches

- Non-reserved traffic support including notification of network congestion for frame relay.

- Relay/ATM and networking efficiency

- Multiple Logical Trunk (MLT) function over a single E1/T1/J1/J2 link reducing access line requirements

- Mixed multiprotocol capabilities on a single adapter for reduced hardware and configuration costs

14.2.6 Functional Comparisons

Table 22 lists the hardware products TCP/IP support for selected connectivity options.

Table 22 (Page 1 of 3). IBM Hardware Platforms TCP/IP Support						
	2210 MRS	Access Utility	2216 MAS	Network Utility	8210/826X MSS	3746 MAE
IP Routing and Management Support						
RIP-1	X	X	X	X	X	X
RIP-2	X	X	X	X	X	X
RIPng	X	X	X	X		
OSPF	X	X	X	X	X	X
BGP-4	X	X	X	X	X	X
CIDR	X	X	X	X		X
DVMRP	X	X	X	X	X	X
MOSPF	X	X	X	X	X	X
PIM-DM for IPv6	X	X	X	X		
IPv4	X	X	X	X	X	X
IPv6	X	X	X	X		
SNMP	X	X	X	X	X	X
Multiprotocol Support						
PPP	X	X	X	X		X

	2210 MRS	Access Utility	2216 MAS	Network Utility	8210/826X MSS	3746 MAE
Table 22 (Page 2 of 3). IBM Hardware Platforms TCP/IP Support						
TN3270E Server	X	X	X	X[1]		
DLSW	X	X	X	X		X
DLUR	X	X	X	X		X
HPR	X	X	X	X	X	X
Enterprise Extender	X	X	X	X	X	X
IPX	X	X	X			X
Apple Talk 2	X	X	X			X
Banyan VINES	X	X	X			X
DECnet IV/V	X	X	X			X
NetBIOS	X	X	X	X		X
Availability, Balancing and QoS						
IND	X	X	X	X		X
TN3270E Sever Advisor for IND				X		
Dual Power Support			X[2]		X[3]	X
N+1 Fans			X[2]			
RSVP	X	X	X	X		
VRRP	X	X	X	X		X
Voice over IP Support						
Voice over Frame Relay	X[4]	X[4]				
Network Security Features						
NAT	X	X	X			X
L2TP	X	X	X			X

Table 22 (Page 3 of 3). IBM Hardware Platforms TCP/IP Support

	2210 MRS	Access Utility	2216 MAS	Network Utility	8210/826X MSS	3746 MAE
IPsec	X	X	X			X
AAA Support	X	X	X	X		X
ATM and Physical Connections						
ATM 155 Mbps Support			X	X	X	X
LE Server				X		
LE Support	X		X	X	X	
IP over ATM	X		X	X	X	X
Token-Ring	X	X	X	X	X	X
Fast Token-Ring			X			
Ethernet	X	X	X	X	X	X
Fast Ethernet			X	X		X
FDDI			X	X	X	X
ESCON channel			X	X		X
Parallel channel			X	X		X
HSSI			X	X		X
ISDN BRI	X	X	X			X
ISDN PRI	X		X			X
Frame Relay	X	X	X	X		X
X.25	X	X	X	X		X

Notes:

1. Supported by the TN1 model

2. Available for 2216-400

3. Available for 8260 and 8265

4. Statement of Direction

Appendix A. Special Notices

This publication is intended to discuss TCP/IP. The information in this publication is not intended as the specification of any programming interfaces that are provided by products mentioned in this book. See the PUBLICATIONS section of the IBM Programming Announcement for mentioned products for more information about what publications are considered to be product documentation.

References in this publication to IBM products, programs or services do not imply that IBM intends to make these available in all countries in which IBM operates. Any reference to an IBM product, program, or service is not intended to state or imply that only IBM's product, program, or service may be used. Any functionally equivalent program that does not infringe any of IBM's intellectual property rights may be used instead of the IBM product, program or service.

Information in this book was developed in conjunction with use of the equipment specified, and is limited in application to those specific hardware and software products and levels.

IBM may have patents or pending patent applications covering subject matter in this document. The furnishing of this document does not give you any license to these patents. You can send license inquiries, in writing, to the IBM Director of Licensing, IBM Corporation, North Castle Drive, Armonk, NY 10504-1785.

Licensees of this program who wish to have information about it for the purpose of enabling: (i) the exchange of information between independently created programs and other programs (including this one) and (ii) the mutual use of the information which has been exchanged, should contact IBM Corporation, Dept. 600A, Mail Drop 1329, Somers, NY 10589 USA.

Such information may be available, subject to appropriate terms and conditions, including in some cases, payment of a fee.

The information contained in this document has not been submitted to any formal IBM test and is distributed AS IS. The information about non-IBM ("vendor") products in this manual has been supplied by the vendor and IBM assumes no responsibility for its accuracy or completeness. The use of this information or the implementation of any of these techniques is a customer responsibility and depends on the customer's ability to evaluate and integrate them into the customer's operational environment. While each item may have been reviewed by IBM for accuracy in a specific situation, there is no guarantee that the same or similar results will be obtained elsewhere. Customers attempting to adapt these techniques to their own environments do so at their own risk.

Any pointers in this publication to external Web sites are provided for convenience only and do not in any manner serve as an endorsement of these Web sites.

The following document contains examples of data and reports used in daily business operations. To illustrate them as completely as possible, the examples contain the names of individuals, companies, brands, and products. All of these names are fictitious and any similarity to the names and addresses used by an actual business enterprise is entirely coincidental.

Reference to PTF numbers that have not been released through the normal distribution process does not imply general availability. The purpose of including these reference numbers is to alert IBM customers to specific information relative to the implementation of the PTF when it becomes available to each customer according to the normal IBM PTF distribution process.

The following terms are trademarks of the International Business Machines Corporation in the United States and/or other countries:

AIX	AIX/6000
AnyNet	APPN
AS/400	Bean Machine
C/370	CICS
DATABASE 2	DB2
DB2 Connect	Deep Blue
DRDA	eNetwork
ESCON	graPHIGS
IBM	IBM Registry
IMS	IPDS
MQSeries	MVS
MVS/ESA	Net.Data
NetView	Nways
OfficeVision/VM	On-Demand Server
Open Blueprint	OS/2
OS/390	OS/400
Parallel Sysplex	RACF
RS/6000	S/390
SP	System/390
Ultimedia	VisualAge
VM/ESA	VTAM

The following terms are trademarks of other companies:

C-bus is a trademark of Corollary, Inc.

Java and HotJava are trademarks of Sun Microsystems, Incorporated.

Microsoft, Windows, Windows NT, and the Windows 95 logo are trademarks or registered trademarks of Microsoft Corporation.

PC Direct is a trademark of Ziff Communications Company and is used by IBM Corporation under license.

Pentium, MMX, ProShare, LANDesk, and ActionMedia are trademarks or registered trademarks of Intel Corporation in the U.S. and other countries.

UNIX is a registered trademark in the United States and other countries licensed exclusively through X/Open Company Limited.

Other company, product, and service names may be trademarks or service marks of others.

Full Copyright Statement as requested by recent RFC and Internet draft documents that are referred to within this publication:

This document and the information contained herein is provided on an
"AS IS" basis and THE INTERNET SOCIETY AND THE INTERNET ENGINEERING
TASK FORCE DISCLAIMS ALL WARRANTIES, EXPRESS OR IMPLIED, INCLUDING
BUT NOT LIMITED TO ANY WARRANTY THAT THE USE OF THE INFORMATION
HEREIN WILL NOT INFRINGE ANY RIGHTS OR ANY IMPLIED WARRANTIES OF
MERCHANTABILITY OR FITNESS FOR A PARTICULAR PURPOSE.

Appendix B. Related Publications

The publications listed in this section are considered particularly suitable for a more detailed discussion of the topics covered in this redbook.

B.1 International Technical Support Organization Publications

For information on ordering these ITSO publications see the IBM ITSO home page at the following URL: `http://www.redbooks.ibm.com`.

- *IBM TCP/IP Version 3 Release 2 for MVS Implementation Guide*, SG24-3687

- *OS/390 eNetwork Communications Server V2R5 TCP/IP, Volume I*, SG24-5227

- *OS/390 eNetwork Communications Server V2R5 TCP/IP, Volume II*, SG24-5228

- *OS/390 eNetwork Communications Server V2R5 TCP/IP, Volume III*, SG24-5229

- *TCP/IP in a Sysplex*, SG24-5235

- *OS/390 Security Services and RACF-DCE Interoperation*, SG24-4704

- *AS/400 TCP/IP Autoconfiguration: DNS and DHCP Support*, SG24-5147

- *Stay Cool on OS/390: Installing Firewall Technology*, SG24-2046

- *AS/400 Internet Security: IBM Firewall for AS/400*, SG24-2162

- *Protect and Survive Using IBM Firewall 3.1 for AIX*, SG24-2577

- *Guarding the Gates Using the IBM eNetwork Firewall for NT*, SG24-5209

- *A Comprehensive Guide to Virtual Private Networks, Volume I: IBM Firewall, Server and Client Solutions*, SG24-5201

- *TCP/IP Implementation in an OS/2 Warp Environment*, SG24-4730

- *Beyond DHCP -- Work Your TCP/IP Internetwork with Dynamic IP*, SG24-5280

- *Network Clients for OS/2 Warp Server*, SG24-2009

- *AIX Version 4.3 Differences Guide*, SG24-2014

- *Network Computing Framework Component Guide*, SG24-2119

- *Publishing Tools in the Network Computing Framework*, SG24-5205

- *IBM Network Computing Framework for e-business Guide*, SG24-5296

- *Internet Security in the Network Computing Framework*, SG24-5220

- *Java Network Security*, SG24-2109

- *Integrating Net.Commerce with Legacy Applications*, SG24-4933

- *Secure Electronic Transactions: Credit Card Payment on the Web in Theory and Practice*, SG24-4978

- *Load-Balancing Internet Servers*, SG24-4993

- *Understanding OSF DCE 1.1 for AIX and OS/2*, SG24-4616

- *Administering DCE and DFS 2.1 for AIX (and OS/2 Clients)*, SG24-4714

- *DCE Cell Design Considerations*, SG24-4746

- *Security on the Web Using DCE Technology*, SG24-4949

- *Understanding LDAP*, SG24-4986

- *IBM 2210 Nways Multiprotocol Router Description and Configuration Scenarios - Volume I*, SG24-4446

- *IBM 2210 and IBM 2216: Description and Configuration Scenarios - Volume II*, SG24-4956

- *3746 Nways Controller Models 900 and 950: Multiaccess Enclosure Primer*, SG24-5238

- *The Technical Side of Being an Internet Service Provider*, SG24-2133

- *IBM Network Station - RS/6000 Notebook*, SG24-2016

- *IBM Network Station Guide for Windows NT*, SG24-2127

- *AS/400 IBM Network Station - Getting Started*, SG24-2153

- *S/390 IBM Network Station - Getting Started*, SG24-4954

- *Internetworking over ATM: An Introduction*, SG24-4699

- *Local Area Network Concepts and Products: Routers and Gateways*, SG24-4755

- *Open Systems Adapter 2 Implementation Guide*, SG24-4770

- *MPTN Architecture Tutorial and Product Implementations*, SG24-4170

B.2 Redbooks on CD-ROMs

Redbooks are also available on CD-ROMs. **Order a subscription** and receive updates 2-4 times a year at significant savings.

CD-ROM Title	Subscription Number	Collection Kit Number
System/390 Redbooks Collection	SBOF-7201	SK2T-2177
Networking and Systems Management Redbooks Collection	SBOF-7370	SK2T-6022
Transaction Processing and Data Management Redbook	SBOF-7240	SK2T-8038
Lotus Redbooks Collection	SBOF-6899	SK2T-8039
Tivoli Redbooks Collection	SBOF-6898	SK2T-8044
AS/400 Redbooks Collection	SBOF-7270	SK2T-2849
RS/6000 Redbooks Collection (HTML, BkMgr)	SBOF-7230	SK2T-8040
RS/6000 Redbooks Collection (PostScript)	SBOF-7205	SK2T-8041
RS/6000 Redbooks Collection (PDF Format)	SBOF-8700	SK2T-8043
Application Development Redbooks Collection	SBOF-7290	SK2T-8037

B.3 Other Publications

Documentation for IBM products is available online and shipped with the products.

These publications are also relevant as further information sources:

- *Internetworking with TCP/IP, Volume I, Principles, Protocols and Architecture*, third edition, Prentice-Hall, Inc., 1995, by Douglas E. Comer; ISBN 0-13-216987-8.

- *Internetworking with TCP/IP, Volume II, Design, Implementation, and Internals*, Prentice-Hall, Inc., 1991, by Douglas E. Comer and David L. Stevens; ISBN 0-13-472242-6.

- *Internetworking with TCP/IP, Volume III, Client Server Programming and Applications, Windows Sockets Version*, Prentice-Hall, Inc., 1997, by Douglas E. Comer and David L. Stevens; ISBN 0-13-848714-6.

- *Applied Cryptography*, second edition, John Wiley & Sons, Inc., 1996, by Bruce Schneier; ISBN 0-471-11709-9.

- *IPng and the TCP/IP Protocols*, John Wiley & Sons, Inc., 1996, by Stephen A. Thomas; ISBN 0-471-13088-5.

- *Internet Routing Architectures*, New Riders Publishing, 1997, by Bassam Halabi; ISBN 1-56205-652-2.

- *HTML 3.2 & CGI Unleashed*, Sams.net Publishing, 1996, by John December and Mark Ginsburg; ISBN 1-57521-177-7.

- *TCP/IP Illustrated, Volume I, The Protocols*, Addison Wesley, 1994, by W. Richard Stevens; ISBN 0-201-63346-9.

- *TCP/IP Illustrated, Volume II, The Implementation*, Addison Wesley, 1995, by W. Richard Stevens; ISBN 0-201-63346-9.

- *TCP/IP Illustrated, Volume III, TCP for Transactions, HTTP, NNTP, and the UNIX Domain Protocols*, Addison Wesley, 1996, by W. Richard Stevens; ISBN 0-201-63346-9.

- *TCP/IP Network Administration*, O'Reilly & Associates, Inc., 1994, by Craig Hunt; ISBN 0-937175-82-X.

- *DNS and BIND*, second edition, O'Reilly & Associates, Inc., 1997, by Paul Albitz and Cricket Liu; ISBN 1-56592-236-0.

- *sendmail*, second edition, O'Reilly & Associates, Inc., 1997, by Bryan Costales with Eric Allman, ISBN 1-56592-222-0.

- *Building Internet Firewalls*, O'Reilly & Associates, Inc., 1995, by D. Brent Chapman and Elizabeth D. Zwicky; ISBN 1-56592-124-0.

- *The Java Handbook*, Osborne McGraw-Hill, 1996, by Patrick Naughton; ISBN 0-07-882199-1.

- *The ABCs of JavaScript*, SYBEX, Inc., 1997, by Lee Purcel and Mary Jane Mara; ISBN 0-7821-1937-9.

- *Communications for Cooperating Systems - OSI, SNA and TCP/IP*, Addison-Wesley, Publishing Company, Inc., 1992, by R. J. Cypser; ISBN 0-201-50775-7.

- *LAN Technical Reference: 802.2 and NetBIOS Application Program Interfaces*, SC30-3587

- *Request For Comments (RFC)* and *Internet Drafts (ID)*

  There are more than 2400 RFCs today. For those readers who want to keep up-to-date with the latest advances and research activities in TCP/IP, the ever-increasing number of RFCs and Internet drafts (ID) is the best source of this information. RFCs can be viewed or obtained online from the Internet Engineering Taskforce (IETF) Web page using the following URL: `http://www.ietf.org`.

- *IBM Software Glossary*

  An excellent collection of definitions of commonly used terms for computer software and communications which are used in many IBM product publications can be found in this document which is available on the World Wide Web at the following URL: `http://www.networking.ibm.com/nsg/nsgmain.htm`

  Note: This glossary is not available through regular publication services.

List of Abbreviations

AAA	Authentication, Authorization and Accounting	*ATM*	Asynchronous Transfer Mode
AAL	ATM Adaptation Layer	*BGP*	Border Gateway Protocol
AFS	Andrews File System	*BIND*	Berkeley Internet Name Domain
AH	Authentication Header	*BNF*	Backus-Naur Form
AIX	Advanced Interactive Executive Operating System	*BRI*	Basic Rate Interface
		BSD	Berkeley Software Distribution
API	Application Programming Interface	*CA*	Certification Authority
APPN	Advanced Peer-to-Peer Networking	*CBC*	Cipher Block Chaining
		CCITT	Comité Consultatif International Télégraphique et Téléphonique (now ITU-T)
ARP	Address Resolution Protocol		
ARPA	Advanced Research Projects Agency	*CDMF*	Commercial Data Masking Facility
AS	Autonomous System	*CERN*	Conseil Européen pour la Recherche Nucléaire
ASCII	American Standard Code for Information Interchange	*CGI*	Common Gateway Interface
		CHAP	Challenge Handshake Authentication Protocol
ASN.1	Abstract Syntax Notation 1		
AS/400	Application System/400	*CICS*	Customer Information Control System

865

CIDR	Classless Inter-Domain Routing	*DFS*	Distributed File Service
CIX	Commercial Internet Exchange	*DHCP*	Dynamic Host Configuration Protocol
CLNP	Connectionless Network Protocol	*DLC*	Data Link Control
CORBA	Common Object Request Broker Architecture	*DLCI*	Data Link Connection Identifier
COS	Class of Service	*DLL*	Dynamic Link Library
CPCS	Common Part Convergence Sublayer	*DLSw*	Data Link Switching
CPU	Central Processing Unit	*DLUR*	Dependent LU Requester
CSMA/CD	Carrier Sense Multiple Access with Collision Detection	*DLUS*	Dependent LU Server
		DME	Distributed Management Environment
DARPA	Defense Advanced Research Projects Agency	*DMI*	Desktop Management Interface
DCE	Distributed Computing Environment	*DMTF*	Desktop Management Task Force
DCE	Data Circuit-terminating Equipment	*DMZ*	Demilitarized Zone
DDN	Defense Data Network	*DNS*	Domain Name Server
DDNS	Dynamic Domain Name System	*DOD*	U.S. Department of Defense
DEN	Directory-Enabled Networking	*DOI*	Domain of Interpretation
DES	Digital Encryption Standard	*DOS*	Disk Operating System
		DSA	Digital Signature Algorithm

DSAP	Destination Service Access Point	*HDLC*	High-level Data Link Control
DSS	Digital Signature Standard	*HMAC*	Hashed Message Authentication Code
DTE	Data Terminal Equipment	*HPR*	High Performance Routing
DTP	Data Transfer Process	*HTML*	Hypertext Markup Language
DVMRP	Distance Vector Multicast Routing Protocol	*HTTP*	Hypertext Transfer Protocol
EBCDIC	Extended Binary Communication Data Interchange Code	*IAB*	Internet Activities Board
		IAC	Interpret As Command
EGP	Exterior Gateway Protocol	*IANA*	Internet Assigned Numbers Authority
ESCON	Enterprise Systems Connection	*IBM*	International Business Machines Corporation
ESP	Encapsulating Security Payload	*ICMP*	Internet Control Message Protocol
FDDI	Fiber Distributed Data Interface	*ICSS*	Internet Connection Secure Server
FQDN	Fully Qualified Domain Name		
FR	Frame Relay	*ICV*	Integrity Check Value
FTP	File Transfer Protocol	*IDEA*	International Data Encryption Algorithm
GGP	Gateway-to-Gateway Protocol		
GMT	Greenwich Mean Time	*IDLC*	Integrated Data Link Control
GSM	Group Special Mobile	*IDRP*	Inter-Domain Routing Protocol
GUI	Graphical User Interface		

IEEE	Institute of Electrical and Electronics Engineers	*IRFT*	Internet Research Task Force
IESG	Internet Engineering Steering Group	*ISAKMP*	Internet Security Association and Key Management Protocol
IETF	Internet Engineering Task Force	*ISDN*	Integrated Services Digital Network
IGMP	Internet Group Management Protocol	*ISO*	International Organization for Standardization
IGN	IBM Global Network	*ISP*	Internet Service Provider
IGP	Interior Gateway Protocol	*ITSO*	International Technical Support Organization
IIOP	Internet Inter-ORB Protocol	*ITU-T*	International Telecommunication Union - Telecommunication Standardization Sector (was CCITT)
IKE	Internet Key Exchange		
IMAP	Internet Message Access Protocol		
IMS	Information Management System	*IV*	Initialization Vector
IP	Internet Protocol	*JDBC*	Java Database Connectivity
IPC	Interprocess Communication	*JDK*	Java Development Toolkit
IPSec	IP Security Architecture	*JES*	Job Entry System
IPv4	Internet Protocol Version 4	*JIT*	Java Just-in-Time Compiler
IPv6	Internet Protocol Version 6	*JMAPI*	Java Management API
IPX	Internetwork Packet Exchange	*JVM*	Java Virtual Machine
		JPEG	Joint Photographic Experts Group

LAC	L2TP Access Concentrator	*MIB*	Management Information Base
LAN	Local Area Network	*MILNET*	Military Network
LAPB	Link Access Protocol Balanced	*MIME*	Multipurpose Internet Mail Extensions
LCP	Link Control Protocol	*MLD*	Multicast Listener Discovery
LDAP	Lightweight Directory Access Protocol	*MOSPF*	Multicast Open Shortest Path First
LE	LAN Emulation (ATM)	*MPC*	Multi-Path Channel
LLC	Logical Link Layer	*MPEG*	Moving Pictures Experts Group
LNS	L2TP Network Server	*MPLS*	Multiprotocol Label Switching
LPD	Line Printer Daemon	*MPOA*	Multiprotocol over ATM
LPR	Line Printer Requester	*MPTN*	Multiprotocol Transport Network
LSAP	Link Service Access Point	*MS-CHAP*	Microsoft Challenge Handshake Authentication Protocol
L2F	Layer 2 Forwarding		
L2TP	Layer 2 Tunneling Protocol	*MTA*	Message Transfer Agent
MAC	Message Authentication Code	*MTU*	Maximum Transmission Unit
MAC	Medium Access Control	*MVS*	Multiple Virtual Storage Operating System
MD2	RSA Message Digest 2 Algorithm	*NAT*	Network Address Translation
MD5	RSA Message Digest 5 Algorithm	*NBDD*	NetBIOS Datagram Distributor

NBNS	NetBIOS Name Server	*NSAP*	Network Service Access Point
NCF	Network Computing Framework	*NSF*	National Science Foundation
NCP	Network Control Protocol	*NTP*	Network Time Protocol
NCSA	National Computer Security Association	*NVT*	Network Virtual Terminal
NDIS	Network Drivere Interface Specification	*ODBC*	Open Database Connectivity
NetBIOS	Network Basic Input/Output System	*ODI*	Open Datalink Interface
		OEM	Original Equipment Manufacturer
NFS	Network File System	*ONC*	Open Network Computing
NIC	Network Information Center	*ORB*	Object Request Broker
NIS	Network Information Systems	*OSA*	Open Systems Adapter
		OSI	Open Systems Interconnect
NIST	National Institute of Standards and Technology	*OSF*	Open Software Foundation
NMS	Network Management Station	*OSPF*	Open Shortest Path First
		OS/2	Operating System/2
NNTP	Network News Transfer Protocol	*OS/390*	Operating System for the System/390 platform
NRZ	Non-Return-to-Zero		
NRZI	Non-Return-to-Zero Inverted	*OS/400*	Operating System for the AS/400 platform
NSA	National Security Agency	*PAD*	Packet Assembler/Disassembler

PAP	Password Authentication Protocol	**QOS**	Quality of Service
PDU	Protocol Data Unit	**RACF**	Resource Access Control Facility
PGP	Pretty Good Privacy	**RADIUS**	Remote Authentication Dial-In User Service
PI	Protocol Interpreter	**RAM**	Random Access Memory
PIM	Protocol Indepedent Multicast	**RARP**	Reverse Address Resolution Protocol
PKCS	Public Key Cryptosystem	**RAS**	Remote Access Service
PKI	Public Key Infrastructure	**RC2**	RSA Rivest Cipher 2 Algorithm
PNNI	Private Network-to-Network Interface	**RC4**	RSA Rivest Cipher 4 Algorithm
POP	Post Office Protocol	**REXEC**	Remote Execution Command Protocol
POP	Point-of-Presence		
PPP	Point-to-Point Protocol	**RFC**	Request for Comments
PPTP	Point-to-Point Tunneling Protocol	**RIP**	Routing Information Protocol
PRI	Primary Rate Interface	**RIPE**	Réseaux IP Européens
PSDN	Packet Switching Data Network	**RISC**	Reduced Instruction-Set Computer
PSTN	Public Switched Telephone Network	**ROM**	Read-only Memory
PVC	Permanent Virtual Circuit	**RPC**	Remote Procedure Call
QLLC	Qualified Logical Link Control	**RSH**	Remote Shell

RSVP	Resource Reservation Protocol	*SNA*	System Network Architecture
RS/6000	IBM RISC System/6000	*SNAP*	Subnetwork Access Protocol
RTCP	Realtime Control Protocol	*SNG*	Secured Network Gateway (former product name of the IBM eNetwork Firewall)
RTP	Realtime Protocol		
SA	Security Association		
SAP	Service Access Point	*SNMP*	Simple Network Management Protocol
SDH	Synchronous Digital Hierarchy	*SOA*	Start of Authority
SDLC	Synchronous Data Link Control	*SONET*	Synchronous Optical Network
SET	Secure Electronic Transaction	*SOCKS*	SOCK-et-S (An internal NEC development name that remained after release)
SGML	Standard Generalized Markup Language		
SHA	Secure Hash Algorithm	*SPI*	Security Parameter Index
S-HTTP	Secure Hypertext Transfer Protocol	*SSL*	Secure Sockets Layer
SLA	Service Level Agreement	*SSAP*	Source Service Access Point
SLIP	Serial Line Internet Protocol	*SSP*	Switch-to-Switch Protocol
SMI	Structure of Management Information	*SSRC*	Synchronization Source
		SVC	Switched Virtual Circuit
S-MIME	Secure Multipurpose Internet Mail Extension	*TACACS*	Terminal Access Controller Access Control System
SMTP	Simple Mail Transfer Protocol	*TCP*	Transmission Control Protocol

TCP/IP	Transmission Control Protocol / Internet Protocol	*VRRP*	Virtual Router Redundancy Protocol
TFTP	Trivial File Transfer Protocol	*VTAM*	Virtual Telecommunications Access Method
TLPB	Transport-Layer Protocol Boundary	*WAN*	Wide Area Network
TLS	Transport Layer Security	*WWW*	World Wide Web
TOS	Type of Service	*XDR*	External Data Representation
TRD	Transit Routing Domain	*XML*	Extensible Markup Language
TTL	Time to Live	*X11*	X Window System Version 11
UDP	User Datagram Protocol		
UID	Unique Identifier	*X.25*	CCITT Packet Switching Standard
URI	Uniform Resource Identifier		
URL	Uniform Resource Locator	*X.400*	CCITT and ISO Message-handling Service Standard
UT	Universal Time	*X.500*	ITU and ISO Directory Service Standard
VC	Virtual Circuit		
VM	Virtual Machine Operating System	*X.509*	ITU and ISO Digital Certificate Standard
VPN	Virtual Private Network		
VRML	Virtual Reality Modeling Language	*3DES*	Triple Digital Encryption Standard

Index

Numerics

2210
  See Data Link Switching:
    Switch-to-Switch Protocol
2210 Nways Multiprotocol Router
  BOOTP forwarding   53, 515
2210/2216 Router   852, 853, 854
  Bandwidth Reservation System
    (BRS)   791
  Enterprise Extender   790
  High Performance Routing (HPR)   790
2216
  See Data Link Switching:
    Switch-to-Switch Protocol
2216 Nways Multiaccess Connector
  BOOTP forwarding   53, 515
3746 Nways Multiaccess Enclosure
6Bone
  See IP Version 6 (IPv6)

A

A5 algorithm   345
AAA security model   442
abbreviations   865
absolute domain name
  See Domain Name System (DNS), fully
    qualified domain name
Abstract Syntax Notation One (ASN.1)   278
accounting   443
acronyms   865
address allocation
  See Dynamic Host Configuration Protocol
    (DHCP)
Address Resolution (ATMARP and
  InATMARP)   762
Address Resolution Protocol (ARP)
  algorithm   91

Address Resolution Protocol (ARP)
  (continued)
    BOOTP   512
    cache   88
    Ethernet   88, 759
    Frame Relay   786
    gratuitous ARP   551
    IEEE 802.2 standard   759
    IEEE 802.x standards   88
    IPv6   478
    Mobile IP   551
    packet   89, 94
    proxy ARP   551
    Proxy-ARP   92
    reply   88
    request   88
adjacent router   151
AFS
  See Andrew File System (AFS)
Agent Solicitation message   543
AH
  See Authentication Header (AH)
AIX   215
AIX V4.3   834, 835, 836, 837, 838, 839,
  840
    CacheFS   830
    CIDR   829
    DCE Client   831
    DHCP   829
    IP security (IPSec)   828
    IPv6   828
    Java   828
    Lightweight Directory Access Protocol
      (LDAP)   828
    Lotus Domino Go Webserver   830
    Netscape FastTrack Server   830
    Netscape Navigator   830
    Network File System   830
    Network Station Manager (NSM)   831

AIX V4.3 *(continued)*
  Secure Sockets Layer (SSL) 829
  Sendmail 8.8.8 830
  Telnet 830
  X11R6 829
algorithm
  block 344
  Diffie-Hellman 349
  Digital Signature 355, 407
  key-exchange 348
  link state
    See algorithm, shortest path first (SPF)
  public-key 346, 347, 348
  RSA 348
  shortest path first (SPF)
    in OSPF 137, 154
  stream 344
  symmetric 344, 345
  TCP congestion control 115
  vector distance
    in BGP 182
all-subnets-directed broadcast address 53
Andrew File System (AFS) 730
  access control list (ACL) 733
  authentication 733
  cell 733
  client cache 733
  Kerberos 733
  management utilities 733
  name space 733
  remote procedure call (RPC) 733
  replication 733
Anonymous FTP 233
AnyNet
  See Multiprotocol Transport Network
  Architecture (MPTN)
Apache 557, 582
API
  See application programming interface
  (API)
application level gateway
  See firewall

application programming interface (API)
  sockets 96
  TCP 114
  UDP 99
application protocols 18
architecture
  application 16
  architectural model 13, 15, 17
  internetwork 16
  layers 15
  network interface 17
  transport 16
area border router 147
areas 146
arithmetic, modular 348
ARP
  See Address Resolution Protocol (ARP)
ARPANET 5
  Network Working Group 4
  protocol suite 4
AS
  See autonomous system (AS)
AS boundary router 147
ASN.1
  See Abstract Syntax Notation One
  (ASN.1)
Assigned Internet Numbers
  See Standard Protocol Numbers (STD), ,
  STD 02
Assigned Numbers RFC 384
Asynchronous Transfer Mode 761
  end system addresses 807
  Open Systems Adapter 2 797
athentication 365
ATM
  See Asynchronous Transfer Mode
  See ATM LAN Emulation
  See Cell
  See Classical IP over ATM
  See LAN Emulation Server
  See Multiprotocol Encapsulation
  See Virtual Connection VC

Defense Communication Agency (DCA)   5
Demilitarized Zone (DMZ)
   See firewall
denial-of-service attack   337, 338, 383, 400,
   448
Department of Defense (DoD)   5
DES   345, 348, 357, 728, 818, 827
   See also Data Encryption Standard (DES)
designated router   152, 161
destination options extension header   387,
   392
DHCP
   See Dynamic Host Configuration Protocol
   (DHCP)
DHCPv6
   See Dynamic Host Configuration Protocol
   (DHCP)
dictionary attack   337
Differentiated Services
   admission control   676
   Behavior Aggregate (BA) classifier   670
   boundary node   675
   byte, DS   672
   class of service   665
   classifier   670, 673
   Differentiated Services CodePoint
      (DSCP)   667
   directory client   677
   directory information   677
   directory server   677
   DS boundary node   670
   DS byte   666, 670, 672, 677, 679
   DS domain   666, 669, 672, 677
   DS marker   670
   DSCP   667
   egress node   670
   Expedited Forwarding (EF) PHB   669
   ingress node   670, 679
   interior component   672
   Internet   676
   IPsec   678
   LDAP   677

Differentiated Services *(continued)*
   multi-field (MF) classifier   670
   packet dropper   671
   packet shaper   671
   Per-Hop Behavior (PHB)   667
   PHB   667
   policing   671
   policy information   677
   predictable performance   665
   QoS   666, 669, 672, 676
   RSVP   675
   scalable service discrimination   665
   security   679
   Service Level Agreement (SLA)   666
   SLA   670, 672, 677
   source domain   673
   token bucket filter   671
   TOS octet   666
   traffic class octet   666
   traffic conditioner   671, 673
   Traffic Conditioning Agreement
      (TCA)   672
   traffic meter   670
   traffic prioritization algorithm   672
   traffic profile   670
Diffie-Hellman   348, 349, 357, 405, 406,
   409, 410, 412, 413, 415
Diffie-Hellman key exchange
   See IP Security Architecture (IPSec)
dig   215
digital certificate   356, 815, 827
digital envelope   353
digital signature   338, 346, 352, 408, 409,
   530
Digital Signature Standard   353, 401
Digital Signature Standard (DSS)
   See IP Security Architecture (IPSec)
Directory Access Protocol (DAP)   735
disconnected use model   271
discrete logarithms   348, 350
diskless host   511

Encapsulating Security Payload (ESP)
(continued)
   Security Parameter Index (SPI) 389
   Sequence Number 389
   transform 379
   transport mode 391, 394
   tunnel mode 391, 394
encapsulation 381
encryption 342, 343, 352, 419, 738, 746
encryption algorithm 358, 404
encryption key 343
encryption: 338
eNetwork Communications Server 582
eNetwork Firewall for AIX
   See firewall
Enterprise Extender 790
Entity
   See SNMPv2 Entity
ephemeral port
   See port
ESP
   See Encapsulating Security Payload (ESP)
Ethernet
   802.2 Logical Link Control (LLC) 758
   ARP 88, 759
   DIX 88, 757
   DSAP 758
   frame formats 757
   header fields 757
   IEEE 802.3 standard 757, 759
   IEEE 802.4 standard 759
   IEEE 802.5 standard 759
   IEEE 802.x standards 513
   IPv6 478
   LSAP 758
   multicasting 594
   Open Systems Adapter 2 796
   protocol-type number 757
   SNAP 758
   SSAP 758
   Sub-Network Access Protocol
    (SNAP) 758

Extended TACACS 443
Extensible Markup Language 569
exterior 177
Exterior Gateway Protocol (EGP) 176
   See also exterior routing protocol
   description 176—177
exterior gateway protocols 126
exterior routing protocol 176
   See also Border Gateway Protocol (BGP)
   See also Exterior Gateway Protocol
   (EGP)
   protocol descriptions 176

F

factoring 347
FDDI 760
File Transfer Protocol (FTP) 226, 696
   Anonymous FTP 233
   end the transfer session 230
   FTP proxy 818
   login 228
   Network Computer 552
   normal mode 366
   operations 228
   OS/2 833
   passive mode 230, 366
   proxy 230
   proxy server 365, 366
   reply codes 230
   scenario 231
   subcommands
    cd 229
    close 230
    dir 229
    get 230
    lcd 229
    ls 229
    mode 229
    open 228
    pass 228
    put 230
    quit 230
    site 229

IP Version 6 (IPv6) *(continued)*
   RIPng 144
   router 458
   site-local unicast address 470, 471
   solicited node multicast address 475
   traffic class octet 666
   transition from IPv4 499
   tunneling 464, 501
      automatic 501
      configured 506
   tunneling over IPv4 networks 501
   VPN 434
IP-FDDI 760
IP: the Next Generation (IPng) 510
   See also IP Version 6 (IPv6)
IP6.INT domain 494
IPC
   See InterProcess Communication (IPC)
IPng
   See IP: the Next Generation (IPng)
IPSec
   See IP Security Architecture (IPSec)
IPv4
   See Internet Protocol (IP)
IPv6 434
   See also IP Version 6 (IPv6)
IPX 381
ISAKMP
   See ISAKMP/Oakley
ISAKMP/Oakley
   application-layer security 410
   authentication 348, 410
   authentication key 407
   authentication mechanism 401, 410
   authentication method 404
   certificate 402, 408, 416
   certificate authority 408
   certificate payload 407, 409
   Certificate Request message 408
   certificates 410
   composite value 406
   cryptographic key 401

ISAKMP/Oakley *(continued)*
   cryptographic keys 405, 407, 410
   denial-of-service 400
   destination port 403
   Diffie-Hellman 402, 405, 406, 409, 410, 412, 415
   Diffie-Hellman algorithm 349
   Digital Signature 408, 409
   Digital Signature Algorithm 355, 407
   Digital Signature Standard 401
   DOI 403, 404
   Domain of Interpretation (DOI) 403, 404, 412
   encryption 410
   encryption algorithm 404
   Encryption Bit 408
   Encryption Flag 412
   encryption key 407
   exponent 405
   Flags field 408
   hash function 410
   Hash Payload 412, 413, 415
   identity 405
   identity payload 407, 408, 409
   Identity Protect exchange 402
   Initiator Cookie 403, 404, 406
   Integrity Check Value (ICV) 414
   ISAKMP Header 403, 404, 408, 410, 412, 415
   Key Exchange attribute 410
   Key Exchange field 406, 411
   Key Exchange Payload 413
   KEY_OAKLEY 404, 405
   keying material 400, 406, 407, 413, 415
   LDAP 408
   man-in-the-middle 400
   master key 402
   master secret 401
   Message 1 403, 411, 415
   Message 2 404, 413, 415
   Message 3 405, 415
   Message 4 406

neighbor routers   150

nested tunneling   394

NetBIOS   381

   Data Link Switching: Switch-to-Switch
Protocol   774

   datagram distributor (NBDD)   313

   DNS encoded format   315

   end node   313

   name server (NBNS)   313

   node status request frame   316

   routing extensions   314

   scope   312

   service   312

Netscape Navigator   557, 575

NETSTAT   310

network access server   444

Network Address Translation (NAT)   682,
826

   address pool   376

   AS/400   826

   FTP packet   377

   IP network design   377

   IPSec   379

   load balancer   708

   non-secure network   376

   private IP address   375

   secure network   376

   TCP packet   377

   timeout value   378

   translation mechanism   376

Network Computer   552, 572

Network Element (NE)

   See Simple Network Management
Protocol (SNMP)

Network File System (NFS)

   AIX V4.3   830

   AS/400   823

   Cache File System   302

   concept   297

   file system   301

   Lock Manager Protocol   301

   MOUNT command   298

     options   298

Network File System (NFS) *(continued)*

   Mount protocol   297

   Network Computer   552

   NFS protocol   300

   NFS URL   303

   Remote Procedure Call   297

   VM   821

Network Information System (NIS)   310

network management

   See also Management Information Base

   See also Simple Network Management
Protocol (SNMP)

   object identifier   283

   SGMP   277

   Structure and Identification of
Management Information   278

Network Management Application (NMA)

   See Simple Network Management
Protocol (SNMP)

Network Management Station (NMS)

   See Simple Network Management
Protocol (SNMP)

Network News Transfer Protocol   584

network object   203

Network Service Access Point (NSAP)

Network Virtual Terminal (NVT)   216

network-directed broadcast address   53

news agent   584

news groups   584

NewsReader/2   584

Next Generation Internet (NGI)

   initiative   590

NFS

   See Network File System (NFS)

NFSNET

   See National Science Founfation Network
(NFSNET)

NIC

   See Internet Network Information Center
(InterNIC)

NIS   310

   See also Network Information System
(NIS)

NIST 353

NMA
 See Simple Network Management
  Protocol (SNMP), Network
  Management Application (NMA)

NMS
 See Simple Network Management
  Protocol (SNMP), Network
  Management Station (NMS)

NNTP 584

nodal information 809

node identifier 808

non-repudiation 338, 344, 347

nonce 405, 406, 411, 412, 413, 415

NSA 353

NSAP
 See Network Service Access Point
  (NSAP)

nslookup 215

NVT 216
 See also TELNET

O

Oakley
 See ISAKMP/Oakley

Oakley Main Mode 410

Oakley Quick Mode 410

Object Management Group (OMG) 576

Object Request Broker (ORB) 575

offline model 270

one-time password 338

one-way function 350

online model 271

OPEN
 See also Open Systems Adapter/Support
  Facility (OSA/SF)
 active/passive 113, 114

Open Look 304

Open Shortest Path First (OSPF) 146

Open Shortest Path First Version 2 (OSPF)
 See also multicast
 area ID 154

Open Shortest Path First Version 2 (OSPF)
(continued)
 directed graph 154
 equal-cost multipath 682, 714
 link-state database 154
 protocol description 156
 router ID 154
 routing table 154
 shortest-path tree 137, 154
 shortest-path tree (SPT) 607
 terminology 146
 topological database 154
 TOS metric 154
 type of service (TOS) metric 154

Open Software Foundation (OSF) 304

Open Systems Adapter/Support Facility
 (OSA/SF) 799

OS/2 834, 835, 836, 837, 838, 839, 840
 BOOTP server 831
 BSD 4.3-compliant stack 831
 DDNS incremental zone transfer 831
 DDNS notify 832
 FTP enhancement 833
 Java 832
 Proxy Dynamic DNS Update 831
 Resource Reservation Protocol
  (RSVP) 832
 virtual private network (VPN) 832
 year-2000 833

OS/2 TCP/IP V4.1 IPSec Client

OS/2 Warp 831

OS/2 Warp Server 215, 831

OS/2 Warp Server SMP 831

OS/390 215, 834, 835, 836, 837, 838, 839,
840
 AnyNet 712
 authentication 815
 certificate authority 817
 cryptographic coprocessor 818
 cryptography 815
 digital certificate 815
 Distributed Computing Environment
  (DCE) Security Server 815

OS/390 *(continued)*
  DNS 713
  eNetwork Communications Server 813
  eNetwork Communications Server
    V2R5 712
  Firewall Technologies 815
  FTP proxy 818
  Host On-Demand 817
  Java 817
  Lightweight Directory Access Protocol
    (LDAP) Server 815
  MVS TCP/IP Version 3 Release 2 814
  Network Computing Services 814
  Open Systems Adapter 2 796
  public key infrastructure 815
  Resource Access Control Facility
    (RACF) 815
  Secure Sockets Layer (SSL) 814
  Sysplex 712, 713
  TCP/IP 712
  TCP/IP High Speed Web Access
    (HSWA) server 813
  TN3270 server 817
  VIPA 716
  virtual device 716
  virtual IP address 716
  VTAM 712
  WebSphere Application Server 814
  workload balancing 713
  Workload Manager (WLM) 707, 712,
    815
OS/400 834, 835, 836, 837, 838, 839, 840
  certificate authority 827
  cryptographic processor 827
  Domain Name Server (DNS) 823
  Dynamic Host Configuration Protocol
    (DHCP) 823
  IBM Firewall for AS/400 826
  Internet Connection Secure Server
    (ICSS) 824
  Java 824
  load balancing 823

OS/400 *(continued)*
  Network Address Translation
    (NAT) 826
  Network File System (NFS) 823
  Secure Sockets Layer (SSL) 824
  Socks 826
  VIPA 823
OSF
  See Open Software Foundation (OSF)
OSI 278
OSI protocol stack 735
OSPF
  See Open Shortest Path First Version 2
    (OSPF)
OSPF protocol description 156
OSPF terminology 146
overlapping fragment attack 383

P

packet-filtering 361
packet-filtering router
  See firewall
partial routing information 45, 124
Party
  See SNMPv2 Party
path aggregation
Path MTU Discovery
  See Internet Control Message Protocol
    (ICMP)
per-session key 356
Perfect Forward Secrecy (PFS) 401, 410
performance-related 809
PFS 401, 410
PGP 345
physical layer 801
Ping 85
point of presence 444
Point-to-Point Protocol (PPP) 444
  authentication 779
  IP Control Protocol (IPCP) 780
  IPCP 780
  L2TP tunnel 446

Point-to-Point Protocol (PPP) *(continued)*
    LCP   778
    Link Control Protocol (LCP)   778
    NCP   778
    Network Control Protocol (NCP)   778
    Synchronous Digital Hierarchy
      (SDH)   787
    Synchronous Optical Network
      (SONET)   787
    Synchronous Payload Envelope
      (SPE)   788
    Van Jacobson header compression   780
Point-to-Point Tunneling Protocol
  (PPTP)   445
Pointer Queries
    See Domain Name System (DNS)
policy-related   809
port   95
    ephemeral   95
    well-known   95
Portmap   300
    See also Remote Procedure Call (RPC)
Post Office Protocol   268
PostScript   239, 252, 260
PPP
    See Point-to-Point Protocol (PPP)
prefix discovery
    See Internet Control Message Protocol
      (ICMPv6)
Pretty Good Privacy (PGP)   345
prime factor   355
prime number   347
principal identifier   435
private IP address   382
private key   346, 355
Private Network-to-Network Interface
  (PNNI)
    integrated PNNI (I-PNNI)   806
Project Athena   304
protocol number
    in an IPv6 header   460

protocol stack   15
protocol suite   4
protocol virtual LAN (PVLAN)   800
proxy   230
    See also firewall
proxy server   417
proxy signalling   809
proxy-ARP   551
    Concept   92
ProxyArec
    See also Dynamic Domain Name System
      (DDNS)
    ProxyArec   540
pseudo-header
    IPv6   461
    TCP checksum   108
    UDP checksum   99
pseudo-random function   404
pseudorandom generator   358
public key   345, 355, 356, 401, 431, 534
public key infrastructure   815
public-key algorithm   347, 348
public-key algorithms   346
PVC   763

Q

QoS
    See Differentiated Services
    See Integrated Services
Quality of Service
    See Differentiated Services
    See Integrated Services

R

RADIUS   443
random function   358
random-number generator   357
RARP
    See Reverse Address Resolution Protocol
      (RARP)

RC2 359
RC4 359
reachability 809
Real-Time Transport Protocol (RTP)
 See multicast
RealAudio 826
Reconfigure, DHCP 498
Record Route
 See Internet Protocol (IP)
refresh keys 410
remote access 416
remote access server (RAS) 341
Remote Authentication Dial In User
 Service 443
remote dial-in 442
Remote Exec Daemon (REXECD) 237
 principle 238
 REXEC command 237
 REXECD 237
Remote Forwarder Functional Group
 (RFFG) 804
remote host 398, 401
Remote Printing (LPR/LPD) 297
Remote Procedure Call (RPC) 324
 See also Network File System (NFS)
 Call Message 325
 concept 324
 Portmap 327
 Reply Message 326
 transport 325
 VM 820
Remote Shell Protocol (RSH) 237
replay attack 337
replay protection 384
Request for Comments (RFC)
 See also For Your Information document
 (FYI)
 See also Standard Protocol Numbers
 (STD)
 referenced in this book
  RFC 652 219
  RFC 653 219
  RFC 654 219

Request for Comments (RFC) *(continued)*
 referenced in this book *(continued)*
  RFC 655 219
  RFC 656 219
  RFC 657 219
  RFC 658 219
  RFC 698 219
  RFC 726 219
  RFC 727 219
  RFC 735 219
  RFC 736 219
  RFC 749 220
  RFC 768 97, 99, 120
  RFC 779 220
  RFC 791 35, 120
  RFC 792 74, 75, 120
  RFC 793 100, 114, 120
  RFC 821 239, 241, 250
  RFC 822 239, 242, 251, 562, 591
  RFC 826 87, 88, 120, 762, 765, 810
  RFC 854 226, 236
  RFC 855 226
  RFC 856 219
  RFC 857 219
  RFC 858 219
  RFC 859 219
  RFC 860 219
  RFC 861 219
  RFC 877 782
  RFC 885 220
  RFC 894 759, 810
  RFC 903 93, 120
  RFC 904 176, 191
  RFC 906 512, 515
  RFC 919 35, 120
  RFC 922 35, 53, 120
  RFC 925 92
  RFC 927 220
  RFC 933 220
  RFC 934 252
  RFC 946 220
  RFC 948 759, 760
  RFC 950 35, 74, 75, 120

Simple Network Management Protocol (SNMP) *(continued)*

Network Management Station (NMS) 284

NMA 284

NMS 284

protocol data unit 286

VM 820

single-homed

SIT

See Simple Internet Transition (SIT)

SKEYID 406, 413

SKEYID_a 407, 412

SKEYID_d 407

SKEYID_e 407

SLIP

See Serial Line IP (SLIP)

SMI

See Structure and Identification of Management Information (SMI)

SMTP

See Simple Mail Transfer Protocol (SMTP)

SMTP Service Extensions 239, 243

SNA

See also Data Link Switching: Switch-to-Switch Protocol

LCP 778

Link Control Protocol (LCP) 778

NCP 778

Network Control Protocol (NCP) 778

SNAlink

VM 821

SNMP

See Simple Network Management Protocol (SNMP)

See Version 2 of the Simple Network Management Protocol (SNMPv2)

SNMPv2

See Version 2 of the Simple Network Management Protocol (SNMPv2)

SNMPv2 Entity 288

SNMPv2 Party 289

socket

address 96

association 96

CICS Socket Interface 333

conversation 96

datagram type 323

definition 96

half-association 97

IMS Socket Interface 333

interface 96

raw type 323

REXX Sockets 334

stream type 323

system call 322

transport address 97

SOCKS

AS/400 826

authentication methods 419

circuit-level gateway 417

encapsulation method 421

encryption standards 419

firewall 369, 417

key management systems 419

method options 420

request detail message 422

SOCKS server 417

SOCKSified client 418

SOCKSified TCP/IP stack 418

SOCKSv4 418

SOCKSv5 418

TCP connection 420

tunneling protocols 419

UDP connection 423

UDP port 423

UDP relay server 424

UDP support 419

version identifier 420

source-routing bridges 277

SPF

See algorithm, shortest path first (SPF)

Trivial File Transfer Protocol (TFTP)
(continued)
   Sorcerer's Apprentice Syndrome   235
   TFTP RFCs   234
trust chain   357
TTL
   See Domain Name System (DNS)
   See IP datagram
   See multicast
   See time-to-live
tunnel   445
   tunnel   449
   tunnel mode   679
tunneling   381, 419, 501, 549, 614
two-way random number handshake   338
Type of Service (TOS)   382
type-length-value (TLV)   464

U

UDP
   See User Datagram Protocol (UDP)
UMOUNT command   299
unicast
   address   51
Uniform Resource Identifier (URI)   562
Uniform Resource Locator (URL)   562
Uniform Resource Name (URN)   562
University Corporation for Advanced
  Internet Development (UCAID)   587
Usenet News   584
User Datagram Protocol (UDP)   97, 696
   application programming interface   99
   checksum   99
   datagram format   98
   port   98
   Traceroute   86
user-to-user supplementary   809

V

value, hash   353

vector distance
   See algorithm
Version 2 of the Simple Network
  Management Protocol (SNMPv2)   287
video   559
VIPA   682
Virtual Connection VC   766
virtual private network
   OS/2   832
   OS/390   817
virtual reality   559
virtual router   683, 685
   See also Virtual Router Redundancy
    Protocol (VRRP)
Virtual Router Redundancy Protocol
  (VRRP)   681
   authentication   689
   default router   683
   election protocol   684
   IP Address Owner   684
   multicast address   687
   Primary IP Address   684
   priority   688
   TTL   687
   Virtual Router   684, 685
   Virtual Router Backup   684
   Virtual Router Identifier   684
   Virtual Router Master   684
   VRRP Router   684
virtualizing   4
virus   337
VM   834, 835, 836, 837, 838, 839, 840
   FTP access capability   819
   line printer daemon (LPD)   820
   line printer router (LPR)   820
   Network File System (NFS)   821
   remote procedure call (RPC)   820
   Simple Network Management Protocol
    (SNMP)   820
   SMTP server   820
   TN3270 support   821

X

Y

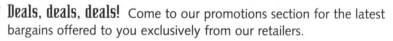